THE BEST OF America's TEST KITCHEN

THE YEAR'S BEST RECIPES, EQUIPMENT REVIEWS, AND TASTINGS

2012

BY THE EDITORS AT
AMERICA'S TEST KITCHEN

PHOTOGRAPHY BY
CARL TREMBLAY, KELLER + KELLER, AND DANIEL J. VAN ACKERE

AMERICA'S TEST KITCHEN
17 Station Street, Brookline, MA 02445

THE BEST OF AMERICA'S TEST KITCHEN 2012
The Year's Best Recipes, Equipment Reviews, and Tastings

1st Edition

Hardcover: $35 US
ISBN-13: 978-1-933615-92-9 ISBN-10: 1-933615-92-3
ISSN: 1940-3925

Manufactured in the United States of America

10 9 8 7 6 5 4 3 2 1

Distributed by America's Test Kitchen
17 Station Street, Brookline, MA 02445

EDITORIAL DIRECTOR: Jack Bishop
EXECUTIVE EDITOR: Elizabeth Carduff
ASSOCIATE EDITOR: Kate Hartke
EDITORIAL ASSISTANT: Alyssa King
DESIGN DIRECTOR: Amy Klee
ART DIRECTOR: Greg Galvan
ASSOCIATE ART DIRECTOR: Matthew Warnick
DESIGNER: Beverly Hsu
FRONT COVER PHOTOGRAPH: Carl Tremblay
STAFF PHOTOGRAPHER: Daniel J. van Ackere
ADDITIONAL PHOTOGRAPHY: Keller + Keller and Carl Tremblay
FOOD STYLING: Marie Piraino and Mary Jane Sawyer
ILLUSTRATOR: John Burgoyne
PRODUCTION DIRECTOR: Guy Rochford
SENIOR PRODUCTION MANAGER: Jessica Quirk
SENIOR PROJECT MANAGER: Alice Carpenter
PRODUCTION AND TRAFFIC COORDINATOR: Kate Hux
ASSET AND WORKFLOW MANAGER: Andrew Mannone
PRODUCTION AND IMAGING SPECIALISTS: Judy Blomquist, Heather Dube, and Lauren Pettapiece
COPYEDITOR: Barbara Wood
PROOFREADER: Jeffrey Schier
INDEXER: Elizabeth Parson

PICTURED ON THE FRONT COVER: Chocolate-Raspberry Torte (page 252)

CONTENTS

America's
TEST KITCHEN
America's
TEST KITCHEN

CHAPTER 1

STARTERS & SALADS

SMOKED SALMON ROLLS

LET'S FACE IT; SMOKED SALMON IS A TRIED-AND-true choice for many a cocktail party spread, and the fact that it is naturally healthy makes it even more appealing. But when you tire of smoked salmon dip or pumpernickel toasts topped with smoked salmon, crème fraîche, and capers, what are the options? After seeing a few recipes for smoked salmon rolls as well as premade versions at the deli counter in our local supermarket, I decided it was time to try my hand at coming up with a smoked salmon roll recipe. I wanted to create a healthy appetizer that was both visually appealing and easy to make.

Many salmon rolls rely on a creamy spread to hold them together, but this component is problematic if you are trying to eat light. Typically dairy-based (cream cheese, sour cream, and not much else), it packs on the calories and lacks flavor, not to mention there's usually so much spread it overwhelms the salmon.

The obvious jumping-off point for a flavorful yet lighter spread was to take out the cream cheese and sour cream and swap in their low-fat counterparts. This worked OK, but I missed the luscious texture of the full-fat versions; this spread was denser, almost pasty. I tried using both low-fat yogurt and part-skim ricotta, but the yogurt was too watery and its tang was too overwhelming, and the ricotta had a grainy texture that didn't work at all. Because I liked the flavor of the light cream cheese and lowfat sour cream combination (tasters approved a 1-to-1 ratio), I decided to move ahead with those ingredients and focus on correcting the texture.

The cream cheese was not incorporating into my mixture well, but when I tried lessening the amount, tasters felt that the flavor balance was off. So first I tried to beat the cream cheese before mixing it with the sour cream, hoping that incorporating some air would lighten the texture. This helped a little, but not enough to justify dirtying my mixer for marginal results. I then tested incorporating various amounts of water to soften the texture, but this only gave the spread an unappealingly loose texture. Ultimately, the answer was simpler than I thought. The whole time I had been working with chilled ingredients. I wanted this appetizer to come together quickly, but I realized it was critical to let the cream cheese come to room temperature first. With that small change, I could move on to boosting the flavor.

My goal was to give the spread a nice, subtle balance of flavors. Too many flavors would overwhelm the salmon; too few, and my appetizer would fall flat. To balance the richness of the cheese and sour cream, this spread needed an acidic component. I tried lemon juice, and white wine, red wine, and cider vinegars, to name a few. Tasters unanimously agreed that ½ teaspoon of lemon juice lent the right clean flavor; it was a logical match for the salmon as well. Minced shallot added depth, capers (also a classic choice for smoked salmon) lent a nice briny bite, and chives added a touch of freshness (though tasters also liked dill, so I left that as an option).

It was time to assemble the rolls. I laid the salmon slices out and topped each one with 1 teaspoon of the cream cheese–sour cream mixture. Originally, I thought

NOTES FROM THE TEST KITCHEN

MAKING SALMON ROLLS

1. After spreading cream cheese mixture over slices of salmon, roll up salmon around filling.

2. Using sharp knife, slice each salmon roll in half.

3. Stand up each roll on cut end and garnish with small leaf of arugula.

SMOKED SALMON ROLLS

this would seem skimpy, but in a side-by-side taste test of a slice of salmon (each was just short of 1 ounce) paired with 1 teaspoon, 2 teaspoons, and 1 tablespoon of filling, tasters preferred the balance of salmon and spread offered by 1 teaspoon. I then gently rolled the salmon into tight cylinders, cut them in half, and stood them on their cut ends.

These rolls looked pretty and tasted great, but something was still missing. In search of both a garnish and a touch of freshness, I landed on one leaf of baby arugula to embellish each roll. Its peppery crunch also lent a new textural element to the dish that tasters unanimously agreed was a welcome addition.

These salmon rolls tasted as fresh and as good as they looked, and with only 50 calories and 2 grams of fat in three rolls, they're about as guilt-free as an appetizer can be.

—JENNIFER LALIME, *America's Test Kitchen Books*

Smoked Salmon Rolls

MAKES ABOUT 18 ROLLS

Be sure to use good-quality, fresh smoked salmon for this recipe; it should glisten and have a bright, rosy color.

1 tablespoon light cream cheese, softened
1 tablespoon low-fat sour cream
½ teaspoon lemon juice
Salt and pepper
1 teaspoon minced shallot
1 teaspoon capers, rinsed and minced
1 teaspoon minced fresh chives or dill
9 slices smoked salmon (8 ounces)
18 small leaves baby arugula

1. Mix cream cheese, sour cream, lemon juice, pinch salt, and pinch pepper together in bowl until uniform, then stir in shallot, capers, and chives.

2. Spread about 1 teaspoon cream cheese mixture evenly over each slice of salmon and roll up salmon around mixture. (Salmon rolls can be made up to this point, covered tightly with plastic wrap, and refrigerated for up to 4 hours.)

3. Slice each salmon roll in half with sharp knife. Stand each roll on its cut end, garnish with 1 arugula leaf, and serve.

MAKE-AHEAD PIGS IN A BLANKET

REMEMBER PIGS IN A BLANKET? THESE HORS d'oeuvres, all the rage in the 1960s, are basically cocktail franks wrapped and baked in store-bought crescent roll dough. Recently, pigs in a blanket have started showing up at parties again. After eating one too many ho-hum versions, I began to wonder when I would encounter a specimen that didn't merely strike a nostalgia chord but actually tasted good. I decided to develop my own recipe, ditching the can in favor of a tasty homemade dough. While I was at it, I would experiment with flavors. But the recipe had to be easy, too—an hors d'oeuvre I could pull from my freezer, bake at a moment's notice, and not be embarrassed to serve.

I ruled out puff pastry, which is daunting to make and seemed excessive, to say the least, for a hot dog. Bread dough wasn't easy or quick enough either. However, pie, buttermilk biscuit, and cream biscuit doughs, each wrapped around tiny hot dogs and baked until golden brown, were all delicious in their own ways. For simplicity's sake, I settled on the last one. Since the cream acts as both liquid and fat, all I had to do was stir it in once I had whisked the flour with salt and baking powder.

I rolled the dough until it was about ¼ inch thick, cut it into many strips, wrapped them around the little hot dogs, and popped them into the oven. Delectable. But would they freeze well before baking? Alas, no. After a week in the freezer, they baked up dry and tough. I should have known: The freezer is notorious for drying things out. Clearly, the dough needed more fat to withstand freezing's detrimental effects. Trial and error showed that adding 4 tablespoons of shortening repaired the dough's texture without requiring significantly more work. Using the food processor, I could incorporate the shortening into the dry ingredients in seconds. When the mixture resembled pebbles, I dumped it into a bowl and stirred in the cream.

Now the texture was a go, but I was having construction problems. As the pigs baked, the biscuit dough unraveled. I brushed the dough with egg wash, which helped slightly. Next, I blotted the hot dogs dry with paper towels and dredged them lightly in flour; together, egg and flour glued the dough to the dog. Great. But rolling these itty-bitty puppies continued to be a pain.

It was much less tedious to wrap full-size hot dogs in dough and then slice each into quarters.

Since I was making my own dough, I stirred in flavor boosters, going for gutsy additions to counteract the dulling effect of the freezer. I added cayenne to the plain biscuit dough and then embellished one version with cheddar cheese and salsa, and another with Swiss cheese, mustard, horseradish, garlic, onion, poppy seeds, and sesame seeds.

Who says you can't teach an old dog new tricks? I admit, my homemade pigs in a blanket are a little more work than tearing open a couple of packages. But they're not that much more work. The hands-on time from start to finish is just 20 minutes—and it's 20 minutes that's very well spent.

—DIANE UNGER, *Cook's Country*

Make-Ahead Pigs in a Blanket

MAKES 24 PIECES

Our favorite brand of hot dogs is Nathan's Famous Beef Franks.

- **2¼ cups (11¼ ounces) all-purpose flour**
- **4 tablespoons vegetable shortening, cut into ½-inch pieces and chilled**
- **2 teaspoons baking powder**
- **1 teaspoon salt**
- **¼ teaspoon cayenne pepper**
- **1½ cups heavy cream**
- **1 large egg, lightly beaten**
- **6 hot dogs**

1. Line rimmed baking sheet with parchment paper. Pulse 2 cups flour, shortening, baking powder, salt, and cayenne together in food processor until mixture resembles coarse meal. Transfer to large bowl. Stir in cream until combined. On lightly floured counter, knead dough until smooth, 8 to 10 times.

2. Roll dough into 15 by 10-inch rectangle. Brush dough with egg and cut into six 5-inch squares. Place remaining ¼ cup flour in shallow dish. Pat hot dogs dry with paper towels and coat with flour, shaking off excess. Arrange 1 hot dog in center of each dough square. Roll dough around hot dog and pinch seam closed. Cut each hot dog into 4 pieces and place on prepared sheet. Freeze until firm, about 30 minutes. Transfer to zipper-lock bag and freeze for up to 1 month.

3. Adjust oven rack to middle position and heat oven to 425 degrees. Arrange wrapped hot dog pieces, seam side down, on parchment-lined rimmed baking sheet. Bake until golden brown, 25 to 30 minutes. Let cool for 10 minutes. Serve warm.

VARIATIONS

Make-Ahead Cheddar and Salsa Pigs in a Blanket

Fold 1 cup shredded sharp cheddar cheese into flour mixture in bowl. Reduce cream to 1 cup. Add ¼ cup brown mustard and ¼ cup hot salsa to cream, then stir into flour mixture.

Make-Ahead Everything-Bagel Pigs in a Blanket

Fold 1 cup shredded Swiss cheese, 2 tablespoons sesame seeds, 2 tablespoons poppy seeds, 1 teaspoon garlic powder, and 1 teaspoon onion powder into flour mixture in bowl. Reduce cream to 1 cup. Add ¼ cup Dijon mustard and ¼ cup drained horseradish to cream, then stir into flour mixture.

NOTES FROM THE TEST KITCHEN

MAKING PIGS IN A BLANKET

1. Brush dough with egg wash to fuse pastry and hot dog together.

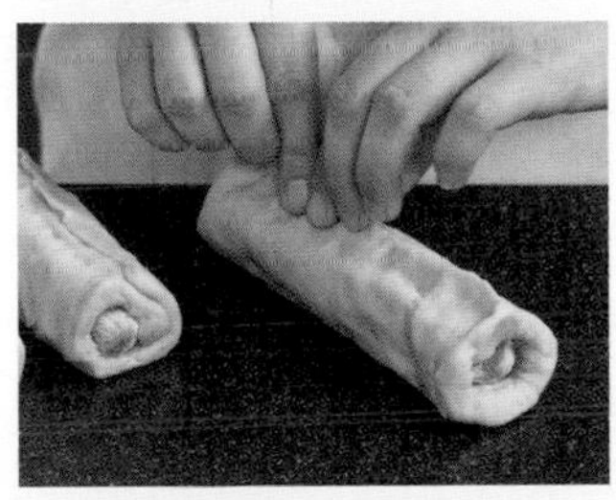

2. After dusting hot dogs with flour, wrap each with dough and pinch seam closed.

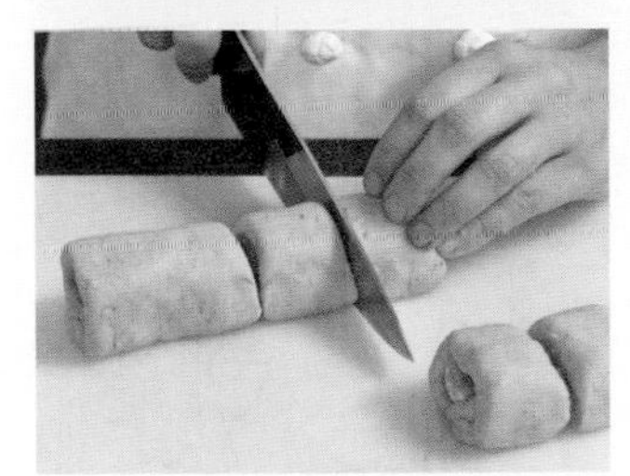

3. Cut wrapped hot dogs into quarters and freeze until ready to bake.

SHU MAI

THE OPEN-FACED DUMPLINGS KNOWN AS *SHU MAI* are as ubiquitous on Cantonese menus as wonton soup and fried rice. These meaty little pouches usually satisfy; the savory-briny combo of pork and shrimp is hard to beat. But the best versions are true standouts that more than live up to their name. (Shu mai translates as "cook and sell," meaning that once they're cooked, they always sell.) Their filling is juicy and tender with a pleasantly springy chew; their flavor is at once salty, sweet, and tangy, as well as faintly smoky from Chinese black mushrooms. These dumplings are too good to be reserved for eating out, so I set myself the task of learning to make them in my own kitchen.

The handful of recipes I found looked surprisingly simple—mix ground pork, shrimp, reconstituted dried mushrooms, and rice vinegar; spoon the mixture into thin-skinned wonton wrappers; crimp; and steam. But my efforts in no way compared to the real thing. Instead of moist, tender, deeply flavorful dumplings, I got beggar's purses of one-dimensional, mealy meatballs.

The obvious move was to head to the source for a few lessons on making dumplings. I finagled my way into the kitchen of China Pearl, long one of my favorite dumpling destinations in Boston. After hours of watching the chef expertly turn out hundreds of shu mai, I left with new ideas for what I would do—and a few for what I wouldn't do.

One idea I would definitely try: grinding my own pork from whole cuts. Preground pork is generally a hodgepodge of scraps from different parts of the animal; some batches can be lean and others riddled with fat. Furthermore, the grind is never consistent—one package can be almost pastelike and another may contain visible chunks of meat and fat. As a result, preground pork rarely cooks up exactly the same way from batch to batch.

The China Pearl chef ground pork butt into coarse ¼-inch chunks, but this fatty, flavorful cut wasn't an option for me. I needed only a pound of meat to make dumplings serving six to eight, and the butt comes in much larger sizes. Boneless country-style ribs, another widely available, well-marbled cut (which actually contains part of the butt), were the next best bet. I cut the meat into 1-inch chunks, which would help produce a more uniform grind, and pulsed it in the food processor into ¼-inch bits along with ½ pound of shrimp. Though not perfect, this filling was markedly more moist and tender than the one made with preground meat.

But now I had a new problem: The filling was so chunky that it broke apart mid-bite. I found that if I divided the meat into two batches and ground one batch more finely (to ⅛ inch), the smaller pieces helped hold the larger bits together and added a pleasing textural contrast. I pulsed the shrimp with the more coarsely ground batch, which produced chunks large enough to be discernible but not distracting.

But even with this nice fatty cut, the filling was still not as juicy and tender as I wanted. The smaller bits in particular were noticeably rubbery. The culprit had to be the steam heat. Moist environments conduct heat very efficiently, and just 10 minutes of steaming cooked the pork to above 165 degrees—the point at which its proteins begin to expel water and shrink, turning the texture dry and grainy. To lubricate the meat and make it seem "juicy," the chef at China Pearl incorporates liberal amounts of lard and fatback into his filling. I'm no foe of fat, but I balked at using either of these ingredients in my homemade dumplings.

I racked my brains for a better way to improve the meat's texture. The answer came to me when I riffled through the test kitchen archives and came across a recipe for all-beef meatloaf. Without the usual fattier pork and gelatin-rich veal in the mix, the meatloaf was prone to drying out. Our solution there—powdered gelatin—seemed equally promising in shu mai. Gelatin can hold up to 10 times its weight in water, and when added to meat, it suspends the juice in a meshlike, semisolid state that prevents it from leaching out. This also

NOTES FROM THE TEST KITCHEN

THE BEST STEAMER BASKET

What could be simpler than a steamer basket, whose sole purpose is to sit above simmering water in a pot? Lately we've noticed updated models boasting new innovative features. We rounded up six baskets (in bamboo, stainless steel, and silicone) and used them to steam dumplings, broccoli, and fish fillets. Our top pick is a compact, classic collapsible stainless steel model from Progressive International. The **Easy Reach Steamer Basket**, $8.95, efficiently steams food and has an adjustable center rod that allows for easy removal from the pot.

SHU MAI (STEAMED CHINESE DUMPLINGS)

translates to a luxuriant texture similar to the suppleness contributed by fat. Half a teaspoon of gelatin, bloomed first in a little water, proved plenty to give my dumplings just the moist, tender texture I was looking for. I got even better results by dissolving the gelatin in soy sauce, which amplifies flavor. On a whim, I mixed in 2 tablespoons of cornstarch, which we've found has yet another power besides thickening: It provides a protective sheath to proteins during cooking, staving off moisture loss and shrinkage.

It was time to think about flavorings. The China Pearl chef's liberal dose of toasted sesame oil was a definite, but his use of MSG was a nonstarter. Instead, I punched up flavor with a little extra soy sauce, rice wine, and rice vinegar. I also found that the concentrated, earthy flavor of reconstituted dried shiitake mushrooms made a fine substitute for the Chinese black variety. Though not traditional, minced cilantro, fresh ginger, and the crunch of water chestnuts rounded out the filling's overall flavor and texture.

For wrappers, I was using widely available square egg roll skins, which I cut into rounds with a biscuit cutter. Though I'll never achieve the speed of a practiced Cantonese chef, crimping the wrappers around the filling proved easier than I thought. As a final touch, instead of traditional shrimp paste or roe, I garnished the dumplings' exposed centers with finely grated carrot and steamed them for 10 minutes.

Served with a quick chili oil that I'd whipped up, these were the best juicy, tender, flavorful dumplings I'd tasted outside of China Pearl. Served for dim sum in a restaurant, these shu mai would definitely cook and sell.

—BRYAN ROOF, *Cook's Illustrated*

NOTES FROM THE TEST KITCHEN

FILLING AND FORMING SHU MAI

1. After brushing edges of dumpling wrappers lightly with water, place heaping tablespoon of filling in center of each wrapper.

2. Pinch opposite sides of wrapper together with your fingers. Rotate dumpling 90 degrees and repeat.

3. Continue to pinch dumpling until you have 8 equidistant folds.

4. Gather sides of dumpling and squeeze gently at top to create "waist."

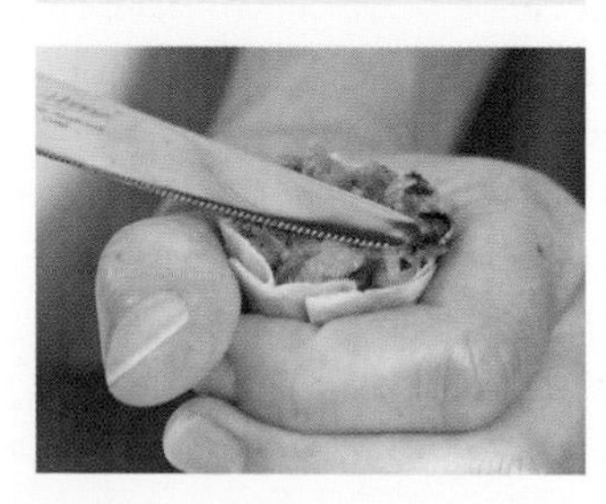

5. Hold dumpling and gently but firmly pack filling into dumpling with butter knife.

Shu Mai (Steamed Chinese Dumplings)

MAKES ABOUT 40 DUMPLINGS, SERVING 6 TO 8

Do not trim the excess fat from the ribs; it contributes flavor and moistness. Use any size shrimp except popcorn shrimp; there's no need to halve shrimp smaller than 26 to 30 per pound before processing. If you do not want to make your own chili oil, you can use store-bought.

- **2 tablespoons soy sauce**
- **½ teaspoon unflavored gelatin**
- **4 dried shiitake mushroom caps (about ¾ ounce)**
- **1 pound boneless country-style pork ribs, cut into 1-inch pieces**
- **8 ounces shrimp, peeled, tails removed, halved lengthwise**
- **¼ cup water chestnuts, chopped**
- **2 tablespoons cornstarch**
- **2 tablespoons minced fresh cilantro**

- 1 tablespoon toasted sesame oil
- 1 tablespoon Chinese rice cooking wine or dry sherry
- 1 tablespoon rice vinegar
- 2 teaspoons sugar
- 2 teaspoons grated fresh ginger
- ½ teaspoon salt
- ½ teaspoon pepper
- 1 (1-pound) package 5½-inch square egg roll wrappers
- ¼ cup finely grated carrot (optional)
- Vegetable oil spray
- 1 recipe Chili Oil (recipe follows)

1. Combine soy sauce and gelatin in small bowl. Set aside to allow gelatin to bloom, about 5 minutes. Microwave ½ cup water and mushrooms in covered bowl until steaming, about 1 minute. Let stand until softened, about 5 minutes. Drain mushrooms in fine-mesh strainer lined with coffee filter, discard liquid, and chop mushrooms finely.

2. Place half of pork in food processor and pulse until coarsely ground into approximately ⅛-inch pieces, about 10 pulses; transfer to large bowl. Add shrimp and remaining pork to food processor and pulse until coarsely chopped into approximately ¼-inch pieces, about 5 pulses. Transfer to bowl with more finely ground pork. Stir in soy sauce mixture, mushrooms, water chestnuts, cornstarch, cilantro, sesame oil, wine, vinegar, sugar, ginger, salt, and pepper.

3. Divide egg roll wrappers into 3 stacks (6 to 7 per stack). Using 3-inch biscuit cutter, cut two 3-inch rounds from each stack of egg roll wrappers (you should have 40 to 42 rounds). Cover rounds with moist paper towels to prevent drying.

4. Working with 6 rounds at a time, brush edges of each round lightly with water. Place heaping tablespoon of filling in center of each round, then form dumplings, crimping wrapper around sides of filling and leaving top exposed. Transfer to parchment paper–lined baking sheet, cover with damp kitchen towel, and repeat with remaining wrappers and filling. Top center of each dumpling with pinch grated carrot, if using.

5. Cut piece of parchment slightly smaller than diameter of steamer basket and place in basket. Poke about 20 small holes in parchment and lightly coat with vegetable oil spray. Place batches of dumplings on parchment liner, making sure they are not touching. Set steamer over simmering water and cook, covered, until no longer pink, 8 to 10 minutes. Serve immediately with chili oil. (Dumplings may be frozen for up to 3 months; cook straight from freezer for about extra 5 minutes.)

Chili Oil

MAKES ABOUT ½ CUP

- 1 tablespoon soy sauce
- 2 teaspoons sugar
- ½ teaspoon salt
- ½ cup peanut oil
- ¼ cup red pepper flakes
- 2 garlic cloves, peeled

Combine soy sauce, sugar, and salt in small bowl; set aside. Heat oil in small saucepan over medium heat until just shimmering and it registers 300 degrees on instant-read thermometer. Remove pan from heat and stir in pepper flakes, garlic, and soy sauce mixture. Let cool to room temperature, stirring occasionally, about 1 hour. Discard garlic before serving.

ARTICHOKE TART

AMONG ALL THE APPETIZERS TO CHOOSE FROM, one of my favorites is the vegetable tart. Guaranteed to stand out on any cocktail party table, it makes a nice break from cheeses and dips. Thinly cut, warm slices of a vegetable tart are sure to impress. Because artichokes are a staple on the party scene, found in many dips and spreads, I had to wonder, Could I find a way to incorporate them into an elegant tart that had big artichoke flavor? I imagined a flavorful alternative to those ubiquitous dips—a creamy artichoke-based filling topped with more artichokes and accented by a crispy crust.

The crust was my first hurdle, but luckily I had a head start. The test kitchen had recently developed a whole-wheat olive oil crust that I thought would provide an interesting alternative to the traditional butter-laden tart crust. After a bit of trial and error, I was able to streamline the method used for conventional rolled-out dough, switching to a much easier press-in method. As an added bonus, the olive oil in the crust provided a subtlety that complemented the Mediterranean flavors of the artichokes. Parbaking the crust before filling it ensured a crisp, evenly baked crust.

With the crust ready to go, I moved on to the tart construction, starting with the filling. In the test kitchen, we often employ a creamy cheese layer in tarts to hold the vegetables in place, but I wanted to lighten this dense layer to allow the flavor of the artichokes to take center stage. I decided that pureeing artichokes with a creamy component would be a good compromise. I tested various combinations of a creamy ingredient (goat cheese, ricotta, cottage cheese, and cream cheese) with artichokes in some form (I tried fresh, canned, and frozen). Fresh artichokes were a lot of work to prepare, but luckily it didn't matter; tasters found the texture of the canned artichokes preferable because they pureed into a velvety smooth spread most easily. As for the binder, the ricotta tasted bland. Tasters thought the cream cheese and sour cream didn't perform any better, creating a strange off-flavor in the filling. The standout was the goat cheese. Tasters overwhelmingly praised it for making a filling with a pleasant tang that didn't overwhelm the artichoke flavor. A little lemon juice and garlic rounded out the flavor of the puree.

With the filling ironed out, I turned my attention to the topping. I needed to determine the best form of artichoke to use. After my filling tests, I decided the limited growing season and labor-intensive nature of fresh artichokes eliminated them from the running. This left canned and frozen artichokes, but even then, neither was without its limitations. While I liked canned artichokes in the filling, when used whole or in chunks on the top of the tart they tasted tinny and a little slimy. They also leached water when baked, which led to a soggy crust.

Frozen artichoke quarters were better, but they tasted a little bland. Because they were baked for only 10 minutes on top of the tart, they didn't have a chance to develop a fuller flavor. I found that roasting them before putting them on the tart helped immensely. They didn't even need to be thawed; they could go straight from freezer to oven and emerge nicely roasted and flavorful after about 20 minutes. For my first test, I arranged the artichokes artfully on the top of the tart. While it looked impressive, the tart was hard to cut into even slices because of the large pieces of artichoke. After a few pulses in the food processor I had a roasted artichoke confetti that could be easily spread over the tart filling. With my topping in place, all I had to do was heat up the assembled tart in the oven for 10 to 15 minutes to warm it through. To round out the flavors, I topped it off just before serving with some shredded basil. This added the touch of freshness my artichoke tart needed.

Satisfied that I had packed as much artichoke flavor into this tart as possible, I developed two variations that would build on the recipe by adding complementary flavors. Sun-dried tomatoes added a rich, briny punch of flavor against the mild artichokes, and sautéed prosciutto added a crisp, salty element when sprinkled on top.

—KELLY PRICE, *America's Test Kitchen Books*

NOTES FROM THE TEST KITCHEN

FORMING A PRESS-IN TART CRUST

1. Transfer processed dough to 9-inch tart pan with removable bottom.

2. Working outward from center, press dough into even layer, sealing any cracks.

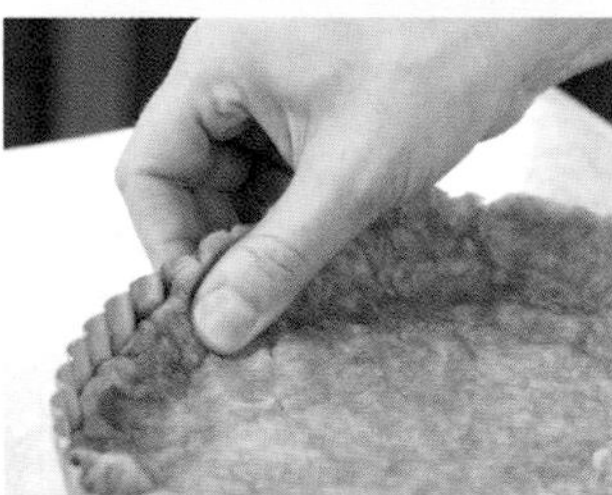

3. Working around edge, press dough firmly into corners of pan, then up sides and into fluted ridges.

4. Lay plastic wrap over dough and smooth out any bumps using your palm.

Artichoke Tart

SERVES 12

The filling in this tart is relatively thin, so you need to press the dough only ¾ inch up the sides of the tart pan. Do not thaw the frozen artichoke hearts before roasting them.

CRUST

- ¾ cup plus 3 tablespoons (4⅔ ounces) all-purpose flour
- ¼ cup plus 1 tablespoon (1¾ ounces) whole-wheat flour
- 1 tablespoon sugar
- ½ teaspoon salt
- 6 tablespoons extra-virgin olive oil
- 4–6 tablespoons ice water

FILLING

- 1 (14-ounce) can artichoke hearts, drained
- 2 ounces goat cheese, crumbled (½ cup)
- 1 teaspoon lemon juice
- 1 garlic clove, minced
- Salt and pepper

TOPPING

- 18 ounces frozen artichoke hearts
- Olive oil spray
- 2 teaspoons extra-virgin olive oil
- Salt and pepper
- 1 tablespoon shredded fresh basil

1. FOR THE CRUST: Process flours, sugar, and salt together in food processor until combined. Drizzle oil over flour mixture and pulse until mixture resembles coarse sand, about 12 pulses. Add 4 tablespoons ice water and process until large clumps of dough form and no powdery bits remain, about 5 seconds. If dough doesn't clump, add remaining 2 tablespoons water, 1 tablespoon at a time, and pulse to incorporate, about 4 pulses. (Dough should feel quite sticky.)

2. Transfer dough to 9-inch tart pan with removable bottom and pat into even layer, then press dough up sides of pan. Lay plastic wrap over dough and smooth out bumps using palm of your hand. Leave plastic wrap on top, place tart pan on large plate, and freeze tart shell until firm, about 30 minutes.

3. Adjust oven rack to middle position and heat oven to 375 degrees. Set tart pan on large baking sheet. Remove plastic, press double layer of aluminum foil into frozen tart shell and over edges of pan, and fill with pie weights. Bake until tart shell is golden brown and set, 40 to 50 minutes, rotating sheet halfway through baking. Transfer baking sheet to wire rack and carefully remove weights and foil. Let tart shell cool on baking sheet while making filling. Increase oven temperature to 450 degrees.

4. FOR THE FILLING: Process canned artichokes, cheese, lemon juice, and garlic together in food processor until smooth, about 1 minute. Transfer to bowl and season with salt and pepper to taste.

5. FOR THE TOPPING: Lightly coat frozen artichokes with olive oil spray. Roast artichokes on baking sheet until browned at edges, 20 to 25 minutes, stirring halfway through cooking time.

6. Transfer roasted artichokes to food processor and pulse until coarsely chopped, about 4 pulses. Transfer to bowl, stir in oil, and season with salt and pepper to taste.

7. Spread artichoke-cheese filling evenly over tart crust, then spread roasted artichoke topping over top. (Assembled tart can be covered with plastic wrap and refrigerated for up to 1 day. To serve, remove plastic wrap and proceed as directed.)

8. Bake tart on baking sheet until heated through, 10 to 15 minutes. Let tart cool on sheet for 5 minutes, then sprinkle with basil. To serve, remove outer metal ring of tart pan, slide thin metal spatula between tart and tart pan bottom, carefully slide tart onto platter or cutting board, and slice. Serve warm.

VARIATIONS

Artichoke Tart with Sun-Dried Tomatoes

Stir ½ cup chopped sun-dried tomatoes into chopped roasted artichokes in step 6.

Artichoke Tart with Crispy Prosciutto

Heat 1 teaspoon canola oil in 10-inch nonstick skillet over medium heat. Cook 2 ounces finely chopped prosciutto until crisp, 3 to 5 minutes. Transfer to paper towel–lined plate and set aside. Sprinkle cooked prosciutto over top of tart when it comes out of oven in step 8.

LIGHTER SEVEN-LAYER DIP

WITH ITS TEX-MEX FLAVORS AND CONTRASTING textures, this classic dip made with layers of refried beans, sour cream, shredded cheese, guacamole, diced tomatoes, scallions, and black olives is easily recognizable to most people. It's a snap to make and has an everyday, football-game-watching "everyman's" appeal that makes it seem like a sure winner. But sadly, it never tastes as good as it sounds or looks. The flavors are always muddled, tired, and bland, and there's nary a hint of freshness. Then there's the fact that seven-layer dip is well known as a real heavyweight, tallying more than 300 calories and 25 grams of fat per ⅓-cup serving—and that's without the chips. I wanted to reevaluate this classic, one layer at a time, to find out if I could breathe new (lighter) life into this staple and at the same time maintain its crowd-pleasing appeal.

I began my overhaul at the bottom, with the beans. Though canned refried beans (made with pinto beans) are the typical choice for this party snack, tasters agreed they tasted stale and tinny, and their dense consistency made them far from dip-friendly. Making my own refried beans from scratch with dried beans would take more time than I wanted to devote to this humble appetizer, so I started with canned beans. At this point, I decided that swapping the pinto beans for black beans would give my dip more appealing color contrast. So I grabbed a can of black beans off the shelf, drained them, and set to work making a flavorful, nicely textured refried black bean layer. To make the beans silky without adding fat, I broke test kitchen protocol by not rinsing them. A simple seasoning of fresh garlic, chili powder, and lime juice gave these quick refried beans the depth and touch of freshness they needed; the five minutes of extra work the beans required was worth it. One layer down, six to go.

Next, I focused on the guacamole. Store-bought guacamole, with its stale (and sometimes rancid) flavor, was a nonstarter. Most guacamole recipes I came across used four avocados, but this was clearly too much fat for my lightened dip. Could I substitute a filler ingredient with a similar texture to avocado but with less fat? I tested cutting the avocados with lima beans, edamame, and peas. Tasters complained that the "mock-a-mole" tasted too lean and that it had an off-putting vegetal flavor. So I settled for less of the real deal, just two avocados mashed with lime juice and salt.

On to the sour cream and cheese layers. For the sour cream, the low-fat variety was the obvious choice, and while it provided plenty of creamy appeal, it was a little bland. Stirring in 1 tablespoon of minced chipotle chile in adobo sauce did the trick. For the cheese, some recipes call for as much as 2 pounds of shredded Monterey Jack or cheddar. I tried making one batch substituting reduced-fat cheddar and another with a lesser amount of the full-fat stuff. To my surprise, tasters were fairly indifferent about the cheese. Amid the beans, avocados, and sour cream, they didn't even know the cheese was there, so I decided to save the calories and forgo the cheese altogether.

Next up was the tomato layer. While a lot of recipes turn to jarred salsa, it just didn't taste fresh, and tasters said straight fresh tomatoes lacked punch. I found my solution in the form of a homemade *pico de gallo*, a relish made with chopped fresh tomatoes, jalapeños, cilantro, scallions, lime juice, and salt. I salted the tomatoes and let them drain before adding them to the dip—this kept

NOTES FROM THE TEST KITCHEN

PREPARING AVOCADOS

1. After slicing avocado in half around pit, lodge edge of knife blade into pit and twist to remove. Use large wooden spoon to pry pit safely off knife.

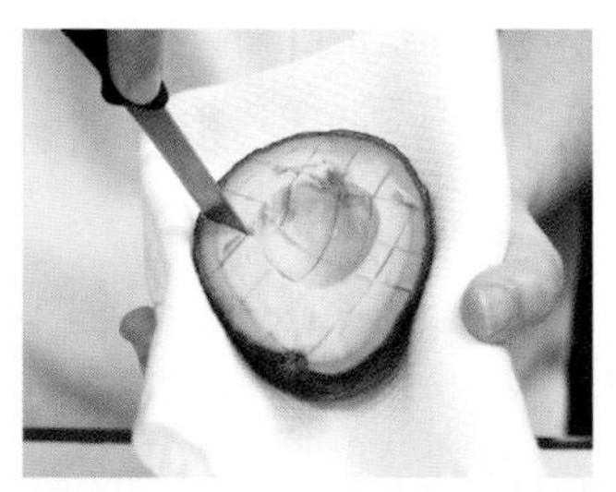

2. Use dish towel to hold avocado steady. Make ½-inch crosshatch incisions in flesh of each avocado half with knife, cutting down to but not through skin.

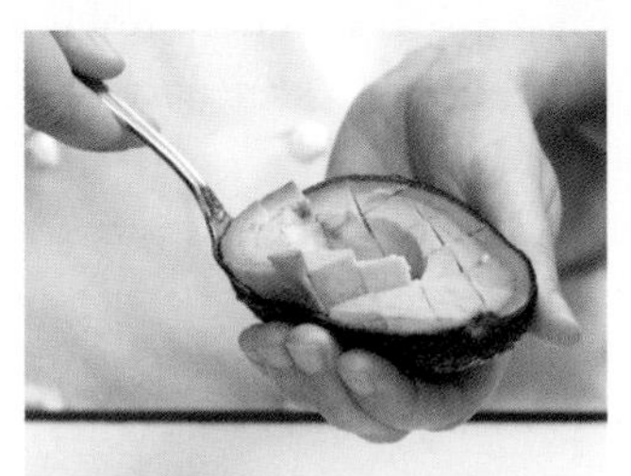

3. Separate diced flesh from skin with soup spoon inserted between skin and flesh, gently scooping out avocado cubes.

excess water from the salsa from diluting the dip and ruining its layers.

After sprinkling on a layer of sliced scallions for fresh bite and good color, I was almost in the end zone. But the final layer of canned sliced black olives needed work. Rinsing the olives helped mitigate their metallic flavor, but they were still bland. After several frustrating rounds of testing, I decided to eliminate the olives.

True, my recipe has just five layers, but with all its textures, flavors, and colors, and just 120 calories and 7 grams of fat per serving, I didn't hear anyone complaining.

—RACHEL TOOMEY KELSEY,
America's Test Kitchen Books

Lighter Seven-Layer Dip

SERVES 12

To make this dip spicier, add the chile seeds. This dip is usually served in a clear dish so you can see the layers.

- **2 pounds tomatoes, cored, seeded, and chopped**
- **Salt**
- **6 scallions, 2 minced and 4, green parts only, sliced thin**
- **5 tablespoons plus 2 teaspoons lime juice (3 limes)**
- **3 tablespoons minced fresh cilantro**
- **2 jalapeño chiles, stemmed, seeded, and minced**
- **1 (15-ounce) can black beans, drained but not rinsed**
- **2 garlic cloves, minced**
- **¾ teaspoon chili powder**
- **1½ cups low-fat sour cream**
- **1 tablespoon minced canned chipotle chile in adobo sauce**
- **2 avocados, pitted and cubed**

1. Place tomatoes in fine-mesh strainer set over bowl, sprinkle with ½ teaspoon salt, and let drain until tomatoes begin to soften, about 30 minutes. Discard liquid and transfer tomatoes to bowl. Stir in minced scallions, 2 tablespoons lime juice, cilantro, and jalapeños. Season with salt to taste and set aside.

2. Pulse 2 teaspoons more lime juice, beans, garlic, and chili powder together in food processor until mixture resembles chunky paste. Season with salt to taste and set aside. Whisk sour cream and chipotle together in bowl and set aside.

3. Combine remaining 3 tablespoons lime juice, avocados, and ¼ teaspoon salt in large bowl and mash with potato masher until smooth. Season with salt to taste.

4. Spread bean mixture evenly over bottom of 8-inch square glass baking dish or 4-cup glass bowl. Spread avocado mixture evenly over bean layer. Spread sour cream mixture over avocado, then top with tomato mixture. Sprinkle with sliced scallions and serve. (Dip can be refrigerated for up to 1 day; let sit at room temperature for 1 hour before serving.)

FRESH SPINACH SALADS

NO SUPERMARKET THESE DAYS IS WITHOUT prewashed baby spinach. But let's face it—as a salad choice, this green is never as flavorful as it is convenient. Unlike sturdier, more mature spinach, the tender, delicate leaves can't support hefty mix-ins like hard-cooked eggs, bacon, or avocado. Worse yet, their smooth, flat surfaces tend to cling together, leaving olives, tomatoes, and nuts drowning in dressing at the bottom of the bowl.

Rather than resign myself to an endless rotation of hardy romaine and red leaf blends, I was determined to make the most of baby spinach. A sturdier element to break up the leaves' fluttery cling was definitely in order—but just about any ingredient can overwhelm baby spinach when chopped into heavy chunks. My first step: Rethink my knifework. Thinly slicing the vegetables (or at least tearing them into small pieces) allowed me to introduce harder, crunchier produce. I shaved fennel, shredded radicchio, tore frilly frisée, and stripped carrot ribbons with a vegetable peeler. Added to individual salads, each fluffed up the spinach leaves considerably and worked in welcome crunch as well as elements of bitterness or sweetness.

The vegetable medleys had shaped up nicely, but I wondered if they weren't a bit one-dimensional. Cheese often pairs well with salad greens, but in this case the spinach leaves were too feathery. Firmer, denser varieties like pecorino and feta sank to the bottom of the bowl, and creamy goat cheese glued the leaves together in slimy clumps. Fresh fruits, I reasoned, would add brighter, cleaner flavors and textural appeal. Orange segments enlivened the carrot salad with acidity and juicy sweetness. Quartered strawberries paired nicely

SPINACH SALAD WITH CARROT, ORANGE, AND SESAME

with assertive frisée; crisp apple matchsticks blended naturally with the fragrant fennel; and ½-inch chunks of sweet mango—just bulky enough to pop through the spinach without plummeting to the bottom of the bowl—mellowed radicchio's bitter edge.

All that was left to do was whisk up a dressing. Anything creamy bogged down the greens, so I stuck with vinaigrette. An earlier test kitchen vinaigrette—which stays perfectly emulsified with just a drop each of mayonnaise and Dijon mustard—was plenty light in terms of texture, but its 3-to-1 oil-to-acid ratio wasn't tart enough for my fruit-filled salads, and it slicked the already slippery leaves. No problem: Two more teaspoons of vinegar (or citrus juice) added just enough tang to bring out the fruits' natural acidity, and a final sprinkling of cilantro, basil, or scallion complemented with fresh bite.

—YVONNE RUPERTI, *Cook's Illustrated*

Spinach Salad with Carrot, Orange, and Sesame

SERVES 6

Even if you buy bagged baby spinach, we recommend washing and drying it.

- **6 ounces baby spinach (6 cups), washed and dried**
- **2 carrots, peeled and shaved with vegetable peeler lengthwise into ribbons**
- **2 oranges, ½ teaspoon finely grated zest from 1, both peeled and segmented**
- **2 scallions, sliced thin**
- **7 teaspoons rice vinegar**
- **1 tablespoon very finely minced shallot**
- **1 teaspoon Dijon mustard**
- **¾ teaspoon mayonnaise**
- **¼ teaspoon salt**
- **3 tablespoons vegetable oil**
- **1½ tablespoons toasted sesame oil**
- **1 tablespoon sesame seeds, toasted**

1. Place spinach, carrots, orange segments, and scallions in large bowl.

2. In small nonreactive bowl, combine vinegar, shallot, mustard, mayonnaise, salt, and orange zest. Whisk until mixture appears milky and no lumps remain. Place oils in liquid measuring cup. Whisking constantly, very slowly drizzle oils into mixture. If pools of oil gather on surface, stop addition of oils and whisk mixture well to combine, then resume whisking in oils in slow stream. Vinaigrette should be glossy and lightly thickened.

3. Pour dressing over spinach mixture and toss to coat; sprinkle with sesame seeds and serve immediately.

VARIATIONS

Spinach Salad with Frisée and Strawberries

Substitute 1 medium head frisée, torn into 2-inch pieces, for carrots; ½ pint hulled and quartered strawberries for oranges; and 2 tablespoons chopped fresh basil for scallions. Substitute balsamic vinegar for rice vinegar, ½ teaspoon pepper for orange zest, and 4½ tablespoons extra-virgin olive oil for vegetable and sesame oils. Omit toasted sesame seeds.

Spinach Salad with Fennel and Apples

Substitute 1 halved, cored, and thinly sliced fennel bulb for carrots; 2 Golden Delicious apples, cored and cut into ¼-inch matchsticks, for oranges; and ¼ cup chopped fennel fronds for scallions. Substitute lemon juice for rice vinegar, 1½ teaspoons finely grated lemon zest for orange zest, 1 tablespoon whole-grain mustard for Dijon mustard, and 4½ tablespoons extra-virgin olive oil for vegetable and sesame oils. Omit toasted sesame seeds.

Spinach Salad with Radicchio and Mango

Substitute 1 small head radicchio (6 ounces), halved, cored, and sliced very thin, for carrots; 1 mango, peeled and cut into ½-inch pieces, for oranges; and ¼ cup minced fresh cilantro for scallions. Substitute lime juice for rice vinegar, 1 teaspoon finely grated lime zest for orange zest, and 4½ tablespoons extra-virgin olive oil for vegetable and sesame oils. Whisk 1 tablespoon honey into vinaigrette with shallot and mustard. Omit toasted sesame seeds.

TOFU SALAD WITH VEGETABLES

ALL TOO OFTEN TOFU IS A SUPPORTING PLAYER AND not the star of the show—witness pad thai, where the tofu is often greasy and buried under mounds of noodles and sauce, or a curry or stir-fry where the sauce and vegetables really shine but the tofu is just thrown in to appease the health-conscious. I wanted to develop a recipe that was all about the tofu and where its most admirable qualities would really stand out. After all, it's a great source of protein, creamy but low in fat, and it marries well with lots of different flavors. Could I develop a satisfying salad that put the tofu front and center?

I began my testing with the tofu. I cut extra-firm, firm, and soft tofu into ¾-inch pieces and dressed them with a basic working dressing. Tasters all agreed that the extra-firm and firm tofus were too firm, almost rubbery, in this context. They unanimously chose soft tofu for its creamy, custardlike texture. To eliminate excess moisture, I simply cut the tofu into cubes and placed them on multiple layers of paper towels to drain.

While tofu would be the star, I needed other vegetables to round out my salad. I wanted the vegetables to be crisp and bright, a nice counterpoint to the creamy texture of the tofu, so I knew they would remain raw. Without any cooking involved, I found that vegetables like broccoli and green beans lent an unappealing toughness, and mild vegetables like zucchini and squash did not offer enough flavor. Tasters liked carrots, snow peas, and bell peppers for both their crisp textures and bright colors, so all three made the cut. Bean sprouts, which are often used in Asian cooking, added a nice crunch and clean flavor that everyone approved.

It was time to move on to the dressing. I limited my scope to creating a boldly flavored Asian-inspired dressing and started by testing three basic flavor profiles: peanut butter, sesame paste (tahini), and soy sauce. The soy sauce made for a dressing that didn't coat the tofu well, and the sesame dressing was a little overpowering. However, the peanut butter flavor held its own with the tofu and vegetables, adding just the right sweetness and nutty flavor. To balance out the dressing and bring in some Asian flavors, I favored a blend of peanut butter, hoisin sauce, lime juice, sesame oil, and garlic, a combination that created the right balance of salty, acidic, and savory. A little chili-garlic sauce added just a touch of heat. To achieve the consistency I wanted, I found that 3 tablespoons of hot water thinned the dressing out perfectly for coating the tofu and vegetables. This bold dressing tasted great, but once it was tossed with the tofu and vegetables, the tofu seemed washed out.

In the test kitchen, we have developed ways to boost the flavor of tofu, including glazing, marinating, and broiling. I immediately eliminated the glazing technique since it requires oil to create a crisp coating on the tofu (so that the glaze can cling), and I wanted to keep my salad on the lighter side. To compare the other two methods, I marinated one batch in half of the dressing for an hour; I brushed the other batch with some of the dressing and broiled it until it turned spotty brown. Tasters barely noticed a benefit from the marinating; even after an hour the flavors had barely penetrated the tofu. But the broiled tofu emerged lightly charred and flavorful. I had my winner.

The tofu now had great flavor and gave the salad more of an identity. After broiling the tofu, I gently tossed it with the crisp, colorful vegetables and remaining dressing. Thinly sliced scallions, minced cilantro, and toasted sesame seeds gave my salad just the right finishing touches.

—SUZANNAH MCFERRAN,
America's Test Kitchen Books

Tofu Salad with Vegetables

SERVES 6

We prefer the texture of soft tofu in this recipe; however, firm tofu may be substituted.

DRESSING

- **3 tablespoons creamy peanut butter**
- **3 tablespoons hot water**
- **¼ cup hoisin sauce**
- **4 teaspoons fresh lime juice**
- **2 teaspoons toasted sesame oil**
- **1 garlic clove, minced**
- **¾ teaspoon Asian chili-garlic sauce**
- **½ teaspoon salt**

SALAD

- **28 ounces soft tofu, cut into ¾-inch pieces and drained**
- **8 ounces snow peas, strings removed, trimmed and cut into ½-inch pieces**

TOFU SALAD WITH VEGETABLES

- 1 **red or yellow bell pepper, stemmed, seeded, and cut into ½-inch pieces**
- 2 **cups bean sprouts**
- 2 **carrots, peeled and shredded**
- 2 **scallions, sliced thin on bias**
- 3 **tablespoons minced fresh cilantro**
- 1 **tablespoon sesame seeds, toasted**
- **Salt and pepper**

1. FOR THE DRESSING: Whisk peanut butter and water together in bowl until smooth, then whisk in hoisin, lime juice, sesame oil, garlic, chili-garlic sauce, and salt until combined; set aside.

2. FOR THE SALAD: Adjust oven rack 6 inches from broiler element and heat broiler. Line rimmed baking sheet with aluminum foil.

3. Toss tofu with half of dressing and spread on prepared baking sheet. Broil until spotty brown, 5 to 6 minutes.

4. Meanwhile, toss snow peas, bell pepper, bean sprouts, carrots, and scallions with remaining dressing in large bowl until well combined. Gently fold in broiled tofu, cilantro, and sesame seeds. Season with salt and pepper to taste and let sit until flavors have blended, about 15 minutes, before serving.

CHICKEN AND WHITE BEAN PANZANELLA SALAD

THE IDEA OF USING BREAD AS ONE OF THE MAJOR components in a salad (and we're not talking croutons) may be unfamiliar to some, but bread salad, or *panzanella*, is not uncommon in Italy. There, stale bread is typically combined with fresh ingredients—tomatoes, onions, and basil—and a simple oil and vinegar dressing. The result is a simple meal that is light yet satisfying, one that is far more than the sum of its parts. I wanted to take this classic recipe one step further and create a complete one-dish meal by including juicy pieces of chicken, white beans, fresh arugula, and shaved Parmesan.

For the chicken, I immediately decided to use boneless, skinless breasts. I started by trimming and pounding the breasts to an even thickness (this ensured that they would cook through at the same rate), seasoned them with salt and pepper, and browned them in the skillet. Dredging the chicken in flour to help create a golden crust wasn't necessary for this recipe because I was going to chop the chicken after it was cooked and incorporate it with so many other flavorful components. After sautéing the chicken, I set it aside and turned my focus to the bread.

I knew the quality of the bread would be fundamental to the success of this dish, so I tried several varieties. Sliced supermarket sandwich bread was immediately out. Its overly smooth texture meant it turned to mush when tossed with the vinaigrette (at this point a simple combination of red wine vinegar and extra-virgin olive oil), and its slightly sweet flavor clashed with the savory flavors of the salad. I thought breads containing dried fruits or nuts might add a nice touch to my salad, but in fact, their garnishes seemed random and out of place. In the end, a high-quality rustic loaf or baguette worked the best. The sturdy texture and strong wheaty flavor paired well with the other flavors, and it held up reasonably well in the dressing.

Panzanella traditionally relies on stale bread, which helps the bread hold up once dressed, but many people don't typically have stale bread on hand, so I set out to make my recipe work with fresh bread. To keep with the rustic nature of the dish, I wanted to streamline my recipe and limit it to one pan, so I nixed the thought of toasting the bread on its own in the oven (two pans to clean) and instead considered ways to combine cooking the chicken and the bread. What if I quickly browned the chicken in the skillet, then placed the cubes of bread underneath the chicken and moved it all to the oven? Though a little far-fetched, it certainly seemed like the most efficient approach possible, so I gave it a shot. I was surprised at how well it worked. After less than 15 minutes, the chicken was cooked through and the bread had toasted nicely, and at the same time it had absorbed the flavorful drippings from the chicken.

Now all I needed to do was put the finishing touches on my vinaigrette and assemble the salad. Keeping with my Mediterranean theme, I started with a basic combination of red wine vinegar and extra-virgin olive oil, seasoned it with salt and pepper, and added some chopped basil for freshness. I tossed the dressing with the bread and pieces of tender chicken, then added my arugula, tomatoes, white beans (canned for convenience), red onion, and Parmesan shavings—all traditional Mediterranean ingredients that worked well here.

After a few forkfuls, tasters agreed that my salad was very close, but everyone had two small complaints: They wanted a bit more flavor, and they thought the bread was too dry. In reviewing my method, an idea came to mind. Why not mix the tomatoes and beans with the dressing and let them marinate while the chicken and bread were in the oven? I whipped up another salad with this method and found that not only did the dressing give the tomatoes and beans more flavor, but the salt in the dressing drew out the tomato juice, thereby creating a more flavorful, juicy dressing. The vinaigrette now lent the bread cubes the moisture they needed and wilted the arugula slightly, creating a flavorful, cohesive dish. Letting the salad sit for 5 to 10 minutes before serving helped improve the final texture even more.

—SUZANNAH MCFERRAN,
America's Test Kitchen Books

Chicken and White Bean Panzanella Salad

SERVES 4 TO 6

Be sure to use high-quality bread here—it is important for both flavor and texture in the salad. To pound the chicken, place each breast between two sheets of plastic wrap, with the smooth side down, and pound gently, making sure that each breast has the same thickness from end to end. Do not discard the seeds or juice as you chop the tomatoes because they add important moisture to the recipe.

- **6 ounces French or Italian bread, cut into ½- to ¾-inch cubes (4 cups)**
- **½ cup extra-virgin olive oil**
- **Salt and pepper**
- **3 (6-ounce) boneless, skinless chicken breasts, trimmed and lightly pounded to uniform thickness**
- **3 tablespoons red wine vinegar**
- **1½ pounds tomatoes, cored and chopped medium, seeds and juice reserved**
- **1 (15-ounce) can cannellini beans, rinsed**
- **1 small red onion, halved and sliced thin**
- **¼ cup chopped fresh basil**
- **3 ounces baby arugula (3 cups)**
- **2 ounces Parmesan cheese, shaved (½ cup)**

1. Adjust oven rack to lowest position and heat oven to 450 degrees. Toss bread cubes with 1 tablespoon oil, ¼ teaspoon salt, and pinch pepper.

NOTES FROM THE TEST KITCHEN

MAKING PARMESAN SHAVINGS

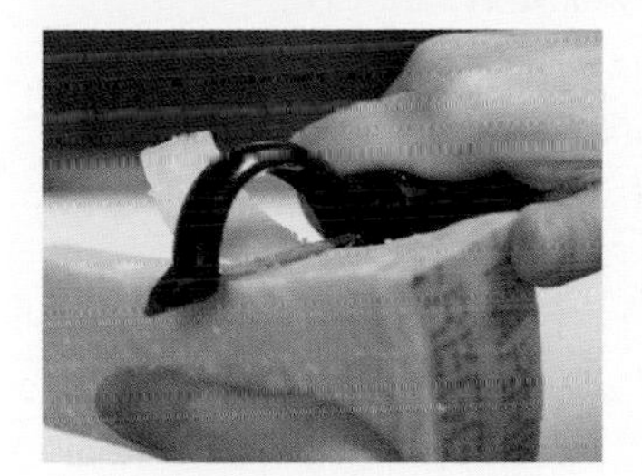

To achieve paper-thin slices of Parmesan, use your vegetable peeler. Run peeler over block of Parmesan, using light touch for thin shavings.

THE BEST RED WINE VINEGAR

Red wine vinegar has a sharp but clean flavor, making it the most versatile choice in salad dressings. While acidity is the obvious key factor in vinegar, it is actually the inherent sweetness of the grapes used to make the vinegar that makes its flavor appealing to the palate. After tasters sampled 10 red wine vinegars plain, in vinaigrette, and in pickled onions, it was clear that they found highly acidic vinegars too harsh; brands with moderate amounts of acidity scored higher. Tasters also preferred those brands that were blends—either blends of different grapes or blends of different vinegars—as they offered more complex flavor. In the end, tasters ranked French import **Laurent du Clos Red Wine Vinegar** first. Made from a mix of red and white grapes, this vinegar won the day with its "good red wine flavor." (See page 291 for more information about our testing results.)

2. Pat chicken dry with paper towels and season with salt and pepper. Heat 1 tablespoon more oil in 12-inch ovensafe skillet over medium-high heat until just smoking. Carefully lay chicken in skillet and brown lightly on both sides, about 2 minutes per side, then transfer to plate.

3. Off heat, spread bread cubes evenly in skillet. Lay chicken on top of bread and transfer skillet to oven. Bake until breast registers 160 degrees and bread is browned in spots, 12 to 15 minutes.

4. Meanwhile, whisk remaining 6 tablespoons oil, vinegar, and ¼ teaspoon salt together in large bowl. Stir in tomatoes with their seeds and juice, beans, onion, and basil and set aside to allow flavors to develop.

5. Transfer chicken to carving board, let cool slightly, then cut into 1-inch pieces. Gently fold chicken, toasted bread cubes, and arugula into tomato mixture. Season with salt and pepper to taste, sprinkle with Parmesan, and let sit for 5 to 10 minutes before serving.

CREAMY EGG SALAD

CREAMY EGG SALAD

EGG SALAD IS ABOUT AS SIMPLE AS RECIPES COME: Mix together chopped hard-cooked eggs, mayonnaise, onion, salt, and pepper, and serve. Do you even need a recipe? Turns out you do—if you can find a good one. The five recipes I prepared were described variously as greasy, bland, watery, rubbery, and chalky. How could such a straightforward recipe be so problematic?

If I were going to fix this recipe—and I was going to fix this recipe—I would have to begin with the eggs. Starting with the test kitchen's foolproof method for hard-cooked eggs, I made two batches, covering 10 eggs (for four generous servings) with an inch of water in each pot, bringing them to a boil, then covering the pots and letting them sit off the heat for 10 minutes. I drained the eggs and chilled them in an ice bath, then peeled and chopped the eggs, finely for one batch, roughly for the other. Finally, I mixed each with ½ cup of mayonnaise and a few tablespoons of chopped onion and celery.

Tasters had strong opinions about how the eggs were chopped. When the pieces were too small, they missed the chunks of egg whites. When the eggs were too large, they complained about the chalky bits of yolk. What to do? For my next batch, I separated the yolks and whites and treated them as separate elements. I chopped the whites into ¼ inch pieces, and then finely mashed the yolks before stirring both into the mayo. I was making progress, but tasters thought the salad could be creamier. Next I tried mixing the mashed yolks directly into the mayonnaise. This new approach not only reduced the overall amount of mayonnaise needed to bind the salad, but it also helped smooth out most of the yolk bits.

But some small bits of yolk remained, and since I was after the creamiest possible egg salad, this wouldn't do. I tried an old test kitchen trick: adding boiling water to the yolks. This made the yolks ultra-smooth, but it also diluted their flavor (no surprise there). I reconsidered my cooking method. The test kitchen technique I'd been using produces perfect hard-cooked eggs, but would slightly undercooking the eggs make for creamier, smoother yolks? Yes. After a few tests, I landed on eight minutes (and an immediate bath in ice to stop the cooking) as the right cooking time for firm whites and yolks that blended easily into the mayonnaise.

I then did some final fine-tuning. Replacing the chopped onion with chives gave the salad better balance—and eliminated the onion water leached by the juicy onions. A tablespoon of Dijon mustard lent kick. Tasters wanted acid to cut the richness, so I tried a handful of different vinegars. In the end, we preferred lemon juice for its fresh taste, the same reason we liked a few pinches of minced parsley.

—CAROLYNN PURPURA, *Cook's Country*

Creamy Egg Salad

MAKES ABOUT 3½ CUPS, ENOUGH FOR 4 SANDWICHES

We prefer Hellmann's Real Mayonnaise (also known as Best Foods). You can substitute Hellmann's Light, but avoid Hellmann's Low Fat Mayonnaise. Minced scallions can be substituted for the chives.

10 large eggs
⅓ cup mayonnaise
1½ tablespoons lemon juice
1 tablespoon Dijon mustard
Salt and pepper
1 celery rib, chopped fine
2 tablespoons minced fresh chives
1 tablespoon minced fresh parsley

1. Combine 4 cups water and 4 cups ice cubes in large bowl; set aside. Place eggs in large saucepan, add water to cover by 1 inch, and bring to boil over high heat. Remove pan from heat, cover, and let stand for 8 minutes. Pour off water from saucepan and gently shake pan back and forth to crack eggshells. Transfer eggs to ice water and cool for 5 minutes.

NOTES FROM THE TEST KITCHEN

THE SECRET TO CREAMY EGG SALAD

We found the key to great egg salad was "undercooking" the eggs by two minutes and immediately shocking them in ice water (to prevent carryover cooking). This gave us a creamy yolk, which we then mashed with the mayonnaise to make a creamy "dressing" for our egg salad.

2. Peel eggs and halve lengthwise. Transfer yolks to large bowl. Using potato masher, mash yolks with mayonnaise, lemon juice, mustard, ¼ teaspoon salt, and ⅛ teaspoon pepper. Whisk mixture until smooth; set aside.

3. Chop whites into ¼-inch pieces. Fold whites, celery, chives, and parsley into yolk mixture and refrigerate for 30 minutes. Season with salt and pepper to taste. Serve. (Salad can be refrigerated for up to 2 days.)

VARIATIONS

Deviled Egg Salad

Reduce mayonnaise to ¼ cup. Replace Dijon mustard with 2 tablespoons spicy brown mustard. Add ½ teaspoon paprika and ¼ teaspoon hot sauce to egg yolk dressing in step 2. Omit celery and parsley.

Olive and Oregano Egg Salad

Omit celery, chives, and parsley. Add ¼ cup chopped pitted kalamata olives and 3 tablespoons minced fresh oregano with egg whites in step 3.

Radish and Arugula Egg Salad

Omit celery, chives, and parsley. Add ½ cup thinly sliced radishes and ½ cup chopped baby arugula with egg whites in step 3.

BEST TUNA SALAD

YOU MIGHT BE THINKING TO YOURSELF, WHAT ARE they smoking in the test kitchen? (And you don't mean ribs.) Why would anyone need a recipe for tuna salad? Because in our experience, even a simple tuna salad has its problems, from being simultaneously watery (the salad) and chalky dry (the tuna) to flavorless, drowning in mayonnaise, or overpowered by raw onion. Over several weeks of testing, I discovered a few surprising techniques that really do make a difference.

I started at the supermarket, where it seemed there were nearly as many tuna choices as fish in the sea: solid (also called fancy), chunk, or flaked; white (from albacore tuna) or light (counterintuitively from darker, stronger-tasting varieties of tuna, such as skipjack, yellowfin, or bigeye); oil or water; sodium or no; and every combination thereof. I purchased as many cans as I could carry, lugged them back to the test kitchen, and arranged a taste test. My team of tasters voted solidly for solid white tuna, with its consistently firm fish and pleasant, mild flavor. Based on our results, I started with three 5-ounce cans of solid white tuna. A little research revealed why tuna salad, despite the mayonnaise, so often tastes dry: Most brands of canned tuna have actually been cooked twice. Whole tuna are baked, boned, packed into cans, and then cooked again for up to four hours to eliminate bacteria. Manufacturers add water, oil, or sometimes vegetable broth to the can in an attempt to keep the tuna moist. In the case of water-packed tuna, this dryness was an issue.

To solve this problem, I tried dribbling oil over drained cans of tuna and letting it sit for a few minutes. The oil beaded up. The next time, I pressed the tuna dry first with a paper towel (ignoring ridicule from my colleagues). It worked (so there!), and just 2 tablespoons of oil moistened the tuna nicely. I tested both vegetable oil and olive oil, and found that the olive oil provided a nice, rich background and lush flavor.

Next I measured the mayonnaise, eventually landing on ½ cup plus 2 tablespoons; any more made the tuna salad soggy. Now that I was drying the tuna, watery tuna salad was a thing of the past. I added lemon juice, salt, pepper, and a pinch of sugar to balance the lemon. This tuna salad was—well, underwhelming. A colleague suggested that I add the seasoning with the oil and let the tuna sit for 10 minutes to pick up flavor. Amazingly, this small step really did yield a more deeply seasoned tuna salad.

The onion presented its own challenges. Scallions weren't quite the taste I sought. Chives were too mild and minced onion too strong. What if I cooked the minced onion in the olive oil I was using to marinate the tuna? I pulled out a skillet—and not only did the harsh flavor soften, but the onion infused the olive oil, which, in turn, seasoned the tuna further. Much as I liked the result, this technique was fussy for tuna salad. When I got it to work in the microwave, I relented. To finish, I added crunch to the tuna salad with minced celery.

—DIANE UNGER, *Cook's Country*

Best Tuna Salad

MAKES ABOUT 2 CUPS, ENOUGH FOR 4 SANDWICHES

We prefer Hellmann's Real Mayonnaise (also known as Best Foods).

- **3 (5-ounce) cans solid white albacore tuna packed in water**
- **¼ cup minced onion**
- **2 tablespoons olive oil**
- **2 teaspoons lemon juice**
- **½ teaspoon sugar**
- **Salt and pepper**
- **½ cup plus 2 tablespoons mayonnaise**
- **1 celery rib, minced**

1. Place tuna in fine-mesh strainer and press dry with paper towels. Transfer to medium bowl and mash with fork until finely flaked. Microwave onion and oil in small bowl until onion begins to soften, about 2 minutes. Cool slightly, about 5 minutes. Combine onion mixture, lemon juice, sugar, ½ teaspoon salt, and ½ teaspoon pepper with tuna and let sit for 10 minutes.

2. Stir mayonnaise and celery into tuna mixture. Season with salt and pepper to taste and serve. (Salad can be refrigerated for up to 1 day.)

VARIATIONS

Best Tuna Salad with Sweet Pickle and Egg

Add ¼ cup sweet pickle relish to tuna with cooked onion mixture in step 1. Stir 2 chopped hard-cooked eggs into salad in step 2.

Best Tuna Salad with Lemon and Dill

Increase lemon juice to 1 tablespoon. Add 1 tablespoon minced fresh dill and ½ teaspoon grated lemon zest to tuna with cooked onion mixture in step 1.

Best Tuna Salad with Roasted Red Peppers and Capers

Add ¼ cup finely chopped jarred roasted red peppers, patted dry, and 2 tablespoons drained and minced capers to tuna with cooked onion mixture in step 1.

NOTES FROM THE TEST KITCHEN

KEYS TO BEST TUNA SALAD

1. Pat tuna dry with paper towels to prevent watery tuna salad.

2. Microwave olive oil with minced onion to flavor oil and soften onion.

3. Marinate tuna in onion-oil mixture to season it, then stir in mayonnaise.

THE BEST CANNED TUNA

Canned tuna is a great pantry staple, but it shouldn't be mushy or bland. In past tastings, we've preferred tuna packed in cans to tuna packed in pouches (which can be mushy) and solid white albacore to "chunk light" style. We gathered eight brands of canned solid white albacore packed in water and sampled them in tuna salad sandwiches to find the best one. Though Starkist, Bumblebee, and Chicken of the Sea dominate the market, none of these came out on top. Tasters preferred **Wild Planet Wild Albacore Tuna**, which they found to be "rich and flavorful." Most large seafood producers cook their fish twice: once before it's canned, then again when it's heated inside the sealed can to kill harmful bacteria. Wild Planet, however, cooks its tuna just once, which preserves the fresh flavor and texture of the fish. It also doesn't pack tuna in any liquid, thus preventing its flavor from becoming diluted.

CHAPTER 2

SOUPS & STEWS

CREAMY GAZPACHO ANDALUZ

YOU COULD SAY THAT "AUTHENTIC" GAZPACHO IS more Old World concept than precise recipe. Centuries ago, Spanish field-workers cobbled together leftover odds and ends—yesterday's bread, almonds, garlic, olive oil, water—and mashed the whole lot together into a humble potage. (Even the term's etymology is fuzzy, though most authorities suggest it derives from words for "fragments," "remainder," and "soaked bread.") Adding a bumper crop of summer produce is a relatively recent adaptation; the tomato didn't make an appearance until explorers brought it back from the New World.

These days, just about every part of Spain prides itself on its gazpacho, but most sources still point to Andalusia, Spain's southernmost region, as the soup's home. Like the chunky, liquid-salsa interpretation popular in the States, the soup is a combination of cucumber, bell pepper, onion, and tomatoes, but bread is added (for body—and historical precedent), as well as a generous glug of extra-virgin olive oil and a bracing shot of sherry vinegar, and the whole thing is pureed in a blender. The result? A creamy, startlingly complex soup that I was determined to add to my recipe file.

I began by preparing a typical recipe, gathering 3 pounds of tomatoes along with a cucumber, a red bell pepper, and a red onion. I finely diced a portion of each vegetable, setting the miniature cubes aside to use as a colorful garnish and then roughly chopping and pureeing the remainder in a blender along with two cloves of garlic, a slice of bread softened in water, and 2 tablespoons of sherry vinegar. With the blender still running, I slowly drizzled in ½ cup of extra-virgin olive oil until the soup was smooth and emulsified. After seasoning and chilling my concoction, I ladled out samples. As my colleagues slurped away, their faces began to register the same unexcited expression. The consensus? The soup tasted so bland, it might as well have been made with just bread. I can't say that I was too surprised. Supermarket vegetables, particularly tomatoes, can be nearly tasteless.

Before I addressed the problematic tomatoes, I made some refinements to the other vegetables. Seedless English cucumbers seemed like the easy choice at first, but the test kitchen has found that they have a higher water content than regular cucumbers. Extra water would only dilute flavor, so ordinary cukes were the way to go (and scooping out seeds takes only a few seconds anyway). And while the red pepper gave the soup an attractive, bright hue, its distinct sweetness was distracting, so I swapped it for a slightly bitter green pepper. Finally, a single serrano chile added a touch of heat.

Now the tough part: the tomatoes. Those that come still attached to the vine (often labeled "vine-ripe") fared better than the beefsteaks I'd been using, but only slightly. Expensive tomatoes packed in plastic clamshells or individual protective foam wrappers were equally unimpressive, leaving tasters cold. I even blended up a batch using canned tomatoes (which are packed when ripe), but the hallmark of the soup—bright, fresh flavor—was absent.

Why are supermarket tomatoes so consistently disappointing? To withstand the rigors of travel, the fruit is picked when still hard and green. It is then treated with ethylene gas, which accelerates ripening. These tomatoes are bright red and thus look ripe, but they lack the deep, sweet flavor that develops only in true vine-ripened fruit.

Looking for solutions to my tomato conundrum, I stepped out of the test kitchen and into the library for some research into the science of taste. What makes one tomato taste more tomatoey than another? It has to do with microscopic flavor molecules that stimulate taste buds. The more of these molecules that are exposed to your tongue, the stronger the signal to the brain, and the more intense the flavor experience. My faux-ripened tomatoes clearly had fewer of these molecules than real vine-ripened specimens. An even bigger problem was that any flavor molecules that a hard, unripe tomato does have are trapped within its firm cell structure, bound to proteins, and can't be tasted. The key to improving the taste of an inferior supermarket tomato, it seemed, would be to burst those cells.

My first thought: Forget coaxing and start with brute force. I cranked my blender to its highest setting, letting a batch of tomatoes whirl for a full five minutes, then eagerly dipped my spoon in for a taste. No luck—the mixture was bland and watery with only a hint of tomato flavor. Our science editor conjectured that even after vigorous blending, most of the flavor molecules were still clinging to proteins, making them

CREAMY GAZPACHO ANDALUZ

unavailable to taste and smell. He suggested a different approach: salting.

Curious about what effect something as simple as salting could have on freeing up flavor molecules, I chopped 2 pounds of tomatoes and tossed them with 1½ teaspoons of kosher salt. An hour later, the tomatoes were swimming in juice. I then pureed these salted specimens along with their exuded liquid. As a control, I also pureed 2 pounds of unsalted chopped tomatoes, stirring in 1½ teaspoons of salt after blending. To my surprise, the salted puree boasted a deep, full flavor; the control paled in comparison. Figuring the same process could only improve the cucumbers, onions, and bell peppers, I made another batch in which I salted them as well, yielding my finest soup yet. It turns out that salt pulls out water-soluble flavor compounds as it forces the proteins to separate from the flavor molecules, releasing more flavor.

Then I thought of one more way to maximize flavor. I'd been soaking the bread for the soup in water. Wouldn't it make better sense to use the exuded vegetable liquid? After salting the vegetables, I put them in a strainer set over a bowl to collect their juices, which I then reserved to soak the bread. Sure enough, this soup tasted even better, especially when I took care to properly season it with more salt before serving. In addition to the diced-vegetable garnish, I gussied up each bowl with sprinkles of minced fresh herbs (parsley, chives, and basil all worked well) and ground black pepper plus more extra-virgin olive oil and sherry vinegar.

Who knew that with a bit of salt and time, even supermarket vegetables could give the best gazpacho a run for its money?

—J. KENJI LOPEZ-ALT, *Cook's Illustrated*

Creamy Gazpacho Andaluz

SERVES 4 TO 6

For ideal flavor, allow the gazpacho to sit in the refrigerator overnight before serving. Red wine vinegar can be substituted for the sherry vinegar. Although we prefer to use kosher salt in this soup, half the amount of table salt can be used. Serve the soup with additional extra-virgin olive oil, sherry vinegar, pepper, and diced vegetables for diners to season and garnish their own bowls as desired.

3 pounds (8 medium) ripe tomatoes, cored
1 small cucumber, peeled, halved lengthwise, and seeded
1 green bell pepper, stemmed, halved, and seeded
1 small red onion, halved
2 garlic cloves, peeled and quartered
1 small serrano chile, stemmed and halved lengthwise
Kosher salt
1 slice hearty white sandwich bread, crust removed, torn into 1-inch pieces
½ cup extra-virgin olive oil, plus extra for serving
2 tablespoons sherry vinegar, plus extra for serving
2 tablespoons finely minced fresh parsley, chives, or basil
Pepper

1. Roughly chop 2 pounds tomatoes, half of cucumber, half of bell pepper, and half of onion and place in large bowl. Add garlic, chile, and 1½ teaspoons salt and toss to combine.

2. Cut remaining 1 pound tomatoes, cucumber, and bell pepper into ¼-inch dice and place in medium bowl. Mince remaining onion and add to diced vegetables. Toss with ½ teaspoon salt and transfer to fine-mesh strainer set over medium bowl. Let drain for 1 hour. Transfer drained diced vegetables to medium bowl and set aside, reserving exuded liquid (there should be about ¼ cup; discard extra liquid).

3. Add bread pieces to exuded liquid and soak for 1 minute. Add soaked bread and any remaining liquid to roughly chopped vegetables and toss thoroughly to combine.

4. Transfer half of vegetable-bread mixture to blender and process for 30 seconds. With blender running, slowly drizzle in ¼ cup oil and continue to blend until completely smooth, about 2 minutes. Strain soup through fine-mesh strainer into large bowl, using back of ladle or rubber spatula to press soup through strainer. Repeat with remaining vegetable-bread mixture and ¼ cup olive oil.

5. Stir vinegar, parsley, and half of diced vegetables into soup and season with salt and pepper to taste. Cover and refrigerate overnight or for at least 2 hours to chill completely and develop flavors. Serve, passing remaining diced vegetables and additional olive oil, sherry vinegar, and pepper separately.

KOREAN SPICY BEEF SOUP

THE KEY COMPONENTS OF THE KOREAN SOUP called *yukgaejang* are as follows: fall-apart-tender beef brisket, lots of hot red pepper, and an ample dose of scallions. This intensely spicy soup exemplifies the philosophy of "fight fire with fire"; it is served in the winter to combat the cold, and it also encourages sweating to cool off on the hottest summer days. Although recipes I found varied in ingredient lists, some calling for obscure additions such as fernbrake (an edible fern), sweet potato noodles, and tripe, as well as more familiar Asian ingredients such as bean sprouts, egg, and soy sauce, I thought it would be simple enough to re-create this fiery soup in the test kitchen.

I soon came across a few roadblocks. First of all, in most of the recipes the brisket was simmered by itself for several hours before being shredded and continuing to cook with the soup for an additional half-hour or so. While I wasn't demanding a quick soup (brisket takes some time to get tender), I also didn't want to be standing over a pot all day. Second, although not all recipes called for tripe and fernbrake, they all relied on Korean red pepper powder, a specialty product that not everyone can find easily. I set out to come up with a streamlined version of this fiery Korean soup that would cook in little over an hour and rely—if possible—solely on supermarket ingredients.

I first addressed the cooking liquid and the beef. Some recipes start with a homemade broth, and others start with water, but either way, the brisket is then simmered in the liquid for a few hours before being removed, shredded, and returned to the pot to cook with the other ingredients. The water method was appealingly easy, but the resulting broth was weak and, not surprisingly, watery. Clearly water was not a sufficient cooking liquid for this recipe; however, making a broth from scratch was contrary to my time-saving mission. Plus, for a soup with such bold heat and seasonings, a homemade broth seemed unnecessary.

Therefore, I started with store-bought broth and focused on boosting its flavor. I knew that sautéed aromatics would help, but to get deep flavor, I decided to depart from the traditional recipes for this soup and brown the brisket in oil before adding any liquid to the pot. This step took only a few minutes, but the resulting fond, or flavorful browned bits, packed the broth with rich, slow-cooked flavor. To further save time, I opted to forgo cooking the brisket whole in favor of cutting it into thin strips that would replicate the shape of the shredded beef in the original dish. These small pieces cooked much faster, and their increased surface area maximized browning and therefore flavor.

After browning the beef in a Dutch oven, I set it aside and sautéed some onion and a generous amount of garlic—six cloves. I then added the store-bought broth (a combination of chicken and beef broth produced the most balanced flavor) and brought it to a simmer before returning the beef to the pot. With this method, I had tender, perfectly cooked brisket in only an hour. Plus, I could skip the step of fishing the meat out of the hot broth to shred it into bite-size pieces.

When it came to seasoning, it was paramount that I find a substitute for Korean red pepper powder. Although referred to as "powder," the type of Korean red pepper powder that is commonly used for cooking actually has a consistency somewhere between that of cayenne pepper and red pepper flakes. It doesn't contain the seeds of the peppers and has a milder heat and sweeter pepper flavor than either cayenne or pepper flakes. Most recipes that I found for this soup required several tablespoons of the powder. Using a lesser amount of cayenne or pepper flakes gave me a soup with comparable heat, but it lacked the pepper flavor and deep color. After some experimentation, I settled upon a combination of 1 tablespoon of red pepper flakes (for heat) and 3 tablespoons of sweet paprika (for pepper flavor and color). In addition to a tablespoon of soy sauce, 2 tablespoons of toasted sesame oil rounded out the flavors. I found it best to add the seasonings to the soup during the last 20 minutes of cooking. This way their flavors had time to meld but their brightness wasn't dulled.

The major components of my soup decided, I looked at other ingredients I'd come across in my research. After some testing, I decided that the slightly exotic additions of fernbrake, sweet potato noodles, and Korean radish were unnecessary, but a generous quantity (two bunches) of scallions was crucial, providing a freshness that offset the heat of the soup. I found it best to cut the

NOTES FROM THE TEST KITCHEN

HOW TO CUT BRISKET FOR SOUP

1. Cut brisket, against grain, into 1½-inch-wide strips.

2. Holding knife parallel to cutting board, slice each strip of meat into 2 thin pieces.

3. Slice each thin strip crosswise into thin strips.

THE BEEFIEST BEEF BROTH

In the past, we've found beef broths to be light on beefy flavor, but with a few flavor additives, beef broth can pull off a deeply flavorful soup or stew. We gathered 13 beef stocks, broths, and reconstituted bases to find out which one could stand in for homemade. We tasted them plain, then the top eight were sampled in French onion soup and gravy. What did we find? Generally, you should note the ingredients on the label; we found that the best broths had flavor-amplifying ingredients, such as yeast extract and tomato paste, near the top of the list. Our winner, **Rachael Ray Stock-in-a-Box All-Natural Beef Flavored Stock**, also included concentrated beef stock, which is made with twice as much fresh meat as beef stock, the primary ingredient in the runners-up. Tasters found that the winning broth boasted a "steak-y" flavor and "thick" body. (See page 292 for more information about our testing results.)

scallions into 2-inch lengths and add them to the soup with the seasonings. Many recipes included bean sprouts and wisped egg; tasters liked both. To incorporate the egg, I mixed it with a small amount of cornstarch to stabilize the proteins before stirring the mixture into the hot soup, resulting in wispy, soft ribbons. The bean sprouts were best added just before serving to maintain their crunchy texture.

My soup had the bracing heat, deep brick red color, and distinct pepper flavor of the real thing, and tasters were surprised to learn it contained no Korean red pepper or other specialty ingredients. Although this soup may be meant for extreme weather, my recipe is easy and flavorful enough that I'll be making it year-round.

—ADELAIDE PARKER, *America's Test Kitchen Books*

Korean Spicy Beef Soup

SERVES 6 TO 8

To make slicing the beef easier, freeze it for 15 minutes. This soup is very spicy; for a less spicy soup, reduce the quantity of red pepper flakes. Serve with Basic White Rice (page 40), if desired.

SOUP

- **1 pound beef brisket, trimmed and cut into thin strips**
- **Salt and pepper**
- **2 tablespoons vegetable oil**
- **1 onion, chopped**
- **6 garlic cloves, minced**
- **4 cups low-sodium chicken broth**
- **4 cups beef broth**
- **3 tablespoons sweet paprika**
- **2 tablespoons toasted sesame oil**
- **1 tablespoon red pepper flakes**
- **1 tablespoon soy sauce**
- **2 bunches scallions, cut into 2-inch pieces**

EGG AND BEAN SPROUTS

- **1 teaspoon water**
- **½ teaspoon cornstarch**
- **1 large egg**
- **2 cups bean sprouts**

1. FOR THE SOUP: Pat beef dry with paper towels and season with salt and pepper. Heat 2 teaspoons oil in Dutch oven over medium-high heat until just smoking. Add half of meat and cook, stirring occasionally, until well browned, 5 to 7 minutes. Transfer browned beef to medium bowl. Repeat with 2 teaspoons more oil and remaining beef; transfer to bowl.

2. Add remaining 2 teaspoons oil to pot and place over medium heat until shimmering. Add onion and cook until softened, 5 to 7 minutes. Stir in garlic and cook until fragrant, about 30 seconds. Stir in chicken broth, beef broth, and browned meat with any accumulated juice. Bring to boil, cover, reduce to gentle simmer, and cook for 45 minutes.

3. Stir in paprika, sesame oil, pepper flakes, soy sauce, and scallions, cover partially (leaving pot open by about 1 inch), and simmer gently until beef is tender, 15 to 25 minutes. Remove soup from heat (do not let it cool) and season with salt to taste.

4. FOR THE EGG AND BEAN SPROUTS: Whisk water and cornstarch together in small bowl, then whisk in egg until combined. Use a spoon to slowly drizzle very thin streams of egg mixture into hot soup in circular motion. Without stirring soup, let it continue to sit off heat for 1 minute.

5. Briefly return soup to simmer over medium-high heat without stirring, then remove from heat immediately. Gently stir in bean sprouts and serve immediately.

CHICKEN AND SLICKS

MANY REGIONS PUT THEIR OWN STAMP ON CHICKEN and dumplings. The Appalachian version is chicken and "slicks." The slicks are made from flour, lard (or oil), and water; leavener rarely sneaks in. The dough is rolled out, cut into fat noodles, and dropped into simmering chicken stew. The late Cissy Gregg, food columnist for the *Louisville Courier-Journal* in the 1940s and 1950s, distinguished fluffy, leavened "pillows" from slicks, or "sad flats," as she termed them. "Those who call fat bits of fluff-duff with stewed chicken by the name of dumplings are one kind of people, while those who make slick dumplings to go with their chicken are another kind."

We're not sure which kind of folks we are, but one thing we are sure of: We love chicken and slicks. (The name, by the way, refers to the fact that the cooked dumplings are slippery, says Mark Sohn in *Appalachian Home Cooking: History, Culture, & Recipes.*) To make the dish, pieces of chicken, or sometimes the whole bird, are poached in water. The cook then removes and shreds the cooked chicken and returns it to the pot with noodles that she's made while the chicken was simmering. The slicks should be tender with just the slightest bit of chew, and the broth lies partway between a soup and a stew—more body than the former, less than the latter—and has intense chicken-y flavor and a nice peppery kick. This simple dish, by the way, gives the cold shoulder to vegetables (mostly): It's made up of chicken, slicks, a bit of onion, and homey goodness, period.

Because this dish relies on chicken for just about all its flavor, the recipes I tested using modern (read: mild to the point of bland) supermarket birds were disappointing. Without free-range, older, tastier chickens at my disposal, I would have to figure out another way to deepen flavors. A second challenge lay in getting the texture of both broth and noodles right. I headed into the test kitchen and began assembling ingredients and pots and pans.

Using chicken broth as the basis for the stew in place of water was a no-brainer. In Appalachia back in the day, I doubt that canned chicken broth was in the pantry, but I had it, and I'd use it. Instantly, both stew and chicken had more depth. Rather than simply throwing the chicken parts into the simmering broth, I browned them first, to boost the flavor further. (I used both white and dark meat to please fanciers of each, and bone-in for best flavor.) The savory bits (fond) that stuck to the pot went into my broth, fortifying its flavor—but not until I'd taken the opportunity to sauté a chopped onion in the fat, for (you guessed it) yet more savory flavor, and to add flour, for thickening. I discarded the chicken skin—its work was done—and only now tossed the chicken pieces into the broth. I also opted to add thyme and a couple of bay leaves; neither violated the simple spirit of chicken and slicks, and both supplied needed seasoning.

For the sake of simplicity, I was making the dough for the slicks in the food processor, combining water, oil (instead of lard, which most of us don't keep around), flour, and salt, and then kneading the dough briefly before forming the slicks. Obviously, the water added no flavor, so in its place I tried chicken broth. This improvement led me to an even better idea: I set aside some of the rendered chicken fat (from browning the meat) and added that to the dough, too.

Now the dumplings had loads of flavor, and I should have let well enough alone. But I'd seen a couple of recipes that called for baking powder and a few that abhorred its use; one even branded it "scandalous." I was curious (as I'm paid to be). I don't know if baking powder rises to the level of a scandal, but it did make the slicks spongy. After one test, I abandoned it.

I rolled and cut the slicks and then dropped them into the simmering, thickening chicken broth–flour base for about 15 minutes. When the noodles failed to cook through in the thick, soupy base, I turned up the heat. They broke apart. What if, instead of adding the flour to the stew at the start, I made a slurry of flour and chicken broth, set it aside so I could cook the slicks in thin, simmering broth, and added the slurry back at the end? This time, the slicks cooked perfectly, but the base tasted like raw flour. I brought the liquid to a boil to cook out the floury taste and—whoops—the slicks blew out again. A colleague suggested that I make the slurry with toasted flour (heating it in a pot until its color changed). That did it: The dish had no floury taste, and the slicks were mostly intact.

Mostly—there was the rub. To nudge "mostly" to "entirely," I chilled the slicks before cooking them and noticed a slight improvement. To better my odds, I froze them. This time, the slicks were savory, tender, and shapely. Even just 10 minutes in the freezer had firmed and dehydrated the dough (some of the liquid evaporating, some soaked up by the starch) so that the slicks held up in the simmering broth. To finish, I added the chunks of moist chicken back into the golden broth, stirred in a handful of parsley, and watched as cooks battled to snag bowls of the homey, cheering, and wholly delicious stew.

—LYNN CLARK, *Cook's Country*

Chicken and Slicks

SERVES 4 TO 6

If you're short on chicken fat at the end of step 1, supplement it with vegetable oil.

- **1½ pounds bone-in chicken thighs, trimmed**
- **1½ pounds bone-in split chicken breasts, trimmed, halved crosswise**
- **Salt and pepper**
- **2 cups plus 6 tablespoons all-purpose flour**
- **3 tablespoons vegetable oil**
- **1 onion, chopped**
- **2 teaspoons minced fresh thyme**
- **7½ cups low-sodium chicken broth**
- **2 bay leaves**
- **¼ cup minced fresh parsley**

1. Pat chicken dry with paper towels and season with salt and pepper. Toast 6 tablespoons flour in Dutch oven over medium heat, stirring constantly, until just beginning to brown, about 5 minutes. Transfer flour to medium bowl and wipe out pot. Heat 1 tablespoon oil in now-empty Dutch oven over medium-high heat until just smoking. Cook chicken until well browned on both sides, about 10 minutes; transfer to plate. When chicken is cool enough to handle, remove and discard skin. Pour fat (you should have about 2 tablespoons) into small bowl; set aside.

2. Add onion and 1 tablespoon more oil to now-empty pot and cook over medium heat until softened, about 5 minutes. Stir in thyme and cook until fragrant, about 30 seconds. Add 7 cups broth, chicken, and bay leaves and bring to boil. Reduce heat to low and simmer, covered, until breasts register 160 degrees and thighs register 175 degrees, 20 to 25 minutes. Remove from heat and transfer chicken to clean plate; remove and discard bay leaves. When chicken is cool enough to handle, shred into bite-size pieces and set aside, discarding bones.

3. Meanwhile, combine remaining ½ cup chicken broth, reserved fat, and remaining 1 tablespoon oil in liquid measuring cup. Process remaining 2 cups flour and ½ teaspoon salt in food processor until combined. With machine running, slowly pour in broth mixture and process until mixture resembles coarse meal. Turn dough onto lightly floured counter and knead until

CHICKEN AND SLICKS

smooth. Divide in half. (Dough can be wrapped in plastic wrap and refrigerated for up to 1 day; let sit at room temperature for 15 minutes before proceeding with step 4.)

4. Roll each dough half into 10-inch square. Cut each square into twenty 5 by 1-inch rectangles. Place handful of noodles in single layer on parchment paper–lined plate, cover with another sheet of parchment, and repeat stacking with remaining noodles and additional parchment, ending with parchment. Freeze until firm, at least 10 minutes or up to 30 minutes.

5. Return broth to simmer and add noodles. Cook until noodles are nearly tender, 12 to 15 minutes, stirring occasionally to separate. Remove 1 cup broth from pot and whisk into reserved toasted flour. Stir broth-flour mixture into pot, being careful not to break up noodles, and simmer until slightly thickened, 3 to 5 minutes. Add shredded chicken and parsley and cook until heated through, about 1 minute. Season with salt and pepper to taste. Serve.

NOTES FROM THE TEST KITCHEN

MAKING SLICKS

1. After kneading dough briefly, roll each dough half into 10-inch square of ⅛-inch thickness.

2. Using sharp knife or pizza wheel, cut dough into 5 by 1-inch rectangles.

3. Stack slicks between layers of parchment paper and freeze briefly before simmering.

BRAZILIAN FISH STEW WITH COCONUT MILK

BRAZIL IS HOME TO A HOST OF CELEBRATED FISH stews. Of these traditional offerings, none is more beloved and respected than *moqueca* (pronounced moh-KEH-kah), a mix of local white fish, tomatoes, onions, cilantro, and coconut milk. Cooked in a thick, covered pot made of black clay and mangrove tree sap, moqueca is undeniably Brazilian and deeply satisfying. While there are countless variations on moqueca, two regions lay claim to the stew's origin: Bahia in the northeast of Brazil and Espírito Santo in the south. *Moqueca baiana* (from Bahia) is a decidedly earthy, spicy rendition that employs a liberal amount of an unrefined, pulpy palm oil called *dendê* and includes sliced peppers in the aromatic mix. Hailing from Espírito Santo, *moqueca capixaba* eschews dendê in favor of olive oil and offers a cleaner, more nuanced expression of the sea. After a visit to a local Brazilian restaurant, where I was able to try both styles side by side, I knew I wanted to develop an authentic recipe for the lighter moqueca capixaba. Without a clay pot or easy access to traditional ingredients, I had my work cut out for me in bringing this Brazilian national treasure stateside.

Traditional moqueca capixaba starts with heating a clay pot (the size of which depends upon the number of diners) over an open flame. Olive oil is then added, along with a generous amount of chopped onion, tomato, and cilantro. Once these aromatics become slightly softened, firm white fish is added, followed by another layer of onion, tomato, and cilantro. The pot is then covered with a hot clay lid and allowed to stew and bubble away until the fish is just cooked through. When the lid is removed, the flaky white fish is sitting in a substantial broth of its own juice, infused with the heady aroma of cilantro and onion. A splash of coconut milk is then added and allowed to briefly simmer and meld with the fish broth. Brought to the table with white rice and a thick hot pepper sauce, this stew can be transcendent. Unfortunately, as I found while researching recipes, it can also be cloyingly sweet, harsh-tasting, and even bland. Vowing to create a stew worthy of moqueca's reputation, I ordered some fish and headed into the kitchen.

In Brazil, the fish of choice for moqueca is a type of sand perch. Favored for its firm, mild white flesh, the fish releases considerable juice as it cooks, eliminating the need to add broth to the moqueca pot. While I had plenty of firm white fish available to me, none of the species I tested released nearly enough juice to make a moqueca of the proper consistency. Resigned to the fact that I would need to add some liquid to the pot, I chose my fish based on taste and texture alone. Haddock, cod, halibut, striped bass, and hake all received high marks, gently flaking into tender pieces as they cooked. In the end, haddock won for its slightly superior texture and sweeter flavor. I knew that larger pieces of fish were less likely to dissolve into tiny flakes when cooked in liquid, so I cut the fillets into sizable 3-inch pieces. By the time they were cooked through, the fillets had separated into hearty chunks that tasters liked. With the fish component settled, I started to build my moqueca.

Without a local source for black clay pots, I looked around the test kitchen for an alternative that would deliver a comparable kind of even heat and settled on a Dutch oven. Usually crafted from thick, enameled cast iron, Dutch ovens absorb and conduct heat in much the same way as a thick clay pot—albeit slightly faster. To my new moqueca vessel I added a splash of olive oil and a generous amount of chopped tomatoes, onion, and cilantro leaves. Once they were softened and fragrant, I added my seasoned fish fillets and another layer of this same aromatic mix. To compensate for the lack of moisture in my native fish, I added a couple of cups of water, brought everything to a simmer, and threw on the lid. After about five minutes of gentle simmering, I removed the lid, added a can of coconut milk, and let the flavors blend while the fish cooked through. While the aroma of this stew had tasters' mouths watering, the flavor and consistency left much to be desired. The broth, which was overly sweet and creamy, featured little fish flavor. In addition, the stew was pockmarked with bits of raw-tasting onion that overpowered the flavor of tomato and cilantro. I decided to tackle the broth issues first.

The 2 cups of water were providing ample cooking liquid for the fish but, unfortunately, little else. It was clear that we needed a more flavorful replacement. Given that I needed only 2 cups of liquid, and that this stew takes just minutes to cook, preparing fish broth from scratch was out of the question. Searching for a quicker way to infuse my moqueca with briny depth, I looked to bottled clam juice. Substituting 1 cup of clam juice for 1 cup of the water was good, but switching to all clam juice was even better. I then looked at scaling back the coconut milk. While the recipes I had consulted suggested using at least a full can of the creamy stuff, this had produced a heavy, one-dimensional stew. To find the right balance, I started with just ¼ cup of coconut milk and slowly added more until tasters were pleased. At ¾ cup, the resulting broth was slightly sweet and rich, but not creamy, offering subtle, supporting flavor. With my broth in order, I targeted the tomato, onion, and cilantro.

Often seen as simply supporting characters that should dissolve into the background, aromatics take center stage in moqueca. Chopped coarse and added in two stages, they provide depth of flavor and freshness, as well as contrasting textures. To correct the raw bits of onion that tasters complained about, I cut it smaller, finely chopping it instead. Now the onions softened just enough to provide freshness, without a harsh finish. To bump up the cilantro flavor, I took a page from many South American cuisines and chopped both the leaves and the stems together. Cut this way, the cilantro provided great flavor and even better texture. Tasters preferred the freshness of raw cilantro, so I reserved the second addition to finish the soup. Finally, I addressed the accompaniments.

Along with white rice, moqueca is often served with a creamy, vinegary pepper sauce made from native malagueta peppers packed in olive oil. Unable to find malagueta or any other peppers packed in olive oil at my local market, I looked to other options. With a wide range of hot peppers preserved in vinegar available to me, it made sense to start there. I pureed vinegar-preserved jalapeños, banana peppers, and hot cherry peppers with olive oil and salt. Tasters unanimously preferred the batch made with hot cherry peppers for its robust pepper flavor and heat. To balance the vinegar and spice, I added a little onion and sugar to the mix. Dolloped onto a serving of moqueca and rice, my creamy pepper sauce was the crowning jewel on this robust dish. Sans clay pot or Brazilian heritage, I had managed to create an inspired, authentic-tasting version of one of the world's truly great fish stews.

—DAN SOUZA, *America's Test Kitchen Books*

Brazilian Fish Stew with Coconut Milk

SERVES 6 TO 8

Pickled hot cherry peppers are usually sold jarred, next to the pickles or jarred roasted red peppers at the supermarket. Serve with Basic White Rice (page 40).

PEPPER SAUCE

- **4 pickled hot cherry peppers (3 ounces), stemmed, seeded, and chopped coarse**
- **½ cup coarsely chopped onion**
- **¼ cup olive oil**
- **⅛ teaspoon sugar**
- **Salt**

STEW

- **2 tablespoons olive oil**
- **1¼ pounds plum tomatoes, cored and cut into ½-inch pieces**
- **2 onions, chopped fine**
- **1 cup coarsely chopped fresh cilantro leaves and stems**
- **3 pounds skinless haddock fillets, ¾ to 1 inch thick, cut into 3- to 4-inch pieces**
- **Salt and pepper**
- **2 (8-ounce) bottles clam juice**
- **¾ cup coconut milk**

1. FOR THE PEPPER SAUCE: Process peppers, onion, oil, and sugar together in food processor until smooth. Season with salt to taste and set aside.

2. FOR THE STEW: Heat oil in Dutch oven over medium-high heat until shimmering. Add half of tomatoes, half of onions, and half of cilantro and cook until vegetables are softened, 5 to 7 minutes.

3. Pat fish dry with paper towels and season with salt and pepper. Place fish on top of softened vegetables and sprinkle remaining tomatoes and onions over top. Add clam juice and bring to gentle simmer. Cover and simmer gently, stirring gently a few times, until fish is almost cooked through, about 4 minutes.

4. Add coconut milk and continue to simmer gently until fish is just cooked through, 1 to 2 minutes longer. Sprinkle with remaining cilantro and season with salt and pepper to taste. Serve, passing pepper sauce separately.

VARIATION

Brazilian Fish and Shrimp Stew with Coconut Milk

Reduce haddock to 2 pounds. Add 8 ounces peeled and deveined large shrimp (31 to 40 per pound) to stew with coconut milk.

GUMBO

PEEK INTO A POT OF GUMBO, AND YOU'LL SEE THE influence of the many groups who have settled in New Orleans. The base, a roux, arrived with the French; smoked sausage was brought by Germans and Acadians (from northeastern Canada); and the piquant peppers tagged along with the Spanish. Okra came from Africa, and ground sassafras (filé powder) was used by Native Americans. Many Louisiana natives fondly remember waking up to the smell of cooking roux, which Mom would stir for hours over low heat until it was chocolate-colored. Aromatic vegetables were stirred in, then homemade stock, and finally the meat: Poultry, sausage, game, and seafood are all traditional. The process takes the better part of an afternoon—but time is not the only problem. There's also what New Orleans chef Paul Prudhomme refers to as "Cajun napalm."

Roux is made by cooking equal parts fat and flour until colored. Light roux is the base of many cheese sauces and gravies, but dark roux is used almost exclusively in Cajun and Creole cooking. To achieve the requisite dark brown color and toasted flavor, the flour and fat (usually vegetable oil today) are cooked over low heat for a bare minimum of 30 minutes (and often more than an hour). But dark roux not only requires time, it practically requires a hazmat suit. To avoid burning the flour, the cook must stir constantly, and even over low heat, temperatures in the pot can reach 500 degrees—one splatter and you're reaching for the burn cream. Worse, after a steady hour of stirring, the roux can go from toasty brown to burnt in seconds. Is it any wonder some cooks have been scared off making gumbo at all? But hey, if the long-suffering New Orleans Saints could win the Super Bowl, surely I could find an easier, safer, quicker way to make an authentic-tasting gumbo.

My testing started with a handful of recipes for "faster" roux. Those that didn't give the roux time to darken made for insipid gumbo. Others, like Prudhomme's version, turned up the heat to accelerate the process, with explosive and scary results. I did find one unusual recipe, though, that offered the promise of both ease and safety. Three-quarters of a cup each of flour and vegetable oil were mixed together in a large pot and moved to a 350-degree oven to cook—sans stirring—for just under two hours. This hands-off roux sounded too good to be true. The same recipe called for homemade shrimp stock, so before getting started on the gumbo, I painstakingly peeled a pound of shrimp and simmered the shells with onion and peppercorns. When, some two hours later, I peered into the pot, my jaw went slack: The roux looked (and smelled) perfect. The closed lid and gentle heat had provided the perfect no-stir environment for it to brown. How would it hold up in the gumbo?

Traditional gumbos start with sautéing onion, celery, green bell pepper, and garlic in the dark roux, and mine would be no exception. Thyme and cayenne pepper were essential seasonings. For the chicken, I turned to dark-meat thighs because of their rich flavor. Simmering them in the gumbo for 30 minutes before chopping the meat and returning it to the pot ensured that the meat stayed moist. As for tomatoes and okra, Louisianians either love 'em or loathe 'em in gumbo. I included both on the basis of the "more is more" theory. Finally, stirring in the spicy andouille sausage, okra, and shrimp at the end kept them from overcooking. When the gumbo was done, I was amazed at the rich, toasty, silky taste. The oven roux had worked. But don't cue the singing angels just yet: It wasn't as speedy as I'd hoped.

Cranking up the oven temperature shortened the cooking time, but at a cost: The roux required stirring or it scorched. Starting the roux on the stovetop before placing it in the oven would require high heat and constant stirring, so I ruled it out. I did try heating the oil on the stovetop before stirring in flour and moving it to the oven, but the splattering made it messy and dangerous. What about toasting just the flour in a dry pot on the stove? After five minutes (yes, I had to stir) the flour began to brown, so I added the oil and put the pot in the oven. Forty-five minutes later, the roux was beautifully dark brown, and it made a gumbo with toasted, smoky flavor. Meanwhile, I had time to prepare the other ingredients. I fine-tuned the roux, which was a tad thin and greasy, by cutting back the oil by ¼ cup and adding a tablespoon of flour.

I had been making my own shrimp stock, but peeling a pound of shrimp and then simmering and straining stock were neither fast nor easy. I switched to store-bought chicken broth, but it lacked the rich, briny depth of the shrimp stock. Would mixing the broth with clam juice do the trick? Nope—this also lacked complexity and punch. In the test kitchen, we sometimes add a slug of soy sauce or Worcestershire sauce to give depth and richness to stews and sauces, so I made two gumbos and added soy sauce to one and Worcestershire to the other. These improved the taste, but I still missed the shrimp flavor. Then I had an idea I hoped just might be crazy enough to work: adding Asian fish sauce, which is complex, intensely flavored, and made from fish. I snuck some into my next batch without telling tasters, and they unanimously agreed that this gumbo was the best yet; the fish sauce added briny depth without being identifiable. Sure, some may view it as heretical to authentic gumbo. I prefer to look at it as yet another culture stirred into an already diverse pot.

—LYNN CLARK, *Cook's Country*

NOTES FROM THE TEST KITCHEN

A SAFER, FASTER, EASIER ROUX—IN THE OVEN

Traditionally, long-cooked roux gives gumbo its toasty depth, but it requires constant stirring and carries the danger of splatter burns. We developed a quicker and safer alternative by pretoasting the flour and moving the roux from the stovetop to the oven. After 45 minutes in the oven, the roux is deep brown (the shade of an old copper penny), fragrant, and ready to be used in gumbo.

SECRET INGREDIENT: FISH SAUCE

Widely used throughout Asia, this potent seasoning is made from salted, fermented fish. It lends depth and complexity to our gumbo in a fraction of the time it would take to make shrimp stock. In a tasting of different brands, we preferred Thai Kitchen, but all sauces were acceptable in our recipe for gumbo. If you have a choice of brands, buy the one with the least sodium.

Gumbo

SERVES 6 TO 8

This recipe is engineered for efficiency: Get the roux into the oven and then prep the remaining ingredients. A heavy, cast-iron Dutch oven yields the fastest oven roux. If a lightweight pot is all you have, increase the oven time by 10 minutes. The chicken broth must be at room temperature to prevent lumps from forming. Fish sauce lends an essential savory quality. It can be found with the Asian ingredients at the supermarket, but if you can't find it, substitute ¼ cup soy sauce combined with 4 minced anchovy fillets; add the soy-anchovy mixture with the garlic in step 2. Since the salt content of fish sauce varies among brands, taste the finished gumbo before seasoning with salt.

- **¾ cup plus 1 tablespoon all-purpose flour**
- **½ cup vegetable oil**
- **1 onion, chopped fine**
- **1 green bell pepper, stemmed, seeded, and chopped**
- **1 celery rib, minced**
- **5 garlic cloves, minced**
- **1 teaspoon minced fresh thyme**
- **¼ teaspoon cayenne pepper**
- **1 (14.5-ounce) can diced tomatoes, drained**
- **3¾ cups low-sodium chicken broth, room temperature**
- **¼ cup fish sauce**
- **2 pounds bone-in chicken thighs, skin removed, trimmed**
- **Salt and pepper**
- **8 ounces andouille sausage, halved lengthwise and sliced thin**
- **2 cups frozen okra, thawed (optional)**
- **2 pounds extra-large shrimp (21 to 25 per pound), peeled and deveined**

1. Adjust oven rack to lowest position and heat oven to 350 degrees. Toast ¾ cup flour in Dutch oven on stovetop over medium heat, stirring constantly, until just beginning to brown, about 5 minutes. Off heat, whisk in oil until smooth. Cover, transfer pot to oven, and cook until mixture is deep brown and fragrant, about 45 minutes. (Roux can be refrigerated for up to 1 week. To proceed, heat in Dutch oven over medium-high heat, whisking constantly, until just smoking, and continue with step 2.)

2. Transfer Dutch oven to stovetop and whisk cooked roux to combine. Add onion, bell pepper, and celery and cook over medium heat, stirring frequently, until softened, about 10 minutes. Stir in remaining 1 tablespoon flour, garlic, thyme, and cayenne and cook until fragrant, about 1 minute. Add tomatoes and cook until dry, about 1 minute. Slowly whisk in broth and fish sauce until smooth. Season chicken with pepper. Add chicken to pot and bring to boil.

3. Reduce heat to medium-low and simmer, covered, until chicken is tender, about 30 minutes. Skim fat and transfer chicken to plate. When chicken is cool enough to handle, cut into bite-size pieces and return to pot; discard bones. (Gumbo can be refrigerated for up to 3 days. To serve, bring to simmer, covered, in Dutch oven; remove lid and proceed with recipe.)

4. Stir in sausage and okra, if using, and simmer until heated through, about 5 minutes. Add shrimp and simmer until cooked through, about 5 minutes. Season with salt and pepper to taste. Serve. (Gumbo can be refrigerated for up to 1 day.)

Basic White Rice

SERVES 6 TO 8

White rice is the traditional accompaniment for gumbo. Rinsing the rice, which removes much of the exterior starch, produces the lightest, fluffiest result. Lundberg Organic Long-Grain White Rice is the test kitchen's top-rated brand.

- **2 cups jasmine or long-grain white rice**
- **1 tablespoon unsalted butter**
- **3 cups water**
- **1 teaspoon salt**

1. Place rice in fine-mesh strainer set over large bowl. Rinse under running water until water runs clear, about 1 minute. Drain rice well.

2. Melt butter in large saucepan over medium heat. Add rice and cook, stirring frequently, until edges begin to turn translucent, about 2 minutes. Add water and salt, increase heat to high, and bring to boil.

3. Cover, reduce heat to low, and simmer until liquid is absorbed and rice is tender, about 20 minutes. Off heat, remove lid and place kitchen towel folded in half over saucepan. Cover and let stand for 10 minutes. Fluff with fork. Serve.

SPLIT PEA AND HAM SOUP

SPLIT PEA SOUP USED TO BE THE THING TO MAKE after serving a roast ham for Sunday supper. Once you were done frying ham and eggs for breakfast and shaving off meaty slabs for ham sandwiches at lunch, you would drop the bone (with hunks of meat still clinging to it) into a big soup pot with a bag of split peas and cover it with water. After hours of simmering, the meat would fall off the bone, the fat would melt into the broth, and the peas would disintegrate and thicken the rib-sticking potage.

That was the idea, anyway. But in my experience, this thrifty dish has never amounted to anything greater than the sum of its parts. Too often it turns into an overly thick—dare I say sludgy—green mash with bland flavor. Plus, these days, I rarely serve roast ham, so procuring a leftover bone is not as simple as reaching into my refrigerator. But the thought of what this dish is meant to be—a spoon-coating, richly flavorful broth studded with tender shreds of sweet-smoky meat—was enough to send me back to the kitchen.

Without a ham bone, I had to find an equally flavorful replacement. Most of the recipes I came across swapped in ham hocks, but these fatty, sinewy knuckle pieces (I tried both fresh and smoked) only rendered my soup greasy. Plus, unless you find a particularly substantial specimen, hocks tend to be skimpy on meat, making a supplemental form of pork necessary.

My tasters wanted plenty of ham strewn throughout the pot, so I made a point of shopping for meatier alternatives and returned to the test kitchen with Canadian bacon and ham steak. The former was disappointing. Unlike regular strip American bacon made from fat-streaked (read: flavorful) pork belly, the Canadian version comes from the lean loin region of the pig, and its meek flavor barely broke through the thick fog of peas. Ham steak, however, was a welcome addition to the pot; after I quartered the slab and let it simmer in the broth (a classic base of water fortified with sautéed onion and garlic, carrots and celery added midway through cooking to preserve their texture, bay leaves, and a pair of thyme sprigs) for about 45 minutes, the liquid had taken on significantly fuller pork flavor, and the ham itself was tender enough to pull into meaty shreds with a pair of forks.

But as my tasters rightly pointed out, the ham steak was hardly an equal substitute for bone. We all agreed that the soup was still lacking richness and could use more smokiness—a perfect job for American bacon, I figured. (Apparently, two forms of pork were going to be necessary after all.) But the quick fix I was hoping for proved elusive. I crisped a few strips and added them to the pot only to find that they overwhelmed the ham and peas. Instead, I slid raw bacon into the soup along with the ham steak, which offered subtler flavor, and the slices could be fished out right before serving.

As for the peas, I knew from experience that the presoaking step in many recipes was unnecessary. Unsoaked peas break down just as readily as soaked peas, and the resulting soup is actually more flavorful, since they absorb the pork-enriched broth.

All that was left to do was work up a few garnishes. A handful of fresh peas seemed appropriate; their sweetness popped against the hearty, smoky broth. Minced mint leaves and a drizzle of good balsamic vinegar added freshness and sweetness, respectively, and punched up the flavors even more. Finally, I floated gently fried croutons on the surface. As my tasters ladled out second (and even third) helpings, I knew that I'd reworked this stodgy supper into an updated classic.

—KEITH DRESSER, *Cook's Illustrated*

NOTES FROM THE TEST KITCHEN

THE BEST LIQUID MEASURING CUP

The liquid measuring cup is a basic kitchen tool, where accuracy matters more than looks, and form should follow function. But when we perused stores recently, we found cup after wacky cup, with silly shapes and candy colors, made of materials that are flimsy, with markings that run from minimal (no quarter-cups or thirds) to ridiculously excessive (pints, tablespoons, and cubic centimeters). Unsure whether any of these innovative shapes or features might prove useful, we gathered 15 glass, silicone, and plastic 2-cup liquid measures and tested them for accuracy, durability, resistance to heat, and user-friendliness. Some cups were downgraded because they gave us inaccurate measurements; others resulted in inaccurate measurements simply because they were too difficult to read, with small type and busy designs. In the end, we liked the **Good Cook by Bradshaw International 2-Cup Measuring Cup**, $3.99. While we'd prefer a more substantial glass cup, this lightweight, crisply marked plastic model was accurate and easy to read and provided all the measurements we need. (See page 300 for more information about our testing results.)

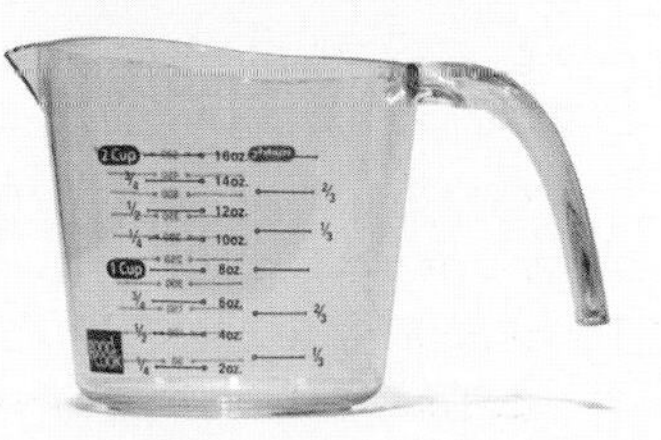

SPLIT PEA AND HAM SOUP

Split Pea and Ham Soup

SERVES 6 TO 8

Four slices of regular bacon can be used, but the thinner slices are a little harder to remove from the soup. Depending on the age and brand of split peas, the consistency of the soup may vary slightly. If the soup is too thin at the end of step 3, increase the heat and simmer, uncovered, until the desired consistency is reached. If it is too thick, thin it with a little water. In addition to sprinkling the soup with Buttery Croutons, we like to serve it with fresh peas and minced fresh mint and drizzled with aged balsamic vinegar.

- **2 tablespoons unsalted butter**
- **1 large onion, chopped fine**
- **Salt and pepper**
- **2 garlic cloves, minced**
- **7 cups water**
- **1 pound ham steak, rind removed, cut into quarters**
- **1 pound green split peas (2 cups), picked over and rinsed**
- **3 slices thick-cut bacon**
- **2 sprigs fresh thyme**
- **2 bay leaves**
- **2 carrots, peeled and cut into ½-inch pieces**
- **1 celery rib, cut into ½-inch pieces**
- **1 recipe Buttery Croutons (recipe follows)**

1. Melt butter in Dutch oven over medium-high heat. Add onion and ½ teaspoon salt and cook, stirring frequently, until softened, about 3 to 5 minutes. Add garlic and cook until fragrant, about 30 seconds. Add water, ham steak, peas, bacon, thyme, and bay leaves. Increase heat to high and bring to simmer, stirring frequently to keep peas from sticking to bottom. Reduce heat to low, cover, and simmer until peas are tender but not falling apart, about 45 minutes.

2. Remove ham steak, cover with foil to prevent drying out, and set aside. Stir in carrots and celery; continue to simmer, covered, until vegetables are tender and peas have almost completely broken down, about 30 minutes longer.

3. When cool enough to handle, shred ham into small bite-size pieces with two forks. Remove and discard thyme sprigs, bay leaves, and bacon slices. Stir ham back into soup and return to simmer. Season with salt and pepper to taste, sprinkle with croutons, and serve. (Soup can be refrigerated for up to 3 days; if necessary, thin with water when reheating.)

Buttery Croutons

MAKES 2 CUPS

- **3 tablespoons unsalted butter**
- **1 tablespoon olive oil**
- **3 slices hearty white sandwich bread, cut into ½-inch cubes**
- **Salt**

Heat butter and oil in 12-inch skillet over medium heat. When butter has melted, add bread cubes and cook, stirring frequently, until golden brown, about 10 minutes. Transfer croutons to paper towel–lined plate and season with salt to taste.

SLOW-COOKER LENTIL SOUP

LENTIL SOUP—WHEN DONE WELL—IS RICH AND hearty, with a satisfying mélange of textures and flavors. I thought the slow cooker would be the perfect vessel to prepare this classic soup, as lentils need a gentle simmer to properly break down—and using the slow cooker to do this would free me up to do other things. But when I gathered and prepared a variety of recipes, I was severely disappointed; so many were lackluster, calling for canned tomatoes and a hodgepodge of vegetables. I wanted a deeply flavorful, slow-cooker lentil soup, with tender lentils that were still intact—neither blown-out nor mushy—and well-chosen vegetables that retained their character after a long simmer. I decided to start with the lentils and then begin work on creating a flavorful base.

I began by checking out the varieties of lentils available at my local supermarket. Brown, green, and red lentils were the most common choices. At specialty markets and high-end supermarkets, I also found yellow lentils and French green lentils (lentilles du Puy). Because I wanted an easy, straightforward recipe, I gave a thumbs-down to the less accessible yellow and French lentils and chose red, brown, and green for my initial tests.

Remarkably, the three varieties offered minimal flavor differences. Texture, however, was a different story. Red lentils, traditionally used in Indian cooking, quickly turned to mush. But the green and brown lentils fared well, the brown lentils holding their shape and texture slightly better. Plus, the brown lentils maintained their integrity once the soup was finished cooking—they continued to soften but did not fall apart. My lentil of choice in hand, I examined the cooking method.

Many of the recipes I came across in my research recommended simply adding the lentils to the slow cooker along with the aromatics and cooking liquid, but while this dump-and-cook method was effortless, it produced a soup with weak flavor. Looking for a way to bolster the flavor, I tried sautéing the aromatics before adding them to the slow cooker. I began with a basic combination of onions, garlic, and thyme, allowing the aromatics to soften and begin to brown in a skillet. Then I transferred the mixture to the slow cooker and stirred in the cooking liquid (a combination of water and chicken broth), lentils, and carrots (I'd worry about other vegetables later). Tasting the results, I discovered that this step had made a huge difference, creating a robust background for my soup. But as I surveyed my stovetop—and the extra pan I now had to clean—I wondered if there was a quicker, neater way to jump-start the cooking of the aromatics. What if I used the microwave instead?

For my next test, I combined the onions, garlic, and thyme, along with some olive oil, in a bowl, transferred the bowl to the microwave, and hit the start button. After about five minutes, the onions had softened nicely. I combined this mixture in the slow cooker with the other ingredients, set the cooker, and waited. Surprisingly, this batch of soup was every bit as flavorful as the previous batch—but it was easier and I had fewer dishes to do. I was sold.

But although my lentil soup was good, the broth was slightly one-note at this point. Looking to add some complexity, I decided to add tomato paste and minced dried mushrooms—both favorites in the test kitchen for amping up flavor—to the microwaved aromatics. The tomato paste added a deep, round flavor, and the mushrooms added a surprising amount of richness. One more simple move—swapping the water for vegetable broth—brought a nice sweetness to the soup's base.

Many of the recipes I'd come across included bacon for some smoky depth, but again, I didn't want to drag out the skillet to crisp a few slices. Instead, I opted to simply add the bacon slices—whole—to the slow cooker. When the soup was done, the slices were easy enough to fish out, and they had instilled the broth with a solid backbone of smoky flavor.

My soup was coming along, yet there was still the issue of the vegetables. Tasters liked the carrots, but they clamored for a more robust soup—with more veggies. I gave the usual canned diced tomatoes a spin, but—no pun intended—no dice with this one; the tomatoes broke down too much and disintegrated after their time in the slow cooker. I also tried adding white mushrooms, but after the long stint in the slow cooker, they turned slimy. Turning to sturdier portobellos instead, I found that they retained their texture and provided a missing heartiness to the soup. Searching for a hearty green to offer an earthy and colorful contrast to the brown lentils, I settled on Swiss chard and added it during the last half-hour of cooking.

NOTES FROM THE TEST KITCHEN

PREPARING HEARTY GREENS

1. To prepare Swiss chard, kale, and collard greens, cut away leafy green portion from either side of stalk or stem using chef's knife.

2. Then stack several leaves, and either slice leaves crosswise or chop into pieces (as directed in recipe). Wash and dry leaves after they are cut, using salad spinner.

My lentil soup was now plenty rich and flavorful. And though it was slow-cooked, it was quickly devoured in the test kitchen—which I took as a resounding endorsement.

—DAN ZUCCARELLO, *America's Test Kitchen Books*

Slow-Cooker Lentil Soup

SERVES 8

Removing the portobello gills ensures that the soup doesn't take on a muddy flavor or unattractive hue. To do this, simply scrape the gills off the underside of the mushroom with a spoon.

- **2 onions, chopped fine**
- **4 garlic cloves, minced**
- **2 tablespoons extra-virgin olive oil, plus extra for serving**
- **1 tablespoon tomato paste**
- **½ ounce dried porcini mushrooms, rinsed and minced**
- **1½ teaspoons minced fresh thyme or 1 teaspoon dried**
- **4 cups low-sodium chicken broth**
- **4 cups vegetable broth**
- **4 slices bacon**
- **3 carrots, peeled and cut into ½-inch pieces**
- **2 medium portobello mushroom caps, gills removed, cut into ½-inch pieces**
- **7 ounces brown lentils (1 cup), picked over and rinsed**
- **2 bay leaves**
- **8 ounces Swiss chard, stemmed, leaves sliced ½ inch thick**
- **Salt and pepper**

1. Microwave onions, garlic, oil, tomato paste, porcini mushrooms, and thyme in bowl, stirring occasionally, until onions are softened, about 5 minutes; transfer to slow cooker.

2. Stir chicken broth, vegetable broth, bacon, carrots, portobello mushrooms, lentils, and bay leaves into slow cooker. Cover and cook until lentils are tender, 9 to 11 hours on low or 5 to 7 hours on high.

3. Stir in chard, cover, and cook on high until chard is tender, 20 to 30 minutes. Discard bacon and bay leaves. Season with salt and pepper to taste and serve with additional olive oil.

OUR FAVORITE BEEF CHILI

CHILI DEVOTEES (OR "CHILIHEADS," AS THEY ARE known) are an opinionated, even cheerily belligerent bunch. Each cook swears that the only chili worth eating is his or her own: rich with slow-cooked meat and redolent with chile peppers and spices, all bound in an unctuous sauce. But chili is basically just meat cooked with ground chiles; how could one be so much better than another? The key, any chilihead will tell you, lies in the all-powerful "secret ingredients."

I lost count of the references unearthed in my research to the intriguing additions that could magically improve a humble pot of chili, but the specifics were hard to nail down. (Chiliheads are as secretive as they are argumentative.) It took a lot of digging to compile a list. The Internet yielded fascinating new leads, such as prunes floated atop the simmering chili (removed before serving), and obscure cookbooks revealed a couple of others (chocolate, beer). Chiliheads were reluctant to reveal the key to their own success; luckily, they could occasionally be coaxed to divulge the details of other cooks' recipes, including one chili that was thickened with "just a touch of peanut butter." The chili cook-off circuit, however, proved to be something of a dead end; my sleuthing in this arena yielded little in the way of practical instruction.

Although my list of secret ingredients was slowly growing, it was getting me nowhere until I developed a basic recipe that these strange additions could embellish. Adopting the opinionated swagger of a veteran chili cook, I brashly laid down my own ground rules: To live up to my high expectations, my chili would have to be all beef (diced, not ground), and it would have pinto beans, tomatoes, onions, and garlic. These last four ingredients are actually highly controversial in some parts of the United States, but—my recipe, my rules. It's the chilihead way.

I began by testing five different cuts of beef: flap meat, brisket, chuck-eye roast, skirt steak, and short ribs, all in ¾-inch dice, and all browned before going into the pot with sautéed onions, jalapeños, and garlic; diced tomatoes; beef broth; and quick-soaked pinto beans. For the sake of simplicity, I seasoned each pot with ⅓ cup of chili powder.

Though the short ribs were extremely tender, some tasters felt that they tasted too much like pot roast (plus they were pricey). The brisket was wonderfully beefy but lean and a bit tough. The clear winner was chuck-eye roast, favored for its tenderness and rich flavor. The beans were praised for their soft, creamy texture (attributed to the hour-long soak in salt water), and tasters embraced the addition of the tomatoes and aromatics. But I was far from home free: My tasters also complained that the chili powder gave the dish a gritty, dusty texture, and the flavor was "less than vibrant."

Making my own chili powder seemed the best way to solve both of those problems, so I decided to give it a try. Of all the dried chiles that are available in most supermarkets, I chose anchos for their earthiness and árbols for their smooth heat. I removed the stems and seeds, then toasted the anchos in a dry skillet until they were fragrant (the thin árbols burned when I tried to toast them). After cooling the anchos, I ground them in a spice grinder along with the árbols and 2 teaspoons each of cumin and oregano, both common seasonings in commercial chili powder blends. The sauce in chili made with my own blend was not only much more deeply flavored but also remarkably smooth. Why was the batch made with the supermarket chili powder so gritty in comparison?

Research revealed that at many processing plants dried chiles are ground whole—stems, seeds, and all. The stems and seeds never break down completely, and that's what gives some commercial powders that sandy texture. Making chili powder is undeniably a time-consuming step, but for my ultimate chili it was worth it.

Nevertheless, before venturing into the world of secret ingredients, I wondered if I could streamline my recipe a bit. I was spending too much time trimming my roast of fat, so I switched to blade steak, which also comes from the chuck and took much less time to break down into ¾-inch chunks. Rather than grind the chiles in batches in a spice grinder, I pulverized them all at once in the food processor, adding a bit of broth to encourage the chile pieces to engage with the blade rather than simply fly around the bowl. The puree wasn't quite as fine as I wanted it to be, but I'd address that later. I also used the food processor to chop the onions and jalapeños. Since stovetop cooking required occasional stirring to prevent scorching, I moved the bulk of the cooking to the gentler heat of the oven, where the chili could simmer unattended.

Happy with my basic recipe, I was ready to spring a series of unlikely ingredients on my colleagues. My research had indicated that chili cooks' secret weapons tend to fall into five categories: cooking liquids, complexity builders, sweeteners, meat enhancers, and thickeners. In a series of blind tastings, I set out to separate the wonderful from the simply weird.

At this point, the only liquid in my recipe was the predictable beef broth. To my next four pots of chili I added Guinness, red wine, coffee, and lager. The stout flattened out the bright notes of the jalapeños and tomatoes, and the wine was too tangy. Tasted just 30 minutes into the cooking time, the coffee seemed promising, but later on it became as bitter and acidic as the dregs in the office urn. The lightly hoppy flavor of the lager, however, complemented the tomatoes, onions, and jalapeños beautifully—not so surprising, perhaps, since chili and beer pair well by tradition. Lager was in.

Next up: the complexity builders, ingredients that add depth without being readily discernible. Cloves and cinnamon were deemed too identifiable and sweet, but members of the chocolate family—unsweetened chocolate, unsweetened cocoa, and bittersweet chocolate—performed well; tasters appreciated the complexity that each provided. Since I would be sweetening the pot in the next test, I selected the unsweetened cocoa.

The aim of adding a sweet ingredient to chili is to smooth out any sharp or acidic flavors without making the dish noticeably sweet. I had high hopes for the two prunes left to float on the top of the simmering chili, but that technique was too subtle for my tasters. Some Coca-Cola had the surprising effect of enhancing the tomato flavor too much, and brown sugar was "OK but kind of boring." The winner in this round? Molasses, which lent the chili an "earthy, smoky depth."

The next category, meat enhancers, yielded the most surprising results. Many cooks swear by the practice of augmenting their chili with "umami bombs" in the form of anchovies, soy sauce, mushrooms, or even Marmite. I found that adding such ingredients dramatically increased the meaty flavor of the chili, but in doing so they threw the balance of chiles, aromatics, and spices out of whack. It was just too meaty. Tasters even persuaded me to switch from beef broth to chicken broth, citing better balance. Good-quality meat was meaty enough, thanks.

On to the most eagerly anticipated test of them all: peanut butter. Intended to thicken the chili, it's not as

OUR FAVORITE BEEF CHILI

bizarre as you might think. Mexican cooks often add ground seeds and nuts to mole to give it richness, texture, and depth, so why not add peanut butter to chili? I tested more prosaic thickeners as well: flour and the traditional masa (dough made with limed corn, which is then dried and ground). The flour subtly thickened the chili, but it didn't offer anything in terms of flavor. The peanut butter, on the other hand, lent a "big roasted flavor" to the chili, but it also left a strange aftertaste. The masa was well received for its thickening properties and the subtle corn flavor it contributed, but buying a 4-pound bag of masa just to use 3 tablespoons seemed silly. This is where I introduced my own quirky ingredient to the pantheon of secret ingredients. I found that when I added 3 tablespoons of cornmeal to my food processor chili paste, its bulk helped me achieve a finer grind, and it accomplished the thickening goal admirably.

Other cooks might accuse me of being full of beans, but this chili, with its tender beef and complex sauce, plus its own secret ingredients, is one I will defend with the vigor of the most seasoned chilihead.

—ANDREA GEARY, *Cook's Illustrated*

Our Favorite Beef Chili

SERVES 6 TO 8

A 4-pound chuck-eye roast, well trimmed of fat, can be substituted for the steak. Because much of the chili flavor is held in the fat of this dish, refrain from skimming fat from the surface. Wear gloves when working with both dried and fresh chiles. Dried New Mexican or guajillo chiles make a good substitute for the anchos; each dried árbol may be replaced by ⅛ teaspoon cayenne pepper. If you prefer not to work with any whole dried chiles, you can substitute ½ cup commercial chili powder and ¼ to ½ teaspoon cayenne pepper for the anchos and árbols, though the texture of the chili will be slightly compromised. Good choices for condiments include diced avocado, chopped red onion, chopped cilantro leaves, lime wedges, sour cream, and shredded Monterey Jack or cheddar cheese.

Salt
8 ounces dried pinto beans (1¼ cups), picked over and rinsed
6 dried ancho chiles (1¾ ounces), stemmed, seeded, and torn into 1-inch pieces
2–4 dried árbol chiles, stemmed, halved, and seeded
3 tablespoons cornmeal
2 teaspoons dried oregano
2 teaspoons ground cumin
2 teaspoons cocoa
2½ cups low-sodium chicken broth
2 onions, cut into ¾-inch pieces
3 small jalapeño chiles, stemmed, seeded, and cut into ½-inch pieces
3 tablespoons vegetable oil
4 garlic cloves, minced
1 (14.5-ounce) can diced tomatoes
2 teaspoons light molasses
3½ pounds blade steak, ¾ inch thick, trimmed and cut into ¾-inch pieces
1 (12-ounce) bottle mild lager, such as Budweiser

1. Combine 16 cups water, 3 tablespoons salt, and beans in Dutch oven; bring to boil over high heat. Remove pot from heat, cover, and let stand for 1 hour. Drain and rinse well.

2. Adjust oven rack to lower-middle position and heat oven to 300 degrees. Toast ancho chiles in 12-inch skillet over medium-high heat, stirring frequently, until fragrant, 4 to 6 minutes, reducing heat if chiles begin to smoke. Transfer to food processor and let cool. Do not wash skillet.

3. Add árbol chiles, cornmeal, oregano, cumin, cocoa, and ½ teaspoon salt to food processor with toasted ancho chiles; process until finely ground, about 2 minutes. With processor running, very slowly add ½ cup broth until smooth paste forms, about 45 seconds, scraping down sides of bowl as necessary. Transfer paste to small bowl. Place onions in now-empty processor bowl and pulse until roughly chopped, about 4 pulses. Add jalapeños and pulse until consistency of chunky salsa, about 4 pulses, scraping down bowl as necessary.

4. Heat 1 tablespoon oil in Dutch oven over medium-high heat. Add onion mixture and cook, stirring occasionally, until moisture has evaporated and vegetables are softened, 7 to 9 minutes. Add garlic and cook until fragrant, about 1 minute. Add chili paste, tomatoes, and molasses; stir until chili paste is thoroughly combined. Add remaining 2 cups broth and drained beans; bring to boil, then reduce heat to simmer.

5. Meanwhile, pat beef dry with paper towels and sprinkle with 1 teaspoon salt. Heat 1 more tablespoon oil in 12-inch skillet over medium-high heat until shimmering. Add half of beef and cook until browned on all sides, about 10 minutes. Transfer meat to Dutch oven. Add half of lager to skillet, scraping bottom of pan to loosen any browned bits, and bring to simmer. Transfer lager to Dutch oven. Repeat with remaining 1 tablespoon oil, beef, and lager. Once last addition of lager has been added to Dutch oven, stir to combine and return mixture to simmer.

6. Cover pot; transfer to oven. Cook until meat and beans are fully tender, 1½ to 2 hours. Let chili stand, uncovered, for 10 minutes. Stir well, season with salt to taste, and serve. (Chili can be refrigerated for up to 3 days.)

NOTES FROM THE TEST KITCHEN

CHILI FUNDAMENTALS: GETTING IT RIGHT

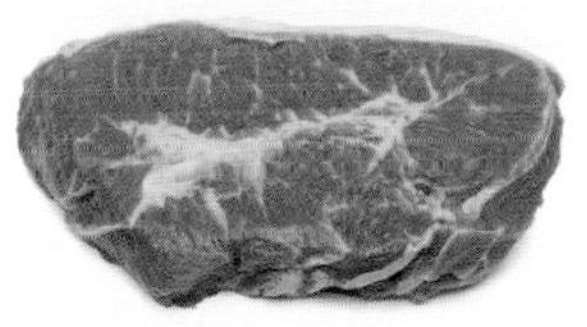

WHOLE BLADE STEAK
Starting with a whole steak allowed us to cut the meat into beefy chunks that stayed moist and tender.

THREE KINDS OF CHILES
For complex chile flavor, we used dried ancho and árbol chiles, which we ground into a paste. Fresh jalapeños contributed a grassy heat.

BRINED DRIED BEANS
Soaking dried beans in salt water before cooking ensured that they were well seasoned and had a creamy texture.

OUR SECRET WEAPONS
We combed the Internet and cookbooks for "secret" ingredients to see if any would actually improve our chili. While peanut butter, red wine, cola, prunes, coffee, mushrooms, and anchovies were a bust, we did hit on a few secret weapons worth deploying. Cornmeal brought great body to the sauce, and beer, molasses, and unsweetened cocoa added depth and complexity.

BLACK BEAN CHILI

BLACK BEAN CHILI IS THE VEGETARIAN'S ANSWER TO hearty, satisfying chili, but so often it can turn out dull and unremarkable. Most versions I've come across over the years either tasted like warmed black beans straight from the can, or they took a kitchen-sink philosophy and included a hodgepodge of vegetables. I wanted a chili that was primarily about the beans, which should be creamy, tender, and well seasoned. It should have enough complexity and depth to hold your interest for a whole bowl; although not meaty, it needed to taste rich and satisfying. With these goals in mind, I headed into the test kitchen.

Since beans were to be the core of my chili, that's where I started testing. The first question was what type to use: canned or dried. One test pitting canned beans against dried beans made it clear that, in this case, convenience wasn't worth it. Dried beans—with their superior texture and flavor—were the only way to go, especially since this was a dish that was all about the beans.

In the test kitchen, we prefer to soak dried beans in a saltwater solution (or brine them) prior to cooking, as this step softens the tough bean skins and evens out the cooking time, so that fewer beans burst open. But when it comes to black bean chili, a few broken beans wouldn't be a bad thing; I wanted a thick chili, and a portion of burst beans would only contribute to the desired texture. I could skip the soaking and move on to the method.

When cooking unbrined beans, it's particularly important to use a flavorful liquid to ensure well-seasoned interiors. In this case, I found that a combination of equal parts vegetable broth and water gave the beans a flavorful backbone. I also wanted to include tomatoes, a traditional ingredient that lends brightness and acidity to chili. After testing fresh chopped tomatoes, canned diced tomatoes, and canned crushed tomatoes, tasters preferred the smooth texture of the crushed tomatoes. One 28-ounce can, combined with the single pound of beans I was working with, provided a solid tomato base without treading into marinara territory. Since acidic ingredients can toughen beans by preventing their cells from absorbing water, I added the tomatoes to the pot halfway through cooking. A small amount of baking soda, stirred in at the beginning of

NOTES FROM THE TEST KITCHEN

THE SECRET TO MEATY-TASTING BLACK BEAN CHILI

Casting about for an ingredient to impart an uber-meaty richness to our black bean chili, we hit on mushrooms, known for their high level of glutamates, a class of amino acids that give meat its savory taste. Breaking the mushrooms down into small pieces in the food processor ensured that they added textural interest but didn't steal the show from the black beans.

SORTING DRIED BEANS

Before cooking any dried beans, pick them over for any small stones or debris. To do this, spread beans out over large plate or rimmed baking sheet.

THE BEST OVEN THERMOMETER

Fact: Ovens are inaccurate. Since all ovens cycle on and off to maintain temperature, even the best models periodically deviate from the desired heat by at least a few degrees. And we've found they can be off by as much as 50 degrees unless they're recalibrated regularly. It doesn't make sense not to have an oven thermometer—they don't cost a lot, and a good one can literally save your dinner (plus everything else you cook or bake).

Overall, we prefer dial-face to bulb-style thermometers; the tinted alcohol used in bulb models can get stuck, compromising accuracy. The thermometer should be accurate, durable, easy to read, and able to be mounted securely out of the way of pans. We recently tested five brands of dial-face thermometers to find the best one. We used a super-precise instant-read thermocouple to check high and low readouts given by each thermometer. We also maneuvered baking dishes in and out of the oven. Finally, we left a thermometer in every oven in the test kitchen and asked test cooks to provide feedback over six months of daily use.

After several months, a few of the models developed fogged or discolored faces (on one model the numbers faded), got in the way of cooking vessels, and were off by as much as 10 degrees. In the end, the **Cooper-Atkins Oven Thermometer**, $5.95, impressed us most. It's accurate, hangs or stands freely on oven racks, and after months of testing, its numbers remained clear and readable.

cooking, ensured that my beans stayed dark and didn't turn gray or drab. To ensure that the beans cooked through evenly, I transferred the pot to the oven, which provides a more uniform, consistent heat than can be found on the stovetop.

Confident that I had solved my bean-cooking method, I looked for ways to boost the meaty flavor of the chili. Searching for something that would complement but not overwhelm the black beans, I hit on mushrooms, known for their high level of glutamates, a class of amino acids that give meat its savory taste. I made three batches of beans, adding a different sliced mushroom to each; I tried white, cremini, and portobello mushrooms. While tasters found that the portobellos' bold, earthy flavor dominated the chili, they praised the cremini and white mushrooms for complementing the beans with their meaty texture and rich flavor. Since it was a tie between the two, I opted to go with the more readily available white mushrooms.

To further ensure that the mushrooms played a supporting role to the beans—and didn't take over the pot of chili—I chopped them fine, then sautéed them with some onion to drive off moisture and create a flavorful fond on the bottom of the pot. The chopped pieces of mushroom were now hard to identify as mushrooms given the rich, dark color of the chili, but they still provided plenty of flavor, texture, and body. An additional test determined that pulsing the mushrooms in the food processor produced the same results as chopping by hand but took a fraction of the time.

As for aromatics and spices, in addition to onion, I stirred in a generous quantity of garlic, chili powder, and a couple of bay leaves. Whole cumin seeds and minced chipotle added depth and smokiness. So far, so good, but something was missing. Looking for another way to deepen the flavor of the chili, I reviewed existing recipes for black bean chili again, hoping for inspiration. I noticed a few that called for mustard seeds. It seemed a bit odd for chili, but I was curious and gave it a shot, adding a few tablespoons with the other aromatics. I found that the chili now had an appealing pungency and an additional level of complexity that tasters immediately noticed but couldn't identify. I eventually settled on 1 tablespoon of mustard seeds (more than this, and the chili took on a bitter taste) rounded out with a tablespoon of brown sugar. To enhance the flavor of the mustard seeds, I employed the technique of "blooming," a common test kitchen practice for bringing out the flavor of dried spices by briefly sautéing them. Sautéing the seeds in oil proved to be a minor disaster, however, causing them to pop out of the pot. Toasting them in a dry pan, along with the cumin seeds, achieved the same goal but with less drama.

Finally, for some textural contrast and a bit of sweetness, I added two red bell peppers, cut into ½-inch pieces; stirring them in with the tomatoes preserved their color and texture. With a spritz of lime and a sprinkling of minced cilantro, this rich, hearty chili was so satisfying, no one even missed the meat.

—ADELAIDE PARKER, *America's Test Kitchen Books*

Black Bean Chili

SERVES 6 TO 8

We strongly prefer the texture and flavor of mustard seeds and cumin seeds in this chili; however, ground cumin and dry mustard can be substituted—add ½ teaspoon ground cumin and/or ½ teaspoon dry mustard to the pot with the chili powder in step 3. Serve with sour cream, shredded Monterey Jack or cheddar cheese, chopped tomatoes, and/or chopped onion.

- **1 pound white mushrooms, trimmed and broken into rough pieces**
- **1 tablespoon mustard seeds**
- **2 teaspoons cumin seeds**
- **3 tablespoons vegetable oil**
- **1 onion, chopped medium**
- **9 garlic cloves, minced**
- **1 tablespoon minced canned chipotle chile in adobo sauce**
- **3 tablespoons chili powder**
- **2½ cups vegetable broth**
- **2½ cups water, plus extra as needed**
- **1 pound dried black beans (2½ cups), picked over and rinsed**
- **1 tablespoon light brown sugar**
- **⅛ teaspoon baking soda**
- **2 bay leaves**
- **1 (28-ounce) can crushed tomatoes**
- **2 red bell peppers, stemmed, seeded, and cut into ½-inch pieces**
- **½ cup minced fresh cilantro**
- **Salt and pepper**
- **Lime wedges**

1. Adjust oven rack to lower-middle position and heat oven to 325 degrees. Pulse mushrooms in food processor until uniformly coarsely chopped, about 10 pulses; set aside.

2. Toast mustard seeds and cumin seeds in Dutch oven over medium heat, stirring constantly, until fragrant, about 1 minute. Stir in oil, onion, and processed mushrooms, cover, and cook until vegetables have released their liquid, about 5 minutes. Uncover and continue to cook until vegetables are dry and browned, 5 to 10 minutes longer.

3. Stir in garlic and chipotle and cook until fragrant, about 30 seconds. Stir in chili powder and cook, stirring constantly, until fragrant, about 1 minute (do not let it burn). Stir in broth, water, beans, sugar, baking soda, and bay leaves and bring to simmer, skimming surface if necessary. Cover, place pot in oven, and cook for 1 hour.

4. Stir in crushed tomatoes and bell peppers, cover, and continue to cook in oven until beans are fully tender, about 1 hour longer. (If chili begins to stick to bottom of pot or looks too thick, stir in additional water as needed.)

5. Remove pot from oven and remove bay leaves. Stir in cilantro, season with salt and pepper to taste, and serve with lime wedges.

CHAPTER 3

VEGETABLES & SIDE DISHES

ROASTED SMASHED POTATOES

WHEN IT COMES TO POTATOES, THERE'S NOTHING I like better than the silky creaminess of mashed potatoes—except for the satisfying crispness you get when they're fried. So when I recently discovered a quirky recipe for something called crispy smashed potatoes, which promised an abundance of both textures in the same spud, I had to try it. The approach looked simple and straightforward: Whole skin-on potatoes are parcooked, then squashed with a masher until about a half-inch thick. These pattylike disks are then coated in oil or butter and cooked at a high enough heat to render the roughened edges and torn skin browned and crispy and the interior flesh creamy and sweet. The results aren't the prettiest, but if you can bring out the best in a potato's flavor and texture, aesthetics are moot, right? The question was exactly how to bring out those ideals.

In every recipe I consulted the potatoes were parcooked by simmering them in water. From there, the techniques were divided. Some recipes called for pan-frying; others advocated roasting. Pan-frying produced nice crispness but required close supervision and lots of fat. I opted for the oven's more even heat and a baking sheet's roomier surface, which allowed me to cook enough potatoes for four in a single batch.

But when it came time to start smashing, some spuds cooperated better than others. Thick, oblong russets wouldn't budge under the press of a potato masher and needed the smack of a heavy skillet, at which point their starchy interiors crumbled into messy piles. Smaller Yukon Golds and red potatoes (no more than 2 inches in diameter) worked far better, flattening into disks that held their shape. I also liked the way their thinner skins crisped up nicely in the oven. In the end, I preferred the red potatoes for their slightly moister, less starchy flesh.

As for cooking fat, I first tried melted butter but found that its milk solids burned long before the potatoes fully crisped, leaving them marred by bitter black patches. I settled on olive oil; applying half before smashing and drizzling on the rest after smashing ensured that it reached every nook and cranny.

So far, I'd managed to achieve creamy-crispy textures and pretty good flavor. But a certain rich earthiness still eluded me. Was I washing away some of the potato flavor during parcooking? Simmering was standard among existing recipes, but let's be honest: When does boiling really improve taste? I tried spiking the cooking water with bay leaves, smashed garlic, various herbs and spices, and even bacon slices, but no hint of these came through.

Giving drier heat a try, I placed the potatoes in a large bowl and microwaved them until tender before roasting. These tasted better—but now the skins were tough and rubbery. Meanwhile, my preheated 500-degree oven was at the ready; why not just cook the potatoes in there from start to finish? I spread them on a baking sheet and let them cook until tender on the oven's bottom rack, closest to the heating element, then proceeded with my recipe. The results were the best yet: Without the diluting effect of boiling, the creamy flesh tasted sweet, deep, and earthy.

But roasting the potatoes took a good hour, and by now dinnertime had come and gone. Trapping some steam would help break down their flesh faster, so I wrapped the baking sheet in foil. This cut the cooking time by 15 minutes. Adding a splash of water to the pan created even more steam and eliminated another 15 minutes. After a 10-minute rest (very hot potatoes crumbled apart when smashed), I simply pressed the potatoes right on the sheet tray. I then returned them to the oven for an additional 35 to 45 minutes to finish, first on the top rack, where the ambient heat would

NOTES FROM THE TEST KITCHEN

MAKING ROASTED SMASHED POTATOES

1. After rolling cooled, oven-steamed potatoes in olive oil, space potatoes evenly on baking sheet and place second baking sheet on top; press down uniformly on baking sheet until potatoes are ⅓ to ½ inch thick.

2. Sprinkle smashed potatoes with thyme, season with salt and pepper, and drizzle evenly with remaining oil. Roast as directed.

ROASTED SMASHED POTATOES

thoroughly brown their exposed surfaces, then back to the bottom rack, to crisp their undersides.

These were the creamy spuds encased in rough, crispy skin I'd been after, but individually smashing nearly 20 potatoes was a pain. As I glanced around the kitchen for a more efficient tool, I found the answer right in front of me: another baking sheet. I balanced it on top of another batch of parcooked potatoes and then pushed down evenly and firmly. In one fell swoop, I had perfect cracked patties—and, once they were browned and crunchy, a great new potato dish to add to my starch rotation.

—MATTHEW CARD, *Cook's Illustrated*

Roasted Smashed Potatoes

SERVES 4 TO 6

This recipe is designed to work with potatoes 1½ to 2 inches in diameter; do not use potatoes any larger. It is important to thoroughly cook the potatoes so that they will smash easily. Remove the potatoes from the baking sheet as soon as they have finished browning—they will toughen if left too long. A potato masher can also be used to "smash" the potatoes.

- **2 pounds small red potatoes**
- **6 tablespoons extra-virgin olive oil**
- **1 teaspoon minced fresh thyme**
- **Kosher salt and pepper**

1. Adjust oven racks to top and lowest positions and heat oven to 500 degrees. Arrange potatoes on rimmed baking sheet, pour ¾ cup water into baking sheet, and wrap tightly with aluminum foil. Cook on lowest rack until paring knife or skewer slips in and out of potatoes easily (poke through foil to test), 25 to 30 minutes. Remove foil and cool for 10 minutes. If any water remains on baking sheet, blot dry with paper towel.

2. Drizzle 3 tablespoons oil over potatoes and roll to coat. Space potatoes evenly on baking sheet and place second baking sheet on top; press down firmly on baking sheet, flattening potatoes until ⅓ to ½ inch thick. Sprinkle with thyme and season generously with salt and pepper; drizzle evenly with remaining 3 tablespoons oil. Roast potatoes on top rack for 15 minutes. Transfer potatoes to lowest rack and continue to roast until well browned, 20 to 30 minutes longer. Serve immediately.

WHIPPED POTATOES

MOST CHEFS AND MANY COOKBOOKS WILL TELL YOU that anything but the gentlest treatment turns mashed potatoes into wallpaper paste. My very own *Joy of Cooking*, for one, sternly warns that "whipping or beating hard results in gummy potatoes." But while leafing through a 1950s cookbook not long ago, I came across a recipe that called for beating potatoes in the mixer for five minutes. Indoctrinated by the "never whip" mantra, I was skeptical. But a colleague confirmed that her own grandmother made whipped potatoes for Thanksgiving, and she swore that no mashed potato had ever tasted as fluffy and ethereal.

I did a little digging (which seemed appropriate for potatoes) and learned that these potatoes supposedly develop their lovely texture from whipping rather than from adding gobs of butter and cream. Recipes for whipped potatoes started to appear in cookbooks in the late 1870s; an 1881 recipe (from *Tasty Dishes, Made from Tested Recipes*) described their texture flatteringly as "almost like a meringue." (Naturally, at that time, they were whipped with a fork, not a mixer.)

Wanting to see what all the fuss was about, I started by picking a handful of recipes. They varied mostly in the ratio and type of boiled potatoes to milk (not cream) and butter; as a group, they used considerably less butter than modern recipes. To my astonishment, not one of the batches I produced—whipped anywhere from one to five minutes—was gluey. Instead, they had the exact fluffy texture the old recipe had predicted. Once I got over the shock, I felt an itch to make improvements. I wondered if it were possible to combine the lovely texture of these mixer-whipped potatoes with the ultra-rich, super-creamy style that's popular today.

I began with our favorite recipe from my first round of tests. A test kitchen colleague had supplied it—well, her mother, actually, who still uses both her 1950 Mixmaster and the recipe booklet that came with it. The Mixmaster recipe called for 4 pounds of hot boiled potatoes, 1 cup of hot milk, a mere 2 tablespoons of butter, and salt and pepper, whipped together for three minutes. I tested Yukon Gold, russet, red, and all-purpose potatoes to see which would make the fluffiest mash; it was the russets, no contest. Our science editor explained that russets have more starch in their cells, which swells when cooked, causing the cells to separate and puff. Waxy varieties have less starch, so they hold together when cooked and have a denser texture.

Now I looked for the best way to cook the potatoes. Most recipes called for boiling, but the russets, which I'd peeled and diced, absorbed a lot of water. If I could get rid of that excess water, might the potatoes be both fluffier and better able to absorb butter and milk? For the next batch, I dried the diced, boiled potatoes over low heat on the stovetop, and sure enough, they pouffed higher than before as they whipped. I next tried cutting them into larger chunks before boiling, figuring they'd absorb even less water. A few tasters detected a slight difference, but when I got a better idea—or so I thought—I changed tack.

What if instead of merely getting rid of excess water, I prevented it from reaching the potatoes in the first place? The heck with boiling; I'd steam them. As soon as they came out of the steamer, I could see there was a flaw in my logic: The potatoes were gluey and sticky to the touch, and even gummier once they were whipped. I put in another call to our science editor, who explained that now that I was no longer boiling them, I was no longer washing away the exterior starch. I fixed the problem by giving the raw, cut russets a good rinse under running water before steaming. They still benefited from a quick stovetop drying session after steaming.

The fluffy cloud of potatoes that came out of the mixing bowl was very nice indeed, and since they weren't wet, I hoped they'd now lap up extra butter and milk. Tablespoon by tablespoon, I added to the recipe to figure out just how much. The answer: 6 more tablespoons of butter and another ½ cup of whole milk. These whipped potatoes were satisfyingly buttery yet perfectly light and fluffy.

—KRIS WIDICAN, *Cook's Country*

NOTES FROM THE TEST KITCHEN

FOR FLUFFY SPUDS, MIX—DON'T PROCESS

We found that the key to light and fluffy whipped potatoes was using the whisk attachment of the stand mixer; the beating motion of the mixer makes smooth, fluffy potatoes every time. If you don't have a stand mixer, a hand-held mixer can be used. Just don't try this recipe in the food processor—the sharp blades will cut open the starch granules and turn the potatoes to glue.

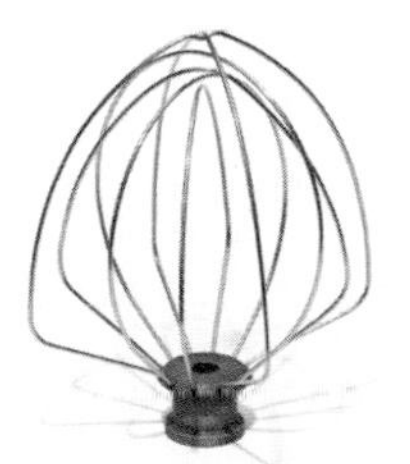

WHIP RIGHT
Use the stand mixer for light, fluffy whipped potatoes.

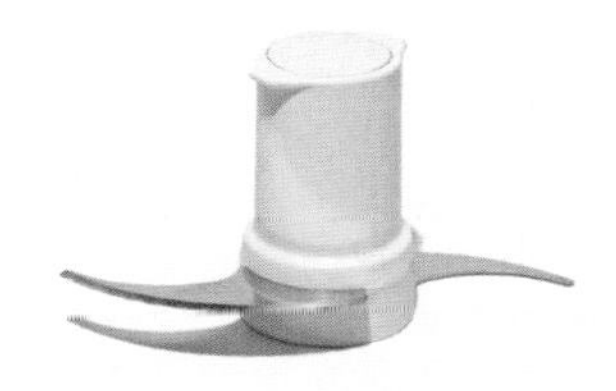

DON'T BOTHER
Don't use a food processor; its blade makes gluey mashed potatoes.

Whipped Potatoes

SERVES 8 TO 10

If your steamer basket has short legs (under 1¾ inches), the potatoes will sit in water as they cook and get wet. To prevent this, use balls of aluminum foil as steamer basket stilts. A stand mixer fitted with a whisk attachment yields the smoothest potatoes, but a hand mixer may be used as well.

- **4 pounds russet potatoes, peeled and cut into 1-inch pieces**
- **1½ cups whole milk**
- **8 tablespoons unsalted butter, cut into pieces**
- **2 teaspoons salt**
- **½ teaspoon pepper**

1. Place potatoes in colander and rinse under cold running water until water runs clear, about 1 minute. Drain potatoes. Fill Dutch oven with 1 inch water and bring to boil. Place steamer basket in Dutch oven and fill with potatoes. Reduce heat to medium and cook, covered, until potatoes are tender, 20 to 25 minutes.

2. Heat milk, butter, salt, and pepper in small saucepan over medium-low heat, whisking until smooth, about 3 minutes; cover and keep warm.

3. Pour contents of Dutch oven into colander and return potatoes to dry pot. Stir over low heat until potatoes are thoroughly dried, about 1 minute. Using stand mixer fitted with whisk, break potatoes into small pieces on low speed, about 30 seconds. Add milk mixture in steady stream until incorporated. Increase speed to high and whip until potatoes are light and fluffy and no lumps remain, about 2 minutes. Serve.

POTATO GALETTE

ABOUT ONCE A YEAR, I FEEL COMPELLED TO MAKE pommes Anna, the classic French potato cake in which thin-sliced potatoes are tossed with clarified butter, tightly shingled in a skillet, and cooked slowly on the stovetop. The results can be glorious: a crisp, deeply bronzed crust encasing a creamy center that tastes of earthy, well-seasoned potatoes and sweet butter. It's about as good as non-deep-fried potatoes can get.

But despite my fondness for it, the galette is strictly special-occasion fare in my house. It's not the ingredient list—that part is brief. But thinly slicing and then diligently layering all those potato disks take more time and attention to detail than I usually want to spend. That said, plenty of existing recipes promise to make the dish "easy," "simple," and "foolproof," but I have yet to find one that really delivers on all counts. Only one that I've tried produced anything resembling the classic potato galette, and it differed from the others in two ways: First, the potatoes were roasted in a very hot (450-degree) oven, where the steady, ambient heat cooked the 3-odd pounds of potatoes evenly (no chalky bits of raw tuber) and colored them nicely brown. Second, only the first layer of ⅛-inch-thick potato slices was neatly arranged; the rest were casually packed into the pan, eliminating most of the usual tedious layering work. Then, following tradition, the cooked galette was inverted out of the skillet, its crisp, golden exterior hiding the haphazard arrangement within.

But the recipe got me only halfway to my goal. The whole operation was still fussier than I wanted, and while the exterior of this improvised galette more or less looked the part, the tightly fused, striated layers that are the hallmark of classic pommes Anna were gone. And as soon as the knife hit the crust, the underlying slices slid apart.

So, there was obvious potential in roasting, and I had a simple (if not totally foolproof) assembly method for the cake—but everything else in the recipe was up for consideration. For starters, there was the pan. Pommes Anna is traditionally cooked in a cast-iron skillet, which absorbs heat beautifully and turns out a galette with a substantial, deeply browned crust. But considering that this new iteration was cooked in the oven—and that inverting the already heavy vessel when it's full and searing hot can be intimidating—wasn't a baking pan worth a try? But as I tested my way through square, round, ovoid, rectangular, and springform pans, every one either warped in the hot oven or failed to generate much of a crust. A skillet really was the best tool for the job, though for convenience's sake—and to avoid the risk of the cake sticking to the pan bottom—I opted to forgo cast iron in favor of an ovensafe nonstick model.

Of course I'd need to compensate for the lighter, thinner pan's browning inadequacies, so I started fiddling with the placement of the oven rack on which the potatoes were cooking. Not surprisingly, the farther I lowered the rack toward the main heating element, the deeper the spuds browned. On the advice of several colleagues, I tried to eke out even more color and flavor by placing a pizza stone under the skillet. Sure enough, the thick slab (which absorbs heat in much the same way as a cast-iron skillet) guaranteed even browning—but it also required preheating for an hour and more heavy lifting than I wanted. Ultimately, I devised a much simpler two-pronged approach that worked equally well: First I got the galette cooking on the stovetop (where the direct flame jump-started the browning process), then I slid the pan onto the bottom rack of the hot oven. That gave me great browning with no stone.

Next up—the laborious clarifying step required by most recipes. This traditional technique involves barely simmering the butter until its water has just cooked off, then removing the milk solids. The idea is that the milk solids in whole butter can cause the potatoes to stick to the bottom of the pan. But when I whipped up batches of my working recipe with clarified and whole butter, I couldn't tell the difference between the two. One more complication out of the way.

NOTES FROM THE TEST KITCHEN

FASTER AND MORE UNIFORM THAN A CHEF'S KNIFE

To make quick work of thin-slicing the potatoes in our galette, we turned to a mandoline. Our favorite model, the **OXO Good Grips V-Blade Mandoline Slicer**, $49.99, sports a razor-sharp V-blade that easily pierces foods; a wide, sturdy gripper guard that keeps your hands out of harm's way; and a measurement-marked dial for accuracy.

POTATO GALETTE

At this point, I was pleased with my progress—the galette was deeply bronzed—but one lingering problem remained: How to keep the potatoes from sliding away from each other into a messy heap when I sliced the cake? One contributing factor, I realized, was my informal assembly method. Simply dumping most of the potatoes into the skillet may have been easy, but the bond between the piled-on slices was fairly haphazard. Still, the lack of adhesiveness often seemed exacerbated by the potatoes themselves. Sometimes they seemed to have more starchy glue, and other times they cooked up overly dry. Up to this point, I'd been using russet potatoes, which virtually every pommes Anna recipe, classic or otherwise, calls for. Switching to Yukon Golds didn't help. Though tasters preferred their buttery, sweet flavor, their texture was just as unreliable as that of the russets, and they weren't any better at keeping the layers together.

After giving it some thought, I realized that the variable "stick-ability" of the potatoes—whether Yukons or russets—had a simple explanation: The starch in any potato is always a wildcard, since it changes considerably depending how long the potato has been out of the ground. To eliminate this factor as a variable, I knew I needed to first wash away the potato starch and then find another means of gluing the slices together. Though counterintuitive, this two-pronged approach was not entirely unfamiliar. A few years back the test kitchen developed a recipe for potato roesti (pommes Anna's Swiss cousin, made with shredded spuds) in which we first rinsed the potatoes of their surface starch, then tossed them with cornstarch to ensure cohesion.

Hopeful that the technique might transfer to my sliced potatoes—I decided to stick with the more flavorful Yukons—I proceeded with my working recipe, swirling the slices in a bowl of cold water to wash away their starch, then thoroughly patting them dry. (Excess moisture also impedes bonding.) Then I added a tablespoon of cornstarch to the melted butter, tossed the two components together, and proceeded with assembly. The result? Big improvement. Though the galette still wasn't quite as dense and compact as a meticulously layered pommes Anna is, at least the slices adhered to one another more reliably.

So what could I do about that loose layering of potatoes? Some recipes suggest occasionally tamping down on the galette as it cooks to compress the slices, but I wondered if more constant contact might be better. I placed a foil-wrapped brick on top of the cake for the first part of the cooking, and the layers did indeed stick together somewhat better, but unevenly—the outer rim was still loose. Rummaging around for something broader and rounder, I spied the cake pan I'd discarded earlier in my testing and thought of a novel deployment. I filled the center with pie weights, placed it on the cake, pressed down firmly, and left it on during the first 20 minutes of baking (with a sheet of oil-sprayed aluminum foil in between to prevent the pan bottom from sticking). After removing the cake pan halfway through cooking to allow the top layer of potatoes to take on a little color, I was delighted to find the cake not only uniformly browned, but nicely compacted as well.

The exhaustive testing paid off. Once flipped out of the pan, my crispy potato cake revealed itself to be perfectly browned and, better yet, perfectly whole. A few cuts with a serrated knife and it was ready to serve—completely looking the part of a classic pommes Anna. I, however, knew the truth: It took an easy few minutes to assemble, cooked largely unattended, and, best yet, was foolproof.

—MATTHEW CARD, *Cook's Illustrated*

Potato Galette

SERVES 6 TO 8

In order for the potato cake to hold together, it is important to slice the potatoes no more than ⅛ inch (3 mm) thick and to make sure the slices are thoroughly dried before assembling the cake. Use a mandoline slicer or the slicing attachment of a food processor to slice the potatoes uniformly thin. Be sure to use a heavy-bottomed ovenproof nonstick skillet for this recipe. A pound of dried beans, rice, or coins can be substituted for the pie weights.

2½ pounds Yukon Gold potatoes, sliced ⅛ inch thick
5 tablespoons unsalted butter, melted
1 tablespoon cornstarch
1½ teaspoons minced fresh rosemary (optional)
1 teaspoon salt
½ teaspoon pepper
Vegetable oil spray

1. Adjust oven rack to lowest position and heat oven to 450 degrees. Place potatoes in large bowl and fill with cold water. Using hands, swirl to remove excess starch, then drain in colander. Spread potatoes on kitchen towels and dry thoroughly.

2. Whisk 4 tablespoons butter, cornstarch, rosemary (if using), salt, and pepper together in large bowl. Add dried potatoes and toss until thoroughly coated. Place remaining 1 tablespoon butter in 10-inch ovenproof nonstick skillet and swirl to coat. Place 1 potato slice in center of skillet, then overlap slices in circle around center slice, followed by outer circle of overlapping slices. Gently place remaining sliced potatoes on top of first layer, arranging so they form even thickness.

3. Place skillet over medium-high heat and cook until sizzling and potatoes around edge of skillet start to turn translucent, about 5 minutes. Spray 12-inch square of aluminum foil with vegetable oil spray. Place foil, sprayed side down, on top of potatoes. Place 9-inch cake pan on top of foil and fill with 2 cups pie weights. Firmly press down on cake pan to compress potatoes. Transfer skillet to oven and bake for 20 minutes.

4. Remove cake pan and foil from skillet. Continue to cook until potatoes are tender when paring knife is inserted in center, 20 to 25 minutes longer. Return skillet to medium heat on stovetop and cook, gently shaking pan (using potholder, as handle will be hot), until galette releases from sides of pan, 2 to 3 minutes. Carefully slide galette onto large plate, place cutting board over galette, and gently invert plate and cutting board together; remove plate. Using serrated knife, gently cut galette into wedges and serve immediately.

NOTES FROM THE TEST KITCHEN

MAKING POTATO GALETTE

1. Place 1 potato slice in center of skillet, then overlap potato slices in circle around center slice.

2. Continue to layer potato slices in overlapping fashion to form layer that covers bottom of pan. Then gently place remaining potatoes on top to form second layer, making sure to form cake of even thickness.

3. After cooking potatoes for 5 minutes, place foil on top and press down on galette with cake pan full of pie weights. Transfer skillet to oven, keeping cake pan on top for first 20 minutes of baking.

INVERTING POTATO GALETTE

1. Slide loosened galette out of skillet onto large plate.

2. Gently place cutting board over galette. Do not use overly heavy board, which may crush it.

3. Carefully flip plate over so board is on bottom. Remove plate and slice and serve galette.

BARBECUE FRENCH FRIES

I'VE TRIED EVERY PERMUTATION OF FRENCH FRIES: Cajun, Buffalo, rosemary-Parmesan, garlic, and even butterscotch (don't ask). But my favorite variation is barbecue french fries, which should be crispy on the outside, light and fluffy within, and freckled with sweet and tangy barbecue spices. I set out to create a recipe that I could call on whenever the craving hit.

Since there was no getting around peeling and cutting russet potatoes (which fry up crisp and creamy) into fries, the cooking would have to be dead simple. Most french fry recipes call for double-frying: an initial fry cooks the interior, and a second, higher-temperature fry crisps the outside. Hoping to avoid frying twice, I boiled the potatoes to cook the interiors and then fried them just once to crisp the outside. Unfortunately, potatoes wet from boiling translate to mealy fries. Next, I precooked the fries in the microwave so they wouldn't be submerged in water. I drained and cooled them thoroughly before they hit the hot oil. The payoff? Fluffy interior, crispy exterior.

Frying the potatoes in two batches also proved key, since one big batch (I was using 3 pounds of potatoes to serve four) cooled down the oil and gave me soggy fries. After much trial and error, I landed on a method of frying half the potatoes until almost done, removing them, and adding the other half to the oil. Then, when the second batch was almost done, I returned the first batch to the pot briefly so all the fries were done at the same time.

I turned my attention to the spices. Working from a classic barbecue spice rub, I tossed a batch of cooked fries with paprika, chili powder, salt, brown sugar, onion powder, and cayenne. These fries were OK, but the spices tasted raw and a little rough around the edges. Toasting the spices in a dry skillet helped round out their flavor.

These fries had good barbecue flavor on the outside, but my tasters challenged me to get that smoky, spicy flavor all the way through. I tried adding the spices to the raw potatoes and microwaving them together, but the spices burned as soon as they hit the hot oil. I got the same result with adding bottled barbecue sauce to the potatoes in the microwave—the sauce burned in the oil. But one ingredient in the bottled sauce held promise: liquid smoke. I added a few drops to the cut potatoes before microwaving and then fried and tossed the fries with spices at the end. The smoke flavor permeated the flesh of the potato, perfectly complementing the spices on the exterior.

—MEGHAN ERWIN, *Cook's Country*

Barbecue French Fries

SERVES 4

Our top-rated brand of liquid smoke is Wright's All Natural Hickory Seasoning Liquid Smoke; it contains only smoke and water.

- **3 pounds russet potatoes, peeled and cut into ½-inch-thick fries**
- **¼ teaspoon liquid smoke**
- **½ teaspoon chili powder**
- **½ teaspoon paprika**
- **¼ teaspoon salt**
- **⅛ teaspoon brown sugar**
- **⅛ teaspoon cayenne pepper**
- **⅛ teaspoon onion powder**
- **3 quarts peanut oil or vegetable oil**

NOTES FROM THE TEST KITCHEN

BUILDING BIG BARBECUE FLAVOR

We season our fries inside and out with barbecue smoke and spice. Microwaving the potatoes with liquid smoke first infuses them with pungent smoke flavor, and tossing the fried potatoes with our own toasted spice blend ensures that their exteriors are well seasoned with barbecue flavor.

SMOKE

SPICE

1. Toss potatoes with liquid smoke in large bowl. Cover tightly with plastic wrap and microwave until potatoes are tender but not falling apart, 6 to 8 minutes, shaking bowl to redistribute potatoes halfway through cooking. Drain potatoes and arrange on paper towel–lined baking sheet. Cool until firm, about 10 minutes. (Potatoes can be stored at room temperature, covered, for up to 2 hours.)

2. Toast chili powder, paprika, salt, sugar, cayenne, and onion powder in dry skillet over medium heat, stirring frequently, until fragrant, 1 minute; transfer to bowl.

3. Heat oil in Dutch oven over high heat to 375 degrees. Fry half of potatoes, stirring occasionally, until golden brown, 5 to 6 minutes. Replace paper towels on baking sheet and drain fries. Return oil to 375 degrees and add remaining fries. When second batch is golden brown, return first batch to oil and fry until all fries are deep golden brown and crisp, 1 to 3 minutes. Drain on paper towels and transfer to bowl. Add spice mixture and toss to coat. Serve.

ASPARAGUS GRATIN

IN A TRADITIONAL GRATIN, VEGETABLES ARE swaddled in a creamy, cheesy sauce. This approach works wonders for hardy potatoes and cauliflower—the mild vegetables get a boost from the strong cheese sauce while providing starch that thickens the sauce as they slowly bake and soften. Asparagus, by contrast, has a bright flavor and takes mere minutes to cook, so I wasn't surprised when I dug into an asparagus gratin and pulled out a brown, lifeless stalk. What a shame to smother this delicate spring vegetable. For a dish more like a light spring jacket than a bulky woolen coat, I'd approach the asparagus and sauce separately, and then bring them together for a quick broil to brown the top.

I trimmed the tough bottom ends off two bunches of asparagus, steamed the stalks until barely tender, and then set to work on the sauce. I made a roux with 2 tablespoons each of butter and flour and whisked in a cup of half-and-half (heavy cream was stifling), followed by Parmesan and Gruyère, two classic gratin cheeses. The sauce was slightly gritty and squelched the vegetable's flavor. Tests showed that the Gruyère was to blame for the grit, so I traded it for milder, smoother Monterey Jack. I poured this new sauce over steamed asparagus and summoned tasters. The grit was gone and the cheese flavor was well calibrated. Unfortunately, the half-and-half still muffled the fresh asparagus flavor.

To give the asparagus more breathing room, I made three different sauces: my working recipe (with the half-and-half), a version in which I replaced half of the half-and-half with water, and a third in which I used all water. "A cheese sauce with no milk or cream?" asked some incredulous tasters. But much to our surprise, we

NOTES FROM THE TEST KITCHEN

MAKING A LIGHTER, LIVELIER SAUCE

For a richly flavored but not-so-heavy sauce for our Asparagus Gratin, we started by making a five-minute vegetable stock from the woody asparagus ends. Then we simmered the asparagus spears in the stock, creating a double-concentrated liquid that we used in our cheese sauce in place of the usual (smothering) heavy cream.

TRIMMED ASPARAGUS ENDS

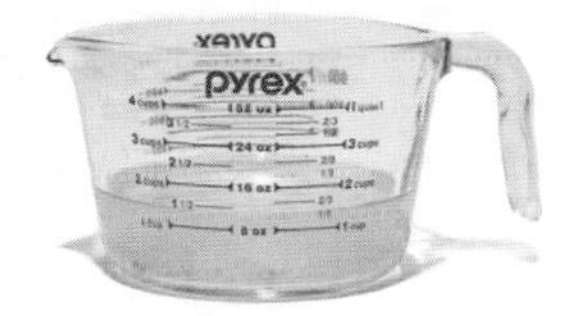

ASPARAGUS STOCK

THE BEST BROILER-SAFE BAKING DISH

When it comes to casseroles, our favorite pan is the Pyrex Bakeware 13 by 9-inch Baking Dish. But this essential dish shouldn't go under the broiler; abrupt temperature changes can cause it to crack or shatter. We wanted an alternative with roughly the same dimensions and capacity, since many recipes are sized to fit the Pyrex, but it had to be able to handle the heat. We gathered seven rectangular broiler-safe baking dishes and cranked up the heat. We tested two dishes made of enameled cast iron and five made of ceramic, including two of porcelain, which is lighter, harder, and less porous than many other ceramics.

Because heat comes from above during broiling, the pan's conductivity has less effect on cooking performance than it would if used in baking; therefore, design and shape were just as important when it came to our testing. We preferred the lightweight porcelain dishes, which were easy to carry, even when full. Large, easy-to-grip handles were also important, and straight sides ensured that the capacity of the baking dish wasn't cut short and that the food was easy to slice. Our winner was the **HIC Porcelain Lasagna Baking Dish**, $37.49, which has large handles and straight sides. (See page 310 for more information about our testing results.)

ASPARAGUS GRATIN

liked that version best. For the first time in weeks, we could really taste the asparagus. True, the sauce was now anemic, but I could fix that: I'd replace the water with vegetable stock. Scrounging around the test kitchen for scraps to make stock, I remembered the asparagus trimmings. Perfect—I'd use those.

For clean, pure asparagus flavor, I'd make the stock with nothing but the trimmings. After just five minutes of simmering, I had a decidedly asparagus-flavored stock. I made a new sauce using 1 cup of my five-minute stock in place of the original half-and-half and was pleased by how it brought the asparagus and cheese flavors into balance.

At this point, I happened to notice that when I drained the water from cooking the asparagus, it was pale green—I had been pouring flavor down the drain. To harness it, I first simmered the asparagus ends in water to make my five-minute stock, and then simmered the spears in the stock instead of in plain water. After the spears were cooked, I reserved the now-double-concentrated stock and used it to make the sauce. I sauced the asparagus, sprinkled extra Parmesan on top, and broiled the gratin to crisp the cheese. This asparagus gratin was dressed for spring.

—SARAH GABRIEL, *Cook's Country*

Asparagus Gratin

SERVES 8

For even cooking, buy asparagus spears that are between ¼ and ½ inch thick.

- **2 pounds thin asparagus**
- **2½ cups water**
- **Salt and pepper**
- **2 tablespoons unsalted butter**
- **2 tablespoons all-purpose flour**
- **2 ounces Monterey Jack cheese, shredded (½ cup)**
- **1½ ounces Parmesan cheese, grated (¾ cup)**

1. Adjust oven rack to upper-middle position and heat broiler. Line broiler-safe baking dish with paper towels. Trim 1½ inches from stem end of asparagus and reserve ends. Bring water to boil in 12-inch skillet over medium-high heat. Add asparagus ends and ¼ teaspoon salt and cook, covered, for 5 minutes. Using slotted spoon, remove asparagus ends and discard. Add asparagus stalks to skillet, cover, and cook, stirring occasionally, until nearly tender, 2 to 4 minutes. Transfer asparagus to paper towel–lined baking dish. Pour asparagus water into liquid measuring cup; reserve 1 cup.

2. Melt butter in now-empty skillet over medium heat. Add flour and cook, stirring constantly, until golden, about 1 minute. Whisk in reserved asparagus water and bring to boil. Reduce heat to medium-low and simmer until thickened, 3 to 5 minutes. Off heat, whisk in Monterey Jack and ½ cup of Parmesan until smooth. Season with salt and pepper to taste. Cover and let stand for 5 minutes.

3. Remove paper towels from baking dish. Drizzle sauce over center of asparagus and top with remaining ¼ cup Parmesan. Broil until cheese is golden and asparagus is tender, 6 to 8 minutes. Serve.

BUTTERED CARROTS

CARROTS ARE ALWAYS ON MY EASTER TABLE, RIGHT next to the ham, asparagus, and a lemon dessert of some sort. Over the years, I've glazed them with marmalade; simmered them with chicken stock, honey, and butter; and roasted them in a very hot oven. As I put together this year's holiday menu, I found myself thinking, "Been there, done that." That's when I remembered reading about an intriguing method for "waterless carrots." It's an adaptation of a French technique in which finely sliced, or "ribboned," carrots are cooked in a covered saucepan with butter, salt, pepper, and nothing else. While I liked the idea of a simple recipe showcasing the natural sweetness and earthiness of carrots, I admit I was skeptical. Was it possible to cook this hard root vegetable well with no liquid at all? I decided to find out.

Following an old recipe, I peeled and "scraped" 2 pounds of medium carrots with a vegetable peeler, into what resembled a pile of carrot ribbons. I put them in a saucepan with 4 tablespoons of butter and the seasonings, and then covered the pot. After they'd cooked for 10 minutes over low heat, I lifted the lid and was surprised to find the carrot ribbons simmering in very buttery, orange liquid. The salt was apparently drawing out the natural moisture as the carrots cooked. I dipped a spoon into the carrot liquid and was delighted by its sweet, concentrated flavor. Unfortunately, the carrots themselves had cooked down into a greasy mound of vegetable mush.

For my next test, I abandoned the ribbons (they were labor-intensive and, truth be told, a little too frou-frou for my tastes anyway) and instead sliced the carrots into ¼-inch pennies. I also cut the butter back to 3 tablespoons—just enough to coat the carrots without making them greasy. To speed things along, I started cooking them over medium heat. When steam began coming from the saucepan, indicating that the carrots were producing their own liquid (after about five minutes), I reduced the heat to low and let them simmer in their juice until tender, 15 to 20 minutes more. Now I helped myself to a bowl. Utterly undiluted by any water or chicken broth, the sweet, pure carroty flavor was intense—and the very essence of carrot. Some of the slices remained slightly crunchy, however, so I transferred the operation to a skillet for my next test. Spread out on the larger surface, the carrot pennies could cook more evenly.

At this point, the carrots were really good, especially considering that I'd hardly done any work. There was still carrot liquid left in the skillet, so I uncovered it and turned up the heat. As the carrot juice reduced and concentrated, the milk solids in the butter began to brown. What luck! The browning butter added an unexpected and utterly delicious, nutty, caramelized dimension to the dish.

These carrots were so naturally concentrated and sweet, they needed almost no seasoning: just a hit of fresh chive, and they tasted fantastic. Still, variety is the spice of life, and my tasters demanded some. I developed three simple variations. To one batch of carrots I added sliced shallots and tarragon. To a second I added freshly grated ginger and cilantro, and to a third a bit of orange juice and minced parsley. The technique is so simple that I'd urge every home cook to come up with his or her own personalized variation on this easy recipe.

—DIANE UNGER, *Cook's Country*

Buttered Carrots

SERVES 6 TO 8

Slice the carrots as evenly as you can so they cook at the same rate.

- **3 tablespoons unsalted butter**
- **2 pounds carrots, peeled and sliced ¼ inch thick on bias**
- **Salt and pepper**
- **2 tablespoons minced fresh chives**

1. Melt butter in 12-inch skillet over medium heat. Add carrots and ½ teaspoon salt and cook, covered, until steam begins to escape from under lid, about 5 minutes. Reduce heat to low and continue to cook, covered, stirring occasionally, until carrots are just tender, 15 to 20 minutes longer.

2. Remove lid, add ¼ teaspoon pepper, and cook, stirring occasionally, until liquid is evaporated and butter begins to brown, about 5 minutes. Sprinkle with chives and season with salt and pepper to taste. Serve.

VARIATIONS

Buttered Carrots with Shallots and Tarragon

Add 2 thinly sliced shallots with carrots in step 1. Substitute 1 tablespoon minced fresh tarragon for chives.

Buttered Carrots with Ginger and Cilantro

Add 2 teaspoons grated fresh ginger with carrots in step 1. Substitute 1 tablespoon minced fresh cilantro for chives.

Buttered Carrots with Orange and Parsley

Add 1 teaspoon grated orange zest with carrots in step 1. Substitute 1 tablespoon minced fresh parsley for chives.

WILD RICE DRESSING

WILD RICE DRESSING IS USUALLY JUST ANOTHER name for pilaf: The rice is cooked in chicken broth or water, then flavorings and vegetables are sautéed and stirred in. That's fine for stuffing a Cornish hen, but I wanted to add bread and make the mixture cohesive, bringing wild rice dressing closer to classic Thanksgiving stuffing.

Before I even started on the dressing, though, I bought several brands of wild rice to familiarize myself with the star ingredient. Some recipes called for boiling the rice for up to an hour, others for just 30 minutes. The liquid-to-rice proportions on the back of the boxes were as inconsistent as the times. After making a few batches of different brands, I learned that the reason for these disparities was that wild rice varies, well, wildly in its absorbency. Since I couldn't know exactly how much water would be absorbed by the rice, I'd have to cook the grains in extra liquid, draining them and discarding the liquid once the rice was tender. To feed 12, I settled on 4 cups of water to 2 cups of rice. For extra flavor, I replaced half the water with chicken broth.

I added the boiled rice to sautéed celery, herbs, and onions, as is usual for a dressing, and then tossed in 10 slices' worth of stale bread cubes for good measure. To make the dressing cohesive and rich, I decided on that most satisfying of combinations—cream and eggs, aka custard. I poured custard I'd made with heavy cream over the stuffing base. The bread cubes drank it up. But while the baked dressing held together, it was so rich that tasters could barely eat two forkfuls. I was about to replace some of the cream with chicken broth when I got a better idea: I'd use the liquid left from cooking the rice. I saved 1½ cups and used it to dilute the same amount of heavy cream. Now the stuffing's nutty, earthy flavor was spot-on, plus the starchy cooking liquid made the casserole even more cohesive.

A few nagging problems remained. The big cubes of bread overpowered the bitty grains of rice. Easy—I processed the cubes into pea-size pieces. Next, the grains of rice at the surface of the casserole were inedibly crunchy. To fix this, I covered the casserole with aluminum foil. The grains cooked through, but the dressing was now pale and squishy. By toasting the bread, I got a semblance of color and crunch on top (and no longer needed stale bread). I then reinforced both by drizzling melted butter over the casserole before baking it. Yes, it's unconventional, but this dressing is rich, nutty, buttery, savory, and wholly delicious, fit for any holiday table.

—IAN KNAUER, *Cook's Country*

Wild Rice Dressing

SERVES 10 TO 12

Depending on the brand, wild rice absorbs varying quantities of liquid. If you have less than 1½ cups of leftover cooking liquid, make up the difference with additional low-sodium chicken broth.

- **2 cups low-sodium chicken broth**
- **2 cups water**
- **1 bay leaf**
- **2 cups wild rice**
- **10 slices hearty white sandwich bread, torn into pieces**
- **8 tablespoons unsalted butter**
- **2 onions, chopped fine**
- **3 celery ribs, minced**
- **4 garlic cloves, minced**
- **1½ teaspoons dried sage**
- **1½ teaspoons dried thyme**
- **1½ cups heavy cream**
- **2 large eggs**
- **¾ teaspoon salt**
- **½ teaspoon pepper**

1. Bring broth, water, and bay leaf to boil in medium saucepan over medium-high heat. Add rice, reduce heat to low, and simmer, covered, until rice is tender, 35 to 45 minutes. Strain contents of pan through fine-mesh strainer into liquid measuring cup. Transfer rice to bowl; discard bay leaf. Measure out and reserve 1½ cups cooking liquid.

2. Adjust oven racks to upper-middle and lower-middle positions and heat oven to 325 degrees. Pulse half of bread in food processor into pea-size pieces and transfer to rimmed baking sheet. Repeat with remaining bread and second rimmed baking sheet. Bake bread crumbs until golden, about 20 minutes, stirring occasionally and switching and rotating sheets halfway through baking. Cool completely, about 10 minutes.

3. Melt 4 tablespoons butter in 12-inch skillet over medium heat. Cook onions and celery until softened and golden, 8 to 10 minutes. Add garlic, sage, and thyme and cook until fragrant, about 30 seconds. Stir in reserved cooking liquid, remove from heat, and let cool for 5 minutes.

4. Whisk cream, eggs, salt, and pepper together in large bowl. Slowly whisk in warm broth-vegetable mixture. Stir in rice and toasted bread crumbs and

NOTES FROM THE TEST KITCHEN

HARVESTING RICE WATER

Instead of letting the flavorful, starchy rice cooking liquid go down the drain, we reserved it and used it in our dressing, which amplified the earthy, nutty flavor of our casserole and made the dressing more cohesive.

transfer to 13 by 9-inch baking dish. (Dressing can be refrigerated for up to 1 day. To serve, proceed with recipe, increasing baking time by 20 minutes.)

5. Melt remaining 4 tablespoons butter in now-empty skillet and drizzle evenly over dressing. Cover dish with aluminum foil and bake on lower-middle rack until set, 45 to 55 minutes. Remove foil and let cool for 15 minutes. Serve.

VARIATIONS

Dried Fruit and Nut Wild Rice Dressing

Add 1½ cups chopped dried apricots, cranberries, or cherries and 1½ cups chopped toasted pecans with bread crumbs in step 4.

Leek and Mushroom Wild Rice Dressing

Substitute 4 leeks (white and light green parts only), halved lengthwise and sliced thin, and 10 ounces thinly sliced cremini mushrooms for onions and celery.

BUTTERED SPAETZLE

SLIGHTLY CHEWY, LIGHT, AND BUTTERY, SPAETZLE are a homey cross between egg noodles and dumplings that are often served with sauerbraten. And while the idea of making homemade noodles (or dumplings) is daunting, spaetzle (pronounced SHPEHT-sel) are pretty simple. A batter of nothing more than flour, eggs, and water or milk is pushed through the holes of a spaetzle-making gadget (what, you don't have one?) into boiling water, then drained and buttered.

I tested several recipes and, based on the results, started with 2 cups of seasoned flour, 3 eggs, and about ¾ cup of liquid—which gave me a batter stiff enough to form cohesive dumplings yet loose enough to pass through a spaetzle press or whatever I came up with as a substitute. My next test showed that milk produced richer, lighter spaetzle than water. Some recipes advise resting the batter before forming the dumplings; if the gluten can relax, the spaetzle will be tender. Did I have to? I made five batches, cooking one right away and letting the others rest for varying lengths of time. A 15- to 30-minute rest proved ideal.

Originally, spaetzle were formed by hand into pieces of dough that resembled small sparrows (spaetzle in German). They became considerably quicker to make after the invention of the spaetzle press. What's an American cook to do without one? I tried scraping the batter off the edge of a cutting board into boiling water (a method many recipes suggest); the spaetzle from the front of the board were done before I'd finished scraping. The holes in both a potato ricer and a colander were too small to form good-sized dumplings.

I'd have to jury-rig a spaetzle press. I poked holes in a disposable aluminum pie plate, scooped in the batter, and pushed it through. The pie plate folded, and I'd have needed an extra set of hands to hold it steady while pushing. Next, I tried a lasagna-size aluminum pan, which was big enough to rest on the rim of the pot. I learned from experience to work with half the batter at a time. Otherwise the batter fuses into one gigantic noodle. As soon as the spaetzle floated to the surface, I drained them and tossed them with butter. They were even better when crisped in an oiled skillet (butter burned) with shallots. Off the heat, I stirred in a tasty pat of butter—and gave myself a pat on the back for a recipe I knew I'd be making again soon.

—DIANE UNGER, *Cook's Country*

Buttered Spaetzle

SERVES 6 TO 8

Three tablespoons of finely chopped red onion can be substituted for the shallot.

- **2 cups all-purpose flour**
- **Salt and pepper**
- **¼ teaspoon ground nutmeg**
- **¾ cup whole milk**
- **3 large eggs**
- **1 (13 by 9-inch) disposable aluminum roasting pan**
- **2 tablespoons vegetable oil**
- **1 shallot, minced**
- **2 tablespoons unsalted butter**

1. Combine flour, ¾ teaspoon salt, ½ teaspoon pepper, and nutmeg in large bowl. Whisk milk and eggs until combined in bowl. Slowly whisk milk mixture

BUTTERED SPAETZLE

NOTES FROM THE TEST KITCHEN

MAKING SPAETZLE

1. Set disposable aluminum pan over empty Dutch oven and poke about forty ¼-inch holes into bottom of pan with paring knife. Remove pan and boil water.

2. Then set pan with holes over pot and use spatula to scrape batter through holes into boiling water to form spaetzle.

into flour mixture until smooth. Cover and let rest for 15 to 30 minutes.

2. Meanwhile, set disposable pan over empty Dutch oven and poke about forty ¼-inch holes into bottom; set aside. Bring 4 quarts water to boil in Dutch oven. Add 1 tablespoon salt and set prepared pan on Dutch oven. Transfer half of batter to prepared pan and use spatula to scrape batter across holes, letting it fall into water. Boil until spaetzle float, about 1 minute. Using slotted spoon, transfer spaetzle to paper towel–lined baking sheet to drain. Repeat with remaining batter. Pat spaetzle dry with paper towels. (Spaetzle can be tossed with 1 tablespoon vegetable oil and refrigerated for up to 1 day. To serve, proceed with step 3.)

3. Heat oil in 12-inch nonstick skillet over medium-high heat until shimmering. Stir in shallot and cook until softened, about 2 minutes. Add spaetzle and cook, stirring occasionally, until golden and crisp at edges, 5 to 7 minutes. Off heat, stir in butter. Season with salt and pepper to taste and serve.

MEATY BAKED BEANS

ONCE UPON A TIME, HOME COOKS PUT MORE MEAT in their baked beans than we do today. A whole lot more. For a single quart of beans, the great Fannie Farmer used to call for an entire pound of "mixed pork." (Apparently, 19th-century butchers didn't specialize in shrink-wrapped packages of just pork shoulder or ham hocks.) Blame it on economics or the vegetarian revolution, but nowadays you're lucky to find a few strips of bacon or a token cube of salt pork in that same quart of cooked legumes. And that is a darn shame.

I wanted to restore meat to its proper status as an equal partner in this pork-and-beans duo. What I had in mind was a hearty, satisfying dish: creamy, well-seasoned beans and loads of rich, meltingly tender pork simmered together in a thick, balanced sauce as porky as it was sweet and tangy.

After trying out a few recipes to get my bearings, I learned there were as many interpretations of this dish as beans in a bag—and as many pitfalls. Beans ended up overcooked and blown out—or as crunchy as raw peanuts. I tasted my way through cloying, syrupy sauces and stringy, chewy, and/or flavorless meat.

First up, the beans. In most recipes the beans are simmered for hours in the oven, but the details were legion. To soak or not to soak? For how long and how hot? Times and temperatures varied from a 450-degree power sprint to a daylong, 250-degree affair. Starting with 1 pound of dried beans (I used navy), 6 cups of water, a couple of ham hocks (which I'd definitely bump up later), and ½ cup each of molasses and barbecue sauce (for sweetness and zip), I made several batches, testing every variable. Just before serving, I stirred the meat pulled from the hocks into the saucy beans.

Moderation proved key: The beans were creamy and evenly cooked after three to four hours in a 350-degree oven. Regarding soaking, I liked what an overnight soak did to pare down the cooking time. The tiny navy beans I'd been using were perfectly tasty, but given the pork-apalooza I had in store, I wondered if a heartier bean might be better. In a side-by-side comparison of navy beans, pink beans, pintos, and kidney beans, our favorite turned out to be the meatier pinks (with pintos a close runner-up), for their luxuriously creamy interiors.

Finally, the pork. While ham hocks were providing pretty good flavor, I didn't end up with nearly enough pullable meat. I wanted a morsel in every bite! Bumping up the number of ham hocks so that I could get enough meat left hardly enough room in the pot for the beans. But the smoky taste was a keeper, so I tried several other options, most of which were ill suited to the four-hour simmer: ham steak (spongy), smoked pork chops (rubbery), bacon (it simply melted into the sauce). The prize pig was a boneless smoked pork shoulder cut into hefty chunks. With the average supermarket shoulder weighing in at almost 3 pounds, the smoky taste infused every bean, and I had more than enough succulent meat in the end.

Turning my attention to the sauce, I found that sweet, tangy ketchup beat out the smoky barbecue sauce I was using (now that I had smoked flavor in spades), dark brown sugar balanced out the strong flavors best, a quarter-cup of spicy brown mustard provided a welcome punch of heat, and a bit of sautéed onion and garlic added fragrant complexity. I gave the beans one more taste. Every forkful was packed with tender, smoky meat and lusciously creamy beans, and the sweet-smoky-tangy liquid reduced to a silky sauce. Fannie would be pleased.

—DIANE UNGER, *Cook's Country*

NOTES FROM THE TEST KITCHEN

MORE OF A GOOD THING

Most recipes for baked beans flavor lots of beans with only a smidgen of pork. For truly meaty baked beans, we reversed the usual meat-to-bean ratio, using just a small hill of beans to a pile of pork.

1 POUND OF BEANS

3 POUNDS OF PORK

Meaty Baked Beans

SERVES 6

Begin checking for doneness after 2 hours of uncovered baking. If the sauce has thickened but the beans are not yet tender, add up to 1½ cups water and continue baking. You can substitute boneless smoked ham for the boneless smoked pork shoulder.

- **1 pound dried pink beans (2½ cups), picked over and rinsed**
- **1 tablespoon vegetable oil**
- **1 onion, chopped fine**
- **4 garlic cloves, minced**
- **6 cups water**
- **1 (2½- to 3-pound) boneless smoked pork shoulder roast, cut into 4 pieces**
- **1 cup ketchup**
- **½ cup packed dark brown sugar**
- **¼ cup spicy brown mustard**
- **Pepper**

1. Place beans in Dutch oven and add water to cover by 1 inch. Let stand overnight; drain well.

2. Adjust oven rack to middle position and heat oven to 350 degrees. Heat oil in Dutch oven over medium heat until shimmering. Add onion and cook until softened, about 5 minutes. Stir in garlic and cook until fragrant, about 30 seconds. Add water, pork, and beans and bring to boil. Cover, transfer to oven, and cook until beans are just beginning to soften, about 1 hour.

3. Stir in ketchup, sugar, and mustard. Bake, uncovered, until beans are completely tender and sauce is slightly thickened, 2 to 3 hours. Remove pork from pot and transfer to plate. When cool enough to handle, cut pork into bite-size pieces and return to pot; discard fat. Season with pepper to taste. Serve. (Beans can be refrigerated for up to 3 days.)

TO CAT

CHAPTER 4

BREAKFAST & BREADS

DEEP-DISH QUICHE LORRAINE

THERE ARE ANY NUMBER OF REASONS THAT "REAL" men don't eat quiche, but here's mine: Unlike the authentic version, composed of a crisp, flaky shell that stands tall and is filled to the brim with plush, silky custard, typical wedges suffer one of several classic flaws. Some feel so slight on the plate they're more tart than main-course material, and others are so overaccessorized with add-ins that the carefully bound egg-cream mixture either breaks into a curdled puddle or fades into the background.

That's why I used to avoid quiche altogether. Given all the effort that goes into turning out a homemade version—and from-scratch versions don't come together quickly—it seemed like a waste of both my kitchen time and my appetite. But recently I came across a recipe in *Bouchon*, the bistro cookbook by famed chef Thomas Keller, that gave me pause. From the description and photos alone—Keller dedicates eight pages to the subject—I could see that this was a quiche I could get behind. Thick-crusted and baked in a ring mold standing 2 inches tall, it brimmed with creamy custard in which healthy (but not heavy-handed) doses of fillings—the bacon, onion, and shredded Gruyère of the classic Lorraine version—were perfectly suspended. In fact, this might have become my go-to recipe, save for the extreme labor (the onions alone take two hours to prepare) and the ring mold, essentially a specialty tool. After one bite, though, I knew it would be my model as I developed a streamlined version.

First things first: If I wanted more custard, I needed a taller vessel. The typical choices—a 1-inch-deep tart pan with flared sides or a similarly shaped 1½-inch-deep pie plate—can't accommodate more than 4 cups of filling once lined with pastry. (I was aiming for the 8 cups called for in Keller's quiche.) Scaling up to a 2-inch-tall deep-dish pie pan wasn't enough. The straight sides of the ring mold in Keller's recipe give it more volume, but since I didn't have one, I fished around in my bakeware cabinet for something comparable and pulled out my 9-inch springform pan. Its 2½-inch removable walls offered plenty of capacity and easily unfastened from the base when it came time to unmold the tart. Unfortunately, those perks came with problems of their own: Namely, the custard had a tendency to leak through the thin gap between the springform's base and ring, and fitting my pastry dough up the exceptionally tall sides without tearing it took some practice. The other option on hand—a 9 by 2-inch round cake pan—more closely approximated the ring mold without the architectural and plumbing issues.

For extra insurance against leaks and tearing, I employed three more tricks. First, I lined the pan with a foil "sling" to help extract the pastry from its mold. Second, I picked up a handy pastry technique from Keller's recipe: Using most of a double-crust pastry (the test kitchen's regular pie dough proved too malleable here, so I opted for our favorite all-butter pastry), I rolled out a 15-inch round and draped a generous amount of dough up and over the sides of the pan, which helped to anchor the crust in place, preventing it from sagging or shrinking when prebaked. And third, I glazed the baked crust with an egg white wash before adding the filling, which helped seal any would-be cracks. Rich with butter, supremely flaky, and strong enough to hold the custard without turning soggy, this crust was the perfect bowl for satiny custard.

Unfortunately, my custard still resembled a soupy omelet—not the quivering, barely set pudding I was after. Like all gels, custard is a delicate matter, and its success depends on just the right ratio of eggs to liquid (including any excess moisture exuded by watery ingredients like onions) plus gentle, even heat. I baked off dozens of quiches, taking the eggs and dairy up and down and fiddling with the oven's temperature dial. Too few eggs left the custard loose and runny, and too many lent it a scrambled-egg flavor and rubbery chew. I finally settled on eight whole eggs, plus the extra yolk left over from sealing the crust (which contributed more fat and emulsifiers for a creamier texture), and 3 cups of dairy (I got the best results with a 50–50 split of whole milk and heavy cream). I baked the quiche in a 350-degree oven until it was just barely firm in the center (about 160 degrees); any hotter and the custard started to curdle.

Now came the really tricky part: introducing the fillings. Never mind that I had just refined the fragile suspension of the custard to a tee (though, admittedly, it wouldn't be sliceable until it had chilled overnight in the fridge); tossing in other ingredients, specifically watery onions, broke it apart in seconds. To mitigate this effect, I needed to understand how heat turns eggs from liquid to solid in the first place. According to our science editor, heat breaks the tight bonds inside the individual egg proteins, allowing them to unravel. When these stretched-out proteins encounter one another, they bond to produce a three-dimensional network. Inside that web are smaller compartments of the liquid that previously surrounded the proteins. The result is the conversion of a protein-rich liquid (raw eggs, milk, and cream) into a moist, solid protein network (custard).

But when onions enter the equation, the weak acid they release produces electrical charges on the proteins, causing them to fuse and squeeze out the suspended liquid in the process; in other words, the custard curdles. To prevent this, our science editor suggested, we should add a little cornstarch. One large spoonful (1½ tablespoons) whisked into the dairy kept the custard glossy and rich from one edge of the pastry to the other. Better yet, it allowed me to bake the quiche longer, until it reached 170 degrees at its center, which resulted in a slightly firmer, more foolproof custard that could be sliced cleanly on the day it was baked.

Finally, more than 50 quiches (and untold hundreds of eggs) later, I sat down to a hearty, clean-cut slice: The wall of butter-rich, flaky crust gave way to lush, shiny custard packed with the salty-sweet-nutty mix of flavors that defines a good Lorraine-style quiche. Any man (or woman) could happily sink a fork into this—and proudly serve it to company.

—ANDREW JANJIGIAN, *Cook's Illustrated*

NOTES FROM THE TEST KITCHEN

USING A CAKE PAN FOR DEEP-DISH QUICHE

1. Unlike a pie plate, a deep cake pan requires foil sling (made from two lengths of foil) to remove quiche. Crimp ends of foil around rim of cake pan to secure.

2. Instead of 12-inch round, roll out dough to 15-inch circle big enough to fit in cake pan with plenty of overhang.

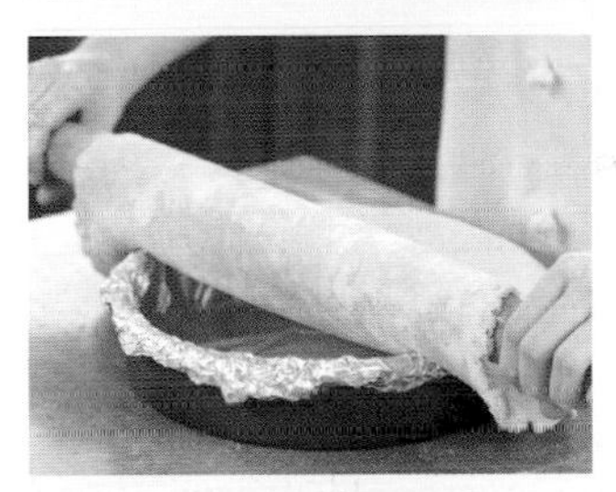

3. Roll dough loosely around rolling pin and unroll it into foil-lined cake pan.

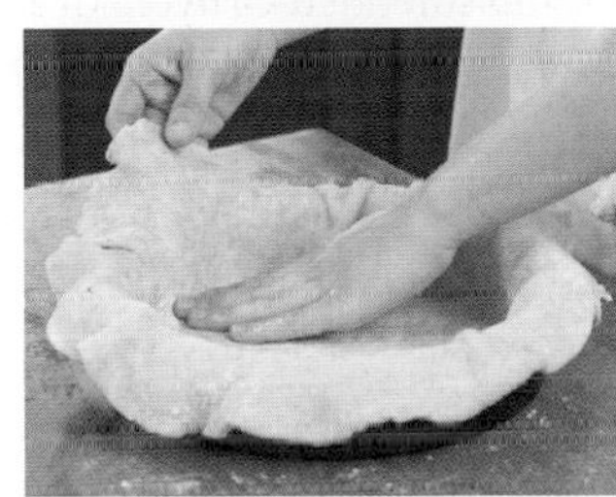

4. Gently ease dough into pan. Trim, leaving generous 1-inch overhang to anchor dough.

Deep-Dish Quiche Lorraine

SERVES 8 TO 10

To prevent the crust from sagging during blind baking, make sure it overhangs the pan's edge and use plenty of pie weights (about 3 to 4 cups). To reheat the whole quiche, place it on a rimmed baking sheet on the middle rack of a 325-degree oven for 20 minutes; slices can be reheated in a 375-degree oven for 10 minutes.

PASTRY DOUGH

- **1¾ cups (8¾ ounces) all-purpose flour, plus extra for counter**
- **½ teaspoon salt**
- **12 tablespoons unsalted butter, cut into ½-inch pieces and chilled**
- **3 tablespoons sour cream**
- **¼–⅓ cup ice water**
- **Vegetable oil spray**
- **1 large egg white, lightly beaten**

CUSTARD FILLING

- **8 slices thick-cut bacon, cut into ¼-inch pieces**
- **2 onions, chopped fine**
- **1½ tablespoons cornstarch**
- **1½ cups whole milk**
- **8 large eggs plus 1 large yolk**
- **1½ cups heavy cream**
- **½ teaspoon salt**
- **¼ teaspoon pepper**
- **⅛ teaspoon ground nutmeg**
- **⅛ teaspoon cayenne pepper**
- **6 ounces Gruyère cheese, shredded (1½ cups)**

1. FOR THE PASTRY DOUGH: Process flour and salt together in food processor until combined, about 3 seconds. Add butter and pulse until butter is size of large peas, about 10 pulses.

2. Combine sour cream and ¼ cup ice water in bowl. Add half of sour cream mixture to flour mixture; pulse 3 times. Repeat with remaining sour cream mixture. Pinch dough with fingers; if dough is floury and dry and does not hold together, add 1 to 2 tablespoons more ice water and pulse until dough forms large clumps and no dry flour remains, 3 to 5 pulses.

3. Turn dough out onto counter and flatten into 6-inch disk; wrap disk in plastic wrap and refrigerate until firm but not hard, 1 to 2 hours, before rolling. (Dough can be refrigerated for up to 1 day; let stand at room temperature for 15 minutes before rolling.)

4. Cut two 16-inch lengths of aluminum foil. Arrange foil pieces, perpendicular to each other, in round 9 by 2-inch cake pan, pushing them into corners and up sides of pan; press overhang against outside of pan. Spray foil lightly with vegetable oil spray.

5. Roll out dough on generously floured counter to 15-inch circle about ¼ inch thick. Roll dough loosely around rolling pin and unroll into prepared cake pan. Working around circumference, ease dough into pan by gently lifting edge of dough with one hand while pressing into pan bottom with other. Trim any dough that extends more than 1 inch over edge of pan. Patch any cracks or holes with dough scraps as needed. Refrigerate any remaining dough scraps. Refrigerate dough-lined pan until dough is firm, about 30 minutes, then freeze for 20 minutes.

6. Adjust oven rack to lower-middle position and heat oven to 375 degrees. Line dough with aluminum foil or parchment paper and fill completely with pie weights or dried beans, gently pressing weights into corners of shell. Bake on rimmed baking sheet until exposed edges of dough are beginning to brown but bottom is still light in color, 30 to 40 minutes. Carefully remove foil and pie weights. If any new holes or cracks have formed in dough, patch with reserved scraps. Return shell to oven and bake until bottom is golden brown, 15 to 20 minutes longer. Remove shell from oven and brush interior with egg white. Set aside while preparing filling. Reduce oven temperature to 350 degrees.

7. FOR THE CUSTARD FILLING: Cook bacon in 12-inch skillet over medium heat until crisp, 8 to 12 minutes. Transfer to paper towel–lined plate and discard all but 2 tablespoons bacon fat from skillet. Return to medium heat, add onions, and cook, stirring frequently, until softened and lightly browned, about 12 minutes. Set aside to cool slightly.

8. Whisk cornstarch and 3 tablespoons milk together in large bowl to dissolve cornstarch. Whisk in remaining milk, eggs, egg yolk, cream, salt, pepper, nutmeg, and cayenne until smooth.

9. Scatter onions, bacon, and cheese evenly over crust. Gently pour custard mixture over filling. Using fork, push filling ingredients down into custard and drag gently through custard to dislodge air bubbles. Gently tap pan on counter to dislodge any remaining air bubbles.

10. Bake until top of quiche is lightly browned, toothpick inserted into center comes out clean, and center registers 170 degrees, 1¼ to 1½ hours. Transfer to wire rack and let stand until cool to touch, about 2 hours.

11. When ready to serve, use sharp paring knife to remove any crust that extends beyond edge of pan. Lift foil overhang from sides of pan and remove quiche from pan; gently slide thin-bladed spatula between quiche and foil to loosen, then slide quiche onto serving plate. Cut into wedges. Serve warm or at room temperature. (Quiche can be refrigerated for up to 3 days.)

VARIATIONS

Deep-Dish Quiche with Leeks and Blue Cheese

Omit bacon and onions. Melt 1 tablespoon unsalted butter in 12-inch skillet over medium heat. Add 4 large leeks, white and light green parts only, halved lengthwise and sliced ¼ inch thick, and cook, stirring frequently, until softened, 10 to 12 minutes. Increase heat to medium-high and continue to cook, stirring constantly, until leeks are beginning to brown, about 5 minutes longer. Transfer leeks to plate lined with triple layer of paper towels; press with double layer of paper towels to remove excess moisture. Increase salt in filling to 1 tablespoon. Substitute 1½ cups crumbled blue cheese for Gruyère; scatter blue cheese and sautéed leeks over crust before adding custard. Reduce baking time to 1 to 1¼ hours.

Deep-Dish Quiche with Sausage, Broccoli Rabe, and Mozzarella

Omit bacon and onions. Cook 8 ounces hot or sweet Italian sausage, casings removed, in 12-inch skillet over medium heat, breaking sausage into ½-inch pieces, until no longer pink, 5 to 7 minutes. Transfer to paper towel–lined plate and discard all but 2 tablespoons fat from skillet. Return skillet to medium heat, add 8 ounces broccoli rabe, cut into ½-inch pieces, and cook, stirring occasionally, until slightly softened, about 6 minutes. Transfer rabe to plate lined with triple layer of paper towels; press with double layer of paper towels to remove excess moisture. Increase salt in filling to 1 tablespoon. Substitute 1½ cups shredded low-moisture whole milk mozzarella cheese for Gruyère; scatter mozzarella and cooked sausage and broccoli rabe over crust before adding custard. Reduce baking time to 1 to 1¼ hours.

EGG ROULADE

FOR MANY OF US, SUNDAY BRUNCH IS A CHANCE to serve something a step beyond our normal weekday breakfast roster. But juggling sauté pans to make individual omelets or frittatas is certainly daunting for anyone who hasn't spent years as a short-order cook. Could I come up with an impressive egg dish that would simplify the brunch frenzy by feeding several people at once? During my research I spotted recipes for a super-size rolled omelet where eggs are poured onto a rimmed baking sheet, a filling of gooey cheese and fresh vegetables is added, and then the whole thing is baked and rolled up like a jellyroll. This dish had all the appeal of a loaded omelet, with the additional benefit of feeding several people. It was a perfect candidate for a lighter, crowd-pleasing egg dish. All you need to do is roll, slice, and serve. I knew my challenge would be fine-tuning the cooking method and keeping things light.

First I turned my attention to the cooking method, keeping the filling out of the picture until I perfected the eggs themselves. I knew I wanted to feed six people with this dish, so I whipped up 15 eggs (an appropriate number to feed six, though I would need to lighten this base later) with ¼ cup of milk, poured the mixture into my rimmed baking sheet, and baked it in the oven at 375 degrees. After about 10 minutes, the eggs were nicely cooked, but the whole thing stuck to the baking sheet, making it impossible to roll. In search of a solution, I cooked batch after batch of eggs and eventually found my answer. I lined the rimmed baking sheet with a large enough piece of greased parchment to come up the sides, a precaution that prevented the eggs from running under the parchment. It was crucial that the parchment be liberally sprayed with vegetable oil spray; if I skimped even a little bit, my eggs stuck, making rolling the omelet impossible. Additionally, the parchment aided the rolling process; I used it as a guide to roll the eggs into a tight pinwheel.

With a successful cooking method in place, it was time to lighten my roulade. I decided to begin by removing yolks. I started with a ratio of two whites to one yolk, increasing the number of whites incrementally by one in each test. I wanted my eggs to have enough structure to be rollable, but not so much that they were rubbery and bland. It did not take long to reach the threshold of how many I could add. A ratio of four whites to one yolk went too far and yielded an egg roulade that tasted overly lean and was rubbery and split when rolled. While a ratio of three whites to one yolk (5 whole eggs plus 10 whites) provided the best balance of flavor—these eggs tasted rich but remained lean—unfortunately it produced a roulade that also split when rolled.

Looking back at the rolled omelet recipes I had found, I noticed that in some flour was incorporated into the eggs. I hadn't analyzed why before, but now I understood its addition. The flour was there to strengthen the eggs and provide structure, allowing the roulade to be rolled without cracking. I prepared several batches of eggs (using my determined ratio), incorporating flour in 1-tablespoon increments by whisking it with the milk before adding it to the eggs. Two tablespoons proved to be the magic number—eggs prepared with this amount cooked through and rolled seamlessly. Any more flour produced pasty, gummy eggs.

At this point, my method and egg mixture worked like a charm, so I moved on to the filling. Off the

EGG ROULADE WITH SPINACH AND GRUYÈRE

bat, cheese struck me as a natural fit, and it took only one test to prove that low-fat cheeses did not provide enough flavor to warrant their inclusion. I moved on to boldly flavored, full-fat cheeses. Parmesan and Gruyère both worked well, and a little bit went a long way, boosting the flavor immensely and allowing me to keep the fat down. Tasters slightly preferred the Gruyère. For a healthy complement to the cheese, tasters agreed that spinach, with its earthy flavor and bright color, would do the job nicely. I tested roulades made with baby spinach and frozen chopped spinach; the subtler flavor of baby spinach won out, but it leached water into my eggs, ruining the texture. Microwaving the spinach until wilted, then squeezing it dry before sprinkling it over the eggs just before baking, fixed this issue. Just one clove of garlic added the depth my roulade needed. Once rolled, my spinach and Gruyère egg roulade was flecked with green, full of flavor, and an elegant presentation for Sunday brunch (not to mention easy to make).

For a few variations, a combination of ham, Parmesan, and scallion was a hit, as was the trio of sun-dried tomatoes, Parmesan, and scallion. These roulades looked fantastic and tasted great, but best of all, none of our brunch guests would know how easy they were to put together.

—CHRIS O'CONNOR, *America's Test Kitchen Books*

Egg Roulade with Spinach and Gruyère

SERVES 6

To avoid having extra yolks left over, you can use 5 whole eggs and 1¼ cups store-bought egg whites.

- **Vegetable oil spray**
- **5 ounces baby spinach (5 cups)**
- **¼ cup water**
- **¼ cup 1 percent low-fat milk**
- **2 tablespoons all-purpose flour**
- **10 large egg whites**
- **5 large eggs**
- **1 small garlic clove, minced to paste**
- **¼ teaspoon salt**
- **⅛ teaspoon pepper**
- **2 ounces Gruyère cheese, shredded (½ cup)**

NOTES FROM THE TEST KITCHEN

MINCING GARLIC TO A PASTE

After mincing garlic, sprinkle with pinch salt, then drag side of chef's knife over mixture to make fine paste. Continue to mince and drag knife as necessary until paste is smooth.

MAKING EGG ROULADE

1. Coat rimmed baking sheet with vegetable oil spray, then press piece of parchment paper into sheet, making sure to get paper into corners and up sides. Coat parchment with vegetable oil spray.

2. Pour egg mixture into prepared baking sheet, then sprinkle spinach and cheese over top. Bake until cheese is melted and eggs are set.

3. Once eggs are cooked, starting at one short end, roll eggs into tidy cylinder, using parchment paper to lift and roll eggs.

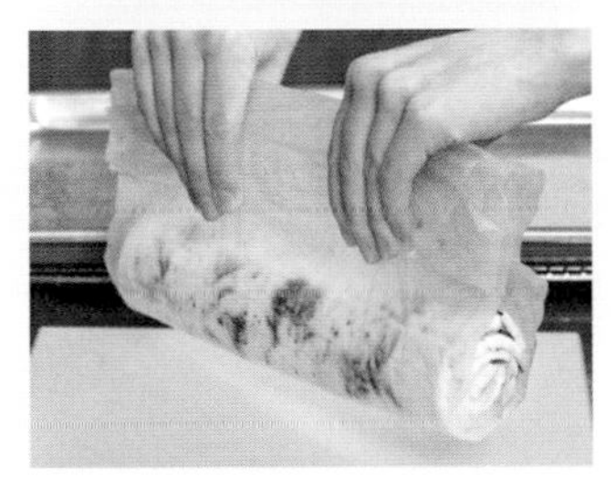

4. Gently roll roulade backward into middle of parchment paper, then use parchment as sling to transfer roulade to cutting board.

1. Adjust oven rack to middle position and heat oven to 375 degrees. Spray 18 by 13-inch rimmed baking sheet with vegetable oil spray, line with parchment paper, liberally coat parchment paper with vegetable oil spray, and set aside.

2. Place spinach and water in bowl. Cover bowl and microwave until spinach is wilted and decreased in volume by half, 3 to 5 minutes. Using potholders, remove bowl from microwave, then transfer spinach to colander set over bowl and press with spatula to release excess liquid.

3. Whisk milk and flour together in bowl. In large bowl, whisk egg whites, eggs, garlic, salt, and pepper together, then whisk in milk-flour mixture until uniform. Carefully pour egg mixture into prepared baking sheet, sprinkle drained spinach and cheese on top, and bake until cheese is melted and eggs are just set, about 11 minutes, rotating pan halfway through baking.

4. Remove baking sheet from oven and, beginning at one short end, use parchment paper to roll egg over itself into tight cylinder. Roll roulade backward into middle of parchment paper and transfer to cutting board, using parchment as sling. Slice and serve.

VARIATIONS

Egg Roulade with Ham, Parmesan, and Scallion

Omit spinach and water. Substitute ½ cup grated Parmesan cheese for Gruyère. Sprinkle 2 ounces finely chopped ham steak and 1 minced scallion over eggs before baking.

Egg Roulade with Sun-Dried Tomatoes, Parmesan, and Scallion

Omit spinach and water. Substitute ½ cup grated Parmesan cheese for Gruyère. Sprinkle ⅓ cup chopped oil-packed sun-dried tomatoes and 1 minced scallion over eggs before baking.

SLOW-COOKER BREAKFAST STRATA WITH SAUSAGE

HERE IN THE TEST KITCHEN, WE'RE BIG FANS OF strata, the hearty breakfast casserole that's composed of bread, eggs, cheese, and milk or cream. Not only is this creamy, custardy casserole incredibly satisfying, but it's also easy to assemble ahead of time, and it can be baked at the last minute—perfect for a weekend brunch. But this seemingly ideal brunch offering has a few negatives; strata hogs a good amount of space in the oven, and it requires almost an hour of baking time. Plus, it has to be served immediately, lest it lose its creamy texture. I hoped for an easier path to strata heaven, one that would be fuss-free and leave the oven available for other tasks—so I looked to my slow cooker.

Although it wasn't hard to find recipes for slow-cooker strata, I worried that the moist cooking environment of the slow cooker would be problematic when it came to achieving just the right creamy, custardy texture. After testing a few recipes in which bread chunks were basically tossed into the slow cooker, covered with a mixture of heavy cream, eggs, shredded cheddar, chopped onion, and minced garlic and thyme, and left to cook, I knew I'd been right to worry. The resulting casseroles were overly dense, moist, and gummy, and they offered little in the way of flavor; the onion tasted raw and didn't contribute any savory depth. My slow-cooker strata would need a hand if it was to turn out every bit as creamy and satisfying as a traditional strata.

My first move was to toast the bread until it was thoroughly dry, which would provide some insurance against an overly wet, gummy strata. After about 40 minutes in the oven, my bread pieces were well toasted; using a large baking sheet ensured that the hot air of the oven could circulate evenly around it. Layering the bread and cheese in the slow cooker before pouring the cream and egg mixture over the top helped to form separate, distinct layers instead of one single, dense layer.

Next, I reconsidered my choice of dairy. Heavy cream had given me strata that was incredibly rich—too rich, in fact. Would using half-and-half or milk help to lighten it? Even when combined with the eggs and a good dose of cheese, whole milk resulted in strata that tasted slightly lean. Half-and-half worked much better, providing some richness without giving me strata that tasters pushed away after one forkful.

The texture of my strata was now rich and custardy, not dense and heavy, but the flavor was still lacking. In the test kitchen, we almost always sauté onion and garlic to deepen their flavors and tame their harsh notes; while I hoped to avoid this extra step, I found that the extra 10 minutes spent cooking my aromatics on the stovetop was well worth it. Now my strata had the right texture and a well-rounded, complex flavor to back it up.

This slow-cooker strata was shaping up, but I was on the lookout for something to add some meaty heartiness. Breakfast sausage, with its savory, spicy flavor, was an ingredient that popped up in a number of recipes; I found it enriched the dish nicely. To make things easier, I simply browned the sausage in the pan before sautéing the aromatics. To prevent a greasy strata, I drained some of the rendered fat, saving just 2 tablespoons to sauté the aromatics. I added the sausage (combined with the aromatics) as its own layer, between the cheese and bread, so it had a distinct presence in my strata. Tasters were pleased.

I was almost at the finish line, but in each test, I noticed that one edge of the strata was overbrowning and burning slightly. We've found that slow-cooker inserts can have "hot spots," generally found on the side opposite the control panel. To insulate my strata and prevent it from coming into direct contact with the back of the slow-cooker insert, I lined the insert with an aluminum foil collar. Problem solved.

I had nailed the texture and flavor of my slow-cooker strata, but one nagging issue remained: When the strata was done, no matter which serving utensils I used, I ended up with somewhat messy pieces. This was fine for a more casual breakfast, but for an elegant brunch with friends, I wanted picture-perfect slices of strata. By lining the slow cooker with a foil sling—something we frequently use for brownies and bar cookies—I could remove the entire strata at once, before cutting and plating attractive slices. My slow-cooker strata tasted every bit as good as the traditional version. Scratch that—it tasted better.

—CHRIS O'CONNOR, *America's Test Kitchen Books*

NOTES FROM THE TEST KITCHEN

PREPARING THE SLOW COOKER FOR STRATA

1. Make foil collar by layering and folding sheets of heavy-duty aluminum foil to create six-layered rectangle that measures roughly 16 inches long by 4 inches wide. Press collar into back side of slow-cooker insert.

2. Then fit 2 large sheets of heavy-duty foil into and across bottom of slow-cooker insert, perpendicular to each other, with extra hanging over edges. To serve, use edges of foil sling to remove strata fully intact.

THE BEST SLOW COOKER

Gone are the days of merely picking out a slow cooker based on size. We found dozens of models, varying not only in size but also in price—from $20 up to a staggering $200. We tested seven slow cookers to find out which one was best (and whether we really had to shell out $200). We limited our lineup mainly to oval slow cookers, which can fit a large roast, with capacities of 6 quarts or more, so we could feed a crowd.

Six of the seven models had programmable timers and warming modes, features we liked. Clear glass lids were also helpful, as they allowed us to see through to assess the food as it cooked. Dishwasher-safe inserts with handles, which made it easy to remove the insert from the slow cooker, earned extra points.

To test performance, we made pot roast, meaty tomato sauce, and French onion soup. Ideally, a slow cooker should produce perfect results on all settings. Unfortunately, few of our models did just that—some just didn't get hot enough, and others reached the boiling point. That's the reason some of the models variously gave us pot roast with dry, tough meat or juicy, sliceable meat, and tomato sauces that were extra-thick or thin and watery. However, a few models did produce good food consistently. Our winner, the **Crock-Pot Touchscreen Slow Cooker**, $129.99, cooked our dinner perfectly. (See page 309 for more information about our testing results.)

Slow-Cooker Breakfast Strata with Sausage

SERVES 8 TO 10

Don't let this strata cook longer than 4 hours or it will become dried out and rubbery.

- **Vegetable oil spray**
- **12 ounces supermarket French or Italian bread, cut into ½-inch pieces**
- **1 tablespoon vegetable oil**
- **8 ounces bulk breakfast sausage**
- **1 onion, chopped fine**
- **2 garlic cloves, minced**
- **2 teaspoons minced fresh thyme or ½ teaspoon dried**
- **6 ounces sharp cheddar cheese, shredded (1½ cups)**
- **2½ cups half-and-half**
- **9 large eggs**
- **1 teaspoon salt**
- **¼ teaspoon pepper**

1. Line slow cooker with aluminum foil collar, then line with foil sling and coat with vegetable oil spray. Adjust oven rack to middle position and heat oven to 225 degrees. Spread bread on baking sheet and bake, shaking pan occasionally, until dry and crisp, about 40 minutes, rotating pan halfway through baking.

2. Heat oil in 12-inch skillet over medium-high heat until just smoking. Brown sausage well, breaking up large pieces with wooden spoon, about 5 minutes; transfer to medium bowl. Pour off all but 2 tablespoons of fat left in skillet. Add onion, garlic, and thyme and cook over medium-high heat until onion is softened and lightly browned, 8 to 10 minutes; transfer to bowl with sausage and toss to combine.

3. Spread half of dried bread in prepared slow cooker and sprinkle with half of sausage mixture and ½ cup cheese. Layer remaining dried bread, sausage mixture, and 1 cup cheese into slow cooker. Whisk half-and-half, eggs, salt, and pepper together in bowl, then pour mixture evenly over bread. Press gently on bread to submerge. Cover and cook until center of strata is set, about 4 hours on low.

4. Let strata cool for 20 minutes. To serve, either spoon strata onto individual plates or remove strata from slow cooker using sling and transfer to serving platter.

MORNING BUNS

ONE MORNING IN THE MID-1970s, A BAKER AT THE Ovens of Brittany restaurant in Madison, Wisconsin, sprinkled cinnamon sugar on a strip of croissant dough, rolled it up, and baked it; the morning bun was born. Daily sales soon soared to the thousands, and the buns were even distributed to airlines. It's no wonder they took off. What's not to love about a buttery, flaky croissant with cinnamon sugar? Nothing—unless you're the person making them. Making croissant dough is the brain surgery of the pastry world, so if that dough is a prerequisite for this treat, a team of Viennese pastry chefs is, too. I set out to translate morning buns for the home cook without losing any of their appeal.

My mission was clear: to develop a recipe that yielded flaky, crackly, perfectly sugared buns without assistance from a trained professional. Laminating, or inserting a layer of butter between two layers of dough and then folding, gives croissant pastry its hundreds of flaky layers. But the process of making this pastry is intense. First, you must press many sticks of butter into a large, flat square that is warm enough to be pliable yet cool enough not to melt as you work with it. Then you must mix the yeast dough, wait for it to rise, punch it down, roll it out, chill it, seal the sheet of butter inside it, roll it out again, fold it up and chill it, and then repeat the rolling, folding, and chilling three times. Just describing the process is exhausting, and it can go wrong at any moment if the butter gets too warm. I wanted a dough that was easy and fast enough to keep the butter (and the baker) cool.

I started by experimenting with pastries that achieve flakiness through simpler methods than lamination. Pie crusts, biscuits, scones, rugelach, and "blitz," or quick, puff pastry get their layers when the baker coats pieces of cold butter in the dry ingredients and uses only enough liquid to bring the dough together. Unfortunately, morning buns made with biscuit, scone, and rugelach doughs had the flavor and texture of the pastries they're intended for, not what I was aiming for. Buns made with blitz puff pastry, however, were closer to the real thing: many-leaved and very buttery. But the buns I made using blitz dough lacked the yeasty flavor of croissant dough and required a complex regimen of rolling, folding, and resting in the refrigerator.

MORNING BUNS

NOTES FROM THE TEST KITCHEN

MAKING FAUX PUFF PASTRY

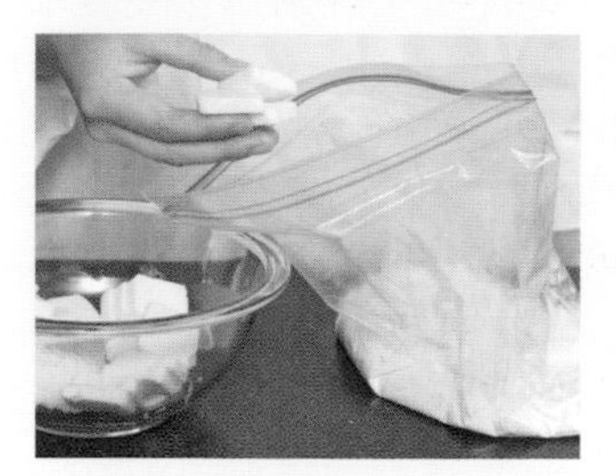

1. Toss slices of butter with flour in zipper-lock bag and shake until butter is coated with flour.

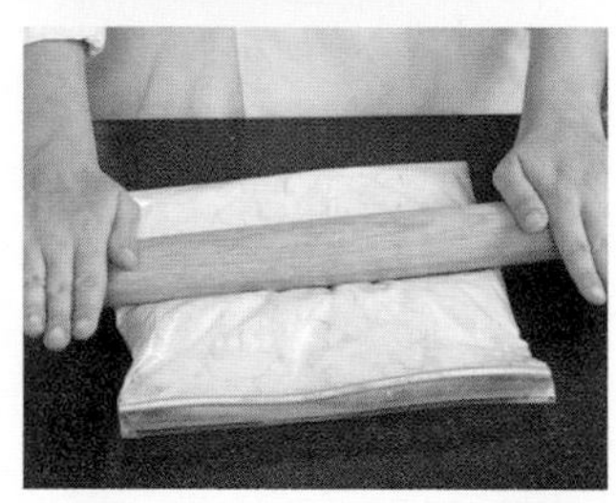

2. Flatten butter into long, flaky pieces easily, neatly, and quickly by pressing air out of bag, sealing it, and rolling over it a few times with rolling pin.

3. Dump butter-flour mixture into bowl; stir in sour cream, orange juice, water, and egg yolk.

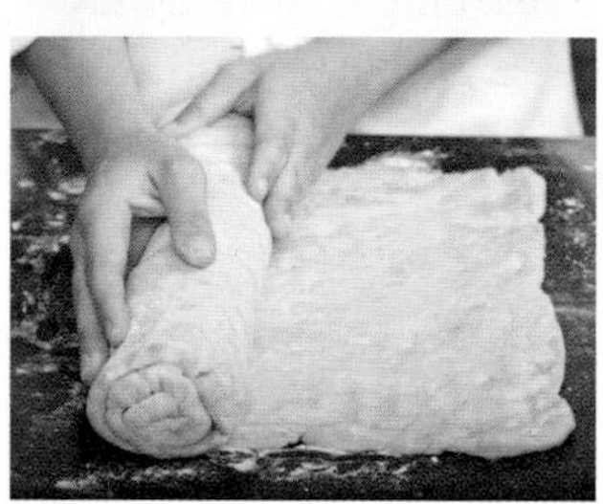

4. Knead mixture briefly, form into ball, and roll dough into rectangle. Then, starting at short end, roll dough up into tight cylinder.

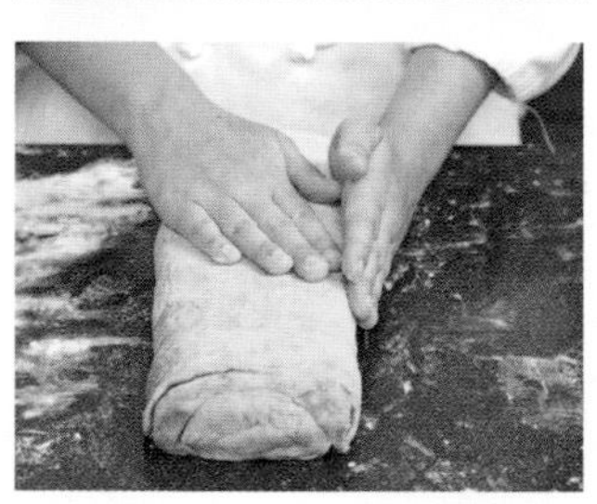

5. Flatten cylinder gently and freeze for 15 minutes; roll chilled dough into rectangle again and fill.

ASSEMBLING MORNING BUNS

1. After sprinkling dough rectangle with filling, roll filled dough into cylinder, starting at long edge.

2. Divide cylinder into quarters, then cut each quarter into thirds to make 12 buns total.

3. Place buns in muffin tin lined with lightly greased foil liners. Chill to firm up butter (which will result in flakier buns). Let buns rise, then bake them.

THE BEST MUFFIN TIN

With the price tags of muffin tins ranging from $13 to $30, we wondered if there was a good reason for shelling out big bucks. We gathered eight tins and cranked out more than 300 muffins and cupcakes. The best tins browned the muffins evenly and turned out well-shaped cupcakes and muffins; the worst tins browned unevenly and gave us squat baked goods. Nonstick coatings ensured easy release of muffins and cupcakes, although some coatings were more effective than others. Our top-ranking muffin tin was the **Wilton Avanti Everglide Metal-Safe Nonstick 12-Cup Muffin Pan**, $13.99. Its nonstick coating consistently released muffins and cupcakes. (See page 311 for more information about our testing results.)

Still, tangling with those problems was preferable to the much more complicated lamination. If I could get back that nice yeasty flavor and simplify the rolling and folding, morning buns would be within my grasp.

My blitz puff pastry recipe called for dumping the dry ingredients and butter onto the counter and rolling over the pile with a rolling pin to flatten the butter into long sheets. It sounds logical—until you're chasing the pile across the kitchen counter and scraping half-melted butter flakes off the rolling pin. In search of a tidier, easier method, I tried shaving the butter on a box grater instead of rolling it, but it was a finger-endangering mess. Freezing the butter before shaving produced shards instead of flakes, and trying to get flakes of butter by slicing with a knife was greasy and dangerous. The rolling pin method was a mess and a hassle, but at least it worked—if only I could speed it up (so the butter wouldn't have time to melt) and contain the pile.

The solution turned out to be the freezer bag in which I was storing the dry ingredients for future tests. What if, instead of taking the dry ingredients out of the bag to mix with the butter, I threw the butter in? I put the flour and salt in a gallon-size zipper-lock bag, threw in quarter-inch butter slices, and sealed and shook the bag. Once the butter was coated in flour, I rolled over the bag a few times with a rolling pin. When I opened the bag, I had long, thin, still cool sheets of butter.

In addition to these flat pieces of butter, folding (or "turning") gives blitz puff pastry its layers. My recipe called for four intricate folds, with two 30-minute and two 1-hour rests between them. Clearly, this would not do. I found I could get away with just three folds with no harm done. Any fewer, though, and the buns were noticeably less flaky. What to do?

After all the folding is done, morning buns are shaped by rolling the dough into a rectangle, sprinkling it with cinnamon sugar, and then rolling it up like a jellyroll. That gave me an idea. I rolled out the dough into a rectangle, then into a cylinder, and gently patted it flat. This method produced instant multiple layers in one step and required just one 15-minute rest in the freezer to cool the butter down enough that I could proceed to filling and shaping the buns.

With the flakiness under control, I started adjusting the flavor of the dough. Blitz puff pastry calls for sour cream, ice water, and salt, but I wanted the yeasty flavor of a croissant. Luckily, it was as easy as adding a packet of yeast and a tablespoon of sugar (to feed it) to the bag of dry ingredients and subsequently letting the buns rise in a warm oven before baking. Croissant dough contains eggs, so I wondered what effect eggs would have on my hybrid dough. One yolk tenderized and added richness.

Relieved to be finished with the dough, I experimented with fillings. In the cinnamon sugar, tasters loved a blend of brown and white sugar for its subtle molasses flavor. Orange zest, a recent addition in many café and bakery versions, has become popular enough to nearly eclipse the original filling, and the bright citrus aroma won everyone over. In fact, I liked it so much I exchanged some of the water in the dough for orange juice. Vanilla extract balanced the citrusy brightness.

Admittedly, these buns are still a project. But they're far quicker to make than croissant dough, and what was even faster was the speed with which they disappeared from the test kitchen.

—SARAH GABRIEL, *Cook's Country*

Morning Buns

MAKES 12 BUNS

If the dough becomes too soft to work with at any point, refrigerate it until it's firm enough to handle. To prevent sticking, bake the morning buns in lightly greased foil muffin-tin liners—paper liners will stick; remove the buns from the liners while they're still warm.

DOUGH

- **3 cups (15 ounces) all-purpose flour**
- **1 tablespoon granulated sugar**
- **2¼ teaspoons instant or rapid-rise yeast**
- **¾ teaspoon salt**
- **24 tablespoons unsalted butter (3 sticks), cut into ¼-inch-thick slices and chilled**
- **1 cup sour cream, chilled**
- **¼ cup orange juice, chilled**
- **3 tablespoons ice water**
- **1 large egg yolk**

FILLING

- **Vegetable oil spray**
- **½ cup (3½ ounces) granulated sugar**
- **½ cup packed (3½ ounces) light brown sugar**
- **1 tablespoon grated orange zest**
- **2 teaspoons ground cinnamon**
- **1 teaspoon vanilla extract**

1. FOR THE DOUGH: Combine flour, sugar, yeast, and salt in large zipper-lock bag. Add butter to bag, seal, and shake to coat. Press air out of bag and reseal. Roll over bag several times with rolling pin, shaking bag after each roll, until butter is pressed into large flakes. Transfer mixture to large bowl and stir in sour cream, orange juice, water, and egg yolk until combined.

2. Turn dough out onto floured counter and knead briefly to form smooth, cohesive ball. Roll dough into 20 by 12-inch rectangle. Starting at short edge, roll dough into tight cylinder. Pat cylinder flat to 12 by 4-inch rectangle and transfer to parchment paper–lined rimmed baking sheet. Cover with plastic wrap and freeze for 15 minutes.

3. FOR THE FILLING: Line 12-cup muffin tin with foil liners and spray liners with vegetable oil spray. Combine granulated sugar, brown sugar, orange zest, cinnamon, and vanilla in bowl. Remove dough from freezer and place on lightly floured counter. Roll dough into 20 by 12-inch rectangle and sprinkle evenly with filling, leaving ½-inch border around edges. Starting at long edge, roll dough into tight cylinder and pinch lightly to seal seam. Trim ½ inch of dough from each end and discard. Cut cylinder into 12 pieces and transfer, cut sides up, to prepared muffin cups. Cover loosely with plastic wrap and refrigerate for at least 4 hours or up to 24 hours. (Alternatively, buns can be frozen in muffin tin until firm, about 30 minutes; transfer buns, with liners, to zipper-lock bag and freeze for up to 1 month. To serve, return buns to muffin tin and refrigerate for at least 8 hours or up to 24 hours; proceed with recipe.)

4. Adjust oven rack to middle position and heat oven to 200 degrees. When oven reaches 200 degrees, turn it off. Remove muffin tin from refrigerator and discard plastic. Place in turned-off oven until buns are puffed and doubled in size, 20 to 30 minutes. Remove buns from oven and heat oven to 425 degrees. Bake until buns begin to rise, about 5 minutes, then reduce oven temperature to 325 degrees. Continue to bake until deep golden brown, 40 to 50 minutes longer. Cool buns in tin for 5 minutes, then transfer to wire rack and discard liners. Serve warm.

ULTIMATE BANANA BREAD

THE TRADITION OF BAKING BANANA BREAD IS more heavily steeped in parsimony than indulgence: When bananas get covered with brownish-black spots, the frugal alternative to pitching them in the trash has always been to mash them up, add them to a quick bread batter, and bake.

I'm all for thrift in the kitchen, but I've yet to come across a banana bread recipe that actually makes me glad I saved those overripe specimens. Depending on the fat-to-flour ratio—and just how spotty those bananas really are—the crumb varies from cottony and tough to dense and damp, with a typically overbaked ring crusting over the exterior. Even more discouraging, all that ripe banana flavor somehow seems to vaporize during baking, leaving me with a ho-hum loaf that just begs for the added oomph of chocolate chips, coconut, rum, or gobs of cream cheese slathered on top. Without upsetting the humble charms of this bread, what would it take to create a moist, tender loaf that really tasted like bananas? I decided to find out.

Just to reacquaint myself with the core problems, I cherry-picked a few promising-looking recipes to make in the test kitchen, most of which followed a formula along these lines: Combine mashed, ripe bananas with vegetable oil, eggs, and sugar; fold that into a dry mix of flour, baking soda, and salt; and scrape the batter into a loaf pan before popping it into a 350-degree oven for about an hour. I suppose the breads were passable as PTA-meeting handouts—sweet-smelling and pleasant enough to eat while warm and fresh—but their banana flavor was utterly forgettable.

Except for one loaf, that is. With a stature that was a good half-inch shorter than the other breads and an interior crumb that was fairly wet, it wasn't much to look at. (One taster actually used the word "sludgy.") But after only a couple of bites my colleagues and I were returning for seconds, declaring that this loaf had unprecedented true fruit flavor. Why the drastic difference? Simple: This recipe called for roughly the same amount of flour, sugar, fat, and eggs as all the others but twice the number of bananas—six instead of the usual three. Their effect was both a blessing and a curse; doubling the bananas may have doubled the flavor, but it also oversaturated the batter. My task was clear: Figure out how to cram as many bananas as possible into the loaf without sinking its cakelike structure.

Since it was obvious that simply mashing up more bananas to add to the batter compromised the crumb, I decided to try alternative avenues to ratcheting up the flavor. In a few of the more inventive recipes I came across, crushed banana chips were stirred into the batter; presumably, the chips' toasty, concentrated flavor would pick up where the fresh fruit left off. Wrong. The loaf I made with ½ cup of ground chips had no more flavor than previous batches; in fact, it was even a bit drier. It turns out that banana chips are made from underripe bananas (because they withstand processing better than ripe fruit), and underripe bananas are largely composed of moisture absorbing starch. Scratch that off the list.

If banana chips were too dehydrated, maybe the answer to bigger banana flavor was to start at the source—actual ripe bananas—and drain their liquid myself. That way, I'd get all the benefits of the fruit's creamy sweetness and be able to control the moisture level. Flipping through the test kitchen archives for ideas, I came across a recipe for low-fat banana bread, where we discovered that roasting the fruit not only helped some of the excess moisture evaporate but also concentrated its rich brown-sugar notes. My goal was to remove enough moisture so that two more bananas (for a total of five) wouldn't overwhelm the batter. Unsure how much moisture would escape through the skin, I roasted batches of bananas three different ways—peels intact, peels split, and peels removed—and then incorporated them into the batter. No matter what the roasting method, five bananas still produced an unacceptably wet loaf, so I scaled back to four. This time around, the split-peel loaf stood out with a nice, moist (but not puddinglike) crumb and a fruity flavor that was a significant step up from any three-banana loaf I'd made. But roasting tacked 45 minutes onto the recipe. And were four bananas really as high as I could go?

My patience with this process was growing thin. Then a thrifty colleague mentioned that in lieu of throwing out bananas that are too ripe to eat, she saves them in the freezer, though she has seen them exude quite a lot of liquid when thawed. Armed with this promising nugget, I thawed some very ripe bananas I had stored in the freezer; sure enough, five of them yielded around ⅔ cup of liquid. I pureed the fruit, added it to my bread, and was rewarded with a flavor-packed loaf boasting a moist, fully baked crumb. My enthusiasm was renewed—until I realized this discovery would be moot if I had no frozen ripe bananas at the ready.

I had no choice but to return to trying to cook off extra moisture. This time around, I moved my efforts out of the oven and onto the stove: I tried simmering the mashed bananas as well as dicing and sautéing them, but the direct heat in both attempts gave the fruit an overcooked, jamlike flavor. I was stumped until I remembered a solution for removing moisture from waterlogged eggplant: microwaving it. I placed five bananas in a glass bowl, zapped them on high power for about five minutes, then transferred the now-pulpy fruit to a sieve to drain. Bingo! This caused them to release as much liquid as the thawed frozen bananas. Furthermore, since the bananas were heated for only a short time, they didn't take on the overly cooked flavor of the simmered puree or sautéed bananas.

NOTES FROM THE TEST KITCHEN

BANANAS—THE RIPER, THE BETTER

Don't even think of making banana bread with anything less than very ripe, heavily speckled fruit—unless you're fine with a bland loaf. As bananas ripen, their starch converts to sugar at an exponential rate. In lab tests, we found that heavily speckled bananas had nearly three times the amount of fructose (the sweetest of the sugars in fruit) than less spotty bananas. (The exact percentage will vary from fruit to fruit.) But the impact of ripeness only goes so far: We found little difference in sweetness between loaves baked with completely black bananas and those made with heavily speckled ones.

1.8% FRUCTOSE = TOO SOON
A lightly speckled banana has only a little fructose, the sweetest sugar in fruit.

5.3% FRUCTOSE = JUST RIGHT
A heavily speckled banana has a lot more fructose.

SHINGLING THE LOAF

Layering thin banana slices on either side of loaf adds even more banana flavor. To ensure loaf rises evenly, leave 1½-inch-wide space down center.

But what to do about the banana liquid I'd collected? I couldn't bear the thought of pouring all that sweet flavor down the drain. (In cooking terms, it seemed as blasphemous as throwing away the fond.) I transferred this liquid to a saucepan, cooked it down to 2 ounces, and then added it back to the mashed bananas (along with another ¼ cup of flour to compensate for the extra liquid). As crazy as it sounded to extract banana liquid only to put it back (albeit in concentrated form), the result was a revelation. Not only did this step infuse the bread with ripe, intensely fruity banana flavor, but it also assuaged my frugal Yankee conscience. Furthermore, the extra moisture in the batter helped to create a crumb that was tender through and through, without being framed by overly crusty sides.

With the flavor problem solved, a few minor tweaks completed the recipe. I exchanged the granulated sugar for light brown sugar, finding that the latter's molasses notes better complemented the bananas. A teaspoon of vanilla rounded out the bananas' faintly boozy, rumlike flavor, as did swapping out the oil for the nutty richness of butter. I also added ½ cup of toasted walnuts to the batter, finding that their crunch provided a pleasing contrast to the rich, moist crumb.

This banana bread was a true showpiece, from its deep golden crust to the center's velvety crumb, yet lingering in the back of my mind was the urge to actually double the number of bananas in the conventional recipe. Wondering if the crust might benefit from a little embellishment, I sliced a sixth banana and shingled it on top of the batter. A final sprinkle of sugar helped the buttery slices caramelize and gave the loaf an enticingly crisp, crunchy top. In fact, I started craving thick slices of this bread so often, I now make a point of always having a bunch of ripe bananas waiting in the wings.

—ANDREA GEARY, *Cook's Illustrated*

Ultimate Banana Bread

MAKES ONE 8-INCH LOAF

Be sure to use very ripe, heavily speckled (or even black) bananas in this recipe. This recipe can be made with 5 thawed frozen bananas; since they release a lot of liquid naturally, they can bypass the microwaving in step 2 and go directly into the fine-mesh strainer. Do not use a thawed frozen banana in step 4; it will be too soft to slice. Instead, simply sprinkle the top of the loaf with sugar. This recipe was developed using a loaf pan that measures 8½ by 4½ inches; if you use a 9 by 5-inch loaf pan, start checking for doneness 5 minutes earlier than advised in the recipe.

Vegetable oil spray
1¾ cups (8¾ ounces) all-purpose flour
1 teaspoon baking soda
½ teaspoon salt
6 large very ripe bananas (2¼ pounds), peeled
8 tablespoons unsalted butter, melted and cooled
2 large eggs
¾ cup packed (5¼ ounces) light brown sugar
1 teaspoon vanilla extract
½ cup walnuts, toasted and chopped coarse (optional)
2 teaspoons granulated sugar

1. Adjust oven rack to middle position and heat oven to 350 degrees. Spray 8½ by 4½-inch loaf pan with vegetable oil spray. Whisk flour, baking soda, and salt together in large bowl.

2. Place 5 bananas in bowl, cover with plastic wrap, and cut several steam vents in plastic with paring knife. Microwave until bananas are soft and have released liquid, about 5 minutes. Transfer bananas to fine-mesh strainer placed over medium bowl and allow to drain, stirring occasionally, for 15 minutes (you should have ½ to ¾ cup liquid). Transfer bananas to bowl.

3. Transfer liquid to medium saucepan and cook over medium-high heat until reduced to ¼ cup, about 5 minutes. Remove pan from heat, stir reduced liquid into bananas, and mash with potato masher until fairly smooth. Whisk in butter, eggs, brown sugar, and vanilla.

4. Pour banana mixture into flour mixture and stir until just combined with some streaks of flour remaining. Gently fold in walnuts, if using. Scrape batter into prepared pan. Slice remaining banana diagonally into ¼-inch-thick slices. Shingle banana slices on top of either side of loaf, leaving 1½-inch-wide space down center to ensure even rise. Sprinkle granulated sugar evenly over loaf.

5. Bake until toothpick inserted in center of loaf comes out clean, 55 to 75 minutes, rotating pan halfway through baking. Cool bread in pan on wire rack for 15 minutes, then remove loaf from pan and continue to cool on wire rack. Serve warm or at room temperature. (Banana bread can be stored for up to 3 days.)

SWEDISH PANCAKES

THEIR NUMBERS MAY NOT RANK UP THERE WITH the Irish diaspora, but when all was said and done 100 years ago, some 1.3 million Swedes had settled in America. Like all immigrants, they brought their cultural and religious traditions with them. More to the point for us, they brought their recipe for Swedish pancakes. A cousin of the French crêpe, a Swedish pancake is lighter and more delicate than an American pancake, with lacy, buttery edges and a barely custardy middle. According to tradition, the very thin batter is poured into a special pan, which makes silver-dollar-size pancakes that are typically eaten with lingonberry jam. If these delicious pancakes are new to you, maybe it's time to channel your inner Swede.

Swedish pancakes—maybe you've had them at IHOP—are made from a batter of eggs, melted butter, flour, sugar, and milk or cream. Unlike American pancakes, they don't contain baking soda, baking powder, or buttermilk. And unless you are the proud possessor of a Swedish plett pan, chances are you will be making your Swedish pancakes one at a time in a nonstick skillet. Made this way, they're rolled or folded into quarters and served with a dollop of jam.

I tested several existing recipes (including one purported to be the secret IHOP recipe). As a group, they called for vigorously whisking the ingredients together, pouring a thin layer of batter into a buttered pan, browning it on both sides, and repeating until the batter was used up. After weighing tasters' comments, I put together a batter from 2 cups of flour, 2 tablespoons of sugar, 5 eggs, 1 tablespoon of butter, and 3 cups of milk. As several of the recipes suggested, I rested the batter for one hour to relax the gluten in the flour and thus produce tender pancakes.

These pancakes tasted fine, but if I had to stand at the stove making one pancake at a time, fine wouldn't cut it. While a flapjack can be a vehicle for butter and syrup, Swedish pancakes need to taste sweet and rich on their own. These didn't. Also, a one-hour rest was out of the question.

I gradually increased the sugar, stopping at ¼ cup. For richness, I replaced the milk first with half-and-half, then heavy cream. Both yielded dense pancakes. I stuck with milk and upped the butter instead to 4 tablespoons for delicious, golden brown pancakes. Next, after a taster complained that my pancakes tasted like omelets, I tried the batter with every possible combination and number of whole eggs, yolks, and whites, the last stiffly beaten and not. Two whole eggs and two yolks made rich, tender pancakes.

At this point, my pancakes were, proverbially, flat as pancakes—they needed a little lift. Bucking tradition, I tested them with a scant amount of baking powder, then baking soda. Neither produced the desired result. My next gambit, using fizzy club soda for some of the milk (think tempura batter), produced the right texture, but now that half of the liquid in the batter was water, I revisited the milk, replacing it with half-and-half.

Ignoring the resting period produced, as I'd feared, tough pancakes. I remembered that Julia Child used

NOTES FROM THE TEST KITCHEN

MAKING SWEDISH PANCAKES

1. Slowly pour ⅓ cup batter into hot, buttered skillet, tilting pan to coat evenly.

2. Swirl batter to evenly cover bottom of skillet. Cook until pancake appears dry.

3. To turn pancake, loosen edge with rubber spatula, grab it, and flip.

SWEDISH PANCAKES

instant flour in crêpe batter as a way to bypass the rest. Because superfine instant flour dissolves "instantly," you needn't whisk it much, so the gluten doesn't develop. In turn, it doesn't have to relax. If the French Chef could use instant flour in her French pancakes, surely I could use it in my Swedish pancakes. I tried it. After just a few turns of the whisk, the batter was lump-free. I immediately poured the batter into a hot, buttered skillet and cooked a test pancake. *Min Svenska är dålig!* According to a page of Swedish phrases I found on the Internet, that means "My Swedish is bad." No matter. My Swedish pancakes were very, very good.

LYNN CLARK, *Cook's Country*

Swedish Pancakes

MAKES 15 PANCAKES, SERVING 4 TO 6

This recipe calls for instant flour, such as Wondra or Pillsbury Shake & Blend. Serve with the traditional lingonberry jam or your favorite jam and a pat of butter.

- **2 cups instant flour**
- **¼ cup sugar**
- **1 teaspoon salt**
- **1½ cups half-and-half**
- **1½ cups club soda**
- **5 tablespoons unsalted butter, melted and cooled**
- **2 large eggs plus 2 large yolks, lightly beaten**

1. Adjust oven rack to middle position and heat oven to 200 degrees. Combine flour, sugar, and salt in large bowl. Slowly whisk half-and-half, club soda, 4 tablespoons melted butter, eggs, and yolks into flour mixture until smooth.

2. Brush surface and sides of 10-inch nonstick skillet with 1 teaspoon more butter and heat over medium heat. When butter stops sizzling, pour ⅓ cup batter into skillet, tilting pan to evenly coat bottom with batter. Cook until golden brown, 1 to 2 minutes per side. Transfer to baking sheet and place in oven. Repeat with remaining butter and remaining batter. Roll up pancakes or fold into quarters and serve. (Cooled pancakes can be layered between sheets of parchment paper, wrapped in plastic wrap, transferred to zipper-lock bag, and refrigerated for up to 3 days or frozen for up to 1 month. To serve, microwave stacks of 3 pancakes on 50 percent power until heated through, 10 to 20 seconds.)

HEAVENLY HOTS

THE APTLY NAMED HEAVENLY HOTS FIRST GAINED recognition at the Bridge Creek Restaurant in Berkeley, California, but they were immortalized (in the eyes of pancake lovers everywhere, anyhow) in Marion Cunningham's *The Breakfast Book*. These tiny, delicate pancakes are loaded with sour cream—2 cups to four eggs, with a mere ¼ cup of cake flour to (barely) hold the batter together. There's also baking soda and sugar. Together, the unlikely proportions account for the pancakes' incredibly tender texture, which is as much tangy, golden brown soufflé as flapjack. Heavenly Hots live up to their name.

That is, if you work the griddle station in a restaurant and are adept at flipping them in the pan without turning their insides out. This, incidentally, is what happened to me the first time I made them. Dejectedly, I ate what I could of the pancake carnage and was amazed at how delicious it nevertheless tasted. I wanted a foolproof method for these pancakes.

It was not hard to see that the proportion of eggs to flour was off the charts. But as I gradually added more flour to give the pancakes more structure, they lost their ethereal texture and increasingly resembled traditional flapjacks. I switched the tender cake flour that the recipe called for to all-purpose flour plus a teaspoon of cornstarch. This made the pancakes sturdier but not dense. The batter was slightly easier to flip, but not much.

Next, I tried separating the eggs and whipping the whites, folding them in after I'd combined all the other ingredients. This batter showed promise: It was much thicker, and I could spoon it into the skillet instead of pouring it. But once it came time to flip, I was yet again scraping pancake guts out of the pan.

Next, I tried to eliminate flipping altogether. I slid the buttered, pancake-laden skillet under a hot broiler and held my breath. By the time the pancakes had browned on top, they were tragically overcooked inside. What if I covered the pancakes in the skillet, creating, in effect, a gentle mini oven? After about two minutes, the bottoms were golden brown and the centers had partially cooked. They still needed a turn to brown their second side, but flipping the firmer pancakes was a breeze.

Unfortunately, covering the skillet trapped the moisture from the wet batter, causing the pancakes to come out soggy. I already knew that adding more flour would harm their tender texture, so I removed an egg instead. Sigh. While significantly less wet, the pancakes now lacked the lift that fourth egg had provided. So I replaced some of the baking soda (which reacted quickly when it came in contact with the acidic sour cream) with baking powder (which provides a rise activated by heat). Not only did I get an airier pancake, but I fortuitously underlined the tanginess of the sour cream (the soda had been neutralizing it). I added a dash of vanilla to round out this pleasant sourness. With a dusting of confectioners' sugar, these pancakes were—I'll say it—heavenly.

—ERIKA BRUCE, *Cook's Country*

Heavenly Hots

MAKES 32 PANCAKES, SERVING 4

Serve these pancakes plain or dusted with a bit of confectioners' sugar.

- **¼ cup all-purpose flour**
- **3 tablespoons sugar**
- **1 teaspoon cornstarch**
- **1 teaspoon baking powder**
- **½ teaspoon salt**
- **¼ teaspoon baking soda**
- **2 cups sour cream**
- **3 large eggs, lightly beaten**
- **½ teaspoon vanilla extract**
- **3 tablespoons unsalted butter**

1. Adjust oven rack to middle position and heat oven to 200 degrees. Combine flour, sugar, cornstarch, baking powder, salt, and baking soda in bowl. Whisk sour cream, eggs, and vanilla in large bowl until smooth. Gently fold flour mixture into sour cream mixture until incorporated.

2. Heat 2 teaspoons butter in 12-inch nonstick skillet over medium-low heat until butter begins to sizzle. Place five 1-tablespoon scoops of batter in pan, cover, and cook until tops appear dry and bottoms are golden brown, 1½ to 2 minutes.

3. Gently flip pancakes and cook, uncovered, until golden brown, about 30 seconds. Transfer to baking sheet and place in oven. Repeat with remaining batter, using remaining butter as needed. Serve.

APPLE FRITTERS

IN 1880, MARK TWAIN, WRITING IN *A TRAMP ABROAD,* bellyached for more than 10 pages about the lousy food on his trip: "A man accustomed to American food and American domestic cookery would not starve to death suddenly in Europe; but I think he would gradually waste away, and eventually die." Twain proceeded to pen a lengthy list of dishes that he hoped would await him, hot, when he reached home: fried chicken, corn-pone, Boston bacon and beans, . . . and apple fritters. You definitely wouldn't catch me grousing about the food in Europe. But maybe, just maybe, I'd cut my vacation a few days short if I knew a plate of warm, sweet apple fritters would be waiting for me when I got home.

Apple fritters should be crisp on the outside and moist within, and they should sing out apple flavor. I started my testing with a delicious recipe for drop doughnuts that the test kitchen developed several years back: I combined milk, eggs, flour, sugar, cinnamon, nutmeg, and baking powder and then stirred in grated apples. (I figured the apples would distribute better if they were grated.) I heated the oil, scooped out batter, and got down to the business of frying.

When I pulled the fritters out of the oil, they looked pretty good. But when tasters bit in, it turned out the crispy exteriors enclosed heavy, wet goo—more raw batter than light, fluffy fritter. And so much for even distribution of the apples: If I hadn't stirred them in myself, I never would have known they were in there.

I made up a new batch of fritters using chopped apples, which I hoped would be drier and more conspicuous. My tasters weren't impressed, as these fritters weren't much better. The apple chunks were identifiable, sure, but also crunchy and raw. And yet again the insides of the fritters hadn't cooked. "Fritter flops," a colleague announced to my embarrassment.

No matter what variety of apple I tried, the fruit caused trouble. Moist to begin with, the apple chunks became even wetter as the fritters fried. (As anyone who has ever baked a fruit pie knows, fruit oozes water as it cooks.) Consequently, the fritters were too wet on the inside to cook through.

I refused to cut back on the apples (two for 2 cups of flour)—these were apple fritters, after all. Instead, I tried both salting and sugaring the chopped apples to

APPLE FRITTERS

NOTES FROM THE TEST KITCHEN

FORMING APPLE FRITTERS

1. Use ⅓-cup measure and spoon to carefully and gently portion batter into hot oil.

2. Then use spoon to gently press on and flatten each fritter to help interior cook through.

THE BEST SPIDER SKIMMER

Trying to pull fritters from bubbling oil with a spoon or a pair of tongs may leave you with mangled pastries, an oily mess, burns—or all three. The best tool for the job is a type of skimmer that chefs call a "spider." Essentially a shallow basket at the end of a long handle, a spider lets boiling fat or water safely drain away while you lift food comfortably from a pot. We tested five spiders while boiling wontons and frying apple fritters and french fries. All were about 5 inches in diameter and cost from $6.95 to $19.95.

Each spider handled wontons and french fries with relative ease. But the fritters, which we shallow-fried, were another story. We like to fry in a deep Dutch oven to reduce splattering, but getting under the fritters posed a problem. Some skimmers were awkward to use and had us chasing finished fritters around the Dutch oven while the rest of the batch burned. We prefer longer metal handles with extreme angles that keep our hands away from hot edges and don't absorb odors. We also prefer woven wire baskets to solid perforated or slotted ones, which tend to bring oil with them, and we like baskets with shallower, flatter lips that get underneath food easily. Our winner, the **WMF Profi Plus 13-cm Wok Mesh Strainer**, $18, has all of these features, plus it's dishwasher-safe for easy cleanup.

draw out their moisture before stirring them into the batter. Both methods did draw out liquid, but I couldn't seem to shut off the spigot, even after the fritters hit the hot oil. At that point, the weeping liquid prevented the insides from cooking through. If I simply fried the fritters longer, the outsides burned, yet the interiors still didn't cook. I was running out of ideas.

I dispiritedly blotted the chopped apples dry with paper towels and made a new batch. In all honesty, I didn't expect this to do much, but it did produce marginally drier fritters. Tossing the towel-dried apples with the dry ingredients had a bigger impact. Our science editor explained that the dry ingredients soaked up moisture that would otherwise migrate out from the inside of the finished fritters as they cooled, making them soggy.

Maybe I could get the insides to cook through if I made flatter fritters. I'd been deep-frying the fritters, dropping the batter into 4 quarts of peanut oil, and getting big, round fritters. I cut back the oil to just 3 cups and tried shallow-frying the fritters in large scoopfuls, lightly pressing the batter against the bottom of the Dutch oven. With this method, the fritters (and the apple chunks) cooked through, and as a bonus the edges were beautifully crunchy, almost caramelized.

Now it was time to bump up the apple flavor. I replaced the milk in the batter with, in turn, apple juice, apple butter, and apple cider. The juice was wimpy and the apple butter weighed down the batter, but the apple cider got the nod of approval. I added dashes of nutmeg and cinnamon to the batter and stirred in 2 tablespoons of melted butter for richness. Serendipitously, the butter helped the fritters crisp.

I had one final decision to make: Should I crown my fritters with a dusting of powdered sugar or a glaze? The shell-like, translucent glaze gave a little snap to the fritter's craggy exterior, contrasting nicely with the fluffy interior, so I went with that. To make the glaze, I mixed confectioners' sugar with more spices and more apple cider, which gave these warm, sweet, apple-imbued fritters one final layer of apple flavor.

—DIANE UNGER, *Cook's Country*

Apple Fritters

MAKES 10 FRITTERS

We prefer Granny Smith apples in these fritters for their tart flavor and crisp texture.

FRITTERS

- **2 Granny Smith apples, peeled, cored, and cut into ¼-inch pieces**
- **2 cups (10 ounces) all-purpose flour**
- **⅓ cup (2⅓ ounces) granulated sugar**
- **1 tablespoon baking powder**
- **1 teaspoon salt**
- **1 teaspoon ground cinnamon**
- **¼ teaspoon ground nutmeg**
- **¾ cup apple cider**
- **2 large eggs, lightly beaten**
- **2 tablespoons unsalted butter, melted and cooled**
- **3 cups peanut oil or vegetable oil**

GLAZE

- **2 cups (8 ounces) confectioners' sugar**
- **¼ cup apple cider**
- **½ teaspoon ground cinnamon**
- **¼ teaspoon ground nutmeg**

1. FOR THE FRITTERS: Spread prepared apples in single layer on paper towel–lined baking sheet and pat thoroughly dry with paper towels. Combine flour, sugar, baking powder, salt, cinnamon, and nutmeg in large bowl. Whisk cider, eggs, and melted butter together in bowl until combined. Stir apples into flour mixture. Stir in cider mixture until incorporated.

2. Heat oil in Dutch oven over medium-high heat to 350 degrees. Use ⅓-cup measure to transfer 5 heaping portions of batter to oil. Press batter lightly with back of spoon to flatten. Fry, adjusting burner as necessary to maintain oil temperature between 325 and 350 degrees, until deep golden brown, 2 to 3 minutes per side. Transfer fritters to wire rack set inside rimmed baking sheet. Return oil to 350 degrees and repeat with remaining batter. Let fritters cool for 5 minutes.

3. FOR THE GLAZE: Meanwhile, whisk together glaze ingredients in bowl until smooth. Top each fritter with 1 heaping tablespoon glaze. Let glaze set for 10 minutes. Serve.

ROSEMARY FOCACCIA

IN THE PANTHEON OF ARTISAN BREADS, FOCACCIA has a looser history than most. Centuries ago, it began as a by-product: When Italian bakers needed to gauge the heat of the wood-fired oven—"focaccia" stems from *focolare*, meaning "fireplace"—they would tear off a swatch of dough, flatten it, drizzle it with olive oil, and pop it into the hearth to bake as an edible oven thermometer. Because the technique was handy with just about any bread, there evolved countless variations on the theme. That said, it's the deep-dish Genovese interpretation that most Americans recognize: dimpled, chewy, and thick with a smattering of herbs. I'm sure a slab from the mother country would do this version justice—plenty of Italian bakeries and cafés capitalize on its denser texture by slicing the bread in half to make hearty sandwiches—but most stateside breads I've tasted are leaden, oil-slicked, and strewn with pizzalike toppings. Personally, I never understood the appeal.

Before I considered trying to improve on the Genovese adaptation, I happened upon an entirely different style of focaccia in a bakery called Annarosa's in Newburyport, Massachusetts. The crisp-crusted loaves that co-owner Bill Malatesta pulled from his brick oven were round instead of flat and rectangular, and more delicately scented with herbs and olive oil than any focaccia I'd ever encountered. Biting into one revealed an interior that was also lighter, airier, and slightly less chewy than other versions I'd had. In fact, the only familiar elements were the chopped rosemary and flecks of salt on top. Intrigued, I asked him to walk me through his method, a series of kneading, rising, and shaping steps that I was determined to reproduce in my own kitchen. True, I didn't have a heavy brick steam-injected oven to guarantee earthy flavor and an ultra-crisp crust. But with a little research and experimentation, I hoped I could redefine my notion of focaccia with a close replica. I wanted bread with a crackly exterior, a more bubbly interior than the doughier Genovese focaccia, and just enough chew throughout.

A brush of fruity olive oil and heady seasonings gave the Annarosa's breads an addictive savory edge, but that wouldn't mean a thing if the dough itself lacked flavor. The biggest key here is fermentation—the process by which long chains of carbohydrates with little taste convert to sugars, alcohol, and carbon dioxide. And like many other organic processes, it's most effective over a long period of time. A slow ferment—usually several hours—not only allows the yeast to give the dough its lofty rise but also produces a multitude of aromatic molecules that contribute to the flavor of the bread.

To get the benefits of long fermentation with minimal effort, many bakers, Malatesta included, use a "preferment" (also known as a sponge, starter, or *biga* in Italian): a mixture of flour, water, and a small amount of yeast that rests (often overnight) before being incorporated into a dough either in place of or along with more yeast. Time is the main factor here. That little bit of yeast in the biga grows as the hours go by, and the flavor that slowly develops is stronger and more complex than you would get by simply adding yeast to flour and water and kneading.

Cobbling together a basic recipe, I mixed up a biga (⅓ cup of water and ½ cup of flour, plus ¼ teaspoon of yeast) the night before I wanted to bake the loaf, covered the bowl tightly, and let it ferment on the counter. The next morning, it looked bubbly, smelled faintly boozy, and boasted a ripe, slightly sour tang. I added the biga to a basic lean dough—flour, water, salt, and yeast—and went through the typical motions of kneading in a stand mixer, then rising (or "proofing"), dividing, shaping, proofing again, brushing with olive oil, and sliding the dough onto a preheated pizza stone in a blazing-hot oven. Many focaccia recipes include oil in the dough, but I left it out; from personal experience, I knew that it could make the bread dense and greasy. What emerged 40 minutes later was already a significant improvement over other recipes: flavorful, golden loaves perfumed—rather than saturated—with olive oil.

What I hadn't quite nailed on a first take was the tender, airy interior I was after. My fast, powerful stand mixer was developing too much gluten, the strong, elastic network of cross-linked proteins that gives bread its crumb structure. Hand-kneading produced loaves that were even chewier.

Figuring a gentler approach was warranted, I immediately recalled an almost no-knead bread recipe we'd published. This no-knead system, originally developed by Sullivan Street Bakery owner Jim Lahey, relies on the ability of gluten to assemble into large networks on its own, given enough moisture in the dough and sufficient time. Here's how it works: When water and flour are mixed, the proteins in the flour initially combine to form many tightly balled-up units of gluten. Rather than relying on kneading to mechanically unravel each of these gluten units and link them together into larger networks, the no-knead process takes advantage of the enzymes naturally present in the wheat to produce the same effect. During the dough resting process called autolysis (or *autolyse* in French), these enzymes (known as proteases) snip the tiny nests of gluten into shorter strands, which quickly unravel and link together into the more organized sheets of gluten that exist in a well-developed dough.

The sticking point, however, is the hydration of the dough—in other words, the weight of the water in relation to the weight of the flour. Enzymes need water to work their magic, and the more of it in the mix, the more efficient the snipping process. Thus no-knead dough is often wetter than machine-mixed dough. My working recipe rang in at 68 percent hydration (meaning that by weight, it had 6.8 ounces of water for every 10 ounces of flour), whereas no-knead breads tend to work with hydrations in the 75 to 90 percent range. Water also makes dough more capable of expanding without tearing, promoting the formation of larger bubbles. I figured that adapting my focaccia to a no-knead method would improve its texture twice over: A higher hydration—I finally settled on 84 percent—helped to open up the crumb structure, and the lack of handling kept it tender, light, and airy.

But to be effective, the standard no-knead method requires a long rest—anywhere from 12 to 18 hours—after the dough is mixed, during which the gluten develops. And even then the loaves were squatter than I'd hoped. But from experience baking bread, I had a trick to try: "turning" the dough while it proofs.

A standard no-knead dough develops structure gradually because the individual gluten clusters are relatively slow to combine into larger units. But gently turning the dough over itself at regular intervals accomplishes three things: It brings the wheat proteins into closer proximity to one another, keeping the process going at maximum clip; it aerates the dough, replenishing the oxygen that the yeasts consume during fermentation; and it elongates and redistributes the bubbles.

While my next batch of dough proofed, every 30 minutes I gently lifted and folded the edges of the dough toward the middle and then let it rest. Roughly three hours (and five sets of turns) later, the dough was a soft, supple, bubbly mass that had more than doubled in volume. Once it was baked, the results were even better than I had hoped for: From the oven's heat, the dough rounds had leaped twice as tall and bronzed beautifully. Inside, a maze of bubbles punctuated the tender, moist crumb, for focaccia that was as light as the air it contained.

Still, I hoped I could further abbreviate the three-hour proofing and gluten development stage. Some research turned up a second approach to autolysis that supposedly hastens gluten development. Here, a freshly mixed dough is allowed to rest briefly before the salt is added, since salt inhibits the ability of flour to absorb water and prevents its enzymes from breaking down proteins to help form strong gluten networks. I gave it a whirl—and was stunned by the dramatic results. When I let the dough rest for 15 minutes before stirring in the salt, it was already supple and not at all sticky. With this new approach, I not only shaved an hour off the gluten development but also got away with just three sets of turns.

While my bread had just enough rich olive oil taste, the crust lacked the crunchy, almost fried bottom that most oiled-dough focaccia recipes produce. Going against my instincts, I incorporated some olive oil into my dough, and the bottom did crisp up, but the bread's interior turned dense and cakelike. (Just as with shortbread, fat "shortens" the dough by blocking the gluten's ability to form continuous networks.) Instead, I moved my free-form breads into round cake pans, where a few tablespoons of oil coating the exterior would be contained. After swirling the bottom in the oil and some coarse salt, I flipped the dough, gently stretched it to the pan's edges, let it proof for just a few extra minutes, and scattered a healthy dose of chopped fresh rosemary over the top before sliding it onto the hot pizza stone. This focaccia was a revelation: crackly crisp on the bottom, deeply browned on top, and an interior that was open and airy.

With a loaf this good, I'll never go back to any other style of focaccia again.

—ANDREW JANJIGIAN, *Cook's Illustrated*

Rosemary Focaccia

MAKES TWO 9-INCH ROUND LOAVES

If you don't have a baking stone, bake the bread on an overturned, preheated rimmed baking sheet set on the upper middle oven rack.

BIGA

- **½ cup (2½ ounces) all-purpose flour**
- **⅓ cup water, heated to 110 degrees**
- **¼ teaspoon instant or rapid-rise yeast**

DOUGH

- **2½ cups (12½ ounces) all-purpose flour, plus extra for counter**
- **1¼ cups water, heated to 110 degrees**
- **1 teaspoon instant or rapid-rise yeast**
- **3 teaspoons kosher salt**
- **Vegetable oil spray**
- **4 tablespoons extra-virgin olive oil**
- **2 tablespoons minced fresh rosemary**

1. FOR THE BIGA: Combine flour, water, and yeast in large bowl and stir with wooden spoon until uniform mass forms and no dry flour remains, about 1 minute.

NOTES FROM THE TEST KITCHEN

FOR BIG FLAVOR, A LONG REST IS BEST

Creating a small batch of starter dough (also known as a preferment, or a *biga* in Italian) boosts the flavor in our bread dramatically. A starter is made by combining small amounts of flour and water with a little yeast and allowing it to ferment overnight. With a lengthy rest, long carbohydrate chains that have little taste break down into a multitude of sugars and alcohol with lots of flavor.

THIS BAKING STONE TAKES THE HEAT

Baking stones simulate a brick oven in your home oven, absorbing and radiating intense, consistent heat to produce crisp, golden-brown crusts on pizza, calzones, and bread. Of the five stones we tested, the **Baker's Catalogue Pizza Baking Stone by Old Stone Oven**, $54.95, won out for being roomy but not cumbersome, with ridged "feet" that lifted the edge for a comfortable grip. Pizzas and calzones emerged evenly golden brown and crisp.

NOTES FROM THE TEST KITCHEN

MAKING FOCACCIA

1. Fold partially risen dough over itself by gently lifting and folding edge of dough toward middle. Turn bowl 90 degrees; fold again. Turn bowl and fold dough 6 more times (for total of 8 turns).

2. Cover with plastic wrap and let rise for 30 minutes. Repeat lifting, folding, and rising 2 more times, for total of three 30-minute rises.

3. Dust dough with flour and divide in half. Shape halves into 5-inch rounds. Place in oiled pans and slide around to coat bottom and sides of dough. Flip and repeat. Cover pans; let rest briefly.

4. Using your fingertips, press dough out toward edges of pan, taking care not to tear it. (If dough resists stretching, let it relax briefly before trying to stretch again.)

5. Using fork, poke surface of dough 25 to 30 times. Deflate any large bubbles with fork. Sprinkle rosemary over top of dough and let rest until slightly bubbly, 5 to 10 minutes, before baking.

Cover bowl tightly with plastic wrap and let stand at room temperature (about 70 degrees) overnight (at least 8 hours or up to 24 hours). Use immediately or store in refrigerator for up to 3 days (let stand at room temperature for 30 minutes before proceeding with recipe).

2. FOR THE DOUGH: Stir flour, water, and yeast into biga with wooden spoon until uniform mass forms and no dry flour remains, about 1 minute. Cover with plastic wrap and let rise at room temperature for 15 minutes.

3. Sprinkle 2 teaspoons salt over dough; stir into dough until thoroughly incorporated, about 1 minute. Cover with plastic wrap and let rise at room temperature for 30 minutes. Spray rubber spatula or bowl scraper with vegetable oil spray; fold partially risen dough over itself by gently lifting and folding edge of dough toward middle. Turn bowl 90 degrees; fold again. Turn bowl and fold dough 6 more times (total of 8 turns). Cover with plastic wrap and let rise for 30 minutes. Repeat folding, turning, and rising 2 more times, for total of three 30-minute rises. Meanwhile, adjust oven rack to upper-middle position, place baking stone on rack, and heat oven to 500 degrees at least 30 minutes before baking.

4. Gently transfer dough to lightly floured counter. Lightly dust top of dough with flour and divide in half. Shape each piece of dough into 5-inch round by gently tucking under edges. Coat two 9-inch round cake pans with 2 tablespoons olive oil each. Sprinkle pans with remaining ½ teaspoon salt. Place round of dough in pan, top side down; slide dough around pan to coat bottom and sides, then flip over. Repeat with second piece of dough. Cover pans with plastic wrap and let rest for 5 minutes.

5. Using fingertips, press dough out toward edges of pan. (If dough resists stretching, let it relax for 5 to 10 minutes before trying again.) Using dinner fork, poke surface of dough 25 to 30 times, popping any large bubbles. Sprinkle rosemary evenly over top of dough. Let dough rest until slightly bubbly, 5 to 10 minutes.

6. Place pans on baking stone and reduce oven temperature to 450 degrees. Bake until tops are golden brown, 25 to 28 minutes, switching pans halfway through baking. Transfer pans to wire rack and let cool for 5 minutes. Remove loaves from pans and return to wire rack. Brush tops with any oil remaining in pan. Let cool for 30 minutes before serving. (Bread can be stored, wrapped well in plastic wrap, at room temperature for up to 2 days or frozen, wrapped in aluminum foil and placed in zipper-lock bag, for up to 2 months.)

VARIATIONS

Focaccia with Kalamata Olives and Anchovies

Omit salt from pans in step 4. Substitute ½ cup coarsely chopped, pitted kalamata olives; 4 minced anchovy fillets; and 1 teaspoon red pepper flakes for rosemary. Sprinkle each focaccia with ¼ cup finely grated Pecorino Romano cheese as soon as it is removed from oven.

Focaccia with Caramelized Red Onion, Pancetta, and Oregano

Omit salt from pans in step 4. After preheating oven, cook 4 ounces finely chopped pancetta in 12-inch skillet over medium heat until most of fat has rendered, about 10 minutes. Using slotted spoon, transfer pancetta to paper towel–lined plate. Return skillet to medium heat, add 1 chopped red onion and 2 tablespoons water; cook, stirring frequently, until onion is soft and beginning to brown, about 12 minutes. Remove pan from heat and set aside. Substitute cooked pancetta, red onion, and 2 teaspoons chopped fresh oregano for rosemary.

GARLIC KNOTS

GARLIC KNOTS ARE STRIPS OF PIZZA DOUGH TIED in knots, baked, and tossed in garlic butter. Sometimes they're dusted with cheese or parsley, but garlic is really the main attraction here. I tested a few recipes, intending to bring this popular snack home, but instead of slightly chewy pizza dough and bold, potent garlic flavor, I got fluffy knots or dry, crackerlike ones. Garlic powder tasted musty, and fresh minced garlic was either incinerated or raw, in both cases clinging to the knots in greasy clumps.

Looking for pizza dough that would deliver knots chewier than dinner rolls but fluffier than pizza crust, I tweaked ingredients and mixing methods to get a slightly elastic dough that I could make with all-purpose flour. Dough resolved, I turned to garlic flavor. Minced garlic and garlic powder flopped in the initial tests, so I made a paste of roasted garlic and butter. To get mellow flavor without the hour it takes to roast a head of garlic, I toasted unpeeled cloves in a dry skillet. They never reached the melting, mellow sweetness of oven-roasted garlic. When I cooked halved cloves in butter, the butter burned when the cloves were still crunchy.

Maybe minced garlic was the answer after all. I'd flavor the butter by cooking it with minced garlic, then strain out the bits. Unfortunately, the butter browned faster than the garlic. Butter begins to brown after the water in it evaporates, so I added water to buy time. With 1 teaspoon of water and 1 tablespoon of butter, the garlic was golden brown and the butter wasn't. I stirred in 5 more tablespoons of butter to stop any residual cooking, and I let the mixture steep off the heat to eke out more flavor, then strained it. Smelling the garlicky aroma, I baked a batch of knots and brushed on my new garlic butter—but tasters demanded more garlic.

To boost flavor, I brushed the knots with garlic butter midway through as well as at the end of baking. It helped—a bit. Using more garlic butter made the knots greasy, so for more bang from the same amount, I infused the butter with twice as much garlic: 10 cloves. Surprisingly, doubling the garlic didn't double the flavor. Apparently, the butter had reached its garlic saturation point; the only place left to put garlic was the dough.

NOTES FROM THE TEST KITCHEN

TYING THE KNOT

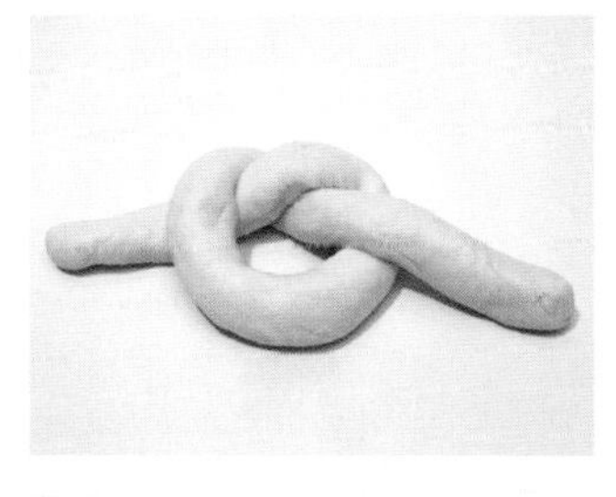

1. Making a 1½-inch loop, tie rope as in first step of tying shoelaces.

2. Then tuck one tail into center of loop from top.

3. Pull other tail up through bottom so end pokes up through center.

GARLIC KNOTS

Ignoring convention, I exchanged the olive oil in the pizza dough for garlic butter and baked a batch of knots. I was ready to hang up my garlic press when one taster chimed in, "I could use a little more garlic." The others agreed. Had I created addicts? I caught sight of the toasty garlic bits I had strained out of the butter. Unappealing on the knots, would they work in the knots? I added them to the dough and baked a batch. Finally, my garlic-crazed tasters got their fix.

—SARAH GABRIEL, *Cook's Country*

Garlic Knots

MAKES 12 KNOTS

You should have 2 tablespoons minced garlic.

- **10 garlic cloves, minced**
- **6 tablespoons unsalted butter**
- **1 teaspoon water, plus ¾ cup water, heated to 110 degrees**
- **1⅛ teaspoons instant or rapid-rise yeast**
- **2 cups (10 ounces) all-purpose flour**
- **1 teaspoon salt**

1. Adjust oven rack to middle position and heat oven to 200 degrees. When oven reaches 200 degrees, turn it off. Grease large bowl.

2. Cook garlic, 1 tablespoon butter, and 1 teaspoon water in 8-inch nonstick skillet over low heat, stirring occasionally, until garlic is straw-colored, 8 to 10 minutes. Add remaining 5 tablespoons butter, stirring until melted. Let stand for 10 minutes off heat. Strain garlic butter through fine-mesh strainer into bowl; reserve garlic solids.

3. Whisk together remaining ¾ cup water, 1 tablespoon garlic butter, reserved garlic solids, and yeast in liquid measuring cup until yeast dissolves. Using stand mixer fitted with dough hook, mix flour and salt together until combined. With mixer on low speed, add water mixture in steady stream and mix until dough comes together, about 1 minute. Increase speed to medium and knead until dough is smooth and comes away from sides of bowl, about 6 minutes. Turn dough out onto counter and knead briefly to form smooth, cohesive ball. Transfer dough to prepared bowl and turn to coat. Cover with plastic wrap and place in turned-off oven until dough has doubled in size, 40 to 50 minutes.

4. Line baking sheet with parchment paper. Punch down dough on lightly floured counter. Roll dough into 12 by 6-inch rectangle and cut into twelve 6-inch strips. With flat hands, roll each strip into 12-inch ropes and tie each rope into knots, tucking tails. Place on prepared baking sheet. (Shaped knots can be refrigerated, covered with plastic wrap, for up to 24 hours. To finish, let sit at room temperature for 30 minutes. Meanwhile, heat oven to 200 degrees and turn off. Proceed with recipe.)

5. Cover knots loosely with plastic wrap and return to turned-off oven until doubled in size, about 20 minutes. Remove knots from oven and discard plastic. Heat oven to 500 degrees. Return knots to oven and bake until set, about 5 minutes. Remove knots from oven and brush with 2 tablespoons more garlic butter. Rotate sheet, return to oven, and bake until golden, about 5 minutes. Brush knots with remaining garlic butter and cool for 5 minutes. Transfer to wire rack. Serve warm.

WHOLE WHEAT SANDWICH BREAD

MOST RECIPES FOR WHOLE WHEAT SANDWICH bread lead to one of two pitfalls. They either pay lip service to being "whole wheat," yielding loaves containing so little of the whole grain stuff that they resemble the fluffy, squishy bread you find at the supermarket; or they call for so much whole wheat that the loaves bake up coarse and dense, crumbling as soon as you slice into them. These squat breads may boast strong wheat flavor, but it's often accompanied by a bitter, musty edge. I wanted to create sandwich bread with a full-blown nutty—but not bitter—taste and a hearty yet soft crumb that sliced neatly.

The cornerstone of any good bread is gluten—the network of proteins that forms when the flour is kneaded with water and provides structure for the loaf. The challenge when making whole wheat bread is that the very thing that gives it character and distinguishes it from white bread—the presence of bran, the outer layer of the cereal grain that's stripped away in refined flour—is also an impediment to gluten development. The fiber in bran has sharp edges that tend to cut the gluten strands, weakening their bonds and making the dough less able to contain gases during proofing and baking. When there's too much whole wheat in the mix, the upshot is a heavy, crumbly loaf. Bran is also what makes whole wheat bitter.

Since baking with whole wheat flour leads to a minefield of issues, I decided to start with a known quantity—a good white-flour recipe—and then work my way backward to "unrefine" it. I consulted my friend Richard Miscovich, a baking instructor at Johnson & Wales University in Providence, Rhode Island, who gave me his trusted recipe for a white-flour *pain de mie,* the French equivalent of our sandwich bread.

To see firsthand the effects of swapping in whole wheat flour, I made a series of loaves, replacing a portion of the 3 cups of all-purpose white flour in Miscovich's recipe with whole wheat in amounts from 25 to 100 percent. Because whole wheat flour absorbs more liquid than its refined counterpart, I incrementally increased the amount of water as well to keep the dough pliant and workable. Per Miscovich's method, I mixed the dough, turned it midway through the first rise to remove large gas bubbles and promote even fermentation, and shaped it into loaves. Before putting the bread in the oven, I poured boiling water into an empty loaf pan that I'd positioned on the bottom rack. The water would supply steam—a common bread baker's technique that prevents the crust from drying out before the loaves have fully expanded. I then placed the loaves in the oven on a preheated baking stone (its heat would help ensure a maximum amount of rise before the crumb set, locking in volume).

Once the breads' crusts turned a burnished mahogany color, I pulled them from the oven and let them cool. I'm not exaggerating when I say that these loaves were a motley crew—they ranged from tall, airy beauties to compact bricks. In fact, the results followed my expectations exactly: The higher the percentage of whole wheat flour, the squatter the loaf and the denser the crumb.

After sampling slices from each loaf, my tasters and I concluded that 40 percent whole wheat flour was as high as I could go before the texture began to take a turn for the worse. But I was facing a catch-22: The flavor contributed by this amount of whole wheat—while decent—was still far from the full-fledged wheat taste I was after; but if I added any more whole wheat flour, the lack of gluten would interfere with the bread's structure.

There was one immediate idea I could try to get the proportion of whole wheat up a notch without impacting the height of the bread or its texture: Substitute bread flour for all-purpose flour. Thanks to the boost in gluten development from its extra protein, I was able to bump up the amount of whole wheat flour to 50 percent. But if I wanted to up the count even further, I'd need another approach.

Delving into more bread research, I uncovered a crucial piece of information: Many whole grain bread recipes require soaking the grains in some of the water or other liquid from the recipe before incorporating

NOTES FROM THE TEST KITCHEN

THE BEST TOASTER

Today, even the simplest toasters come with fancy features like digital countdown timers, bagel buttons, "hi-lift" levers to remove hot toast, and defrost functions. But have more than 80 years of innovations accomplished the basic goal of golden brown toast, fast? To find out, we gathered seven 2-slice toasters priced from $30 to almost $70 and tried them out.

After toasting dozens of loaves of bread (and piles of toaster pastries, frozen waffles, and bagels), we could see that not every model was up to par when it came to the essential tasks of making evenly toasted bread and doing so quickly. Most machines toasted single slices of bread darker on one side than the other. Threading temperature probes into slices of bread revealed that the heating elements in some models reached distinctly uneven temperatures. Compounding this problem was the fact that the wires in the empty slot often overheated the nearer side of the single piece of toast, causing it to darken more rapidly. (When we toasted two slices at once, we got bread that was more evenly toasted.) As for speed, few contenders in our lineup managed to perform quickly and also produce acceptable toast; most models could do one but not the other. Beyond performance and speed, good design was also important. We preferred toasters with slots big enough to fit toaster pastries and bagels and those with dials, which were simpler to read and set than digital controls. We also liked models that stayed cool to the touch. In the end, we found our winner in the **Kalorik Aqua 2-Slice Toaster**, $59.99, which was easy to use and stayed cool while properly heating waffles and pastries, toasting bagels, and making nice-looking toast quickly. (See page 304 for more information about our testing results.)

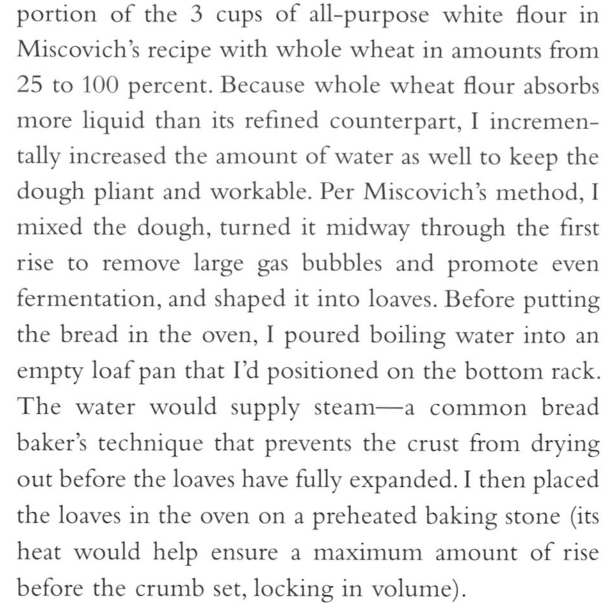

them into the dough. A prolonged soak—most sources recommended overnight—accomplishes three things: First and foremost, it softens the grains' fiber, thereby preventing the sharp edges from puncturing and deflating the dough. Second, the hydrating effect also prevents the grains from robbing moisture from the dough, which would toughen the crumb. Third, steeping the grains activates the wheat's enzymes, converting some starches into sugars and, in turn, reducing bitterness and coaxing out a sweet flavor.

A soaker dough might be just the thing that would allow me to ramp up the percentage of whole wheat flour without any negative impact. I made another series of breads, incrementally increasing the whole wheat as far as I dared beyond 40 percent. This time I mixed the wheat flour in each batch with the milk I was already using until it formed a rough dough. I kneaded it briefly, then covered the bowl and let it rest on the counter overnight. The next morning, I broke each soaker dough into small pieces that would be easier to knead with the remaining ingredients (bread flour, water, yeast, sugar, butter, and salt) and baked off the loaves. The results were even better than I had hoped: I was able to bring the total proportion of wheat flour up to 60 percent—a full 10 percent more than in my last attempt—with no decrease in loaf volume. Even better, the flavor of this bread was considerably more wheaty than that of any loaf I'd baked so far and boasted just the right hint of bitterness.

To add even more wheat flavor to the bread, I made another batch, mixing a small amount of wheat germ into the soaker. The germ, which is removed along with the bran during the milling process, is a significant source of not only the whole grain's nutrition but also its sweet flavor. Just as I'd hoped, the wheat germ strengthened the bread's wheat taste even further, and everyone agreed that I'd taken that flavor as far as it could go. But my work was not yet done. I wanted this loaf to be the best it could be.

I'd baked enough bread over the years to know that the difference between a good tasting loaf and one that offers the most robust, well-developed flavor can boil down to the use of a biga (also known as a starter or preferment). When left to sit overnight, this mixture of flour, water, and yeast develops a full range of unique flavors that give bread even more character.

My recipe was already an overnight process, so just before making the soaker I mixed the bread flour and water with a small amount of yeast and left the two bowls to sit at room temperature. But then I thought of something: The biga had used up all the remaining liquid in my dough.

Usually when I make bread, I use cold water to help keep the dough cool during the kneading process—the friction causes the dough's temperature to rise and can lead to an overproofed product whose flavor and texture both suffer. But all the liquid in my recipe was now incorporated into either the biga or the soaker—and after their overnight rest, both would be at room temperature.

There was nothing I could do about the biga—it needed to rest at around 75 degrees to properly ferment. But I wondered if I could get away with refrigerating the soaker as it sat overnight and then using it to keep the final dough's temperature cool.

Fortunately, the refrigerator did not inhibit the soaking process one bit, and when I kneaded the chilled soaker with the room-temperature biga the next morning, the finished dough came out of the mixer at an ideal 75 degrees. I then proofed, shaped, and baked the dough as before. The result? A unanimous thumbs-up from my tasters, all of whom appreciated the bread's newfound complexity.

Now that I had my basic recipe figured out, there were just two minor tests to sort through. White sugar had been working fine, but when I experimented with brown sugar, molasses, and honey, my tasters voted for the honey, citing superior flavor and complexity. And then there was the fat. Butter was making the bread just a tad too tender and rich. No problem: Cutting back on the fat by more than half was a good start, and then swapping out even more of the butter for vegetable oil was an easy fix.

That was the last batch I pulled out of the oven—a hearty yet soft-textured loaf that sliced cleanly and offered up an earthy, faintly sweet flavor with just a hint of bitterness. And just to be sure it functioned well in all applications, I made toast, grilled cheese sandwiches, and tuna melts, all with great success. Admittedly, making this bread was not a speedy process, but the results were worth the wait.

—ANDREW JANJIGIAN, *Cook's Illustrated*

Whole Wheat Sandwich Bread

MAKES TWO 8-INCH LOAVES

You can hand-knead the dough, but we've found that it's easy to add too much flour during the kneading stage, resulting in a slightly tougher loaf. Wheat germ is usually found either in the baking aisle near the flours or with hot cereals such as oatmeal.

BIGA

- **2 cups (11 ounces) bread flour**
- **1 cup water, heated to 110 degrees**
- **½ teaspoon instant or rapid-rise yeast**

SOAKER

- **3 cups (16½ ounces) whole wheat flour, plus extra for counter**
- **½ cup wheat germ**
- **2 cups whole milk**

DOUGH

- **¼ cup honey**
- **2 tablespoons instant or rapid-rise yeast**
- **4 teaspoons salt**
- **6 tablespoons unsalted butter, softened**
- **2 tablespoons vegetable oil**
- **Bread flour for counter**
- **Vegetable oil spray**

1. FOR THE BIGA: Combine flour, water, and yeast in large bowl and stir with wooden spoon until uniform mass forms and no dry flour remains, about 1 minute. Cover bowl tightly with plastic wrap and let stand at room temperature (70 degrees) overnight (at least 8 hours or up to 24 hours). Use immediately or store in refrigerator for up to 3 days (let stand at room temperature for 30 minutes before proceeding with recipe).

2. FOR THE SOAKER: Combine flour, wheat germ, and milk in large bowl and stir with wooden spoon until shaggy mass forms, about 1 minute. Turn dough out onto lightly floured counter and knead until smooth, 2 to 3 minutes. Return soaker to bowl, cover tightly with plastic wrap, and refrigerate overnight (at least 8 hours or up to 24 hours).

3. FOR THE DOUGH: Tear soaker apart into 1-inch pieces and transfer to stand mixer fitted with dough hook. Add biga, honey, yeast, salt, butter, and oil. Mix on low speed until cohesive mass starts to form, about 2 minutes. Increase speed to medium and knead until dough is smooth and elastic, 8 to 10 minutes. Turn dough out onto lightly floured counter and knead for 1 minute. Shape dough into ball and place in lightly greased bowl. Cover tightly with plastic wrap and let rise at room temperature for 45 minutes.

4. Gently press down on center of dough to deflate. Holding edge of dough with fingertips, fold partially risen dough over itself by gently lifting and folding edge of dough toward middle. Turn bowl 90 degrees; fold again. Turn bowl and fold dough 6 more times (total of 8 folds). Cover with plastic wrap and let rise at room temperature until doubled in volume, about 45 minutes.

5. Adjust oven racks to middle and lowest positions, place baking stone on middle rack, and heat oven to 400 degrees. Spray two 8½ by 4½-inch loaf pans with vegetable oil spray. Transfer dough to well-floured counter and divide into 2 pieces. Working with 1 ball of dough at a time, pat each into 8 by 17-inch rectangle. With short side facing you, roll dough toward you into firm cylinder, keeping roll taut by tucking it under itself as you go. Turn loaf seam side up and pinch it closed. Place loaf seam side down in prepared loaf pan, pressing gently into corners. Repeat with second ball of dough. Cover loaves loosely with plastic wrap and let rise at room temperature until almost doubled in size, 60 to 90 minutes (top of loaves should rise about 1 inch over lip of pan).

6. Place empty loaf pan or other heatproof pan on lowest oven rack and bring 2 cups water to boil on stovetop. Using sharp serrated knife or single-edge razor blade, make one ¼-inch-deep slash lengthwise down center of each loaf. Pour boiling water into empty loaf pan in oven and set loaves on baking stone. Reduce oven temperature to 350 degrees. Bake until crust is dark brown and bread registers 200 degrees, 40 to 50 minutes, rotating pans 180 degrees and side to side halfway through baking.

7. Transfer pans to wire rack and let cool for 5 minutes. Remove loaves from pans, return to rack, and cool to room temperature, about 2 hours. (Bread can be stored, wrapped in double layer of plastic wrap, at room temperature for up to 3 days or frozen, wrapped in additional layer of aluminum foil, for up to 1 month.)

NOTES FROM THE TEST KITCHEN

MAKING SERIOUSLY WHEATY SANDWICH BREAD

1. Combine bread flour, water, and yeast and let mixture rest overnight to create bubbly, aromatic starter dough, or biga.

2. Create soaker by steeping whole wheat flour and wheat germ in milk. This hydrates the bran and helps to reduce its bitterness.

3. Briefly knead soaker, then chill overnight to ensure that final dough reaches proper temperature.

4. Tear soaker into 1-inch pieces and mix with biga (and remaining ingredients). Knead, then let rise for 45 minutes.

5. Deflate center of dough, then fold it in on itself. Turn bowl 90 degrees; fold again. Repeat 6 more times (for total of 8 folds). Let rise for 45 minutes before shaping into loaves.

SHAPING WHOLE WHEAT LOAVES

1. After halving dough, pat each portion into 8 by 17-inch rectangle, with short side facing you.

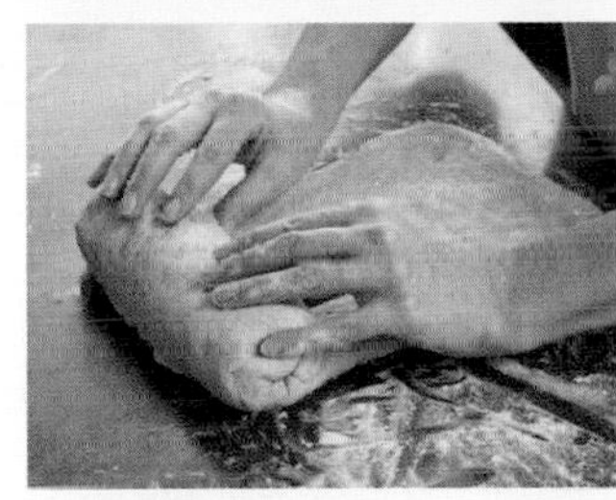

2. Roll each sheet toward you into tight cylinder. Keep roll taut by tucking it under itself as you go. Pinch seams to seal.

3. Place each loaf seam side down in prepared loaf pans. Let dough rise until almost doubled in size, 60 to 90 minutes, before baking.

THE BEST WHOLE WHEAT FLOUR

Whole wheat flour boasts a brown color and more pronounced wheat flavor than the refined white stuff derived from just the grain's stripped-down inner layer, or endosperm. We chose five brands, tasting them in our recipes for whole wheat sandwich bread and pancakes. The flours were milled in a range of grain sizes, from coarse to fine. Their textures in bread corresponded, with coarse flour giving us coarse and crumbly loaves and more finely milled flour producing a finer crumb. In pancakes, the coarsely ground flours won favor for their bold wheat taste. In the end, finely ground **King Arthur Premium Whole Wheat Flour** won out for its sweet, nutty flavor and hearty but not overly coarse texture in both bread and pancakes.

CHAPTER 5

PASTA & PIZZA

CHICKEN RIGGIES

AROUND UTICA, NEW YORK, THE WORD "RIGGIES" refers to the city's signature dish: rigatoni with tender boneless chicken and vegetables in a spicy, creamy tomato sauce. Brimming with hometown pride for this Italian-American specialty, locals advocate enthusiastically for their favorite versions, and anyone within earshot is apt to weigh in. Along the main drag, Genesee Street, I queried a woman in a gray business suit. "Georgio's has the best, hands down," she responded. A man in a stark white lab coat stopped short. "Georgio's is good," he said, "but Dominique's Chesterfield has the original." That assertion caught the attention, or should I say contention, of a third person, delivering FedEx packages. "Nah," he said. "You really want to go to Teddy's, up in Rome. They won RiggieFest a few years running."

RiggieFest? You read that right. It's an annual competition for restaurants and home cooks that fills the Utica Memorial Auditorium. The fest had come and gone for the year, but I spent 24 carbo-loaded hours running around Utica to seven different restaurants, from pizza joint to white-tablecloth establishment, tasting riggies. Made well, riggies offer a cascade of bold flavors—garlic! onions! spicy pickled peppers! Romano cheese!—enriched with cream, fortified with white-meat chicken, and set against the winning backdrop of pasta. My favorite versions included mushrooms and black olives. I wanted to develop a recipe for riggies that would enable me to skip the four-hour drive from Boston to Utica the next time the craving hit.

Every recipe I found was essentially the same: Brown the chicken, then add the vegetables and sauce ingredients, and simmer the sauce for up to an hour—with the chicken and vegetables sitting in it. This explained why the chicken was often rubbery and the vegetables mushy. The remedy for both problems was shorter cooking time. Eight minutes proved perfect for tenderizing the mushrooms and bell peppers without obliterating their texture. To spare them from stewing in the sauce, I removed them from the pan after cooking and added them back at the very end. A similar treatment for the chicken—brown it and remove it from the pan—improved its texture as well.

It was time to move on to the basics of the sauce (to dress 1 pound of rigatoni and feed six). Since there are no tomato chunks in riggies, I skipped canned diced tomatoes and cycled through tomato puree, tomato paste, plain canned sauce, jarred marinara sauce, and crushed tomatoes. Tasters preferred the last for their bright flavor and rustic texture. Many recipes include white wine or sherry, and some recommend chicken broth, but tasters voted them off the ingredient list because they muted the other flavors without adding much. One onion contributed enough sweetness, and five cloves of garlic, some dried oregano, and a hefty dose of grated Romano cheese gave the sauce real Italian attitude.

Hot pickled cherry peppers are essential in riggies for both heat and vinegary tang. A quarter cup of chopped peppers lent just enough punch (you can always add more for a spicier dish), and I reinforced their telltale flavor by adding a mere tablespoon of the pepper brine. A relatively conservative ¾ cup of heavy cream balanced the high-impact ingredients without turning the dish into a full-fledged cream sauce.

But the chicken still didn't taste like much. Spying the jar of cherry peppers on the counter, I got the idea to make a marinade with some of the brine. I added salt and a little olive oil to just 2 tablespoons of brine, tossed in the chicken, and waited. A modest 30 minutes in the briny, salty vinaigrette hugely improved the chicken's flavor. (The oil helps protect the chicken from "cooking" in the brine's vinegar; still, avoid mushy chicken by marinating for less than one hour.) The chicken was so flavorful, in fact, that I questioned the extra step of browning it. It may be unorthodox (sorry, Uticans), but I found that poaching the marinated chicken in the sauce at the end of cooking kept it extra-tender and tasting great.

Maybe I will make that drive to Utica one more time—to enter my recipe in next year's RiggieFest.

—ADAM RIED, *Cook's Country*

NOTES FROM THE TEST KITCHEN

SECRET INGREDIENT: JARRED CHERRY PEPPERS

Riggies just wouldn't be riggies without jarred cherry peppers. Normally, they are used to flavor the sauce. To also flavor the chicken with their spicy tang, we marinated it with olive oil and brine from the cherry pepper jar.

CHICKEN RIGGIES

Chicken Riggies

SERVES 6

If you find only sweet cherry peppers, add ¼ to ½ teaspoon red pepper flakes with the garlic in step 2. Parmesan cheese can be substituted for the Pecorino Romano.

- **1½ pounds boneless, skinless chicken breasts, trimmed, cut into 1-inch pieces**
- **¼ cup finely chopped jarred sliced hot cherry peppers, plus 3 tablespoons cherry pepper brine**
- **3 tablespoons olive oil**
- **Salt and pepper**
- **10 ounces white mushrooms, trimmed and quartered**
- **2 red bell peppers, stemmed, seeded, and cut into 1-inch pieces**
- **1 onion, cut into 1-inch pieces**
- **5 garlic cloves, minced**
- **1½ teaspoons dried oregano**
- **1 (28-ounce) can crushed tomatoes**
- **¾ cup heavy cream**
- **¾ cup pitted kalamata olives, halved lengthwise**
- **1 pound rigatoni**
- **2½ ounces Pecorino Romano cheese, grated (1¼ cups)**

1. Combine chicken, 2 tablespoons cherry pepper brine, 1 tablespoon oil, and 1 teaspoon salt in zipper-lock bag and refrigerate for at least 30 minutes or up to 1 hour.

2. Heat 1 tablespoon more oil in Dutch oven over medium-high heat until shimmering. Stir in mushrooms, bell peppers, and ½ teaspoon salt and cook until browned, about 8 minutes. Transfer vegetables to bowl; set aside. Add onion and remaining 1 tablespoon oil to now-empty pot and cook over medium heat until softened, about 5 minutes. Stir in cherry peppers, garlic, and oregano and cook until fragrant, about 30 seconds. Add tomatoes, cream, and ½ teaspoon pepper and bring to boil. Reduce heat to medium and simmer, stirring occasionally, until sauce is very thick, 10 to 15 minutes. Stir in chicken and reserved vegetables and simmer, covered, until chicken is cooked through, 6 to 8 minutes. Add olives and remaining 1 tablespoon cherry pepper brine. Cover to keep warm.

3. Meanwhile, bring 4 quarts water to boil in large pot. Add pasta and 1 tablespoon salt and cook, stirring often, until al dente. Reserve ½ cup cooking water, then drain pasta and return it to pot. Add sauce and cheese and toss to combine, adding reserved cooking water as needed to adjust consistency. Season with salt and pepper to taste. Serve.

CREAMY ORZO WITH CHICKEN

ORZO IS OFTEN PIGEONHOLED IN ITS CULINARY roles: It's typically served as either a cold pasta salad or a quick side dish. While both have their merits, I wondered if I could promote this quick-cooking, ricelike pasta from supporting player to star of the show for an easy weeknight dinner. In the past, the test kitchen has had success cooking orzo like risotto, gently but quickly so that the grains are coated in a creamy sauce that develops from the grains' own starch. With the simple additions of tender poached chicken and fresh vegetables to this style of orzo, I felt I could have the makings of an elegant yet quick-to-prepare meal. I wanted tender, flavorful chicken and carefully selected, perfectly cooked vegetables—all married with my perfectly cooked orzo risotto. I set out to see what I could do.

First up was the chicken. Similarly to how I would incorporate a protein into a traditional rice-based risotto, my plan for this recipe was to cook the chicken separately, then shred it and stir it into the orzo once the orzo was done. Quick-cooking boneless, skinless breasts were the obvious choice, and for the cooking method, I considered broiling, sautéing, and poaching. Broiling was the easiest method, but it gave the chicken a leathery exterior that tasters rejected. I liked the color and deeper flavor of the sautéed chicken, but at the same time tasters preferred the tender, juicy meat of the poached chicken. I decided my best route was to merge the two techniques, so I began by browning both sides of the chicken breasts in a skillet, then moved them to a saucepan to gently poach until they cooked through (this freed up the skillet to start cooking aromatics for the orzo). Cooking the chicken in chicken broth rather than water gave the meat another boost of flavor. Once the chicken was cooked, I let it cool a bit and then shredded it into bite-size pieces. Now it was ready for the orzo.

The test kitchen had previously developed a reliable procedure for cooking orzo that is very much like the method for making the traditional rice-based risotto. I started by sautéing aromatics, then added the orzo to the skillet to toast, giving it a deeper flavor. I then deglazed the skillet with wine, added liquid to the skillet with the pasta, and cooked, stirring frequently, until it was creamy and tender. It was key here (just as it is when making risotto) to determine the correct ratio of liquid to orzo. I had found in the previous tests that a ratio of roughly 3 to 1 gave me orzo that after about 25 minutes was perfectly tender and swathed in a creamy sauce that was neither gluey nor watered down. For the liquid, water would have been an easy choice, but I realized that using the broth from poaching the chicken would give my pasta another boost of chicken-y flavor and help to unify the dish even more.

It was time to move on to the vegetables and other final additions. I sampled a number of vegetable combinations, and while everyone liked the duo of artichokes and peas, as well as summer squash and tomatoes, tasters were quick to put the pairing of fresh, clean-tasting asparagus and rich, sweet sun-dried tomatoes at the top of their lists. I sliced the asparagus on the bias into ¼-inch pieces, and rather than deal with cooking the asparagus separately, I found I could simply stir it into the pot with the orzo. Adding it halfway through the orzo's cooking time ensured that the asparagus was tender yet crisp by the end. Stirring in the sun-dried tomatoes at the end, along with the chicken, was easy enough. Tasters also wanted a little more richness and depth, and looking to traditional risotto recipes, I thought Parmesan might do the trick. A couple of ounces amplified the creaminess of my recipe and added just the nutty flavor it needed.

At this point my recipe was close, but tasters noted that the shredded chicken seemed unappealingly long and stringy when matched with the short, stubby orzo. I found that by cutting the cooked chicken breasts in half crosswise before shredding, I got smaller shreds of chicken that were much better matched to the pasta. After stirring in some fresh basil, I had an elegant skillet meal that took weeknight cooking to the next level.

—KELLY PRICE, *America's Test Kitchen Books*

Creamy Orzo with Chicken, Asparagus, and Sun-Dried Tomatoes

SERVES 4

The orzo in this dish cooks until tender and will take on a creamy texture similar to that of risotto.

- **2 (6-ounce) boneless, skinless chicken breasts, trimmed**
- **Salt and pepper**
- **1 tablespoon olive oil**
- **4 cups low-sodium chicken broth**
- **1 onion, chopped fine**
- **1¼ cups orzo**
- **4 garlic cloves, minced**
- **½ cup dry white wine**
- **1 pound asparagus, trimmed and cut on bias into ¼-inch pieces**
- **2 ounces Parmesan cheese, grated (1 cup)**
- **¼ cup oil-packed sun-dried tomatoes, rinsed, patted dry, and chopped fine**
- **2 tablespoons chopped fresh basil**

1. Pat chicken dry with paper towels and season with salt and pepper. Heat 2 teaspoons oil in 12-inch nonstick skillet over medium-high heat until shimmering. Carefully lay chicken in skillet and cook until golden brown on first side, about 5 minutes. Flip chicken and cook until lightly browned on second side, about 3 minutes. Transfer chicken to medium saucepan.

2. Pour broth over chicken, bring to simmer, and cook over medium-low heat until chicken registers 160 degrees, 18 to 25 minutes. Transfer chicken to plate, reserving broth. When cool enough to handle, cut chicken breasts in half crosswise and shred meat into bite-size pieces. Set aside.

3. Combine remaining 1 teaspoon oil, onion, and ⅛ teaspoon salt in skillet. Cover and cook over medium-low heat until softened, 8 to 10 minutes. Uncover, increase heat to medium-high, and continue to cook, stirring occasionally, until onion is lightly browned, 4 to 6 minutes longer.

4. Stir in orzo and cook over medium heat until lightly golden, 2 to 3 minutes. Stir in garlic and cook until fragrant, about 30 seconds. Stir in wine, scraping up any browned bits, and cook until evaporated.

5. Add reserved broth to skillet, bring to simmer, and cook over medium heat, stirring frequently, until liquid is almost absorbed and orzo is almost tender, 12 to 15 minutes. Add asparagus and continue to cook, stirring frequently, until asparagus is crisp-tender and orzo is creamy, about 10 minutes longer.

6. Off heat, stir in shredded chicken, Parmesan, sun-dried tomatoes, and basil. Season with salt and pepper to taste and serve.

PASTA ROLL-UPS WITH CHICKEN

WHILE IT'S UNDENIABLY HOMEY AND COMFORTING, baked manicotti, which appears on the menu of just about every old-school Italian restaurant, can be a bit mundane. I wanted a new take on the pasta casserole, one that was a little more upscale. I decided to turn manicotti on its head and swap the red sauce for a rich (but not heavy) white sauce and the simple cheese stuffing for a more substantial filling.

Right off, I started with the filling. Italians typically use leftover meat to stuff their pasta (a recipe I'd seen called for a pound of any combination of cooked meat), but I wanted to build my sauce from the ground up without precooked ingredients. As I considered my options, chicken seemed like the best choice: It's quick-cooking and mild enough to pair with a variety of ingredients. I knew that poaching boneless, skinless chicken parts in broth was efficient and produced good results, so I proceeded in this fashion. In addition to being fast and easy, this method gave me a flavorful mix of dark and white meat, which I could assemble into portions as I pleased. Another bonus of this method was that the leftover poaching broth, infused with flavor by the chicken, gave me the perfect base for my sauce.

But before I could jump ahead to the sauce, I had to finish the filling. For the cheese, I knew I wanted something more intensely flavored than ricotta to pair with the chicken, so I tested a few possibilities. Gorgonzola was overpowering and fontina was dull and grainy. Goat cheese, however, was perfect. It was more flavorful than ricotta but still creamy, and I found that its flavor was nicely brightened by the addition of lemon zest and juice. A little Parmesan sharpened the goat cheese and lent some bite, as did briny olives. I tried black and green olives and quickly discovered that the black olives turned the filling an unappealing purple hue. Luckily, tasters were in favor of the cleaner flavor of the green olives anyway. A touch of minced garlic and a generous amount of chopped fresh basil finished the filling perfectly.

Next I addressed the sauce. With the reserved poaching broth ready to go, I had the base of a classic French sauce called *velouté,* which is basically roux-thickened broth. Deciding to start bare-bones and build the flavor of the sauce as needed, I made a roux by cooking equal parts butter and flour. I then whisked in the reserved broth and a cup of heavy cream and simmered until thickened. The sauce was rich and appropriately clingy, but—no surprise—it tasted a little dull. White wine cut the richness and started building depth. For more complexity, I added finely chopped onion and garlic (sautéing them in the butter before adding the flour). A couple of bay leaves and ground nutmeg imparted a delicate but noticeable enhancement. As a final addition, I stirred some Parmesan and chopped basil into the thickened sauce off the heat. Satisfied with the flavor of both the filling and the sauce, I was ready to roll.

I started out with no-boil lasagna noodles, which we've found have a texture superior to that of traditional noodles once cooked. I soaked them in boiling water to make them pliable before spreading the filling over them and rolling them up pinwheel-style. I spread some of the sauce in the bottom of a 13 by 9-inch baking dish, then nestled in the rolled pasta. After a few rounds, I decided to modify the manicotti rolling technique; spreading the chicken filling out over the noodle meant that the meat ended up in unappealing small bits. So instead of rolling the noodles up like pinwheels, I mounded the chicken filling on one end of the pasta and rolled the pasta around it (more like a sushi roll).

I then covered the pasta with the remaining sauce and baked it until the noodles were fully softened and the filling was hot throughout. Though the overall flavor was spot-on, the filling was separated and loose. It lacked cohesion, and tasters thought it had more in common with warm chicken salad than a filling suitable to a pasta dinner. To make my filling more cohesive, I tried adding some mozzarella, which proved key to marrying the ingredients and transforming them from chicken salad territory to pasta filling.

Despite my progress, the filling was still a little loose and separating slightly, and tasters found it a tad dry. In the next test, I incorporated some of my cream sauce, which contained a fair amount of flour, hoping it would

PASTA ROLL-UPS WITH CHICKEN, SUN-DRIED TOMATOES, AND PINE NUTS

add moisture as well as starch to bind the filling and prevent separation. I was thrilled to find that with that addition, the filling was moist and no longer curdled. Increasing the quantity of flour in the sauce (from ¼ cup to ⅓ cup) created a thick binder that provided enough heft to keep the filling together as well as set up around the rolled pasta.

Baking my casserole took some finesse, as the bright and subtle flavors of the filling were easily killed with extended stints in the oven. After some experimentation, the key proved to be using a low-heat/high-heat method. I baked the casserole, covered, at 350 degrees until it just started to bubble around the edges. I then removed the cover and quickly broiled the casserole to brown the top. This last technique was the final touch needed to perfect my fresh take on pasta casserole.

—ADELAIDE PARKER, *America's Test Kitchen Books*

Pasta Roll-ups with Chicken and Goat Cheese

SERVES 6 TO 8

We prefer Barilla no-boil lasagna noodles for their delicate texture that resembles that of fresh pasta. Other brands of no-boil noodles contain only 12 noodles per package; note that this recipe requires 16 noodles. It's important not to overbake this dish; be sure to remove the casserole from the oven once the sauce begins to bubble around the edges in step 8.

CHICKEN AND SAUCE

- **1 pound boneless, skinless chicken breasts and/or thighs, trimmed**
- **2½ cups low-sodium chicken broth**
- **4 tablespoons unsalted butter**
- **1 onion, chopped fine**
- **4 garlic cloves, minced**
- **⅓ cup all-purpose flour**
- **¼ cup dry white wine**
- **1 cup heavy cream**
- **2 bay leaves**
- **½ teaspoon ground nutmeg**
- **1 ounce Parmesan cheese, grated (½ cup)**
- **2 tablespoons chopped fresh basil**
- **Salt and pepper**

FILLING AND NOODLES

- **10 ounces goat cheese (2½ cups)**
- **6 ounces whole-milk mozzarella cheese, shredded (1½ cups)**
- **2 ounces Parmesan cheese, grated (1 cup)**
- **1 large egg, lightly beaten**
- **1 teaspoon grated lemon zest plus 1 tablespoon juice**
- **1 garlic clove, minced**
- **Salt and pepper**
- **½ cup plus 2 tablespoons chopped fresh basil**
- **⅓ cup pitted green olives, chopped**
- **16 no-boil lasagna noodles**
- **Vegetable oil spray**

1. FOR THE CHICKEN AND SAUCE: Adjust oven rack to middle position and heat oven to 350 degrees. Combine chicken and broth in large saucepan, cover, and simmer over medium heat until breasts register 160 degrees and/or thighs register 175 degrees, 8 to 12 minutes.

2. Remove chicken from pot and pour liquid into measuring cup. Let chicken cool slightly, then shred into bite-size pieces.

3. Wipe pot dry, add butter, and melt over medium heat. Add onion and cook until softened, 5 to 7 minutes. Stir in garlic and cook until fragrant, about 30 seconds. Stir in flour and cook for 1 minute. Slowly whisk in white wine and simmer until nearly evaporated, about 30 seconds.

4. Gradually whisk in reserved broth and cream. Stir in bay leaves and nutmeg and simmer, whisking often, until sauce is thickened and measures about 3½ cups, about 10 minutes. Off heat, remove and discard bay leaves. Whisk in Parmesan and basil and season with salt and pepper to taste. Cover sauce to keep warm; set aside.

5. FOR THE FILLING AND NOODLES: In large bowl, combine goat cheese, mozzarella, ½ cup Parmesan, egg, lemon zest and juice, garlic, ½ teaspoon salt, and ½ teaspoon pepper until uniform. Gradually stir ½ cup of sauce into cheese mixture, then fold in shredded chicken, ½ cup basil, and olives; set aside.

6. Pour 1 inch of boiling water into 13 by 9-inch broiler-safe baking dish and slip noodles into water, one at a time. Let noodles soak until pliable, about 5 minutes, separating noodles with tip of knife to prevent sticking. Remove noodles from water and place in single layer on clean kitchen towels; discard water and dry baking dish.

7. Spread 1 cup more sauce over bottom of baking dish. Mound ¼ cup of chicken-cheese mixture evenly over bottom of each noodle and compact into tidy log. Roll noodle up around filling and lay seam side down in baking dish. Spoon remaining sauce evenly over filled noodles, covering pasta completely. (Assembled roll-ups can be refrigerated, covered with plastic wrap, for up to 1 day. Remove plastic wrap and bake as directed, increasing covered baking time to 45 to 55 minutes.)

8. Cover dish tightly with aluminum foil that has been sprayed with vegetable oil spray. Bake until edges are just bubbling, 25 to 30 minutes, rotating pan halfway through baking.

9. Remove baking dish from oven. Adjust oven rack 6 inches from broiler element and heat broiler. Remove foil from dish, sprinkle with remaining ½ cup Parmesan, and broil until top is spotty brown, 4 to 6 minutes. Let casserole cool for 10 minutes, then sprinkle with remaining 2 tablespoons basil and serve.

VARIATION

Pasta Roll-Ups with Chicken, Sun-Dried Tomatoes, and Pine Nuts

Substitute ½ cup oil-packed sun-dried tomatoes, rinsed and chopped fine, for olives. Add ¼ cup toasted pine nuts and 2 teaspoons minced fresh oregano to filling with chicken in step 5.

NOTES FROM THE TEST KITCHEN

MAKING PASTA ROLL-UPS

1. Using spoon, mound ¼ cup of chicken-cheese mixture over bottom of each noodle, then compact filling into tidy log.

2. Roll noodle up and around filling, then lay roll-up, seam side down, in baking dish.

WEEKNIGHT BOLOGNESE WITH LINGUINE

BOLOGNESE IS OFTEN CONSIDERED THE KING OF Italian meat sauces. The classic Bolognese preparation starts with sautéing finely chopped onion and carrot until softened. Ground beef, pork, and veal are then browned in the pan before liquids (often milk, wine, and pureed tomatoes) are added in stages and slowly simmered. The process can take several hours, but the result is a rich, complex, balanced, and meaty sauce. Wishing for similar results with a fraction of the effort, I hoped to develop a one-pot recipe for authentic-tasting Bolognese that could be prepared on a weeknight. My biggest challenge would be achieving complex flavor without the long simmering time. In addition, I would need to find a way to cook the pasta in the same pot as the sauce.

The test kitchen's traditional, slow-cooked Bolognese recipe starts with softening onion and carrot in butter in a large Dutch oven; meatloaf mix (a combination of ground beef, pork, and veal) is then added and browned to develop rich, meaty flavor. Next, 2 cups of milk, 1½ cups of white wine, and a 28-ounce can of whole tomatoes (processed until almost smooth) are added successively and gently reduced until the pot is almost dry—a process that takes two hours.

My first idea for cutting down on cooking time was to reduce the liquids at a rolling boil. Not surprisingly, this technique left me with stringy meat and a muddied sauce. Next, I tried lowering the amounts of the liquid components. This worked to a point—my cooking time was obviously shorter, but the meat was still tough. It turns out that simmering Bolognese gently over a long period of time accomplishes two things. First, it draws out maximum flavor from the meat and vegetables while evaporating moisture and concentrating the flavors of each liquid. Second, it tenderizes the meat. But given that ground meat is naturally tender, I questioned why anything less than two hours of simmering produced tough meat. Then it hit me: Browning the meat to develop flavor created a formidable crust—one that took hours of gentle cooking to become tender again. What if I skipped the browning entirely?

For my next batch I cooked the ground meat for just one minute before adding the milk, followed by the wine and tomatoes. To my delight, the meat was

WEEKNIGHT BOLOGNESE WITH LINGUINE

supremely tender after just 45 minutes of simmering. But now I had a new problem: By skipping the browning step, I had lost all of the meaty essence that defines Bolognese.

To boost the meatiness of a dish, the test kitchen frequently turns to glutamate-rich ingredients that can quickly add savory richness (a trait known as umami) to any dish. Among these are cured pork products (salt pork, bacon, and pancetta), anchovies, and dried porcini mushrooms. After experimenting with each, I settled on a winning blend. Tasters preferred the clean flavor of pancetta to both bacon and salt pork. Combining the pancetta with ½ ounce of porcini and a minced anchovy, I had a pungent mix that returned my quick Bolognese to exalted, meaty heights. For maximum flavor, I browned the minced pancetta, porcini, and anchovy in butter before adding the onion and carrot to the pot. This sauce tasted great, but considering that my goal was to make Bolognese easier, it seemed counterproductive to add several new ingredients, each of which required its own prep. Some simplifying was in order.

Since I already had my food processor out to blend the tomatoes, I decided to put it to work. First, I processed the onion and carrots; after transferring them to a bowl, I added the porcini, pancetta, and anchovy. Thirty seconds was sufficient to turn this bold combo into a finely ground mixture that browned quickly in the hot pot. Finally I had a great-tasting, quick, and easy Bolognese sauce.

To stay true to my one-pot pasta goal, I had to find the best way to cook the noodles directly in the finished sauce. Since dried pasta absorbs considerable liquid as it cooks, I would have to add water to compensate. To determine how much water was needed to achieve al dente linguine and a properly thickened sauce, I added a pound of pasta and varying amounts of water to finished batches of my Bolognese. After adding the pasta and water, I covered the pot and vigorously simmered (again, a rolling boil proved disastrous for the sauce) the pasta until al dente. Three cups of water was just right, producing nicely cooked pasta and a starchy, but not gluey, sauce. To save time, I tried adding the linguine at the same time as the processed tomatoes. This adjustment easily recouped a quarter of an hour but prevented the tomatoes from reducing and concentrating. To add back concentrated tomato flavor, I stirred in 2 tablespoons of tomato paste.

Bolognese should offer sweet resonance to balance the richness of the meat and the acidity of the wine and tomatoes. The veal provides much of this sweetness, but since tasters wanted more, I added a couple of teaspoons of sugar with the garlic. Rich, meaty, complex, and slightly sweet, my Bolognese sauce delivers on all of the promises of a traditional slow-cooked version. You'd never guess it took one pot and less than an hour to put it on the table.

—DAN SOUZA, *America's Test Kitchen Books*

Weeknight Bolognese with Linguine

SERVES 6

If you can't find meatloaf mix, you can substitute 8 ounces each of 85 percent lean ground beef and ground pork. When adding the linguine in step 5, stir gently to avoid breaking the noodles; after a minute or two they will soften enough to be stirred more easily. If necessary, add hot water, 1 tablespoon at a time, to adjust the consistency of the sauce before serving.

- **2 carrots, peeled and cut into 1-inch pieces**
- **1 onion, cut into 1-inch pieces**
- **3 ounces pancetta, cut into 1-inch pieces**
- **½ ounce dried porcini mushrooms, rinsed**
- **1 anchovy fillet, rinsed**
- **1 (28-ounce) can whole peeled tomatoes**
- **2 tablespoons unsalted butter**
- **2 teaspoons sugar**
- **1 garlic clove, minced**
- **1 pound meatloaf mix**
- **1½ cups whole milk**
- **2 tablespoons tomato paste**
- **½ cup dry white wine**
- **3 cups water**
- **1 pound linguine**
- **Salt and pepper**
- **Grated Parmesan cheese**

1. Pulse carrots and onion in food processor until finely chopped, 10 to 15 pulses; transfer to bowl. Process pancetta, porcini, and anchovy until finely chopped, 30 to 35 seconds; transfer to separate bowl. Pulse tomatoes until mostly smooth, about 8 pulses; transfer to separate bowl.

2. Melt butter in Dutch oven over medium heat. Add processed pancetta mixture and cook until browned, about 2 minutes. Stir in processed carrot mixture and cook until softened, 5 to 7 minutes.

3. Stir in sugar and garlic and cook until fragrant, about 30 seconds. Stir in meatloaf mix, breaking up meat with wooden spoon, and cook for 1 minute. Stir in milk, scraping up any browned bits, and simmer until nearly evaporated, 18 to 20 minutes.

4. Stir in tomato paste and cook for 1 minute. Stir in wine and simmer until nearly evaporated, 8 to 10 minutes.

5. Stir in processed tomatoes, water, and linguine and bring to rapid simmer. Cover and simmer vigorously, stirring often, until pasta is tender and sauce is thickened, 12 to 16 minutes. Off heat, season with salt and pepper to taste and serve with Parmesan.

NOTES FROM THE TEST KITCHEN

THE BEST TOMATO PASTE

Tomato paste is basically tomato puree with most of the moisture cooked out. It adds body, color, and intensity to many dishes, including pastas, stews, and soups. To find out which brand is best, we gathered 10 brands for a tasting: nine in small cans and one in a toothpaste-like tube. We had tasters sample the paste straight from the container, cooked by itself, and cooked in marinara sauce.

When the brands were sampled uncooked, tasters were split between those that tasted bright and acidic, like fresh tomatoes, and those with deep "cooked" tomato flavor. Many tasters downgraded brands for "dried herb" notes, including oregano. Because tomato paste is usually cooked, we sautéed each brand in a skillet and tasted again. Some pastes became dull; others sprang to life. In the marinara sauce, tasters leaned toward those pastes that provided long-simmered flavor and depth. But ultimately, we found that while better tomato pastes improved the taste of the marinara, no single brand ruined the dish. Overall scores were relatively close, but one paste came in slightly ahead of the pack. **Goya** tomato paste was praised for its "bright, robust tomato flavor." Tasters like its sweetness, yet found it was well-balanced. (See page 289 for more information about our testing results.)

SHELLS WITH MEAT SAUCE

PREDICTABLY, GIVEN THEIR GREAT FLAVOR BUT high fat and calorie content (49 grams of fat and 860 calories per serving), stuffed shells have inspired no shortage of lower-fat recipes. Some use novelty ingredients like pureed beans or squashed tofu as a primary filling. When I made these for my tasters, they put down their forks in boredom. Other versions resort to such unfortunate options as grainy diet ricotta, chalky ground turkey, or plasticky fat-free cheese. These caused tasters to wonder suspiciously if they were eating "real" food. Clearly, I'd have to forge my own path to make low-fat stuffed shells taste as good as the full-fat versions.

As a starting point, I used a full-fat test kitchen recipe for the filling, which uses ricotta, Parmesan, shredded mozzarella, and two eggs. I'd slice and whittle where I could. Fortunately, in the process of trying the low-fat versions, I had come across one "diet" ingredient that really worked: fat-free cottage cheese. We usually prefer reduced-fat products to fat-free in the test kitchen because they have better texture and no aftertaste from the stabilizers often added to nonfat ingredients. But in this case we found that when the fat-free cottage cheese was processed to a creamy puree, its smooth texture was indistinguishable from that of the higher-fat versions, its flavor clean and mild. I substituted fat-free cottage cheese for the full-fat ricotta, and the dish remained fully satisfying.

Next, I cut the Parmesan down little by little until I was left with half the starting amount—its flavor is so strong, it didn't take much to make an impact. Using part-skim mozzarella was an easy switch from the full-fat version, and tasters thought it also offered up plenty of flavor even when I'd reduced the amount by half a cup to 1½ cups. Together these changes saved a whopping 130 calories and 15 grams of fat per portion without compromising the flavor or texture.

The filling was delicious at this point but too soupy—it ran right out of the shells. I drained the cottage cheese, but even this was runnier than the ricotta had been, and adjusting the amount and types of shredded cheeses in the filling had reduced their binding power as well.

REDUCED-FAT STUFFED SHELLS WITH MEAT SAUCE

Removing the eggs made the raw filling firmer (and saved some calories), but it still wasn't firm enough to pipe into the shells. One at a time, I added a handful of various low-fat ingredients such as cooked rice, instant potato flakes, and bread crumbs. Each gave the filling body, but in every case either the taste or the texture of these ingredients was notably wrong for stuffed shells. Finally, I reached for a box of saltines. I thought their relatively bland flavor might work in my favor. It did. When ground fine in the food processor with the cheeses, they disappeared into the filling, firming it up nicely and adding only a few calories and no fat per portion.

Now for the sauce. From the first round of testing, I knew that I needed to stick with beef for flavor. Most full-fat recipes use a pound or so of 85 percent lean ground beef. When I reduced the amount to 6 ounces, there was still enough beefy flavor but too much fat. Once I switched to 93 percent lean ground beef, I hit my calorie mark, but the beef flavor was wan, and the texture was tough with so little fat. Adding a tablespoon of savory soy sauce to the raw meat boosted the beef flavor but failed to improve its texture.

A colleague pointed out that browning could be making the meat tough. Indeed, cooking the meat gently until it was no longer pink (but not yet browned) did help a little. Not completely satisfied, I whirled the raw beef in the food processor with the soy, thinking the blades might tenderize it. The technique worked. Our science editor helped me understand why: The blades cut the collagen into shorter fibers, he said. Shorter fibers equal more tender meat.

Since the rest of the sauce was so low in fat, and the stuffed shells finally had rich, beefy flavor combined with good texture, I called it a day. I had cut the calories to 510 and the fat to 15 grams per portion of four stuffed shells. True, the amount of work involved in making the dish hadn't been reduced, but neither had the flavor of the creamy filling and hearty sauce.

—KRIS WIDICAN, *Cook's Country*

NOTES FROM THE TEST KITCHEN

KEYS TO REDUCED-FAT SHELLS

1. Use a small amount of beef and process it with soy sauce to amplify its flavor and make it tender.

2. Cook beef gently and briefly, just until no longer pink, to keep it tender.

3. Puree saltines with drained cottage cheese to mimic creamy texture of full-fat fillings.

THE BEST DICED TOMATOES

We rely on diced tomatoes for everything from tomato sauce to chili to soups and stews. But supermarket shelves are teeming with different brands of diced tomatoes. To make sense of the selection, we gathered 16 widely available styles and brands and tasted them plain and in tomato sauce, rating them on tomato flavor, saltiness, sweetness, texture, and overall appeal.

To our surprise, nearly half of the brands fell short. The lowest-rated tomatoes were awful, eliciting complaints like "mushy, gruel-like texture" and "rubbery and sour." We found that various factors, such as geography and additives, played into whether a sample rated highly. Our top-ranked tomatoes were grown in California, source of most of the world's tomatoes, where the dry, hot growing season develops sweet, complex flavor; the bottom-ranked brands came from the Midwest and Pennsylvania. We tasted tomatoes that were too sweet or too acidic (from not enough or too much citric acid) or bland from lack of salt. Tasters overwhelmingly favored those brands with more salt. In fact, the tomatoes with the least salt—125 mg per serving compared to 310 mg in the top-rated brand—ranked last. In the end, one can stood out from the pack. **Hunt's Diced Tomatoes** were our tasters' favorite, praised for being "fresh" and "bright," with a "sweet-tart" flavor and "juicy," "firm, crisp-tender chunks." (See page 288 for more information about our testing results.)

Reduced-Fat Stuffed Shells with Meat Sauce

SERVES 6

You'll need a 24-ounce container of fat-free cottage cheese (don't use whipped). If it appears watery, drain it in a fine-mesh strainer for 15 minutes before you use it. Separate the shells after draining them to keep them from sticking together.

MEAT SAUCE

- **6 ounces 93 percent lean ground beef**
- **1 tablespoon soy sauce**
- **3 (14.5-ounce) cans diced tomatoes**
- **1 tablespoon olive oil**
- **1 onion, chopped fine**
- **2 tablespoons tomato paste**
- **3 garlic cloves, minced**
- **¼ teaspoon red pepper flakes**
- **½ teaspoon salt**
- **¼ cup finely chopped fresh basil**

STUFFED SHELLS

- **1 (12-ounce) box jumbo pasta shells**
- **Salt**
- **12 saltines, broken into pieces**
- **2½ cups fat-free cottage cheese**
- **8 ounces part-skim mozzarella cheese, shredded (2 cups)**
- **1 ounce Parmesan cheese, grated (½ cup)**
- **2 tablespoons chopped fresh basil**
- **2 garlic cloves, minced**

1. FOR THE MEAT SAUCE: Adjust oven rack to upper-middle position and heat oven to 375 degrees. Pulse beef and soy sauce in food processor until well combined; transfer to medium bowl. Add tomatoes to processor and pulse until coarsely ground.

2. Heat oil in large saucepan over medium heat until shimmering. Add onion and cook until softened, about 5 minutes. Stir in beef mixture, breaking up meat with wooden spoon, and cook just until no longer pink, about 3 minutes. Add tomato paste, garlic, and pepper flakes and cook until fragrant, about 1 minute. Stir in processed tomatoes and salt and simmer until sauce is slightly thickened, about 25 minutes. Off heat, stir in basil; set aside. (Sauce can be refrigerated for up to 3 days.)

3. FOR THE STUFFED SHELLS: Meanwhile, bring 4 quarts water to boil in large pot. Add shells and 1 tablespoon salt and cook, stirring often, until al dente, 12 to 15 minutes. Drain shells and transfer to kitchen towel–lined baking sheet. Reserve 24 shells, discarding any that have broken.

4. Pulse saltines in clean food processor until finely ground. Add cottage cheese, 1½ cups mozzarella, Parmesan, basil, garlic, and ½ teaspoon salt and process until smooth; transfer to large zipper-lock bag. Using scissors, cut off 1 corner of bag and pipe 2 tablespoons filling into each shell.

5. Spread half of meat sauce over bottom of 13 by 9-inch baking dish. Arrange filled shells, seam side up, over sauce in dish. Spread remaining sauce over shells. (Unbaked shells can be refrigerated, covered with plastic wrap, for up to 2 days. To finish, discard plastic and bake as directed, increasing baking time to 45 to 50 minutes.)

6. Cover with aluminum foil and bake until bubbling around edges, 35 to 40 minutes. Remove foil and sprinkle with remaining ½ cup mozzarella. Bake until cheese is melted, about 5 minutes. Let cool for 15 minutes. Serve.

MUSSELS MARINARA WITH SPAGHETTI

THERE'S A LOT TO LIKE ABOUT MUSSELS: THEY'RE quick-cooking, flavorful, and relatively inexpensive. And since most mussels at the market nowadays are rope-cultured and virtually free of sand and grit, they require minimal prep. All of these characteristics make mussels the perfect foundation for a simple one-pot supper. One of my favorite preparations is mussels marinara, where mussels are draped in a spicy tomato sauce and served with crusty bread or pasta. I decided to focus on developing a recipe for this dish. Before choosing the pasta and determining the best way to cook the mussels, I set about developing my sauce.

While the term "marinara" generally conjures images of a thick, smooth tomato sauce, most of the recipes I tested for mussels marinara were brothy and chunky. The few versions that did feature a smooth sauce were generally panned by tasters, who felt this style lacked contrast and texture. After tasting a half-dozen variations on the mussels marinara theme, I found that my ideal sauce was indeed brothy with tender chunks of tomato, relatively spicy, and rich with seafood brininess. Examining my notes, I realized that this sauce has much in common with classic puttanesca sauce, which is also spicy and composed of tomatoes, olives, capers, red pepper flakes, garlic, and anchovies. I began by narrowing down the tomato options and found that processing whole tomatoes with their juice produced a better sauce than diced tomatoes, crushed tomatoes, or tomato puree. Then I made a modified version of an earlier test kitchen puttanesca. In addition to my two 28-ounce cans of whole tomatoes, I included eight anchovies, six cloves of garlic, and ¾ teaspoon of red pepper flakes; I ditched the olives and capers, which were clearly out of place in this dish. Using this sauce as the base of my working recipe, I turned my attention to the pasta.

For the pasta, I added a variety of pasta shapes and sizes (with enough water for them to cook properly) to batches of my sauce and simmered them vigorously until the pasta was tender and the sauce was thickened. Tasters immediately showed a preference for long noodles, which seemed to grab more of the sauce when twirled onto a fork. After testing linguine, spaghetti, vermicelli, cappellini, and bucatini, I settled on spaghetti as the best complement to my marinara sauce. With my pasta of choice and a working tomato sauce recipe, I tackled the true star of this dish: the mussels.

Starting with 2 pounds of mussels (enough for six servings), I examined my options for cooking them. A typical approach for clams and mussels is to steam them open in a large pot using a little water or wine. This method allows the bivalves' liquor to be strained of grit before finishing the dish. This is an important step for clams in particular, but since mussels contain very little sand, I wondered if I could use a different, simpler technique. In keeping with my one-pot approach, I tried adding the mussels directly to the pot as the pasta finished simmering. After a few tests, I found that it took just a couple of minutes for the shells to open and for the mussels to release their briny juice into the pot. This technique resulted in perfectly cooked mussels and pasta, with no additional cooking steps. With my goal of one-pot mussels marinara in sight, I took a final look at the flavors of my sauce.

While tasters liked the texture of my sauce, many found the anchovies and heat to be overpowering. To ensure that the mussels remained in the foreground, I cut the anchovies to just one fillet and reduced the red pepper flakes to ½ teaspoon. This sauce offered better balance but lacked the brininess that tasters expected. Substituting a bottle of clam juice for some of the cooking water was the clear and simple solution; it bolstered the dish's brininess without overpowering the flavor of the mussels. A handful of minced fresh parsley added some color and freshness, and I now had a simple yet sensational one-pot mussels marinara.

—DAN SOUZA, *America's Test Kitchen Books*

Mussels Marinara with Spaghetti

SERVES 6

When adding the spaghetti in step 3, stir gently to avoid breaking the noodles; after a minute or two they will soften enough to be stirred more easily. If necessary, add hot water, 1 tablespoon at a time, to adjust the consistency of the sauce before serving. Drizzle with extra-virgin olive oil and serve with Garlic Toasts for dipping in the flavorful sauce.

- **2 (28-ounce) cans whole peeled tomatoes**
- **3 tablespoons extra-virgin olive oil**
- **1 onion, chopped fine**
- **6 garlic cloves, minced**
- **1 anchovy fillet, rinsed and minced**
- **½ teaspoon red pepper flakes**
- **2 cups water**
- **1 (8-ounce) bottle clam juice**
- **1 pound spaghetti**
- **2 pounds mussels, scrubbed and debearded**
- **¼ cup minced fresh parsley**
- **Salt and pepper**
- **1 recipe Garlic Toasts (recipe follows)**

1. Pulse tomatoes, 1 can at a time, in food processor until coarsely chopped and no large pieces remain, 6 to 8 pulses; transfer to bowl.

2. Heat 2 tablespoons oil in Dutch oven over medium heat until shimmering. Stir in onion and cook until softened, 5 to 7 minutes. Stir in garlic, anchovy, and pepper flakes and cook until fragrant, about 30 seconds. Stir in processed tomatoes and simmer gently until tomatoes no longer taste raw, about 10 minutes.

3. Stir in water, clam juice, and spaghetti and bring to rapid simmer. Cover and simmer vigorously, stirring often, for 12 minutes. Stir in mussels and continue to simmer vigorously, covered, until pasta is tender and mussels have opened, about 2 minutes longer.

4. Uncover, reduce heat to low, and stir in remaining 1 tablespoon oil and parsley. Cook, tossing pasta gently, until it is well coated with sauce, 1 to 2 minutes. Season with salt and pepper to taste and serve with Garlic Toasts.

Garlic Toasts

MAKES 8 SLICES

Be sure to use a high-quality, crusty bread, such as a baguette; do not use sliced sandwich bread.

- **8 (1-inch-thick) slices rustic bread**
- **1 large garlic clove, peeled**
- **3 tablespoons extra-virgin olive oil**
- **Salt and pepper**

Adjust oven rack 6 inches from broiler element and heat broiler. Spread bread on rimmed baking sheet and broil until golden brown on both sides, about 2 minutes per side. Briefly rub one side of each toast with garlic. Drizzle toasts with oil, season with salt and pepper to taste, and serve.

NOTES FROM THE TEST KITCHEN

DEBEARDING MUSSELS

Occasionally, mussels have a harmless weedy piece, or beard, protruding from shells; it's fairly small and can be difficult to tug out of place. To remove it easily, trap beard between side of small paring knife and your thumb and pull.

SPANISH-STYLE NOODLES WITH SEAFOOD

IN SPAIN, *FIDEOS* ARE VERY SHORT NOODLES similar to vermicelli, but the word also refers to a classic Valencian dish in which these noodles are toasted to a golden brown and simmered in a flavorful, saffron-spiked broth until they have soaked up most of the broth and are tender and only lightly sauced. With the addition of chorizo and shellfish, it becomes a hearty meal that is similar to paella but with noodles instead of rice. It's an elegant yet satisfying dinner, but it isn't without its challenges. Labor-intensive homemade stock and oil-slicked noodles plagued many of the recipes I found. And then there were the issues with timing the noodles and seafood so they were properly cooked simultaneously and ending up with just the perfect amount of sauce to coat the noodles. I headed to the kitchen to see if I could create a streamlined fideos with each component perfectly cooked.

My first hurdle was the noodles. Traditional fideos are very thin noodles that are about 2 inches long. Because I couldn't find them at my grocery store, I needed an alternative. I settled on similarly thin vermicelli, which I could easily and tidily break into 2-inch lengths by placing them in a zipper-lock bag and breaking them over the edge of the counter.

Just as toasting the rice is key to paella, toasting the noodles is an integral part of what gives fideos its signature flavor. Traditionally, the uncooked noodles are tossed with several tablespoons of oil and toasted in a skillet until golden brown. I found that I could achieve acceptable browning with much less oil (just 2 teaspoons), and it took just five minutes over medium heat for the noodles to turn the right deep golden color.

After toasting the noodles, I set them aside so I could focus on the noodles' cooking liquid. Homemade fish stock was common to many of the recipes I had found, but I wanted a dish I could make any night of the week. I turned to clam juice, an ingredient we often use in the test kitchen when looking for an easy alternative to stock. But before I could add the clam juice, I took a few extra steps to ensure that the flavor of the cooking liquid would be well rounded. First, I sautéed the chorizo, which, though not always included in fideos recipes, I felt was key for adding smoky flavor and complexity to the dish. If I cut the sausage into small ¼-inch pieces, just 2 ounces was enough to infuse its smoky flavor throughout. After it had browned, I set it aside and sautéed my aromatics, a mixture of garlic and onion, in the flavorful oil left behind from browning the chorizo. Once the aromatics were softened, the clam juice went into the skillet along with some crumbled saffron, a signature ingredient of fideos that adds grassy, flowery notes, and I also stirred in a combination of diced tomatoes and white wine, both of which gave the dish an acidic brightness. Then I added the noodles and chorizo to the mixture, gave it all a stir, covered the skillet, and let it simmer until the noodles were tender. Unfortunately, by the time they were done (it took about 15 minutes), my skillet was completely dry and all I had was gummy noodles. I had started with 2 cups of clam juice, so for my next test I tried upping the amount to 3 cups. This produced the tender noodles I was after, but now the flavor was too salty. Using water rather than clam juice for the additional cup of liquid was an easy fix. These noodles were tender, nicely flavored, and just slightly saucy.

When it comes to fish and shellfish, fideos can contain anything and everything from shrimp, clams, and mussels to calamari, monkfish, and octopus. To keep things simple, I limited myself to clams and shrimp. But because both are quick-cooking, I gave the noodles a five-minute head start before adding the clams and shrimp to the pan. However, one test proved that the shrimp needed even less time. Adding the clams five minutes into the noodles' cooking time and the shrimp three minutes after that did the trick. Now every component was perfectly cooked.

Tasters liked everything about the recipe, but still, I felt it was missing something. Traditionally fideos is served with a garlicky aïoli, but I didn't want to fuss with another recipe at this point. I tried adding extra olive oil to boost the richness, but everyone agreed it fell a little flat. Though not traditional, I found my solution in a pat of butter. It added not just richness but also a sweetness that echoed that of an aïoli. A sprinkling of parsley added a bright, fresh flavor and a pop of color. With that, I had a recipe for Spanish-style noodles that was festive enough for company but easy enough for a fun family dinner, no trip to Spain required.

—KELLY PRICE, *America's Test Kitchen Books*

Spanish-Style Noodles with Seafood

SERVES 4

You can substitute andouille or linguiça for the chorizo if preferred. Be sure to discard any clams that are open or have broken shells prior to cooking.

- **1 pound extra-large shrimp (21 to 25 per pound), peeled and deveined**
- **Salt and pepper**
- **1 tablespoon olive oil**
- **12 ounces vermicelli, broken into 2-inch pieces**
- **2 ounces chorizo sausage, cut into ¼-inch pieces**
- **1 onion, chopped fine**
- **3 garlic cloves, minced**
- **1 (14.5-ounce) can diced tomatoes**
- **2 (8-ounce) bottles clam juice**
- **1 cup water**
- **½ cup dry white wine**
- **½ teaspoon saffron threads, crumbled**
- **1 pound littleneck clams, scrubbed**
- **1 tablespoon unsalted butter**
- **2 tablespoons minced fresh parsley**
- **Lemon wedges**

1. Toss shrimp with ¼ teaspoon salt and ⅛ teaspoon pepper in bowl and set aside.

2. Heat 2 teaspoons oil in 12-inch nonstick skillet over medium heat. Add vermicelli and cook, stirring frequently, until golden, 4 to 6 minutes. Transfer noodles to plate.

3. Add remaining 1 teaspoon oil to skillet and return to medium-high heat until just smoking. Add chorizo and cook, stirring occasionally, until lightly browned, 2 to 4 minutes. Transfer chorizo to paper towel–lined plate.

NOTES FROM THE TEST KITCHEN

BREAKING NOODLES

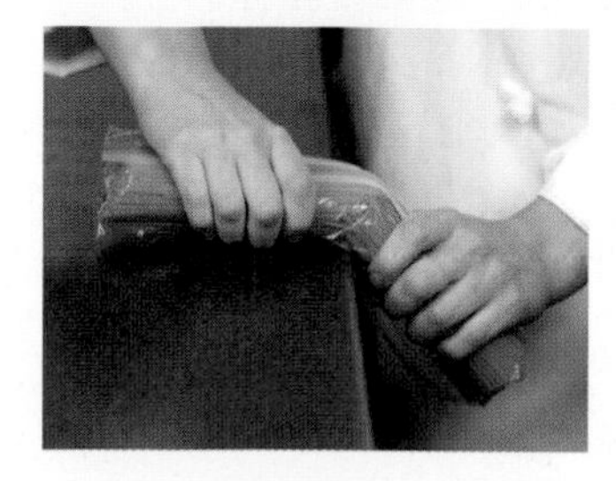

To break noodles evenly and neatly, put them in a zipper-lock bag (or wrap them in a clean kitchen towel), then press against corner of counter.

4. Add onion and ⅛ teaspoon salt to oil left in skillet and return to medium-low heat. Cover and cook, stirring occasionally, until onion is softened, 8 to 10 minutes. Uncover, stir in garlic, and cook until fragrant, about 30 seconds. Stir in tomatoes with their juice, clam juice, water, wine, and saffron and bring to simmer.

5. Return vermicelli and chorizo to skillet. Cover, increase heat to medium-high, and cook for 5 minutes, stirring often and adjusting heat to maintain vigorous simmer. Nestle clams, hinge side down, into vermicelli. Cover and simmer for 3 minutes. Sprinkle shrimp over top, cover, and cook until shrimp are translucent and clams have opened, 5 to 7 minutes.

6. Gently stir in butter, sprinkle with parsley, and season with salt and pepper to taste. Serve with lemon wedges.

THIN-CRUST PIZZA

PIZZA WAS THE FIRST FOOD I LEARNED TO MAKE AS a kid, and I've been determined to perfect it ever since. Over the years, my dogged pursuit of the ideal crust—thin, crisp, and spottily charred on the exterior; tender yet chewy within—has led me into exhaustive research and experiments, and even compelled me to extremes. I've been known to override the lock on my oven during its white-hot cleaning cycle. I've even built a wood-fired oven in my backyard.

But despite those efforts, I had yet to produce a recipe that was both reliable and reasonable for someone baking in a conventional oven. After the 10 to 12 minutes necessary to crisp the crust, the interior inevitably turns dry and tough. Plus, the raw dough itself is a devil to work with: Too wet and it becomes sticky; too dry and it's a stiff, dense wad. And forget stretching it into a neat circle; most of the time it either rips or springs back like a rubber band. If I were really going to bring home the kind of pizza I've come to crave when dining out, I'd have to take each element back to the drawing board, starting with the dough.

Like other lean doughs, pizza tends to have a short ingredient list (often just flour, water, salt, and yeast), so each element counts for a lot. Flour was the obvious first consideration, and I opted for high-protein (about 13 percent by weight) bread flour. It's a typical choice when a chewy, nicely tanned crust is the goal, since the proteins both encourage gluten development and brown easily.

The other major factor is the hydration level of the dough—in other words, the weight of the water in relation to the weight of the flour. From my recent work on focaccia (see page 95), I knew that low-hydration doughs (55 to 70 percent water) generally result in the type of tight, even crumb you might find in sandwich bread, whereas a higher hydration (70 percent and up) produces the looser, airier, more bubbly crumb typical of rustic artisan-style breads. Figuring my goal was somewhere in the middle, I started my testing by mixing together five moderately wet doughs (from 58 to 67 percent hydration), kneading all the ingredients with our preferred food-processor method. (It might take 15 to 20 minutes for a more conventional stand-mixer method to turn the dough into a shiny, elastic mass, but we've found that a food processor turns out comparably kneaded results in less than two minutes.) I let the dough proof at room temperature for a few hours, shaped and topped the pies with a quick no-cook pizza sauce (a placeholder at this stage) and a generous handful of shredded mozzarella, and shuttled them onto blazing-hot (500-degree) baking stones to cook. I pulled them out roughly 10 minutes later, once the crusts had puffed up a bit and blistered in spots and the cheese was melted and spotty brown.

Just as I'd expected, the lower-hydration doughs were not only stiff and difficult to shape into even rounds when raw but also tough to chew once baked. But really wet doughs weren't ideal either; though they emerged significantly more tender from the oven, all that water had made the raw dough so sticky and soft that it tended to tear when stretched. The best of the bunch fell at about 61 percent—enough to stretch easily without ripping or sticking to my fingers and retain moisture as it baked. With further experimentation, I found that I could raise the hydration level to 63 percent and still be able to handle this stickier dough by adding a little extra flour to the exterior as I shaped and stretched the pie. Such a judicious use of "bench flour" allowed me to increase the hydration of the dough while still maintaining the ability to shape it easily.

With this dough I had a good jumping-off point, but pizza perfection was still a long way away. First off, instead of being thin and just a bit floppy, like a good parlor pie, my crust was bready and overinflated—more like focaccia than pizza—even when stretched as

THIN-CRUST PIZZA

thinly as possible. Even more troubling, the dough was lacking in flavor, save for a strong yeastiness.

Simply dialing back on the yeast seemed like an obvious test—and it did help deflate the too-puffy crust a bit. But it also wiped out what little flavor the dough had. Since keeping the yeast to a minimum was a given, I needed a totally different approach to fermentation.

First, a little background on the relationship between fermentation and dough's texture and flavor. When dough is first mixed, tiny "seed" bubbles form that expand with carbon dioxide at two different junctures: once when the bread is proofed and again when a last burst of carbon dioxide is produced during the first few minutes of baking. The larger the bubbles in the dough prior to baking, the more open and puffy the final dough will be. One way to minimize the size of the bubbles is to chill the dough as it proofs. Aside from producing finer, tighter air bubbles, cold fermentation has the added benefit of creating more flavorful dough. Why? Because at lower temperatures, yeast produces less carbon dioxide and more of the initial side products of fermentation: flavorful sugars, alcohol, and acids.

With that in mind, I mixed up a new batch of dough and immediately placed it in the refrigerator to proof. The next day, I pulled it out, divided and shaped it into rounds, and let it warm to room temperature while I preheated my baking stone. I was skeptical at first; unlike the room temperature–proofed batch, this dough showed none of the telltale signs of active fermentation such as an airy, bubbly structure. But one sniff of its heady, slightly boozy aroma clearly indicated that plenty had been happening beneath the surface. Furthermore, this tighter, smoother dough proved much easier to work with, pulling effortlessly into a circle that gradually tapered in thickness from edge to center. I shouldn't have been surprised by this latter development. Besides slowing carbon dioxide production, chilling dough slows down gluten development so that dough literally stays looser, making it easier to stretch and hold its shape without snapping back. And the pizza it produced? Vastly better than previous attempts. Though not perfect, the dough was more complexly flavored and crisp than in any other pie I'd made, with an interior that boasted decent tenderness and chew. Even the rim offered just the right degree of puffiness and functioned as an ample handle.

I had to wonder: If 24 hours of cold fermentation had such a dramatic effect on the dough, what would happen if I left it in the fridge even longer? Three days later, I had my answer. I'd mixed and chilled a batch of dough each day over a 72-hour period, and the pizza bake-off proved that its flavor improved as time went by. (Push the fermentation beyond three days, however, and the yeast finally starts to produce a surplus of carbon dioxide, rendering the dough puffy.) True, cold-fermented dough wasn't exactly quick, but the recipe was a snap to make. Plus, the long rest wasn't altogether inconvenient; with a little planning, this dough had great make-ahead potential.

But the crust's crispness—or lack thereof—continued to nag me. Adding a tablespoon of oil to the dough helped a bit, but not enough. I had one other idea about how to encourage more crunch and color: sugar. We often sprinkle a spoonful over poultry skin to help it darken and crisp up in the oven, and I saw no reason the same trick couldn't be used here. I worked 2 teaspoons into the dough and, sure enough, the next pizza I pulled from the oven was tinged a slightly deeper shade of brown. But it still wasn't enough.

The real problem was the same one I'd been trying to address with all of my radical pizza-baking experiments over the years: the fact that home ovens simply don't get hot enough to produce a deeply browned crust before the interior crumb dries out and toughens. The best solution has always been the hottest setting on the oven dial and a pizza stone, which soaks up the radiating heat like a sponge. Following that logic, most recipes call for the stone to be placed as low in the oven as possible, where it gets maximum exposure to the main heating element. But when I thought about it, that technique didn't really make sense—and I even had an industry clue to prove it: commercial pizza ovens. These wide, shallow chambers quickly reflect heat from the floor back onto the top of the pie as it cooks, preventing the crust from drying out before the toppings have browned. Obviously I couldn't alter the shape of my oven—but I could move the stone up closer to the top to narrow the gap between the stone and the ceiling. After a series of tests with thermocouples and an infrared thermometer, I found that the best position for the stone is really as close to the top of the oven as possible—about 4 inches or so from the ceiling, which left just enough headroom to comfortably house the pie. When I pulled this latest attempt from my newfangled setup, the results were a revelation: Everything had baked in sync, producing a pizza that was thoroughly crisp, well browned on both top and bottom, and slightly chewy, just like a good parlor slice.

I had my perfect foundation; all I had left to do was tweak the toppings. The no-cook sauce I'd been using—canned tomatoes, garlic, olive oil, and spices pureed in the food processor—needed a quick jolt of flavor, so I added a splash of red wine vinegar. As for the cheese, I supplemented the mozzarella with a bit of sharp, salty, finely grated Parmesan. And that's where I stopped. Of course, additional toppings are fine (provided one doesn't use too heavy a hand); but for me, this simple-to-make, simply dressed pie bakes up perfectly as is.

—ANDREW JANJIGIAN, *Cook's Illustrated*

Thin-Crust Pizza

MAKES TWO 13-INCH PIZZAS

You can shape the second dough ball while the first pizza bakes, but don't top the pizza until right before you bake it. If you don't have a baking stone, bake the pizzas on an overturned and preheated rimmed baking sheet. It is important to use ice water in the dough to prevent overheating the dough while in the food processor. Semolina flour is ideal for dusting the peel; use it in place of bread flour if you have it. The sauce will yield more than needed in the recipe; extra sauce can be refrigerated for up to 1 week or frozen for up to 1 month.

DOUGH

- **3 cups (16½ ounces) bread flour, plus extra for counter**
- **2 teaspoons sugar**
- **½ teaspoon instant or rapid-rise yeast**
- **1⅓ cups ice water**
- **1 tablespoon vegetable oil, plus extra for counter**
- **1½ teaspoons salt**
- **Vegetable oil spray**

SAUCE

- **1 (28-ounce) can whole peeled tomatoes, drained**
- **1 tablespoon extra-virgin olive oil**
- **1 teaspoon red wine vinegar**
- **2 garlic cloves, minced**
- **1 teaspoon salt**
- **1 teaspoon dried oregano**
- **¼ teaspoon pepper**

CHEESE

- **1 ounce Parmesan cheese, finely grated (½ cup)**
- **8 ounces whole-milk mozzarella cheese, shredded (2 cups)**

1. FOR THE DOUGH: Process flour, sugar, and yeast in food processor until combined, about 2 seconds. With machine running, slowly add water through feed tube; process until dough is just combined and no dry flour remains, about 10 seconds. Let dough stand for 10 minutes.

2. Add oil and salt to dough and process until dough forms satiny, sticky ball that clears sides of workbowl, 30 to 60 seconds. Remove dough from bowl and knead briefly on lightly oiled counter until smooth, about 1 minute. Shape dough into tight ball and place in large, lightly oiled bowl. Cover tightly with plastic wrap and refrigerate for at least 24 hours or up to 3 days.

3. FOR THE SAUCE: Process all ingredients in food processor until smooth, about 30 seconds. Transfer to bowl or container and refrigerate until ready to use.

4. TO MAKE THE PIZZAS: One hour before baking pizza, adjust oven rack to upper-middle position (about 4 to 5 inches below broiler), set pizza stone on rack, and heat oven to 500 degrees. Remove dough from refrigerator and divide in half. Shape each half into smooth, tight ball. Place on lightly oiled baking sheet, spacing balls at least 3 inches apart. Cover loosely with plastic wrap coated with vegetable oil spray and let stand for 1 hour.

5. Coat 1 ball of dough generously with flour and place on well-floured counter. Using fingertips, gently flatten into 8-inch disk, leaving 1 inch of outer edge slightly thicker than center. Using hands, gently stretch disk into 12-inch round, working along edges and giving disk quarter turns as you stretch. Transfer dough to well-floured peel and stretch into 13-inch round. Using back of spoon or ladle, spread ½ cup tomato sauce in thin layer over surface of dough, leaving ¼-inch border around edge. Sprinkle ¼ cup Parmesan evenly over sauce, followed by 1 cup mozzarella. Slide pizza carefully onto stone and bake until crust is well browned and cheese is bubbly and beginning to brown, 10 to 12 minutes, rotating pizza halfway through baking. Remove pizza and place on wire rack for 5 minutes before slicing and serving. Repeat step 5 to shape, top, and bake second pizza.

MAKING THIN-CRUST PIZZA DOUGH

1. Create a relatively wet dough, which stretches without tearing and stays tender once baked.

2. Chill dough in refrigerator for at least 24 hours, which ensures less rise, a more flexible dough that holds its shape, and thinner (and more flavorful) crust.

3. Halve dough and shape into balls. Place on lightly oiled baking sheet and cover with oiled plastic wrap. Let rest for 1 hour to allow dough to return to room temperature.

4. On well-floured surface and using fingertips, gently flatten dough into 8-inch disk, leaving outer edge slightly thicker than center to create fatter "handle."

5. With hands, stretch dough into 12-inch round, working along edges and giving dough quarter turns. Transfer to well-floured peel and stretch to 13-inch round, then top with sauce and cheese.

TOPPING TIPS

We like our Thin-Crust Pizza simply dressed with tomato sauce and handfuls of shredded mozzarella and Parmesan, but additional toppings are always an option—provided they're prepared correctly and added judiciously. (An overloaded pie will bake up soggy.) Here are a few guidelines for how to handle different types of toppings:

HEARTY VEGETABLES

Aim for a maximum of 6 ounces per pie, spread out in a single layer. Vegetables such as onions, peppers, and mushrooms should be thinly sliced and lightly sautéed (or microwaved for a minute or two along with a little olive oil) before using.

DELICATE VEGETABLES AND HERBS

Leafy greens and herbs like spinach and basil are best placed beneath the cheese to protect them or added raw to the fully cooked pizza.

MEATS

Proteins (no more than 4 ounces per pie) should be precooked and drained to remove excess fat. We like to poach meats like sausage (broken up into ½-inch chunks), pepperoni, or ground beef for 4 to 5 minutes in a wide skillet along with ¼ cup of water, which helps to render the fat while keeping the meat moist.

THE BEST SUPERMARKET PEPPERONI

You may think of it as a greasy flavor bomb atop a slice of pizza, but pepperoni dates back to ancient Rome, where it was a convenient food for soldiers on the march. It crossed time—and the Atlantic Ocean—to reach America with the Italian immigrants who arrived on these shores around 1900. Pepperoni met pizza in New York City, underwent a total transformation from artisanal to commercial, and the rest, as they say, is history.

Pepperoni is made from cured and fermented pork with just a little beef and is seasoned with pepper, sugar, anise, cayenne, paprika (the source of its orange color), and lots of salt. Twenty-one tasters sampled six national brands of sliced pepperoni, straight from the package as well as baked on cheese pizza. We sought spice, heat, meat, and chew. Our winner, **Margherita Italian Style Pepperoni**, boasted a nice balance of "meatiness and spice" and tasted as though it had been "sliced off a pepperoni stick at an Italian market."

CHAPTER 6

MEAT

CLASSIC POT ROAST

THERE IS NO SHORTAGE OF WAYS TO COOK A POT roast, typically a tough cut made tender after hours of cooking in a covered vessel. Italians favor a nice bottle of Barolo for the braising liquid. The French supplement the beef with veal and cognac-soaked salt pork. Central Europeans might turn to flavorings like beer and orange peel. Here in the United States, styles range from Tex-Mex, with chili powder and jalapeños in the mix, to teriyaki renditions flavored with sugar and soy sauce.

These jazzed-up iterations have their place, but to me there's something equally appealing about the simplest approach: Throw the meat into a pot with liquid, a few basic seasonings, carrots, and onions; cover and place in a low oven; then walk away until dinner. My goal was to make this no-frills recipe the best it could be: a meltingly tender, sliceable roast sauced in a full-bodied gravy. I wanted it to be good enough for Sunday supper, of course—but also ready for prime time on Saturday night.

As I pulled together a file of recipes to try, I came across a strikingly minimalist take on the dish in *Mrs. Lincoln's Boston Cook Book* (1884), the precursor to Fannie Farmer's *The Boston Cooking-School Cook Book* (1918). The recipe listed just two ingredients: a large roast and a cup of water. Bigger, clearer beef flavor was definitely one of my goals, so it couldn't hurt to try it. But one thing gave me pause: Mrs. Lincoln suggested either a rump or a round roast, but I knew these cuts from the back leg of the cow to be somewhat lean and lacking in both flavor and the collagen that is key to turning a tough cut tender. Instead, I opted for a cut from the shoulder, the chuck eye. This well-marbled roast is full of collagen and particularly suited to braising, with a long, tapered shape that slices easily.

I followed the rest of her sparse instructions to the letter: Sear the roast, cover tightly (I even sealed my Dutch oven with aluminum foil before adding the lid to trap as much liquid as possible), and place it "where it will just keep below the boiling point." For me, this meant the 300-degree oven specified in most modern pot roast recipes.

After 4½ hours of cooking, much of the collagen in the roast had broken down into gelatin, a stand-in for the moisture wrung out of the meat by the long cooking, which turns it tender and thickens the braising liquid. This gravy, while not complex, was surprisingly beefy. Maybe Mrs. Lincoln was onto something with the scant 1 cup of liquid she added to the pot. Many modern recipes I found called for three times that amount; she must have realized the beef would contribute enough of its own juice to fill out a decent gravy.

But this bare-bones recipe could never give me the full-flavored dish I had in mind. To rectify that, I began by salting the meat before cooking. Salting draws moisture out of the meat, forming a shallow brine that, over time, migrates back into the meat to season it throughout rather than just on the exterior. With roasts, we often advocate letting the salted meat rest for several hours. Since I didn't want to turn this dish into a prolonged affair, I tried just an hour. Although the roast wasn't quite as beefy as one salted for six hours, it was pretty darn good, and I knew that my flavorful gravy would make up for any minor shortcomings.

I also wanted to do something about the pesky globs of interior fat that stubbornly refused to render, a common problem with pot roast. I opened the roast along its natural seam and trimmed away the excess. I was about to tie the two lobes together when I thought better: Why not just leave them as two separate roasts? When I double-checked with a follow-up test, the benefits were twofold: Using these smaller roasts shaved about an hour off the cooking time, from roughly 4½ hours to 3½ hours. Plus, all that exposed surface area meant the salt penetrated even further in just an hour.

In the interest of more streamlining, I wondered if the initial sear called for in not only Mrs. Lincoln's recipe but every other pot roast recipe I found was really necessary. Browning meat, of course, sets off the Maillard reaction, creating thousands of new compounds that intensify flavor. But in a recent low-liquid beef braise, the test kitchen found that the "dry" part of the meat that stayed above the liquid eventually browned, even without searing. Since much of my roast sat well above the braising liquid, similar low-temperature browning should occur here as well. I prepared two roasts, one seared and one not. When the unseared roast tasted almost as beefy as the seared one, I knew I'd found a way to make a simple recipe even simpler.

It was time to think about the gravy. The first thing I did to beef up its flavor was to trade the water for 1 cup of beef broth. Some amount of red wine was also a given. Not only would it add needed depth to the braise, but it contains glutamates that significantly enhance meaty flavor. I added a half-cup to keep liquid to a minimum, along with a tablespoon of tomato paste, another glutamate-rich ingredient. A couple of cloves of garlic and some herbs were obvious additions; I chose bay leaf and thyme, both excellent flavorings in meaty dishes. The standard mirepoix trio of onions, carrots, and celery was also a must. Sautéing them in a couple tablespoons of butter instead of oil brought extra richness.

By the time I pulled the roasts out of the pot, the vegetables had broken down and started to thicken the gravy. I couldn't resist eking out every bit of their flavor, so I tossed them into the blender with the defatted cooking liquid and extra beef broth (to thin the consistency). Just before serving, I stirred in a spoonful of balsamic vinegar and a bit more wine for brightness. The resulting gravy was exceptionally rich and full-bodied, the perfect complement to ladle over the meat, which was now rested and sliceable.

By Mrs. Lincoln's standards, this pot roast might not qualify as the most basic. But I know of very few recipes that taste as good with so little effort.

—ANDREW JANJIGIAN, *Cook's Illustrated*

NOTES FROM THE TEST KITCHEN

KEYS TO FLAVORFUL POT ROAST

1. Sprinkling roast halves with salt and resting them for 1 hour improves meaty flavor.

2. Adding small amount of liquid to pot (just 1½ cups) leads to more intensely flavored gravy.

3. Sealing pot with aluminum foil before covering locks in valuable juice and ensures that roasts have enough liquid for braising.

4. Pureeing onions, carrot, and celery cooked with roast and adding beef broth creates gravy with body and flavor.

Classic Pot Roast

SERVES 6 TO 8

You can substitute table salt for the kosher salt; use 1½ teaspoons to season the meat in step 1. Chilling the whole cooked pot roast overnight improves its flavor and makes it moister and easier to slice.

- **1 (3½- to 4-pound) boneless beef chuck-eye roast, pulled into 2 pieces at seams and trimmed**
- **Kosher salt and pepper**
- **2 tablespoons unsalted butter**
- **2 onions, halved and sliced thin**
- **1 large carrot, chopped**
- **1 celery rib, chopped**
- **2 garlic cloves, minced**
- **2–3 cups beef broth**
- **¾ cup dry red wine**
- **1 tablespoon tomato paste**
- **1 bay leaf**
- **1 sprig fresh thyme plus ¼ teaspoon minced**
- **1 tablespoon balsamic vinegar**

1. Season meat with 1 tablespoon salt, place on wire rack set inside rimmed baking sheet, and let stand at room temperature for 1 hour.

2. Adjust oven rack to lower-middle position and heat oven to 300 degrees. Melt butter in Dutch oven over medium heat. Add onions and cook, stirring occasionally, until softened and beginning to brown, 8 to 10 minutes. Add carrot and celery; continue to cook, stirring occasionally, about 5 minutes longer. Add garlic and cook until fragrant, about 30 seconds. Stir in 1 cup broth, ½ cup wine, tomato paste, bay leaf, and thyme sprig; bring to simmer.

3. Pat beef dry with paper towels and season generously with pepper. Tie each piece of meat using 3 pieces of kitchen twine.

4. Nestle meat on top of vegetables. Cover pot tightly with large piece of aluminum foil and cover with lid; transfer pot to oven. Cook beef until fully tender and sharp knife easily slips in and out of meat, 3½ to 4 hours, turning meat halfway through cooking.

5. Transfer roasts to carving board and tent loosely with foil. Strain liquid through fine-mesh strainer into 4-cup liquid measuring cup. Discard bay leaf and thyme sprig. Transfer vegetables to blender. Let liquid settle for 5 minutes, then skim any fat off surface. Add beef broth as necessary to bring liquid amount to 3 cups. (Pot roast, vegetables, and liquid can be transferred to bowl and refrigerated for up to 2 days. After transferring to bowl, let cool for 1 hour, cover with plastic wrap, and cut vents in plastic before refrigerating. To serve, proceed with recipe, blending vegetables and liquid and slicing roasts as directed; reheat in 13 by 9-inch baking dish, covered, on middle rack of 325-degree oven until heated, about 45 minutes.)

6. Add liquid to blender and blend until smooth, about 2 minutes. Transfer gravy to medium saucepan and bring to simmer over medium heat.

7. Meanwhile, remove twine from roasts and slice against grain into ½-inch-thick slices. Transfer meat to large serving platter. Stir minced thyme, remaining ¼ cup wine, and vinegar into gravy and season with salt and pepper to taste. Spoon half of gravy over meat. Serve, passing remaining gravy separately.

CHUCK ROAST IN FOIL

THIS RECIPE SWEPT THE COUNTRY IN THE 1950s. Whether called "Chuck Roast Winner Dinner," "Beef in Foil," "Foil-Baked Pot Roast," or "Sweep Steak," it always followed the same formula: Rub a chuck roast with dehydrated onion soup mix, seal it in aluminum foil, and cook until tender. Its attractions were obvious: It's quick, it's easy, it makes its own jus, and there's no pan to scrub. Given those virtues, it's no surprise that Peg Bracken featured the recipe (as Sweep Steak) in her 1960 *The I Hate to Cook Book*, intended for frustrated housewives seeking merely to survive cooking, not revel in it. But that's not the whole story. At about the same time, a new current was entering the American culinary mainstream. In 1961, Julia Child published *Mastering the Art of French Cooking*, then she went on to create her hit PBS series encouraging cooks to try their hand at complex dishes. My idea was to marry these two seemingly contradictory trends. I wanted to make the super-easy chuck roast in foil recipe so good that even Julia would have wanted to make it.

There's no question that rubbing a chuck roast with onion soup mix and wrapping it in foil is easy, but what does it taste like? The recipes I tried produced dry, stringy meat and greasy, salty, artificial-tasting drippings. But there were two pleasant surprises. First, after steaming in their own juice for almost six hours, the roasts were (somehow) well browned. And second, although none of the recipes called for any liquid, there was over a cup of jus in the foil packet at the end of cooking. I liked the idea of a pot roast that required no stovetop browning or added liquid, and if I could just get the meat to cook properly and develop a tasty homemade seasoning mix, I'd have a great lazy cook's pot roast.

I looked at the ingredients on the packet of onion soup mix—as I suspected, onion powder and salt were high on the list, closely followed by sugar and monosodium glutamate (MSG). My homemade mix, then, would start with onion powder, salt, and sugar, just like the original, as well as black pepper, thyme, and celery seed. As for the MSG, I hoped that ground, dried porcini mushrooms would impart the meaty savoriness that MSG gave the Lipton packet. I rubbed a chuck roast with this mix, sealed it in foil, and roasted it.

Tasters found the mushroom flavor sour, and as for the roast, it was suspiciously pale—not nicely browned like the ones made with the packaged mix. Working on the flavor first, I tried replacing the dried mushrooms with a paste of sautéed fresh mushrooms, but it didn't bring much flavor. Shifting gears, I turned to soy sauce: Like MSG and mushrooms, it's rich in glutamates, the compounds responsible for savory, meaty flavor (called umami). With a huge boost from soy sauce, my jus was definitely improving. Exchanging the white sugar for light brown added more depth, and an offbeat ingredient, espresso powder, added the last bit of toasty complexity.

To fix the browning, I revisited the ingredient list on the packaged soup mix. Amid vaguely menacing-sounding ingredients such as "disodium inosinate," I spied cornstarch. I assumed it was there as a thickener, but our science editor explained that the cornstarch reacts with the meat juice to form sugars (like glucose and maltose) that brown—even at a low temperature in a moist environment. Surprisingly, 3 tablespoons in my "soup mix" helped the roast brown perfectly.

Although the roast was now well browned, it was still dry and stringy. I had been following the protocol from earlier recipes of roasting at 350 degrees, but I wondered if cooking for longer at a lower temperature would improve the texture. Three hundred degrees was indeed an improvement, and by cutting the roast in half, I trimmed the cooking time from 6 hours to only 4½ hours or so. As a bonus, the increased surface area allowed me to apply more of my flavorful soup mix.

Some recipes call for adding carrots and potatoes to the foil packet. I liked this idea, but I expected the vegetables to be overcooked and mushy after hours of roasting. I was happily surprised that, with a few tests of different-size cuts, the vegetables cooked perfectly—and added flavor and volume to the meat drippings, too. (I threw in a couple of onions to flavor the sauce.) Finally, my pot roast was easy enough for those who hate cooking—and tasty enough for those who love it.

—SARAH GABRIEL, *Cook's Country*

Chuck Roast in Foil

SERVES 6 TO 8

You will need an 18-inch-wide roll of heavy-duty aluminum foil for this recipe. We prefer to use small red potatoes, measuring 1 to 2 inches in diameter, in this recipe.

RUB

- **3 tablespoons cornstarch**
- **4 teaspoons onion powder**
- **2 teaspoons light brown sugar**
- **2 teaspoons salt**
- **1 teaspoon pepper**
- **1 teaspoon garlic powder**
- **1 teaspoon instant espresso powder**
- **1 teaspoon dried thyme**
- **½ teaspoon celery seed**

CHUCK ROAST

- **2 onions, quartered**
- **1 pound small red potatoes, quartered**
- **4 carrots, peeled and cut into 1½-inch pieces**
- **2 bay leaves**
- **2 tablespoons soy sauce**
- **1 (4-pound) boneless beef chuck-eye roast, pulled into 2 pieces at seams, trimmed, each piece tied at 1-inch intervals**

1. FOR THE RUB: Adjust oven rack to lower-middle position and heat oven to 300 degrees. Combine rub ingredients in bowl. (Rub can be stored for up to 1 month.)

2. FOR THE CHUCK ROAST: Fit two 30 by 18-inch sheets of heavy-duty aluminum foil, perpendicular to each other, inside large roasting pan. Place onions, potatoes, carrots, and bay leaves in center; drizzle with soy sauce. Set roasts on top of vegetables. Rub roasts all over with rub. Fold opposite corners of foil toward each other; crimp edges tightly to seal. Transfer pan to oven; cook until meat is completely tender, about 4½ hours.

3. Remove roasts from foil and place on carving board. Tent loosely with foil and let rest for 20 minutes. Discard onions and bay leaves. Using slotted spoon, place carrots and potatoes on serving platter. Strain contents of roasting pan through fine-mesh strainer into fat separator. Let liquid settle for 5 minutes, then pour defatted pan juices into serving bowl.

4. Remove twine from roasts and slice meat thinly against grain. Transfer meat to platter with vegetables. Pour ½ cup pan juices over meat. Serve, passing remaining pan juices separately.

NOTES FROM THE TEST KITCHEN

THE BEST FAT SEPARATOR

Before a broth can be used or a gravy made from pan juices, the fat must be removed. If you have the time to wait, the fat will naturally rise to the top, where it can be spooned off. A faster method involves a specially designed fat separator. There are three distinct styles: pitcher-type measuring cups with sharply angled spouts; ladles with slots around the perimeter; and "fat mops," brushes with long, soft bristles made from plastic fibers.

Our favorite style of fat separator is the pitcher cup because of its efficiency and ability to handle fairly large volumes of stock. The **Trudeau Gravy Separator**, $12.95, is our favorite because of its large, 4-cup capacity; its wide mouth that makes for easy filling; and its integrated strainer.

GRANDMA'S ROAST BEEF

WHEN I WAS GROWING UP, WE FOLLOWED AN unwavering routine on Sundays: supper with my grandmother. No one ever had to ask what was for dinner—it was inevitably roast beef. It's not surprising, since this is the classic "company dinner" in the United States, where beef enjoys a popularity unrivaled in the rest of the world. Early colonists brought their English love of beef with them, but throughout the early history of our country, it remained a luxury available only to the wealthy, except on very special occasions. After the Civil War, though, the opening of vast cattle-grazing lands in the West coincided with the invention of refrigerated railway cars to make roast beef a weekly, if still celebratory, event for many middle-class Americans. My grandmother's rendition was iconic, with a deep brown exterior and juicy, rare meat that she carved into thin slices. It was my job to shake flour and water in the aluminum gravy shaker, a device that my grandmother used to thicken her silken, deeply flavored gravy. I still have that shaker. What I don't have is her recipe.

Hoping to replicate her roast, I purchased a top round, which is cheap, easy to find—and what my grandmother used. To get a good seared crust, I started the roast in a hot 500-degree oven, then finished at a moderate 350 degrees. This treatment produced a dry, tough roast with a gray ring of overcooked meat on the outside. But a fast stovetop sear followed by a few hours in a low, slow oven (275 degrees) yielded a more tender roast that was a pretty pink from center to rich, dark crust. Curious how low I could go, and what impact it would have, I knocked down the temperature another 25 degrees, and then 25 more; the last roast was the most tender by far.

To develop its flavor, I salted the meat and let it sit overnight. Osmosis, our science editor explained, causes the salt to travel from the outside of the meat (high salt concentration) to the inside (low salt concentration). Overnight was best, but even as little as one hour was sufficient to begin to season the meat. Time to make the gravy.

I noticed that many older recipes specify dredging the roast in flour (and even flouring the pan) before roasting, to get both a good crust and a head start on gravy. Because my oven temperature was so low, the flour just sat on the roast, remaining pasty and raw. But the flour in the roasting pan did brown, jump-starting a thick, toasty, if lumpy, base for gravy that was then stretched with water. To enhance its flavor, after browning the next roast, I added chopped celery, carrot, and onion to the fat in the skillet. I stirred in the flour at this point (lumps solved), as well as tomato paste for more depth. Normally, I'd roast beef on a V-rack, but it occurred to me to simply set the roast on top of the vegetables in a roasting pan, and so avoid washing an extra item.

Over about three hours in the oven, the meat turned pink and tender; the vegetables softened and deepened; the flour browned. As the meat rested, I poured the flavorful juices into a skillet. To get even more flavor, I whisked canned beef broth instead of water into the drippings, let the gravy thicken, and then strained it, chucking the vegetables now that they'd done their work. Not bad, but not all I remembered. Scanning the pantry, I found a can of beef consommé, which I reconstituted with just half the amount of water suggested, as I was after a power player. I'd found it—with this double-strength beef broth, my gravy turned dark, glossy, and deeply beefy.

My roast beef and gravy tasted fabulous, but the mechanics of the recipe were irksome. I had to brown the roast and vegetables in a skillet, move them to a roasting pan, and three hours later pour the drippings into a saucepan for gravy. I wondered, Could I simply roast the beef in the very same skillet in which I browned it, and then make the gravy in that pan, too? Done. Now the recipe was not only delicious, but dead easy as well.

—DIANE UNGER, *Cook's Country*

Grandma's Roast Beef with Gravy

SERVES 6 TO 8

You can substitute top sirloin for the top round. Look for an evenly shaped roast with a ¼-inch fat cap. We prefer this roast cooked to medium-rare, but if you prefer it more or less done, see our guidelines in the chart on page 162.

1 (4- to 5-pound) boneless top round roast, tied at 1-inch intervals
Salt and pepper
1 tablespoon vegetable oil
4 tablespoons unsalted butter
2 carrots, peeled and cut into 2-inch pieces

GRANDMA'S ROAST BEEF WITH GRAVY

- 1 onion, cut into ½-inch rounds
- 1 celery rib, cut into 2-inch pieces
- ½ cup all-purpose flour
- 1 teaspoon tomato paste
- 2 (10.5-ounce) cans beef consommé
- 1½ cups water

1. Pat roast dry with paper towels and rub with 2 teaspoons salt. Wrap in plastic wrap and refrigerate for at least 1 hour or up to 24 hours.

2. Adjust oven rack to middle position and heat oven to 225 degrees. Pat roast dry with paper towels and rub with 2 teaspoons pepper. Heat oil in 12-inch ovensafe skillet over medium-high heat until just smoking. Brown roast all over, 8 to 12 minutes; transfer to plate.

3. Pour off all but 2 tablespoons fat from pan. Add butter and melt over medium heat. Add carrots, onion, and celery and cook until lightly browned, 6 to 8 minutes. Add flour and tomato paste and cook until flour is golden and paste begins to darken, about 2 minutes. Off heat, push vegetables to center of pan. Place roast on top of vegetables and transfer skillet to oven. Cook until meat registers 120 to 125 degrees (for medium-rare), 2½ to 3½ hours. Transfer roast to carving board, tent loosely with foil, and let rest for 20 minutes.

4. Meanwhile, return skillet with vegetables to medium-high heat; cook, stirring occasionally, until vegetables are deep golden brown, about 5 minutes. Slowly whisk in consommé and water, scraping up any browned bits; bring to boil. Reduce heat to medium and simmer until thickened, 10 to 15 minutes. Strain gravy through fine-mesh strainer into serving bowl; discard vegetables. Season with salt and pepper to taste.

5. Remove twine from roast and thinly slice crosswise against grain. Serve, passing gravy separately.

NOTES FROM THE TEST KITCHEN

MAKING GRANDMA'S ROAST BEEF WITH GRAVY

1. Pat roast dry with paper towels, season, and brown in hot skillet. Then brown vegetables.

2. Set roast on top of vegetables, which take place of V-rack.

3. Cook roast in low-temperature oven for 2½ to 3½ hours.

4. Use beef consommé and a little water to deglaze pan and make rich, beefy gravy.

BEEF TENDERLOIN WITH POTATO FANS

WHEN YOU'RE COOKING TO IMPRESS A CROWD, few cuts can top a whole beef tenderloin. This elegant roast cooks relatively quickly, and its rich, buttery slices are incredibly fork-tender. But given its high price tag, it's a cut home cooks can find intimidating. I wanted to settle the best way to cook a perfect beef tenderloin. If I could add an equally impressive side dish that could be cooked along with the meat, I'd have the perfect dinner to serve company.

I started my testing with a trip to the butcher. A whole beef tenderloin can be purchased "unpeeled," which means it has a thick layer of exterior fat still attached, but more often it is sold "peeled," or stripped of this fat. I found that the peeled roasts were the more economical choice once you factor in usable meat and time spent if you have to strip the fat.

Now I was ready to start roasting. The problem is that while the tenderloin's sleek, boneless form makes for quick cooking, it is shaped like a torpedo—thick at one end and gradually tapering at the other—which leads to uneven roasting. To fix this, I folded the tip end underneath and tied it in place, which bulked up that end to almost the same thickness as the more substantial butt end. I also tied the roast at 1½-inch intervals, further guaranteeing uniformity. I knew from experience that if left as is, the translucent silver skin encasing the tenderloin would shrink during cooking and cause the meat to bow, so I made sure to cut it at several points.

To determine the ideal roasting temperature, I tested two extremes, roasting one tenderloin at 200 degrees and the other at 500. As expected, the roast cooked at 500 degrees not only created a smoky kitchen from the rendering fat (despite its being a lean roast, this is still an issue), but it was also overcooked at each end and around the perimeter. However, the high oven heat did have one upside: It gave my tenderloin a thick, flavorful crust, critical for boosting the appeal of this ultra-tender but mildly flavored cut. That trait was missing from my tenderloin cooked at 200 degrees; despite its even, rosy-pink interior, that roast lacked the all-important crust.

I didn't want my roast to take all day, so I decided to work my way down from the top. A 450-degree oven still gave me smoke and uneven cooking, so I moved down to 425 degrees. This roast emerged from the oven looking beautiful, and it took just 45 minutes. I felt like I had found the winner, but I decided to run just one more test. Often I cook roasts at two temperatures, a low temperature to gently cook through the interior and a briefer stint at a higher temperature to develop a crust. So I roasted another tenderloin, which I started in a 200-degree oven, increasing to 425 degrees at the end of cooking to develop a crust. To my surprise, this roast looked and tasted almost identical to the roast cooked at 425 the whole time. Because the slow-roasted tenderloin was a hair more fussy and took about twice as long, I settled on the high-heat method and moved on to the side dish.

Since the flavor of tenderloin is relatively mild, I knew it would play well with a side dish that had a strong presence. So far the meal required little kitchen work other than tying the roast, freeing me up to spend a few extra minutes on creating a flavorful, unique side. Not long ago the test kitchen had developed a recipe for baked potato fans, which combine the fluffy interior of a baked potato, the crisp, golden exterior of an oven fry, and a cheesy spiced topping—all with a distinctive, fanned-out presentation. They struck me as a perfect fit here, and with the tenderloin occupying the center of a rack set in a large rimmed baking sheet, I had two vacant aisles on either side; 10 potatoes (one for each guest), lined up in two diagonal rows, fit perfectly.

The fanning of the potatoes is done by slicing almost all the way through a whole potato crosswise at narrow intervals along its length. Leaving the bottom of the potato intact allows the slices to gently fan open like an accordion as the potato bakes. The skin crisps while the fans create openings into which seasonings, cheese, and bread crumbs can be sprinkled before a final pass in the oven. Earlier testing had worked out most of the tricky details already. For the type of potato, the russet was the right choice here, as its starchy flesh translated into a fluffy texture when baked; red potatoes and Yukon Golds both dried out.

I cut my russets crosswise into ¼-inch slices but did not slice all the way through. At first this was a challenge, but after some experimentation I hit upon some tricks that made it nearly foolproof. Slicing off a thin layer lengthwise from each potato created a stable base, or bottom, and placing a chopstick on either side prevented the knife from slicing all the way through. To avoid sticking between slices, caused by the starch in the potatoes, it was key to give them a quick rinse after slicing. And finally, taking a slice off of each end of the potato would give the remaining slices more room to fan out as they baked.

In the original recipe, the prepped potatoes were parcooked in the microwave (a less drying environment than the oven), baked for about 30 minutes in a 450-degree oven, then garnished with the topping and finished under the broiler. So my trick would be to find a way to get perfect baked potato fans cooked along with my beef, and at the same time keep the method as straightforward as possible.

I thought perhaps I could simply cook entrée and side together start to finish, but I was surprised to find that the potatoes still hadn't cooked through by the time the beef was done. I decided to parcook the potatoes in the microwave, then cook them through (without the topping) alongside the beef. By the time the beef was cooked through, the potatoes were crispy outside and tender inside. I then removed the beef from the rack to rest and topped my potatoes with a combination of Parmesan (for nutty flavor), Monterey Jack (because it melts well), and homemade bread crumbs mixed with a little melted butter. Fresh garlic didn't have enough time to cook and mellow, but garlic powder (mixed with some paprika) worked nicely. As a final step, I broiled the potatoes to make the topping irresistibly crunchy.

This was a truly impressive dinner to feed a crowd, and not only was it surprisingly simple to prepare, but perhaps the biggest achievement was that there was only one pan to clean up.

—ADELAIDE PARKER, *America's Test Kitchen Books*

NOTES FROM THE TEST KITCHEN

PREPPING BAKED POTATO FANS

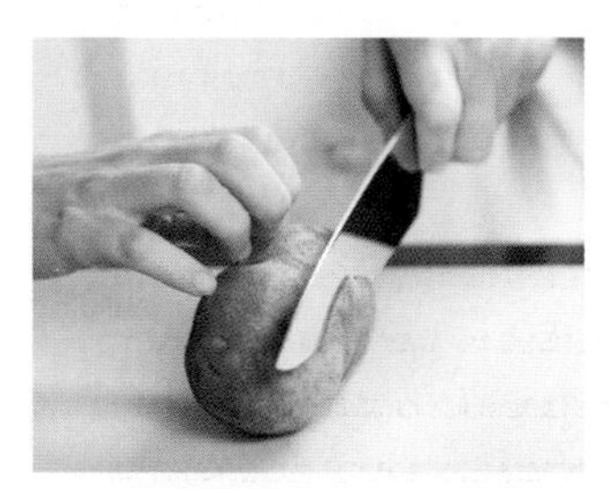

1. Trim ¼-inch slices from bottom and ends of each potato so they sit flat and to give slices extra room to fan out during baking.

2. Place chopstick snugly on either side of potato, running lengthwise. Slice potatoes crosswise at ¼-inch intervals, leaving bottom ¼ inch of potato intact (chopsticks will stop knife from cutting through).

3. Gently flex fans open while rinsing under cold running water to rid potatoes of excess starch, which can impede fanning.

TUCKING AND TYING A TENDERLOIN

To promote even cooking, tuck tail of tenderloin under and tie roast with kitchen twine every 1½ inches.

Classic Beef Tenderloin with Crispy Baked Potato Fans

SERVES 10

Unpeeled whole beef tenderloins are cheaper by the pound than peeled but have a thick layer of exterior fat that must be removed; we prefer to buy peeled beef tenderloins that already have this fat removed. To keep the meat from bowing as it cooks, nick the silver skin 5 or 6 times along the length of the roast. To ensure that the potatoes fan out evenly, look for uniformly shaped potatoes. We prefer this roast cooked to medium-rare, but if you prefer it more or less done, see our guidelines in the chart on page 162. If desired, serve with Horseradish Sauce (recipe follows).

POTATOES

- **2 slices hearty white sandwich bread, torn into quarters**
- **8 tablespoons unsalted butter, melted**
- **4 ounces Monterey Jack cheese, shredded (1 cup)**
- **1 ounce Parmesan cheese, grated (½ cup)**
- **1 teaspoon paprika**
- **1 teaspoon garlic powder**
- **Salt and pepper**
- **Vegetable oil spray**
- **10 medium russet potatoes (7 to 9 ounces each)**
- **6 tablespoons extra-virgin olive oil**

BEEF

- **1 (5- to 6-pound) whole peeled beef tenderloin, trimmed, silver skin cut, tail end tucked, tied at 1½-inch intervals**
- **2 tablespoons olive oil**
- **Salt and pepper**

1. FOR THE POTATOES: Adjust oven rack to lower-middle position and heat oven to 200 degrees. Pulse bread in food processor until coarsely ground, about 8 pulses. Bake bread crumbs on rimmed baking sheet until dry, about 20 minutes. Let bread crumbs cool slightly, then toss with butter, cheeses, paprika, garlic powder, ½ teaspoon salt, and ½ teaspoon pepper in bowl. (Bread-crumb topping can be refrigerated for up to 2 days.)

2. Increase oven temperature to 425 degrees. Place wire rack inside aluminum foil–lined rimmed baking sheet and coat with vegetable oil spray. Trim ¼-inch slice off bottom and both ends of each potato. Place each potato on cut base, place chopstick snugly on either side, and cut into fan by slicing potato crosswise at ¼-inch intervals, leaving bottom ¼ inch intact. Gently rinse potato fans under running water, then let drain. (Potato fans can be covered with water and refrigerated for up to 1 day; drain before proceeding.)

3. Working with half of potatoes at a time, place them, sliced side down, on large plate and microwave until slightly soft, 6 to 12 minutes, flipping them halfway through cooking. Brush potatoes thoroughly with oil (skin and flesh) and season with salt and pepper.

4. FOR THE BEEF: Pat roast dry with paper towels, coat with oil, and season with salt and pepper. Lay roast down center of rack on prepared baking sheet. Arrange potato fans, sliced side up, on sheet on either side of beef, angling potatoes as needed to fit. (Beef and potato fans can sit at room temperature for up to 1 hour before roasting.)

5. Roast until beef registers 120 to 125 degrees (for medium-rare), skin of potatoes is crisp, and potatoes are beginning to brown, 45 to 60 minutes. Remove baking sheet from oven. Transfer roast to carving board and let rest for 20 minutes.

6. Meanwhile, adjust oven rack 9 inches from broiler element and heat broiler. Carefully top potatoes with bread-crumb mixture, pressing gently to adhere. Return potatoes to oven and broil until topping is deep golden brown, about 3 minutes. Remove from oven and tent loosely with foil.

7. Remove twine from beef and cut meat crosswise into ½-inch-thick slices. Serve with potatoes.

Horseradish Sauce

MAKES ABOUT 1¾ CUPS

Brands of prepared horseradish can vary dramatically in flavor and intensity; season with additional horseradish to taste.

- **1 cup sour cream**
- **¼ cup mayonnaise**
- **½ cup prepared horseradish, plus extra to taste**
- **½ teaspoon sugar**
- **Salt and pepper**

Mix all ingredients together in serving bowl. Season with additional horseradish, salt, and pepper to taste. Cover with plastic wrap and refrigerate for 30 minutes before serving.

PAN-SEARED STEAKS WITH RESTAURANT-STYLE SAUCE

IT'S EASY ENOUGH TO FINISH A SEARED STEAK WITH a quick pan sauce or a knob of flavored butter, but anyone who's dined in a fine French restaurant knows that nothing compares to a sauce made with the ultra-savory, full-bodied reduction known as demi-glace. The preparation has been a hallmark of haute cuisine since the days of the 19th-century French chef Auguste Escoffier, and chefs trained in classic French technique tend to keep a supply on hand not only to dress up steak, but as a meaty flavor foundation for numerous soups, sauces, and sautés.

But making demi-glace is another matter. The time-consuming process is really feasible only in a restaurant kitchen. The process in a nutshell: Veal bones are roasted for a couple of hours with aromatics; the roasting pan is deglazed, releasing all the flavorful browned bits that will help enrich the stock; the whole works are transferred to a stockpot with wine and several quarts of water, where it all gurgles gently for at least six hours. The stock is then strained and reduced to an ultra-concentrated, glossy, silky essence.

I wasn't about to delve into such fussy work in my own kitchen. But this rich, velvety sauce is too good to be left only to restaurant chefs. Surely with some experimenting I could find a shortcut.

I immediately got to work on the demi-glace (I could refine my steak-cooking method later). I started by browning carrot, onion, and garlic chunks in a Dutch oven before deglazing with red wine and beef broth. Once the mixture had boiled down and thickened a bit, I took a taste. The result wasn't terrible, but its flavor was thin and it had no real body to speak of—hardly something that could stand as the backbone to a sauce.

I had one quick idea for amping up the flavor: In a traditional demi-glace, the vegetables are usually cut into large chunks, which break down and release flavor over the course of roasting and simmering. But since I needed big flavor fast, I pulsed the aromatics in the food processor until they were roughly chopped, figuring their increased surface area would offer more opportunity for flavorful browning. I also added mushrooms and tomato paste (another component common in traditional demi-glace), knowing that both ingredients' meat-mimicking glutamates would increase the savory flavor. Sure enough, this batch—which I further enhanced with thyme, bay leaves, and peppercorns; deglazed with red wine and a quart of beef broth; and reduced for about 25 minutes—showed definite flavor improvement. But it still didn't win over my tasters. Even after I'd worked this latest version into a classic herb pan sauce, they unenthusiastically pushed pieces of steak around in the still-thin reduction. My faux base still wasn't fooling anybody.

There was no doubt what was missing: Without the meatiness and unctuous gelatin given up by roasted veal bones, my attempt would never be as savory or silky-textured as the real deal. I was at a loss for my next move when a colleague reminded me of a similar conundrum when we tried to make full-bodied chicken soup without the time-consuming step of slow-simmering a chicken carcass. Our secret there? Ground chicken. The choice actually makes a lot of sense, as the goal with any stock is to extract as much flavor from the meat as possible—and the finer the bits, the quicker the flavor is extracted. Figuring the same principle would apply here, I grabbed a half-pound of ground beef and browned it along with tomato paste for about 10 minutes before adding the vegetables. This was the breakthrough I'd been looking for. Though still not as full-bodied as I would have liked, this base more than hinted at the flavor of roasted bones.

The consistency issue was a little trickier. Calves' bones are particularly rich in collagen, which prolonged roasting and simmering break down into rich gelatin. Even when I reduced my base to a near-syrupy consistency, the effect wasn't at all the same. But I did have something in my kitchen cupboard that might help: powdered gelatin. I stirred two packages into the final reduction (after straining the solids) and boiled it down to half a cup. As I'd hoped, this was all it took to turn my quick demi-glace silky and viscous.

Now, I turned to the steaks themselves. Tasters exhibited a clear preference for well-marbled, beefy-tasting cuts; strip and rib-eye were the top picks. Once a nice crust had formed on both sides, I set the steaks aside and built my sauce using the fond and demi-glace, along with an assortment of other ingredients for flavor variations; fresh herbs, brandy with green peppercorns, and port wine were our favorites. This time, my tasters mopped up every drop of sauce left on their plates.

—ANDREW JANJIGIAN, *Cook's Illustrated*

NOTES FROM THE TEST KITCHEN

THE BEST WINE OPENER

Lever-style corkscrews are designed to use leverage rather than muscle power to pull the cork, but many such models are unwieldy and bulky. We wanted a wine opener that could cleanly and effortlessly remove any type of cork, took minimal cajoling (the fewer steps, the better), and would fit neatly in a drawer. So we gathered 17 models ranging in price from $8 to $100—everything from lever-style openers to waiter's corkscrews (in which the lever rests on one side of the lip of the bottle), twisting pull models, and winged designs—and opened cases of wine until we narrowed our choices to seven. After wine-opening novices and experts alike test-drove our finalists on both natural and synthetic corks, the sleek, economical, lever-style **Oggi Nautilus Corkscrew**, $24.99, was dubbed the premier pick. And because we paid a fraction of the cost of some of its competitors, we had more to spend on a good bottle.

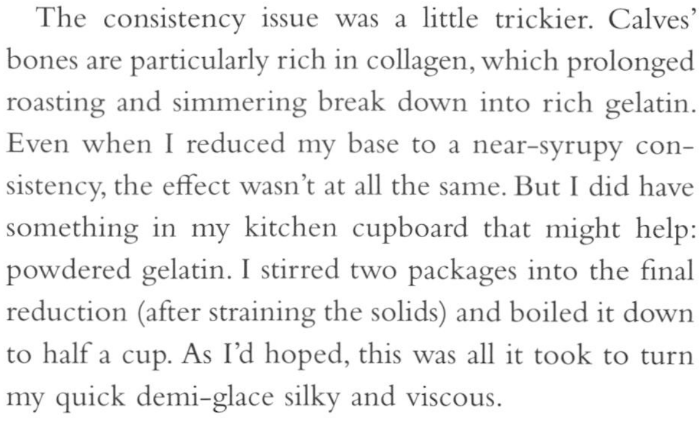

Ultimate Pan-Seared Steaks with Herb Sauce

SERVES 4

We like this sauce with strip or rib-eye steaks, but it will work with any type of pan-seared steak. We prefer these steaks cooked to medium-rare, but if you prefer them more or less done, see our guidelines in the chart on page 162.

STEAKS

4 (8-ounce) boneless strip or rib-eye steaks, 1 to 1¼ inches thick
Salt and pepper
1 tablespoon vegetable oil

HERB SAUCE

1 small shallot, minced
½ cup white wine
¼ cup Steak Sauce Base
¼ teaspoon white wine vinegar
1 tablespoon unsalted butter
1½ teaspoons minced fresh chives
1½ teaspoons minced fresh parsley
1 teaspoon minced fresh tarragon
Salt and pepper

1. FOR THE STEAKS: Pat steaks dry with paper towels; season both sides with salt and pepper. Heat oil in

12-inch skillet over medium-high heat until smoking. Lay steaks in pan, leaving ¼ inch between them. Cook, not moving steaks, until well browned, about 4 minutes. Using tongs, flip and continue to cook until steaks register 120 to 125 degrees (for medium-rare), 3 to 7 minutes longer. Transfer to platter; tent loosely with foil.

2. FOR THE HERB SAUCE: Return now-empty skillet to medium-low heat; add shallot and cook, stirring constantly, until lightly browned, about 2 minutes. Add wine and bring to simmer, scraping bottom of pan to loosen browned bits. Add Steak Sauce Base, vinegar, and any accumulated juice from steaks; return to simmer and cook until slightly reduced, about 1 minute. Off heat, whisk in butter, chives, parsley, and tarragon; season with salt and pepper to taste. Spoon sauce over steaks and serve immediately.

Steak Sauce Base

MAKES ½ CUP

The Steak Sauce Base recipe yields more than called for in the steak recipes; leftover sauce can be refrigerated for up to 3 days or frozen for up to 1 month.

- **1 small onion, cut into rough ½-inch pieces**
- **1 small carrot, peeled and cut into rough ½-inch pieces**
- **8 ounces cremini mushrooms, trimmed and halved**
- **2 garlic cloves, peeled**
- **1 tablespoon vegetable oil**
- **8 ounces 85 percent lean ground beef**
- **1 tablespoon tomato paste**
- **2 cups dry red wine**
- **4 cups beef broth**
- **4 sprigs fresh thyme**
- **2 bay leaves**
- **2 teaspoons whole peppercorns**
- **5 teaspoons unflavored gelatin**

1. Pulse onion, carrot, mushrooms, and garlic in food processor into ⅛-inch pieces, 10 to 12 pulses, scraping down bowl as needed.

2. Heat oil in Dutch oven over medium-high heat until shimmering; add beef and tomato paste and cook, stirring frequently, until beef is well browned, 8 to 10 minutes. Add vegetable mixture and cook, stirring occasionally, until any exuded moisture has evaporated, about 8 minutes. Add wine and bring to simmer, scraping bottom of pan to loosen browned bits. Add broth, thyme, bay leaves, and peppercorns; bring to boil. Reduce heat and gently boil, occasionally scraping bottom and sides of pot and skimming fat from surface, until reduced to 2 cups, 20 to 25 minutes.

3. Strain mixture through fine-mesh strainer set over small saucepan, pressing on solids to extract as much liquid as possible (you should have about 1 cup). Sprinkle gelatin over top and stir to dissolve. Bring to boil over medium-high heat and boil gently, stirring occasionally, until reduced to ½ cup, 5 to 7 minutes. Remove from heat and cover to keep warm.

VARIATIONS

Ultimate Pan-Seared Steaks with Brandy and Green Peppercorn Sauce

Substitute brandy for white wine and red wine vinegar for white wine vinegar. Omit butter, chives, parsley, and tarragon. In step 2, add ¼ cup heavy cream, 2 tablespoons rinsed green peppercorns, and ¼ teaspoon minced fresh thyme to skillet along with Steak Sauce Base and vinegar.

Ultimate Pan-Seared Steaks with Port Wine Sauce

Substitute ruby port for white wine and balsamic vinegar for white wine vinegar. Substitute ¼ teaspoon minced fresh thyme for chives, parsley, and tarragon.

GRILLED ARGENTINE STEAKS WITH CHIMICHURRI

OF ALL THE COOKING TRADITIONS INVOLVING LIVE fire and a piece of meat, none is more sacred than preparing the perfect grilled steak. In Argentina especially, where cattle farming is a major industry and the per-capita beef consumption is the highest in the world (roughly 150 pounds annually), grilling steaks over burning embers is not just a means of getting dinner on the table, but a nationwide ritual.

All this I learned as I made my way to the Jackson Heights neighborhood of Queens, New York, where the large Argentine population is served by numerous *churrascarias*, or steakhouses, serving up huge slabs of *churrasco* (which refers to both the technique and the grilled meat itself). As a diehard carnivore, I was intrigued by a culture that prides itself on the pleasures

GRILLED ARGENTINE STEAKS WITH CHIMICHURRI SAUCE

of a great grilled steak and curious to see how its technique would measure up to my own.

Differences were apparent not 10 minutes after I arrived at the first restaurant, La Porteña. First, this was anything but fast food. Here (and everywhere else I ate), the waiter warned me that the steak would take at least 30 minutes to prepare. In contrast to the American method of slapping meat over a blazing fire to sear hard and fast, Argentine steaks are grilled low and slow over hardwood logs, not charcoal (and never over gas), which imbues them with a smokiness that is subtler and more complex than the typical "barbecue" flavor one comes to expect of grilled meat here in the States. The resulting steak tastes the way a roaring fireplace smells: warm (not hot) and woody (not smoky).

Second, Argentines scoff at American steakhouse advertisements for "flame-broiled" meats; to them, burning the steak distracts from its prized beefy flavor. Instead, the cuts I was served boasted a mahogany-hued char that snapped with each bite, almost as if the meat were sheathed in an invisible layer of breading. And finally, there was size. Quite frankly, these extra-thick (1½- to 2-inch), nearly 2-pound slabs looked monstrous by my standards, but their immensity had more to do with cooking technique than gluttony. It was simple logic: With thick steaks, the meat could remain on the grill (called a *parrilla* in Argentina) long enough to absorb smoke flavor and avoid the risk of overcooking. With the piquant parsley, garlic, and olive oil sauce known as *chimichurri* served alongside, they added up to some of the best eating I've ever done and persuaded me to race back to the test kitchen, where I would try to duplicate this way of cooking steaks.

The first order of business was sorting out which cut of meat to use. In truth, there is no one cut that can be considered a "typical" Argentine steak. Instead, churrasco is a method that can be applied to just about any grill-worthy piece of meat. Still, many of the cuts popular in Argentina—including *vacio* (a type of flank steak), *bife ancho* (prime rib steaks), and *tira de asado* (strips of meat and bone from the rib section, similar to short ribs)—aren't available in this country. In lieu of these, the restaurants I visited in Queens offered a wide selection of the steaks Americans like, from porterhouse to T-bone. All were large and boasted either lots of marbling or a substantial layer of external fat to lubricate and moisten the beef during its long stay over the fire.

After scanning my supermarket butcher case, I selected four flavorful steaks that met my basic height and weight criteria (about 1½ inches thick, but well under 2 pounds—after all, Americans aren't quite the avid carnivores that the people of Argentina are): strip steak, shell steak, tri-tip, and bottom round, the last an attempt to replicate rump cap steak, an oblong cut from the top round portion of the hind leg that's another favorite choice among Argentine grill cooks, or *parrilleros*. I built a medium fire by spreading a full chimney's worth of charcoal around the bottom of my grill (tactics for pumping up wood-grilled flavor would come later), salted each of the steaks generously, cooked them to medium-rare, let them rest briefly, and then sliced them across the grain. Tri-tip and bottom round were out. Though each offered decent flavor, tasters found them to be just a tad tough and dry. Meanwhile, well-marbled strip steak boasted big beefy flavor, not to mention an interior that was both moist and tender and pleasantly chewy. (Shell steak, a flavorful sirloin cut located just to the rear of the strip loin, lost a few votes for its stringier texture, but it makes a good bargain alternative.)

My steaks selected, I moved on to Meaty Matter No. 2: building up the essential wood-smoke flavor. Cooking over actual logs was out of the question; the amount of wood required to build a hot enough fire would not fit in the average kettle grill. Instead, I tried various wood chunk and chip alternatives (soaked and unsoaked, foil-wrapped and unwrapped). Unsoaked chunks proved best. Four pieces nestled around the perimeter of the fire lasted long enough to tinge the steaks with a subtle essence of burning wood. Placing the lid on the grill for the first few minutes of cooking helped to quickly trap smoke flavor.

Unfortunately, I still hadn't nailed the requisite deep brown char without overcooking the interior. Without resorting to dry-aging my steaks for days (not even the Jackson Heights restaurants went to that trouble), I needed to figure out a way to drive off their exterior moisture so that a deep crust could form. Salting the steaks overnight in the fridge helped—after first being drawn out by the salt, the juice gradually is pulled back in, leaving the exterior of the meat drier than before—but I hated adding this lengthy extra step. Then I thought of something else. In the test kitchen, we're always talking about how the severely dry environment of the freezer robs food of its moisture. Usually that's an effect we're trying to prevent, but could it work in my favor? To find out, I salted the meat and then left it uncovered in the freezer for an hour. Sure enough, the meat emerged from the icebox practically bone-dry, and it browned within moments of hitting the grill. Even better, these partially frozen steaks could stand about five more minutes of fire, adding up to more char and more flavor.

NOTES FROM THE TEST KITCHEN

KEYS TO ARGENTINE-STYLE GRILLED STEAKS

Here's how we produced our own brand of smoky charred churrasco—without the aid of a wood-burning Argentine grill.

1. Rubbing steaks with cornstarch and salt seasons meat and expedites crust formation by drying meat's exterior; cornstarch also enhances browning.

2. Freezing steaks for 30 minutes drives off exterior moisture and chills steaks' interiors, so they can stay on grill longer, soaking up more smoke flavor.

3. Adding four large chunks of unsoaked wood to single-level fire infuses meat with wood-grilled flavor.

Nearly satisfied with my Argentine facsimile, I focused my last few tests on that distinctive crunch I remembered from the restaurant steaks. Inspired by the "nano-breaded" quality of their crusts, I added a small amount of cornstarch to my salt rub—a trick we've used in the past to crisp up everything from turkey skin to potatoes. This twist had two results: I was able to cut the freezing time to 30 minutes, since cornstarch is another moisture-eating powerhouse, and I got steaks with all the color and snap I was looking for, because its starches enhance browning.

All my churrasco needed was the requisite chimichurri dressing, the sharp, grassy flavors of which are designed to offset the rich, unctuous qualities of the steak. My tasters leaned toward one of the most traditional forms: fresh parsley, cilantro, oregano, garlic, red wine vinegar, red pepper flakes, and salt—all emulsified with fruity extra-virgin olive oil. As I pulled the crisp-crusted, wood-smoked steaks off the grill, splashed on a little chimichurri, and took my first bite—near-perfect, if I did say so myself—I decided to make this new American spin on an age-old Argentine tradition my go-to technique.

—ANDREW JANJIGIAN, *Cook's Illustrated*

Grilled Argentine Steaks with Chimichurri Sauce

SERVES 6 TO 8

Our preferred steak for this recipe is strip steak, also known as New York strip. A less expensive alternative is a boneless shell sirloin steak (or top sirloin steak). We prefer oak, but other types of wood chunks can be used. Flipping the steaks three times during cooking allows for even cooking and limits flare-ups. You can substitute table salt for the kosher salt; use 1 teaspoon in the chimichurri sauce and 1 tablespoon in the rub. We prefer these steaks cooked to medium-rare, but if you prefer them more or less done, see our guidelines in the chart on page 162.

CHIMICHURRI SAUCE

- **¼ cup hot water**
- **2 teaspoons dried oregano**
- **2 teaspoons kosher salt**

- **1⅓ cups loosely packed fresh flat-leaf parsley**
- **⅔ cup loosely packed fresh cilantro**
- **6 garlic cloves, minced**
- **½ teaspoon red pepper flakes**
- **¼ cup red wine vinegar**
- **½ cup extra-virgin olive oil**

STEAKS

- **2 tablespoons kosher salt**
- **1 tablespoon cornstarch**
- **4 (1-pound) boneless strip steaks, 1½ inches thick**
- **4 (2-inch) unsoaked wood chunks**
- **1 (9-inch) disposable aluminum pie plate, if using gas**
- **Pepper**

1. FOR THE CHIMICHURRI SAUCE: Combine hot water, oregano, and salt in bowl; let stand for 5 minutes. Pulse parsley, cilantro, garlic, and pepper flakes in food processor until coarsely chopped, about 10 pulses. Add water mixture and vinegar and pulse briefly to combine. Transfer mixture to medium bowl and slowly whisk in oil until incorporated and mixture is emulsified. Cover with plastic wrap and let stand at room temperature for at least 1 hour. (Sauce can be refrigerated for up to 3 days; bring to room temperature before using.)

2. FOR THE STEAKS: Combine salt and cornstarch in bowl. Pat steaks dry with paper towels and place on wire rack set inside rimmed baking sheet. Rub both sides of steaks with cornstarch mixture and place steaks, uncovered, in freezer until very firm, about 30 minutes.

3A. FOR A CHARCOAL GRILL: Open bottom vent halfway. Light large chimney starter filled with charcoal briquettes (6 quarts). When top coals are partially covered with ash, pour evenly over grill. Place wood chunks directly on coals, spacing them evenly around perimeter of grill. Set cooking grate in place, cover, and open lid vent halfway. Heat grill until hot and wood chunks are smoking, about 5 minutes.

3B. FOR A GAS GRILL: Turn all burners to high, cover, and heat grill until hot, about 15 minutes. Place wood chunks in perforated aluminum pie plate and set on cooking grate. Close lid and heat until wood chunks begin to smoke, about 5 minutes. Leave all burners on high.

4. Clean and oil cooking grate. Season steaks with pepper. Place steaks on grill, cover, and cook until steaks begin to char, 2 to 3 minutes. Uncover grill, flip steaks, and cook on second side until beginning to char, 2 to 3 minutes. Flip again and cook first side until well charred, 2 to 3 minutes. Flip 1 last time and continue to cook until second side is well charred and steak registers 120 degrees (for medium-rare), about 4 minutes. Transfer to large plate and tent loosely with foil. Let rest for 10 minutes. Slice and serve, passing chimichurri sauce separately.

GRILLED STEAKHOUSE STEAK TIPS

YOU CAN SMELL THEM COMING FROM THE KITCHEN before your server even sets the plate in front of you: a pile of big chunks of beef sirloin flap meat, loaded with flavor from both a potent marinade and a high-sear crust. I wanted to re-create this steakhouse classic for home cooks, so I phoned a few steakhouses and rooted around our cookbook library for recipes. Most sources stressed the importance of two things: high heat (for maximum char) and a "secret" marinade ingredient—beer, ketchup, barbecue sauce, Italian dressing, or cola. I was intrigued and eager to put these recipes to the test.

I whisked together marinades and fired up the grill. The beer-based marinade produced tips that were bitter and soggy, not charred. Italian dressing left behind a sour flavor and mushy texture. Both ketchup and barbecue sauce produced significant char because they contain sugar, but these distinctively seasoned condiments produced tips that tasted as though they belonged in a barbecue joint, not a steakhouse. For my money, the only "secret" ingredient that promoted the right sort of char was cola, but the cola marinade was a drippy mess, necessitating sloppy drying between refrigerator and grill.

While none of these marinades was very good, at least I'd learned that sugar would play an important role. I whisked together a working marinade of garlic, paprika, cayenne, pepper, vegetable oil, soy sauce (which adds salt and boosts meaty flavors), and a tablespoon each of light brown sugar and (sugary) tomato paste.

I cut a large flap steak into 2½-inch chunks: A few tests had already shown that smaller chunks overcooked by the time they were well charred, and larger chunks were more like mini roasts than tips. I marinated the chunks for an hour—the minimum time called for in many recipes.

I prepared the grill—a single-level fire was in order here. Generally speaking, we usually like our steak cooked to medium-rare, so I pulled the tips off the grill when they reached 120 degrees. They were OK, but the char needed a boost and the tips were a little chewy. Flap meat has more connective tissue than other steaks, so it can be tough when cooked rare or medium-rare. I found that cooking the tips to medium (about 130 degrees) provided the best meeting point of tenderness and juiciness. The combination of slightly longer cooking (to medium) and upping the brown sugar to 3 tablespoons gave me the smoky, crusty char I'd been looking for. Trading the light brown sugar for dark brown lent extra flavor without being cloying.

The tips tasted great, but more than one taster joked about jaw fatigue—the meat was still a little tough. I tried the common trick of poking the meat with a fork before cutting it into chunks. It worked: The poking breaks long, tough muscle fibers into shorter, more tender pieces. Fork-tenderizing had the added advantage of exposing more surface to soak up the marinade. Before hanging up my tongs, I did a final round of time tests. They revealed that two hours of marinating time was far superior to one, but also that there was no harm (nor great advantage) in soaking the tips for up to one day.

—SARAH GABRIEL, *Cook's Country*

NOTES FROM THE TEST KITCHEN

COMMON INGREDIENTS, UNCOMMON RESULTS

We engineered the marinade to give our steak tips maximum meaty flavor and a satisfying texture. These familiar ingredients make a strong team, each with its own part to play. Vegetable oil distributes the flavors and activates oil-soluble flavor compounds, such as those found in garlic. Soy sauce penetrates the meat to season it deeply, and its glutamates boost meaty flavor. Dark brown sugar ensures a caramelized, crusty char, and tomato paste adds a savory backbone and enough body to help the marinade cling.

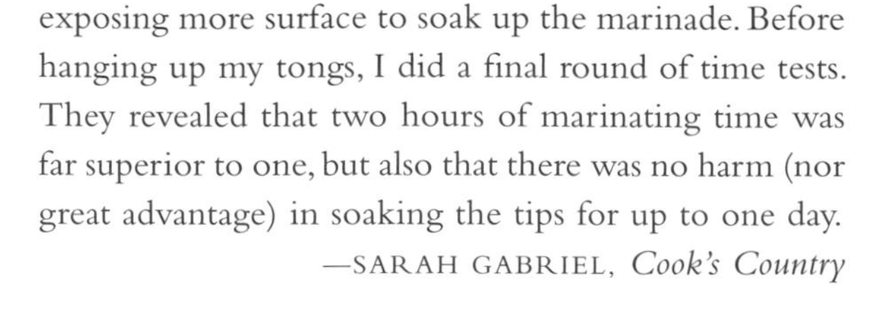

Grilled Steakhouse Steak Tips

SERVES 4 TO 6

Be sure to coat the meat evenly with the marinade before sealing it in a zipper-lock bag. We prefer these steak tips cooked to medium, but if you prefer them more or less done, see our guidelines in the chart on page 162.

- **⅓ cup soy sauce**
- **⅓ cup vegetable oil**
- **3 tablespoons packed dark brown sugar**
- **5 garlic cloves, minced**
- **1 tablespoon tomato paste**
- **1 tablespoon paprika**
- **½ teaspoon pepper**
- **¼ teaspoon cayenne pepper**
- **1 (2½-pound) beef flap steak**

1. Whisk soy sauce, oil, sugar, garlic, tomato paste, paprika, pepper, and cayenne together in bowl until sugar dissolves; transfer to zipper-lock bag. Pat beef dry with paper towels. Prick beef all over with fork and cut into 2½-inch pieces. Add meat to bag with soy sauce mixture, seal, turn to coat meat, and refrigerate for 2 hours or up to 24 hours, turning occasionally.

2A. FOR A CHARCOAL GRILL: Open bottom grill vent completely. Light large chimney starter filled with charcoal briquettes (6 quarts). When top coals are partially covered with ash, pour evenly over grill. Set cooking grate in place, cover, and open lid vent completely. Heat grill until hot, about 5 minutes.

2B. FOR A GAS GRILL: Turn all burners to high, cover, and heat grill until hot, about 15 minutes. Leave all burners on high.

3. Clean and oil cooking grate. Grill beef until charred and it registers 130 to 135 degrees (for medium), 8 to 10 minutes. Transfer meat to platter, tent loosely with foil, and let rest for 5 minutes. Serve.

GRILLED STEAKHOUSE STEAK TIPS

JUICY PUB-STYLE BURGERS

MAKING HAMBURGERS FROM PREGROUND BEEF sure gets dinner on the table in a hurry. But when my goal is a memorably thick, juicy burger full of big, beefy flavor—the kind served in the best high-end pubs—I wouldn't dream of using the preground stuff. The fact is, supermarket ground beef is mediocre. Because it's typically purchased in bulk from beef processing plants, supplemented with meat scraps, and then reground, the flavor and texture vary from package to package. More often than not, I find that the beef has literally been ground to a pulp that cooks up dry and pebbly, no matter how much care I take. And it never has the rich, meaty flavor I crave.

So when I received an assignment to create a thick, pub-style burger, I knew that grinding my own beef was a given. What I didn't yet know was which cut of beef I would use, how coarsely or finely I would process the meat, and what cooking method would produce a well-seared, thickly crusted burger that was juicy and evenly rosy inside from center to edge.

Standing at the butcher case, I was first inclined to reach for a chuck roast. This popular burger cut boasts a robust amount of fat that lubricates and flavors the meat as it cooks. But it also contains a fair amount of sinew—no problem for a dedicated meat grinder, but more work than my food processor (the test kitchen's reliable alternative to a meat grinder) could handle. Instead, I settled on sirloin steak tips. While not quite as rich as chuck, this cut offers supremely beefy flavor without gristly sinew.

As for the grinding process itself, I already had a good lead to follow in a previously published test kitchen recipe. It calls for cutting the meat into 1-inch chunks, freezing it until just firm, and then pulsing it in the food processor in batches into rough ¹⁄₁₆-inch bits. This relatively coarse grind, coupled with a light touch when packing the meat into disks, is the key to a tender burger. However, when I applied the technique to my heftier, pub-size patties, it didn't translate perfectly. The patties broke apart when I tried to flip them in the skillet. The problem proved easy to solve by cutting the meat into smaller ½-inch chunks before processing, which helped create a more even grind that stuck together better. I also adjusted how I shaped the burgers, first forming the beef into loosely packed meatballs, which I then flattened into patties. Both measures gave the burgers just enough structure to hold their shape when flipped.

On to the next issue: More than a few tasters hinted that they missed the richness of well-marbled chuck. Supplementing the steak tips with another, fattier cut of beef—a common restaurant trick—would be one way to boost flavor, but I wasn't wild about adding more butchering work to the process. Instead, I experimented with adding straight fat. First I tried olive oil, which was a flop; it seeped out once the burgers started to cook and did little to flavor the meat. But melted butter, which solidified as it hit the cold meat, created pinhead-size particles of fat strewn throughout the patties, which improved the burgers' flavor and juiciness. Even better, the extra fat boosted the browning on the exterior.

But good browning was about the only thing the exterior had going for it. Between their crisp, craggy shells and deep pink centers, the patties were marred by a thick band of gray meat that no amount of extra fat was going to help. Clearly, I needed to rethink my cooking method. Up to now, I had been following a pretty standard approach for pan-fried burgers: preheating a skillet over high heat until it was good and hot, then cooking the patties to medium-rare for about four minutes per side.

But I had an alternative method in mind—one we developed for cooking thick-cut steaks. In that recipe, we used a combination stove-oven technique, in which the intense heat of the burner produced a great crust and the gentler, more ambient heat of the oven prevented the gray band of meat from forming beneath it. I followed suit here, quickly searing the burgers in a skillet and then transferring them (in the pan) to a 350-degree oven. But the results were only marginally better. The problem was that the portion of the burgers in direct contact with the skillet continued to cook faster than the top half. Lowering the oven temperature to 300 degrees helped, but only a little. That's when I decided to transfer the burgers after searing from the skillet to a cool baking sheet for finishing in the oven. That did it. After about five minutes, the burgers emerged with perfect interiors—juicy and rosy throughout.

This being a premium pub-style burger, it needed a few premium (yet simple) toppings. I threw together a quick tangy-sweet sauce to smear on each bun and combined it with crispy shallots and blue cheese in one variation and aged cheddar and peppercorn-crusted bacon in another.

Admittedly, this burger required a bit more time and effort than your average patty fashioned from regular supermarket ground beef. But my tasters and I needed only one bite to confirm that the fresh, deeply beefy-tasting, insanely juicy results were well worth the extra trouble.

—BRYAN ROOF, *Cook's Illustrated*

Juicy Pub-Style Burgers

SERVES 4

Sirloin steak tips are also sold as flap meat. When stirring the butter and pepper into the ground meat and shaping the patties, take care not to overwork the meat or the burgers will become dense. For the best flavor, season the burgers aggressively just before cooking. We like these burgers topped with our Pub-Style Burger Sauce, but traditional toppings work well, too. We prefer these burgers cooked to medium-rare, but if you prefer them more or less done, see our guidelines in the chart on page 162.

- **2 pounds sirloin steak tips, trimmed and cut into ½-inch chunks**
- **4 tablespoons unsalted butter, melted and cooled slightly**
- **Salt and pepper**
- **1 teaspoon vegetable oil**
- **4 hamburger buns, toasted and buttered**
- **1 recipe Pub-Style Burger Sauce (optional; recipe follows)**

1. Place beef chunks on baking sheet in single layer. Freeze meat until very firm and starting to harden around edges but still pliable, about 35 minutes.

2. Place one-quarter of meat in food processor and pulse until finely ground into ¹⁄₁₆-inch pieces, about 35 pulses, stopping and redistributing meat around bowl

NOTES FROM THE TEST KITCHEN

KEYS TO THICK, JUICY, PERFECTLY COOKED BURGERS

1. Processing beef chunks into ¹⁄₁₆-inch pieces after chilling them until firm ensures a coarse grind that stays loosely packed.

2. Coating raw ground beef with melted butter not only ensures that burgers cook up super juicy but also encourages flavorful browning.

3. Searing burgers first, then finishing them in low-heat oven trades usual overcooked exterior for well-browned crust and juicy center.

A GREAT GRINDER

Meat lovers who appreciate a great burger know that grinding your own meat is totally worth the effort—provided you're using a well-made machine. Hoping to single out a worthwhile contender, we processed 1-inch chunks of sirloin steak tips and pork butt using four models. The lone hand-cranked apparatus performed the worst, repeatedly becoming jammed with stringy, fatty wads of meat. The other three models, all motorized, ground both cuts faster than our favorite food processor (our usual tool for grinding meat). The winner was the **Waring Pro Professional Meat Grinder**, which costs a pretty penny at $199. If you already own a KitchenAid stand mixer, we have a more affordable suggestion: the KitchenAid Food Grinder Attachment, which costs just $48 and rivaled the brawnier Waring Pro.

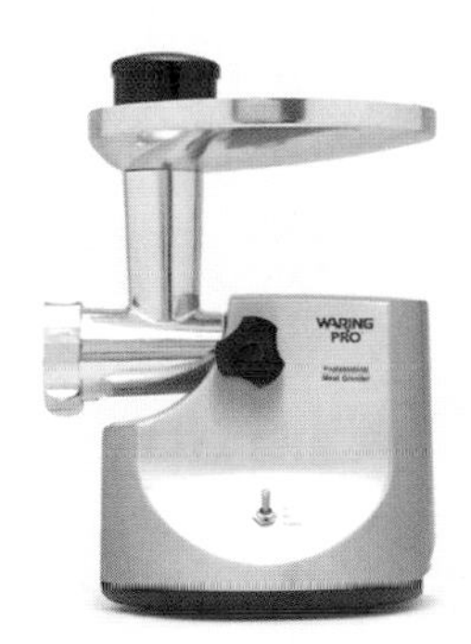

as necessary to ensure beef is evenly ground. Transfer meat to second baking sheet. Repeat grinding with remaining 3 batches of meat. Spread meat on sheet and inspect carefully, discarding any long strands of gristle or large chunks of hard meat or fat.

3. Adjust oven rack to middle position and heat oven to 300 degrees. Drizzle melted butter over ground meat and add 1 teaspoon pepper. Gently toss with fork to combine. Divide meat into 4 lightly packed balls. Gently flatten into patties ¾ inch thick and 4½ inches wide. Refrigerate patties until ready to cook. (Patties can be refrigerated for up to 1 day.)

4. Season both sides of patties liberally with salt and pepper, using spatula to flip patties. Heat oil in 12-inch skillet over high heat until just smoking. Using spatula, transfer burgers to skillet and cook without moving for 2 minutes. Using spatula, flip burgers and cook for 2 minutes longer. Transfer patties to rimmed baking sheet and bake until burgers register 125 degrees (for medium-rare), about 3 minutes.

5. Transfer burgers to plate and let rest for 5 minutes. Transfer to buns, top with Pub-Style Burger Sauce, if using, and additional toppings, and serve.

NOTES FROM THE TEST KITCHEN

THE BEST YELLOW MUSTARD

Many folks think a hamburger or hot dog isn't complete without a squirt of yellow mustard. But beyond the usual burgers and dogs, we use the yellow stuff in salad dressings and marinades for chicken or pork. To determine which yellow mustard is best, we bought seven nationally available brands and tasted them plain and with steamed hot dogs.

Yellow mustard is made from white (also called yellow) mustard seed, which is flavorful but doesn't cause any of the nasal burn of brown or black mustard seed; these last two are used in Dijon, Chinese, and other spicy mustards. Our tasters wanted to actually taste the mustard seed; both brands they judged to have the most mustard flavor list mustard seed second in their ingredients (the other brands list it third). The amount of salt also proved key. We often prefer saltier foods in our tastings, but this time the mustards with the least sodium tended to score higher. Why the break in preference? Vinegar adds so much pungency, these yellow mustards didn't need extra seasoning.

Two top-selling, familiar mustards scored well, as we'd expect, but surprisingly they were edged out of the winner's circle by a small organic brand that tied for having the least sodium. Tasters appreciated the heat and tang of **Annie's Naturals Organic Yellow Mustard** as well as its relatively complex but well-balanced flavor. (See page 290 for more information about our testing results.)

Pub-Style Burger Sauce

MAKES ABOUT 1 CUP

- **¾ cup mayonnaise**
- **2 tablespoons soy sauce**
- **1 tablespoon packed dark brown sugar**
- **1 tablespoon Worcestershire sauce**
- **1 tablespoon minced fresh chives**
- **1 garlic clove, minced**
- **¾ teaspoon pepper**

Whisk all ingredients together in bowl. (Sauce can be refrigerated for up to 5 days.)

VARIATIONS

Juicy Pub-Style Burgers with Crispy Shallots and Blue Cheese

While beef is in freezer in step 1, heat ½ cup vegetable oil and 3 thinly sliced shallots in medium saucepan over high heat. Cook, stirring frequently, until shallots are golden, about 8 minutes. Using slotted spoon, transfer shallots to paper towel–lined plate, season with salt, and set aside. Top each burger with 1 ounce crumbled blue cheese (¼ cup) before transferring to oven. Top with Pub-Style Burger Sauce and crispy shallots just before serving.

Juicy Pub-Style Burgers with Peppered Bacon and Aged Cheddar

While beef is in freezer in step 1, adjust oven rack to middle position and heat oven to 375 degrees. Arrange 6 bacon slices on baking sheet and sprinkle with 2 teaspoons coarsely ground pepper. Place second baking sheet on top of bacon and bake until bacon is crisp, 15 to 20 minutes. Transfer bacon to paper towel–lined plate and let cool. Cut bacon in half crosswise. Top each burger with 1 ounce grated aged cheddar cheese (¼ cup) before transferring to oven. Top with Pub-Style Burger Sauce and bacon just before serving.

MAKE-AHEAD MEATLOAF

STASHING A MEATLOAF IN THE FREEZER SOUNDS like a great idea—until you factor in the hours of defrosting before baking and the washed-out flavor and dry-as-sawdust consistency you can expect from it. The problem is that the freezer robs food of moisture and flavor. In hopes of making a frozen meatloaf that rivaled a freshly made one, I consulted freezer cookbooks. Alas, none offered strategic advice to prevent the degradation of flavor and texture. And most recipes called for 12 to 24 hours of defrosting in the refrigerator (didn't that miss the point?). More promising were no-defrost, straight-from-the-freezer recipes that simply called for increasing the cooking time by 50 percent. I figured I'd give this method a try with the test kitchen's core meatloaf recipe.

Our meatloaf is baked free-form on a rack to promote browning. It uses half ground beef and half ground pork, eggs, panade (a paste made from crushed crackers and milk), browned onion and garlic, and seasonings. I assembled a loaf, wrapped it well, and stowed it in the freezer. A few days later, I unwrapped the frozen loaf, put it in the oven, and set the timer for an hour and a half. (Our recipe bakes for an hour, but this one needed an extra 30 minutes to get to 160 degrees.) It came out of the oven shrunken, twisted, dry, and bland; it hardly resembled meatloaf. Obviously, I'd need a recipe for a loaf engineered to survive freezing not to mention a quicker cooking method.

Our science editor gave me three key pieces of information. First, meat gets dry after freezing and cooking because the water in it crystallizes when frozen, punching holes in the cell walls of the meat. When the ice melts during defrosting and cooking, the meat weeps liquid. So in this case, counterintuitively, a drier raw mix should yield a juicier cooked meatloaf because less water should mean less ice damage. Second, fat is less susceptible than meat to ice damage, so I'd have to add extra fat to my raw mixture. And third, salt makes it harder for water to freeze, thereby reducing damage by ice crystals (and helping offset the freezer flavor loss). Armed with science, I set out to make my raw mix drier, fattier, and saltier.

Using less milk in the panade improved the texture of the meatloaf a little by reducing moisture. But trading the milk for heavy cream made a significantly juicier loaf because it contributed both less water and more fat. Unfortunately, with less liquid, the panade was too stiff to easily incorporate into the meat. So I mixed the meat and crushed crackers first, and then added the cream, onion, and seasonings.

To add even more fat, I tried mixing in grated butter and cheese, but they just didn't taste right. Adding an extra egg yolk improved the texture a bit; any more and the loaf tasted, well, eggy. I had better luck trading ground pork for fatty, salty sausage. I tested several types of sausage: breakfast, sweet and hot Italian, and bratwurst. They all vastly improved the texture, but the relatively neutral-tasting bratwurst did the best job of blending into the meatloaf, adding its fat and salt almost undetected. Now I needed to devise a fast, gentle cooking method for the frozen loaf.

We sometimes use a water bath for finicky baking: The bath promotes gentle, even, and efficient cooking. Would it work here? I couldn't plunk my frozen, free-form loaf into the water—I'd need a loaf pan. I found that using two 8-inch pans made for quicker cooking (and more serving options) than a single 9-inch pan. I could still get a flavorful crust on these loaves if I took them out of the pans and glazed and broiled them at the end of cooking. Finally, my meatloaf was moist and tasty enough to actually look forward to.

—SARAH GABRIEL, *Cook's Country*

Make-Ahead Meatloaf

MAKES TWO 8-INCH LOAVES, EACH SERVING 4 TO 6

If you're baking both loaves at once, increase the cooking time in step 4 by 20 minutes and double the glaze.

MEATLOAF

- **2 teaspoons vegetable oil**
- **1 onion, chopped fine**
- **3 garlic cloves, minced**
- **28 saltines**
- **1¾ pounds 85 percent lean ground beef**
- **8 ounces bratwurst, uncooked, casings removed**
- **½ cup heavy cream**
- **⅓ cup minced fresh parsley**
- **3 large eggs plus 1 large egg yolk, lightly beaten**
- **1 tablespoon Dijon mustard**

1 **tablespoon Worcestershire sauce**
1 **teaspoon salt**
1 **teaspoon pepper**
½ **teaspoon dried thyme**
2 **(8-inch) disposable aluminum loaf pans**

GLAZE

½ **cup ketchup**
2 **tablespoons packed brown sugar**
1 **tablespoon cider vinegar**
¼ **teaspoon hot sauce**

1. FOR THE MEATLOAF: Heat oil in nonstick 12-inch skillet over medium heat until shimmering. Add onion and cook until browned, 6 to 8 minutes. Add garlic and cook until fragrant, about 30 seconds. Transfer to large bowl.

2. Process saltines in food processor until finely ground; transfer to bowl with onion mixture. Pulse beef and bratwurst in food processor until just combined. Add meat mixture, cream, parsley, eggs and yolk, mustard, Worcestershire sauce, salt, pepper, and thyme to bowl and knead gently until combined.

3. Press meatloaf mixture into loaf pans. Freeze, uncovered, until firm, at least 1 hour. Tightly wrap pans with plastic wrap, pressing plastic directly on surface of meat, then wrap with aluminum foil. Freeze for up to 1 month.

4. Adjust oven rack to middle position and heat oven to 350 degrees. Unwrap 1 meatloaf and set in roasting pan. Place roasting pan on rack and pour boiling water into pan until water reaches 1 inch from top of loaf. Bake until center of meatloaf registers 150 degrees, 40 to 50 minutes.

5. FOR THE GLAZE: Meanwhile, whisk all glaze ingredients together in saucepan until sugar dissolves. Simmer glaze over medium heat until slightly thickened, about 2 minutes. Cover and keep warm.

6. When meatloaf registers 150 degrees, remove pan from oven. Turn meatloaf out onto foil-lined rimmed baking sheet and brush 2 tablespoons glaze over top and sides of loaf. Adjust oven rack to upper-middle position and heat broiler. Broil until glaze begins to brown and center of loaf registers 160 degrees, 5 to 10 minutes. Transfer to serving platter, tent loosely with foil, and let rest for 20 minutes. Slice and serve, passing remaining glaze separately.

GRILLED THIN-CUT PORK CHOPS

SINCE SELECTION IS LIMITED IN MOST SUPERMARKETS, the time has come to befriend the ½-inch-thick pork chop. Not only are these lean chops widely available, but they cook in the blink of an eye. Unfortunately, because they are so thin, by the time they pick up any crusty char and distinctive grill flavor, they've become tough and dry. I wanted these quick-cooking chops to achieve the same golden-brown crust and juicy, flavorful meat of chops twice their size.

Since I knew I'd want a hot fire to achieve browning, I needed some insurance against dry chops. Brining—soaking in a saltwater solution—helps meat retain moisture, so I brined bone-in, ½-inch-thick rib chops (both rib and center-cut chops work in this recipe) and then put them on the grill. After a couple of minutes per side they were cooked to 145 degrees and ready to eat. But while they were juicy, they hadn't spent enough time over the fire to get a distinct char. I needed a way to accelerate the formation of a good crust.

I wondered if partially freezing the chops would solve these problems, since the dry environment of a freezer causes rapid evaporation on the surface of the meat. I also figured that partially frozen chops could stay on the grill longer. I didn't want to have to both brine (30 minutes) and freeze (yet more time), so to shortcut, I instead sprinkled the chops with salt before freezing them for 30 minutes. The salting, which works like a brine, would, I hoped, ensure a well-seasoned, juicy chop. When I put these chops over the coals, after four minutes per side (about twice as long as for chops from the refrigerator) they were juicy. Still, despite the extra time on the grill, they were only starting to caramelize when it was time to take them off.

I tried sprinkling brown sugar on them before grilling, which was a step toward adding good caramel flavor. But it offered only a slight improvement of the char. Oil, which I thought might attract heat to the meat to accelerate browning, instead dripped off the firm, frozen chops. Melted butter did the same. As a last-ditch effort, I used softened butter, which I hoped would stay on the chops longer. I mixed 2 tablespoons with the brown sugar (and pepper) and brushed the sweetened butter on both sides of each chop. I grilled the first side and held my breath as I flipped them over.

GRILLED THIN-CUT PORK CHOPS

I needn't have worried. The chops were golden brown with crusty char, and the butter greatly improved the otherwise lean meat.

I decided to finish the cooked chops with even more butter and add some zip while I was at it. I mixed 2 more tablespoons of softened butter with chives, mustard, and lemon zest. After grilling the pork, I placed a pat of the butter on each hot chop, where it melted into a bright, buttery sauce. Now I could make juicy, crusty chops from whatever the supermarket had to offer.

—LYNN CLARK, *Cook's Country*

Grilled Thin-Cut Pork Chops

SERVES 4 TO 6

Cutting slits in the fat around the outside of each raw chop prevents the chops from curling as they cook.

- **6 bone-in pork rib or center-cut chops, ½ inch thick**
- **¾ teaspoon salt**
- **4 tablespoons unsalted butter, softened**
- **1 teaspoon brown sugar**
- **½ teaspoon pepper**
- **1 teaspoon minced fresh chives**
- **½ teaspoon Dijon mustard**
- **½ teaspoon grated lemon zest**

1. Pat chops dry with paper towels and cut 2 slits about 2 inches apart through fat on edge of each chop. Rub chops with salt. Place on wire rack set inside rimmed baking sheet and freeze until chops are firm, at least 30 minutes or up to 1 hour. Combine 2 tablespoons butter, sugar, and pepper in bowl; set aside. Mix remaining 2 tablespoons butter, chives, mustard, and zest in second bowl and refrigerate until firm, about 15 minutes. (Butter-chive mixture can be refrigerated, covered, for up to 1 day.)

2A. FOR A CHARCOAL GRILL: Open bottom vent completely. Light large chimney starter filled with charcoal briquettes (6 quarts). When top coals are partially covered with ash, pour evenly over grill. Set cooking grate in place, cover, and open lid vent completely. Heat grill until hot, about 5 minutes.

2B. FOR A GAS GRILL: Turn all burners to high, cover, and heat grill until hot, about 15 minutes. Leave all burners on high.

3. Clean and oil cooking grate. Pat chops dry with paper towels and spread softened butter-sugar mixture evenly over both sides of chops. Place chops on grill, cover, and cook until well browned and chops register 145 degrees, 3 to 4 minutes per side. Transfer chops to platter and top with chilled butter-chive mixture. Tent loosely with foil and let rest for 5 minutes. Serve.

VARIATIONS

Spicy Thai Grilled Thin-Cut Pork Chops

Substitute 1½ teaspoons Asian chili-garlic sauce, 1 teaspoon minced fresh cilantro, and ½ teaspoon grated lime zest for chives, mustard, and lemon zest.

Caribbean Grilled Thin-Cut Pork Chops

Substitute 1 teaspoon grated fresh ginger, ½ teaspoon minced fresh thyme, and ½ teaspoon grated orange zest for chives, mustard, and lemon zest.

Mediterranean Grilled Thin-Cut Pork Chops

Substitute 1½ teaspoons black olive tapenade and ½ teaspoon minced fresh oregano for chives and mustard.

NOTES FROM THE TEST KITCHEN

THIN IS THE NEW THICK

For juicy, nicely charred thin pork chops, we came up with a new method: salting, freezing, and brushing with softened butter before grilling. Salting ensures juicy chops; freezing promotes crust formation by drying the exterior and adding valuable minutes to the cooking time; butter accelerates browning and adds richness to the lean meat.

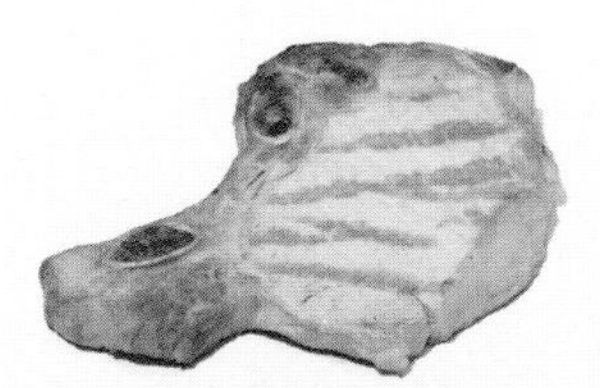

NO PREP? NO THANKS
Grilled straight from the package, this chop is dry, pale, and bland.

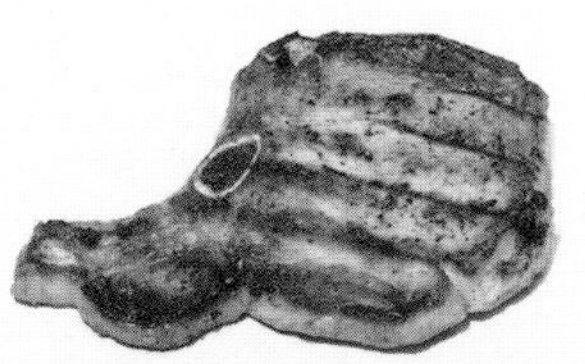

NOW YOU'RE TALKING
Salted, frozen, buttered, then grilled, this chop is juicy, browned, and flavorful.

OKLAHOMA BARBECUE CHOPPED PORK

OKLAHOMANS, BY NATURE, LIKE TO KEEP THINGS close to the vest. Which is why you've probably never heard of Oklahoma barbecue. While their smoke-scented, apron-stained brethren from the Carolinas, Texas, Kansas City, and Memphis will boast about their 'cue for as long as you care to listen, Sooner State pit masters seem content to let their meat—most often pork shoulder, simply seasoned, heavily smoked, and chopped into big chunks—do the talking for them. When pressed, however, an Oklahoma pit master might divulge what Mike Davis, owner of the award-winning Lotta Bull BBQ in Marietta, recently told me. "In Oklahoma," he said, "if your pork is smothered in sauce, it means you're trying to cover something up." Smoke, it seemed, would have to do the heavy lifting.

After calling around to pry as much information as I could out of several professional Oklahoma pit masters, I had a decent understanding of the basics. Oklahoma barbecue starts with a 16- to 18-pound bone-in pork shoulder; the bone adds flavor during the long cooking. The meat is rubbed with salt, black and white pepper, brown sugar, and paprika. It's then smoked with mild hickory wood (no brash mesquite or fancy fruitwood here) for 12 to 15 hours in a big smoker until the meat is tender and redolent with smoke and the outside has developed a crusty, flavorful bark. The meat is then chopped—not shredded—and spooned over soft white buns; it's served with tangy relish and sauce on the side.

My research set my mouth watering, but since I don't have a commercial-size smoker, I'd have to make this recipe work on a backyard kettle grill. But to go low and slow for 12 hours would mean adding charcoal and wood chips to the grill five or six times—no easy feat with a hot grate and a big hunk of meat—and a gas grill would go through a couple of tanks of propane. The test kitchen's method for pulled pork gets around the refueling issue by smoking a 4- or 5-pound boneless pork butt (a smaller shoulder cut) for two hours—the time it takes for one batch of coals and chips to burn—before the meat goes into a low oven to finish cooking. Could I combine the two methods to make authentic-tasting Oklahoma barbecue in half the usual time?

A bone-in shoulder roast was absolutely essential, so I decided to go with a bone-in pork butt, which typically weighs a manageable 7 pounds or so. I rubbed it with the classic Oklahoma seasoning mixture and set it on the grill to smoke. A few early tests confirmed what I'd feared: This cut needed more than two hours on the grill to develop smoky flavor throughout. How could I keep the pork on the grill longer without the hassle of refueling?

During my research, I'd come across a fire configuration called the Minion method (named after its inventor, Washington State competitive barbecuer Jim Minion) in which lit coals are combined with unlit coals to burn longer without refueling. With this method, unlit coals are dumped onto one side of the grill first. Then wood is added, and lit coals are placed on top of that. I set up my grill accordingly but with one modification: I layered in an extra packet of wood chips so that I'd have both smoke and indirect heat for longer. I set the pork butt on the grate opposite the coals and took a seat. The smoky, low fire burned for four-plus hours (and I didn't need to replenish it even once), which meant the pork was exposed to twice as much sweet hickory smoke as before. Now I could transfer the pork to a roasting pan, wrap it in foil, and bring it inside to finish cooking.

After a few hours in a low oven, the pork was finally fork-tender. I let it rest for 30 minutes, then chopped it into substantial chunks. Now it was time to eat. Talk about meaty flavor! The big nubs of pork were tender and juicy with plenty of smoke flavor. My tasters liked the fact that the meat wasn't smothered in sauce. So did I. This meat had nothing to hide.

—DIANE UNGER, *Cook's Country*

Oklahoma Barbecue Chopped Pork

SERVES 8

If you can't find bone-in pork shoulder, substitute a 4- to 5-pound boneless pork roast and begin checking for doneness after 1 hour in step 5. We like hickory wood chips best for this recipe; avoid mesquite. If there are pan juices left behind at the end of step 5, you can defat them and add them back to the chopped pork. Serve on hamburger buns with Oklahoma Barbecue Sauce and Oklahoma Barbecue Relish (recipes follow).

- **2 tablespoons packed brown sugar**
- **2 tablespoons paprika**
- **Salt and pepper**
- **1 tablespoon white pepper**
- **1 (6- to 8-pound) bone-in pork shoulder roast**
- **4 cups wood chips, soaked in water for 15 minutes and drained**

1. Combine sugar, paprika, 1 tablespoon salt, 2 tablespoons pepper, and white pepper in bowl. Pat pork dry with paper towels and rub spice mixture all over pork. (Pork can be refrigerated, covered with plastic wrap, for up to 24 hours.)

2. Using large piece of heavy-duty aluminum foil, wrap 2 cups soaked chips into foil packet and cut several vent holes in top. Repeat with remaining chips.

3A. FOR A CHARCOAL GRILL: Open bottom vent halfway. Place one foil packet on one side of grill, cover with 3 quarts charcoal briquettes (half of large chimney starter), and place second foil packet on top. Light large chimney starter three-quarters full with charcoal briquettes (4½ quarts). When top coals are partially covered with ash, pile on top of second foil packet. Set cooking grate in place, cover, and open lid vent halfway. Heat grill until hot, about 5 minutes.

3B. FOR A GAS GRILL: Add ½ cup ice cubes to one foil packet. Place both wood chip packets directly over primary burner. Turn all burners to high, cover, and heat grill until hot, about 15 minutes. Turn primary burner to medium-high and turn off other burner(s). (Adjust primary burner as needed to maintain grill temperature of 275 to 300 degrees.)

4. Clean and oil cooking grate. Place pork on cool side of grill and cook, covered, until pork is lightly charred and smoky, about 4 hours.

5. Adjust oven rack to middle position and heat oven to 325 degrees. Transfer smoked pork to roasting pan and cover pan tightly with foil. Bake until pork is tender and pulls away from bone, 2 to 3 hours. Remove from oven, tent loosely with foil, and let rest for 30 minutes.

6. Transfer pork to carving board. When cool enough to handle, pull into large chunks. Roughly chop pork and transfer to bowl. Season with salt and pepper to taste and serve. (Pork can be refrigerated for up to 3 days.)

NOTES FROM THE TEST KITCHEN

MAKING OKLAHOMA BARBECUE IN A BACKYARD GRILL

1. Lay packet of wood chips on one side of grill and cover with 3 quarts unlit coals.

2. Lay second packet of wood chips on unlit coals and top with 4½ quarts lit coals.

3. Gently smoke pork on cool side of grill, covered and undisturbed, for 4 hours.

4. Transfer pork to roasting pan, cover with aluminum foil, and continue cooking in 325-degree oven for 2 to 3 hours.

5. After meat has rested for 30 minutes, pull it into large chunks and chop it, discarding fat.

ICE IS NICE

Our Oklahoma Barbecue Chopped Pork is best prepared on a charcoal grill, but if gas is your only option, we found that adding ½ cup of ice cubes to one of the foil packets of wood chips works to slow down the smoke.

Oklahoma Barbecue Sauce

MAKES ABOUT 1½ CUPS

- **1 tablespoon vegetable oil**
- **½ small onion, chopped fine**
- **1 tablespoon tomato paste**
- **2 teaspoons paprika**
- **1 cup ketchup**
- **¾ cup cider vinegar**
- **3 tablespoons packed brown sugar**
- **1 tablespoon Worcestershire sauce**
- **½ teaspoon celery salt**
- **Salt and pepper**

1. Heat oil in medium saucepan over medium heat until shimmering. Add onion and cook until softened, about 3 minutes. Stir in tomato paste and paprika and cook until paste begins to darken, about 1 minute.

2. Add ketchup, vinegar, sugar, Worcestershire sauce, and celery salt and bring to boil. Reduce heat to medium-low and simmer until slightly thickened, 8 to 10 minutes. Transfer to bowl and let cool to room temperature. Season with salt and pepper to taste. Serve with Oklahoma Barbecue Chopped Pork. (Sauce can be refrigerated for up to 5 days.)

Oklahoma Barbecue Relish

MAKES ABOUT 4 CUPS

- **½ head green cabbage, cored and chopped fine (5 cups)**
- **1½ cups sweet pickle relish**
- **½ cup cider vinegar**
- **3 tablespoons yellow mustard**
- **¾ teaspoon celery salt**
- **¼ teaspoon white pepper**

Combine all ingredients in bowl. Cover with plastic wrap and refrigerate until chilled, at least 30 minutes. Serve with Oklahoma Barbecue Chopped Pork. (Relish can be refrigerated for up to 5 days.)

GRILL-ROASTED BONE-IN PORK RIB ROAST

MOST OF US CONSIDER BONELESS PORK ROASTS TO be a welcome modern convenience, like automatic transmissions. Why deal with a clutch and a stick shift—or with bones—if you don't have to? I can't complain about the convenience of a boneless pork roast—little to no butchering on the front end, and fuss-free slicing at the table—but I also know that meat cooked on the bone just tastes better. Plus, for many people, gnawing on the bone is a satisfying way to finish off a meal.

With those reflections in mind, I decided to reacquaint myself with the pleasures of grilling a bone-in roast. I wanted a succulent, flavor-packed roast with a thick, well-browned crust and subtle smokiness. And while I figured out the best way to achieve those results, I also hoped to learn exactly why it is that bones make meat taste juicier and richer.

The obvious starting place was my supermarket butcher case, where I focused on tender, quick-cooking roasts from the loin section of the animal. From this region I had my choice of three roasts: the blade-end (sometimes called the rib-end) roast, the center-cut rib roast, and the confusingly named center cut loin roast. From all the taste tests done in our test kitchen over the years, I already knew that the center-cut loin roast offers the least impressive flavor of the three. So I narrowed my choices to the blade-end and center-cut rib roasts, settling on the center-cut roast for its greater ease of preparation: Because the meat is a single muscle attached along one side to the bones, there is no need to tie the roast for a tidy presentation.

I began by rubbing the meat with a generous handful of kosher salt and letting it rest in the refrigerator for six hours before starting the fire—a technique we've found works better than soaking the meat in a brine when the goal is a deeply browned, crisp crust. Next I built a modified two-level fire, banking all the coals on one side of the kettle. This leaves a cooler area where the meat can cook through slowly by indirect heat without risk of burning the exterior. Then I threw the roast on the grate, covered the grill, and walked away.

A little more than an hour later, the roast's internal temperature registered 140 degrees (I knew it would rise

GRILL-ROASTED BONE-IN PORK RIB ROAST

to the requisite 150 degrees as it rested). I expected to pull the roast over to the grill's hot side for a quick sear before I took it off the grill, but to my delight the meat's exterior had already formed a thick mahogany crust.

Now that I'd picked the best cut and cooking method for the job, I moved on to consider possible tweaks to the flavorings—though, to be honest, I wasn't sure that the roast needed much improvement. The meat was tender and remarkably juicy, and it had plenty of rich, deep flavor. Even my dead-simple salt rub enhanced the pork's taste without distraction.

But, being a skeptic and a perfectionist, I wanted to rule out all other options. So I set up a side-by-side test for my colleagues, pitting my plain salt-rubbed roast against identical specimens crusted with pepper and a range of other spices and herbs. I also tested varying strengths of wood smoke. When the votes were tallied, my original intuition was confirmed: Simpler was better. My tasters opted for nothing more than a little pepper just before cooking and a subtle tinge of smoke flavor. The latter was easy enough: I created a wood chip packet, cut vent holes in the top, placed the packet on the hot coals, positioned the lid vent over the meat, and opened it halfway to draw smoke over the roast.

My testing was all but wrapped up, but I still wanted to know exactly what makes a bone-in roast so flavorful and juicy. I consulted our science editor as well as a number of unaffiliated meat scientists and industry experts, and several of them advanced similar theories about the enhanced juiciness and flavor of bone-in meat.

First, there is extra fat and connective tissue around the bones. As the roast cooks, that fat melts and bastes the meat while the connective tissues break down into gelatin, lending the meat perceived juiciness. (We score the fat on the surface of the roast for exactly the same reason.) Second, the bones act as insulation. They conduct heat poorly, inhibiting evaporation and moisture loss from the meat, keeping it juicier. Our science editor also pointed out that many of the flavor compounds in smoke vapor are fat-soluble, and since there is extra fat in the roast—courtesy of the bones—the meat is likely to absorb and retain more flavor from the smoke.

But another, more intriguing theory, and one I had never heard before, credited the bone marrow. Two experts thought some of the flavorful compounds of the marrow might migrate through the porous bone and into the surrounding meat, though they knew of no experiments that proved it. This hypothesis seemed promising, so our science editor helped devise an experiment to test it. As it turned out, they were onto something—his experiment proved that this theory held water. Bone-in was clearly the way to go.

With all the flavor and tenderness those bones provided, all that this roast needed was a simple orange salsa to provide a counterpoint to its richness. As the man once said, "If it ain't broke, don't fix it."

—ADAM RIED, *Cook's Illustrated*

Grill-Roasted Bone-in Pork Rib Roast

SERVES 6

We prefer natural to enhanced pork (pork that has been injected with a salt solution to increase moistness and flavor), though both will work in this recipe; if using enhanced pork, skip step 1 and season the roast generously with salt before grilling. If you buy a blade-end roast (sometimes called a "rib-end"), tie it into a uniform shape with kitchen twine at 1-inch intervals; this step is unnecessary with a center-cut roast. For easier carving, ask the butcher to remove the tip of the chine bone and to cut the remainder of the chine bone between each rib.

- **1 (4- to 5-pound) bone-in pork center-cut rib- or blade-end roast, tip of chine bone and membrane removed, fat trimmed to ¼-inch thickness**
- **4 teaspoons kosher salt**
- **2 cups wood chips, soaked in water for 15 minutes and drained**
- **1½ teaspoons pepper**
- **1 recipe Orange Salsa with Cuban Flavors (optional; recipe follows)**

1. Pat roast dry with paper towels. Using sharp knife, score fat layer of roast at 1-inch intervals in crosshatch pattern, being careful not to cut into meat. Season roast with salt. Wrap tightly with plastic wrap, place on rimmed baking sheet, and refrigerate for at least 6 hours or up to 1 day.

2. Using large piece of heavy-duty aluminum foil, wrap soaked chips into foil packet and cut several vent holes in top.

NOTES FROM THE TEST KITCHEN

TESTING MEAT FOR DONENESS

An instant-read thermometer is the most reliable method for checking the doneness of chicken, beef, and pork. To use an instant-read thermometer, simply insert it through the side of a chicken breast, steak, or pork chop. The chart below lists temperatures at which the meat should be removed from the heat (the temperature of the meat will continue to climb another 5 to 10 degrees as it rests before serving).

WHEN IS IT DONE?

MEAT	COOK UNTIL IT REGISTERS	SERVING TEMPERATURE
Chicken and Turkey Breasts	160 to 165 degrees	160 to 165 degrees
Chicken Thighs	175 degrees	175 degrees
Duck Breasts		
Medium-rare	120 to 125 degrees	130 degrees
Medium	130 to 135 degrees	140 degrees
Medium-well	140 to 145 degrees	150 degrees
Well-done	150 to 155 degrees	160 degrees
Pork	140 to 145 degrees	150 degrees
Beef and Lamb		
Rare	115 to 120 degrees	125 degrees
Medium-rare	120 to 125 degrees	130 degrees
Medium	130 to 135 degrees	140 degrees
Medium-well	140 to 145 degrees	150 degrees
Well-done	150 to 155 degrees	160 degrees

REMOVING MEMBRANE OF PORK RIB ROAST

Nick membrane at edge of roast with tip of knife to loosen it, then grab loose bit using paper towel and slowly pull off membrane.

3A. FOR A CHARCOAL GRILL: Open bottom vent halfway. Light large chimney starter filled with charcoal briquettes (6 quarts). When top coals are partially covered with ash, pour over one-third of grill with coals steeply banked against side of grill. Place wood chip packet on coals. Set cooking grate in place, cover, and open lid vent halfway. Heat grill until hot and wood chips are smoking, about 5 minutes.

3B. FOR A GAS GRILL: Place wood chip packet over primary burner. Turn all burners to high, cover, and heat grill until hot and wood chips are smoking, about 15 minutes. Turn primary burner to medium-high and turn off other burner(s).

4. Clean and oil cooking grate. Season roast with pepper. Place roast on grill near, but not over, coals and flames. Cover (with vent over meat if using charcoal) and grill-roast until meat registers 140 degrees, 1¼ to 1½ hours.

5. Transfer roast to carving board, tent loosely with foil, and let rest for 30 minutes. Carve into thick slices by cutting between ribs. Serve immediately, passing salsa separately, if using.

Orange Salsa with Cuban Flavors

MAKES ABOUT 2½ CUPS

To make the salsa spicier, add the reserved chile seeds.

- **½ teaspoon finely grated orange zest, plus 5 oranges, peeled and segmented, segments quartered crosswise**
- **½ red onion, chopped fine**
- **1 jalapeño, stemmed, seeded, and minced**
- **2 tablespoons lime juice**
- **2 tablespoons minced fresh parsley**
- **1 tablespoon extra-virgin olive oil**
- **2 teaspoons packed brown sugar**
- **1½ teaspoons white vinegar**
- **1½ teaspoons minced fresh oregano**
- **1 garlic clove, minced**
- **½ teaspoon ground cumin**
- **½ teaspoon salt**
- **½ teaspoon pepper**

Combine all ingredients in bowl. (Salsa can be refrigerated for up to 1 day.)

SLOW-ROASTED PORK SHOULDER

IT'S BEEN MORE THAN 20 YEARS SINCE THE National Pork Producers Council launched a campaign to persuade poultry-loving Americans to eat more pig—specifically the lean "other white meat" between the pig's shoulder and leg known as the loin—and producers began developing new breeds of slimmer pigs. Ever since, consumers have been flocking to butcher cases to buy up the loin and then heading home to try everything under the sun to improve the almost-fat-free meat's bland flavor and stringy chew.

But this premise—cut the fat, then jump through hoops to make lean meat taste less dull—never made sense to me. I wanted to explore the glories of old-fashioned, better-tasting (read: less lean) pork. One such cut, the shoulder roast (also called Boston butt or pork butt), has found new life in both restaurants and supermarket butcher cases. I decided to ditch the loin in favor of this cut, which not only is loaded with flavorful intramuscular fat but also boasts a thick fat cap that renders to a bronze, baconlike crust. A bonus: Pork butt is cheap. True, it would take several hours of roasting before the well-worked shoulder muscle broke down and became fork-tender. But the rewards of richly flavored, crisp-crusted roast would make it time well spent.

The rectangular slab known as pork butt—not to be confused with the cone-shaped, more sinewy "picnic" roast that comes from just below the shoulder blade—can be purchased either boneless or bone-in. Both have their advantages: Boneless cuts typically cook faster than bone-in and come partially butterflied, which leaves plenty of interior meat exposed and available for seasoning. Meanwhile, bone-in roasts take longer to cook and restrict seasoning to the exterior but retain more moisture and cook more evenly. Test kitchen precedent had me leaning toward the latter, and one side-by-side comparison was all I needed to confirm my decision.

Since this wasn't my usual pork roast, I used my knowledge of what it takes to roast large, tough cuts of meat to put together a basic working recipe. First, I salted the meat and left it to rest. We frequently use this technique to allow the seasoning to penetrate deep beneath the surface of a large, tough roast and break down its proteins for improved texture, not to mention bigger flavor. A few tests confirmed that an overnight rest (versus two, four, or even six hours) worked best. Then I set my oven to the same temperature I use to barbecue pork butt on the grill, 275 degrees; covered the roast with aluminum foil to trap the damp, collagen-melting heat; and let the meat go until the barest prick of my fork cleaved the roast into rough hunks along its seams. According to my timer, that was right around the seven-hour mark, and the results weren't bad for a first stab.

The pork was tender, for sure—my instant-read thermometer registered about 190 degrees. Just as with barbecue, slowly and gently taking the pork well beyond its 145-degree "done" stage not only melts fat but also breaks down collagen and tenderizes the meat. Its flavor was also fuller and had more character than that of any loin roast I'd ever cooked. Yet for all the time this meat had spent in the oven, it actually tasted more steamed than roasted. Predictably, given the aluminum foil shield, the exterior was also pale and soggy.

First things first: I'd been eyeing that thick fat cap as crispy skin fodder, so the foil cover had to go. (Plus, with so much fat marbling, I figured the pork wouldn't dry out very quickly.) What's more, I needed to get my roast to taste like, well, a roast, so I spent my next several tests turning the oven dial up notch by notch to instill oven-concentrated, meaty flavor and boost browning. At 325 degrees I stopped. After about five hours, the meat's collagen had broken down and rendered the interior meltingly tender yet sliceable.

The higher heat also crisped up the crust—though not quite as much as I'd hoped. While decently rendered and copper-colored, the exterior fat was not sufficiently crunchy and brittle. I wondered if I should be rubbing the roast's exterior with more than just a handful of salt. I thought back to the crispest, most irresistibly savory pork crust I could remember, and my mind immediately zeroed in on Chinese barbecue, in which the pigs are heavily seasoned with equal parts salt and sugar to encourage caramelization and a crackly-crisp, salty-sweet crust.

The idea seemed promising and perfectly applicable to my simple roast, so I rubbed sugar over the salted pork butt just before putting it in the oven. As I expected, the sugar caramelized and helped crisp the fat cap. I got even deeper browning when I rubbed ⅓ cup of sugar on the meat together with the salt and left it to rest overnight. Because sugar is hygroscopic, over time it pulls water from the outer layers of the meat, drying out the exterior and boosting browning. But to ensure that the meat didn't get too dark, I brushed off some of the sugar-salt rub with a clean towel before roasting. When I switched from white sugar to brown, tasters praised the crust's subtle molasses flavor and hints of caramel.

While the cooked pork rested for about an hour (a necessary step that allows the juice to redistribute in the meat), I noticed the roasting pan was coated with a dark layer of drippings. Ordinarily, I wouldn't think twice about scraping up these flavorful bits of fond and turning them into a sauce, but in this case I had reason to pause. The drippings from this particular roast burned quickly, thanks to their high sugar content. This was easily fixed with a V-rack and a quart of water poured into the bottom of the pan. Once the roast was perched higher up, its fat dripped down and mixed with the water, all of which pooled into a significant jus, with no burning.

With just the pork, salt, sugar, heat, and time, I'd produced a roast that far outdid the fussier, less flavorful specimens I was used to preparing, so any sauce I made would have to be simple. My first inclination: something fruity, with sweet and sour elements to cut the meat's richness. I combined ¼ cup of the defatted pork jus (this was potent stuff) with peaches, white wine, sugar, vinegar, and a couple of sprigs of fresh thyme and reduced the mixture to a thin syrup. To round out the sweetness, I finished it with a spoonful of whole grain mustard.

This meat spoke for itself—particularly the fat responsible for its richness and twofold texture. (Each slice was at once meltingly tender within and almost like cracklings at the surface.) In fact, it was head and (pardon the pun) shoulders above any pork loin I'd ever tasted and would join my Sunday roast rotation for good.

—BRYAN ROOF, *Cook's Illustrated*

Slow-Roasted Pork Shoulder with Peach Sauce

SERVES 8 TO 12

We prefer natural to enhanced pork (pork that has been injected with a salt solution to increase moistness and flavor), though both will work in this recipe. Add more water to the roasting pan as necessary during the last hours of cooking to prevent the fond from burning. Serve the pork with the accompanying Peach Sauce or Cherry Sauce (recipe follows) or with a sweet-tart chutney.

PORK ROAST

- **1 (6- to 8-pound) bone-in pork butt**
- **⅓ cup kosher salt**
- **⅓ cup packed light brown sugar**
- **Pepper**
- **Vegetable oil spray**

PEACH SAUCE

- **10 ounces frozen peaches, cut into 1-inch chunks (2 cups), or 2 fresh peaches, pitted and cut into ½-inch wedges**
- **2 cups dry white wine**
- **½ cup granulated sugar**
- **¼ cup plus 1 tablespoon rice vinegar**
- **2 sprigs fresh thyme**
- **1 tablespoon whole grain mustard**

1. FOR THE ROAST: Pat pork dry with paper towels. Using sharp knife, score fat cap of roast at 1-inch intervals in crosshatch pattern, being careful not to cut into meat. Combine salt and sugar in bowl. Rub salt mixture over entire pork shoulder and into slits. Wrap tightly in plastic wrap, place on rimmed baking sheet, and refrigerate for at least 12 hours or up to 1 day.

2. Adjust oven rack to lowest position and heat oven to 325 degrees. Unwrap roast, brush off excess salt mixture, and season with pepper. Transfer roast to V-rack coated with vegetable oil spray set inside large roasting pan and add 4 cups water to roasting pan.

3. Cook roast, basting twice during cooking, until meat is extremely tender and meat near but not touching bone registers 190 degrees, 5 to 6 hours. Transfer roast to carving board. Tent loosely with foil and let rest for 1 hour. Transfer liquid in roasting pan to fat separator and let stand for 5 minutes. Pour off ¼ cup jus; discard fat and reserve remaining jus for another use.

4. FOR THE SAUCE: Bring peaches, wine, sugar, ¼ cup vinegar, ¼ cup defatted jus, and thyme to simmer in small saucepan; cook, stirring occasionally, until reduced to 2 cups, about 30 minutes. Stir in remaining 1 tablespoon vinegar and mustard. Remove thyme, cover, and keep warm.

5. Using sharp paring knife, cut around inverted T-shaped bone and pull free from roast. Using serrated knife, slice roast. Serve, passing sauce separately.

VARIATION

Slow-Roasted Pork Shoulder with Cherry Sauce

Omit thyme and mustard. Substitute 10 ounces fresh or frozen pitted cherries for peaches, red wine for white wine, and red wine vinegar for rice vinegar. Add ¼ cup ruby port along with defatted jus and increase granulated sugar to ¾ cup. Reduce mixture to 1½ cups.

GLAZED PICNIC HAM

YOUR GARDEN-VARIETY SUPERMARKET HAM— a lean cut from the rear leg of a pig—gets its complex salty savor from curing and smoking. But many cooks are unaware of an even more flavorful cut, the picnic ham, that's given the same treatment. Picnic hams, which come from the lower part of a hog's shoulder, are pleasantly smoky and salty like leg hams, but they taste richer and meatier because they have a lot more fat. Most of the recipes I found for picnic ham called for simmering the meat for hours. But boiling wasn't what I had in mind. I wanted to roast this exceptionally flavorful cut of meat to present as the centerpiece of my Easter table.

Since we've never cooked a picnic ham in the test kitchen, I started with our basic method for spiral-sliced ham: After trimming off most of the tough rind (a step not needed for spiral-sliced hams), I slipped the ham into an oven bag, shut the bag, cut slits in it to vent the steam, and baked the ham in a 300-degree oven until it registered 100 degrees. A couple hours later, I had high hopes as I carved samples for my tasters, but my optimism was short-lived. The meat was unpleasantly chewy, and it was riddled with pockets of fat. Lesson learned: Although picnic hams are technically fully cooked, the extra fat means they need extra cooking (not just heating through, like leg ham) to become palatable.

For my next test, I upped the cooking time to three hours (still in the oven bag) to give the connective tissue enough time to render. The outside of the ham was leathery, and the meat was overcooked, dry, and still pocked with chunks of fat and gristle. Adding insult to injury, since the meat had dried out and concentrated, it was also too salty. Picnic ham was proving to be no picnic in the kitchen.

Was the oven bag actually hurting me here? Through years of smoking similarly large, fatty cuts on the grill, we've learned that collagen (the tough, fatty connective tissue) renders most effectively in a moist, steamy environment (that's why we often use a drip pan when slow-smoking on the grill). But the vented oven bag, which traps enough moisture to keep a leg ham moist when reheating, wasn't trapping enough moisture to keep the picnic ham moist through the necessary extra cooking. I decided to bag the bag and instead placed the ham directly on a rack in a large roasting pan. To create a contained moist environment (akin to covering the grill when smoking), I wrapped the whole roasting pan tightly with foil.

In a single test, the picnic ham improved dramatically. I sorted through the cooking details in subsequent tests and found that cooking the meat to 140 degrees in a 325-degree oven (which took anywhere from two to three hours, depending on the size of the ham) produced the best results—consistently moist, tender meat with much of the fat rendered out.

To balance the salty richness of the meat, I opted for a sweet, spicy glaze. As soon as I put the ham in the oven, I got to work simmering a simple mixture of brown sugar, Dijon mustard, cloves, cayenne pepper, and apple cider vinegar. When the ham was almost done cooking, I carefully removed and discarded the foil, slathered the ham with the sticky glaze, and cranked the heat to 450 degrees so the glaze could caramelize (it took about 25 minutes). The glaze nicely countered the ham's salinity, but tasters wanted more depth. Switching from cider vinegar to balsamic did the trick (and had the added benefit of giving the glaze a deep, rich color), and I thinned out a little extra glaze to a pourable consistency for ladling on at the table.

This ultra-savory ham was better than any I'd ever tasted—and is primed to be my Easter centerpiece for many years to come.

—DIANE UNGER, *Cook's Country*

GLAZED PICNIC HAM (SMOKED SHOULDER)

Glazed Picnic Ham (Smoked Shoulder)

SERVES 12 TO 16

We like the larger whole smoked picnic ham when we're cooking for a crowd, but you can also use a shankless roast (sometimes labeled "smoked shoulder picnic" or "smoked Boston butt"). Crimp the foil tightly around the roasting pan to keep the ham moist and help the collagen render.

- **1 (8- to 10-pound) bone-in smoked picnic ham, skin removed and fat trimmed to ¼-inch thickness**
- **3 tablespoons dry mustard**
- **1 teaspoon pepper**
- **1 cup packed dark brown sugar**
- **½ cup Dijon mustard**
- **½ cup balsamic vinegar**
- **¼ teaspoon cayenne pepper**
- **⅛ teaspoon ground cloves**
- **1 tablespoon apple cider or water**

1. Adjust oven rack to lowest position and heat oven to 325 degrees. Line large roasting pan with aluminum foil. Using sharp knife, score fat layer of ham at 1-inch intervals in crosshatch pattern. Combine 1 tablespoon dry mustard and pepper in small bowl. Rub pepper mixture over entire ham. Set ham on V-rack set inside prepared pan and cover pan tightly with foil. Bake until ham registers 140 degrees, 2 to 3 hours.

2. Meanwhile, bring sugar, Dijon mustard, vinegar, remaining 2 tablespoons dry mustard, cayenne, and cloves to boil in medium saucepan. Reduce heat to low and simmer until reduced to 1 cup, 15 to 20 minutes. (Glaze can be refrigerated for up to 3 days; microwave until hot before using.)

3. Remove ham from oven and let rest for 5 minutes. Increase oven temperature to 450 degrees. Discard foil and brush ham evenly with ½ cup glaze. Return ham to oven and bake until dark brown and caramelized, 25 to 30 minutes. Stir cider into remaining glaze. Transfer ham to carving board, tent loosely with foil, and let rest for 30 minutes. Carve and serve, passing glaze separately.

NOTES FROM THE TEST KITCHEN

SCORING MEAT

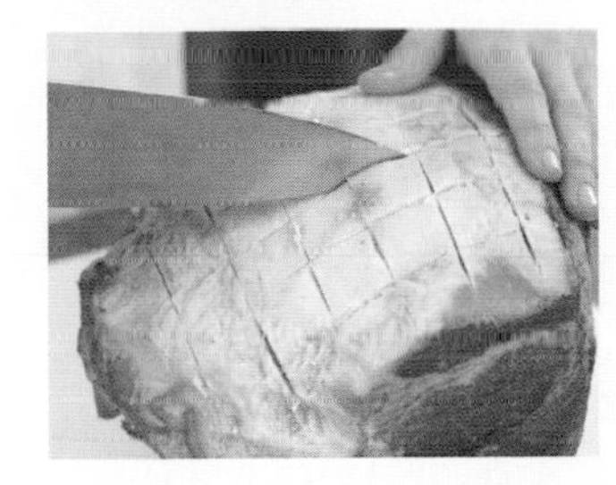

To score a ham or other roast, first trim fat layer as directed. Then use sharp knife to score remaining fat at 1-inch intervals in crosshatch pattern.

CARVING PICNIC HAM

Using a sharp knife, and securing ham by holding largest protruding bone, cut along length of bone to remove large sections of meat, rotating roast slowly as you cut and discarding any pockets of fat.

A TALE OF TWO HAMS

A picnic ham is cut from the shoulder of the front leg of the pig, as opposed to a true ham, which is cut from the pig's back leg. They are both smoked and cured. The picnic ham is available either with the shank and hock attached (the full image) or as the smaller "shankless" cut (everything to the right of the dotted line). For feeding a crowd, we like the larger whole picnic ham.

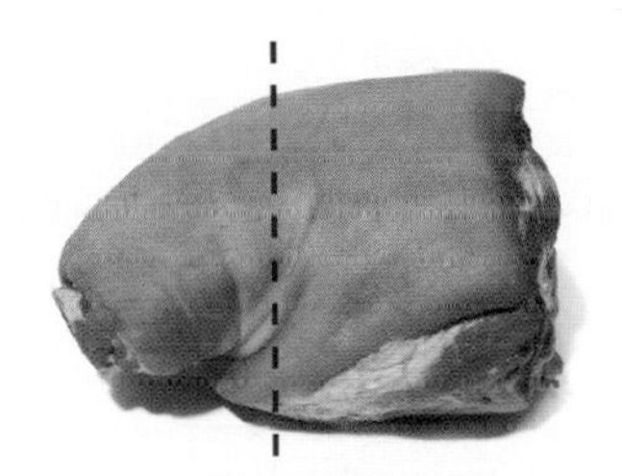

WHOLE SMOKED PICNIC HAM
The shankless version would consist of everything to the right of the line.

CHAPTER 7

POULTRY

CRUNCHY BUTTERMILK BAKED CHICKEN

THERE'S NOTHING ESOTERIC OR MYSTERIOUS about buttermilk baked chicken: You soak bone-in chicken pieces in buttermilk, roll them in crumbs, and bake them, undisturbed, for 40 to 45 minutes at 375 degrees. Just as appealing as the tangy flavor and crunchy coating is the uncomplicated, weeknight-friendly nature of the dish. My tasters were excited when I called them to sample the half-dozen recipes I'd prepared, but their excitement was short-lived. In some of the versions, the chicken was bland and dry with nary a hint of buttermilk bite. Worse still were pasty, soggy, and sandy coatings. Were these from the frozen-food section? tasters asked.

I learned an important lesson from this initial test—it doesn't pay to shortchange the buttermilk soak, since a quick dip imparted zero tang. In my favorite recipe eight pieces of chicken (one cut-up bird) were soaked in a whopping 2 quarts of buttermilk for a full two hours; this gave the meat some, but not enough, buttermilk zip. And the chicken skin was flabby and chewy. While this same recipe had the most promising coating—toasted fresh bread crumbs—it was soggy underneath and wouldn't stay on.

My first task was to bump up the buttermilk flavor while, if possible, shortening the soaking time. Adding salt to the soak seasoned the meat and kept it juicy, but it also helped carry the buttermilk tang into the meat in just 30 minutes. So I wasn't pouring 2 quarts of buttermilk down the drain, I cut back to 2 cups. To add extra flavor, I had a secret ingredient up my sleeve: buttermilk powder. For even more flavor, I replaced the buttermilk powder with powdered ranch seasoning mix (basically buttermilk powder plus seasonings).

I'd been coating the chicken with toasted bread crumbs made from white sandwich bread. My tasters wanted a livelier coating—and more of it (they still weren't sticking). Using some of the ranch dressing mix with the crumbs gave them the flavor boost they sorely needed. To help the crumbs stick, I tried slathering the chicken with mayonnaise (a common "glue" in the test kitchen) after its buttermilk bath, but this turned the coating gummy. I had better luck stirring the mayonnaise into the buttermilk mixture—the thicker liquid held the crumbs much better. To further enhance the buttermilk tang, I replaced the mayonnaise with sour cream. Last, I discarded the chicken skin before soaking, because it couldn't possibly render and crisp when saturated with marinade.

I needed to iron out a few cooking details. The crumb coating was crispy on the top and sides of the chicken but soggy on the bottom. Even when baked elevated on a rack, the chicken pieces didn't crisp underneath. For the next half-dozen tests, I placed oven racks high, low, and in the middle, and I fiddled continually with the temperature dial. Finally, I arrived at a solution: To crisp the bottom, I sprayed the breaded chicken pieces with vegetable oil spray, then started them directly on a baking sheet on the lowest rack in a scorching-hot 450-degree oven. After about 10 minutes, I moved the chicken to the middle rack and turned down the oven to 400 so the chicken could cook through more gently. I gathered my tasters once again. This time, they were too busy devouring the crispy, piquant, flavorful chicken to make wisecracks.

—MEGHAN ERWIN, *Cook's Country*

Crunchy Buttermilk Baked Chicken

SERVES 4

Ranch seasoning mix can be found with the salad dressings and oils at the supermarket.

- **2 cups buttermilk**
- **¼ cup sour cream**
- **1 (1-ounce) envelope ranch seasoning mix**
- **1 tablespoon salt**
- **3 pounds bone-in chicken pieces (breasts, thighs, and drumsticks, or mix, breasts cut in half), skin removed, trimmed**
- **5 slices hearty white sandwich bread, torn into pieces**
- **Vegetable oil spray**

1. Adjust oven racks to lowest and middle positions and heat oven to 450 degrees. Whisk buttermilk, sour cream, 2 tablespoons ranch seasoning mix, and salt together in large bowl until salt dissolves. Add chicken and toss to coat. Refrigerate, covered, for at least 30 minutes or up to 1 hour.

2. Meanwhile, pulse bread and remaining ranch seasoning mix in food processor until finely ground. Bake bread crumbs on baking sheet on middle rack, stirring occasionally, until light golden, about 5 minutes. Transfer to shallow dish or pie plate.

NOTES FROM THE TEST KITCHEN

BUTTERMILK BRINE

Most recipes have you simply dip the chicken in buttermilk—which adds no discernible buttermilk flavor. We soaked the chicken in a seasoned buttermilk brine, which included ranch seasoning mix and sour cream, to flavor the chicken deeply.

BOLD BRINE

This combo spelled success for juicy, flavorful chicken.

3. Line baking sheet with aluminum foil and spray lightly with vegetable oil spray. Remove chicken from brine, allowing excess to drip back into bowl, and dredge in bread crumbs, pressing to adhere. Transfer to prepared baking sheet and spray lightly with vegetable oil spray. Discard brine.

4. Bake on lowest rack until bottom of chicken is golden brown, about 10 minutes. Move baking sheet to middle rack and reduce oven temperature to 400 degrees. Bake until chicken is golden brown and breasts register 160 degrees and legs/thighs register 175 degrees, 20 to 25 minutes. Serve.

EASIER FRIED CHICKEN

HERE'S ONE THING WE CAN ALL AGREE ON: FRIED chicken is great. Crackling crisp, golden brown, and juicy—what's not to love? Here's something else we can all agree on: Heating more than a quart of fat on the stovetop is too much trouble for most home cooks, never mind finding a way to dispose of it. These two premises have spawned a slew of recipes for "oven-fried" chicken designed to deliver one (the chicken) without the other (the hot fat). Using bread crumbs, crushed Melba toasts, or even cereal, these versions certainly deliver crunch and even moist, juicy meat. But they are at best a substitute for and not a replica of the real deal.

With many such recipes, reducing fat is the overriding goal. Not for me. Fried chicken should be an occasional indulgence, and I'm not going to settle for second-rate flavor for the sake of a few calories. My goal was to achieve true fried chicken—golden brown and crisp with a buttermilk-and-flour-based coating—without having to heat up a pot full of fat.

Fried chicken recipes often call for soaking the chicken pieces in buttermilk—it has just enough acid to help tenderize mainly the outer layers of the meat without turning them mushy—then dredging them in seasoned flour before deep-frying. Over the years, we've discovered a few other tricks to help ensure moist meat and an extra-crisp crust. They would make good jumping-off points, I thought.

First, we heavily salt the buttermilk before soaking the chicken pieces, turning the buttermilk into a brine to help the meat retain moisture. We also add baking powder to the seasoned dredging mixture. As the chicken fries, the baking powder releases carbon dioxide, leavening the crust and increasing its surface area, keeping it light and crisp. Finally, while traditional fried chicken recipes call for only dry ingredients in their dredging mixture, we've found that adding buttermilk to the dry ingredients before dredging the chicken creates small clumps of batter that become super-crisp as they fry.

I figured I'd be better able to replicate deep fat frying if I first reviewed what exactly it accomplishes. Just like any other high-heat cooking method, it facilitates the Maillard reaction and the creation of hundreds of new flavor compounds that are the hallmark of properly browned food. It also dehydrates. As the water in the coating reaches 212 degrees (its boiling point), it converts to steam and is expelled from the food (this is what causes the bubbles you see when food is dropped into hot fat). It is this dehydration, along with the hardening of the protein structure in the flour and chicken skin triggered by heat, that give fried chicken its crisp crust. Last, deep-fat frying cooks the food; the trick when frying chicken is finding the right oil temperature to cook the meat through without burning the exterior.

An oven could obviously reach hot enough temperatures to produce browning and cause dehydration. So could I get oven-fried chicken closer to the deep-fried original if I simply ditched the bread crumbs and crushed crackers as a coating and went with traditional flour-dredged pieces? The idea was a shot in the dark—and it totally missed. After an hour in the oven, the

EASIER FRIED CHICKEN

chicken was spotty brown, with some regions coated in raw flour and others nearly burnt. Biting into the meat revealed a powdery, brittle crust, not a moist, crisp one. There had to be something else about deep frying that I was missing.

The answer to the coating question lay in a discovery we made in an earlier recipe for french fries. It turns out that, contrary to popular belief, the higher the temperature of the frying fat, the more it is absorbed by the food being fried. So as a piece of chicken cooks at a relatively hot 300 to 350 degrees, almost all of the moisture in the coating is expelled and replaced with oil. That oil is essential to the flavor and texture of a really good crisp crust—and its absence in the breaded and baked chicken explained the dry, floury results. When the coating's moisture evaporated, there was nothing to replace it. It seemed at least some form of frying was necessary.

Our standard fried chicken recipe calls for 5 cups of oil (we prefer peanut but vegetable oil works, too). To achieve fully cooked chicken, we cover the Dutch oven for part of the time and carefully monitor the temperature throughout using a deep-fat thermometer. Could I significantly reduce the volume of oil and still achieve great results? I tested my way down to 1¾ cups—just enough oil that when I nestled the chicken pieces into it they would raise the level to help cook their sides. Then, all I'd have to do was flip them over to finish cooking once the first side was golden brown. Simple, right?

Wrong. If I'd been using 5 cups, the oil's temperature would have stayed roughly the same after the addition of the chicken. With only 1¾ cups in the pot, however, the temperature dropped dramatically when the chicken was added, to just over 200 degrees from 375. To get the oil back up to the optimal range, I had to crank the flame too high—which fueled a new problem: burnt patches on the parts of the chicken that had been in direct contact with the bottom of the pan (and without a full pot of oil to keep the chicken afloat, this meant a lot of the pieces). To avoid burning, the chicken couldn't stand much more than three or four minutes of frying per side, not enough time for it to cook through. Furthermore, much of the chicken never quite caught up after the big temperature drop; even after being flipped, the pieces were still dead cold in the center and pale golden brown instead of deeply bronzed.

I began to wonder if I'd discounted the oven prematurely. Radiant, circulating heat might be just the ticket to replace the even heating of a deep, hot oil bath and allow my chicken to brown and cook through properly. I decided to try a hybrid method: I'd start by frying the chicken on the stovetop until it formed a light brown crust, then finish it in a hot oven (perched on a wire rack set in a sheet pan to prevent burnt spots and promote air circulation all around the meat) to both cook it through and deepen its color.

I had just one more question to answer: Would there be enough fat left on the surface of the chicken after its initial fry to fully permeate the crust as it dehydrated, as in traditionally fried chicken? In a word, yes. Fifteen minutes in the oven was all it took to give my shallow-fried chicken a golden brown crust that was crisp and craggy enough to make the Colonel blush.

When I tasted it side by side with fried chicken cooked in the usual quart-plus of oil, I couldn't tell the two batches apart. But their differences were very apparent when it came time to take care of the cooking fat. Oil crisis? Solved.

—J. KENJI LOPEZ-ALT, *Cook's Illustrated*

Easier Fried Chicken

SERVES 4 TO 6

Skinless chicken pieces are also an acceptable substitute, but the meat will come out slightly drier. Smaller pieces of chicken may cook faster than larger pieces. A Dutch oven with an 11-inch diameter can be used in place of the straight-sided sauté pan.

1¼ cups buttermilk
Salt and pepper
Hot sauce
1 teaspoon garlic powder
1 teaspoon paprika
¼ teaspoon cayenne pepper
3½ pounds bone-in chicken pieces (breasts, thighs, and drumsticks, or mix, breasts cut in half), trimmed
2 cups all-purpose flour
2 teaspoons baking powder
1¾ cups peanut or vegetable oil

1. Whisk 1 cup buttermilk, 1 tablespoon salt, 1 teaspoon pepper, dash hot sauce, ¼ teaspoon garlic powder, ¼ teaspoon paprika, and pinch cayenne together in large bowl. Add chicken and turn to coat. Refrigerate, covered, for at least 1 hour or up to 24 hours.

NOTES FROM THE TEST KITCHEN

AN EASIER APPROACH TO FRIED CHICKEN

1. Soaking chicken in seasoned buttermilk both enhances flavor and ensures that meat retains moisture.

2. Adding buttermilk to dry ingredients creates irregular texture, which translates to extra crunch.

3. Frying in smaller amount of oil jump-starts super-crisp coating and minimizes cleanup.

4. Transferring chicken to 400-degree oven allows it to cook through without overbrowning.

OIL SHORTAGE

Properly frying chicken from start to finish using traditional methods requires lots of messy oil. Our hybrid stove-to-oven method cuts it way back.

TRADITIONAL WAY
5 cups oil

OUR WAY
1¾ cups oil

2. Adjust oven rack to middle position and heat oven to 400 degrees. Whisk flour, baking powder, 2 teaspoons pepper, 1 teaspoon salt, remaining ¾ teaspoon garlic powder, remaining ¾ teaspoon paprika, and remaining cayenne together in large bowl. Add remaining ¼ cup buttermilk and mix with fingers until combined and small clumps form. Working with 1 piece at a time, dredge chicken pieces in flour mixture, pressing mixture onto pieces to form thick, even coating. Place dredged chicken on large plate, skin side up.

3. Heat oil in 11-inch straight-sided sauté pan over medium-high heat to 375 degrees. Carefully place chicken pieces in pan, skin side down, and cook until golden brown, 3 to 5 minutes. Carefully flip and continue to cook until golden brown on second side, 2 to 4 minutes longer. Transfer chicken to wire rack set inside rimmed baking sheet. Bake chicken until breasts register 160 degrees and legs/thighs register 175 degrees, 15 to 20 minutes. Let chicken rest for 5 minutes before serving.

NUT-CRUSTED CHICKEN CUTLETS

INCORPORATING CHOPPED NUTS INTO THE coating of a boneless, skinless chicken breast not only adds a new, more robust flavor element but also boosts the crust's crunch factor. But in my experience this technique comes with some problems: The crust becomes dense and leaden, and the rich flavor of the nuts rarely comes through. Plus it's all too easy to dry out a lean, boneless breast.

Ensuring juicy, flavorful meat was a simple fix: I salted the cutlets (poking them with a fork first helped the salt penetrate) and rested them briefly before dredging and frying. For the crust, I wondered if a simple "breading" of nuts would help, but when I dredged the cutlets in flour, dipped them in beaten eggs, and dragged them through chopped almonds, the crushed pieces barely adhered to the meat. Using bread crumbs in the final dredge, which would absorb liquid from the eggs to help act as glue, was definitely going to be necessary. A mixture of half nuts and half Japanese panko—coarser and crunchier than conventional bread crumbs—gave me just the light, crisp texture I wanted. To improve flavor, I added Dijon mustard to the egg

NUT-CRUSTED CHICKEN CUTLETS WITH LEMON AND THYME

FILLING

- 2 tablespoons vegetable oil
- 1 onion, chopped fine
- 3 carrots, peeled and cut into ¼-inch-thick slices
- 2 small celery ribs, minced
- Salt and pepper
- 10 ounces cremini mushrooms, trimmed and sliced thin
- 1 teaspoon soy sauce
- 1 teaspoon tomato paste
- 4 tablespoons unsalted butter
- ½ cup all-purpose flour
- 1 cup whole milk
- 3 tablespoons minced fresh parsley
- 2 teaspoons lemon juice
- ¾ cup frozen baby peas

1. FOR THE CHICKEN: Bring chicken and broth to simmer in covered Dutch oven over medium heat. Cook until chicken is just done, 8 to 12 minutes. Transfer chicken to large bowl. Pour broth through fine-mesh strainer into liquid measuring cup and reserve. Do not wash Dutch oven. Meanwhile, adjust oven rack to upper-middle position and heat oven to 450 degrees.

2. FOR THE TOPPING: Combine flour, baking powder, salt, pepper, and cayenne in large bowl and sprinkle butter pieces over top. Using fingers, rub butter into flour mixture until it resembles coarse cornmeal. Stir in Parmesan. Add cream and stir until just combined. Crumble mixture into irregularly shaped pieces, ½ to ¾ inch wide, onto parchment-lined baking sheet. Bake until fragrant and starting to brown, 10 to 13 minutes. Set aside.

3. FOR THE FILLING: Heat 1 tablespoon oil in now-empty Dutch oven over medium heat until shimmering. Add onion, carrots, celery, ¼ teaspoon salt, and ¼ teaspoon pepper; cover and cook, stirring occasionally, until just tender, 5 to 7 minutes. Meanwhile, shred chicken into bite-size pieces. Transfer cooked vegetables to bowl with chicken; set aside.

4. Heat remaining 1 tablespoon oil in now-empty Dutch oven over medium heat until shimmering. Add mushrooms; cover and cook, stirring occasionally, until mushrooms have released their juice, about 5 minutes. Remove cover and stir in soy sauce and tomato paste. Increase heat to medium-high and cook, stirring frequently, until liquid has evaporated, mushrooms are well browned, and dark fond begins to form, about 5 minutes. Transfer mushrooms to bowl with chicken and vegetables. Set aside.

5. Melt butter in now-empty Dutch oven over medium heat. Stir in flour and cook for 1 minute. Slowly whisk in reserved chicken broth and milk. Bring to simmer, scraping pan bottom to loosen browned bits, and continue to simmer until sauce fully thickens, about 1 minute longer. Season with salt and pepper to taste. Off heat, stir in 2 tablespoons parsley and lemon juice.

6. Stir chicken-vegetable mixture and peas into sauce. Pour mixture into 13 by 9-inch baking dish or casserole dish of similar size. Scatter crumble topping evenly over filling. Bake on baking sheet until filling is bubbling and topping is well browned, 12 to 15 minutes. Sprinkle with remaining 1 tablespoon parsley and serve.

NOTES FROM THE TEST KITCHEN

ENSURING A CRISP CRUMBLE TOPPING

To guarantee a crisp topping, crumble it into small pieces and prebake it before sprinkling it over pot pie.

BARBECUED CHICKEN KEBABS

IN THEORY, BARBECUED CHICKEN KEBABS SOUND pretty great: char-streaked chunks of juicy meat lacquered with sweet-sharp barbecue sauce. Using skewers sounds easy, too—a fast-and-loose sort of way to capture the charms of barbecued chicken without the time and patience needed to cook a whole bird or the focus essential to tending a host of mixed parts. Ah, if only the kebabs lived up to that promise. The quandary is that without an insulating layer of skin, even the fattiest thigh meat can dry out and toughen when exposed to the blazing heat of the grill. And forget about ultra-lean, skinless breast meat: It's a lost cause. Simply slathering barbecue sauce onto skewered chicken chunks—the approach embraced in most recipes—does little to address this fundamental problem. In fact, it's often one of the ruining factors: If applied too early or in too great a volume, the sauce drips off the meat, burns, and fixes the chicken fast to the grill.

My goal was simple: juicy, tender chicken with plenty of sticky-sweet, smoke-tinged flavor. I wanted an everyday sort of recipe, one that would work equally well with white or dark meat (skewered separately since they cook at different rates), and I wanted to use a no-nonsense homemade barbecue sauce. But before I got to the sauce (I would use a simple ketchup-based placeholder for now) I had to ensure that the meat was as moist and tender as possible. Brining was the natural next step.

When meat soaks in salty water, the salt helps pull the liquid into the meat, plumping the chicken and thoroughly seasoning it. The salt also denatures the meat proteins, creating gaps that trap water and guard against drying out. But brining isn't a cure-all: When I made kebabs with chicken breasts and thighs that I had brined after cutting them into pieces (1-inch chunks cooked through relatively quickly yet required enough time on the grill to pick up smoky flavor), the brine made the meat slick, which meant that any barbecue sauce I brushed on toward the end of cooking dribbled off.

Would a dry method work better? Sure enough, a heavily salted dry spice mixture (I let the rubbed chicken sit for 30 minutes before grilling) was just the ticket. As the mixture sat, the salt drew the juice to the surface of the chicken pieces, where it mixed with the seasonings and then flowed back into the chicken. The rub also crisped up on the chicken's exterior as it cooked, forming a craggy surface that the sauce could really cling to. To avoid overpowering the chicken, I steered clear of outspoken spices, settling on both sweet and smoked paprika, the former contributing depth and the latter helping to boost the overall smokiness of the dish. Sugar aided in browning, pleasantly complicating the flavor.

With its ruddy exterior, my chicken now looked the part, but the meat was still not quite moist enough and, despite the improvements made by the spices, lacked sufficient depth of flavor. In a hunt for a solution, I read up on Middle Eastern kebab cookery. I learned that Turkish chefs skewer slices of pure lamb fat between lamb chunks before grilling. The fat melts during cooking, continually basting the lean meat.

Using musky lamb fat in a chicken recipe seemed too weird, but what about another fatty yet more complementary meat: smoky bacon? I cut several strips into 1-inch pieces and spliced the chicken pieces with the fatty squares before putting the kebabs on the grill. Unfortunately, by the time the chicken was cooked through, the bacon tightly wedged between the chicken chunks—had failed to crisp. For my next attempt, I tried wrapping strips of bacon around the kebabs in a spiral-like helix. This time, the bacon turned crunchy, but its flavor overwhelmed that of the chicken.

If strips didn't work, how about rendered bacon fat? I liberally coated the prepared kebabs with bacon drippings and set them on the grill. Within minutes, the fat trickled into the coals and prompted flare-ups, blackening most of the chicken. What wasn't burned, however, was moist and tasted addictively smoky.

If raw strips were too much of a good thing and rendered fat dripped off too quickly, was there an in-between solution? This time around, I finely diced a few slices of bacon and mixed them with the chicken chunks, salt, and spices. After giving the kebabs a 30-minute rest in the refrigerator, I grilled them over a modified two-level, moderately hot fire. (I had piled all of the coals on one side of the grill and left the other half empty to create a cooler "safety zone" on which to rest the kebabs in the event of a flare-up.) Once the chicken was browned on each side (this took about two minutes), I gave it a quarter turn, which resulted in nearly done meat in about eight minutes. At this point, I brushed barbecue sauce on the kebabs, leaving them on the grill for a minute or two longer to give the sauce a chance to caramelize. The bacon bits clung tenaciously to the chicken, producing the best results yet.

But I wasn't finished. The bacon hadn't cooked evenly: Some bits were overly crisp and others still a little limp. I had an idea that would take care of the problem: grinding the bacon into a spreadable paste. Admittedly, the concept was a bit wacky, but I'd come this far, so why not? I tossed a couple of strips of raw bacon into a food processor and ground them down to a paste, which I then mixed with the chicken chunks and dry rub. As before, I rested the coated chicken in the refrigerator for half an hour before grilling. The chicken looked beautiful when it came off the fire: deeply browned and covered in a thick, shiny glaze, with no burned bacon bits in sight. But to my great disappointment, not to mention puzzlement, the chicken was now dry and had lost flavor. I repeated the test to make sure this batch wasn't a fluke and got the same results.

BARBECUED CHICKEN KEBABS

What could be going on? The only thing I was doing differently was coating the chicken in paste rather than simply mixing it with diced bacon combined with the rub. Then it occurred to me: Maybe the fatty ground-up bacon was adhering so well to the chicken that it was acting as a barrier to the salt, which now couldn't penetrate the meat. What if I first salted the meat for 30 minutes, then tossed it with the sugar, spices, and bacon paste right before I put it on the grill? This simple change was the answer: The chicken was juicy, tender, and full-flavored, with a smoky depth that complemented the barbecue sauce.

Now about that sauce. To enliven my classic ketchup, mustard, and cider vinegar mixture, I stirred in some grated onion and a bit of Worcestershire sauce. Brown sugar and a little molasses added just enough bittersweet flavor to counter the tanginess. Simmered for a few minutes, the mixture tasted bright and balanced and boasted a thick, smooth texture that clung well. As I watched this final batch of supremely moist, smoky, perfectly cooked kebabs disappear as fast as I could pull them off the grill, I knew that this recipe had realized its full potential.

—MATTHEW CARD, *Cook's Illustrated*

Barbecued Chicken Kebabs

SERVES 4 TO 6

We prefer flavorful thigh meat for these kebabs, but you can use white meat. Whichever you choose, don't mix white and dark meat on the same skewer since they cook at different rates. If you have thin pieces of chicken, cut them larger than 1 inch and roll or fold them into approximately 1-inch cubes. Use the large holes of a box grater to grate the onion.

NOTES FROM THE TEST KITCHEN

BACON PASTE: WEIRD, BUT IT WORKS

To create a protective coating that keeps the chicken moist on the grill, we chop bacon, pulse it in the food processor until smooth, and then toss the resulting paste (along with sugar and spices) with raw chicken chunks.

SAUCE

- **½ cup ketchup**
- **¼ cup light or mild molasses**
- **2 tablespoons grated onion**
- **2 tablespoons Worcestershire sauce**
- **2 tablespoons Dijon mustard**
- **2 tablespoons cider vinegar**
- **1 tablespoon packed light brown sugar**

KEBABS

- **2 pounds boneless, skinless chicken thighs or breasts, trimmed and cut into 1-inch cubes**
- **2 teaspoons kosher salt**
- **2 tablespoons sweet paprika**
- **4 teaspoons sugar**
- **2 teaspoons smoked paprika**
- **2 slices bacon, cut into ½-inch pieces**
- **4 (12-inch) metal skewers**

1. FOR THE SAUCE: Bring all ingredients to simmer in small saucepan over medium heat; cook, stirring occasionally, until sauce reaches ketchup-like consistency and is reduced to about 1 cup, 5 to 7 minutes. Transfer ½ cup sauce to small bowl; set aside remaining sauce for serving.

2. FOR THE KEBABS: Toss chicken and salt together in large bowl; cover with plastic wrap and refrigerate for at least 30 minutes or up to 1 hour.

3A. FOR A CHARCOAL GRILL: Open bottom vent completely. Light large chimney starter three-quarters full with charcoal briquettes (4½ quarts). When top coals are partially covered with ash, pour evenly over half of grill. Set cooking grate in place, cover, and open lid vent completely. Heat grill until hot, about 5 minutes.

3B. FOR A GAS GRILL: Turn all burners to high, cover, and heat grill until hot, about 15 minutes. Leave primary burner on high and turn off other burner(s).

4. Clean and oil cooking grate. Pat chicken dry with paper towels. Combine sweet paprika, sugar, and smoked paprika in bowl. Process bacon in food processor until smooth paste forms, 30 to 45 seconds, scraping down bowl twice during processing. Add bacon paste and spice mixture to chicken; mix with hands or rubber spatula until ingredients are thoroughly blended and chicken is completely coated. Thread meat onto skewers, rolling or folding meat as necessary to maintain 1-inch cubes.

5. Grill kebabs (covered if using gas), turning one-quarter turn every 2 to 2½ minutes until well browned and slightly charred, 8 minutes for breasts and 10 minutes for thighs. (If flare-ups occur, slide kebabs to cool side of grill until fire dies down.) Brush top surface of kebabs with ¼ cup sauce; flip and cook until sauce is brown in spots, about 1 minute. Brush second side with remaining ¼ cup sauce; flip and continue to cook until brown in spots and breasts register 160 degrees and thighs register 175 degrees, about 1 minute longer. Remove kebabs from grill and let rest for 5 minutes. Serve, passing reserved barbecue sauce separately.

GRILLED STUFFED CHICKEN BREASTS

FOR BETTER OR WORSE, EVERY DISH THAT'S A good idea inside the kitchen seems eventually to make its way outside onto the grill. The transition is not always successful. Take the classic dish chicken cordon bleu. Baked in the oven, the stuffing of sharp, nutty melted cheese and salty sliced ham deftly solves the problem of dry, bland chicken breasts, lending both moisture and flavor to this otherwise lean cut. But try bringing it out to the grill, and that same stuffing introduces more problems than it solves. The threat of leaky cheese causing flare-ups as it drips from the chicken and into the coals compounds the standard grilling difficulties: evenly cooking the meat and avoiding a tough, leathery exterior.

Of the many existing recipes I tried, all called for boneless, skinless breasts, though each had its own stuffing method. One required tediously cramming the filling into a narrow pocket. In another the breast was split like a hot dog bun and heaped with a filling that spilled from the top like a mound of sauerkraut. In one notable failure the filling was sandwiched between two breasts but not sealed in, producing a brilliant burned-cheese fireball on the grill. The most successful approach was to butterfly the meat by splitting the breast horizontally and leaving it hinged like a book, but even that didn't completely manage to keep the filling in place.

Still, the promise of moist, smoky chicken wrapped around a meaty, cheesy filling that stayed where it was put was too appealing to pass up. To make good on this dish, I decided to work from the inside out, starting with perfecting my filling.

Grilled chicken, with its smokiness, requires stronger flavors than the deli ham and Swiss cheese in most cordon bleu recipes. I opted instead for more flavorful prosciutto and fontina, a moist melting cheese with moderate tang. Butterflying seemed like my best bet, so I sliced a breast nearly in half horizontally, splayed it open, layered on prosciutto, then sprinkled it with grated fontina. I rolled the breast around the filling like a jellyroll and secured it with kitchen twine. So far, so good, but I was curious to see how it would fare on the grill.

Disaster started as a tiny drop of cheese oozed out the end and grew into a lavalike eruption, dropping onto the coals and flaring up. The result: chicken with a blackened, sooty exterior and no cheese left in the center. Adding more twine to the bundle did nothing to hold the melting cheese in place. Soaking toothpicks in water, then using them to secure the seams of the chicken, was like trying to plug a dam with chewing gum.

Then a thought struck me: Maybe the key was not to rely on the cumbersome chicken to keep the cheese in place, but to use something more flexible: the prosciutto. For my next test, I tightly wrapped the prosciutto around the cheese before I placed the whole bundle inside the chicken cavity. It worked like a charm. To make wrapping and stuffing even easier, instead of grating the fontina, I cut it into 3-inch-long, ½-inch-wide sticks.

As for the stuffing, the only thing remaining was to add a bit of moisture and flavor. A simple compound butter enlivened by shallots and tarragon did the trick; I spread it over the inside of the chicken before adding the prosciutto and cheese. I was now ready to turn my attention to the exterior, which, despite the success of the filling, was still tough to chew.

The problem was that while boneless, skinless chicken breasts are easy to butterfly and stuff, the lean, exposed meat rapidly dries out in the intense heat of a grill. Brining the chicken in a saltwater solution for 30 minutes can help it retain more moisture with any cooking method, and it certainly helped in this case. Switching from a standard one-level fire to a modified two-level

GRILLED STUFFED CHICKEN BREASTS WITH PROSCIUTTO AND FONTINA

fire (in which all the coals are banked on one side of the grill) was also an improvement, allowing me to first sear the breasts over the hot coals for color and flavor, then finish cooking them over more moderate indirect heat. But the fact remained that my chicken was dry and leathery, and the most flavorful stuffing in the world wasn't going to cure it.

What I needed was some kind of protective wrapping to shield the delicate meat from the direct heat of the flames. I tried wrapping the chicken with bacon, pancetta, and some of the prosciutto that I used to wrap the cheese. But on the grill, these fatty meats caused flare-ups, and they also shrank and crumbled off the chicken long before it hit the table. But hold on—why was I spending time trying to create an artificial skin for the chicken? I'd been so focused on the traditional recipe and its use of skinless breasts that the most obvious solution failed to occur to me: starting with skin-on breasts.

Skin-on breasts almost always come bone-in, but any concerns I had that the presence of the bone would make the meat difficult to butterfly proved unfounded: The only modification I needed to make was to slice from the thicker side of the meat, near the breastbone. Since bone-in breasts are larger than their boneless cousins, I anticipated a longer cooking time on the grill. Again I seared the breasts on both sides over the hot side of the grill until well colored, then moved them to the cooler side of the grill to finish cooking. To my delight, the skin protected the exterior of the chicken, releasing fat and basting the breast as it cooked. Even better, the bone also worked to my advantage, helping to prevent shrinkage and shielding the underside of the meat from the direct heat of the grill. While the cooking time had been extended by 10 minutes, the finished chicken was well worth the wait.

For serving, I opted to remove the chicken from the breastbone, which allowed me to slice it and display the stuffing. This proved remarkably easy (and didn't disturb the filling at all), requiring just the slide of a knife blade under the meat and against the ribs. Then voilà—a boneless stuffed breast that I could enjoy straight through the grilling season.

—BRYAN ROOF, *Cook's Illustrated*

NOTES FROM THE TEST KITCHEN

ASSEMBLING STUFFED CHICKEN BREASTS

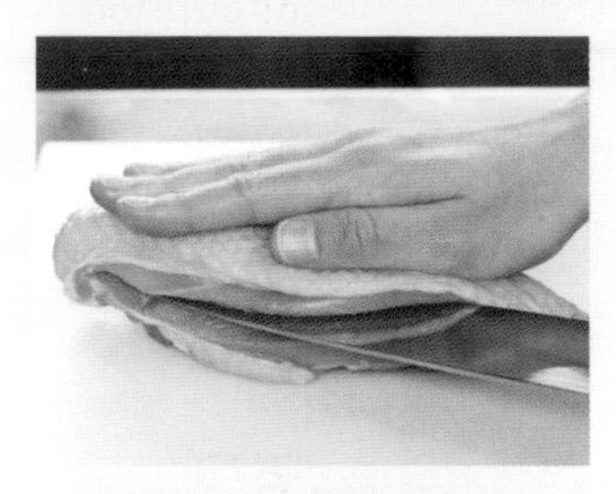

1. Starting on thick side closest to breastbone, cut horizontal pocket in each breast, stopping ½ inch from edge.

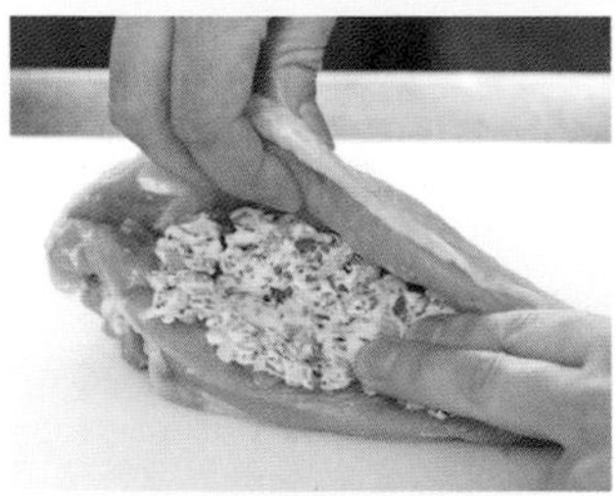

2. Spread equal amount of compound butter inside each breast.

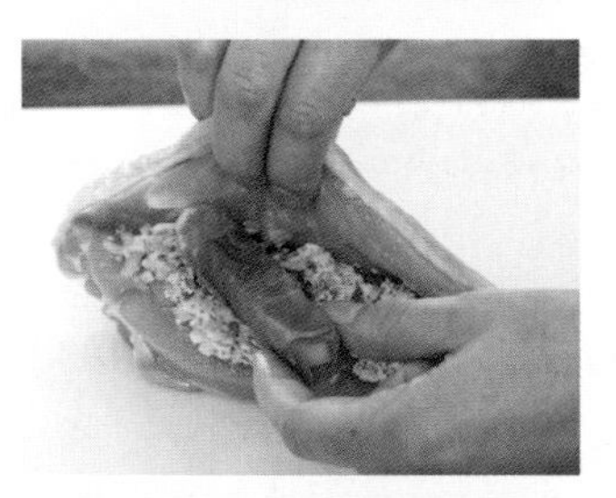

3. Place 1 prosciutto-wrapped piece of cheese inside each breast and fold breast over to enclose.

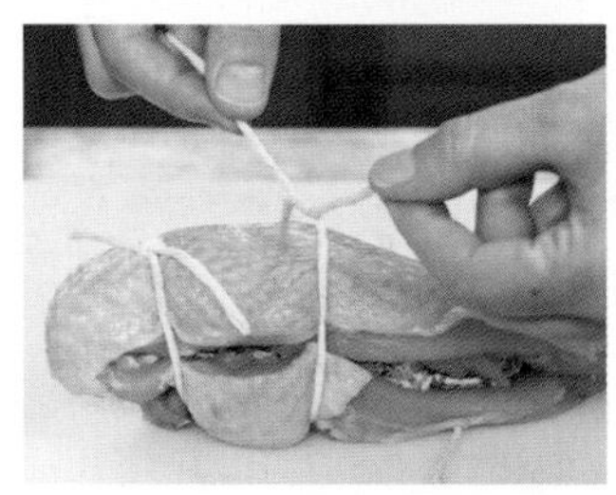

4. Tie each breast with three 12-inch pieces of kitchen twine at even intervals.

CARVING STUFFED CHICKEN BREASTS

Insert tip of chef's knife into chicken breast just above breastbone. While gently lifting breast meat away from rib cage, cut with tip of knife against ribs, following contour, to separate meat.

Grilled Stuffed Chicken Breasts with Prosciutto and Fontina

SERVES 4

You can serve the chicken on the bone, but we prefer to carve it off and slice it before serving.

- **4 (12-ounce) bone-in split chicken breasts, trimmed**
- **Salt and pepper**
- **4 tablespoons unsalted butter, softened**
- **1 shallot, minced**
- **4 teaspoons minced fresh tarragon**
- **2 ounces fontina cheese, rind removed, cut into four 3 by ½-inch sticks**
- **4 thin slices prosciutto (2 ounces)**

1. Cut horizontal pocket in each breast. Dissolve 3 tablespoons salt in 1 quart cold water in large container. Add chicken and refrigerate, covered, for 30 minutes.

2A. FOR A CHARCOAL GRILL: Open bottom vent completely. Light large chimney starter filled with charcoal briquettes (6 quarts). When top coals are partially covered with ash, pour evenly over half of grill. Set cooking grate in place, cover, and open lid vent completely. Heat grill until hot, about 5 minutes.

2B. FOR A GAS GRILL: Turn all burners to high, cover, and heat grill until hot, about 15 minutes. Leave primary burner on high and turn off other burner(s).

3. Clean and oil cooking grate. Combine butter, shallot, and tarragon in bowl. Roll each piece of cheese in 1 slice prosciutto. Remove chicken from brine, dry thoroughly inside and out with paper towels, and season inside and out with pepper. Spread equal amount of butter mixture inside each breast. Place 1 prosciutto-wrapped piece of cheese inside each breast and fold breast over to enclose. Evenly space three 12-inch pieces of kitchen twine beneath each breast and tie, trimming any excess.

4. Place chicken breasts, skin side down, over hot part of grill and cook (covered if using gas) until well browned, 3 to 5 minutes. Flip chicken and cook until second side is just opaque, about 2 minutes. Move chicken, skin side up, to cool side of grill, with thicker side facing fire. Cover grill and continue to cook until chicken registers 160 degrees, 25 to 30 minutes longer (30 to 40 minutes if using gas). Transfer chicken to carving board and let rest, tented loosely with foil, for 10 minutes. Remove twine, then carve meat from bone. Carve into ½-inch-thick slices and serve.

VARIATION

Grilled Stuffed Chicken Breasts with Black Forest Ham and Gruyère

Substitute 1 teaspoon minced fresh thyme for tarragon and add 1 tablespoon Dijon mustard to butter in step 3. Substitute 4 slices Black Forest ham for prosciutto and Gruyère cheese for fontina.

BARBECUED DRY-RUBBED CHICKEN

WHEN IT COMES TO FLAVORING BARBECUED chicken, there are two schools of thought: those who rely on sauce, and those, including many pro pit masters, who put their faith in a mixture of spices known as a dry rub.

The barbecue sauce is easy—slather it on near the end of cooking and it turns into an attractive, tasty glaze. On the downside, the sauce never flavors the meat deeply, it can make the skin soggy, and it requires more time and a slew of ingredients. You could use the bottled stuff, but it's rarely great. In contrast, dry rubs, which are rubbed into the chicken, do flavor the meat well and don't result in soggy skin. Unfortunately, neither do they provide the glaze that results when barbecue sauce meets heat. I sought to develop a dry rub to do double duty, both flavoring and glazing the chicken.

A couple of factors were a given. First, with both white and dark meat fans to please, I'd use drumsticks, split breasts, and thighs. Next, I'd include sugar to duplicate the sweetness of barbecue sauce and to help form a glaze. I skipped over Demerara and turbinado sugars, whose large crystals are less likely to melt into a glaze. I tested white sugar (too sweet in the quantity necessary), light brown sugar (not bad), and more complexly flavored dark brown sugar (the hands-down winner). Dark brown sugar has almost 20 percent more moisture than white sugar, which helped it melt reliably.

The spices were a matter of taste, and we were after classic barbecue. Chili powder and paprika helped define that flavor. Onion powder mimicked the fresh onion in homemade barbecue sauces, and dry mustard lent brightness. Salt, pepper, and cayenne rounded out the rub.

A single coating of my dry rub resulted in a skimpy, blotchy glaze. I handled that problem by dredging the

BARBECUED DRY-RUBBED CHICKEN

chicken pieces in the dry rub again halfway through cooking, when the sugar began to melt. The second coating adhered to the sticky, partially melted "base coat," and together they melted into a very nice lacquer. Early on I learned the benefits of allowing the raw chicken to rest, 30 minutes at least, in its initial rub coating. First, it was juicier and tasted better because the salt and brown sugar in the rub seasoned the meat. Second, the salt and sugar also drew some of the moisture in the chicken to its surface, which jump-started the glazing process.

Now I had to engineer a grilling technique that would cook the chicken through without burning its sugary coating. Testing every possible combination of heat, position, and time showed that grilling the chicken directly over medium-low heat (about 325 degrees) let the skin slowly render. As the melting fat blended with the dry rub and enriched the glaze, the meat gently cooked through. I let the cooked chicken rest, covered with foil; the residual heat melted any grains of sugar that had survived the grill.

Granted, the recipe and technique are unconventional, but this chicken is juicy with a full barbecue flavor and a light, lacquered, even glaze. Bottled barbecue sauce just lost its place in my pantry.

—ADAM RIED, *Cook's Country*

Barbecued Dry-Rubbed Chicken

SERVES 4 TO 6

Apply the second coating of spice with a light hand or it won't melt into a glaze.

- **3 tablespoons packed dark brown sugar**
- **2 teaspoons chili powder**
- **2 teaspoons paprika**
- **1½ teaspoons pepper**
- **1 teaspoon dry mustard**
- **1 teaspoon onion powder**
- **1 teaspoon salt**
- **¼ teaspoon cayenne pepper**
- **3 pounds bone-in chicken pieces (breasts, thighs, and drumsticks, or mix, breasts cut in half), trimmed**

1. Combine sugar, chili powder, paprika, pepper, dry mustard, onion powder, salt, and cayenne in bowl. Transfer half of dry rub to shallow dish; set aside. Pat chicken dry with paper towels and coat over and under skin with remaining rub. Transfer to plate and refrigerate, covered, for at least 30 minutes or up to 1 hour.

2A. FOR A CHARCOAL GRILL: Open bottom vent completely. Light large chimney starter half full with charcoal briquettes (3 quarts). When top coals are partially covered with ash, pour evenly over grill. Set cooking grate in place, cover, and open lid vent completely. Heat grill until hot, about 5 minutes.

2B. FOR A GAS GRILL: Turn all burners to high, cover, and heat grill until hot, about 15 minutes. Turn all burners to medium-low.

3. Clean and oil cooking grate. Arrange chicken skin side down and grill until skin is well browned and crisp, 15 to 20 minutes.

4. Lightly coat skin side of chicken with reserved rub and return to grill, skin side up. Continue to grill, covered, until rub has melted into glaze and breasts register 160 degrees and thighs/drumsticks register 175 degrees, 15 to 20 minutes longer. Transfer chicken to platter, tent with foil, and let rest for 5 minutes. Serve.

NOTES FROM THE TEST KITCHEN

TURNING A RUB INTO A GLAZE

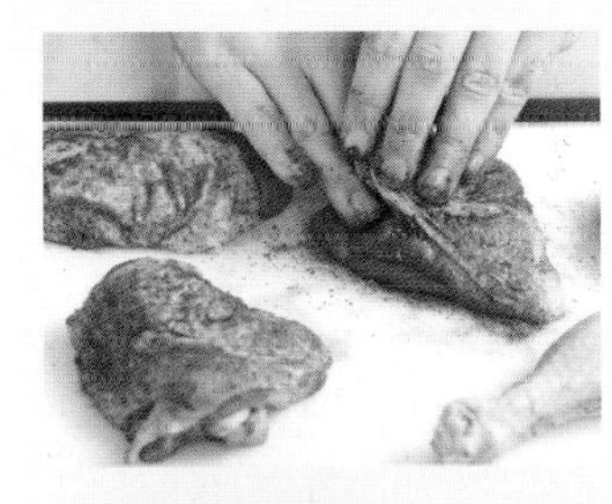

1. To season meat and jump-start glaze, put half of rub over and under skin. Then let chicken rest 30 minutes before grilling.

2. Cook chicken on grill until skin is nicely browned and crisp. Then dredge skin side of chicken in remaining rub.

3. Return chicken to grill, skin side up, and continue cooking until rub melts into glaze and chicken has cooked through.

CHAPTER 8

SEAFOOD

STIR-FRIED SHRIMP

HERE IN THE TEST KITCHEN, WE'VE ALREADY established and perfected a stir-frying technique for the flat American stovetop: Batch-sear marinated meat and vegetables in a hot skillet, not a wok (its concave shape is designed to sit in a cylindrical pit); add aromatics; and finish with a flavorful, quick-simmered sauce. It works with just about any type of protein—beef, chicken, pork, even tofu—so how could it fail with shrimp?

That was the question—after the first tightly curled, rubbery shrimp we choked down proved that meat and shrimp are not interchangeable. To begin with, shrimp cook faster than meat. Second, marinades seem to roll right off their tightly grained flesh and end up merely burning in the hot skillet.

Chinese cooks often work around the problem of tough stir-fried shrimp by cooking them shell-on to protect their delicate flesh, but neither crunching into shrimp shells nor peeling them at the table appealed to us. A better approach would be to modify our stir-fry technique, customizing it to produce plump, juicy, well-seasoned shrimp in a balanced, flavorful sauce.

Most stir-fry recipes suffer from a basic flaw: They don't account for the fact that home cooks lack high-output, restaurant-style burners. Without this blazing heat, recipes that call for cooking all the meat in a single batch turn out lackluster results: The pan can't maintain temperatures hot enough to effectively sear the food before the whole mess overcooks in a cloud of steam.

That's where our batch-cooking method comes in. To keep the pan good and hot throughout the process, we use a large, shallow nonstick skillet (which, on a Western range, heats more efficiently than a wok and provides maximum surface area for evaporation), crank up the flame to high, and cook each component separately and in small quantities so that the pieces have a chance to thoroughly brown. The meat is browned first, then set aside while vegetables are seared and aromatics such as garlic, ginger, and scallions are briefly sautéed, after which the protein goes back in, a sauce is added, and everything simmers until just cooked through.

In this case, however, I needed a buffer between the heat and the shrimp. Cooking them shell-on was out, but I wondered if the solution was as simple as fabricating an artificial "shell" to help protect the peeled shrimp. With one such technique, a traditional Chinese method known as "velveting," the protein is coated in a starch-egg-oil slurry before cooking to set up a barrier between the meat and the pan. I tried every iteration of this approach I could think of: cornstarch, flour, whole eggs, and egg whites. Some of the dishes showed slight improvements, but overall they were uninspiring.

If the problem was overcooking, maybe I needed to step back even further to reconsider the super-hot fire. Traditionally, high heat serves two purposes: speed and flavorful browning. The time and temperature window for perfectly plump, just-firm shrimp, however, is narrow. An internal temperature of 140 degrees is ideal, but at even a few degrees beyond that the shrimp turn to rubber, so high heat is actually hazardous. Substantial browning, meanwhile, doesn't occur until well above 300 degrees—a surefire path to overcooking. Since shrimp stir-fries usually call for an assertive sauce, and the vegetables could still develop deep color, I wondered what would happen if I skipped the browning.

Abandoning the high-heat method, I turned the burner down to medium-low, gently parcooked a batch of shrimp, removed them from the skillet, then turned up the heat to sear the vegetables, sauté the aromatics, and finish cooking the shrimp with the sauce. This worked beautifully. Not a single taster missed a browned exterior, instead commenting on the shrimp's supreme tenderness. Reversing the approach—cooking the veggies and aromatics over high heat, then turning the heat down for the shrimp—made the process more efficient.

It was time to think more deeply about the marinade. The test kitchen's standard Chinese rice wine–soy sauce mixture for beef, chicken, and pork wasn't doing much for the shrimp; in fact, it merely overwhelmed its sweet taste. Instead, I tried another common Chinese texture-boosting technique, which I hoped would also improve flavor: soaking the shrimp in a saltwater brine, which both seasons and hydrates the flesh. Their texture became noticeably juicier, but I still wanted more flavor in the shrimp themselves. I knew infusing the brine with aromatics—garlic, specifically—wouldn't work, since the clove's flavorful compounds are mostly oil-soluble and thus don't come through in a watery solution.

So was there any need to introduce water at all? A few years back when I developed a recipe for Spanish-style garlic shrimp, I marinated the shrimp in a combination of oil, salt, and minced garlic. The salt not only helped the shrimp retain moisture as they cooked, but it also drew flavorful compounds out of the garlic's cells, which then dissolved in the oil and spread evenly around the shellfish. Sure enough, this method worked like a charm for my shrimp. Even better, the technique lent itself to a flavor variation with ginger.

As for an assertive sauce, the heavily soy-based brews we turn to for meat stir-fries were runny and salty. Better suited to the shrimp (and more traditional in Chinese cuisine) were sweeter or spicier sauces flavored with garlic and chiles and reduced to a consistency that tightly adhered to the shellfish. I tweaked my vinegar-based hot and sour sauce and whipped up a spicy Sichuan-style sauce along with an intense garlic sauce, all of which complemented the shrimp perfectly. By combining Chinese traditions with new techniques, these from-the-sea stir-fries would no longer play second fiddle to their land-based counterparts.

—J. KENJI LOPEZ ALT, *Cook's Illustrated*

Stir-Fried Shrimp with Snow Peas and Red Bell Pepper in Hot and Sour Sauce

SERVES 4

Serve with Basic White Rice (see page 40).

- **1 pound extra-large shrimp (21 to 25 per pound), peeled, deveined, and tails removed**
- **3 tablespoons vegetable oil**
- **2 garlic cloves, 1 minced and 1 thinly sliced**
- **1 tablespoon grated fresh ginger**
- **½ teaspoon salt**
- **3 tablespoons sugar**
- **3 tablespoons white vinegar**
- **1 tablespoon Asian chili-garlic sauce**
- **1 tablespoon dry sherry or Shaoxing wine**
- **1 tablespoon ketchup**
- **2 teaspoons toasted sesame oil**
- **2 teaspoons cornstarch**
- **1 teaspoon soy sauce**
- **1 large shallot, sliced thin**
- **8 ounces snow peas or sugar snap peas, strings removed**
- **1 red bell pepper, stemmed, seeded, and cut into ¾-inch pieces**

1. Combine shrimp, 1 tablespoon vegetable oil, minced garlic, ginger, and salt in bowl. Let sit at room temperature for 30 minutes.

2. Meanwhile, whisk sugar, vinegar, chili-garlic sauce, sherry, ketchup, sesame oil, cornstarch, and soy sauce together in second bowl. Combine sliced garlic with shallot in third bowl.

3. Heat 1 tablespoon more vegetable oil in 12-inch nonstick skillet over high heat until just smoking. Add snow peas and bell pepper and cook, stirring frequently, until vegetables begin to brown, 1½ to 2 minutes. Transfer vegetables to bowl.

4. Add remaining 1 tablespoon vegetable oil to now-empty skillet and heat until just smoking. Add garlic-shallot mixture and cook, stirring frequently, until just beginning to brown, about 30 seconds. Add shrimp, reduce heat to medium-low, and cook, stirring frequently, until shrimp are light pink on both sides, 1 to 1½ minutes. Whisk soy sauce mixture to recombine and add to skillet; return to high heat and cook, stirring constantly, until sauce is thickened and shrimp are cooked through, 1 to 2 minutes. Return vegetables to skillet, toss to combine, and serve.

NOTES FROM THE TEST KITCHEN

DEVEINING SHRIMP

1. After removing shell, use paring knife to make shallow cut along back of shrimp so that vein is exposed.

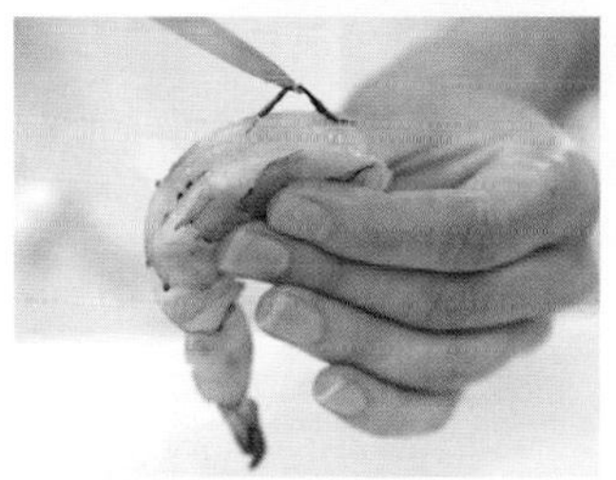

2. Use tip of knife to lift vein out of shrimp. Discard vein by wiping blade against paper towel.

FOR TENDER STIR-FRIED SHRIMP, LOWER THE HEAT

For perfectly plump, juicy shrimp, we cook the vegetables first—and then turn the heat way down when the shrimp are added to the pan.

VARIATIONS

Stir-Fried Shrimp with Garlicky Eggplant, Scallions, and Cashews

SERVES 4

Do not peel the eggplant as the skin helps hold it together during cooking. Serve with Basic White Rice (see page 40).

- **1 pound extra-large shrimp (21 to 25 per pound), peeled, deveined, and tails removed**
- **3 tablespoons vegetable oil**
- **6 garlic cloves, 1 minced and 5 thinly sliced**
- **½ teaspoon salt**
- **2 tablespoons soy sauce**
- **2 tablespoons oyster sauce**
- **2 tablespoons dry sherry or Shaoxing wine**
- **2 tablespoons sugar**
- **1 tablespoon toasted sesame oil**
- **1 tablespoon white vinegar**
- **2 teaspoons cornstarch**
- **⅛ teaspoon red pepper flakes**
- **6 scallions, greens cut into 1-inch pieces and whites sliced thin**
- **½ cup unsalted cashews**
- **12 ounces eggplant, cut into ¾-inch dice**

1. Combine shrimp, 1 tablespoon vegetable oil, minced garlic, and salt in bowl. Let sit at room temperature for 30 minutes.

2. Meanwhile, whisk soy sauce, oyster sauce, sherry, sugar, sesame oil, vinegar, cornstarch, and pepper flakes together in second bowl. Combine scallion whites, sliced garlic, and cashews in third bowl.

3. Heat 1 tablespoon more vegetable oil in 12-inch nonstick skillet over high heat until just smoking. Add eggplant and cook, stirring frequently, until lightly browned, 3 to 6 minutes. Add scallion greens and continue to cook until scallion greens begin to brown and eggplant is fully tender, 1 to 2 minutes longer. Transfer vegetables to bowl.

4. Add remaining 1 tablespoon vegetable oil to now-empty skillet and heat until just smoking. Add garlic-scallion-cashew mixture and cook, stirring frequently, until just beginning to brown, about 30 seconds. Add shrimp, reduce heat to medium-low, and cook, stirring frequently, until shrimp are light pink on both sides, 1 to 1½ minutes. Whisk soy sauce mixture to recombine and add to skillet; return to high heat and cook, stirring constantly, until sauce is thickened and shrimp are cooked through, 1 to 2 minutes. Return vegetables to skillet, toss to combine, and serve.

Stir-Fried Sichuan-Style Shrimp with Zucchini, Red Bell Pepper, and Peanuts

SERVES 4

This recipe is spicy. If you can find a Chinese long pepper, use it in place of the jalapeño. Broad bean chili paste is also referred to as chili bean sauce or horse bean chili paste. If you can't find it, increase the amount of Asian chili-garlic sauce by 1 teaspoon. Serve with Basic White Rice (see page 40).

- **1 pound extra-large shrimp (21 to 25 per pound), peeled, deveined, and tails removed**
- **3 tablespoons vegetable oil**
- **2 garlic cloves, 1 minced and 1 thinly sliced**
- **½ teaspoon salt**
- **2 tablespoons dry sherry or Shaoxing wine**
- **1 tablespoon white vinegar or Chinese black vinegar**
- **1 tablespoon broad bean chili paste**
- **1 tablespoon Asian chili-garlic sauce**
- **2 teaspoons soy sauce**
- **2 teaspoons Chinese hot chili oil or toasted sesame oil**
- **1 teaspoon sugar**
- **1 teaspoon cornstarch**
- **½ teaspoon Sichuan peppercorns, toasted and ground (optional)**
- **1 jalapeño chile, stemmed, halved, seeded, and sliced thin on bias**
- **½ cup roasted unsalted peanuts**
- **1 small zucchini, cut into ¾-inch dice**
- **1 red bell pepper, seeded and cut into ¾-inch dice**
- **½ cup lightly packed cilantro**

1. Combine shrimp, 1 tablespoon vegetable oil, minced garlic, and salt in bowl. Let sit at room temperature for 30 minutes.

2. Meanwhile, whisk sherry, vinegar, chili paste, chili-garlic sauce, soy sauce, chili oil, sugar, cornstarch, and ground peppercorns, if using, in second bowl. Combine jalapeño, sliced garlic, and peanuts in third bowl.

3. Heat 1 tablespoon more vegetable oil in 12-inch nonstick skillet over high heat until just smoking. Add zucchini and bell pepper and cook, stirring frequently, until zucchini is tender and well browned, 2 to 4 minutes. Transfer vegetables to bowl.

4. Add remaining 1 tablespoon vegetable oil to now-empty skillet and heat until just smoking. Add garlic-jalapeño-peanut mixture and cook, stirring frequently, until just beginning to brown, about 30 seconds. Add shrimp, reduce heat to medium-low, and cook, stirring frequently, until shrimp are light pink on both sides, 1 to 1½ minutes. Whisk soy sauce mixture to recombine and add to skillet; return to high heat and cook, stirring constantly, until sauce is thickened and shrimp are cooked through, 1 to 2 minutes. Return vegetables to skillet, add cilantro, toss to combine, and serve.

GRILLED SHRIMP TACOS

IF IT'S A HEALTHY AND FLAVORFUL DINNER OFF the grill you're looking for, you can't go wrong with a shrimp taco paired with a fruit salsa. Easy, refreshing, and quick to make, this dish should be in everyone's recipe repertoire. But after trying a few existing recipes, I discovered that most out there are riddled with problems. Underseasoned, overcooked shrimp paired with a salsa that was either watery or cloyingly sweet was not something I wanted to have for dinner, healthy or not. I headed to the test kitchen to see what I could do.

Based on past experience, I already knew the best way to tackle the overcooked shrimp issue. Small shrimp on a hot grill cook so quickly that it is tricky to keep them from becoming tough and dry. The test kitchen has found that threading the shrimp tightly on skewers helps slow down the cooking process enough to let the outside develop a slight char while the inside remains tender. Sprinkling a small amount of sugar over one side of the skewered shrimp promotes browning and complements their briny sweetness. I also knew I'd need the grill set up with a hot side for a quick sear and a cooler side for cooking the shrimp through gently. I grilled my shrimp, sugared side down, over the hot side for a few minutes. When a nice crust had developed, I flipped the skewers and moved them to the cool part of the grill to finish up. This method gave me perfect results. The shrimp had a smoky crust on the outside and were tender and moist on the inside.

With my technique settled, I began working on the flavor of the shrimp. Borrowing again from proven test kitchen techniques, I knew that butterflying and marinating the shrimp would boost their flavor considerably. I tested a number of different marinade ingredients, but tasters settled on a combo of garlic, cayenne, chili powder, cumin, and coriander as their favorite. A colleague suggested quickly cooking the spices in a small amount of oil before tossing them

NOTES FROM THE TEST KITCHEN

BUTTERFLYING AND SKEWERING SHRIMP

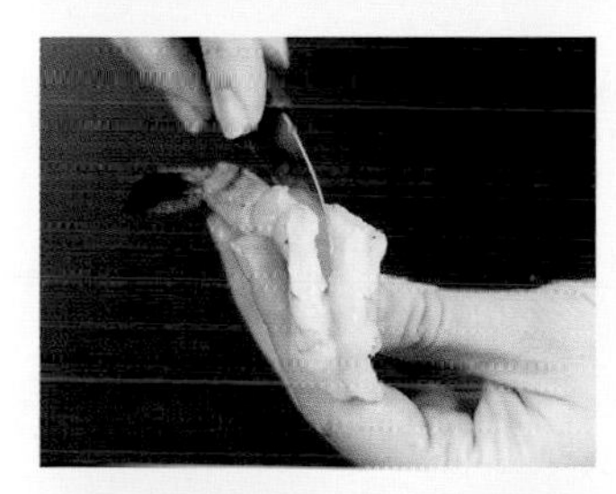

1. After deveining shrimp, use knife to deepen cut slightly along outside curve of shrimp.

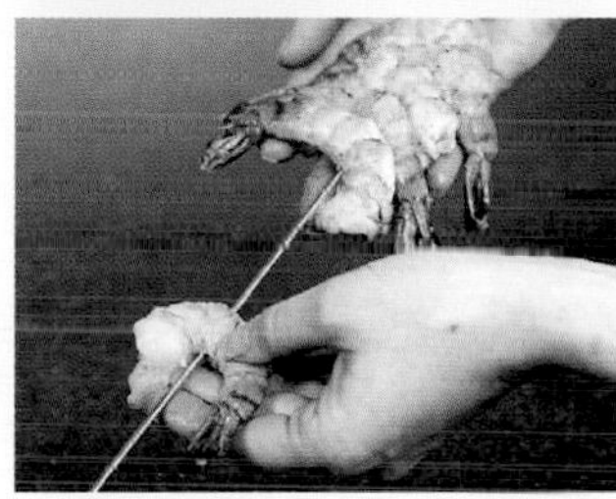

2. Pack shrimp tightly on skewer, alternating direction of shrimp so about 12 will fit snugly on each skewer.

CUTTING PINEAPPLE FOR FRUIT SALSA

1. After trimming off bottom and top of pineapple, set fruit on its bottom and cut off skin in strips, top to bottom, with sharp knife.

2. Quarter pineapple lengthwise, then cut tough core from each quarter and chop pineapple as directed in recipe.

GRILLED SHRIMP TACOS WITH PINEAPPLE-JÍCAMA SALSA

with the shrimp to marinate. This bloomed the spices and helped deepen the flavor of the shrimp even more.

With the shrimp ready to go, it was time to work on the fresh fruit salsa. I chopped up all the fruits I could get my hands on that I thought might work in a salsa: oranges, papayas, mangoes, and kiwis, to name a few. I liked a number of combinations, but ultimately the duo of pineapple and jícama (a refreshing, slightly sweet root vegetable with white crunchy flesh that is grown in Mexico and South America) won the day. Minced jalapeño gave my salsa a touch of heat to cut the sweetness, and cilantro and lime juice added the right tang and herbal flavors.

Excited to try my creation, I fired up the grill. I wrapped my shrimp in a lightly charred tortilla and topped them with the salsa. It took only one bite to realize something was missing. The tacos were flavorful, no doubt, but something was amiss with the texture. Tasters wanted something smooth to balance all of the crunch. I lightly mashed an avocado with some lime juice and salt to make a quick guacamole. After topping each taco with a spoonful of the avocado mixture, I knew I had done it. Tasters agreed; these tacos were so good and full of flavor, they'd make them again and again.

—KELLY PRICE, *America's Test Kitchen Books*

Grilled Shrimp Tacos with Pineapple-Jícama Salsa

SERVES 6

Don't let the shrimp marinate for longer than 15 minutes or the acid marinade will begin to "cook" the shrimp and turn them rubbery. To make this dish spicier, add the chile seeds. Be sure to use a ripe avocado for this recipe.

- **1 avocado, peeled and pitted**
- **¼ cup lime juice (2 limes)**
- **Salt**
- **10 ounces jícama, peeled and cut into ¼-inch pieces**
- **2 cups pineapple, cut into ¼-inch pieces**
- **2 tablespoons minced fresh cilantro**
- **1 jalapeño chile, stemmed, seeded, and minced**
- **2 tablespoons vegetable oil**
- **3 garlic cloves, minced**
- **2 teaspoons chili powder**
- **1 teaspoon ground coriander**
- **1 teaspoon ground cumin**
- **¼ teaspoon cayenne pepper**
- **1½ pounds extra-large shrimp (21 to 25 per pound), peeled, deveined, butterflied, and tails removed**
- **3–4 (12-inch) metal skewers**
- **½ teaspoon sugar**
- **12 (6-inch) corn tortillas**

1. Mash avocado with 1 tablespoon lime juice in bowl until some small chunks remain. Season with salt to taste. Refrigerate, covered, until ready to serve.

2. Combine 2 tablespoons more lime juice, jícama, pineapple, cilantro, and jalapeño in bowl. Season with salt to taste. Cover and refrigerate until ready to serve.

3. Heat oil in 8-inch skillet over medium heat. Add garlic, chili powder, coriander, cumin, and cayenne and cook until fragrant, about 1 minute. Transfer to medium bowl and let cool to room temperature, then stir in remaining 1 tablespoon lime juice and ½ teaspoon salt.

4. Add shrimp to spice mixture and toss to coat. Refrigerate, covered, for 15 minutes. Thread shrimp onto skewers, then sprinkle one side of shrimp with sugar.

5A. FOR A CHARCOAL GRILL: Open bottom grill vent completely. Light large chimney starter filled with charcoal briquettes (6 quarts). When top coals are partially covered with ash, pour evenly over half of grill. Set cooking grate in place, cover, and open lid vent completely. Heat grill until hot, about 5 minutes.

5B. FOR A GAS GRILL: Turn all burners to high, cover, and heat grill until hot, about 15 minutes. Leave all burners on high.

6. Clean and oil cooking grate. Place shrimp, sugared side down, on hot side of grill and cook (covered if using gas) until lightly charred on first side, 3 to 4 minutes.

7. Flip shrimp; slide to cooler part of grill (turn all burners to low if using gas). Cover and continue to cook until second side is no longer translucent, 1 to 2 minutes longer. Transfer shrimp to platter; remove from skewers.

8. Working in batches, place a few tortillas in single layer on grill (turn all burners to medium if using gas) and cook until warm, about 10 seconds per side. Wrap tortillas in aluminum foil to keep warm.

9. Place 3 shrimp in each tortilla, top with 1 tablespoon avocado mixture and ¼ cup pineapple-jícama salsa, and serve.

INDONESIAN-STYLE FRIED RICE

FRIED RICE HAS ALWAYS BEEN THE FRUGAL CHEF'S template for using up leftovers: Take cold cooked rice, stir-fry it with whatever meat, vegetables, and aromatics are on hand, and toss it in a sauce that lightly coats the mixture and rehydrates the grains. When done well, the result is a satisfying one-dish meal.

And yet after years of eating the typical Chinese take-out versions—in which the rice is chock-full of meat and vegetables cut to the same size, cooked together, and tossed in a garden-variety "brown sauce"—I often crave something a bit more inspired. Indonesia's spin on the approach, *nasi goreng*, provides an answer. In this Southeast Asian rendition, the grains themselves are more thoroughly seasoned with a pungent chili paste called *sambal*, along with fermented shrimp paste and a syrupy-sweet soy sauce known as *kecap manis*. Then, instead of being loaded up with a hodgepodge of meats and vegetables, the rice is garnished with crunchy fried shallots, egg, and crisp fresh vegetables. The final product boasts so much complexity in flavor and texture that it hardly seems like the typical afterthought. But how best to replicate the dish in my own kitchen?

A quick survey of Indonesian fried rice recipes revealed the source of this dish's heady flavor: chili paste. This coarse mixture is nothing more than a puree of shallots, garlic, and fresh Thai chiles. In most recipes, sautéing the chili paste in oil is the first step in the process. This way, the paste develops complexity and heat before the other ingredients hit the pan.

The chili paste, I discovered, isn't hard to reproduce. I easily found the ingredients at the supermarket, and the paste was a snap to make, requiring just a few quick pulses in the food processor. As for duplicating the flavors of the shrimp paste, glutamate-rich anchovies packed a rich, salty punch but were a little too fishy. Pungent fish sauce made a better substitute but didn't single-handedly capture the paste's brininess. For that, I ended up going directly to the source, sautéing 12 ounces of chopped extra-large shrimp with the chili paste.

Bottled versions of kecap manis consist of palm sugar, which has a rich, almost caramelized flavor, and soy sauce. But simply adding brown sugar, which also has caramel notes, to soy sauce didn't quite replicate this condiment's complex flavor and viscosity. I had the best luck sweetening the soy sauce with equal amounts of dark brown sugar and molasses.

In a series of quick motions, I added the shrimp to the pan in which I had been sautéing the paste, followed by the sweet soy mixture (including the fish sauce) and, finally, the rice. Each bite of this fried rice revealed that famously addictive balance of sweetness, heat, and pungency. A scattering of sliced scallions and a squirt of lime juice gave the dish a fresh finish.

With the flavors of this dish locked down, I moved on to tackle a more fundamental fried rice problem: hastening the crucial rice-chilling step. Unlike freshly cooked rice, which forms soft, mushy clumps when stir-fried too soon, chilled rice undergoes a process called retrogradation, in which the starch molecules form crystalline structures that make the grains firm enough to withstand a second round of cooking. That's why this dish is tailor-made for last night's leftover rice: After hours in the fridge, the grains are cold and firm. But since cold cooked rice is something that I rarely have on hand, I had to take the extra step of cooking the rice the day before—a process that required more forethought than I wanted to give the dish.

I wondered: Was the 12 to 24 hours in the fridge really necessary? Hoping that I could get away with less chill time, I tried my recipe with rice that had been refrigerated for two, three, and four hours. While the results weren't bad, they hardly compared with the batches made with stiffer, drier grains that had chilled overnight. The freezer was no help; although the rice felt cold and dry, it cooked up surprisingly mushy. Our science editor offered an explanation: Once the rice freezes, retrogradation comes to a halt, since freezing prevents the starch from crystallizing.

If I couldn't figure out a way to speed up retrogradation, maybe I could produce similarly firm, dry results by cooking the rice in less water. Getting the amount of liquid just right took some fiddling; the standard 3-to-2 ratio of water to rice was saturating the grains too much, so I drained varying amounts of water from the pot before achieving the ideal texture with just a third of a cup less liquid in the mix. Then I briefly rested the pot on the counter with a dish towel under the lid (to absorb excess moisture), spread the rice on a baking sheet, and popped the tray in the fridge. Twenty minutes later, the rice felt almost as firm as the overnight-chilled batches. The only holdup: The grains were a bit sticky. My two-pronged solution? Rinsing the raw rice and

INDONESIAN-STYLE FRIED RICE WITH SHRIMP

then briefly sautéing it in a splash of oil to form a greasy barrier before adding the water.

All that remained was adding the traditional trimmings: a fried egg or omelet, frizzled shallots, and fresh-cut cucumbers and tomatoes. The latter three were no problem, but I had to decide how to prepare the egg, and everyone agreed that avoiding the last-minute work of egg frying would be a plus. With that in mind, I whipped up a quick omelet, which I rolled into a tight log, sliced into spirals, and set aside until I was ready to garnish.

With its sweet-salty flavors, spicy kick, and contrasting textures, this take on fried rice had officially eclipsed the more familiar humdrum versions. And I didn't even have to wait a day to make it.

—YVONNE RUPERTI, *Cook's Illustrated*

NOTES FROM THE TEST KITCHEN

HOW TO MAKE FRIED RICE WITHOUT LEFTOVERS

Leftover white rice that's been thoroughly chilled—essential to making fried rice—is a staple in Asian households but not something that most of us keep on hand. To condense the overnight chilling process, we came up with a three-pronged approach that produces comparably dry, firm rice in less than an hour.

1. Sauté rinsed rice in oil before steaming to help keep grains from clumping.

2. Cook rice in slightly less water to yield more rigid grains that don't require overnight chill.

3. Then rest and briefly refrigerate rice to ensure it is dry and firm enough for second round of cooking.

Indonesian-Style Fried Rice with Shrimp

SERVES 4 TO 6

If Thai chiles are unavailable, substitute 2 serranos or 2 jalapeños. Reduce the spiciness of this dish by removing the ribs and seeds from the chiles. This dish progresses very quickly at step 4; it's imperative that your ingredients be in place by then and ready to go. If desired, serve the rice with sliced cucumbers and tomato wedges.

- **5 green or red Thai chiles, stemmed**
- **7 large shallots, peeled**
- **4 large garlic cloves, peeled**
- **2 tablespoons dark brown sugar**
- **2 tablespoons light or mild molasses**
- **2 tablespoons soy sauce**
- **2 tablespoons fish sauce**
- **Salt**
- **4 large eggs**
- **½ cup vegetable oil**
- **1 recipe Faux Leftover Rice (recipe follows)**
- **12 ounces extra-large shrimp (21 to 25 per pound), peeled, deveined, tails removed, and cut crosswise into thirds**
- **4 scallions, sliced thin**
- **Lime wedges**

1. Pulse chiles, 4 shallots, and garlic in food processor until coarse paste is formed, about 15 pulses, scraping down sides of bowl as necessary. Transfer mixture to bowl; set aside. In second bowl, stir together brown sugar, molasses, soy sauce, fish sauce, and 1¼ teaspoons salt. Whisk eggs and ¼ teaspoon salt together in third bowl.

2. Thinly slice remaining 3 shallots and place in 12-inch nonstick skillet with oil. Fry over medium heat, stirring constantly, until shallots are golden and crisp, 6 to 10 minutes. Using slotted spoon, transfer shallots to paper towel–lined plate and season with salt to taste. Pour off oil and reserve. Wipe out skillet with paper towels.

3. Heat 1 teaspoon reserved oil in now-empty skillet over medium heat until shimmering. Add half of eggs to skillet, gently tilting pan to evenly coat bottom. Cover and cook until bottom of omelet is spotty golden brown and top is just set, about 1½ minutes. Slide omelet onto cutting board and gently roll up into tight log. Using sharp knife, cut log crosswise into 1-inch segments (leaving segments rolled). Repeat with 1 teaspoon more reserved oil and remaining eggs.

4. Remove rice from refrigerator and break up any large clumps with fingers. Heat 3 tablespoons more reserved oil in now-empty skillet over medium heat until just shimmering. Add chile mixture and cook until mixture turns golden, 3 to 5 minutes. Add shrimp, increase heat to medium-high, and cook, stirring constantly, until exterior of shrimp is just opaque, about 2 minutes. Push shrimp to sides of skillet to clear center; stir molasses mixture to recombine and pour into center of skillet. When molasses mixture bubbles, add rice and cook, stirring and folding constantly, until shrimp is cooked, rice is heated through, and mixture is evenly coated, about 3 minutes. Stir in scallions, remove from heat, and transfer to serving platter. Garnish with omelet segments, fried shallots, and lime wedges. Serve immediately.

Faux Leftover Rice

MAKES 6 CUPS

Rinsing the rice, which removes much of the exterior starch, and sautéing it in oil prevents it from being overly sticky once cooked.

- **2 cups jasmine or long-grain white rice**
- **2 tablespoons vegetable oil**
- **2⅔ cups water**

1. Place rice in fine-mesh strainer set over large bowl. Rinse under running water until water runs clear, about 1 minute. Drain rice well.

2. Heat oil in large saucepan over medium heat until shimmering. Add rice and cook, stirring to coat grains with oil, about 30 seconds. Add water, increase heat to high, and bring to boil.

3. Cover, reduce heat to low, and simmer until liquid is absorbed, about 18 minutes. Off heat, remove lid and place kitchen towel folded in half over saucepan. Cover and let stand until rice is just tender, about 8 minutes. Spread cooked rice on rimmed baking sheet, set on wire rack, and let cool for 10 minutes. Transfer to refrigerator and chill for 20 minutes.

GLAZED SALMON FILLETS

THERE ARE FEW BETTER WAYS TO HIGHLIGHT the rich, silky flesh of salmon than offsetting it with a sweet-tart glaze. In most recipes the fish is brushed with a sticky mixture, then placed a few inches from the broiler element and basted every minute or so to ensure a substantial coating. Of course, I didn't relish the idea of repeatedly reaching into a hot oven, but the method seemed viable enough. When I tried it, however, the sugary glaze charred, and as can happen with thick cuts of meat, a band of leathery, overcooked flesh developed on the outside, with only the very center of the salmon exhibiting the translucent, buttery texture I was looking for.

The problem was the broiler. It was simply too hard to pinpoint the proper degree of doneness using such extreme heat, and repeatedly opening and closing the oven door to apply the glaze only complicated matters. But I had another idea: So-called slow-cooked salmon is a popular restaurant dish these days, and the approach reverses the tactic I'd been trying. The fish bakes in a low-temperature oven, which renders its flesh terrifically moist and tender. The likely trade-off would be a well-lacquered exterior, but I thought it was worth a shot. I switched the oven to "bake," moved the rack to the middle position, and gently cooked the fish plain (I'd address the glaze later). After 10 minutes at 300 degrees, the salmon was cooked perfectly.

Now that my salmon was succulent and pink throughout, I had only one problem: Tasters missed the slightly crusty, flavorful browned exterior of the broiled fish. Cranking the heat back up was out of the question. Instead, I briefly seared each side of the fish in a hot skillet before transferring it to the low oven. But while the crust was nicely browned, one bite revealed that I had virtually negated the benefits of my slow-cooking technique. The outer layer of the fish was tough and dry—reminiscent of the broiled recipes I'd tried.

What I needed to do was more rapidly caramelize the fillets before their exteriors had a chance to turn tough and leathery—and that's when I remembered a favorite test kitchen technique: To expedite browning on everything from pork tenderloin to tuna, we lightly sprinkle the flesh with sugar. Here, I tried brown sugar (for its subtle molasses flavor), and it took only a minute for a delicate, flavorful crust to form. I then seared the skin side of the fish for another minute to promote even cooking and transferred the skillet to the oven. Seven minutes later, I had just what I wanted: a golden brown exterior and a pink, wonderfully moist interior.

That left me with just the glaze. I combined more brown sugar with vinegar, then added mirin, soy sauce, and mustard to create a teriyaki-inspired varnish that would serve as a perfect foil to the rich, fatty salmon. I brought the mixture to a boil in a saucepan; reduced it for five minutes, when it was thick enough to coat the back of a spoon; then brushed it over the seared salmon fillets. But even before I got the fish into the oven, much of the glaze slid off and pooled in the bottom of the pan. Basting the salmon every couple of minutes would certainly help, but I hated to go that tedious route.

Another obvious remedy would be to further thicken the glaze, so I tried adding a small amount of cornstarch to the mixture. The result? Better, but too much of the sauce still dribbled down the sides of the fish. Adding more cornstarch was not an option; any more than a teaspoon rendered the mixture gummy and gloppy. I was running out of ideas when a different approach occurred to me: What if instead of trying to create a tackier glaze, I worked on getting the salmon to have more "stickability"? I had a hunch that rubbing cornstarch on the surface of the fish would add texture, creating tiny nooks and crannies to trap the glaze.

Fingers crossed, I combined ¼ teaspoon of cornstarch with the brown sugar I was already rubbing on the fish, plus ½ teaspoon of kosher salt for seasoning, and then seared the fillets. As I'd hoped, the surface was now quite coarse, mottled with tiny peaks and valleys. I proceeded with the recipe, spooning the glaze over the salmon and transferring it to the low oven. This time the mixture stuck, resulting in a glistening, well-lacquered exterior.

With my glaze holding fast to the fillets, I whipped up three more variations: a fruity pomegranate version spiked with balsamic vinegar; an Asian barbecue mixture sweetened with hoisin sauce and made tart with rice vinegar; and a salty, citrusy orange-miso version.

Not only was my technique easier and more foolproof than the frequent basting method in other recipes, but I had dinner on the table in about 20 minutes.

—BRYAN ROOF, *Cook's Illustrated*

Glazed Salmon Fillets

SERVES 4

Use center-cut salmon fillets of similar thickness so that they cook at the same rate. The best way to ensure uniformity is to buy a 1½- to 2-pound whole center-cut fillet and cut it into 4 pieces. Prepare the glaze before you cook the salmon. If your nonstick skillet isn't ovensafe, sear the salmon as directed in step 2, then transfer it to a baking sheet, glaze it, and bake it as directed in step 3.

1 teaspoon packed light brown sugar
½ teaspoon kosher salt
¼ teaspoon cornstarch
4 (6- to 8-ounce) center-cut skin-on salmon fillets
Pepper
1 teaspoon vegetable oil
1 recipe glaze (recipes follow)

1. Adjust oven rack to middle position and heat oven to 300 degrees. Combine sugar, salt, and cornstarch in bowl. Pat salmon dry with paper towels and season with pepper. Sprinkle brown sugar mixture evenly over flesh side of salmon, rubbing to distribute.

2. Heat oil in 12-inch ovensafe nonstick skillet over medium-high heat until just smoking. Place salmon, flesh side down, in skillet and cook until well browned, about 1 minute. Using tongs, carefully flip salmon and cook on skin side for 1 minute.

3. Remove skillet from heat and spoon glaze evenly over salmon fillets. Transfer skillet to oven and cook until fillets are still translucent when checked with tip of paring knife and register 125 degrees (medium-rare), 7 to 10 minutes. Transfer fillets to platter or individual plates and serve.

Soy-Mustard Glaze

MAKES ABOUT ½ CUP

Mirin, a sweet Japanese rice wine, can be found in Asian markets and the international section of most supermarkets.

3 tablespoons packed light brown sugar
2 tablespoons soy sauce
2 tablespoons mirin
1 tablespoon sherry vinegar

1 tablespoon whole-grain mustard
1 tablespoon water
1 teaspoon cornstarch
⅛ teaspoon red pepper flakes

Whisk all ingredients together in small saucepan. Bring to boil over medium-high heat; simmer until thickened, about 1 minute. Remove from heat and cover to keep warm.

Pomegranate-Balsamic Glaze

MAKES ABOUT ½ CUP

Our winning brand of whole-grain mustard is Grey Poupon Harvest Coarse Ground Mustard.

3 tablespoons packed light brown sugar
3 tablespoons pomegranate juice
2 tablespoons balsamic vinegar
1 tablespoon whole-grain mustard
1 teaspoon cornstarch
Pinch cayenne pepper

Whisk all ingredients together in small saucepan. Bring to boil over medium-high heat; simmer until thickened, about 1 minute. Remove from heat and cover to keep warm.

Asian Barbecue Glaze

MAKES ABOUT ½ CUP

2 tablespoons ketchup
2 tablespoons hoisin sauce
2 tablespoons rice vinegar
2 tablespoons packed light brown sugar
1 tablespoon soy sauce
1 tablespoon toasted sesame oil
2 teaspoons Asian chili-garlic sauce
1 teaspoon grated fresh ginger

Whisk all ingredients together in small saucepan. Bring to boil over medium-high heat; simmer until thickened, about 3 minutes. Remove from heat and cover to keep warm.

Orange-Miso Glaze

MAKES ABOUT ½ CUP

Miso, a fermented soybean paste, can be found in Asian markets and the international section of most supermarkets.

1 teaspoon grated orange zest plus ¼ cup juice (2 oranges)
2 tablespoons white miso
1 tablespoon packed light brown sugar
1 tablespoon rice vinegar
1 tablespoon whole-grain mustard
¾ teaspoon cornstarch
Pinch cayenne pepper

Whisk all ingredients together in small saucepan. Bring to boil over medium-high heat; simmer until thickened, about 1 minute. Remove from heat and cover to keep warm.

NOTES FROM THE TEST KITCHEN

THE BEST INEXPENSIVE NONSTICK SKILLET

We've always recommended buying inexpensive nonstick skillets, because with regular use the nonstick coating inevitably scratches, chips off, or becomes ineffective. Why spend big bucks on a pan that will last only a year or two? To find the best nonstick pan on the market, we tested eight contenders under $60 against our longtime favorite, the All-Clad Stainless 12-Inch Nonstick Frying Pan, $129.99. We tested the nonstick effectiveness of each pan by frying eggs and stir-frying beef and vegetables. To see which pans cooked food evenly and had good size and heft but were comfortable to maneuver, we made crêpes in each. We also ran them through a number of durability tests. We'd like to say our new favorite pan, the **T-Fal Professional Total Non-Stick 12½-Inch Fry Pan**, aced every test, but a loose handle that resulted from the durability testing was a sign that it's not high-end cookware. Still, at $34.99, it's a bargain, offering an exceptionally slick, durable nonstick coating and top performance in cooking.

As for the All-Clad, it is a solidly built pan and a great piece of cookware, but its coating became slightly worn (the T-Fal remained perfectly slick). Because the All-Clad boasts a lifetime warranty, we still recommend it, but now we'll be buying the T-Fal for our own kitchens. (See page 306 for more information about our testing results.)

GRILLED SALMON STEAKS

CHOOSING SALMON STEAKS FOR THE GRILL IS a no-brainer: Their bone and thickness make them a far sturdier cut than a fillet. That's good news for a laid-back summer cook like me. I'd rather turn on my oven on a 90-degree day than try to scrape bits and pieces of salmon off the grill grate. Unfortunately, that thickness can also work against grilled salmon steaks: By the time the interior is cooked through, what was a nicely charred exterior will be blackened and dry. Also overcooked and dry are the thin strips of flesh that come down on either side of the bone (the fish's belly flaps). And no matter how much seasoning goes on the outside, it never seems to permeate the whole steak.

My quest began with a much-needed tummy tuck (for the salmon, not me). I gently removed the skin from one of the belly flaps and tucked it in toward the center of the steak, and then wrapped the other flap around it and secured the steak with kitchen twine. Now I had neat medallions that cooked evenly and could be easily maneuvered around the grill.

As much fun as it is to grill with serious fire, I knew that I would have to take a more gentle approach. Cooking over medium-low heat produced moist, cooked interiors—but at the steep cost of a good, flavorful sear. I needed a two-level fire: high heat to sear the steaks, low heat to finish the job. This method took up to 20 minutes total for a 1½-inch steak, but the steaks were now both moist and nicely browned.

Turning to flavor, I thought about how another common cooking method for this cut of salmon—broiling—introduces flavor. The steaks are slathered with a sauce and absorb its flavor as they cook. How could I translate this technique to the grill without risking flare-ups and burned, stuck-on fish? Got it: I'd replace the broiler pan with a disposable aluminum roasting pan and finish cooking the steaks in a sauce over low heat.

A sucker for classics, I made a simple lemon-and-shallot butter sauce directly in the roasting pan while the steaks seared on the hot part of the grill. Then I transferred the browned fish steaks to the pan, coating them with sauce. When they were done, they were flavorful, juicy, and moist. But the delicate sauce needed a boost to compete with the charred grill flavor; more lemon juice, the addition of zest and capers, plus a sprinkling of fresh parsley gave it the necessary fortification. Now I had zesty, succulent salmon steaks, plus built-in insurance against overcooking if I happened to get distracted by my lawn chair and a chilled glass of white wine.

—ERIKA BRUCE, *Cook's Country*

Grilled Salmon Steaks with Lemon-Caper Sauce

SERVES 4

Before eating, lift out the small circular bone from the center of each steak; the thin pinbones attached to it will follow.

4 (10-ounce) skin-on salmon steaks, 1 to 1½ inches thick
Salt and pepper
2 tablespoons olive oil
1 teaspoon grated lemon zest plus 6 tablespoons juice (2 lemons)
1 shallot, minced
3 tablespoons unsalted butter, cut into 3 pieces
1 tablespoon capers, rinsed
1 (13 by 9-inch) disposable aluminum roasting pan
2 tablespoons minced fresh parsley

1. Pat salmon steaks dry with paper towels. Working with one steak at a time, carefully trim 1½ inches of skin from one tail. Tightly wrap other tail around skinned portion; tie steak with kitchen twine. Season salmon with salt and pepper; brush both sides with oil. Combine lemon zest, lemon juice, shallot, butter, capers, and ⅛ teaspoon salt in disposable pan.

2A. FOR A CHARCOAL GRILL: Open bottom vent completely. Light large chimney starter filled with charcoal briquettes (6 quarts). When top coals are partially covered with ash, pour evenly over half of grill. Set cooking grate in place, cover, and open lid vent completely. Heat grill until hot, about 5 minutes.

2B. FOR A GAS GRILL: Turn all burners to high, cover, and heat grill until hot, about 15 minutes. Leave primary burner on high and turn off other burner(s).

3. Clean and oil cooking grate, then repeatedly brush grate with well-oiled paper towels until grate is black

GRILLED SALMON STEAKS WITH LEMON-CAPER SAUCE

and glossy, 5 to 10 times. Place salmon on hot part of grill. Cook until browned, 2 to 3 minutes per side. Meanwhile, set pan on cool part of grill and cook until butter has melted, about 2 minutes. Transfer salmon to pan and gently turn to coat. Cook (covered if using gas) until center of salmon is still translucent when checked with tip of paring knife and salmon registers 125 degrees (medium-rare), 6 to 14 minutes, flipping salmon and rotating pan halfway through grilling. Remove twine and transfer salmon to platter. Off heat, whisk parsley into sauce. Drizzle sauce over steaks and serve.

VARIATIONS

Grilled Salmon Steaks with Lime-Cilantro Sauce

Omit lemon zest, lemon juice, shallot, and capers. Add 1 teaspoon grated lime zest, 6 tablespoons lime juice, 2 minced garlic cloves, and ½ teaspoon ground cumin to pan in step 1. Replace parsley with 2 tablespoons minced fresh cilantro.

Grilled Salmon Steaks with Orange-Ginger Sauce

Omit lemon zest, lemon juice, shallot, and capers. Add 1 teaspoon grated orange zest, 6 tablespoons orange juice, 1 tablespoon grated fresh ginger, and 1 tablespoon soy sauce to pan in step 1. Replace parsley with 1 thinly sliced scallion.

NOTES FROM THE TEST KITCHEN

PREPPING SALMON MEDALLIONS

1. For salmon steaks that are sturdy enough to grill easily, begin by removing 1½ inches of skin from one tail of each steak.

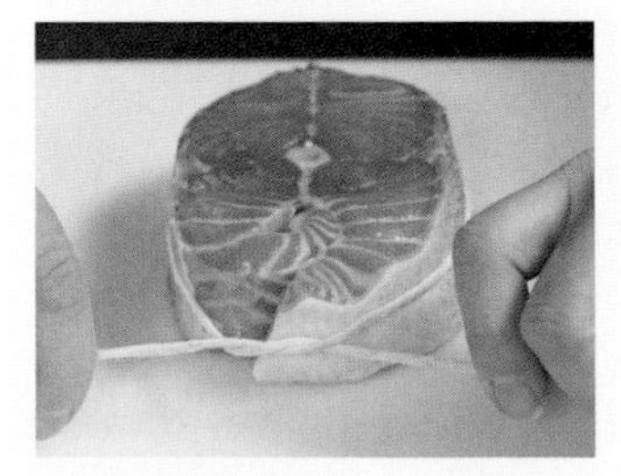

2. Then, tuck skinned portion into center of steak, wrap other tail around it, and tie with kitchen twine.

HALIBUT EN PAPILLOTE

COOKING EN PAPILLOTE—WHERE THE FOOD IS baked in a tightly sealed, artfully folded parchment package that is slit open just before serving for dramatic presentation—may seem as outdated or showy as beef Wellington or pheasant under glass. But there's a practical reason the technique has held its own through countless culinary fads and fashions. It's an easy, mess-free way to enhance delicate flavor, particularly that of fish, since the food is allowed to steam in its own juices. The fish cooks quickly in the moist environment, and because there's no water added to dilute flavors, it's a more flavorful method than ordinary poaching. If you throw vegetables into the package, it adds up to a light but satisfying, and visually appealing, "one-pouch" meal.

But fish en papillote, while delicate and simple in flavor, is not trouble-free in terms of technique. Without the right blend of flavorings, the fish can taste so lean and bland you might as well be dining on diet food. Also, not all vegetables pair well with fish, and careful consideration must be given to their size and their required cooking time, as you can otherwise wind up with fish surrounded by crunchy and undercooked or mushy and overcooked vegetables. I wanted to create an approach worthy of this technique's haute cuisine roots that also produced moist, flaky fish and tender-firm vegetables, all flavored by the rich, aromatic goodness of their mingled juices.

All the classic recipes call for cutting parchment paper into attractive shapes such as teardrops, hearts, and butterflies. The fish is placed between two of these identical shapes, which are then painstakingly crimped together. The results make for a dramatic visual—the paper balloons and browns in the oven, to be slit open just before serving. After some experimentation with parchment, I found that I could achieve the same results as the fussy recipes without a talent for origami. I folded a piece of parchment in half, trimming the corners so it unfolded into a rough heart shape. The vegetables and fish went on one side of the heart, the other half was folded over the fish, and the two sides were folded together to complete the package. With only one shape to cut per fish bundle, eight packets came together quickly, with no awkward parchment pieces to match up, and only one seam to crimp per packet.

My method settled, the next step was to figure out what type of fish worked best. After trying a variety of fish fillets, I determined that tasters favored flaky, mild white fish, like halibut and red snapper, over more assertively flavored salmon and tuna. In the moist atmosphere of the pouch, the oilier fish had a more concentrated flavor that tasters felt would overpower the flavors of the milder vegetables.

Next I needed to determine the best vegetables for the situation. Since the fish and vegetables would have to cook at the same rate, I knew there would be some limitations. Dense vegetables like potatoes were immediately out of the running because they took far too long to cook through, as were absorbent vegetables like eggplant, which would simply cook to mush. Broccoli seemed a little bold for an otherwise delicate dish. Light, clean-tasting zucchini, sliced into thin rounds, was a winner. For sweetness, color, and some more moisture to encourage steaming, I also settled on chopped tomatoes.

Determining when the fish was done proved more challenging: It was hard to nick and peek when the fish was sealed in parchment. The old rule of thumb for fish—10 minutes of cooking time per inch of thickness—failed in this case, as the fish was barely opaque within that period. After experimenting with oven temperatures, I found that 1-inch-thick fillets cooked best at 450 degrees for 15 minutes. While this seemed like a long time for such high heat, I found that the fish cooked in this manner was flaky and moist since it was well insulated within the sealed packets, and the vegetables were likewise perfectly cooked.

But now that I had the textures right, I was ending up with diluted flavor. The solution was to salt and drain the zucchini in a colander before assembling the packet; the moisture from the tomatoes was all I needed for the perfect steamy environment. Cooking the packets on two baking sheets (four packets per sheet) gave them the contact they needed with the hot sheet to concentrate the liquid within and evenly steam the contents.

To boost the flavor of my meal and add a little richness, I turned to a compound butter flavored with garlic, red pepper flakes, and oregano for an assertive kick. For a finishing touch, a sprinkling of chopped basil lent a pleasant fragrance. The flavored butter basted the fish as it cooked and mingled with the juices given off by the vegetables, leaving behind an aromatic, full-flavored sauce that perfectly complemented the fish.

—ADELAIDE PARKER, *America's Test Kitchen Books*

Halibut en Papillote with Zucchini and Tomatoes

SERVES 8

Haddock, red snapper, sea bass, and cod can be substituted for the halibut, as long as the fillets measure 1 to 1¼ inches thick. You will need 8 pieces of 16 by 14-inch parchment paper for this recipe, but it's a good idea to have extra around for practice; do not substitute waxed paper. Dry the vegetables and fish well before assembling the packets as excess moisture can weaken and tear the paper. Cut open each packet promptly after baking to prevent overcooking.

- **4 zucchini (8 ounces each), sliced ¼ inch thick**
- **Salt and pepper**
- **8 tablespoons unsalted butter, softened**
- **4 garlic cloves, minced**
- **2 teaspoons minced fresh oregano**
- **¼ teaspoon red pepper flakes**
- **1 pound plum tomatoes, cored, seeded, and cut into ½-inch pieces**
- **8 (16 by 14-inch) sheets parchment paper**
- **8 (6-ounce) skinless halibut fillets, 1 to 1¼ inches thick**
- **½ cup chopped fresh basil**
- **Lemon wedges**

1. Toss zucchini with 1 teaspoon salt and let drain in colander for 30 minutes. Spread zucchini on several layers of paper towels and thoroughly blot dry. In bowl, combine softened butter, garlic, oregano, pepper flakes, ½ teaspoon salt, and ¼ teaspoon pepper. In separate bowl, season tomatoes lightly with salt and pepper.

2. Fold and cut parchment into 8 rough heart shapes. Adjust oven racks to lower-middle and upper-middle positions and heat oven to 450 degrees.

3. Spread parchment pieces on clean, dry counter. Neatly shingle zucchini into small pile on one side of each parchment sheet. Spoon ¼ cup tomatoes on top of each zucchini pile. Pat fish dry with paper towels, season with salt and pepper, and lay on top of tomatoes. Spread 1 tablespoon butter mixture evenly over top of each piece of fish.

4. Fold cut edges of parchment over to make tidy airtight packets. Place packets on 2 large baking sheets. Bake for 15 minutes, switching and rotating pans halfway through baking.

5. Working quickly, cut *X* in top of each packet with scissors and sprinkle basil over fish. Gently transfer packets to individual plates and serve with lemon wedges.

VARIATION

Halibut en Papillote with Leeks and Carrots

Omit zucchini, tomatoes, and red pepper flakes. Substitute 2 teaspoons minced fresh thyme for oregano; add 2 teaspoons grated lemon zest to butter mixture. Combine 3 leeks, white and light green parts only, cut into matchsticks, rinsed thoroughly, and dried, with 4 carrots, peeled and cut into matchsticks, in bowl and season lightly with salt and pepper. Neatly pile leek-carrot mixture on one side of each parchment sheet, place fish on top, and spread 1 tablespoon butter mixture evenly over top of each piece of fish. Seal packets and bake as directed. Serve, substituting ¼ cup minced fresh parsley for basil.

NOTES FROM THE TEST KITCHEN

MAKING FISH EN PAPILLOTE

1. Fold 16 by 14-inch sheet of parchment in half widthwise. Trim 3 corners so that when paper is unfolded, it has rough heart shape with flat bottom and straightened sides.

2. Unfold paper and pile vegetables on one side of heart, close to fold. Place piece of fish on top of vegetables and spread 1 tablespoon butter mixture over top.

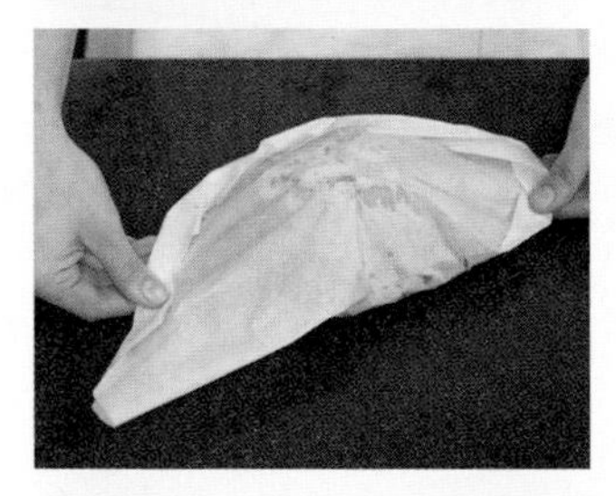

3. Refold paper heart over fish and align edges. Then, starting at top of heart, fold outer 1 inch of parchment over into tight, triangle-shaped fold. Run thumb over edge to seal, then repeat at ¾-inch intervals to seal fish securely in pouch.

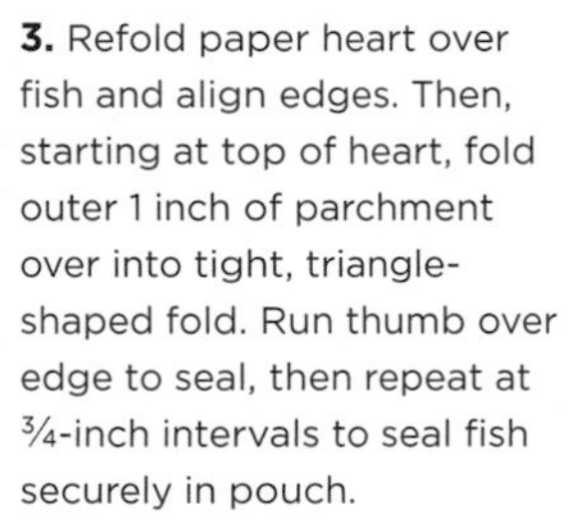

4. When finished crimping, fold final tailpiece of crimped parchment underneath to seal.

CUTTING LEEKS INTO MATCHSTICKS

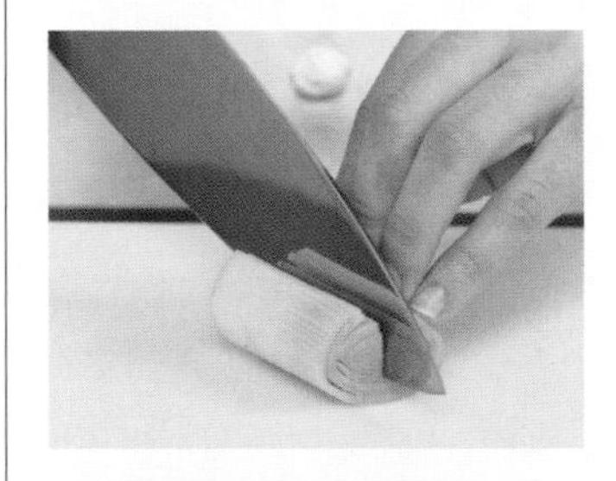

1. After trimming dark green tops and root end, cut leek into 2-inch segments. Then cut each segment in half lengthwise and pull leek apart into smaller stacks of 3 or 4 layers.

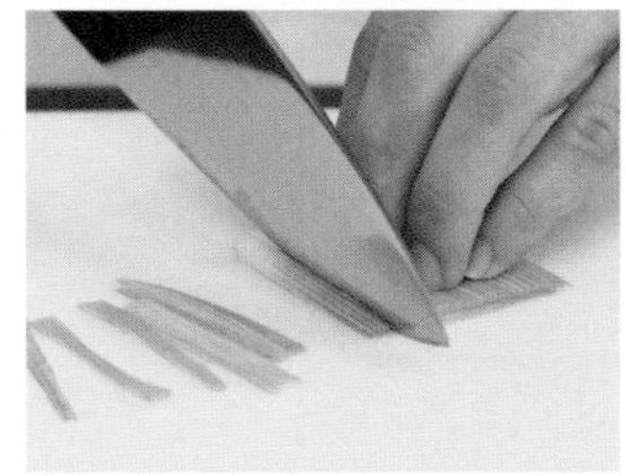

2. Cut smaller stacks into ⅛-inch-thick matchsticks, then rinse and dry thoroughly.

CUTTING CARROTS INTO MATCHSTICKS

1. Slice carrot on bias into 2-inch-long, oval-shaped pieces.

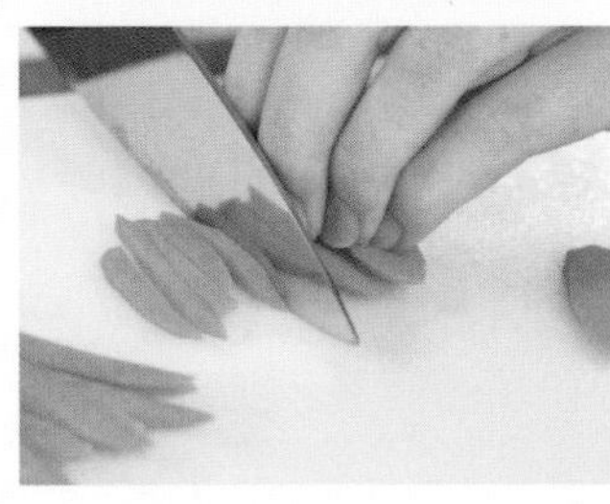

2. Lay ovals flat, then slice into 2-inch-long matchsticks, about ¼ inch thick.

COD FILLETS WITH POTATOES

THE DUO OF COD AND POTATOES IS A CLASSIC pairing, but I wanted a streamlined way to prepare this combo using a single pan, for an easy weeknight supper. Cooking fish fillets and potatoes on a sheet pan is standard practice in the test kitchen—what if I attempted to join cod and spuds into one simple supper, all cooked on a sheet pan? Cooking them together on the same pan at once, though easy, would present a challenge: Fish cooks quickly but potatoes take quite a bit more time. Try to cook them together, and the result is rubbery fish and rock-hard potatoes. And while the clean flavor and lean nature of cod are much of its appeal, it runs the risk of tasting plain. Could I find a way to boost the flavor of mild cod and also cook the fish and potatoes together?

Putting aside flavor for the moment, I focused on finding a cooking method that would deliver perfectly cooked potatoes and fish. I already knew that just throwing them in the oven together wouldn't work. And since chunks of potato would need a significant amount of time in the oven to become tender and spotty brown before the fish fillets could be added, I figured that slicing the potatoes thin would speed up the process. Additionally, slicing the potatoes would allow me to take advantage of the large surface area of the baking sheet, exposing more of the potatoes' flesh to the dry heat of the oven and the hot pan. I hoped this would result in some browning and crisping.

After a few tests, I settled on ¼-inch-thick potato slices—thin enough to cook quickly but thick enough to cut by hand. Instead of spreading the potatoes across the oiled baking sheet in a single layer, I shingled them into four individual piles that would serve as a bed for each piece of cod. When the potatoes were tender and starting to brown (which took about 30 minutes in a 425-degree oven), I placed the fish on top and put the sheet pan back in the oven. Cod is a relatively wet fish, so it stands up well to high heat; 15 minutes later it was perfectly cooked and moist.

In an effort to speed up the cooking time of the potatoes (and thus save time overall), I tried covering them with foil during the initial stint in the oven. This method did cut the cooking time, but it also inhibited browning, so I ditched it. Tasters preferred the textural variation of the uncovered potatoes, which resulted in a combination of the crisp, golden potatoes that remained exposed to the heat of the oven and the creamy, soft potatoes that were under the fish.

Up to this point, russets had been my potato of choice, but I was curious to see if other varieties might be better. I tried red potatoes and Yukon Golds, but tasters found both a bit waxy. The traditional russet, with its tender bite and earthy flavor, was the unanimous favorite. Russets also formed tighter, more cohesive layers owing to their higher starch content. This allowed me to slide a spatula under the potatoes and fish and serve the whole thing intact for an attractive presentation.

Now that my fish and potatoes were cooked to perfection, it was time to focus on infusing them with flavor. I kept the potatoes simple. A little olive oil, garlic, salt, and pepper were all they needed. The lean fish, however, could benefit from a more substantial preparation. I decided that a compound butter would add plenty of flavor and richness. I stirred minced thyme and lemon juice into softened butter and rubbed it on the fish before baking. This kept the fish moist and added flavor, but the thyme didn't spend long enough in the oven to mellow; tasters thought it overwhelmed the mild cod. Nevertheless, they liked the flavor combination, so I just needed an alternative method of incorporating it.

Backing up, I considered the layered arrangement of fish and potatoes. What if I took the components of the

NOTES FROM THE TEST KITCHEN

SHINGLING POTATOES FOR LEMON-HERB COD

1. Shingle potato slices in 3 tight rows, measuring about 4 by 6 inches. Then gently push rows together so that potatoes are tidy and cohesive.

2. Carefully place cod fillet, skinned side down, on top of each set of parcooked potatoes. Top fish with butter pieces, thyme sprigs, and lemon slices.

LEMON-HERB COD FILLETS WITH CRISPY GARLIC POTATOES

herb butter—butter, thyme, and lemon—and layered them on top of the fish? After placing the cod on the potatoes, I scattered pieces of butter on top, then topped each fillet with a sprig of thyme, followed by a few slices of lemon. This technique was a success: The butter and lemon basted the fish as it baked, as the thyme gently flavored the fish. This method not only worked better than the compound butter, but it was easier; no chopping of herbs or waiting for butter to soften. Best of all, the rustic appearance of the dish was impressive—an elegant presentation for an extremely simple meal.

—ADELAIDE PARKER, *America's Test Kitchen Books*

Lemon-Herb Cod Fillets with Crispy Garlic Potatoes

SERVES 4

Halibut or haddock can be substituted for the cod. Use medium potatoes (7 to 9 ounces each) that are uniform in shape.

- **3 tablespoons olive oil**
- **1½ pounds russet potatoes, sliced into ¼-inch-thick rounds**
- **3 garlic cloves, minced**
- **Salt and pepper**
- **4 (6-ounce) skinless cod fillets, 1 to 1½ inches thick**
- **3 tablespoons unsalted butter, cut into ¼-inch pieces**
- **4 sprigs fresh thyme**
- **1 lemon, sliced thin**

1. Adjust oven rack to lower-middle position and heat oven to 425 degrees. Brush large rimmed baking sheet with 1 tablespoon oil.

2. In large bowl, toss potatoes with remaining 2 tablespoons oil and garlic; season with salt and pepper. Shingle potatoes into 4 rectangular piles of 3 rows each, about 4 by 6 inches in size; gently push rows together so potatoes form cohesive pile. Roast potatoes until spotty brown and just tender, 30 to 35 minutes, rotating sheet halfway through roasting.

3. Pat cod dry with paper towels and season with salt and pepper. Carefully place 1 cod fillet, skinned side down, on top of each potato pile. Top fish with butter pieces, thyme sprigs, and lemon slices. Continue to bake fish and potatoes until fish flakes apart when gently prodded with paring knife, about 15 minutes.

4. Slide spatula underneath potatoes and fish, gently transfer to individual plates, and serve.

FISH CAKES

MARYLANDERS MAY RAVE ABOUT THEIR CRAB cakes, but here in New England we love a good cod cake. There is certainly no shortage of recipes, but most I've tried make more of a bread patty or potato cake than fish cake. They are laden with binders that not only mask the flavor of the fish but also create an unappealingly dense texture. I set out to develop a recipe for fish cakes that were moist, delicate, and tender yet still cohesive, and with seasoning and binding that complemented the clean, subtle flavor of the cod.

Initial research turned up two basic approaches to making fish cakes: using cooked cod (usually bound by mashed potatoes) and using raw cod (bound by bread crumbs). After a few tests, tasters agreed that the cakes made with cooked cod and potatoes were heavy and too time-consuming to prepare. The recipes that used raw cod showed more promise—they were light and cleaner-tasting, but they tended to fall apart in the pan. But at least it was a starting point.

The next issue was how to prepare the raw cod before forming the cakes. Early tests told me a combination of textures was best. Finely chopped cod helped bind the cakes (and kept the fish flavor at the forefront), and larger, bite-size chunks added heartiness. I pulsed all the cod in the food processor for just a few pulses and got the inconsistent texture I wanted—a mix of both finely minced and larger pieces of fish.

As for a binder, I wanted to use as little as possible. I had already ruled out mashed potatoes, which created a pasty, heavy cake. Fresh bread crumbs absorbed too much moisture and created doughy, wet pockets in and around the cod—I wanted fish cakes, not dough balls. I ultimately settled on finely ground dry bread crumbs. They didn't have an overwhelming flavor, they were easy to mix in, and they didn't mask the texture of the mild cod. The trickiest part was knowing when to stop. Fish cakes need just enough binder to hold together, but not so much that the filler takes over the flavor. I started with 1 cup of dry bread crumbs and eventually worked my way down to just ¼ cup. This gave me tender cakes in which the cod flavor took center stage. Any less and the cakes could not hold their shape.

Because cod is a lean, flaky fish, I knew I would need some moisture to supplement the bread crumbs and keep the cakes from falling apart. To prevent the cakes from becoming too heavy and rich, I tried a range of low-fat options. Low-fat yogurt and buttermilk were too wet and added too much moisture, and light sour cream and cream cheese added unwanted tang. Finally I tried light mayonnaise, which provided the right amount of moisture but came across as somewhat sweet. Some Dijon mustard added a touch of sharpness to balance it out. Two tablespoons of mayonnaise combined with 4 teaspoons of mustard worked perfectly. To further help the binding, instead of the whole egg that most recipes call for, I added a single egg white and found that's all it took to keep my cod cakes together.

Careful mixing proved a must to avoid a pasty, mushy cake. I found that a rubber spatula worked best, and I used it in a folding, rather than stirring, motion. Handling the mixture as little as possible was also key in keeping my cakes tender and light yet cohesive.

When it came time to cook my cakes, I still had some trouble making them hold together. I didn't want to add more binder, so I tried chilling the cakes before cooking, a technique the test kitchen has used successfully for crab and shrimp cakes. Just half an hour in the refrigerator made a huge difference. I also tried different cooking methods. After baking, pan-frying, and broiling, I settled on sautéing my cod cakes in a nonstick skillet over medium-high heat. It was fast but still gave me complete control over how brown and crisp the cakes got. Dredging them lightly in flour before putting them in the pan helped create a crust and prevented sticking.

For seasonings, tasters preferred simplicity—some minced shallot and parsley, as well as lemon juice, accented the delicate cod and brought out its fresh flavor. These were fish cakes I would happily put head-to-head against the best of the crab cakes.

—SUZANNAH MCFERRAN, *America's Test Kitchen Books*

Fish Cakes

SERVES 4

Be sure to use raw cod; do not substitute cooked cod. Don't overprocess the cod in step 1 or the cakes will be pasty. Serve with tartar sauce (recipe follows).

1 pound skinless cod fillets, cut into 1-inch pieces
¼ cup plain dried bread crumbs
1 large egg white
1 shallot, minced
3 tablespoons minced fresh parsley
2 tablespoons light mayonnaise
4 teaspoons Dijon mustard
1 tablespoon lemon juice
¼ teaspoon salt
⅛ teaspoon pepper
¼ cup all-purpose flour
2 tablespoons vegetable oil
Lemon wedges

1. Pulse half of cod fillets in food processor until they form mix of equal parts finely minced and coarsely chopped pieces, about 4 pulses. Transfer processed cod to large bowl and repeat with remaining cod. Sprinkle bread crumbs over cod.

2. Whisk egg white, shallot, parsley, mayonnaise, mustard, lemon juice, salt, and pepper together in bowl. Using rubber spatula, gently fold mixture into cod and bread crumbs until mixture just holds together.

3. Divide cod mixture into 4 equal portions and shape each into round cake, about 3 inches across and 1½ inches high. Transfer to plate, cover with plastic wrap, and refrigerate for at least 30 minutes or up to 24 hours.

4. Spread flour in shallow dish or pie plate. Dredge fish cakes in flour, shaking off excess. Heat oil in 12-inch nonstick skillet over medium-high heat until shimmering. Carefully lay chilled fish cakes in skillet and cook until well browned on both sides, 8 to 10 minutes, flipping them halfway through cooking. Carefully transfer fish cakes to platter and serve with lemon wedges.

Tartar Sauce

MAKES ABOUT ½ CUP

This is a lighter version of the classic sauce for fried seafood. If cornichons are not available, substitute dill pickles.

¼ cup mayonnaise
2 tablespoons sour cream
4 large cornichons, minced, plus 2 teaspoons cornichon juice
2 tablespoons finely chopped red onion
1 tablespoon capers, rinsed and minced
⅛ teaspoon pepper
Water

Mix all ingredients together in bowl, adding water as needed to thin sauce. Refrigerate, covered, until flavors blend, about 30 minutes. (Sauce can be refrigerated for up to 1 day.)

FISH CAKES WITH TARTAR SAUCE

CHAPTER 9

VEGETARIAN ENTRÉES

EGGPLANT CASSEROLE

EGGPLANT PARMESAN HAS A LOT OF APPEAL because it has the same Italian, tomato-sauced, comfort-food profile as manicotti or lasagna but offers a break from the noodles and meat. But while it is essentially just eggplant, tomato sauce, and cheese, traditional recipes for eggplant Parmesan are notoriously tedious and messy. Typically, sliced eggplant is salted, breaded, and then deep-fried in several batches before being topped with sauce and cheese. Add to this the fact that most versions turn out disappointingly greasy and soggy after all that work. I understood why most people would rather not bother. Could I breathe some life into this classic combination and develop a streamlined technique for a modern, more in-balance take on eggplant Parmesan that was actually worth making?

I decided I needed to break from tradition and look toward a looser interpretation of eggplant Parmesan to meet my goals. Right off the bat I eliminated the breading process. It was simply too fussy, and all the oil the coating absorbed made the dish too greasy. Of course, I would still need to cook the eggplant before putting it in the casserole, so the question was how.

Sautéing or frying eggplant, breaded or unbreaded, is problematic because eggplant is essentially a sponge, ready to absorb anything, and it's packed with water. This one-two punch transforms raw eggplant into oil-soaked mush before it has a chance to caramelize. For this reason, eggplant is often salted before cooking to draw out liquid. While I wasn't limiting myself to 30 minutes for this casserole, standing in the kitchen salting and drying slices of eggplant wasn't really appealing. For a more hands-off route, I wondered if the high heat of the oven could both evaporate the juice and concentrate the vegetable's flavor with a limited quantity of oil.

I tossed sliced eggplant with olive oil and salt, then spread the eggplant on baking sheets and cooked it in the oven until browned (a good indicator that the bulk of the moisture was gone). This initial test was promising—excess moisture had evaporated and the eggplant had even browning—so I focused on fine-tuning the details. For efficiency's sake, I chose globe eggplants since they are a decent size; I didn't want to multiply the number of slices I'd have to prepare by dealing with smaller varieties. For the best appearance, taste, and texture, I settled on unpeeled, ¾-inch-thick rounds. These slices seemed a little on the thick side when raw, but once roasted they shrank to a manageable size for layering in a casserole dish and serving (thinner slices tended to disintegrate). Most eggplant Parmesan recipes I found called for 2 pounds of eggplant, but I found it was necessary to double this amount in order to achieve a proper balance of ingredients.

After some experimentation I found that roasting 4 pounds of eggplant required 3 tablespoons of oil: 2 tablespoons to coat all of the eggplant rounds and 1 tablespoon to coat the two baking sheets and prevent sticking. Rotating the pans and flipping the slices partway through ensured even cooking, and at 450 degrees, the slices became fully tender and golden brown in about 35 minutes.

While the eggplant roasted in the oven, I had time to grate some cheese and whip up a quick tomato sauce. For the cheese, Parmesan was a given, but mozzarella is standard in many eggplant Parmesan recipes as well, serving as the binder for the casserole. I decided to use both.

A heaping tablespoon of minced garlic, sautéed in olive oil, started off my quick sauce, followed by a large can of crushed tomatoes. Ten minutes of simmering cooked out the raw tomato flavor but still left the sauce bright and fresh-tasting. After seasoning it with salt and pepper, I finished the sauce with some chopped fresh basil and moved on to putting the casserole together.

In a 13 by 9-inch baking dish I layered sauce, cooled eggplant, more sauce, then cheese, and repeated the process. The casserole went into a 375-degree oven, covered with foil to keep it from drying out. When the eggplant was hot throughout, I took the foil off so the top of the casserole could brown.

The result? Very close . . . but no cigar. Tasters were impressed by the flavor of this dish but felt it wasn't hearty enough to stand alone as a main course. Thinking that perhaps my efforts to lighten the dish had gone too far, I considered adding a layer of ricotta cheese, a common ingredient in Italian casseroles. I mixed some ricotta with Parmesan, salt, pepper, and an egg for stability before spreading the mixture into two thin but distinct layers in my casserole. The ricotta worked perfectly, imparting richness and body to the casserole while still allowing the eggplant to be the front-runner.

For a final touch, I decided the casserole would benefit from a crisp topping as a nod toward the traditional breaded and fried version of this dish. After the casserole was in the oven, I tossed together some panko, olive oil, Parmesan, and a clove of garlic; when the foil came off the baking dish, I sprinkled on the panko topping so it could get crispy and brown in the oven.

My streamlined take on eggplant Parmesan was just as satisfying as the old-fashioned comfort-food version, but with the additional benefit of being lighter and easier to prepare—traits that are comforting all on their own.

—ADELAIDE PARKER, *America's Test Kitchen Books*

Eggplant Casserole

SERVES 6 TO 8

Leaving the skins on the eggplant keeps the slices intact during roasting.

- **6 tablespoons olive oil**
- **4 pounds eggplant, sliced into ¾-inch-thick rounds**
- **Salt and pepper**
- **5 garlic cloves, minced**
- **1 (28-ounce) can crushed tomatoes**
- **2 tablespoons chopped fresh basil**
- **15 ounces whole-milk or part-skim ricotta cheese (1¾ cups)**
- **3 ounces Parmesan cheese, grated (1½ cups)**
- **1 large egg, lightly beaten**
- **1 pound whole-milk mozzarella cheese, shredded (4 cups)**
- **Vegetable oil spray**
- **1 cup panko bread crumbs**

1. Adjust oven racks to upper-middle and lower-middle positions and heat oven to 450 degrees. Line 2 large rimmed baking sheets with aluminum foil and brush each with 1½ teaspoons oil. Toss eggplant with 2 tablespoons more oil and 1 teaspoon salt and arrange in single layer on prepared baking sheets.

2. Roast eggplant until golden brown, 35 to 45 minutes, flipping eggplant and switching baking sheets halfway through baking. Let eggplant cool until needed. Adjust oven rack to middle position and reduce temperature to 375 degrees.

3. Meanwhile, heat 2 tablespoons more oil and 4 garlic cloves in large saucepan over medium heat until fragrant but not brown, 1 to 2 minutes. Stir in tomatoes and ¼ teaspoon salt and simmer until slightly thickened, about 10 minutes. Off heat, stir in basil and season with salt and pepper to taste. Cover to keep warm; set aside.

4. In bowl, mix ricotta, 1 cup Parmesan, egg, ½ teaspoon salt, and ½ teaspoon pepper together; set aside.

5. Spread ¾ cup of sauce over bottom of 13 by 9-inch baking dish. Fit half of roasted eggplant into dish in single layer, squeezing slices together tightly as needed. Spread ¾ cup more sauce over eggplant. Dollop half of ricotta mixture over sauce, then gently flatten dollops with back of spoon.

6. Sprinkle with 2 cups mozzarella, then dollop ¾ cup more sauce over cheese. Repeat layering process with remaining eggplant, remaining ¾ cup sauce, remaining ricotta mixture, and remaining 2 cups mozzarella. (Assembled casserole can be refrigerated, covered with plastic wrap, for up to 1 day. To finish, discard plastic and bake as directed, increasing covered baking time to 45 minutes.)

7. Cover dish tightly with aluminum foil that has been sprayed with vegetable oil spray. Bake until filling is bubbling, about 25 minutes.

8. Toss panko with remaining ½ cup Parmesan, remaining 1 tablespoon oil, and remaining garlic clove in bowl and season with salt and pepper to taste. Remove foil from casserole, sprinkle with panko mixture, and continue to bake until topping is spotty brown and crisp, 20 to 25 minutes longer. Let casserole cool for 10 minutes and serve.

NOTES FROM THE TEST KITCHEN

THE BEST PANKO BREAD CRUMBS

For a super-crispy finish to our Eggplant Casserole, we sprinkled panko bread crumbs over the top halfway through the baking time. These light, flaky crumbs, which originated in Japan, add big crunch and a neutral flavor to any number of dishes, from casseroles to deep-fried foods. Once the domain of specialty shops and Asian markets, panko are now available in most supermarkets.

When we gathered our tasters and compared a number of brands head to head, we couldn't distinguish any differences in taste, but the tasting did reveal differences in texture and crunch. For a super-crunchy—rather than delicate and crisp—texture, we found that **Ian's Panko Breadcrumbs** stood out from the pack.

LIGHTER TAMALE PIE

LIGHTER TAMALE PIE

TAMALE PIE IS THE SOUTHWEST'S ANSWER TO shepherd's pie. The dish is inspired by Mexican tamales, with their masa coating surrounding a filling of meat, cheese, or vegetables topped with a tomato or chili sauce, but in an easier-to-make, casserole-style version. Typically, a chili-like mixture of ground meat and vegetables is topped with cheese and a cornmeal crust of cornbread or polenta. Tasty and satisfying, yes. Good for you, not so much. Meat- and cheese-heavy pies rank high in flavor but heavy in fat and calories, often pushing 27 grams of fat and 530 calories per serving. All-vegetable tamale pie recipes exist, but those I tested were anything but impressive. The vegetables were a hodgepodge, the filling lacked cohesion, and the tomato-based sauce was muddy-tasting and watery. A heavy hand with ground spices vastly overcompensated for the lack of meat and fat in an attempt to boost flavor. Could I lighten it up and create a tasty vegetarian version? My goal was to create a killer combination of vegetables, beans, and cheese bound together with a flavorful sauce that would satisfy even the most confirmed carnivore—a vegetable-*full*, rather than meat-*less*, tamale pie.

The defining ingredient in tamales is the masa dough exterior, with its soft yet sturdy texture and toasty corn flavor. For tamale pie, the stand-in is most often a polenta-like cornmeal mush, though you'll also find tamale pies topped with a cornbread crust. In a side-by-side tasting, tasters agreed the polenta topping was too soft. They strongly preferred the slightly crunchy, subtle sweetness of the cornbread crust, knowing it would provide a nice textural contrast to the saucy vegetable filling.

My topping settled, I moved on to creating a base, or sauce, for my pie with just the right consistency. Since I was going the cornbread topping route, I needed a filling thick enough to adhere to and support the crust and also hold the vegetables and beans together (I used zucchini and black beans for now) as a unified whole, rather than a medley of juicy vegetables topped with some cornbread. The meatless tamale pie recipes I had tested early on simply relied on the juice in canned tomatoes to moisten and bind the ingredients, which left me with a wet, watery filling. I thought about pureeing tomatoes for a thicker texture, which seemed like a good route to take, but then a colleague suggested, while I was at it, that swapping out the usual red sauce in favor of a brighter-tasting tomatillo-based green sauce might help give my tamale pie a fresh lift. While it's common to see a green (or *verde*) sauce paired with enchiladas, I knew it was a little unorthodox for tamale pie, but that didn't cause me to hesitate.

For my next test I tried convenient canned tomatillos, but they were too acidic; fresh tomatillos, which I would precook to mellow their flavor, were a must. I tried both boiling the tomatillos and roasting them under the broiler, then pureeing each. Roasting softened the acidity of the tomatillos without the waterlogging effect of boiling, so I settled on the former. To smooth out the texture of the pureed tomatillos, I added small amounts of vegetable broth and olive oil, and a teaspoon of sugar nicely balanced the sauce's acidity. The final ingredient, cilantro, provided a bright, herbal burst of freshness and deepened the sauce's already vibrant color.

Now I needed to pick beans and vegetables to complement my sauce. Tasters were united in their preference for white cannellini beans over black beans. The white beans' creamy, mild flavor provided good contrast to the tangy green sauce. When it came to the vegetables, the surprise star turned out to be poblanos, as they added a great smoky flavor and hit of spice that worked perfectly with the sauce. They became the anchor of my filling, followed by corn since it nicely echoed the sweet flavor in my cornbread crust. I considered both butternut squash and zucchini, but the dense winter squash seemed out of place texturally, not to mention it would require precooking before being added to the other vegetables. I kept the zucchini, approved in my preliminary tests for its fresh flavor and chunky texture, adding it at the end of cooking to keep it from turning mushy.

To leave no vegetable unearthed, I also experimented with hearty greens. Swiss chard, though not usually found in tamale pie, is a popular green in Mexican cooking, and I thought it might work well here. However, while tasters liked its flavor, the texture just didn't work with the other vegetables, no matter how big or small I sliced it. The chard came across as slimy, and it muddied the other flavors. Other greens like kale and spinach fared no better. I decided that less was more: It wasn't about how many kinds of vegetables I mixed together; it was finding the right combination. With the addition of a little cumin, cayenne, garlic, and onion, I felt confident my filling hit the mark.

I then turned to the final ingredient: cheese. Though not an essential component of traditional tamales (unless it's the tamale's filling), cheese typically makes an appearance in tamale pie as a thin, melted layer beneath the crust. I didn't want to give up its gooey appeal in my lighter version. I wondered if adding my cheese to the filling would help fully incorporate it into the dish, so I tried mixing queso fresco, a fresh, crumbly Mexican cheese, into the filling. Because this cheese does not melt well, it dispersed in unappealing chunks, and the flavor was lost amid the stronger flavors of the vegetables and sauce. I next tried my favorite low-fat cheddar to see how it would perform. Mixed into the sauce, it produced a thick, gloppy texture tasters disliked. Also, I noticed that the cornbread topping was slightly soggy without the typical barrier of cheese. Maybe tradition is best after all. When I sprinkled the low-fat cheddar on top of the filling before adding the crust, the final pie had good cheese flavor in every bite and an appealing gooey layer that kept my topping from getting waterlogged.

After 15 minutes in the oven, the cornbread topping was cooked through and golden brown, sealing in the filling and melting the cheese underneath. The result? A hearty tamale pie that was chock-full of vegetables and full of fresh, bright flavor, clocking in at just 13 grams of fat and 390 calories. I'd take it over the meaty versions any day.

—CHRISTIE MORRISON, *America's Test Kitchen Books*

NOTES FROM THE TEST KITCHEN

THE BEST FOOD PROCESSOR

These days, food processors are fixtures in most well-equipped kitchens thanks to their ability to chop and slice vegetables, mix pizza dough, and emulsify eggs and oil into mayonnaise—all with the push of a button. We've gladly paid top dollar for our favorite food processor, made by KitchenAid, $180, a 12-cup machine that can handle a wide variety of tasks with ease. It slices and chops as evenly and cleanly as an expertly wielded knife—only much faster—and boasts a compact, intuitive design. To find out if any new contenders could beat our champ, we tested seven models against it.

A food processor should buzz through core cutting tasks—shredding, chopping, slicing, and grinding—with ease, backed by a strong motor and super-sharp blade. But after just a few tests, we realized that the design of the feed tube, which allows food to get to the blade, can be problematic. With a too-large tube, food falls out of position for the blade; with a too-small tube, you find yourself trimming the food extensively—which negates even using the food processor.

As for the cutting tests—slicing tomatoes; grating carrots and cheese; mincing parsley; chopping aromatics; and grinding bread crumbs and nuts—almost all of the machines passed with relative success.

After giving each machine its due process, we're sticking with our established favorite, the **KitchenAid KFP750**, which stood out once again for a compact, intuitive design that handily outperformed newer, pricier rivals. Its feed tube is a simple chute, it boasts sharp blades, and it has a powerful motor that churned through pizza dough effortlessly. (See page 308 for more information about our testing results.)

Lighter Tamale Pie

SERVES 6

Purchase tomatillos with dry outer husks, bright green skin, and a fresh, fruity smell. We prefer to make our own cornbread topping, but you can substitute one (6.5- to 8.5-ounce) package of your favorite cornbread mix if desired; follow the package instructions to make the cornbread batter, then dollop the batter over the filling and bake as directed in step 6. Don't try this recipe with a standard pie plate; substitute a 2-quart baking dish if you don't have a deep-dish pie plate.

- **1 pound tomatillos, husks removed, rinsed**
- **Vegetable oil spray**
- **½ cup packed fresh cilantro**
- **¼ cup vegetable broth**
- **2 tablespoons olive oil**
- **1 teaspoon sugar**
- **2 poblano chiles, stemmed, seeded, and chopped**
- **1 red bell pepper, stemmed, seeded, and chopped**
- **1 onion, chopped fine**
- **Salt and pepper**
- **3 garlic cloves, minced**
- **¼ teaspoon ground cumin**
- **⅛ teaspoon cayenne pepper**
- **1 (15-ounce) can cannellini beans, rinsed**
- **1 zucchini, halved lengthwise, seeded, and chopped**
- **1 cup fresh or frozen corn**
- **4 ounces 50 percent light cheddar cheese, shredded (1 cup)**
- **1 recipe Homemade Cornbread Topping (recipe follows)**

1. Adjust oven rack 6 inches from broiler element and heat broiler. Line rimmed baking sheet with aluminum foil. Arrange tomatillos on prepared baking sheet and lightly coat with vegetable oil spray. Broil until tomatillos blacken and begin to soften, 5 to 10 minutes, rotating baking sheet halfway through cooking.

2. Remove tomatillos from oven and let cool slightly. Adjust oven rack to middle position and heat oven to 450 degrees.

3. Process broiled tomatillos, cilantro, broth, 4 teaspoons oil, and sugar together in food processor until almost smooth, 30 to 60 seconds; set aside.

4. Combine remaining 2 teaspoons oil, poblanos, bell pepper, onion, and ¼ teaspoon salt in Dutch oven. Cover and cook over medium-low heat until vegetables are softened, 8 to 10 minutes. Uncover, increase heat to medium high, and continue to cook, stirring occasionally, until vegetables are lightly browned, 4 to 6 minutes longer.

5. Stir in garlic, cumin, and cayenne and cook until fragrant, about 30 seconds. Stir in tomatillo sauce, beans, zucchini, and corn. Bring to simmer over medium-high heat and season with salt and pepper to taste.

6. Transfer mixture to 9-inch deep-dish pie plate. Sprinkle cheese evenly over top. Dollop cornbread topping evenly over filling, then spread into even layer, covering filling completely. Bake until topping is golden and set, 15 to 20 minutes. Let cool for 10 minutes before serving.

Homemade Cornbread Topping

MAKES ENOUGH FOR ONE 9-INCH PIE

- **¾ cup (3¾ ounces) all-purpose flour**
- **¾ cup (3¾ ounces) yellow cornmeal**
- **3 tablespoons sugar**
- **¾ teaspoon baking powder**
- **¼ teaspoon baking soda**
- **½ teaspoon salt**
- **¾ cup buttermilk**
- **1 large egg**
- **1 tablespoon unsalted butter, melted and cooled**

Whisk flour, cornmeal, sugar, baking powder, baking soda, and salt together in large bowl. In separate bowl, whisk buttermilk and egg together. Stir buttermilk mixture into flour mixture until uniform, then stir in melted butter until just combined. Use as directed.

SPANAKOPITA

SPANAKOPITA'S ROOTS RUN DEEP IN GREEK culture, and it's not hard to understand the enduring appeal. This savory spinach "pie" trades on a flaky phyllo crust—wafer-thin sheets of oven-crisped dough—that gives way to a delectably moist filling of tender greens and salty feta, kicked up with lemon, garlic, herbs, and spices. What's not to love?

Plenty, at least stateside. The lackluster versions served at unambitious Greek-American diners bear more resemblance to lukewarm lawn clippings encased in a wet paper bag than the crispy, pillowy pride of Hellenic home cooking. A step up from there, the tidy spinach-and-phyllo turnovers found in supermarket freezers at least get the crispiness right. Yet the paltry ratio of filling to buttery crust places these tasty bites squarely in hors d'oeuvre territory.

My goal was to bring back the features that made spanakopita such a mealtime favorite in the first place—a casserole-style pie with a perfect balance of zesty spinach filling and shatteringly crisp phyllo crust—and I didn't want it to require an all-day stint in the kitchen. To that end, I decided to go with frozen phyllo sheets rather than homemade pastry: I wanted a weeknight meal, not a weeklong project.

Most recipes for spanakopita follow the same basic series of steps: Transparently thin sheets of phyllo—unleavened dough made from flour, water, and lemon juice or vinegar—are layered to form a bottom crust, usually in a 13 by 9-inch baking pan. Each layer receives a brush of melted butter to contribute rich flavor and boost browning. On top of that goes the cheesy spinach filling, followed by another layering of delicate phyllo sheets, which forms the top crust. After being baked at a high temperature (to ensure a golden brown top), the piping-hot pie is cooled and sliced into serving portions.

To get my bearings, I baked off several versions that I came across in various Greek cookbooks (as well as a few family recipes offered by colleagues), confirming that store-bought frozen phyllo dough (thawed and handled properly) was plenty reliable, save for some niggling texture issues involving the bottom crust. (I would deal with those later.) But the filling, by contrast, needed some serious work.

I decided to start with the main ingredient—the spinach—and come up with the perfect filling from that point. To my surprise, many of the recipes I came across in my research called for canned spinach—but knowing the sad, lifeless state of most canned fruits and vegetables, I refused to go there. Instead, I narrowed my options to frozen spinach, fresh baby leaves, and fresh adult greens. After loading up my cart, I headed back to the test kitchen.

Using a bare-bones filling of spinach, feta, and egg (for binding), I needed but one test to rule out frozen spinach. The weak flavor and woody, stringy texture were nonstarters. In the end, tasters favored the bolder flavor of the mature fresh spinach. Happily, all the methods I tried for precooking it (sautéing, boiling, microwaving, steaming) worked well for these hearty leaves, so I went with the convenience of the microwave. Follow-up tests revealed that coarsely chopping the spinach and thoroughly squeezing out its excess moisture yielded superior texture and maximum flavor.

With the green stuff in good shape, I moved on to the other major component: the dairy. Feta rides shotgun to spinach in spanakopita, and the right amount can make or break the dish. I found that simply crumbling the rich, pungent cheese (in the end, 12 ounces) into fine pieces helped it spread evenly through the sea of green, ensuring a salty tang in every bite. To buffer the assertiveness of the feta and add textural contrast, many recipes incorporate soft dairy into the mix as well. I tried everything. Cream cheese gave the spanakopita the consistency of spinach dip; ricotta and cottage cheese cooked up into rubbery curds. Sour cream and yogurt fared better, but thicker Greek yogurt—go figure!—turned out the best batch to date.

Some of the recipes I tested even included a third dairy component in the filling: a hard sheep's milk cheese called kefalograviera, which builds complexity. I wanted depth of flavor, but not the hassle of scouring specialty markets for such an obscure item. In the end, another, far more readily available hard sheep's milk cheese, Pecorino Romano, made a stand-up substitute.

A few final flavor tweaks: Grassy scallions trumped onions, leeks, and shallots; the more robust flavor of raw minced garlic beat out sautéed; a generous scattering of dill and mint provided a burst of freshness. A little nutmeg, cayenne, and a dose of lemon (juice plus grated zest) added fragrant warmth and brightness, respectively.

With a filling worthy of Mount Olympus, I was ready to move on to that one maddening texture issue: the crust. The top crust was flaky and golden brown. But no matter how I sliced it, the bottom crust ended up soggy. I tried adjusting the oven temperature, to no avail. Had I missed a clue during my initial survey of spanakopita recipes, too distracted by the lousy fillings to pick up on some clever trick? No—reviewing my notes, I realized that every recipe I had tested was plagued by the same problem.

In fact, the store-bought frozen turnovers were the only versions to achieve crispy bottom crusts. Though I was reluctant to take on the labor-intensive task of turning spanakopita into bite-size triangles for the purposes of weeknight dinner, I decided to bake off a batch just to see what made them work so well. Aside from their cunning shape, the big difference here was the ratio of phyllo to filling in each bite. While not nearly enough filling for my taste it was hard to argue with the crispiness of the triangles.

But could adjusting the ratio of phyllo to filling be the key to success in a casserole version as well? Studying my current recipe, I measured the height of the spinach layer: just shy of 2 inches. I supposed dialing it back was worth a shot. But when I tried this, I didn't start seeing increased crispiness on the bottom crust until the filling was reduced to almost half its original volume—and at that point, I was cutting into the number of servings. Plus the bottom, while improved, was still nowhere close to where I wanted it to be.

Then it occurred to me that no matter how much I reduced the filling, the thick, high walls of the baking dish would still trap any moisture coming off it, in effect helping to "steam" the crust instead of crisping it. So, what if I moved the pie to the flat surface of a baking sheet, which would allow excess liquid to evaporate far more readily? Sure enough, this proved to be an excellent move.

For starters, the assembly was easier. In the baking dish, the phyllo sheets, which were bigger than the vessel, would bunch up on the sides and corners. A typical 18 by 13-inch baking sheet, on the other hand, was plenty big enough to accommodate the full size of the 14 by 9-inch dough sheets. I layered 10 pieces of phyllo for the bottom crust, carefully painting each sheet with butter, then spread my spinach filling over the top, which was now about ¾ inch thick—more than the paltry smear in those spanakopita triangles but less than half as much as the filling in the casserole dish. I covered the spinach with eight more buttered layers of phyllo. As a last-minute brainstorm, I also

SPANAKOPITA (GREEK SPINACH AND FETA PIE)

took the grated Pecorino Romano I was using in the filling and sprinkled it between the first six layers instead, which helped glue them together and fixed the annoying, recurrent problem of having this tissue-thin pastry slide off when sliced. I scored the top few layers of phyllo with the tip of my knife to make it easier to cut once cooked and transferred the baking sheet to a 425-degree oven.

Twenty-five minutes later, what emerged from the oven was a beautiful spanakopita with crispiness on the top and—sure enough—on the bottom. In the end, all this classic needed was a modern twist to make it great. What started as a Greek tragedy was now a real showstopper.

—BRYAN ROOF, *Cook's Illustrated*

Spanakopita (Greek Spinach and Feta Pie)

SERVES 6 TO 8

Full-fat sour cream can be substituted for whole-milk Greek yogurt. Phyllo dough is also available in larger 14 by 18-inch sheets; if using, cut them in half to make 14 by 9-inch sheets. Don't thaw the phyllo in the microwave—let it sit in the refrigerator overnight or on the counter for 4 to 5 hours.

FILLING

- **20 ounces curly-leaf spinach**
- **¼ cup water**
- **12 ounces feta cheese, rinsed, patted dry, and crumbled into fine pieces (3 cups)**
- **¾ cup whole-milk Greek yogurt**
- **4 scallions, sliced thin**
- **2 large eggs, beaten**
- **¼ cup minced fresh mint**
- **2 tablespoons minced fresh dill**
- **3 garlic cloves, minced**
- **1 teaspoon grated lemon zest plus 1 tablespoon juice**
- **1 teaspoon ground nutmeg**
- **½ teaspoon pepper**
- **¼ teaspoon salt**
- **⅛ teaspoon cayenne pepper**

PHYLLO LAYERS

- **7 tablespoons unsalted butter, melted**
- **8 ounces (14 by 9-inch) phyllo, thawed**
- **1½ ounces Pecorino Romano cheese, grated fine (¾ cup)**
- **2 teaspoons sesame seeds (optional)**

1. FOR THE FILLING: Place spinach and water in large bowl, cover, and microwave until spinach is wilted and decreased in volume by half, about 5 minutes. Carefully remove bowl from microwave and keep covered for 1 minute. Uncover and transfer spinach to colander set in sink. Using rubber spatula, gently press spinach against colander to release excess liquid. Transfer spinach to cutting board and roughly chop. Transfer spinach to clean kitchen towel and squeeze to remove excess water. Place drained spinach in large bowl. Add remaining filling ingredients and mix until thoroughly combined. (Filling can be refrigerated for up to 24 hours.)

2. FOR THE PHYLLO LAYERS: Adjust oven rack to lower-middle position and heat oven to 425 degrees. Line rimmed baking sheet with parchment paper. Using pastry brush, lightly brush 14 by 9-inch rectangle in center of parchment with melted butter to cover area same size as phyllo. Lay 1 phyllo sheet on buttered parchment and brush thoroughly with melted butter. Repeat with 9 more phyllo sheets, brushing each with butter (you should have total of 10 layers of phyllo).

3. Spread spinach mixture evenly over phyllo, leaving ¼-inch border on all sides. Cover spinach with 6 more phyllo sheets, brushing each with butter and sprinkling each with about 2 tablespoons Pecorino. Lay 2 more phyllo sheets on top, brushing each with butter (these layers should not be sprinkled with Pecorino).

4. Working from center outward, use palms of your hands to compress layers and press out any air pockets. Using sharp knife, score pie through top 3 layers of phyllo into 24 equal pieces. Sprinkle with sesame seeds (if using). (Spanakopita can be frozen whole on baking sheet, wrapped well in plastic wrap, or cut in half crosswise and frozen in smaller sections on plate. To finish, bake spanakopita frozen, increasing baking time by 5 to 10 minutes.)

5. Bake until phyllo is golden and crisp, 20 to 25 minutes. Let cool on baking sheet for 10 minutes or up to 2 hours. Using parchment, slide spanakopita to cutting board. Cut into squares and serve.

SAVORY CRÊPES

WHAT'S NOT TO LOVE ABOUT A THIN CRÊPE wrapped around a savory, simple, yet flavorful filling? The richness and heaviness of most recipes, for one. While these fillings often start with chicken or a mix of vegetables—a healthy way to begin—when hefty amounts of cheese and butter are added they wind up high in fat. To top it off, crêpes are often covered with a heavy cream sauce. These rich crêpes are anything but light fare. I wondered if I could reinterpret this classic dish, updating it into a healthy vegetarian entrée that would highlight a simple yet flavorful vegetable filling.

I began with the crêpes themselves. The test kitchen had already developed an easy crêpe batter recipe, and I saw no reason to reinvent the wheel. In this simple recipe all the ingredients—eggs, milk, water, flour, salt, and melted butter—are combined in a food processor, forming a smooth batter after a few seconds. Many recipes call for resting the batter, but our previous tests had showed that rested crêpe batter yields crêpes that are difficult to roll around filling. Unrested batter was the way to go, yielding sturdier crêpes that were easier to roll, not to mention that skipping the step saved time.

To see if I could cut some fat from our full-fat crêpe recipe, I swapped in skim milk for the whole and was happy that these crêpes turned out well. However, for the butter, I found I didn't have as much leeway; the original recipe used 5 tablespoons, and I found that any less than 4 tablespoons for a batch made texture and flavor suffer.

Turning my attention to the filling, I narrowed my options quickly to a few of the typical choices: ricotta, spinach, and mushrooms, testing each one alone and in combination with another. Tasters preferred the combination of spinach and mushrooms because it was the most substantial. But sautéing ½ pound of white mushrooms, then wilting some baby spinach in the pan, made for a fairly bland filling. Since browning mushrooms deepens their flavor, my first adjustment was to give them more time in the pan to develop more color, and for more impact I upped the amount to a full pound. Adding onion with the mushrooms contributed sweetness, and minced garlic added depth. To incorporate all the highly flavorful fond from browning the mushrooms into the filling, I deglazed the pan with sherry, a classic match for mushrooms that added a nice complementary flavor. Then the spinach was stirred in. This filling had great mushroom flavor but tasters wanted more spinach; unfortunately, there simply wasn't enough room in the pan to wilt a sufficient amount of baby spinach to make everyone happy. The solution was simple; I switched from fresh spinach to frozen, which allowed me to pack more spinach into the pan since it is already cooked.

I had hoped I could skip making a sauce entirely, but my crêpes felt unfinished and slightly dry. A sauce, I realized, was a must. The most common types I found paired with crêpes were béchamel (a sauce of milk thickened with a roux made of butter and flour) and Mornay (béchamel with a rich cheese added), neither of which is traditionally light. Though not as frequently seen, tomato sauces also made an appearance. I started with the tomato sauce since it was the leanest candidate. While tasters liked the moisture that the tomato sauce added to the dish, they felt the acidic flavor competed too much with the filling. So I went back to the béchamel and Mornay sauces, ultimately settling on the béchamel, which would come together more quickly.

But to keep this dish healthy, I couldn't just pour on a sauce made of butter and milk. I tried cutting down on the amount of sauce, but the results were disappointing. It acted more like a garnish and didn't add enough creaminess. I was stumped about what to do until one of my fellow test cooks suggested incorporating a small amount of the béchamel with the spinach and mushrooms, just enough to add the right moisture and creaminess to the filling. Theoretically, I would get more mileage this way, and maybe these crêpes wouldn't even need a sauce to top them off.

For my next test, I made a small batch of béchamel, substituting skim milk for the usual whole, and incorporated it into the filling before stuffing and baking my crêpes. Just as I'd hoped, the lightened béchamel worked wonders, adding the moisture and richness I had missed and turning the filling from slightly dry to creamy and satisfying. To simplify my cooking process, I eliminated the extra saucepan used to make the béchamel and instead built it right in the pan with my filling. After adding the garlic, all I had to do was sprinkle a few teaspoons of flour over the vegetables and allow the flour to combine with the butter left in the skillet from

NOTES FROM THE TEST KITCHEN

MAKING MUSHROOM AND SPINACH CRÊPES

1. Pour ¼ cup of crêpe batter into pan and gently swirl batter to evenly cover bottom. Cook crêpe until spotty golden brown on bottom, 30 to 60 seconds.

2. Loosen edge of crêpe and grasp gently with your fingertips. Quickly flip crêpe and continue to cook until second side is dry, about 30 seconds longer.

3. After preparing filling, place 3 tablespoons of filling on each crêpe, about 1½ inches from bottom. Fold sides over filling, then fold up crêpe bottom and continue to roll into tidy cylinder.

4. Place crêpes, seam side down, in 13 by 9-inch broiler-safe baking dish, sprinkle with remaining cheese, and bake, covered, for 15 minutes. Uncover and broil until cheese is browned.

THE BEST PARING KNIFE

Nothing compares with a chef's knife when it comes to sawing through large cuts of meat or mincing herbs. But for detail work—hulling strawberries, scraping out vanilla beans, or trimming away silver skin on a roast—smaller, more maneuverable paring knives are far better tools. We tested 10 models and subjected them to a range of tasks to determine their maneuverability, comfort, and precision.

The best knives had sharply pointed tips, a good handle-to-blade balance and weight, and a comfortable grip. Our winner, the **Wüsthof Classic PEtec 3½-inch Paring Knife**, $39.95, scored high across the board, boasting a razor-sharp blade and a comfy handle. (See page 303 for more information about our testing results.)

sautéing the vegetables. Then, after I added the sherry and it had evaporated, the milk went into the skillet and I allowed the sauce to thicken. Tasters thought that the crêpes could use just a bit more richness; stirring in a few ounces of grated Parmesan cheese (and a pinch of nutmeg) took this filling from good to great.

With my crêpes made and the filling set, all that was left was to stuff the crêpes and heat them in the oven. I placed 3 tablespoons of filling on each crêpe and rolled them into cylinders, sprinkled them with some more Parmesan cheese, and baked them, covered with foil, for about 15 minutes. Running them under the broiler, uncovered, browned the cheese and gave my lighter crêpes (a mere 330 calories and 15 grams of fat per two crêpes) just the right finishing touch.

—CHRIS O'CONNOR, *America's Test Kitchen Books*

Mushroom and Spinach Crêpes

SERVES 6

It takes a few crêpes to get the heat of the pan right; your first 2 or 3 will almost inevitably be unusable. To allow for practice, the recipe yields about 16 crêpes; only 12 are needed for the dish. Use a ¼-cup dry measuring cup to portion the crêpe batter.

CRÊPES

- **1½ cups (7½ ounces) all-purpose flour**
- **1½ cups skim milk**
- **½ cup plus 2 tablespoons water**
- **3 large eggs**
- **4 tablespoons unsalted butter, melted**
- **½ teaspoon salt**
- **Vegetable oil spray**

FILLING

- **1 pound white mushrooms, trimmed and sliced thin**
- **1 onion, chopped fine**
- **2 tablespoons unsalted butter**
- **Salt and pepper**
- **2 garlic cloves, minced**
- **4 teaspoons all-purpose flour**
- **¼ cup dry sherry**
- **1 cup skim milk**
- **10 ounces frozen chopped spinach, thawed and squeezed dry**
- **3 ounces Parmesan cheese, grated (1½ cups)**
- **Pinch ground nutmeg**

1. FOR THE CRÊPES: Process flour, milk, water, eggs, melted butter, and salt together in food processor until smooth batter forms, 3 to 4 seconds; transfer to bowl.

2. Lightly coat bottom and sides of 10-inch nonstick skillet with vegetable oil spray. Heat skillet over medium heat until hot, about 3 minutes. Remove pan from heat, add ¼ cup of batter, and quickly swirl pan to evenly coat bottom with batter. Return skillet to heat and cook until bottom of crêpe is spotty golden brown, 30 to 60 seconds.

3. Loosen edge of crêpe with rubber spatula, grasp edge, and flip crêpe. Continue to cook until second side is spotty golden brown, about 30 seconds longer. Transfer crêpe to paper towel–lined plate. Repeat with vegetable oil spray and remaining crêpe batter, stacking cooked crêpes.

4. FOR THE FILLING: Combine mushrooms, onion, butter, and ⅛ teaspoon salt in 12-inch skillet over medium-low heat. Cover and cook until vegetables are softened, 8 to 10 minutes. Uncover, increase heat to medium-high, and continue to cook, stirring occasionally, until vegetables are well browned, 8 to 12 minutes longer.

5. Stir in garlic and cook until fragrant, about 30 seconds. Stir in flour and cook for 1 minute. Stir in sherry, scraping up any browned bits, and cook until liquid has almost evaporated, about 30 seconds. Stir in milk, bring to simmer, and cook until thickened, 2 to 3 minutes. Transfer mixture to medium bowl and stir in spinach, 1 cup of Parmesan, and nutmeg. Season with salt and pepper to taste.

6. TO ASSEMBLE THE CRÊPES: Adjust oven rack to upper-middle position and heat oven to 425 degrees. Lightly coat 13 by 9-inch broiler-safe baking pan with vegetable oil spray.

7. Place 3 tablespoons of filling on each crêpe, about 1½ inches from bottom, fold sides over filling, then fold up crêpe bottom and roll crêpe into tidy cylinder. Place rolled crêpes, seam side down, in prepared baking pan and sprinkle with remaining ½ cup Parmesan. Cover with aluminum foil and bake until heated through, about 15 minutes. Uncover, heat broiler, and broil until cheese is browned, about 5 minutes. Serve.

CHICKPEA CAKES

CHICKPEAS APPEAR IN CUISINES AROUND THE world, particularly the Mediterranean, Middle East, and India, gracing tables in everything from hearty soups and salads to spicy curries, creamy hummus, and crispy falafel. Looking for a new way to use this earthy-flavored bean in a vegetarian entrée, I came across several recipes for chickpea cakes in modern Indian cookbooks. I loved the idea of a dish featuring the buttery, nutty flavor of chickpeas that would be satisfying but not too heavy. I knew that my biggest challenge would be creating cakes that were tender but at the same time would hold together, all without going overboard on binders that would take away from the chickpea flavor. I wanted to develop a chickpea cake that was infused with the subtle flavor of Indian spices and had an appealing texture that was neither pasty nor too chunky.

I started with the chickpeas themselves. In the test kitchen, we prefer dried beans in most applications for their superior texture, but since these beans were going to be at least partially mashed, dried beans weren't as critical. Using canned beans was a great timesaver since it would eliminate the steps of soaking and precooking the beans, and two cans of beans would provide the right amount of bulk to make six cakes.

I found there were two main camps when it came to preparing the cakes: Some recipes mash some of the beans and leave some whole; others mash all of the beans. I tried both, combining the chickpeas with shallot, olive oil, and an egg (for binding); forming them into cakes; and pan-searing them on each side (I had more control over the cakes in a skillet rather than the oven). I wasn't surprised when tasters declared the texture of the all-mashed style to be pasty. However, leaving some chickpeas whole did come with problems; the cakes did not hold together well. For my next test, I tried using the food processor to create a blend of small and larger pieces, which avoided the problem of whole beans without making cakes that were pasty. Tasters gave the texture of these cakes the thumbs-up, but even with the texture worked out, I had trouble keeping the cakes from falling apart in the skillet.

I wondered if more eggs would keep my cakes together, so I made two more batches using two and three eggs. The cakes made with three eggs turned out too moist, closer to a dippable hummus than a firm

LANE CAKE

FOR GENERATIONS OF SOUTHERNERS, A LANE CAKE on a table signals a major event. The tall, fluffy, snow-white cake is filled with a rich, sweet mixture of egg yolks, butter, raisins, and "a wine glass full of good whiskey," as the original recipe puts it. The billowy white icing shines like satin. Emma Rylander Lane, of Clayton, Alabama, is credited with creating the cake more than 100 years ago—she won first prize for it at a county fair and later published the recipe in her own cookbook. But delicious as Lane cake is, given the amount of work that goes into baking one, it's no mystery why Southerners save it for celebrations.

Mrs. Lane got the ball rolling, but her eponymous cake truly came into its own when Harper Lee referred to it in *To Kill a Mockingbird*. One character, Maudie Atkinson, is determined to keep the recipe a secret from another, Stephanie Crawford: "That Stephanie's been after my recipe for thirty years," Atkinson says, "and if she thinks I'll give it to her . . . she's got another think coming."

Obviously I wasn't going to get my hands on the fictional Miss Maudie's recipe either, but I did find several others to test, including Mrs. Lane's. Over two long days in the test kitchen, I baked 15 layers of cake, whipping egg whites until stiff and then oh, so carefully folding them into various batters. I fussed over tricky custard fillings, monitored frostings with candy thermometers and kitchen timers, and (finally) wearily assembled and frosted the many-layered cakes. When I sat down at last, exhausted, I was ready to throw in the towel, but then I glanced over at the cakes lined up on the counter: They were stunning. A few forkfuls made it even clearer why Southerners have loved Lane cake for generations. This special cake is worth a little extra effort, I decided, but I still wasn't willing to commit to two days in the kitchen. And while I was simplifying, I figured I'd temper the painfully sweet frostings and ultra-boozy fillings.

The foundation of a Lane cake is a white layer cake. For ease, I decided on just two layers. Most Lane cakes are made by creaming butter and sugar, alternately adding milk and cake flour, and then folding in whipped egg whites. The cake is bright white (it has no yolks to give it color) and delicate. Maybe too delicate: Once I'd layered it with the gooey filling, the cake literally crumbled under pressure, and the filling oozed out the sides when I cut a slice. The test kitchen's recipe for white cake relies on the "reverse creaming" method, in which softened butter followed by milk and egg whites (no whipping necessary) are beaten into the combined dry ingredients. Less air is beaten into the batter, which makes for a sturdier cake that can handle a substantial filling.

What really sets Lane cake apart is the filling. It resembles a thick custard sauce, with bourbon taking the place of the usual milk or cream—my kind of cake! Egg yolks, butter, and sugar thicken on the stovetop, then bourbon and raisins—sometimes nuts and coconut, too—are added. We liked the nuts and coconut, but the bourbon proved polarizing. Whiskey lovers wanted more, teetotalers less. I split the difference and added 5 tablespoons.

But the cooking method was still tricky: Too much heat or time and the egg yolks curdled; not enough and the mixture was too thin to spread. I wondered if I could borrow from German chocolate cake and use sweetened condensed milk in my filling. I melted butter and stirred in the canned milk, bourbon, raisins, nuts, and coconut. The filling was thin, but as rich and buttery as the original. I added a spoonful of cornstarch and let it boil, which thickened it nicely. For speed, I chopped the dried fruit and nuts in the food processor and quickly toasted the nuts and coconut in the butter (instead of in the oven) before adding the bourbon and condensed milk. In just five minutes of cooking and with little to do but stir, I'd wrapped up the signature filling.

Lane cake's crowning touch is a seven-minute frosting made by beating together egg whites, sugar, and vanilla. The mixture must be heated to ensure that the egg whites are safe to eat. Some recipes call for hand-mixing egg whites and sugar in a double boiler until they are thick and glossy. Others call for heating sugar and water to precisely 238 degrees, then pouring this sugar syrup over egg whites and beating them. Without constant attention and the use of a candy thermometer, the egg whites curdle and the mixture crystallizes.

Fortunately, I found a promising "no-cook" seven-minute frosting: Boil water, pour over egg whites and sugar in a mixing bowl, and beat until stiff. The hot water was supposed to heat the egg whites to safety (160 degrees). It sounded so clever I wondered why I'd

LANE CAKE

never heard of it before. Maybe because it doesn't work? Sugar syrup can reach 240 degrees, but water can't go above 212. By the time I'd poured the water into the mixer, it had cooled too much to heat the eggs to safety. I suddenly thought of corn syrup, a ready-made sugar syrup that doesn't crystallize when heated. I worried it would make the frosting too sweet until I remembered that corn syrup is actually less sweet than sugar. I whipped the whites to soft peaks with just a little sugar and then slowly poured in ⅔ cup of boiling corn syrup.

I assembled and frosted my streamlined cake. The cake itself was moist and tender, the frosting balanced and ethereal, and the filling deliciously boozy. Admittedly, my recipe still requires three components, but each is easy and comparatively quick to make, and well worth the elegant, impressive result. Don't worry, Miss Maudie, I won't give Stephanie Crawford the recipe—unless she reads *Cook's Country*.

—LYNN CLARK, *Cook's Country*

Lane Cake

SERVES 8 TO 10

We like bourbon in the filling, but any whiskey will work.

CAKE

- **1 cup whole milk, room temperature**
- **6 large egg whites, room temperature**
- **2 teaspoons vanilla extract**
- **2¼ cups (9 ounces) cake flour**
- **1¾ cups (12¼ ounces) sugar**
- **4 teaspoons baking powder**
- **1 teaspoon salt**
- **12 tablespoons unsalted butter, cut into 12 pieces and softened**

FILLING

- **5 tablespoons bourbon**
- **1 tablespoon heavy cream**
- **1 teaspoon cornstarch**
- **Pinch salt**
- **⅓ cup sweetened shredded coconut**
- **¾ cup pecans**
- **¾ cup golden raisins**
- **4 tablespoons unsalted butter**
- **¾ cup sweetened condensed milk**
- **½ teaspoon vanilla extract**

FROSTING

- **2 large egg whites, room temperature**
- **¼ teaspoon cream of tartar**
- **¼ cup (1¾ ounces) sugar**
- **⅔ cup light corn syrup**
- **1 teaspoon vanilla extract**

1. FOR THE CAKE: Adjust oven rack to middle position and heat oven to 350 degrees. Grease two 9-inch round cake pans, line bottoms with parchment, grease parchment, and flour. Whisk milk, egg whites, and vanilla together in large liquid measuring cup. Using stand mixer fitted with paddle, mix flour, sugar, baking powder, and salt together on low speed until combined. Add butter, 1 piece at a time, and beat until only pea-size pieces remain, about 1 minute. Add half of milk mixture, increase speed to medium-high, and beat until light and fluffy, about 1 minute. Reduce speed to medium-low, add remaining milk mixture, and beat until incorporated, about 30 seconds. Give batter final stir by hand.

2. Scrape equal amounts of batter into prepared pans and bake until toothpick inserted in center of cakes comes out clean, 20 to 25 minutes, switching and rotating pans halfway through baking. Cool cakes in pans on wire rack for 10 minutes. Remove cakes from pans, discarding parchment, and let cool completely, about 2 hours. (Cooled cakes can be wrapped in plastic wrap and stored at room temperature for up to 2 days.)

3. FOR THE FILLING: Whisk bourbon, cream, cornstarch, and salt together in bowl until smooth. Process coconut in food processor until finely ground. Add pecans and raisins and pulse until coarsely ground. Melt butter in 12-inch skillet over medium-low heat. Add processed coconut mixture and cook, stirring occasionally, until golden brown and fragrant, about 5 minutes. Stir in bourbon mixture and bring to boil. Off heat, add condensed milk and vanilla. Transfer to bowl and cool to room temperature, about 30 minutes. (Filling can be refrigerated for up to 2 days. Bring filling to room temperature before using.)

4. FOR THE FROSTING: With stand mixer fitted with whisk, whip egg whites and cream of tartar together on medium-high speed until frothy, about 30 seconds. With mixer running, slowly add sugar and whip until soft peaks form, about 2 minutes; set aside. Bring corn syrup to boil in small saucepan over medium-high heat and cook until large bubbles appear around perimeter of pan, about 1 minute. With mixer running, slowly pour hot syrup into whites (avoid pouring syrup onto whisk or it will splash). Add vanilla and beat until mixture has cooled and is very thick and glossy, 3 to 5 minutes.

5. Place 1 cake round on serving platter. Spread filling over cake, then top with second cake round. Spread frosting evenly over top and sides of cake. Serve. (Cake can be refrigerated, covered, for up to 2 days. Bring to room temperature before serving.)

NOTES FROM THE TEST KITCHEN

THE BEST CAKE CARRIER

Bake a cake for a special occasion, frost it, and once plastic wrap hits the frosting, all your hard work is for naught. Take your cake on the road and a frosting-smeared trunk (or lap) is guaranteed. Safe, secure transport is what cake carriers are all about. We tested four, all plastic and all dishwasher-safe. We baked and frosted chocolate layer cakes and drove down pothole-riddled roads, evaluating the condition of each cake afterward. The integrity of every cake was pristine after these wild rides, so design determined our winner: the **Progressive Collapsible Cupcake and Cake Carrier**, $29.95. With comfortable handles, a sturdy locking system, and a collapsible design for easy storage, this carrier is the one to have if you're traveling with dessert. It can fit 9-inch round or square layer cakes or up to 24 cupcakes (with an included insert).

THE BEST CAKE LIFTER

Handling cakes can be tricky, whether you're stacking fragile, split layers as you frost them or moving an iced cake to a serving platter. In the past, we've used rimless cookie sheets and pizza peels to give us a hand. Now bakeware companies have created cake lifters—large spatula-like devices designed to slip under and support cakes, preventing breakage. We put six lifters, priced from $9.99 to $29, to the test.

Moving unassembled, uniced cake layers of standard thickness posed no problem for any cake lifter. But as we transferred thin, fragile, split layers to assemble a four-layer lemon cake, we were grateful for some extra support.

The greater challenge, we found, was moving cakes after they were assembled and frosted. Thin cake lifters, though easy to slide under cakes, flexed and bounced under the weight. Lifters that were too large or unbalanced felt awkward and heavy, straining our wrists. **Fat Daddio's Cake Lifter**, $11.88, fell right in the middle. It's slightly flexible, small enough to maneuver for stacking cake layers, and plenty sturdy.

STRAWBERRY DREAM CAKE

I FIRST RAN INTO IT AT A BIRTHDAY PARTY FOR a little girl: a bubblegum-pink layer cake with fluffy, pale pink frosting. The cake was shaped like a dome, which formed a skirt for the Barbie doll stuck in its center. When I looked for a recipe, I found a single one duplicated ad infinitum on the Internet. That recipe called itself Strawberry Dream Cake, although the closest it came to a real berry was the picture on the box of strawberry Jell-O. To make the cake, the contents of that box were stirred together with white cake mix and baked. But I dreamed of a cake made from scratch with real berries and real strawberry flavor. Recipes for chocolate, yellow, and lemon layer cakes abound. Where were the recipes for strawberry cake?

I finally uncovered a few from home cooks who, like me, couldn't believe a recipe for real strawberry cake didn't exist, so they had developed their own. One afternoon in the test kitchen, I tested their recipes alongside the Jell-O-and-box-mix version. The latter, not surprisingly, tasted about as much like real strawberries as fake tans look like real ones. But the from-scratch versions didn't measure up either. Some used strawberry jam in the batter—as much as a cupful—but the cakes lacked fresh berry flavor. Others called for stirring in lots of chopped fresh berries. This approach sounded promising, but the layers came out dense and soggy. The frostings, while pink, lacked even the merest hint of berry, and most were too sweet. I was beginning to understand why original recipes were hard to come by, yet I remained determined to fill the gap.

To develop my own recipe, I chose frozen strawberries over fresh. I'd be baking them anyway, plus I wanted to be able to bake this cake year-round. I started with the test kitchen's foolproof white layer cake recipe, which (because it uses an unusual reverse creaming method) produces a tender cake with a fine crumb. Also, I hoped that the lack of rich egg yolks would allow the delicate strawberry flavor to shine.

I began by pureeing thawed frozen berries and adding them to the cake in place of some of the milk. As in my initial tests, the berry solids made the cake soggy and dense. On the bright side, the puree did add flavor. Thinking it was too wet, I cooked it into a thicker "jam." (Since I was cooking it quickly and in a small batch, my jam retained the fresh berry flavor.) This yielded better flavor still but the same gummy layers.

To extract the berry flavor while leaving the pulp behind, I once again thawed the berries (the microwave made quick work of the job) and pressed them through a fine-mesh strainer. (It took a bit of elbow grease.) I discarded the pulp that was in the strainer and stirred the strawberry juice into the batter. Now the cake was light and tender again, but the strawberry flavor was faint. To get supercharged berry flavor, I reduced the juice by more than half on the stovetop until it was thick and syrupy—it took about eight minutes. The cake I made using that syrup had "berrylicious" flavor, as one taster put it, and the syrup turned the cake a pretty shade of pink.

Even the Jell-O-and-cake-mix recipes usually called for from-scratch frosting, in most cases a classic American icing made from confectioners' sugar, butter, and chopped fresh berries. It wasn't bad, but the cream cheese icing used in a few of the recipes was better. Its tang offset the sweet, fruity cake. The final piece of the icing puzzle came together one day while I was pressing juice out of the berries for some additional batter testing. Why, I suddenly wondered, was I discarding the pulp? I tried beating it into the frosting and found that in one pressing, I could flavor both cake and frosting.

I'd come to believe that any self-respecting strawberry cake needs a few fresh berries, so as a final touch I laid sliced fresh berries over the bottom layer. But when I placed the second cake layer over the first, it slid off the slick berries. I was able to prevent the problem by sandwiching the berries between thin coats of frosting.

To confirm that my Strawberry Dream Cake was now in perfect working order, I baked and iced one last cake. The cake was tender and light. Its pale tint was the color of a June rose and its subtle berry flavor was as soft and alive as a June day. It may not have been Barbie's Strawberry Dream Cake, but it was definitely mine.

—LYNN CLARK, *Cook's Country*

NOTES FROM THE TEST KITCHEN

GETTING STRAWBERRIES TO WORK

For great strawberry cake that can be made year-round, we turned to frozen strawberries. But we had to find a way to eliminate their excess moisture and maximize their flavor. To do this, we cooked our berries in the microwave, drained them, and saved the solids for the frosting and the juice for the batter.

FROZEN STRAWBERRIES
Easy to find. Always ripe.

PULP FOR THE FROSTING
We pressed thawed frozen strawberries through a fine-mesh strainer and reserved the solids for the frosting.

SYRUP FOR THE BATTER
Then we concentrated the strained juice on the stovetop and mixed it into the batter.

Strawberry Dream Cake

SERVES 8 TO 10

The strawberries do not need to be thawed in advance for this recipe.

CAKE

- **10 ounces frozen whole strawberries (2 cups)**
- **¾ cup whole milk, room temperature**
- **6 large egg whites, room temperature**
- **2 teaspoons vanilla extract**
- **2¼ cups (9 ounces) cake flour**
- **1¾ cups (12¼ ounces) granulated sugar**
- **4 teaspoons baking powder**
- **1 teaspoon salt**
- **12 tablespoons unsalted butter, cut into 12 pieces and softened**

FROSTING

- **10 tablespoons unsalted butter, softened**
- **2¼ cups (9 ounces) confectioners' sugar**
- **12 ounces cream cheese, cut into 12 pieces and softened**
- **Pinch salt**
- **8 ounces fresh strawberries, hulled and sliced thin (2 cups)**

1. FOR THE CAKE: Adjust oven rack to middle position and heat oven to 350 degrees. Grease two 9-inch round cake pans, line bottoms with parchment paper, grease parchment, and flour.

2. Transfer strawberries to bowl, cover, and microwave until strawberries are soft and have released their juice, about 5 minutes. Place in fine-mesh strainer set over small saucepan. Firmly press fruit dry (juice should measure at least ¾ cup); reserve strawberry solids. Bring juice to boil over medium-high heat and cook, stirring occasionally, until syrupy and reduced to ¼ cup, 6 to 8 minutes. Whisk milk into juice until combined.

3. Whisk strawberry milk, egg whites, and vanilla together in bowl. Using stand mixer fitted with paddle, mix flour, sugar, baking powder, and salt together on low speed until combined. Add butter, 1 piece at a time, and mix until only pea-size pieces remain, about 1 minute. Add half of milk mixture, increase speed to medium-high, and beat until light and fluffy, about 1 minute. Reduce speed to medium-low, add remaining milk mixture, and beat until incorporated, about 30 seconds. Give batter final stir by hand.

4. Scrape equal amounts of batter into prepared pans and bake until toothpick inserted in center of cakes comes out clean, 20 to 25 minutes, switching and rotating pans halfway through baking. Cool cakes in pans on wire rack for 10 minutes. Remove cakes from pans, discarding parchment, and let cool completely, about 2 hours. (Cooled cakes can be wrapped in plastic wrap and stored at room temperature for up to 2 days.)

5. FOR THE FROSTING: Using stand mixer fitted with paddle, mix butter and sugar together on low speed until combined, about 30 seconds. Increase speed to medium-high and beat until pale and fluffy, about 2 minutes. Add cream cheese, 1 piece at a time, and beat until incorporated, about 1 minute. Add reserved strawberry solids and salt and mix until combined, about 30 seconds. Refrigerate until ready to use.

6. Pat strawberries dry with paper towels. When cakes are cooled, spread ¾ cup frosting over 1 cake round. Press 1½ cups strawberries in even layer over frosting and cover with additional ¾ cup frosting. Top with second cake round and spread remaining frosting evenly over top and sides of cake. Garnish with remaining strawberries. Serve. (Cake can be refrigerated for up to 2 days. Bring to room temperature before serving.)

SWEET CHERRY PIE

I'VE OFTEN WONDERED WHY APPLE PIE BEAT OUT cherry as our national dessert. At their best, cherry pies are juicier, more colorful, and, in my opinion, just plain tastier than apple pies. It all boils down to a matter of availability. You can find decent apples year-round in even the most meagerly stocked supermarket, but cherry season is cruelly short—just a brief blossoming period during the early summer. And even when cherries are available, chances are they're a sweet variety (usually crimson-colored Bing or red-yellow-blushed Rainier), not the rare, ruby-hued sour species prized for jams and pie making.

What makes sour cherries such prime candidates for baking (most people find them too tart for snacking purposes) is their soft, juicy flesh and bright, punchy flavor that neither oven heat nor sugar can dull. Plumper sweet cherries, on the other hand, have a mellower flavor and meaty, firm flesh—traits that make them ideal for eating straight off the stem but don't translate well to baking. My challenge was obvious: Develop a recipe for sweet cherry pie with all the intense, jammy flavor and softened but still intact fruit texture of the best sour cherry pie.

Before I abandoned sour cherries altogether, I needed to get my hands on one batch to help me understand how they function in pie compared with their sweeter cousins. With help from the U.S. Postal Service, I obtained a few pounds of the tart variety from an online retailer, baked them into a pie, and tasted it side by side with one made with supermarket sweet cherries. The difference was like night and day. Compared with the sour cherry pie's bracing acidity, the sweet cherry pie's taste was beyond sweet; it was downright cloying. Even more problematic, the sweet cherries' drier, relatively dense flesh failed to break down completely (even after an hour or more of baking) and resulted in a filling that called to mind slightly softened jumbo marbles, not fruit.

So I had two issues to resolve: taming the cherries' sweetness, and getting them to break down to the proper juicy texture. To get my bearings, I made another pie. I combined 2 pounds of pitted fresh Bing cherries and 1 cup of sugar, stirred in 3 tablespoons of ground tapioca (our preferred thickener for juicy fruit pies), poured the filling into a shell, and wove a traditional lattice-top crust to show off the fruit's jewel-like shine. After the pie had baked and cooled, I offered my colleagues a bite. As I expected, nobody could taste past the sweetness. Figuring all that sugar wasn't helping, I tried cutting back a few tablespoons at a time, but that only created a new problem: Sugar draws moisture out of the cherries through osmosis, so less of it made for a less juicy filling. A half cup was as low as I could go without completely ruining the texture, but the filling still verged on candylike sweetness.

My only other option was to add another ingredient to offset the sweetness. A couple of splashes of bourbon—a classic pairing with cherries—helped, as did the acidity of fresh lemon juice, but these were minor tweaks, and adding more of either just made the pies taste boozy or citrusy. I even tried vinegar, hoping to more closely mimic the tartness of sour cherries, but tasters objected to the sharpness of even the smallest drop. As a last-ditch effort, I tried introducing alternative fruits: super-tart fresh cranberries (too bitter), tangy red grapes (too musty), and dried sour cherries (too chewy).

None of these ideas panned out, but the concept did get me thinking about other types of fruit. Cherries fall into the stone-fruit category, along with peaches, nectarines, and plums. Sweet-fleshed peaches and nectarines wouldn't help me, but the tartness of plums might be worth a shot. For my next pie, I sliced a couple of plums into the filling, but their flesh was just as dense and resilient as the cherries'. No problem, I thought; this was nothing my trusty food processor couldn't fix. I made another pie, this time pureeing the plums and mixing the resulting pulp with the cherries. Perfect! The flavor, now tangy and complex, was spot-on, and nobody suspected my secret.

Now that I'd crossed one challenge off my list, I was ready to tackle the sweet cherries' overly firm texture. The problem was twofold: Not only were the cherries refusing to break down, but as a result they also weren't releasing enough juice to amply moisten the filling. As it turned out, the culprit was cellulose, the main structural component of fruit cells: Compared with sour cherries, the sweet variety contains a full 30 percent more cellulose, making the flesh more rigid.

Without a way to rid the cherries of that extra structure, I'd have to rely on more conventional techniques to soften the flesh. I was already macerating them in sugar before baking to help draw out some of their juice, but with their relatively thick skin, this technique wasn't effective. Halving them helped considerably, since their juice was very easily drawn out of the exposed fleshy centers. Even better, the cut cherries collapsed more readily and turned out markedly softer in the finished pie, save for a few too many solid chunks. By tossing a portion of them (1 cup) into the food processor along with the plums (and straining the chewy skins out of the resulting pulp), I got a filling that was ideally soft, if a bit dry, and studded with a few still-intact cherry pieces. As a bonus, the pies I tested using a good brand of frozen sweet cherries—an easier alternative to pitting dozens of the fresh variety—baked up equally well, making this an any-season dessert.

I'd hoped that mashing and precooking the cherries with sugar would help release some fruit juice, but this technique actually caused moisture to evaporate through the crust's ventilated top as it baked, leading to a drier pie. Then I realized: My problem wasn't the fruit itself, but the lattice crust. Juice-gushing sour cherry and berry pies may benefit from the extra evaporation of a woven crust, but with these cherries I needed to keep a tighter lid on the available moisture. Rolling out a traditional disk of dough, I fitted it to the bottom pastry, neatly sealed the edges, and slid the whole assembly onto a preheated baking sheet in the oven to ensure that the bottom crust crisped up before the fruit filling could seep through. An hour or so later, out came a gorgeously golden brown, perfectly juicy (but not runny) pie. When my tasters began to line up for second helpings, I knew I'd finally gotten cherry pie in apple-pie order.

—YVONNE RUPERTI, *Cook's Illustrated*

Sweet Cherry Pie

MAKES ONE 9-INCH PIE, SERVING 8

The tapioca should be measured first, then ground in a coffee grinder or food processor for 30 seconds. If you are using frozen fruit, measure it frozen, but let it thaw before making the filling; if you don't, you run the risk of partially cooked fruit and undissolved tapioca. See page 278 for tips on rolling out pie dough.

1 recipe Foolproof Double-Crust Pie Dough (page 244)
2 red plums, halved and pitted
6 cups (2 pounds) pitted sweet cherries or 6 cups pitted frozen cherries, halved
½ cup (3½ ounces) sugar

SWEET CHERRY PIE

- 1 tablespoon lemon juice
- 2 teaspoons bourbon (optional)
- 2 tablespoons instant tapioca, ground
- ⅛ teaspoon salt
- ⅛ teaspoon ground cinnamon (optional)
- 2 tablespoons unsalted butter, cut into ¼-inch pieces
- 1 large egg, lightly beaten with 1 teaspoon water

1. Remove 1 disk of dough from refrigerator and roll out on generously floured (up to ¼ cup) counter to 12-inch circle about ⅛ inch thick. Roll dough loosely around rolling pin and unroll into pie plate, leaving at least 1-inch overhang. Ease dough into plate by gently lifting edge of dough with one hand while pressing into plate bottom with other hand. Refrigerate until dough is firm, about 40 minutes.

2. Adjust oven rack to lowest position, place baking sheet on oven rack, and heat oven to 400 degrees. Process plums and 1 cup halved cherries in food processor until smooth, about 1 minute, scraping down sides of bowl as necessary. Strain puree through fine-mesh strainer into large bowl, pressing on solids to extract liquid; discard solids. Stir remaining halved cherries, sugar, lemon juice, bourbon (if using), tapioca, salt, and cinnamon (if using) into puree; let stand for 15 minutes.

3. Transfer cherry mixture, including all juices, to dough-lined plate. Scatter butter pieces over fruit. Roll out second disk of dough on generously floured counter (up to ¼ cup) to 11-inch circle about ⅛ inch thick. Roll dough loosely around rolling pin and unroll over pie, leaving at least ½-inch overhang. Flute edges using thumb and forefinger or press with tines of fork to seal. Brush top and edges with egg mixture. With sharp knife, make 8 evenly spaced 1-inch-long vents in top crust. Freeze pie for 20 minutes.

4. Place pie on preheated baking sheet and bake for 30 minutes. Reduce oven temperature to 350 degrees and continue to bake until juices bubble around edges and crust is deep golden brown, 30 to 40 minutes longer.

5. Transfer pie to wire rack; let cool to room temperature so juices have time to thicken, 2 to 3 hours. Cut into wedges and serve.

NOTES FROM THE TEST KITCHEN

KEYS TO JUICY, SWEET-TART CHERRY PIE

1. Halving cherries exposes their dense, meaty flesh and helps them release more juice than if left whole.

2. Pureeing 1 cup cherries with 2 plums and adding strained liquid to halved cherries contributes juiciness and tartness.

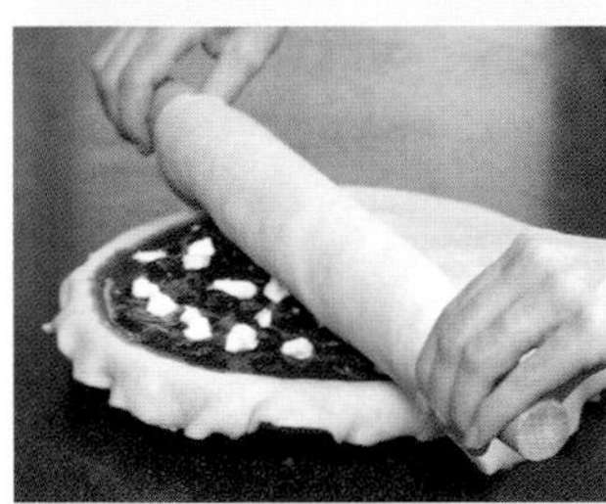

3. Using closed top crust, instead of traditional lattice crust, keeps juices inside and prevents too much moisture from evaporating during baking.

THE BEST FROZEN SWEET CHERRIES

With cherry season so fleeting, a good frozen brand can come in handy. Of the three brands we tasted (Dole, Tree of Life, and Cascadian Farm), only **Cascadian Farm Premium Organic Sweet Cherries** stood out for consistently plump, juicy cherries that rivaled fresh cherries for their firm, not mushy, texture and deep fruity flavor.

Foolproof Double-Crust Pie Dough

MAKES ENOUGH FOR ONE 9-INCH DOUBLE-CRUST PIE

Vodka is essential to the texture of the crust and imparts no flavor. This dough will be moister and more supple than most standard pie doughs and will require more flour to roll out (up to ½ cup).

- 2½ cups (12½ ounces) all-purpose flour
- 2 tablespoons sugar
- 1 teaspoon salt
- 12 tablespoons unsalted butter, cut into ¼-inch pieces and chilled

- ½ **cup vegetable shortening, cut into 4 pieces and chilled**
- ¼ **cup cold vodka**
- ¼ **cup cold water**

1. Pulse 1½ cups flour, sugar, and salt in food processor until combined, about 2 pulses. Add butter and shortening and process until homogeneous dough just starts to collect in uneven clumps, about 15 seconds (dough will resemble cottage cheese curds and there should be no uncoated flour). Scrape down bowl with rubber spatula and redistribute dough evenly around processor blade. Add remaining 1 cup flour and pulse until mixture is evenly distributed around bowl and mass of dough has been broken up, 4 to 6 quick pulses. Empty mixture into medium bowl.

2. Sprinkle vodka and water over mixture. With rubber spatula, use folding motion to mix, pressing down on dough until dough is slightly tacky and sticks together. Divide dough into 2 even balls and flatten each into 4-inch disk. Wrap each disk in plastic wrap and refrigerate for at least 45 minutes or up to 2 days.

Foolproof Single-Crust Pie Dough

MAKES ENOUGH FOR ONE 9-INCH SINGLE-CRUST PIE

Vodka is essential to the texture of the crust and imparts no flavor. This dough will be moister and more supple than most standard pie doughs and will require more flour to roll out (up to ¼ cup).

- 1¼ **cups (6¼ ounces) all-purpose flour**
- 1 **tablespoon sugar**
- ½ **teaspoon salt**
- 6 **tablespoons unsalted butter, cut into ¼-inch pieces and chilled**
- ¼ **cup vegetable shortening, cut into 2 pieces and chilled**
- 2 **tablespoons cold vodka**
- 2 **tablespoons cold water**

1. Pulse ¾ cup flour, sugar, and salt in food processor until combined, about 2 pulses. Add butter and shortening and process until homogeneous dough just starts to collect in uneven clumps, about 10 seconds (dough will resemble cottage cheese curds with some very small pieces of butter remaining and there should be no uncoated flour). Scrape down bowl with rubber spatula and redistribute dough evenly around processor blade. Add remaining ½ cup flour and pulse until mixture is evenly distributed around bowl and mass of dough has been broken up, 4 to 6 quick pulses. Empty mixture into medium bowl.

2. Sprinkle vodka and water over mixture. With rubber spatula, use folding motion to mix, pressing down on dough until dough is slightly tacky and sticks together. Flatten dough into 4-inch disk. Wrap disk in plastic wrap and refrigerate for at least 45 minutes or up to 2 days.

NOTES FROM THE TEST KITCHEN

KEYS TO FOOLPROOF PIE DOUGH

1. Completely blending part of flour with all of butter and shortening ensures consistent amount of fat-coated flour in final dough.

2. Pulsing remaining flour ensures consistent amount of uncoated flour in finished dough.

3. Sprinkling dough with water and vodka ensures even distribution. No need to skimp—unlike water, vodka won't make dough tough.

FRESH STRAWBERRY PIE

GROWING UP IN SOUTHERN CALIFORNIA, I COULD hardly wait for the kickoff of strawberry season. In the late spring months, farm stands overflowed with baskets of ripe red berries, which local bakeries would pile whole into fresh strawberry pies. This sweet, juicy dessert traded on nothing more than the fresh-picked berries, a sheer glaze that just barely held the fruit together while making it sparkle, and a flaky, buttery crust. Serving neat slices was downright impossible—the pie inevitably split into shards of pastry and a tumble of berries—but in a dessert so good, looks hardly mattered. Besides, mounds of whipped cream always covered the mess.

Though strawberry pie was a treat my family indulged in on an annual basis, I never learned to make it myself. When I moved back to California a few years ago, I was determined to nail down my own approach. I figured it couldn't be hard, since, with the best ripe berries, the pie would practically make itself. But to my dismay, most of the recipes I tried were flawed, and the fruit's sweet juice was the culprit. Because the uncooked berries shed so much liquid (even when they were left whole), the filling had to be firmed up with some sort of thickener, producing results that ranged from stiff and bouncy to runny and gloppy—hardly the dessert I remembered.

Clearly, re-creating my ideal—fresh berries lightly held together by a sheer, glossy glaze that would make their flavor pop in the buttery pastry shell—hinged on my getting the thickener just right.

Most recipes attacked the excess liquid problem with cornstarch; I also found a few that called for gelatin. The thickener of choice was simmered in a pan with liquid (often a juice like pineapple or grape, or even water), sugar, and a dash of salt; this mixture was then combined with the fresh whole berries, mounded in a prebaked pie shell, and chilled to set. Predictably, the gelatin produced a stiff and springy filling. The cornstarch was no better, rendering the berry mixture cloudy, gummy, and not at all firm. Adjusting the amount of each type of thickener didn't improve matters much. Ramping up the amount of cornstarch simply led to an increasingly gloppy, dull-tasting filling that never actually firmed up. As for the gelatin, the line between lightly thickened and stiff proved impossible to nail down (⅓ teaspoon, anyone?).

Maybe I was just using the wrong type of thickener. I spent the next few days working through alternatives (flour, arrowroot, potato starch, tapioca), as well as strawberry jam and even a grated apple—a trick from an earlier test kitchen blueberry pie recipe, in which the apple's natural pectin seamlessly jells up the juicy fruit filling. But nothing panned out, and I was left with pies that were off-flavored, unpredictable, or gluey. The jam offered a reasonably thick texture, but its flavor was dull and cloying, and in this (mostly) fresh-fruit filling, bits of grated apple were hardly a subtle fix.

Frustrated, I decided to try a recipe I'd found that didn't use any added liquid or thickener at all. Instead, half of the uncooked berries were turned into a smooth, thick puree in the food processor, mixed with sugar, simmered briefly in a saucepan to thicken, and then combined with the fresh berries. The puree tasted bright and sweet and added body to the cut-up fruit, but I wasn't surprised when it didn't prove to be sufficient. Even after I assembled and chilled the pie for a couple of hours, the filling oozed from each cut slice.

The cooked puree was a keeper, but there was no getting around it: Some form of added thickener was a must. I circled back to my earlier tests. Of all the thickeners I'd tried, jam had been the most promising. The jelling agent in jam, of course, is pectin. What if I made my own jam by adding pectin to the cooked puree? That way I could control how much was added and how long it simmered with the puree, preserving as much fresh flavor as possible. Pectin comes in two varieties, regular and low-sugar, the latter engineered to set without a surplus of sugar or acid. Since I didn't want to overload my sweet berries with excess sugar, I mixed some of the low-sugar product into the puree and proceeded. But as soon as the knife hit the pie's stiff, springy surface, I knew I still hadn't found the solution.

I was tempted to give up on strawberry pie altogether when our science editor suggested something so obvious I couldn't believe I hadn't thought of it before: If I couldn't get the effect I wanted from one thickener, why not try two? After all, combining thickeners to produce a particular effect is exactly what the processed food industry does. Pectin still seemed like my best bet, so I considered what I might use with it. Gelatin was out—it would only exacerbate the pectin's springiness. The "alternative" starches I tried had too many issues, and I crossed them off the list as well. That left cornstarch.

The more I thought about it, the better the idea seemed. Since cornstarch on its own produced a filling that was too loose and pectin produced a filling that was too firm, a combination of the two might actually do the trick. Excited, I headed back into the test kitchen. After some tinkering, I finally hit upon a formula that worked. With ¾ cup of puree, 2 tablespoons of cornstarch, and 1½ teaspoons of pectin, I managed to produce just the right supple, lightly clingy glaze.

I knew the berry juice would leach out eventually (sugar extracts moisture), but that didn't worry me. A pie this irresistible would never sit around for long.

—DAWN YANAGIHARA, *Cook's Illustrated*

Fresh Strawberry Pie

MAKES ONE 9-INCH PIE, SERVING 8

To account for any imperfect strawberries, the ingredient list calls for several more ounces of berries than needed. Seek out ripe, farmers' market–quality berries. Make certain that you use Sure-Jell engineered for low- or no-sugar recipes (packaged in a pink box) and not regular Sure-Jell (in a yellow box); otherwise, the glaze will not set properly. The pie is at its best after 2 or 3 hours of chilling; as it continues to chill, the glaze becomes softer and wetter, though the pie will taste just as good. See page 278 for tips on rolling out pie dough.

1 recipe Foolproof Single-Crust Pie Dough (page 245)

FILLING

3 pounds strawberries, hulled (9 cups)
¾ cup (5¼ ounces) sugar
2 tablespoons cornstarch
1½ teaspoons Sure-Jell for low-sugar recipes
Generous pinch salt
1 tablespoon lemon juice

WHIPPED CREAM

1 cup heavy cream, chilled
1 tablespoon sugar

1. FOR THE PIE DOUGH: Remove dough from refrigerator and roll out on generously floured (up to ¼ cup) counter to 12-inch circle about ⅛ inch thick. Roll dough loosely around rolling pin and unroll into pie plate, leaving at least 1-inch overhang. Ease dough into plate by gently lifting edge of dough with one hand while pressing into plate bottom with other hand. Refrigerate until dough is firm, about 30 minutes.

2. Adjust oven rack to lowest position, place baking sheet on oven rack, and heat oven to 425 degrees. Trim dough overhang to ½ inch beyond lip of pie plate. Fold overhang under itself; folded edge should be flush with edge of pie plate. Flute edges using thumb and forefinger or press with tines of fork to flatten against rim of pie plate. Refrigerate dough-lined plate until firm, about 15 minutes.

3. Remove pie plate from refrigerator, line crust with aluminum foil, and fill with pie weights or pennies. Bake for 15 minutes. Remove foil and weights, rotate plate, and bake until crust is golden brown and crisp, 5 to 10 minutes longer. Let cool to room temperature.

4. FOR THE FILLING: Select 6 ounces misshapen, underripe, or otherwise unattractive berries, halving those that are large; you should have about 1½ cups. In food processor, process berries to smooth puree, 20 to 30 seconds, scraping down bowl as needed (you should have about ¾ cup).

5. Whisk sugar, cornstarch, Sure-Jell, and salt together in medium saucepan. Stir in berry puree, making sure to scrape corners of pan. Cook over medium-high heat, stirring constantly with rubber spatula, and bring to full boil. Boil, scraping bottom and sides of pan to prevent scorching, for 2 minutes to ensure that cornstarch is

NOTES FROM THE TEST KITCHEN

DOUBLING UP TO THICKEN JUICY FRUIT

To create a filling with just enough sticking power to hold the berries together gently, we turned to a thickener more common in jam than in pie—low-sugar pectin—and used it in combination with cornstarch. When used independently, neither product resulted in a suitable pie filling, but together they yielded a glaze with just the right texture.

LOW-SUGAR PECTIN

CORNSTARCH

fully cooked (mixture will appear frothy when it first reaches boil, then will darken and thicken with further cooking). Transfer to large bowl and stir in lemon juice. Let cool to room temperature.

6. Meanwhile, pick over remaining berries and measure out 2 pounds of most attractive ones; halve only extra-large berries. Add berries to bowl with glaze and fold gently with rubber spatula until berries are evenly coated. Scoop berries into pie shell, piling into mound. If any cut sides face up on top, turn them facedown. If necessary, rearrange berries so that holes are filled and mound looks attractive. Refrigerate pie until chilled, about 2 hours. Serve within 5 hours of chilling.

7. FOR THE WHIPPED CREAM: Just before serving, using stand mixer fitted with whisk, whip cream and sugar on medium-low speed until foamy, about 1 minute. Increase speed to high and whip until soft peaks form, 1 to 3 minutes.

8. Cut pie into wedges and serve with whipped cream.

THOROUGHBRED PIE

IN THE FINAL STRETCH OF ANY PROPERLY HOSTED Kentucky Derby party—trailing behind the mint juleps, burgoo, and hot browns—comes a slice of gooey, rich chocolate-nut pie. Although you can find countless recipes for it, the Kern family created the standard-bearer. They began baking it at their inn in Prospect, Kentucky, in 1954 and subsequently trademarked it as "Derby-Pie." It's soft and very sweet and studded with walnuts and chocolate chips; the top of the pie has a sugary, slightly crackly crunch. To this day, the recipe remains a closely guarded Kern family secret, but I was determined to crack the code—or at least create an equally winning pie.

I mail-ordered a "Derby-Pie" from the original makers and, when it arrived, called my fellow test cooks to the table. The pie fell decisively into the classic Southern category of homey, soft, and super-sweet pies; other examples include pecan, chess, vinegar, and transparent pies. All use butter and eggs, as well as flour, cornstarch, or cornmeal to thicken, and all go heavy on the sweetener (variously white or brown sugar, molasses, or Karo syrup). There they diverge. Among the characteristics that distinguish this pie (generically called thoroughbred pie) is its use of bourbon (usually), chocolate, and walnuts, not to mention that signature crackle layer at the top.

I rounded up recipes, dusted off my rolling pin, and rolled up my sleeves. It was hard to imagine how anything made from these tempting ingredients could taste bad, but a few hours later, I found myself surveying a disappointing bunch. As a group, the pies were sweeter than a John Denver tune, and with all that sugar going on, you barely noticed the nuts or the chocolate. On top of that (or, more accurately, below that), the crusts were pale, soggy, and underdone. Well, at least my goals were clear: more flavor, less sugar, and a nicely browned, crisp crust.

As my starting point, I used tasters' top pick from the recipes in my initial test and gradually reduced the amount of sugar, pie by pie, until I was using not much more than half of what many recipes call for. (Thoroughbred pies by definition don't call for liquid sweeteners like corn syrup or molasses.) Next, I did side-by-side tests of pies made with all white sugar, all brown sugar, and a combination (other recipes went in all directions). Brown sugar contributed a hint of spice and depth; more neutral white sugar ensured that the nuts and the chocolate weren't eclipsed. Ultimately, I used a bit of both. The chocolate was also helping to push the sugar level into the stratosphere. To bring more balance, I replaced the semisweet chips with chopped bittersweet chocolate.

Now that I had a handle on the sugar, I could actually taste the other elements. For the first time I noticed that as the pie baked, the layer of walnuts that floated to the top got nice and crisp while those underneath were soggy and bland. So I toasted the nuts before stirring them into the filling, which kept them crisp no matter their location. At the same time, I went up to 1½ cups from the 1 cup called for in most recipes.

But the pie took a giant leap forward when I got the idea to brown the butter. When you brown butter—melt it in a skillet until the milk solids toast—you get a heady, nutty aroma and flavor. You can stop the process when the butter turns golden, but I took it a step further, cooking the butter to a light brown. Now the pie tasted deeply nutty.

The top of my pie had none of the appealing faint crunch that we'd tasted in the trademarked pie.

THOROUGHBRED PIE

Our science editor gave me a couple of helpful hints: Increase the carbohydrates and decrease the protein. In plain English: I switched the flour (which contains protein) that I'd been using as a thickener to cornstarch (which is a carbohydrate). At the same time, I lost an egg white (protein again, and also moist, so it was softening the top) and tested a pie with two whole eggs plus one yolk. Right on cue, that distinctive sugary crunch presented itself.

To avoid underbaking, many pie recipes require parbaking the crusts. But doing so would require that I refrigerate and then freeze the shell to keep it from shrinking, slumping, and toughening, all before I even turned on the oven. Hoping to bypass these steps, I tried a favorite test kitchen method: starting the pie on a low shelf in a very hot oven to take advantage of the blast of heat from the bottom, then immediately lowering the heat to bake the pie through.

Unfortunately, while this method succeeds beautifully for pecan pie, thoroughbred pie simply didn't stay in the oven long enough for it to work. I returned to the blind baking method. As I was taking a warm, golden, parbaked shell from the oven, I got a good idea. I sprinkled the chopped chocolate over the still-warm crust, where it gently melted. I spread the softened chocolate evenly over the bottom crust. Now the pie had a flavorful, browned crust plus a hit of intense chocolate in every bite—an improvement on the usual random smattering of chips.

I baked one last pie. Its delicately crisp top layer contrasted nicely with the soft yet nutty center, and the whole pie had layers of flavor. I called tasters over and watched happily as slices left the gate as fast as any Churchill Downs thoroughbred.

—ERIKA BRUCE, *Cook's Country*

NOTES FROM THE TEST KITCHEN

ENSURING AN EVEN LAYER OF CHOCOLATE

Sprinkle chopped chocolate on warm crust, let sit for 5 minutes to soften, then spread evenly over crust.

Thoroughbred Pie

SERVES 8

We like this pie served with a dollop of Bourbon Whipped Cream (recipe follows). See page 278 for tips on rolling out pie dough.

- **1 recipe Foolproof Single-Crust Pie Dough (page 245)**
- **3 ounces bittersweet chocolate, chopped fine**
- **8 tablespoons unsalted butter, cut into 8 pieces**
- **3 tablespoons bourbon**
- **¾ cup (5¼ ounces) granulated sugar**
- **½ cup packed (3½ ounces) light brown sugar**
- **2 tablespoons cornstarch**
- **½ teaspoon salt**
- **2 large eggs plus 1 egg yolk, lightly beaten**
- **1 teaspoon vanilla extract**
- **1½ cups walnuts, toasted and chopped**

1. Remove dough from refrigerator and roll out on generously floured (up to ¼ cup) counter to 12-inch circle about ⅛ inch thick. Roll dough loosely around rolling pin and unroll into pie plate, leaving at least 1-inch overhang. Ease dough into plate by gently lifting edge of dough with one hand while pressing into plate bottom with other hand. Refrigerate until dough is firm, about 30 minutes.

2. Adjust oven rack to lower-middle position and heat oven to 375 degrees. Trim dough overhang to ½ inch beyond lip of pie plate. Fold overhang under itself; folded edge should be flush with edge of pie plate. Flute edges using thumb and forefinger or press with tines of fork to flatten against rim of pie plate. Refrigerate dough-lined plate until dough is firm, about 15 minutes.

3. Remove pie plate from refrigerator, line crust with aluminum foil, and fill with pie weights or pennies. Bake until surface of dough no longer looks wet, 20 to 25 minutes. Remove pie from oven and reduce oven temperature to 325 degrees. Remove foil and weights and sprinkle chocolate over bottom of hot crust. Let sit for 5 minutes, then spread chocolate into even layer; set aside.

4. Melt butter in small saucepan over medium-low heat. Cook, stirring constantly, until butter is nutty brown, 5 to 7 minutes. Off heat, slowly stir in bourbon (mixture will bubble strongly); let cool for 5 minutes.

5. Whisk granulated sugar, brown sugar, cornstarch, and salt together in large bowl until combined. Add eggs, yolk, and vanilla, whisking until smooth. Slowly whisk in warm butter mixture until incorporated. Stir in walnuts and pour filling into chocolate-lined crust. Bake until filling is puffed and center jiggles slightly when pie is gently shaken, 35 to 40 minutes. Cool on wire rack for 4 hours. Slice and serve. (Pie can be refrigerated, covered, for up to 2 days.)

Bourbon Whipped Cream

MAKES ABOUT 2 CUPS

- **1 cup heavy cream, chilled**
- **2 tablespoons bourbon**
- **1½ tablespoons light brown sugar**
- **½ teaspoon vanilla extract**

Using stand mixer fitted with whisk, whip cream, bourbon, sugar, and vanilla together on medium-low speed until foamy, about 1 minute. Increase speed to high and whip until soft peaks form, 1 to 3 minutes.

CHOCOLATE-RASPBERRY TORTE

NINETEENTH-CENTURY ARISTOCRATS MAY HAVE considered Sachertorte an indulgent dessert, but the Viennese cake has never held the attention of a chocoholic like me. Once you get past its alluring facade—a two-layer chocolate sponge cake sandwiching a spread of apricot jam and covered with a sleek-looking chocolate glaze—the confection's true colors reveal themselves. The cake is usually dry and anemic in flavor, as if the batter were merely tanned with cocoa rather than steeped in creamy bar chocolate. Meanwhile, the jam center adds only sweetness to each bite, not bright, complex fruit flavor. As for the glaze, it's typically nothing more than a thin, overly sugary coating. Perhaps my over-the-top American sensibilities have gotten the better of me, but I expect more from a dessert than good looks and historical precedent. My mission: Create a rich, deeply chocolaty dessert, using the basic layered architecture of the Sachertorte as inspiration. While I was at it, I decided to put my own spin on the dessert and pair the chocolate with my favorite fruit: raspberries.

The cake's biggest problem—weak chocolate flavor—made sense once I started looking at recipes. The sponge cake (or genoise) used in most classic Sachertortes relies on a modest amount of chocolate, typically about 4 ounces. Rather than fiddle with this model, I knew I would do better to start with an entirely different kind of cake. The obvious choice? A rich, fudgy, flourless chocolate cake.

I started by baking a previously published test kitchen recipe for flourless chocolate cake in two 9-inch pans instead of a springform pan. This way, I could sandwich the two cakes together rather than struggle to horizontally halve a single delicate cake. I let the layers cool, then spread raspberry jam on one. So far, so good. But when I picked up the second layer to lay it on top of the first, the dense cake tore and fell apart. Undeterred, I patched the layers together, poured a simple chocolate glaze over the top, and then chilled the assembly. There was no denying the intense chocolate taste, but each forkful crumbled on its way to my mouth. Obviously my cake needed more structure.

I tried to remedy this problem by judiciously mixing flour into the batter, but when I added enough to sufficiently strengthen the cake (about ½ cup), I created a new problem: a heavy, pasty texture. Leaveners proved ineffective at lightening this heavy, chocolate-laden batter. Separating the eggs and folding in the beaten whites did no better.

At a dead end, I went back to the books and came across a technique that I'd initially ignored. Many classic tortes contain either bread crumbs or ground nuts in place of some of the flour. I had thought this was a little off base for modern cooks, but I figured it was worth a shot. In fact, the latter turned out to be a game-changing improvement. While bread crumbs merely created a spongy, mushy cake, substituting ground toasted almonds for half of the flour worked perfectly. The layers were still moist but had enough structure so that a filling could be added and the second layer placed on top of the first without any collateral damage. What's more, the flavor of the cake benefited from the depth provided by toasted nuts.

My only gripe was that this cake—and the eventual cleanup—was turning into quite the project. All along, I had been using a stand mixer to whip the eggs, but now that I was using a food processor to grind the nuts, I wondered if I could consolidate appliances.

I processed the almonds and flour, then transferred the mixture to a bowl. Next, I processed the eggs until they were almost doubled in volume, then added the sugar. After combining the eggs with the melted chocolate and butter, I folded in the almond-flour mixture and baked the cakes. This worked beautifully. The processor aerated the batter just as effectively as the stand mixer, and I now had a recipe that dirtied only one piece of equipment.

As for the filling, the thin veneer of apricot jam in a traditional Sachertorte has always struck me as syrupy and dull, and the raspberry jam I'd been using as a stand-in was equally underwhelming. I needed something with as much complexity as the cake. Plain fresh raspberries lacked sweetness—and tended to tumble from the cut cake slices—and pulverizing them with sugar yielded a soupy mixture. Cooking the berries thickened them so they didn't ooze out of the cake but squelched their bright taste. Ultimately, the winning approach was to combine jam with lightly mashed fresh berries, for a tangy-sweet mixture that clung to the cake.

All I had left to do was apply a glaze. To keep things simple, I melted 5 ounces of bittersweet chocolate with ½ cup of heavy cream to create a rich-tasting, glossy ganache that poured smoothly over the cake. To up the glamour quotient, I dotted fresh raspberries around the top perimeter of the torte and pressed sliced toasted almonds along its sides. My updated torte was a real beauty—inside and out.

—YVONNE RUPERTI, *Cook's Illustrated*

NOTES FROM THE TEST KITCHEN

TORTE REFORM

We're all for restraint—but not when it comes to dessert. Here's how we packed more chocolate flavor and fruitiness into our torte than in the classic European model.

SWAP SPONGE FOR FLOURLESS

A flourless cake holds twice the chocolate of the usual sponge cake base.

ADD GROUND ALMONDS

Ground toasted almonds lend complexity to the rich cake.

GLAZE WITH POTENT GANACHE

A ganache of just chocolate and cream keeps the flavor pure and intense.

FILL WITH TWO KINDS OF BERRIES

Fresh raspberries and raspberry jam make for a bright-tasting filling.

Chocolate-Raspberry Torte

MAKES ONE 9-INCH CAKE, SERVING 12 TO 16

We recommend using either Callebaut Intense Dark L-60-40NV or Ghirardelli Bittersweet Chocolate Baking Bar, but any high-quality bittersweet or semisweet chocolate will work. Be sure to use a cake pan with at least 2-inch-tall sides. If you're refrigerating the cake for more than 1 hour in step 6, let it stand at room temperature for about 30 minutes before serving.

CAKE AND FILLING

- **8 ounces bittersweet chocolate, chopped fine**
- **12 tablespoons unsalted butter, cut into ½-inch pieces**
- **2 teaspoons vanilla extract**
- **¼ teaspoon instant espresso powder**
- **1¾ cups sliced almonds, lightly toasted**
- **¼ cup (1¼ ounces) all-purpose flour**
- **½ teaspoon salt**
- **5 large eggs**
- **¾ cup (5¼ ounces) sugar**
- **2½ ounces fresh raspberries (½ cup), plus 16 berries for garnish**
- **¼ cup seedless raspberry jam**

GLAZE

- **5 ounces bittersweet chocolate, chopped fine**
- **½ cup plus 1 tablespoon heavy cream**

1. FOR THE CAKE: Adjust oven rack to middle position and heat oven to 325 degrees. Line bottoms of two 9-inch round cake pans with parchment paper. Melt chocolate and butter in large bowl set over saucepan filled with 1 inch simmering water, stirring occasionally until smooth. Remove from heat and cool to

room temperature, about 30 minutes. Stir in vanilla and espresso powder.

2. Pulse ¾ cup almonds in food processor until coarsely chopped, 6 to 8 pulses; set aside to garnish cake. Process remaining 1 cup almonds until very finely ground, about 45 seconds. Add flour and salt and continue to process until combined, about 15 seconds. Transfer almond-flour mixture to bowl. Process eggs in now-empty food processor until lightened in color and almost doubled in volume, about 3 minutes. With processor running, slowly add sugar until thoroughly combined, about 15 seconds. Using whisk, gently fold egg mixture into chocolate mixture until some streaks of egg remain. Sprinkle half of almond-flour mixture over chocolate-egg mixture and gently whisk until just combined. Sprinkle in remaining almond-flour mixture and gently whisk until just combined.

3. Divide batter between cake pans and smooth with rubber spatula. Bake until centers are firm and toothpick inserted into center of cakes comes out with few moist crumbs attached, 14 to 16 minutes. Let cakes cool completely in pans on wire rack, about 30 minutes. Run paring knife around sides of cakes, invert onto cardboard rounds cut same size as cakes, and remove parchment. Using plate or wire rack, reinvert 1 cake so top side faces up; slide back onto cardboard round.

4. TO ASSEMBLE TORTE: Place ½ cup raspberries in medium bowl and coarsely mash with fork. Stir in raspberry jam until just combined. Spread raspberry mixture onto cake layer that is top side up. Top with second cake layer, leaving it bottom side up. Transfer assembled cake, still on cardboard round, to wire rack set inside rimmed baking sheet.

5. FOR THE GLAZE: Melt chocolate with cream in medium bowl set over saucepan filled with 1 inch simmering water, stirring occasionally until smooth. Remove from heat and gently whisk until very smooth. Pour glaze onto center of assembled cake. Use offset spatula to spread glaze evenly over top of cake, letting it flow down sides. Spread glaze along sides of cake to coat evenly.

6. Using fine mesh strainer, sift reserved almonds to remove any fine bits. Holding bottom of cake on cardboard round with one hand, gently press sifted almonds onto cake sides with other hand. Set cake on serving platter and arrange individual raspberries around circumference. Refrigerate cake until glaze is set, at least 1 hour or up to 24 hours. Slice and serve.

NOTES FROM THE TEST KITCHEN

ASSEMBLING CHOCOLATE-RASPBERRY TORTE

1. Run paring knife around sides of cakes and invert layers onto cardboard rounds. Then, using a plate or wire rack, reinvert 1 cake so top faces up; slide back onto cardboard round.

2. Spread raspberry filling over cake layer with its top side facing up.

3. Top with second cake, leaving bottom facing up.

4. Pour glaze onto cake and use offset spatula to evenly spread ganache over top and sides.

5. Using cardboard round, lift and hold cake with one hand and gently press chopped nuts onto its sides with other hand.

6. Place 1 raspberry at top of cake at 12 o'clock, then another at 6 o'clock. Place third berry at 9 o'clock and fourth at 3 o'clock. Continue to place berries opposite each other until all are evenly spaced.

BOSTON CREAM PIE

LEGEND HAS IT THAT BOSTON CREAM PIE WAS invented in the 1850s at Boston's landmark Parker House Hotel. A creative baker produced what was to become a wildly popular dessert by simply pouring chocolate glaze onto a cream-filled cake. So why is this dessert called a "pie"? Food historians theorize that home cooks transferred the concept to the most common form of bakeware in the mid-19th-century kitchen: a pie plate.

But today Boston cream pie is rarely made at home, through no fault of its taste: It's hard to beat the trifecta of tender sponge cake layered with vanilla-scented pastry cream and covered in a rich chocolate glaze. The reason home cooks avoid making it is that there are so many opportunities for failure. Sponge cakes are scary: Separating eggs, whipping, folding—this is no easy feat for the uninitiated, and the resulting crumb can be dry and tasteless. And pastry cream? It could curdle—or worse, never thicken. As for the glaze, well, chocolate is famously capricious, at times seizing up unexpectedly, at others looking deceptively glossy going on the cake, only to set up dull and gritty.

But when Boston cream pie hits all the marks, there really is no better dessert. As a native Bostonian, I wanted to pay homage to my roots by leading the dessert's revival with a fail-safe recipe.

Boston cream pie is traditionally made from a genoiselike sponge cake: lean, practically weightless layers leavened only by the air whipped into the eggs in the batter. When I baked the genoise from the Parker House Hotel's own recipe, I identified three problems with this style of cake. First, it's fussy and unreliable. The whipped eggs must be gently folded with the flour so as not to deflate the mixture, leading to a cake that's dense instead of airy. Second, with a high concentration of egg and little fat, the crumb can be too lean and tough for modern tastes. Finally, low-fat cakes require quite a bit of sugar for structure (think angel food cake), and with so little butter to balance it, genoise often ends up tasting overly sweet. While genoise may have satisfied diners in the 1850s, today we crave a soft, moist, tender crumb.

With all that in mind, I baked a traditional American yellow cake containing just over two sticks of butter. I wasn't surprised when tasters heartily approved—the cake was incredibly moist. But there was more work to be done: A truly great Boston cream pie boasts contrasting flavors and textures. With an overly rich cake, the lush pastry cream would be lost, not showcased.

Looking for middle ground, I came across another cake that was actually trendy during Boston cream pie's heyday: the hot-milk sponge cake. This cake contains more butter than a genoise, yielding a tender crumb, but it still has considerably less fat than a traditional yellow cake. The mixing method involves whipping eggs with sugar, then simply stirring in the remaining ingredients (including warm milk)—no finicky folding or separating of eggs required. And because the batter is bolstered with a fair amount of baking powder, it doesn't rely solely on the whipped eggs for lift.

After I baked up a batch and offered slices to tasters, I knew that I'd nailed it. Not only had the cake been supremely easy to prepare, but its light texture and subtle flavor were shaping up to be the perfect platform for a creamy filling. Baking the batter in two pans eliminated the need to slice a single cake horizontally before adding the filling.

Next up: pastry cream. This filling is typically made by bringing dairy (we prefer half-and-half) to a simmer and then using it to temper—or slowly raise the temperature of—a mixture of egg yolks, sugar, and cornstarch or flour. The mixture is then returned to the heat and whisked until it has thickened and the eggs are lightly cooked. But if insufficiently heated or overwhisked, the pastry cream will not reach the proper consistency, which presents a particular problem in Boston cream pie: If its texture is too loose, the cream will squish out when the cake is sliced.

I'd always been under the impression that cornstarch and flour are equally good options in pastry cream. However, when I experimented with both, I found flour to be more reliable. But I still needed pastry cream with a slightly sturdier texture that would stand up to slicing.

After some reflection, I thought of another ingredient that might provide body: butter. I mixed 4 tablespoons (along with a spoonful of vanilla) into the cooked mixture of yolks, sugar, half-and-half, and flour, and then dipped in my spoon for a taste. The butter reinforced the richness of the pastry cream, enhancing its luxurious flavor. And once the butter-enriched cream was spread on the cake and refrigerated, it sliced cleanly and held fast between the layers while still maintaining a silky smoothness.

With a moist, tender cake and perfect pastry cream ready to go, it was time to address the glaze. The key was to create a smooth mixture that would cling to the top of the cake and drip artistically down its sides, retaining softness and shine after refrigeration. The Parker House Hotel recipe calls for melted chocolate thickened with a fondant (water and sugar cooked to the "soft ball" stage). The glaze went on easily but formed a firm shell when chilled. Other glazes made with just chocolate and heavy cream (called ganache) looked beautifully shiny as they were poured on the cake, only to dry to a dull matte brown. And both types of glaze failed to bond with the cake beneath, forming a skin that separated from the cake when it was sliced.

My glaze needed shine and flexibility. Corn syrup held promise, and sure enough, adding a couple of spoonfuls to a mixture of heavy cream and melted chocolate gave the ganache luster with staying power. The glaze also clung nicely to the cake, holding on to the crumb during slicing. It turns out that the sugar molecules in corn syrup form a perfectly smooth surface, reflecting light waves in the same direction, creating shine. Corn syrup also acts as a plasticizer, making the glaze flexible rather than brittle so that it adheres to the cake instead of peeling off.

As I assembled the last in a long series of Boston cream pies, I knew that I'd finally developed a fear-free recipe to make this Bostonian proud. Sure, there are three components, but I'd figured out ways to guarantee success with each.

—ANDREA GEARY, *Cook's Illustrated*

Boston Cream Pie

SERVES 8 TO 10

Be sure to chill the assembled cake for at least 3 hours to make it easy to cut and serve.

PASTRY CREAM

- **2 cups half-and-half**
- **6 large egg yolks**
- **½ cup (3½ ounces) sugar**
- **Pinch salt**
- **¼ cup (1¼ ounces) all-purpose flour**
- **4 tablespoons unsalted butter, cut into 4 pieces and chilled**
- **1½ teaspoons vanilla extract**

CAKE

- **1½ cups (7½ ounces) all-purpose flour**
- **1½ teaspoons baking powder**
- **¾ teaspoon salt**
- **¾ cup whole milk**
- **6 tablespoons unsalted butter**
- **1½ teaspoons vanilla extract**
- **3 large eggs**
- **1½ cups (10½ ounces) sugar**

GLAZE

- **½ cup heavy cream**
- **2 tablespoons light corn syrup**
- **4 ounces bittersweet chocolate, chopped fine**

1. FOR THE PASTRY CREAM: Heat half-and-half in medium saucepan over medium heat until just simmering. Meanwhile, whisk yolks, sugar, and salt together in medium bowl until smooth. Add flour to yolk mixture and whisk until incorporated. Remove half-and-half from heat and, whisking constantly, slowly add ½ cup to yolk mixture to temper. Whisking constantly, return tempered yolk mixture to half-and-half in saucepan.

2. Return saucepan to medium heat and cook, whisking constantly, until mixture thickens slightly, about 1 minute. Reduce heat to medium-low and continue to simmer, whisking constantly, for 8 minutes.

3. Increase heat to medium and cook, whisking vigorously, until bubbles burst on surface, 1 to 2 minutes. Remove from heat; whisk in butter and vanilla until incorporated. Strain pastry cream through fine-mesh strainer set over medium bowl. Press lightly greased parchment paper directly on surface and refrigerate until set, at least 2 hours or up to 24 hours.

4. FOR THE CAKE: Adjust oven rack to middle position and heat oven to 325 degrees. Grease two 9-inch round cake pans, line bottoms with parchment paper, then grease parchment. Whisk flour, baking powder, and salt together in bowl. Heat milk and butter in small saucepan over low heat until butter is melted. Remove from heat, add vanilla, and cover to keep warm.

5. Using stand mixer fitted with whisk, whip eggs and sugar together at high speed until light and airy, about 5 minutes. Add hot milk mixture and whisk by hand until incorporated. Add dry ingredients and whisk by hand until incorporated.

6. Divide batter evenly between prepared pans. Bake until tops are light brown and toothpick inserted in center of cakes comes out clean, 20 to 22 minutes, switching and rotating pans halfway through baking. Let cakes cool completely in pans on wire rack, about 2 hours. Invert cakes onto wire rack, remove parchment, then reinvert cakes.

7. TO ASSEMBLE CAKE: Place 1 cake layer on serving platter. Whisk pastry cream briefly, then spoon onto center of cake. Using offset spatula, spread evenly to edge. Place second layer on pastry cream, bottom side up, and press lightly on cake to level. Refrigerate while preparing glaze.

8. FOR THE GLAZE: Bring cream and corn syrup to simmer in small saucepan over medium heat. Remove from heat and add chocolate. Whisk gently until smooth, 30 seconds. Let stand, whisking occasionally, until thickened slightly, about 5 minutes.

9. Pour glaze onto center of cake. Use offset spatula to spread glaze to edge of cake, letting excess drip down sides. Chill cake before serving, at least 3 hours or up to 24 hours.

CHOCOLATE ÉCLAIR CAKE

CHOCOLATE ÉCLAIR CAKE, ALTHOUGH VIRTUALLY nonexistent in traditional cookbooks, is one of those odd items that, like the video of Belgian commuters dancing to "The Sound of Music" in Antwerp Central Station, has gone viral on the Internet. Confronted with a deluge of electronic recipes and a comparable number of rave reviews, I wondered how it was possible that I hadn't encountered éclair cake before. I soon learned that it's neither an outsize éclair nor a typical baked cake, despite its name. It more closely resembles a classic easy icebox cake, and practically from the moment I began testing in earnest, I succumbed to its mysterious allure.

Of the hundreds of éclair cake recipes I found online, nearly all proceed the same way: Make an ersatz mousse filling by folding Cool Whip into instant vanilla pudding; line a casserole dish with graham crackers; top the graham crackers with half of the "mousse," more grahams, the remaining mousse, and one final layer of grahams. To finish, gild the lily with canned chocolate frosting.

I was skeptical but put together a few chocolate éclair cakes to see for myself what the online hubbub was all about. I predicted that my tasters would be scornful of this junk food assemblage, but then I noticed them eyeing the pans, forks in hand, poised like runners toeing the starting line, as I frosted the last one. I dug in right alongside them. The filling was creamy yet light, the graham crackers just soft enough to scoop with a spoon. This cake was hard to stop eating. It quickly vanished, plates practically licked clean by a mob of former restaurant chefs and alleged food experts. When we finally did stop eating, however, we paid for our enthusiasm—with toothaches and an aftertaste best described as "plasticky." I knew that if I could reform this dessert using homemade substitutions for the processed-food components, chocolate éclair cake would live up to the hype.

To bring this dish a little more in line with its namesake, the éclair, I traded the graham crackers for pâte à choux, the French pastry that's used to make éclairs and cream puffs. My tasters laughed me out of the kitchen. I got the point: This was supposed to be a simple icebox cake. The graham crackers would stay. Next, I replaced the instant pudding with classic egg yolk–thickened pastry cream. This time, I didn't need tasters to tell me that using a sensitive egg-thickened cream, necessitating a fine-mesh strainer and an ice bath to prevent lumps of curdled egg, was too much hassle for this formerly instant dessert.

To simplify, I tried a classic cornstarch-thickened vanilla pudding. I combined 6 tablespoons of cornstarch with 1¼ cups of sugar, poured in 5 cups of milk, and simmered everything in a pot until thick. Then, off the heat, I added butter and vanilla extract. The pudding was perfectly creamy, with subtle vanilla flavor. I assembled the cake, this time using real whipped cream in place of the plasticky Cool Whip. But rather than a perky mousse, I had a runny pool that nearly dissolved the grahams. Fixing flavor, it seemed, was as simple as tossing out the packaged junk food, but getting the filling to set up was proving trickier.

Doubling the cornstarch in the pudding gave me a stiffer filling and restored the soft (not soggy) crackers in the assembled cake. Unfortunately, the pudding was now stodgy and chalky rather than rich and creamy. I had to back down on the cornstarch and find another way to set the filling. Cool Whip is packed with stabilizers; maybe reinforcing the homemade whipped

CHOCOLATE ÉCLAIR CAKE

cream would help. Gelatin was an obvious choice. After about a dozen tests, during which I slowly decreased the cornstarch in the pudding from 12 tablespoons and increased the gelatin from ½ teaspoon in the whipped cream, I eventually found the sweet spot: 6 tablespoons of cornstarch and 1¼ teaspoons of gelatin. Any more cornstarch and a film clung to my tongue. Any more gelatin and the filling was rubbery. Any less of either and the filling didn't set.

Having tossed out the packaged ingredients in the filling to make this already barely resistible dessert downright addictive, I couldn't settle for canned frosting. Ganache—the French way of saying chocolate melted into hot cream—had too strong a flavor for such a mild and creamy cake. Instead, I tried a glaze made of cocoa powder, confectioners' sugar, and milk. It had a shine reminiscent of a true éclair glaze, but now tasters missed the rich melted chocolate. I circled back to the ganache, this time thinning it out and taming the bitterness with extra cream and adding corn syrup for a smooth, shiny finish.

Tasters were coming back for thirds, and colleagues from other departments were sidling up to me in the hallways and asking in hushed tones, "What was that thing? And when are you making another one?" Finally, I had a homemade treat with junk food appeal, only without the junk.

—SARAH GABRIEL, *Cook's Country*

NOTES FROM THE TEST KITCHEN

THE BEST GRAHAM CRACKERS

When Sylvester Graham, a passionate advocate of whole grains, developed graham crackers almost 200 years ago, they were dense—more like hardtack than the sweet wafers we know today. Marketed as "Dr. Graham's Honey Biskets," the crackers were made from unsifted, coarsely ground whole wheat flour. The Rev. Graham might be faintly horrified by what's become of them: Yes, supermarket grahams still incorporate graham (or whole wheat) flour, but white flour is now the primary ingredient. Some graham crackers are sweetened with honey, others with molasses; all include white sugar and corn syrup, as well as oil, salt, and leaveners.

With ingredients so similar, does it matter which brand you buy? We tasted three top-selling national brands—Honey Maid Honey Grahams, Keebler Grahams Crackers Original, and Nabisco Grahams Original—by sampling them first plain, then in our Chocolate Éclair Cake, and finally in the crust of a Key lime pie. All brands fared well enough to earn our recommendation. For straight snacking, we prefer **Nabisco Grahams Original** because of their wheaty flavor and tempered sweetness. In addition, Nabisco's crackers have the highest percentage of graham flour, which contributes to their flavor but also accounts for their turning to mush between our éclair cake's creamy layers. Essentially, they form less gluten and have more bran, which creates a weaker structure. **Keebler's** grahams performed best in baking, holding up in both pie crust and our éclair cake.

Chocolate Éclair Cake

SERVES 15

You can use 6 ounces of finely chopped semisweet chocolate in place of the chips.

- 1¼ cups (8¾ ounces) sugar
- 6 tablespoons cornstarch
- 1 teaspoon salt
- 5 cups whole milk
- 4 tablespoons unsalted butter, cut into 4 pieces
- 5 teaspoons vanilla extract
- 1¼ teaspoons unflavored gelatin
- 2 tablespoons water
- 2¾ cups heavy cream, chilled
- 14 ounces graham crackers
- 1 cup semisweet chocolate chips
- 5 tablespoons light corn syrup

1. Combine sugar, cornstarch, and salt in large saucepan. Whisk milk into sugar mixture until smooth and bring to boil, scraping bottom of pan, over medium-high heat. Immediately reduce heat to medium-low and cook, continuing to scrape bottom, until thickened and large bubbles appear on surface, 4 to 6 minutes. Off heat, whisk in butter and vanilla. Transfer pudding to large bowl and place plastic wrap directly on surface of pudding. Refrigerate until cool, about 2 hours.

2. Sprinkle gelatin over water and let stand until gelatin is softened, about 5 minutes. Microwave until mixture is bubbling around edges and gelatin dissolves, about 30 seconds. Using stand mixer fitted with whisk, whip 2 cups cream on medium-low speed until foamy, about 1 minute. Increase speed to high and whip until soft peaks form, about 2 minutes. Add gelatin mixture and whip until stiff peaks form, about 1 minute.

3. Whisk one-third of whipped cream into chilled pudding, then gently fold in remaining whipped cream, 1 scoop at a time, until combined. Cover bottom of 13 by 9-inch baking dish with layer of graham crackers, breaking crackers as necessary to line bottom of dish. Top with half of pudding–whipped cream mixture (about 5½ cups) and another layer of graham crackers. Repeat with remaining pudding–whipped cream mixture and remaining graham crackers.

4. Microwave chocolate chips, remaining ¾ cup cream, and corn syrup in bowl, stirring occasionally, until smooth, 1 to 2 minutes. Cool glaze to room temperature, about 10 minutes. Cover graham crackers with glaze and refrigerate cake for at least 6 hours or up to 24 hours. Serve. (Éclair cake can be refrigerated for up to 2 days.)

BANANA PUDDING

ABOUT 100 YEARS AGO, ENGLISH TRIFLE TOOK A decidedly American turn and morphed into banana pudding, the cake giving way to cookies, the jam to banana slices. In 1920 or thereabouts, the National Biscuit Co. printed the recipe on its box of vanilla biscuits, and its popularity soared. Today, banana pudding is on the menu of every barbecue restaurant worth its ribs, and it inspires fierce loyalties among Southerners. John Egerton's family recipe "has been handed down through four generations," he wrote in *Southern Food*, "with all the care and attention properly reserved for an heirloom." A Southern gal born and bred, I get it. Creamy, sweet, cold, and fruity, good banana pudding can't be beat. If only it had more bananas.

The dessert is made by layering vanilla pudding with sliced bananas and vanilla wafers. Naturally, the banana slices can turn brown and slimy. The cookies should be pleasantly cakey and plentiful enough to land in every bite but sometimes are soggy and sparse. The pudding tastes like plain-Jane vanilla—no surprise, it is vanilla. So why the heck is this called banana pudding? I wanted a banana pudding that avoided these problems and, most important, put the banana into the pudding itself.

I tested a half-dozen recipes that ranged from the gourmet—using bourbon, genoise, and homemade praline—to the pedestrian. The latter was exemplified by the back-of-the-box version from Jell-O instant vanilla pudding, which also called for Cool Whip; tasters summed it up with a single word: "Yuck!" Most of these recipes were topped with billows of whipped cream; a few had fluffy meringue caps instead.

The homemade puddings I tried were made with the standard method: gently cooking custards of milk or half-and-half, sugar, egg yolks, cornstarch, and flavorings. Remembering past test kitchen work, I made one slight modification, stirring some of the sugar into the egg yolks first, so they'd incorporate more easily. Next, I pushed the warm puddings through a fine-mesh strainer to make them silky smooth. Finally, I assembled the desserts, sometimes using crushed cookies, sometimes whole, and refrigerated the puddings overnight so the flavors could meld.

I made some fast decisions. I would use half-and-half, not milk: Why go to the trouble of making banana pudding unless it's going to be rich and creamy? The same with meringue; whipped cream was easier. Finally, since the crushed cookies disintegrated in the pudding, I'd use whole ones.

I knew that to combine the bananas with the pudding I'd have to cook them first so they'd break down. I sautéed them in butter and sugar, pureed them, and stirred them into the pudding. This version tasted as yummy as it sounded. But though the bananas were soft in the skillet, they never broke down entirely, so the pudding was mealy. Steaming the bananas in the microwave, my next idea, fixed the texture but did nothing for the flavor.

Knowing that roasting intensifies the flavor and sugars of fruits and vegetables, I put the bananas in a 325-degree oven for about 20 minutes until their skins turned black, then placed the peeled bananas in the processor. It occurred to me that I could skip the cumbersome step of pushing the pudding through the fine-mesh strainer and instead process the vanilla pudding right in there with the bananas.

I layered my new and improved banana pudding with wafers and refrigerated it. The next day, I looked at it in horror: The pudding had turned an ugly beige because the bananas had oxidized. So I added a squeeze of lemon juice to the roasted bananas in my next test,

NOTES FROM THE TEST KITCHEN

WE PUT THE BANANA BACK IN BANANA PUDDING

Roasting slightly underripe bananas makes them richer and sweeter and breaks down their fibers, for a smooth banana pudding with true banana flavor.

THE BEST CREAMY PEANUT BUTTER

Selecting a peanut butter used to be an easy task—your choices were basically creamy or crunchy. Not anymore. Scan the aisle at your supermarket and you'll find dozens of different brands and options, such as honey-roasted, no-salt or low-salt, and "whipped." But no option seems to be taking up shelf space like the "natural" peanut butters. We set out to find the best creamy peanut butter and gathered a number of both conventional and natural varieties.

After sampling 10 peanut butters in plain tastings, tasters made it clear that texture was paramount in a great creamy peanut butter (flavor played a role, too, but it wasn't as important). They preferred butters that were smooth, creamy, and spreadable—and both conventional and natural brands (many of which aren't just peanuts and salt but include palm oil to retain a creamy consistency) performed well at this stage. After tasters tried the butters in peanut butter cookies and a spicy satay sauce, we had our winner. Our previous winner, **Skippy Peanut Butter**, came in first again, praised for its supremely "smooth," "creamy" texture. (See page 296 for more information about our testing results.)

THE BEST FINE-MESH STRAINER

Our Rich and Creamy Banana Pudding recipe uses a food processor to achieve a silky texture, but if you don't have a processor you can strain the pudding through a fine-mesh strainer. We last rated fine-mesh strainers almost 10 years ago, but we decided to take a fresh look when we saw that many strainers in the test kitchen were missing handles. We chose five strainers, all about 6 inches in diameter. All strained pudding and berry sauce passably well. The primary distinctions lay in the shape, style, and durability of the handles. To replicate years of use, we boiled, rapidly cooled, and banged each strainer against a counter. Minus a few scuffs, our new favorite was as good as new after our "bang" testing. The **CIA Masters Collection Fine-Mesh Strainer**, $27.49, came in first; it produced the smoothest sauce and silkiest pudding.

which minimized the browning and at the same time brightened and lightened the rich, sweet pudding. For more banana flavor, I sliced extra bananas into the pudding.

It was time to turn to the cookies, which were still sodden and pasty. To fix that, I first tried using stale cookies, and next crisping fresh cookies in the oven. Neither version succeeded. What did work was cooling the pudding somewhat before constructing the layers.

Finally, I did a series of tests on the pudding-to-cookie ratio; tasters weren't satisfied until I was using an entire box of wafers, double the number called for in a typical recipe. I carefully assembled the dessert and left this banana pudding to chill. The next afternoon, I doled out scoops to waiting tasters (with banana pudding, there are always waiting tasters), and I sat down with my own bowlful. Nothing beats good banana pudding.

—CALI RICH, *Cook's Country*

Rich and Creamy Banana Pudding

SERVES 12

If your food processor bowl holds less than 11 cups, puree half the pudding with the roasted bananas and lemon juice in step 3, transfer it to a large bowl, and whisk in the rest of the pudding.

PUDDING

- **7 slightly underripe large bananas**
- **1½ cups (10½ ounces) sugar**
- **8 large egg yolks**
- **6 tablespoons cornstarch**
- **6 cups half-and-half**
- **½ teaspoon salt**
- **3 tablespoons unsalted butter**
- **1 tablespoon vanilla extract**
- **3 tablespoons lemon juice**
- **1 (12-ounce) box vanilla wafers**

WHIPPED CREAM

- **1 cup heavy cream, chilled**
- **1 tablespoon sugar**
- **½ teaspoon vanilla extract**

1. FOR THE PUDDING: Adjust oven rack to upper-middle position and heat oven to 325 degrees. Place 3 unpeeled bananas on baking sheet and bake until skins are completely black, about 20 minutes. Let cool for 5 minutes.

2. Meanwhile, whisk ½ cup sugar, egg yolks, and cornstarch together in medium bowl until smooth. Bring half and half, remaining 1 cup sugar, and salt to simmer over medium heat in large saucepan. Whisk ½ cup of half-and-half mixture into yolk mixture to temper. Slowly whisk tempered yolk mixture into half-and-half mixture in saucepan. Cook, whisking constantly, until mixture is thick and large bubbles appear at surface, about 2 minutes. Remove from heat; stir in butter and vanilla.

3. Transfer pudding to food processor. Add warm peeled roasted bananas and 2 tablespoons lemon juice and process until smooth. Scrape into large bowl and place plastic wrap directly on surface of pudding. Refrigerate until slightly cool, about 45 minutes.

4. Cut remaining bananas into ¼-inch slices and toss in bowl with remaining 1 tablespoon lemon juice. Spoon one-quarter of pudding into 3-quart trifle dish and top with layer of cookies, layer of sliced bananas, and another layer of cookies. Repeat twice, ending with pudding. Place plastic wrap directly on surface of pudding and refrigerate until wafers have softened, at least 8 hours or up to 2 days.

5. FOR THE WHIPPED CREAM: Using stand mixer fitted with whisk, whip cream, sugar, and vanilla together on medium-low speed until foamy, about 1 minute. Increase speed to high and whip until soft peaks form, 1 to 3 minutes. Top banana pudding with whipped cream. Serve.

VARIATIONS

Toasted-Coconut Banana Pudding

Replace 2 cups half-and-half with 1 (16-ounce) can coconut milk. Sprinkle ¼ cup toasted sweetened shredded coconut over whipped-cream-topped pudding before serving.

Peanutty Banana Pudding

In step 4, sandwich 2 vanilla wafers around 1 banana slice and ½ teaspoon creamy peanut butter (you'll need ½ cup peanut butter to make about 50 cookie sandwiches). Assemble by alternating layers of pudding and cookie-banana sandwiches, ending with pudding. Sprinkle ¼ cup chopped salted dry-roasted peanuts over whipped-cream-topped pudding before serving.

GINGERBREAD CAKE

AS I STEPPED THROUGH THE FAUX-VINTAGE GATES of the "living museum" at Plimoth Plantation, I was hoping for salvation—or at least insight into a cake that dates back to the Colonial era. After a week of baking countless batches of uninspired gingerbread cake, I still lacked a workable baseline recipe. The cake I had in mind was moist through and through and utterly simple—a snack cake that would bake in a square pan. But almost without exception, every recipe I tried that had the moistness I wanted also suffered from a dense, sunken center. Equally disappointing, flavors ran the gamut from barely gingery to addled with enough spices to make a curry fan cry for mercy. So much for simple: This cake had me flummoxed.

So, at the urging of well-intentioned colleagues, I had come to spend a day at this circa-1627 Pilgrim village in Plymouth, Massachusetts, hoping to glean some Colonial wisdom that might help my cake bake up both moist and even. When the museum's culinarian showed up bearing a stack of weathered cookbooks, I was sure I'd come to the right place. But as we prepared these vintage recipes, my optimism faded. Apparently, early Americans liked their gingerbread dry and dense as bricks—an effect exacerbated in a few recipes by a curious kneading step. (Kneading helps develop the glutens in flour, providing structure to bread but rendering cakes and cookies tough.) In cakes so dry, the issue of wet, sunken centers never came up. Dejected, I bid my hosts a polite "good-morrow" and headed back to the test kitchen to regroup.

Cobbling together a basic working recipe from the best of the flawed versions I'd come across, I decided to put the structural problems on hold and focus on fixing flavor first. Using a simple dump-and-stir method, I mixed the wet ingredients (molasses, water, melted butter, a couple of eggs) in one bowl and the dry ingredients (flour, baking soda, baking powder, brown sugar, salt) in another. For now, I opted for a purist's approach to the spice rack, expunging all options but a single tablespoon of ground ginger. Gently folding the wets into the drys, I poured the batter into an 8-inch square cake pan and baked it at 350 degrees for 40 minutes.

As expected, the cake's center collapsed. But with the extraneous spices out of the way, I was able to focus on the ginger. Bumping the ground ginger up to

2 tablespoons yielded an assertive bite, though it lacked complexity. I tried folding in grated fresh ginger with the dried. Sure enough, the pungent notes of the fresh root made the flavor sing.

What about the other spices, which I'd left in temporary exile? Options like cardamom, nutmeg, and cloves weren't terrible but shifted the gingerbread too far into spice cake territory. In the end, only two "guest" spices made the cut: cinnamon and, in an unexpected twist, fresh-ground black pepper, which worked in tandem with all that potent ginger to produce a warm, complex, lingering heat.

Eyeing the liquid components, I suspected that using water was a missed opportunity. Buttermilk added tanginess but dulled the ginger. Ginger ale, ginger beer, and hard apple cider all seemed likely contenders, but baking rendered them undetectable. Dark stout, on the other hand, had a bittersweet flavor that brought out the caramel undertones of the molasses. To minimize its booziness, I tried gently heating the stout to cook off some of the alcohol—a somewhat fussy step that side-by-side tests nonetheless proved worthwhile.

Finally, I found that swapping out the butter for cleaner-tasting vegetable oil and replacing a quarter of the brown sugar with granulated cleared the way to let all those spice flavors come through.

Now that the flavor was coming along nicely, I was more determined than ever to solve the sinking problem. Baking the cake in a Bundt pan might have alleviated the collapse, but not without the fussy steps of greasing and flouring the conical center and turning out the finished cake for serving—not to mention the fact that not everybody has this type of pan. But I had another idea: Bucking the usual protocol for cakes, a few of the recipes I tested incorporated the baking soda with the wet ingredients instead of the other dry ones (including the baking powder). The reason? Too much acid in a batter lessens the baking powder's ability to leaven the cake. Baking powder contains just the right amounts of both acid and alkali, which react to produce carbon dioxide for leavening. But if too much acid is present from other sources, it neutralizes some of the acid in the baking powder, reducing its effectiveness. Thus baking soda, an alkali, is used to neutralize acidic ingredients before they get incorporated into the batter. With gingerbread, the typical culprits are molasses and brown sugar, but my recipe also included stout—a triple threat of acidity that might well be thwarting the rise. I made the recipe again, this time stirring the half teaspoon of baking soda right into the warm stout, followed by the molasses and brown sugar. It was a modest success. While the center still fell, it wasn't nearly as drastic—more of a buckle than a crater.

My batter was quite loose, so I wondered if the flour-to-liquid ratio was off. Would a drier gingerbread be a sturdier gingerbread? I tried decreasing the stout and oil. No dice: Though the cake's center stayed mostly propped up, it wasn't worth the marked decrease in moistness. An extra egg made the texture sturdier—but rubbery. Adjusting the amount of leaveners up and down produced cakes that ranged from dense and squat to light and pillowy, but they all shared one trait: that blasted sunken center.

Oof. My kingdom for better structure. I was getting close to calling it quits—or at least calling for some blemish-masking sleight of hand involving powdered sugar—when I reached a breakthrough. It was a casual conversation with a colleague about that fruitless trip (weeks earlier) to Plimoth Plantation that got me thinking about the gingerbread I'd made there. Structure, I mused, was about the only thing those tough little bricks had going for them—which is when I remembered the unusual kneading step.

Kneading—as well as energetic beating—contributes strength and structure by developing the glutens in flour. But gluten development is the enemy of tenderness, which is why flour is generally incorporated gently into cakes at the end of mixing, after the heavy-duty butter creaming is done. Tenderness I had in spades; structure, I could use. Could roughing up the batter a bit strengthen the crumb?

Departing from my current method of delicately folding the wet ingredients into the dry, I added only about a third of the wets, then mixed vigorously to form a smooth paste. I incorporated the remaining wet ingredients in two more installments, mixing until smooth after each addition. I put the cake in the oven, crossed my fingers, and waited. Sure enough, this cake was a real looker—nary a crater in sight. Fragrant, moist, bold-flavored, and beautiful, this was the gingerbread cake I'd been dreaming of.

Silently, I made a mental note to respect my elders. Sometimes, it turns out, history bears repeating.

—YVONNE RUPERTI, *Cook's Illustrated*

Classic Gingerbread Cake

MAKES ONE 8-INCH SQUARE CAKE, SERVING 8

This cake packs potent yet well-balanced, fragrant, spicy heat. If you are particularly sensitive to spice, you can decrease the amount of dried ginger to 1 tablespoon. Guinness is the test kitchen's favorite brand of stout. Avoid opening the oven door until the minimum baking time has elapsed. If your cake pan has thin walls, you might want to wrap it with premade cake strips or make your own from cheesecloth and foil; this extra insulation will help ensure that the edges of the cake don't overbake. To make your own cake strip, soak one 2 by 32-inch piece of cheesecloth or folded newspaper with water. Gently wring it out and fold aluminum foil around it several times to create a 2 by 36-inch strip; wrap the strip around the pan, pinch the ends together, and secure with twine. Serve the gingerbread plain or with lightly sweetened whipped cream.

- **¾ cup stout**
- **½ teaspoon baking soda**
- **⅔ cup mild molasses**
- **¾ cup (5¼ ounces) packed light brown sugar**
- **¼ cup (1¾ ounces) granulated sugar**
- **1½ cups (7½ ounces) all-purpose flour**
- **2 tablespoons ground ginger**
- **½ teaspoon baking powder**
- **½ teaspoon salt**
- **¼ teaspoon ground cinnamon**
- **¼ teaspoon finely ground pepper**
- **2 large eggs**
- **⅓ cup vegetable oil**
- **1 tablespoon finely grated fresh ginger**

1. Adjust oven rack to middle position and heat oven to 350 degrees. Grease and flour 8-inch square baking pan.

2. Bring stout to boil in medium saucepan over medium heat, stirring occasionally. Remove from heat and stir in baking soda (mixture will foam vigorously). When foaming subsides, stir in molasses, brown sugar, and granulated sugar until dissolved; set aside. Whisk flour, ground ginger, baking powder, salt, cinnamon, and pepper together in large bowl; set aside.

3. Transfer stout mixture to separate large bowl.

NOTES FROM THE TEST KITCHEN

KEYS TO RICHER, ZINGIER FLAVOR

We found 4 keys to reinvigorating our gingerbread cake so it lived up to its name.

BITTERSWEET BEER
Dark stout contributes deep, caramelized notes.

FLAVOR-FREE FAT
Clean, neutral-tasting oil brings key flavors into clear relief.

A ROOTY BOOST
Fresh ginger kicks up the fiery, pungent notes of dried ginger.

BACK-SEAT SPICES
Black pepper and cinnamon complement—without overwhelming—the ginger.

THE BEST CAKE STRIP

Cake strips are designed to correct uneven baking by insulating the outside of a cake pan; the more even heat prevents doming and cracking and keeps the edges of the cake from overbaking. We wrapped four strips, made of silicone or damp aluminized fabric, around 8-inch square, 9-inch round, and 13 by 9-inch pans filled with cake batter and compared them with homemade strips. Its ability to be custom-cut to any size pan gave our homemade version an edge. But for greater convenience, our pick is **Rose's Heavenly Cake Strip**, $9.99. This silicone band snapped around 9-inch round and 8- and (with some preheating to stretch the band) 9-inch square pans and turned out cakes that were level and consistently moist from edge to center. Its only downfall? It won't fit a larger pan.

Whisk in eggs, oil, and grated ginger until combined. Whisk wet mixture into flour mixture in thirds, stirring vigorously until completely smooth after each addition.

4. Transfer batter to prepared pan and gently tap pan against counter 3 or 4 times to dislodge any large air bubbles. Bake until top of cake is just firm to touch and toothpick inserted into center comes out clean, 35 to 45 minutes. Cool cake in pan on wire rack, about 1½ hours. Cut into squares and serve warm or at room temperature. (Cake can be stored at room temperature for up to 2 days.)

FAIRY GINGERBREAD

CENTURIES AGO, GINGERBREAD WAS SO POPULAR that cookbooks devoted entire chapters to it—exhaustive catalogs of passed-down recipes, each producing a confection a tad fluffier or chewier, a little thinner or crispier, than the one before. I'd always pegged the recipes as merely subtle variants, but one recipe in an old cookbook I was thumbing through caught my eye: Fairy Gingerbread. Amid the sober likes of Common Gingerbread, Hot Water Gingerbread, Sponge Gingerbread, and so on, the fanciful name stood out like a frivolous bauble. On closer inspection, the curious method—no eggs, no leavener, batter spread "no thicker than a visiting card" on an inverted baking pan—made me suspect there was more afoot than descriptive whimsy. This was no ordinary gingerbread. I had to try it.

It was in Jessup Whitehead's 1893 classic *Cooking for Profit* that I'd stumbled across the recipe. According to the book, it was a popular sweet served between rounds of the card game euchre—especially in Boston, where it was "held in high favor" and considered "a sort of social duty to know how to make it." Given that geographical shout-out, I wasn't surprised to find a similar recipe with the same name in Fannie Merritt Farmer's seminal *Boston Cooking-School Cook Book* (1896).

Following these recipes, I creamed light brown sugar with softened butter (in a roughly 2-to-1 ratio) until it was light and fluffy, and then slowly added the remaining ingredients (bread flour, milk, ground ginger). With some difficulty, I spread the stiff batter with the back of a knife into an ultra-thin layer across a cookie sheet. (Apparently, a "visiting card" was about as thick as a modern business card.) Then I baked it, as directed, in a "slack oven" (I went with a moderate 350 degrees). Fifteen minutes later, I pulled the sheet from the oven and, working quickly, cut the result into rectangles.

These cookies came out unlike any gingerbread cookie I'd ever made. The crisp, feather-light texture shattered in a single bite, then the ginger wafer promptly melted in my mouth. The indulgent recipe title rang true: as delicate as fairy wings, indeed.

Once I got past the ethereal texture, however, the appeal faded. These cookies were pretty bland. Bumping up the ginger flavor was clearly in order, as was rounding out the overall flavor complexity. But the fairy-wing texture had me sold. I was going in.

Taking care of the easy stuff first, I added a bit of vanilla extract and salt, and the flavor started to sing. Then I tried doubling the amount of ground ginger (to 2 teaspoons). But without any competing flavors, the sharp, astringent quality of the dried spice dominated. I tried to mellow it by steeping it in the milk first—to no avail. Retreating to 1½ teaspoons, I toasted the ginger in a dry skillet, hoping to bring out more of its floral qualities. The kitchen quickly filled with a gingery aroma, which I took as a good sign, and the resulting cookies now boasted a welcome aromatic punch. But they needed still more ginger flavor, so I went straight to the source, grating some fresh ginger, right into the batter. With this two-pronged ginger approach, I now had zesty ginger flavor in spades.

I also had heavy batter that was a bear to wrestle into a thin layer across the baking sheet. I'd been using bread flour, as called for in the vintage recipes. Could switching to softer, lower-protein all-purpose flour help? (Bread flour yields stiffer batters than all-purpose.) The batter was a little more malleable but still a struggle, so I reduced the amount of flour by 2 tablespoons (from the full cup I had been using). Now the batter was loose enough to coax over the cookie sheet without a fight, but stiff enough that it didn't drip over the edges.

But the flour adjustment robbed the cookies of some of their crunch and fairy-wing airiness. Adding a modest amount of baking soda (½ teaspoon) made the cookies puff up in the oven just enough that they set with a lighter crumb, hence achieving a sublime crispiness once baked and cooled. Unfortunately, baking soda also promotes browning, and it made the edges of these

FAIRY GINGERBREAD COOKIES

NOTES FROM THE TEST KITCHEN

MAKING FAIRY GINGERBREAD COOKIES

1. To form cookies of requisite thinness, use small offset spatula to spread batter to edges of 15 by 12-inch sheet of parchment paper.

2. Immediately after removing cookies from oven, use pizza wheel or chef's knife to score 3 by 2-inch rectangles. Work quickly to prevent breaking.

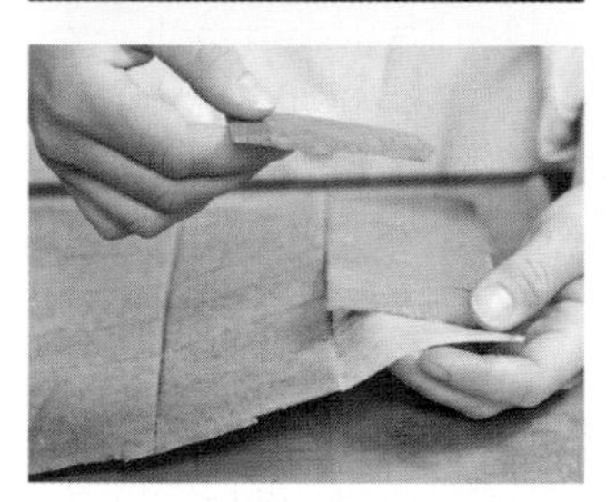

3. Once cookies are cool, trace over scored lines with paring knife and gently break cookies apart along lines.

THE BEST GROUND GINGER

A staple in bakers' pantries, ground ginger adds a warm, spicy flavor and aroma to baked goods and many Asian and Indian dishes. Since ginger is often used in combination with other pungent spices and strong flavors, such as molasses, would it matter which brand we used in recipes like gingerbread? We bought two top-selling national supermarket brands of ground ginger, McCormick and Spice Islands, and compared them with mail-order ground ginger from Penzeys Spices. We tasted each in gingerbread muffins and Fairy Gingerbread Cookies, crisp, wafer-thin cookies in which ginger is the star.

In gingerbread muffins, where cinnamon and allspice muffled our perceptions of the ginger, all three brands received equivalent scores, although a few tasters singled out the more pungent Penzeys for extra praise. But in Fairy Gingerbread Cookies, tasters showed decided preferences. Although we deemed all three brands acceptable, we gave the lowest marks to McCormick, which was quite mild. Once again, a minority preferred Penzeys' potent ginger heat, but the highest scores went to **Spice Islands Ground Ginger**, which straddled the middle ground with full ginger flavor but more moderate heat than Penzeys.

thin cookies dark before their centers were cooked. Thankfully, the solution to this problem was the easiest yet: lowering the oven temperature to 325 degrees. (Apparently, my "slack oven" wasn't quite slack enough.)

My "social duty" fulfilled, I vowed to serve these crisp, gingery, ethereally delicate wafers to whoever comes a-callin'. And I'm thinking of taking up euchre.

—ERIKA BRUCE, *Cook's Country*

Fairy Gingerbread Cookies

MAKES 5 DOZEN COOKIES

Use cookie or baking sheets that measure at least 15 by 12 inches. Don't be disconcerted by the scant amount of batter: You really are going to spread it very thin. Use the edges of the parchment paper as your guide, covering the entire surface thinly and evenly.

- **Vegetable oil spray**
- **1½ teaspoons ground ginger**
- **¾ cup plus 2 tablespoons (4⅜ ounces) all-purpose flour**
- **½ teaspoon baking soda**
- **¼ teaspoon salt**
- **5 tablespoons unsalted butter, softened**
- **½ cup (3½ ounces) plus 1 tablespoon packed light brown sugar**
- **4 teaspoons grated fresh ginger**
- **¾ teaspoon vanilla extract**
- **¼ cup whole milk, room temperature**

1. Adjust oven racks to upper-middle and lower-middle positions and heat oven to 325 degrees. Spray 2 cookie sheets (or inverted baking sheets) with vegetable oil spray and cover each with 15 by 12-inch sheet parchment paper. Toast ground ginger in 8-inch skillet over medium heat until fragrant, about 1 minute. Combine flour, toasted ginger, baking soda, and salt in bowl.

2. Using stand mixer fitted with paddle, beat butter and brown sugar together on medium-high speed until light and fluffy, about 2 minutes. Add grated ginger and vanilla and mix until incorporated. Reduce speed to low and add flour mixture in 3 additions, alternating with 2 additions of milk.

3. Using small offset spatula, evenly spread ¾ cup of batter to cover parchment on each prepared cookie sheet (batter will be very thin). Bake until deep golden brown, 16 to 20 minutes, switching and rotating sheets halfway through baking. Using pizza wheel or chef's knife, immediately score cookies into 3 by 2-inch rectangles. Let cool completely, about 20 minutes. Using tip of paring knife, separate cookies along scored lines. Serve. (Cookies can be stored at room temperature for up to 3 days.)

CHEWY SUGAR COOKIES

THE FIRST CHALLENGE FOR EVERY PROSPECTIVE test cook at *Cook's Illustrated* is to bake a batch of chewy sugar cookies under the watchful eye of the test kitchen director. The task looks simple enough: Cream the fat with sugar; mix in egg and vanilla, followed by the dry ingredients (flour, sugar, salt, and leavener); roll balls of dough in sugar; and bake. But more often than not, the resulting cookies range from stunted and humped to flat and brittle, with a smooth rather than crackly top. With no nuts, raisins, or chunks of chocolate to provide distraction, such flaws become all the more glaring. Indeed, the sugar cookie has been the downfall of many a hopeful applicant.

The truth is, making a just-right version of this humble cookie is far from easy. I was determined to engineer a recipe that would produce my ideal every time: a sugar cookie crisp at the edges, soft and chewy in the center, crackly crisp on top—and, of course, richly flavorful.

I already had a leg up in the chewiness department. While developing an earlier recipe for chewy brownies, I learned that the key to a truly chewy texture is all in the fat. For optimal chew, a recipe must contain both saturated and unsaturated fat in a ratio of approximately 1 to 3. When combined, the two types of fat molecules form a sturdier crystalline structure that requires more force to bite through than the structure formed from a high proportion of saturated fats.

Right away I could eliminate the majority of recipes I'd found in my research; almost all called for butter alone. Butter is predominantly—but not entirely—a saturated fat, and an all-butter cookie actually contains approximately 2 parts saturated fat to 1 part unsaturated fat. For optimal chew, I needed to reverse that ratio and then some.

I got to work adjusting the fat in the recipe that I'd singled out as a baseline for "soft and chewy" sugar cookies. I knocked down the recipe's 8 ounces (16 tablespoons) of butter to 3 ounces (6 tablespoons) and added 5 ounces of mostly unsaturated vegetable oil, which gave me a fat content that was approximately 25 percent saturated and 75 percent unsaturated.

With so little butter in the recipe, there was not enough solid fat to hold the air, so creaming it with the sugar no longer made sense. Instead, I melted the butter and whisked it with the sugar. This simple switch proved to be a boon in more ways than one. First, it eliminated one of the trickier aspects of baking sugar cookies: ensuring that the solid butter is just the right temperature. Second, melted butter would aid in my quest for chewiness: When liquefied, the small amount of water in butter mixes with the flour to form gluten, which makes for chewier cookies. Finally, with creaming out of the equation, I'd no longer need to pull out my stand mixer; I could mix all the ingredients by hand.

But there was a downside to swapping butter for oil. The two doses of liquid fat made the dough so soft that it practically poured onto the baking sheet. Plus, now that I was no longer creaming, there wasn't enough air in the dough, and the cookies were baking up too flat. I spent the next several tests readjusting my ingredients. More flour helped build up structure, and another ½ teaspoon of baking powder added lift. To keep the cookies from being a bit too dry and biscuit-like, I ramped up the sugar, salt, and vanilla and added a tiny bit of milk.

With this new formula, the chewiness of my cookies was spot-on. But I still had a few problems, two of which were mainly cosmetic: The cookies had gone from too flat to a bit more domed than I liked, and they didn't have much of that appealingly crackly top that makes a sugar cookie distinctive. But most important, trading more than half the rich butter for neutral-tasting vegetable oil had rendered the cookies very sweet—and only sweet.

There was no use reducing the amount of sugar: Given the choice between blandness and one-note sweetness, I'd take the latter. Instead, I wondered if I could add something to take the edge off all that sugariness. An acidic ingredient like lemon juice or zest might work. But such assertive citrus flavor took the cookies out of the "sugar" category and dropped them squarely into the lemon family. We often add buttermilk, sour cream, or yogurt to muffins and cakes to round out their flavors. But when I tried each of these in place of the milk in my recipe, I couldn't add more than a tablespoon of any one before it upset the precarious moisture balance, leading to dough that was too soft.

I scanned the supermarket dairy aisle and zeroed in on cream cheese, wondering if it would enrich the dough's flavor without adding much liquid. Of course, the trade-off would be my perfect chewiness ratio: Cream cheese contains less than one-third the amount of overall fat of vegetable oil, but most of it is saturated. With every ounce I added, I would be chipping away at my carefully calibrated ratio of fats, so I traded 1 ounce of oil for a modest 2 ounces of cream cheese. The saturated-fat content increased from 25 percent to 32 percent—and I was thrilled to find that the difference didn't markedly affect the cookies' texture. But flavor-wise, the effect of the cream cheese was dramatic, and my tasters' faces lit up as they bit into this latest batch.

There was more good news: With acidic cream cheese in the mix, I could now add baking soda to the dough. As long as there's an acidic ingredient present, baking soda has all sorts of special powers, including the ability to solve my other two pesky problems: slightly humped cookies with not enough crackle. Just a half teaspoon produced cookies that looked as good as they tasted.

The recipe was in good shape: The butter-oil combination led to satisfying chew, the liquid fats made the dough easy to mix by hand, the cream cheese provided subtle contrast with the sugar, and the baking soda ensured a crackly top and a nicely rounded shape. But when I confidently passed the recipe on to a friend, touting it as "foolproof," I was dismayed to find that when she tried it, her cookies spread all over the pan to form one giant confection.

I asked her to walk me through her process—and I realized I'd taken a crucial test kitchen technique for granted. When baking, we measure our ingredients by weight, but like many home cooks, my friend had measured hers by volume. In the past, we've found that weights of volume-measured ingredients can vary by as much as 20 percent, a particular hazard when too little flour is measured. While a bit too much flour isn't a catastrophe, too little means more flour proteins get coated in fat and can't form structure-building gluten. The result: cookies that spread and bake up flat. For a

NOTES FROM THE TEST KITCHEN

SECRET WEAPONS FOR TASTE AND TEXTURE

Sugar cookies can be cloyingly sweet, and even those billing themselves as chewy rarely are. These two ingredients helped us create the best flavor and chewy texture.

CREAM CHEESE

Cream cheese is an ingredient not often included in sugar cookies. But we found it helps cut their one-note sweetness and round out flavors.

OIL

Swapping some butter (mainly a saturated fat) for vegetable oil (unsaturated fat) boosts chewiness considerably. The combination of fats creates a sturdier structure that requires more force to bite through.

DYNAMIC DUO: BAKING POWDER + BAKING SODA

Many cookie recipes, including our Chewy Sugar Cookies, contain both baking soda and baking powder. Since each is a leavening agent, why do you need both? The answer is that the two work in tandem to create cookies that not only rise, but spread, to the right degree. Plus in our recipe, baking soda has one more purely aesthetic effect: It creates cookies with an appealingly crackly top.

POWDER, NO SODA

With only baking powder in the mix, our cookies bake up humped with less crackly tops.

POWDER + SODA

Both leaveners in the dough lead to cookies that are perfectly mounded and nicely crackly.

truly foolproof recipe, I needed to provide some wiggle room. The solution turned out to be as simple as cutting back a little on the fat, so there would never be too much. Reducing the butter was out of the question—I didn't want to lose its rich flavor. Instead, I took the oil down from ½ cup to ⅓ cup.

This change, of course, rejiggered my fat ratios, with saturated fat now totaling 36 percent and the unsaturated fat 64 percent—closer to a 1-to-2 ratio than a 1-to-3 ratio, but still almost the reverse of the all-butter recipe I began with. Happily, while the cookies were not quite as chewy as before, they still had far more chew than any sugar cookie I've ever eaten.

The only outstanding problem? With such an easy, truly foolproof chewy sugar cookie recipe on record, the test kitchen director will have to find something more challenging to spring on job applicants.

—ANDREA GEARY, *Cook's Illustrated*

Chewy Sugar Cookies

MAKES 2 DOZEN COOKIES

The final dough will be slightly softer than most cookie doughs. For the best results, handle the dough as briefly and gently as possible when shaping the cookies. Overworking the dough will result in flatter cookies.

- **2¼ cups (11¼ ounces) all-purpose flour**
- **1 teaspoon baking powder**
- **½ teaspoon baking soda**
- **½ teaspoon salt**
- **1½ cups (10½ ounces) sugar, plus ⅓ cup for rolling**
- **2 ounces cream cheese, cut into 8 pieces**
- **6 tablespoons unsalted butter, melted and hot**
- **⅓ cup vegetable oil**
- **1 large egg**
- **1 tablespoon milk**
- **2 teaspoons vanilla extract**

1. Adjust oven rack to middle position and heat oven to 350 degrees. Line 2 large baking sheets with parchment paper. Whisk flour, baking powder, baking soda, and salt together in medium bowl. Set aside.

2. Place 1½ cups sugar and cream cheese in large bowl. Place remaining ⅓ cup sugar in shallow baking dish or pie plate and set aside. Pour butter over sugar and cream cheese and whisk to combine (some small lumps of cream cheese will remain but will smooth out later). Whisk in oil until incorporated. Add egg, milk, and vanilla; continue to whisk until smooth. Add flour mixture and mix with rubber spatula until soft, homogeneous dough forms.

3. Divide dough into 24 equal pieces, about 2 tablespoons each (or use #40 portion scoop). Using hands, roll dough into balls. Working in batches, roll balls in reserved sugar to coat and evenly space on prepared baking sheets, 12 dough balls per sheet. Using bottom of drinking glass, flatten dough balls until 2 inches in diameter. Sprinkle tops evenly with 4 teaspoons of sugar remaining in shallow dish (2 teaspoons per tray), discarding any remaining sugar.

4. Bake, one tray at a time, until edges are set and just beginning to brown, 11 to 13 minutes, rotating tray after 7 minutes. Let cookies cool on sheets for 5 minutes. Using metal spatula, transfer cookies to wire rack and let cool to room temperature. Serve.

VARIATIONS

Chewy Chai-Spice Sugar Cookies

Add ¼ teaspoon ground cinnamon, ¼ teaspoon ground ginger, ¼ teaspoon ground cardamom, ¼ teaspoon ground cloves, and pinch pepper to sugar and cream cheese mixture in step 2 and reduce vanilla extract to 1 teaspoon.

Chewy Coconut-Lime Sugar Cookies

Whisk ½ cup sweetened shredded coconut, chopped fine, into flour mixture in step 1. Add 1 teaspoon grated lime zest to sugar and cream cheese mixture in step 2 and substitute 1 tablespoon lime juice for vanilla extract.

Chewy Hazelnut Brown Butter Sugar Cookies

Do not melt butter and omit vanilla extract. Add ¼ cup finely chopped toasted hazelnuts to bowl with sugar and cream cheese in step 2. After placing ⅓ cup sugar in baking dish, melt butter in 10-inch skillet over medium-high heat, about 2 minutes. Cook, swirling pan frequently, until butter is dark golden brown and has nutty aroma, 1 to 3 minutes. Pour butter over sugar and cream cheese mixture and proceed as directed, increasing milk to 2 tablespoons.

TEST KITCHEN RESOURCES

** Every product tested may not be listed in these pages. Please visit www.cooksillustrated.com to find complete listings and information on all products tested and reviewed.*

BEST KITCHEN QUICK TIPS

MAKE-AHEAD PIE DOUGH

Kim Trapp of Feeding Hills, Mass., prefers to make pie dough in multiple batches and freeze it. To minimize the time it takes to thaw and roll the dough, she uses a 9-inch cake pan to create even rounds for freezing.

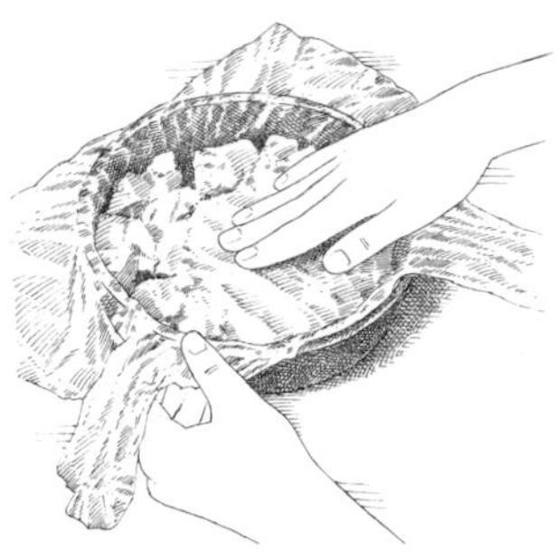

1. Line a 9-inch cake pan with plastic wrap. Gently press pie dough into the pan in an even layer. Wrap the dough in plastic and freeze until firm.

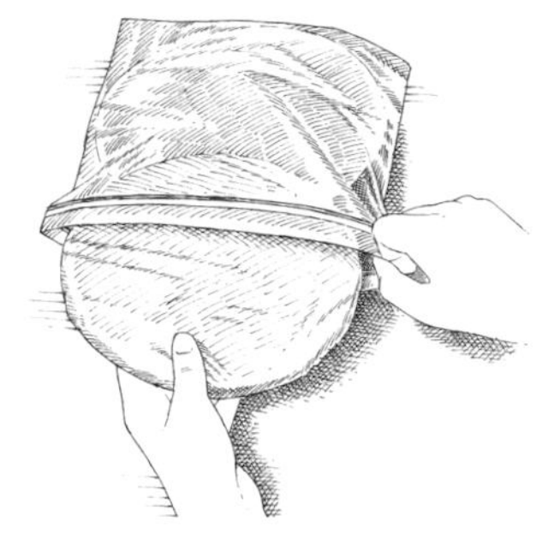

2. Once frozen, the dough rounds can be removed from the cake pan and stored in a large zipper-lock bag until needed.

ICE WATER SHAKE-UP

When recipes like pie dough call for ice water, it can be a challenge to pour just the water, not the cubes as well. Andreas Weiger of Burlington, Wis., uses a tool from his wet bar to ensure a controlled pour.

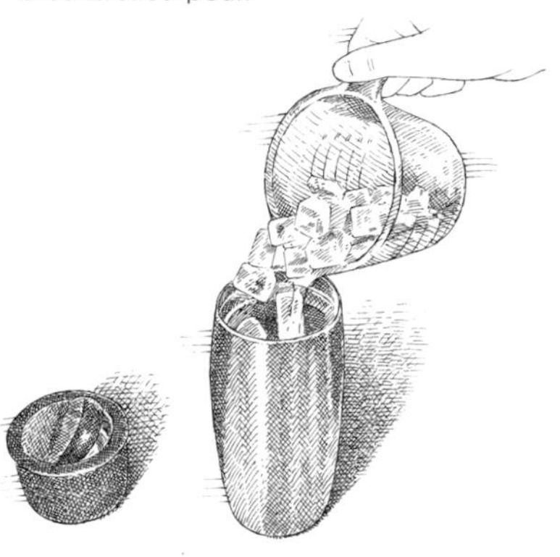

1. Fill a cocktail shaker with the desired amount of water. Add ice and affix the lid.

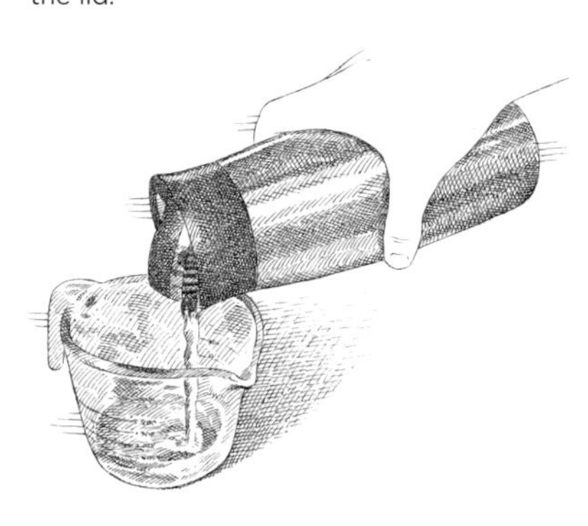

2. Shake vigorously, then pour the water through the strainer, leaving the ice in the base.

PERFECT PIE CRUST IN THE SUMMER

Summer is a mixed blessing for pie bakers. The best fruits are everywhere, but rolling out a nice pie crust on a hot, sticky day can be a challenge. The butter in the pastry melts, the dough becomes too soft to roll out, and there's a good chance that it'll stick to the counter. Leslie Wilson of Albany, N.Y., relies on a cool (pun intended) trick: Fifteen minutes before rolling out the dough, she places a casserole dish filled with ice on the counter. The ice chills the counter briefly—just enough time for her to roll out a pie crust.

KEEPING COOKIE DOUGH ROUND

Leslie Saltsman of Potomac, Md., uses cardboard paper towel rolls to store her refrigerator cookie dough. Once she's formed the dough into a log, she rolls it in plastic wrap and slides the dough inside the cardboard (slit lengthwise) to protect it in the fridge and keep it perfectly round.

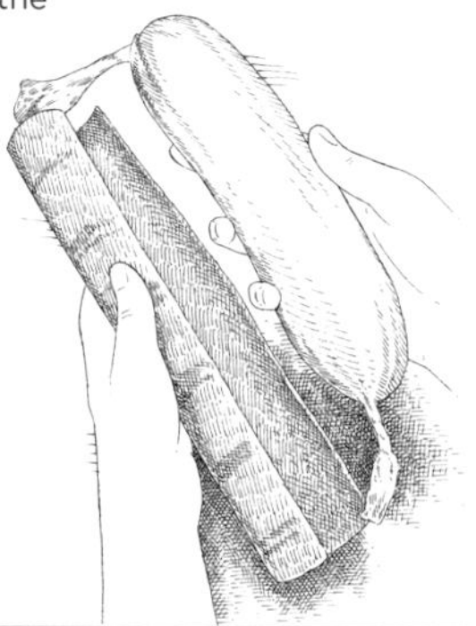

EASIER VINAIGRETTE

To evenly dispense oil when making a vinaigrette or mayonnaise, DeeDee Boies of Incline Village, Nev., measures the oil into a squeeze bottle first. The squeeze bottle is easy to hold and makes adding the oil in a slow, steady stream effortless.

LAZY COOK'S LATTICE

Jane Ikemura of Los Angeles, Calif., has found an easy way to make straight lattice strips to top her pies.

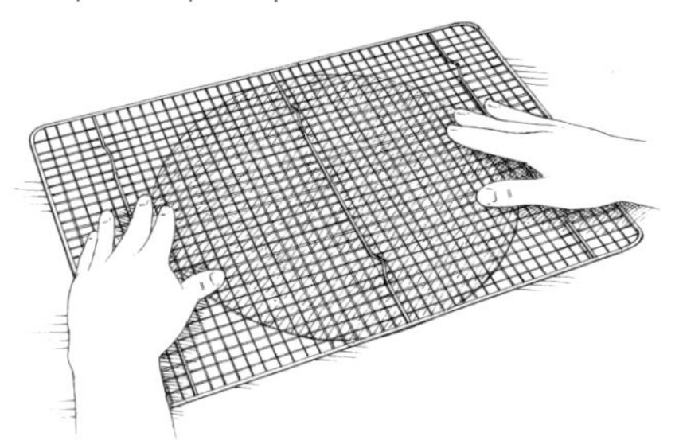

1. Roll out the dough according to the recipe, then lightly press the top of a cooling rack into the dough.

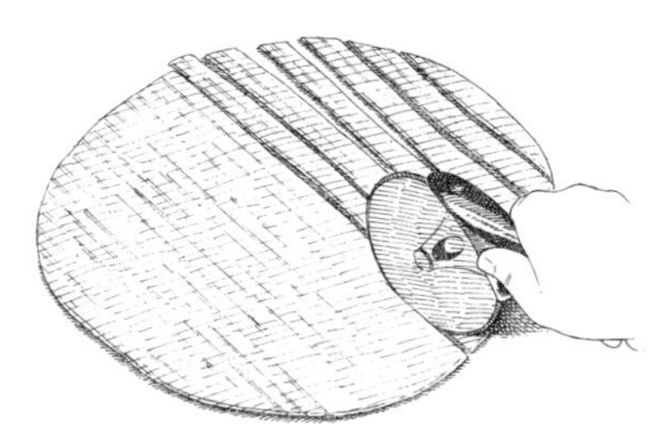

2. Using the rack's indentations as your guide, cut the dough into 1¼-inch strips (every fourth line works with our winning model from CIA Bakeware) with a pizza wheel.

REALLY FAST FRIES

By using his apple slicer, DL Smith of Dexter, Mich., gets his spuds cut and ready for the fryer in no time.

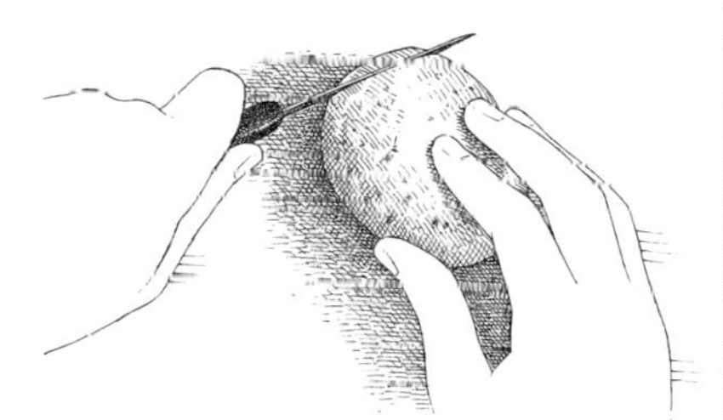

1. Slice one end of the potato to create a stable base. Set the potato cut side down on the cutting board.

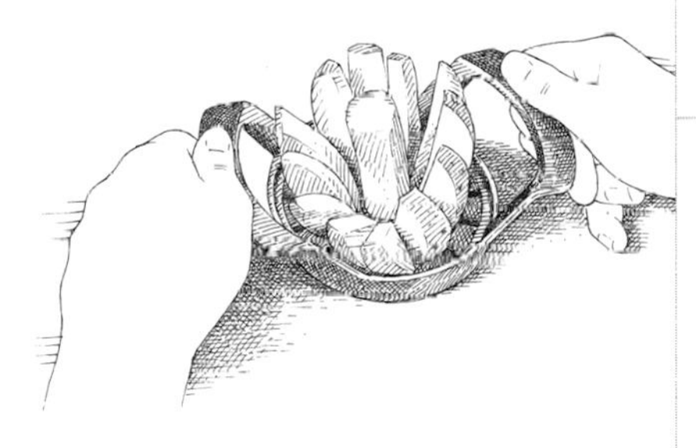

2. Push the apple slicer down over the potato, sectioning it into steak fry-size wedges. Cut the center cylinder in half lengthwise before cooking.

SEEDING PEPPERS

Jeffrey Dunn of Philadelphia, Pa., uses a grapefruit spoon to scrape the seeds and veins out of fiery chiles and mild bell peppers. The spoon's serrated edge pulls the veins from the inner core and walls, and its rounded sides glide around the chile or bell pepper more easily than a knife.

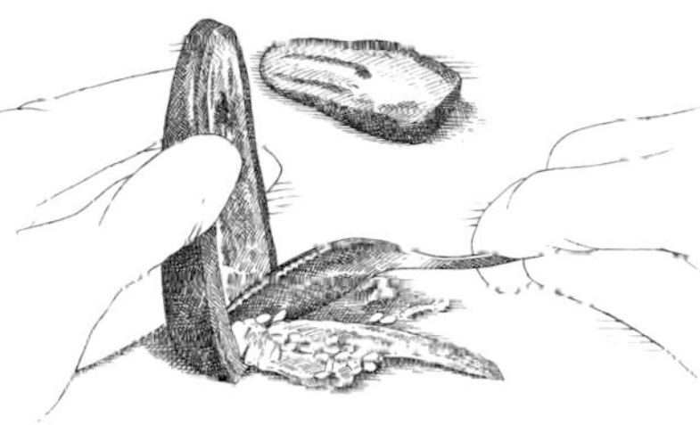

IMPROVISED POTATO MASHER

On a recent vacation, Denise Twist of Portsmouth, Va., found herself in a house without a potato masher. She thought she solved the problem by turning to a hand-held mixer, but even a moderate 2 pounds of potatoes in the bowl proved too thick for the beaters. Her brainstorm: Remove the beaters and grip them in her fist to mash the potatoes.

QUICKER CHERRY PITTING

Alyssa Gilberti of Brighton, Mass., has worked out an efficient way to pit cherries using a takeout utensil and a glass bottle. Place a cherry over the mouth of a clean, empty glass bottle (choose one with a small mouth, such as a wine or soda bottle). Using the blunt end of a chopstick, pierce through the center of the cherry, pushing the pit through the flesh and skin and into the bottle.

SIMPLER SLICING

Unable to slice radishes and carrots thinly and evenly enough for salad with a chef's knife, Thomas Sweeney of Melrose, Mass., discovered a solution buried in his utensil drawer: a vegetable peeler. The sharp blade, he found, makes it easy to cut wafer-thin slices.

CUTTING KERNELS

Paula Osorio of Loveland, Ohio, uses her mandoline to quickly take corn off the cob. After setting the mandoline to ¼-inch thickness and placing a pie plate underneath to catch the kernels, she grips the corn with a kitchen towel for safety, then strips each ear in four quick sweeps down the blade.

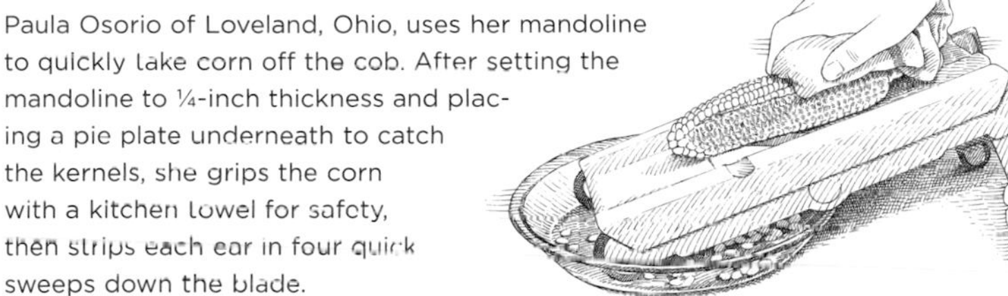

FREEZING CITRUS ZEST

Bob Swander of Allston, Mass., often uses only a teaspoon or so of the zest from a lemon or orange. Here's how he saves the extras:

1. To avoid waste, he removes the zest from the rest of the fruit.

2. He then deposits the grated zest in half-teaspoon increments on a plate and transfers the plate to his freezer.

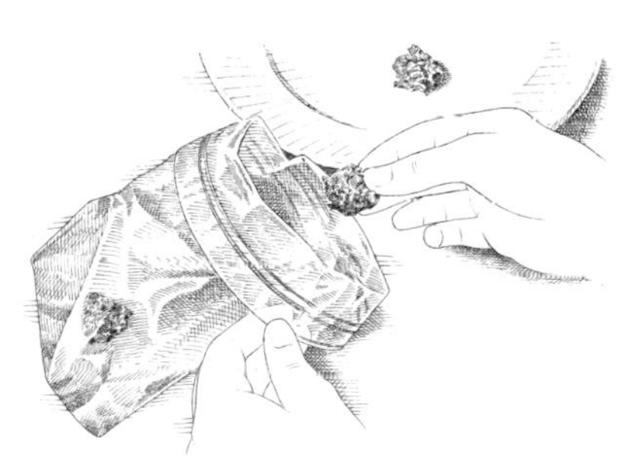

3. Once the piles are frozen, he places them in a zipper-lock bag. Frozen zest keeps for up to 3 weeks.

BEST KITCHEN QUICK TIPS

GREASE, LIGHTNING FAST

Sheila Censorio of Block Island, R.I., has found a smart way to grease cake pans:

1. Save empty butter wrappers in a zipper-lock bag in the freezer.

2. Whenever a recipe calls for a greased pan, pull out one wrapper and wipe it on the pan's surface. Each wrapper usually has just enough butter clinging to it to grease a pan.

CLEANING WAFFLE IRONS

While most waffle irons and panini presses feature an easy-to-clean nonstick cooking surface, Michelle Gate of Fairfield, Conn., finds that food still gets stuck in the deep ridges. A firm bristle toothbrush, she's discovered, is perfect for this cleaning task. The bristles are stiff enough to remove stubborn stuck-on food yet soft enough for a nonstick surface.

SHAKEN, NOT STIRRED

Rather than going out to a coffee shop and spending nearly five bucks for a single iced-coffee drink, Lawrence Tetterson, Albuquerque, N.M., uses a simple bar staple to make it at home. He's found that shaking the ice, coffee, and milk in his cocktail shaker works much better than simply stirring everything together in a glass, giving him a frothy, delicious drink for just pennies.

GREAT PLATE WARMER

Earl Schenberg of St. Louis, Mo., has figured out a way to prevent his room-temperature plates from cooling down his hot breakfast. While his bread is toasting, he places the plates on top of the toaster oven. The radiating heat warms them right up and delivers eggs, pancakes, and other breakfast items to the table still hot.

TRAVELING SPICES

Kathy Bynum of Chocowinity, N.C., frequently cooks while vacationing in rental properties but often finds old, flavorless dried spices gathering dust in the kitchens. Rather than purchasing new spices for every trip, she uses a jumbo pill organizer to transport small amounts of her favorite spices—one in each of the compartments.

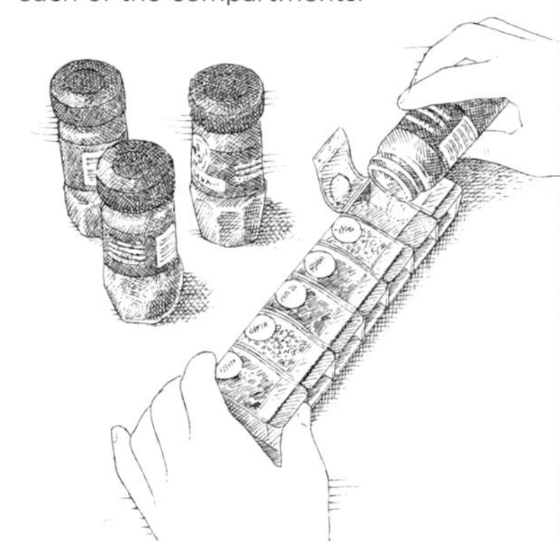

DEVILED EGGS ON THE GO

The deviled egg is all about presentation so packing a dozen for a picnic or a party can be daunting. Errin Chapin of Medfield, Mass., prevents overturned eggs by placing each one in a paper cupcake liner and then arranging them in a single layer in a plastic storage container.

FLIP-FREE CONTAINERS

To keep their plastic storage containers from turning over and filling with water during the wash cycle, Mike and Cindy Ehlenfeldt of Charlestown, N.H., place them on the upper rack of the dishwasher and set a metal wire rack on top. The rack keeps the containers in place while soapy water flows through.

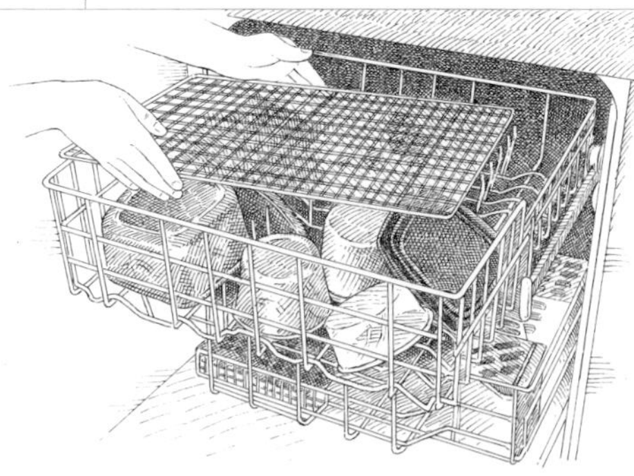

CLEANING CAST IRON

To clean a cast-iron pan without ruining the finish, it is important to avoid using soap and water. Derek Olson of Boulder, Colo., lets the pan cool, then takes a plastic mesh produce bag (the kind that holds lemons or onions) and swipes the pan clean. The mesh bag doesn't damage seasoning the way steel wool will, and he doesn't have to ruin a scrubber pad with grease.

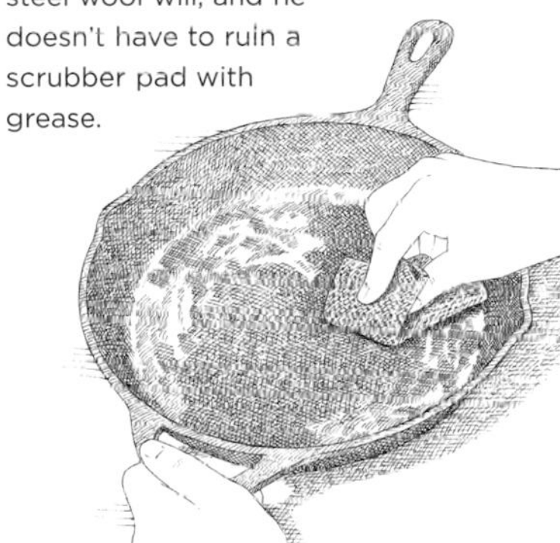

PICTURE-PERFECT RECIPES

Keeping recipes splatter-free is no longer an issue for Maureen Broomall of Pepperell, Mass. She prints them out on water-resistant photo paper so she can wipe away any spills. Plus, its heavy weight makes it more durable than a regular recipe card, and the 4 by 6-inch size fits perfectly in her recipe box.

NO MORE "MYSTERY MEAT"

Gene Koury of Chico, Calif., often freezes raw meat for later use and offers this simple labeling trick. After wrapping the meat in plastic wrap and placing it in a zipper-lock freezer bag, he cuts off the grocery label and puts it inside, facing out. At a glance he knows the exact cut, weight, and—most important—date of purchase, allowing him to gauge how long the meat has been lingering in the freezer.

BIGGER BRINE CONTAINERS

Mike Hocker of Galion, Ohio, saves large pretzel or pickle tubs for brining instead of tying up his large stockpot. He washes them, cuts the necks off, and uses them to brine large birds or cuts of meat—whole chickens, pork roasts, ribs, etc.—that don't easily fit into smaller containers.

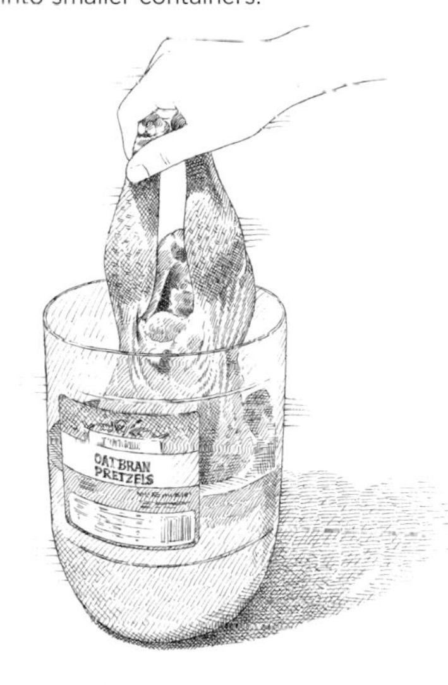

QUICK TRIVET SUBSTITUTE

In the midst of a cooking marathon, Kevin Holland of Palm Coast, Fla., found himself needing a trivet for his hot baking sheet. His solution: He flipped over four spoons and laid them on the counter a few inches apart. Then he set the hot sheet on top to cool.

VERTICAL ROASTER STAND-IN

While we like vertical roasters because they let poultry cook evenly and get the skin crisp, many cooks don't own one. Julianne Douglas of Providence, R.I., has found another stand-in—her Bundt pan. Once the chicken has been seasoned, she slides it onto the center post of the pan, legs facing down, so the chicken stands upright.

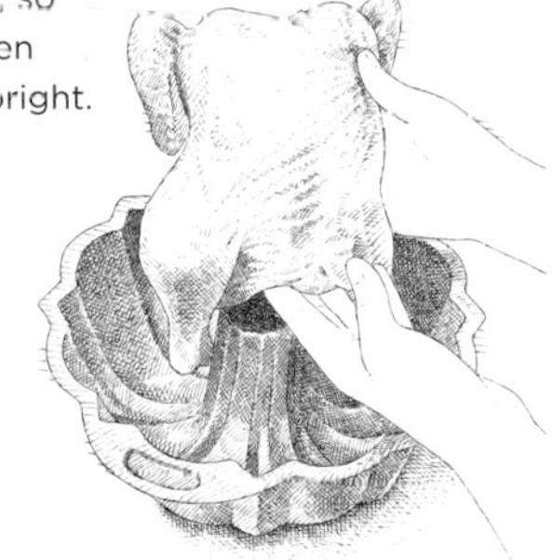

GETTING UNDER THE SKIN

Seasoning a whole chicken or turkey under the skin using your fingers can be tricky, since it's hard to distribute the salt evenly without tearing the skin. Ann Miller of Rochester Hills, Mich., has a long-handled solution: an iced-tea spoon, which also works to loosen the skin first.

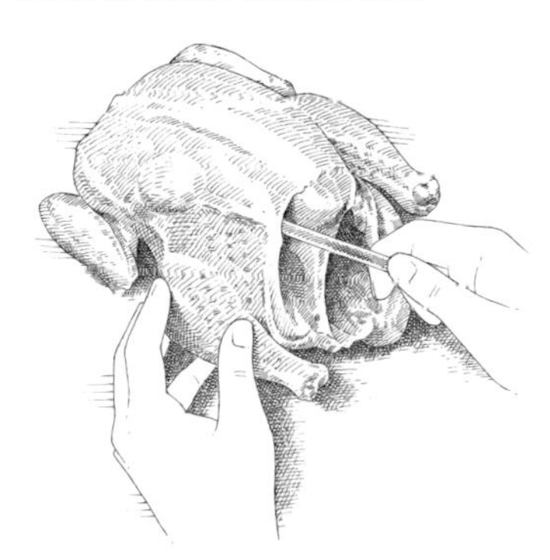

1. Pry the skin from the bird with an iced-tea spoon.

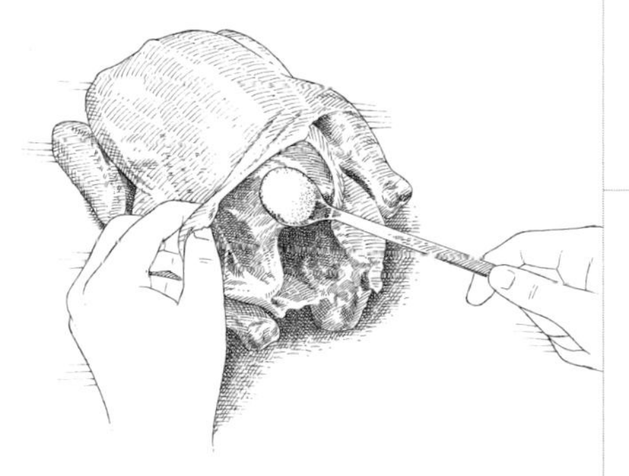

2. Place salt on the spoon and reach under the skin to distribute it evenly.

SPLATTER GUARD SOLUTION

Erica Zito of Cedar Rapids, Iowa, doesn't have a splatter guard—but there are times when she needs one. Fortunately, she discovered she could substitute a metal colander as a splatter guard when frying. Turned upside down, it fits over the pot and keeps the kitchen cleaner.

CHILES 101

There's more to chiles than incendiary punch. From shopping and seeding to toasting and roasting, here's our guide to extracting their full flavor.

COMMON FRESH CHILES

The same chile can go by different names in different parts of the country and can range from green to red, depending on when it was harvested. To ensure that you're buying the chile called for in a recipe, it's a good idea to look at a photo before shopping. Whatever the variety, you should choose chiles with tight, unblemished skin and flesh that's firm to the touch.

	APPEARANCE	FLAVOR	HEAT	SUBSTITUTIONS
Poblano	Large, triangular; green to red-brown	Crisp, vegetal	🌶	Anaheim, bell pepper
Anaheim	Large, long, skinny; yellow-green to red	Mildly tangy, vegetal	🌶🌶	Poblano
Jalapeño	Small, smooth, shiny; green or red	Bright, grassy	🌶🌶 ½	Serrano
Serrano	Small; dark green	Bright, citrusy	🌶🌶🌶	Jalapeño
Thai Bird's Eye	Narrow and petite; bright red	Rich, fruity	🌶🌶🌶 ½	Serrano
Habanero	Bulbous; bright orange to red	Deeply floral, fruity	🌶🌶🌶🌶	Double dose of Thai Bird's Eye

FRESH CHILE PREP

REMOVING SEEDS AND RIBS

To tamp down the fire, remove the seeds and ribs before adding chiles to a dish. Reserve the seeds and add them later to the finished dish.

1. Cut chile in half lengthwise with knife.

2. Starting opposite stem end, run edge of melon baller, teaspoon, or grapefruit spoon along inside of chile, scraping out seeds and ribs.

ROASTING CHILES

Fresh chiles tend to bring bright, floral notes to food. Roasting them releases more flavor compounds and caramelizes their sugars, for a deeper, nuttier taste. Here are two methods for roasting chiles.

STOVETOP METHOD: Small chiles, like jalapeños, can be quickly roasted over a gas burner—but it's a chore to do them one at a time. Here's how we made the process more efficient.

1. Place wire cooling rack over gas burner and turn burner to high.

2. Arrange chiles on wire rack directly over flame and char on all sides, turning with tongs. Steam as with oven method (see step 2 at right); peel skins.

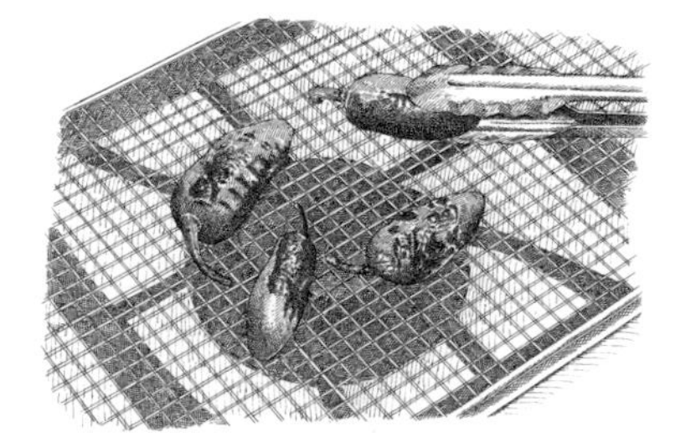

OVEN METHOD: Small chiles can be roasted whole. For large chiles, like poblanos or Anaheims, slice ¼ inch off the top and bottom, pull the core out, make a slit down one side, and then press the chile flat into one long strip.

1. Arrange chiles on foil-lined baking sheet (place skin side up if roasting strips). Broil chiles until charred. Flip small whole chiles over to char both sides.

2. Transfer chiles to bowl and cover with plastic wrap; let steam 20 minutes. Then peel off skins (but not under water, to preserve flavor). Remove seeds from small chiles.

HOT PROPERTIES

ALL FIRED UP

Chiles get their heat from a group of chemical compounds called capsaicinoids, the best known being capsaicin. Most of the capsaicin in a chile is concentrated in the inner whitish pith (also called ribs), with progressively smaller amounts in the seeds and the flesh. In lab tests we conducted on jalapeños, we found the pith contained 100 times the amount of capsaicin in the flesh, while the seeds had 15 times as much.

PUT THE GLOVES ON

In some chiles, the level of capsaicin is so high, it can actually irritate the skin. To protect your hands, wear disposable latex gloves when handling them. This advice holds true whether you're working with fresh or dried chiles.

COMMON DRIED CHILES

Just as dried fruit has a more concentrated taste than its fresh counterpart, chiles gain a more intense character when dried. Because they're allowed to ripen on the plant, many often taste sweeter dried than fresh. For dried chiles with the best flavor, buy ones that are pliable and smell slightly fruity.

	APPEARANCE	FLAVOR	HEAT	SUBSTITUTIONS
Ancho (Dried Poblano)	Wrinkly; dark red	Rich, with raisiny sweetness	🌶	Pasilla, mulato
Mulato (Dried Smoked Poblano)	Wrinkly; deep brown	Very smoky, with hints of licorice and dried cherry	🌶	Ancho
Chipotle (Dried Smoked Jalapeño)	Wrinkly; brownish red	Smoky, chocolaty, with tobacco-like sweetness	🌶🌶	None
Cascabel	Small, round; reddish brown	Nutty, woodsy	🌶🌶	New Mexico
New Mexico	Smooth; brick red	Slightly acidic, earthy	🌶🌶	Cascabel
Árbol	Smooth; bright red	Bright, with smoky undertones	🌶🌶🌶	Pequín
Pequín	Small, round; deep red	Bright, citrusy	🌶🌶🌶	Árbol

DRIED CHILE PREP

TOASTING DRIED CHILES

Just as roasting fresh chiles deepens their flavor, toasting dried ones improves their taste. We either toast chiles in a skillet on the stovetop or in the oven depending on the recipe, although we prefer oven toasting, which is easier and requires less attention.

1. Clean chiles with damp paper towel. Arrange on baking sheet and toast in 350-degree oven just until fragrant and puffed, about 6 minutes.

2. Cool chiles. Break open and brush out seeds and remove stem. Grind in spice grinder or rehydrate and puree.

MAKE YOUR OWN CHILI POWDER

While commercial chili powder is fine in some applications, it usually contains other ingredients (see "Pantry Chile Products," at right) that distract from chile flavor. Grinding your own powder from freshly toasted dried chiles is easy and can make a compelling difference in recipes. Simply tear seeded, stemmed, toasted chiles into pieces, place in a spice grinder, and pulverize for 30 to 40 seconds.

REHYDRATING TOASTED DRIED CHILES

Rehydrating dried chiles will mellow their taste. To concentrate their flavor, puree rehydrated chiles with onions, garlic, and tomatoes and cook in a little oil before adding them to a recipe.

1. To rehydrate, transfer seeded and stemmed toasted chiles to large bowl and cover with boiling water.

2. Let sit, stirring occasionally, until chiles are softened but not mushy, about 20 minutes. Then transfer to blender and puree.

"DRY-CLEAN" YOUR SPICE GRINDER

The oils in dried chiles can cling to a spice grinder, even after you've wiped it with a cloth. Since most grinders can't be immersed in water, we developed a method to "dry-clean" ours: Add several tablespoons of raw white rice to the grinder and pulverize to a fine powder. The powder will absorb residue and oils (discard the powder). Our winning grinder: Krups Fast-Touch Coffee Mill ($19.95).

PANTRY CHILE PRODUCTS

CAYENNE

Contrary to its name, this spice usually contains not only the fiery red cayenne pepper, but also a variety of other ground dried chiles. Like black pepper, it adds kick to food while enhancing other flavors. The volatile oils in cayenne (as in all chiles) lose potency within a few months, so be sure to replenish regularly. In tests, our tasters found brand mattered less than freshness.

CHILI POWDER

Most chili powder is a blend of roasted dried chiles, garlic powder, oregano, ground cumin, and sometimes salt and monosodium glutamate. Our tasters found brand was less of a factor than freshness. Buy at a store with high turnover and discard after six months.

RED PEPPER FLAKES

Made from a blend of roasted, dried, crushed chiles, red pepper flakes are another flavor enhancer that packs heat. Replace every six months.

CHIPOTLES IN ADOBO SAUCE

Cans of these smoky dried chiles packed in a tangy, tomato-and-herb-based adobo sauce are often more readily available than plain dried chipotles. The richly flavored sauce can also be used on its own to bring heat and depth to food.

HOT SAUCE

For complexity and not just heat, bypass Tabasco, which lends a searing, one-note spiciness to foods, and reach for Frank's RedHot Original Cayenne Pepper Sauce.

FOOLPROOF PIE DOUGH 101

The trouble with most pie dough is that it never seems to behave the same way twice. Here's how to create a consistently tender, flaky dough—and get it in the pan in one smooth, even piece.

KEYS TO FOOLPROOF PIE DOUGH

Perfect pie dough has just the right balance of tenderness to structure. The former comes from fat, the latter from long protein chains called gluten that form when flour mixes with water. Too little gluten and the dough won't stick together—but too much and the crust turns tough. We've developed an approach that keeps gluten in check but also allows for an unusually supple dough that's easy to handle and reduces the chance of overworking.

USE TWO FATS

Butter contributes rich taste—but also water, which encourages gluten development. For a crust that's both flavorful and tender, we use a 3:2 ratio of butter to shortening, a pure fat with no water.

USE MORE OF THEM

We incorporate roughly a third more total fat in our dough than the typical recipe, which coats the flour more thoroughly so less of it can mix with water to form gluten.

CREATE LAYERS FOR FLAKINESS

Traditional recipes process all the flour and fat at once, but we add the flour in two batches. We first process the fat with part of the flour to coat it, then give the mixture a few pulses once the remaining flour is added, so less of it is coated. Besides providing protection against toughness, this aids in flakiness by creating two distinct layers of dough—one with gluten and one without.

SWAP WATER FOR VODKA

Gluten forms readily in water, but it won't form in alcohol. By replacing some of the water in our recipe with vodka (which contains 40 percent ethanol but just 60 percent water), we're able to add more liquid to the dough so it stays soft and malleable, but without increasing the danger of the crust turning tough. (Note: Any 80-proof spirit will work. The alcohol burns off in the oven, along with any flavor.)

FOOLPROOF PIE DOUGH

For one 9-inch double-crust pie

- **2½ cups (12½ ounces) all-purpose flour**
- **2 tablespoons sugar**
- **1 teaspoon salt**
- **12 tablespoons unsalted butter, cut into ¼-inch pieces and chilled**
- **½ cup vegetable shortening, cut into 4 pieces and chilled**
- **¼ cup cold vodka**
- **¼ cup cold water**

1. Pulse 1½ cups flour, sugar, and salt in food processor until combined, about 2 pulses. Add butter and shortening; process until homogeneous dough just starts to collect in uneven clumps, about 15 seconds (dough will resemble cottage cheese curds and there should be no uncoated flour). Scrape down bowl with rubber spatula; redistribute dough evenly around processor blade. Add remaining 1 cup flour; pulse until mixture is evenly distributed around bowl and mass of dough has been broken up, 4 to 6 quick pulses. Empty mixture into medium bowl.

2. Sprinkle vodka and water over mixture. With rubber spatula, use folding motion to mix, pressing down on dough until dough is slightly tacky and sticks together. Divide into 2 even balls, flatten each into 4-inch disk, and wrap in plastic wrap; refrigerate for at least 45 minutes or up to 2 days.

THE RIGHT WAY TO ROLL IT OUT

When rolling dough, always work with well-chilled pastry; otherwise, the dough will stick to the counter and tear. Also, never roll out dough by rolling back and forth over the same section; more gluten will develop here, toughening the dough. Here's our method:

1. Place chilled dough on floured counter; sprinkle lightly with flour. Place rolling pin in center, with hands at 9 o'clock and 3 o'clock, and roll dough outward to edge, applying even, gentle pressure.

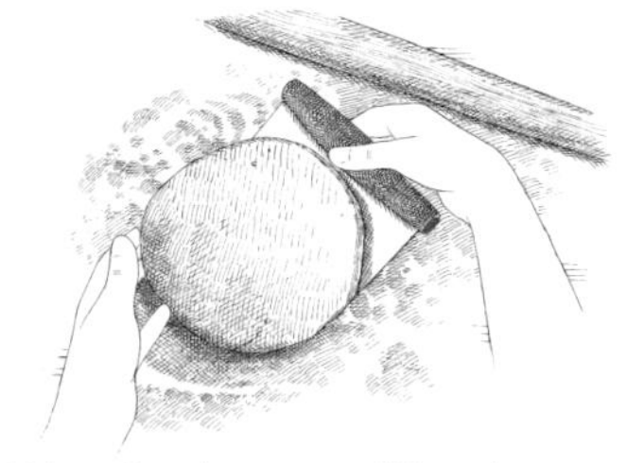

2. Using dough scraper, lift and turn dough 90 degrees. Roll outward again from center, keeping hands at 9 and 3 positions. Lightly flour underneath dough as necessary to prevent sticking.

3. Repeat rolling and turning steps (keeping hands at 9 and 3) until dough is wide enough to overhang pie plate by 4 inches.

TRANSFERRING AND FITTING THE DOUGH

1. Place rolling pin about two inches from top of dough round. Flip top edge of round over rolling pin and turn once to loosely roll around pin. Gently unroll dough over plate.

2. Lift dough around edges and gently press into corners of plate, letting excess dough hang over edge.

FOR A SINGLE-CRUST PIE

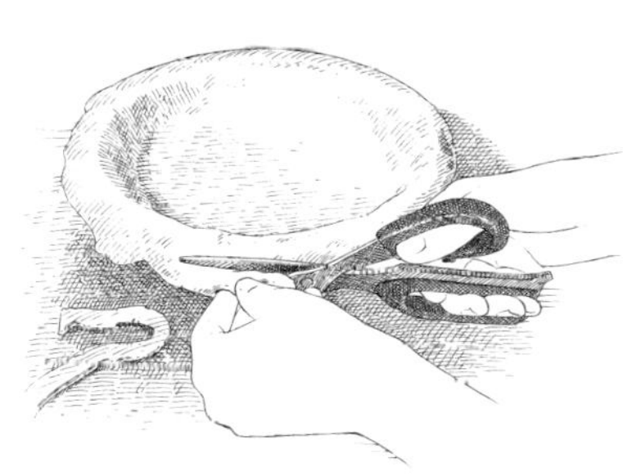

1. Trim dough, leaving ½-inch overhang.

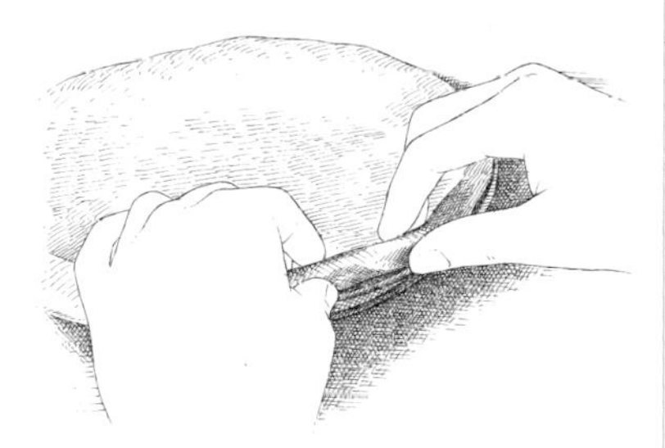

2. Roll overhang under to make flush with lip of pan. Crimp dough evenly around edge of pie using your fingertips or tines of fork.

FOR A DOUBLE-CRUST PIE

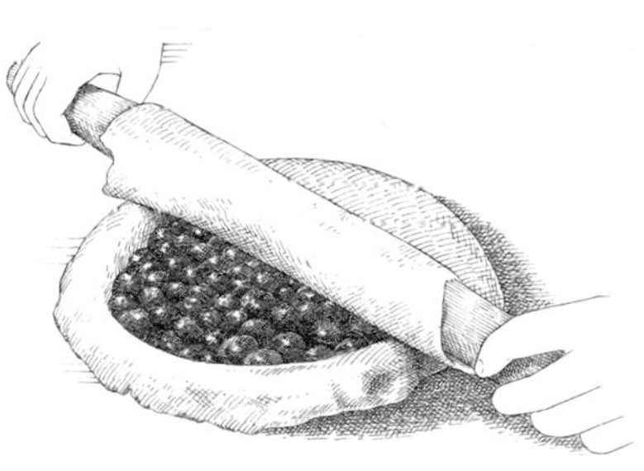

1. Unroll untrimmed top piece of dough over filled pie, taking care not to stretch it and create thin spots. Trim overhanging edges of both crusts to about ½ inch.

2. Press edges of top and bottom crusts together well to prevent leaking, then fold edges underneath to make flush with lip of pan. Crimp dough evenly around edge of pie using your fingertips or tines of fork. Cut 1-inch vents in center of top crust with paring knife (drier pies require only 4 vents while juicy pies require 8 vents).

TROUBLESHOOTING

PROBLEM: Dough sticks to counter.

AVOIDING IT: Start with very cold dough, work as quickly as possible, and make sure to lift and turn dough as you roll.

SOLVING IT: Add more flour to counter each time you lift dough to turn it; add more to top of dough as necessary. If dough still sticks, transfer to rimmed baking sheet and refrigerate until firm, about 15 minutes.

PROBLEM: Dough rips or tears.

AVOIDING IT: Handle dough gently and drape—don't stretch—in pan.

SOLVING IT: Roll or flatten small piece of leftover dough over hole to patch it. With our soft Foolproof Pie Dough, no moistening is necessary.

MAKING A DECORATIVE EDGE

An attractive border is more than window dressing on a pie—it provides support to the edge to prevent leaking. Here are two styles:

FLUTED EDGE
Use thumb and index fingers to create fluted ridges perpendicular to edge of pie plate.

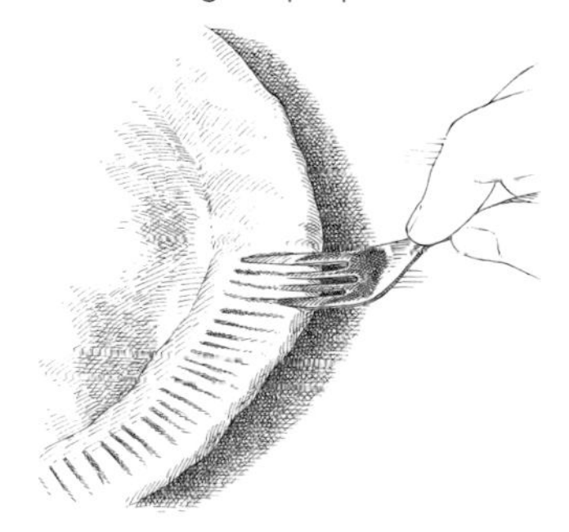

TINE EDGE
Press tines of fork into dough to flatten against rim of pie plate.

SALT 101

Pepper's best mate isn't just for seasoning. This culinary workhorse has a slew of hidden talents—from cleaning cast iron to making scrambled eggs more tender.

TYPES OF SALT

Whether mined from underground salt deposits or obtained by evaporating seawater, salt in its most basic form is the same: sodium chloride. What distinguishes one salt from another is texture, shape, and mineral content. These qualities can affect how a salt tastes as well as how it interacts with other foods.

TABLE SALT

Table salt, also known as common salt, consists of tiny, uniformly shaped crystals created during rapid vacuum evaporation. It usually includes anti-caking agents that help it pour smoothly.

HOW WE USE IT: Fine-grain table salt dissolves easily, making it our go-to for most applications, both sweet and savory.

SHOPPING TIP: Avoid iodized salt, which can impart a subtle chemical flavor.

SEA SALT

Sea salt is the product of seawater evaporation—a time-consuming, expensive process that yields irregularly shaped, mineral-rich flakes that vary in color but only slightly in flavor.

HOW WE USE IT: Don't bother cooking with pricey sea salt; we've found that mixed into food, it doesn't taste any different than table salt. Instead, we use it as a "finishing salt," where its delicate crunch stands out.

SHOPPING TIP: Texture—not exotic provenance—is the main consideration. Look for brands boasting large, flaky crystals such as Maldon Sea Salt.

KOSHER SALT

Coarse-grain kosher salt is raked during the evaporation process to yield flaky crystals originally used for koshering meat. Unlike table salt, kosher salt doesn't contain any additives.

HOW WE USE IT: Kosher salt is our top choice for seasoning meat. The large grains distribute easily and cling well to the meat's surfaces.

SHOPPING TIP: The two major brands of kosher salt—Morton and Diamond Crystal—work equally well; however, their crystal sizes differ considerably (see at left), and this makes a difference when measuring by volume.

HOW MUCH SALT IS IN THAT TEASPOON?

Different types and brands of salt can vary in volume. Here's how they measure up:

1 teaspoon table salt = 1½ teaspoons Morton kosher salt = 2 teaspoons Diamond Crystal kosher salt

BEYOND SEASONING: OTHER GOOD USES FOR SALT

DEEP-CLEANING CAST IRON

The abrasive quality of kosher salt makes it a perfect cleanser for rusty or gummy cast-iron cookware. Our method: Warm ¼ inch vegetable oil in pan 5 minutes; remove from heat and add ¼ cup kosher salt. Scrub salt into pan with paper towels until debris loosens. Rinse well and repeat if necessary.

TENDER SCRAMBLED EGGS

Salt keeps egg proteins from bonding to each other, thereby producing a weaker protein chain and more tender scrambled eggs. We recommend adding ⅛ teaspoon of table salt for every two eggs just prior to cooking.

GREENER GREEN BEANS

Adding salt to the cooking water not only seasons green beans, but also helps them retain their bright color. When green vegetables cook in unsalted water, some of the chlorophyll molecules lose their color-enhancing magnesium atoms. Salt stabilizes the chlorophyll, helping to keep the vegetables green. To maximize color retention without oversalting, use 1½ teaspoons of salt for every quart of water.

MAKING GARLIC PASTE

Garlic paste adds robust garlic flavor to dishes like aïoli and pesto. To ensure that the garlic's texture is smooth and unobtrusive, sprinkle kosher salt over minced garlic and use the side of a knife to reduce the chopped garlic to a fine paste.

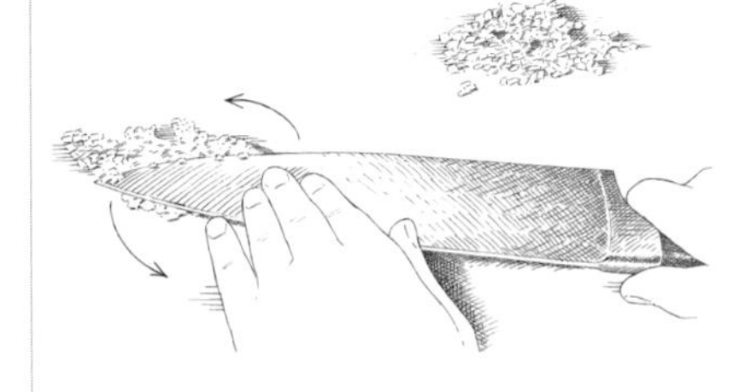

SALTING MEAT

Salting helps proteins retain their own natural juices; it's the best choice for meats that are already juicy and/or well-marbled. When salt is applied to raw meat, juices inside are drawn to the surface. The salt then dissolves in the exuded liquid, forming a brine that is eventually reabsorbed by the meat. We prefer kosher salt for salting meat. Salting is more convenient than brining (no need to fit a big container of salt water in the fridge) and it won't thwart the goal of crispy skin on poultry or well-browned crust on steak, chops, or roasts since no moisture is added to their exteriors, but it takes longer than brining.

CUT	TIME	KOSHER SALT*	METHOD
Steaks, Lamb Chops, Pork Chops	1 hour	¾ teaspoon per 8-ounce chop or steak	Apply salt evenly over surface and let rest at room temperature, uncovered, on wire rack set in rimmed baking sheet.
Beef, Lamb, and Pork Roasts	At least 6 hours and up to 24	1 teaspoon per pound	Apply salt evenly over surface, wrap tightly with plastic wrap, and let rest in refrigerator.
Whole Chicken	At least 6 hours and up to 24	1 teaspoon per pound	Apply salt evenly inside cavity and under skin of breasts and legs and let rest in refrigerator on wire rack set in rimmed baking sheet. (Wrap with plastic wrap if salting for longer than 12 hours.)
Bone-In Chicken Pieces; Boneless or Bone-In Turkey Breast	At least 6 hours and up to 24	¾ teaspoon per pound	If poultry is skin-on, apply salt evenly between skin and meat, leaving skin attached, and let rest in refrigerator on wire rack set in rimmed baking sheet. (Wrap with plastic wrap if salting for longer than 12 hours.)
Whole Turkey	24 to 48 hours	1 teaspoon per pound	Apply salt evenly inside cavity and under skin of breasts and legs, wrap tightly with plastic wrap, and let rest in refrigerator.

* Measurements based on Diamond Crystal

BRINING MEAT

Brining, which works faster than salting, adds moisture, making it the best choice for lean proteins. Salt in the brine not only seasons the meat, but also promotes a change in its protein structure, reducing its overall toughness and creating gaps that fill with water and keep the meat juicy and flavorful. We prefer table salt for brining. Brining can make lean cuts such as chicken breast or pork tenderloin juicier than salting since it adds, versus merely retains, moisture; however, brining can inhibit browning on the skin or exterior, and it requires fitting a big container in the fridge.

CHICKEN	TIME	COLD WATER	TABLE SALT
1 whole chicken (3½ to 4 pounds)	½ to 1 hour	2 quarts	½ cup
2 whole chickens (3½ to 4 pounds each)	½ to 1 hour	3 quarts	¾ cup
4 pounds bone-in chicken pieces	½ to 1 hour	2 quarts	½ cup
4 boneless, skinless chicken breasts	½ to 1 hour	2 quarts	¼ cup
TURKEY			
1 turkey (12 to 17 pounds)	6 to 12 hours	2 gallons	1 cup
1 turkey (18 to 24 pounds)	6 to 12 hours	3 gallons	1½ cups
1 bone-in turkey breast (6 to 8 pounds)	3 to 6 hours	1 gallon	½ cup
PORK			
4 bone-in rib loin chops (12 ounces each), 1½ inches thick	1 hour	1½ quarts	3 tablespoons
1 pork roast (3 to 6 pounds)	1½ to 2 hours	2 quarts	¼ cup

SEASONING STRATEGIES

SAFE SEASONING

To avoid contaminating our salt box when seasoning raw meat, poultry, or fish, we mix pepper and salt in a small bowl. This lets us reach into the same bowl—no hand-washing needed.

AVOIDING OVERSALTING

Because slight variations in ingredients and cooking times affect the saltiness of a dish, it's best to hold back on fully seasoning until the very end of cooking.

SALTY SOAK FOR BEANS

We have found that soaking dried beans in salted water ensures beans that cook up with softer skins. As the beans soak, the sodium ions replace some of the calcium and magnesium ions in the skins, allowing more water to penetrate into the skins, leading to a softer texture. The sodium ions only filter in partway, so their greatest effect is on the outermost part of the beans.

BRINING FORMULA: For 1 pound of dried beans, dissolve 3 tablespoons of table salt in 4 quarts of cold water. Soak at room temperature for 8 to 24 hours. Drain and rinse well before using.

PERFECT COOKIES 101

Cookies couldn't be simpler to make. So why do they so often turn out irregularly shaped, unevenly baked, and lacking the desired texture? Here's everything you need to know to bake the perfect batch.

MAKING THE DOUGH

MEASURE ACCURATELY

In tests, we've found that the most common way of measuring dry ingredients—spooning them into the measuring cup—is also the least accurate. Since even the slightest variation in an amount can have a direct effect on your cookie (too much flour, for example, and the cookie will be dry; too little and the cookie will bake up flat), it's important to measure precisely.

PREFERRED METHOD
For the greatest accuracy, weigh sugar and flour.

SECOND BEST
Dip a measuring cup into flour or sugar and scoop away excess with a straight edge.

USE BUTTER AT OPTIMAL TEMPERATURE

Whether softened or melted, proper butter temperature is as critical in a simple sugar cookie as it is in the fanciest cake.

SOFTENED BUTTER

Properly softened butter (65 to 67 degrees, or roughly room temperature) allows air to be pumped into the butter for tender texture in the final cookie. Two good cues: The butter should give slightly when pressed but still hold its shape, and it should bend without cracking or breaking. Avoid microwaving to soften butter—it's easy to soften it too much. Instead, cut the butter into small pieces. By the time you've preheated the oven and measured the remaining ingredients, the pieces should be near 65 degrees.

MELTED BUTTER

When a recipe calls for melted butter, make sure it's lukewarm (85 to 90 degrees) before adding it to the dough. Butter that's too warm can cook the dough (or the eggs in it) and cause clumps.

PORTIONING THE DOUGH

DROP AND ROLL

With drop cookies, we usually go beyond merely depositing tablespoons of dough on the cookie sheet. Instead, we prefer to roll the dough between our hands to create uniformly shaped balls that bake evenly.

A BETTER WAY TO ROLL

With roll-and-cut cookies, there's always a danger of working too much flour into the dough during rolling and producing dry cookies. We like to roll out the dough between two large sheets of parchment paper instead of on a floured counter. Chill the rolled-out dough in the fridge for 10 minutes to make cutting easier.

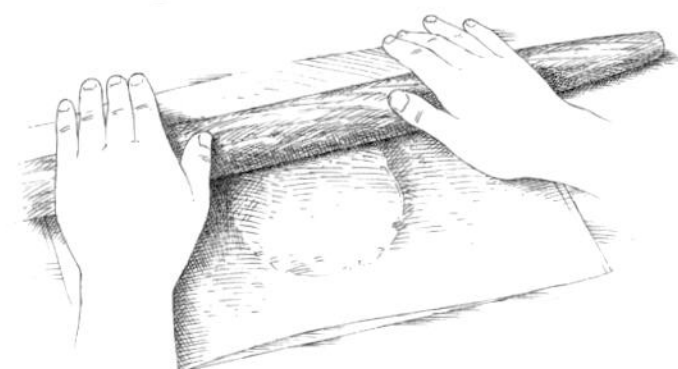

BAKING

ALWAYS PREHEAT

To keep cookies from spreading too much, it is important to expose them to an immediate blast of heat; it can take 15 minutes for an oven to reach the desired temperature.

USE AN OVEN THERMOMETER

Oven temperatures can be off by as much as 50 degrees. Always use an oven thermometer to tell you what's really going on inside.

PREPARING THE PAN

USE A PARCHMENT LINER

Don't grease your sheets—the extra fat can cause cookies to bake unevenly. Instead, line the baking sheet with parchment. Its slick surface allows cookies to easily release. (Waxed paper isn't a good substitute—high temperature can make the wax coating melt.) To keep parchment flat on the pan, put a small dab of dough on each corner of the baking sheet.

MAKE A SLING

It's nearly impossible to remove some bar cookies from the pan without tearing or crumbling. Here's our easy solution:

1. Place two sheets of parchment paper or aluminum foil perpendicularly in the baking pan, pushing into the corners and up the sides. Spray with vegetable oil spray.

2. After the bar cookies have baked and cooled, use the overhang to lift the whole thing from the pan. Cut into portions.

TROUBLESHOOTING

THE LAST COOKIES ALWAYS SEEM SHORT ON CHIPS

SOLUTION: Reserve some morsels to add later

When chocolate chips, nuts, or raisins are in the mix, the last few cookies from a batch never seem to have as many of these goodies as the first few. To get around this, reserve some of the mix-ins and stir them into the dough after about half of it has been scooped out.

COOKIES DON'T ADD UP TO THE CORRECT YIELD

SOLUTION: Use a portion scoop

When cookies are portioned out larger or smaller than the recipe directs, they may not produce the intended texture. To ensure consistent size and the proper yield, we use a portion scoop. (We keep many different sizes on hand for just this purpose. A typical cookie requires a #30 scoop.)

CHEWY COOKIES THAT AREN'T CHEWY

SOLUTION: Underbake

To ensure a chewy texture, take cookies out of the oven when they are still slightly underdone, which often means they will droop over the end of a spatula. Crevices should appear moist and edges on smooth cookies should be lightly browned.

COOKIES RUN TOGETHER

SOLUTION: Bake in staggered rows

When scoops of dough are placed too close together on the sheet, the cookies can fuse together. To ensure enough space between cookies, alternate the rows. For example, place three cookies in the first row, two in the second, three in the third, and so on.

UNEVENLY BAKED BATCHES

SOLUTION: Rotate during baking

The temperature in most ovens varies from front to back, top to bottom—even side to side. To prevent uneven baking, rotate the cookie sheet partway through baking so that the back side faces front.

COOKIES KEEP BURNING ON BOTTOM

SOLUTION: Use a light-colored baking sheet and line with parchment paper

We typically don't like light-colored bakeware since it doesn't absorb heat as well as darker finishes, leading to spotty browning. But the cookie sheet is the exception. All of the dark nonstick cookie sheets we've tested consistently overbrown the bottoms of cookies. Light-colored sheets, on the other hand, prevent overbrowning but are prone to sticking. We get around this by baking cookies on parchment paper.

IT'S HARD TO TELL WHEN DARK CHOCOLATE COOKIES ARE DONE

SOLUTION: Press the middle

Most cookies, irrespective of texture, are done when pressing them lightly with your finger leaves just a slight indentation.

COOKIES LEFT IN OVEN TOO LONG

SOLUTION: Cool immediately on rack

If you become distracted and leave your cookies in the oven a minute or two too long, all is not lost. Remove the baking sheet from the oven and, instead of allowing the cookies to set on the sheet, immediately transfer them to a wire rack, where they will cool more quickly.

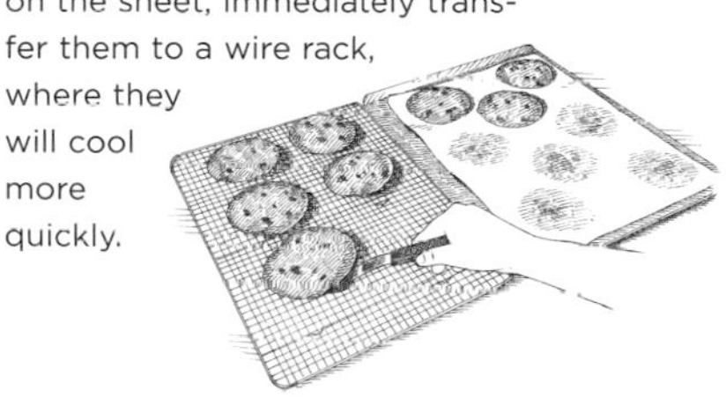

OVERLY CRISP EDGES

SOLUTION: Briefly chill dough and don't use a hot sheet

If your kitchen is particularly hot, the butter in the dough can start to melt, softening the dough and leading to overcooked edges. If the dough seems too soft, chill it for 10 to 15 minutes before portioning.

Putting raw dough on cookie sheets still warm from the oven can cause them to begin spreading, leading to burnt edges. Always allow baking sheets to cool completely before adding more batches. To expedite cooling, rinse warm—but not hot—sheet under cold tap water.

BUTTER 101

We don't just slather it on toast or whip it into cakes. In the test kitchen, butter is what makes for juicier chicken breasts, more tender omelets, and creamier mashed potatoes.

BUYING AND STORING BASICS

SALTED OR UNSALTED?

In the test kitchen, we use unsalted butter almost exclusively and add our own salt to recipes. Why? First, the amount of salt in salted butter varies from brand to brand—on average ⅓ teaspoon a stick—which makes offering a universal conversion impossible. Second, salted butter almost always contains more water, which can interfere with gluten development—particularly important in baking. (Biscuits made with salted butter were noticeably mushy.) Third, salt masks butter's naturally sweet, delicate flavors; in butter-specific recipes like beurre blanc and buttercream frosting, we found that extra salt to be overwhelming.

FAVORITE EVERYDAY BUTTER
Land O'Lakes Unsalted Butter

PLAIN OR PREMIUM?

While you hear a lot about the higher fat content in premium butters, they actually contain only about a gram more per tablespoon than regular butter, and even our tasters had trouble telling the difference. The real distinction is culturing—the process of fermenting the cream before churning it that builds tangy, complex flavors. That said, these nuances are subtle in most cooked applications, so we save the expensive cultured stuff for spreading on toast.

FAVORITE PREMIUM BUTTER
Lurpak Unsalted Butter

STORING

Placed in the back of the fridge where it's coldest (not in the small door compartment), butter will keep for 2½ weeks. In tests we've found that any longer and it can turn rancid as its fatty acids oxidize. For longer storage (up to four months), move it to the freezer. Also, since butter quickly picks up odors and flavors, we like to slip the sticks into a zipper-lock bag.

CLARIFYING CLARIFIED BUTTER AND GHEE

CLARIFIED BUTTER

Butter is mostly made up of fat, but it also contains small amounts of proteins, carbohydrates, minerals (the milk solids), and water, all of which are distributed throughout the fat in an emulsion. When butter is heated, this emulsion is broken, causing the different components to separate. The pure fat left standing is called clarified butter.

Since clarified butter has a higher smoke point than whole butter (clarified ranges from 350–375 degrees, whole butter from 250–300 degrees), food can be seared in it without the danger of milk solids burning.

GHEE

Ghee, a butter product used throughout Indian cooking, takes clarification a step further by simmering the butter until all the moisture is evaporated and the milk solids begin to brown, giving the fat a slightly nutty flavor and aroma. You can find ghee in unrefrigerated jars (100 percent fat is shelf stable) at Indian and Middle Eastern markets, as well as in natural foods stores. The two products can be used interchangeably, but ghee will lend foods cooked in it a slightly richer, more buttery flavor.

GAUGING BUTTER TEMPERATURE

Butter temperature can dramatically affect the texture of baked goods. For the most accurate results, we check the temperature with an instant-read thermometer. The following tactile clues will also provide a good gauge.

CHILLED
(about 35 degrees)

METHOD: Cut butter into small pieces; freeze until very firm, 10 to 15 minutes.

HOW TO TEST IT: Press with a finger—it should be cold and unyielding.

WHY IT MATTERS: Cold butter melts during baking, leaving behind small pockets of air that create flaky layers in recipes like pie dough and croissants.

SOFTENED
(65 to 67 degrees)

METHOD: Let refrigerated butter sit at room temperature for about 30 minutes.

HOW TO TEST IT: The stick will easily bend without breaking and give slightly when pressed.

WHY IT MATTERS: Softened butter is flexible enough to be whipped but firm enough to retain the incorporated air—vital to making cakes with a tender crumb.

MELTED AND COOLED
(85 to 90 degrees)

METHOD: Melt butter in a small saucepan or microwave-safe bowl; cool about 5 minutes.

HOW TO TEST IT: The butter should be fluid and slightly warm.

WHY IT MATTERS: Butter is roughly 16 percent water; when it's melted, the water breaks from the emulsion and helps create gluten for chewier cookies.

COOKING TIPS AND TECHNIQUES

WAIT FOR BUTTER TO STOP FOAMING BEFORE SAUTÉING

Sautéing is best done in hot fat. When foaming subsides, it's an easy visual cue that the melted butter is hot enough for cooking. More specifically, it indicates that all the water in the butter (about 16 percent by weight) has evaporated, and the temperature can rise above water's boiling point of 212 degrees. As foaming subsides, butter continues heating and finally smokes at 250 to 300 degrees. (To sauté in butter at higher temperatures, use clarified butter.)

SLIP BUTTER UNDER THE SKIN OF CHICKEN BREASTS

Notoriously dry and chalky, roast chicken breasts can be transformed with softened butter. Two tablespoons of unsalted butter mixed with ½ teaspoon salt and spread underneath the skin of a whole breast before roasting will baste the white meat, keeping it juicy while adding flavor.

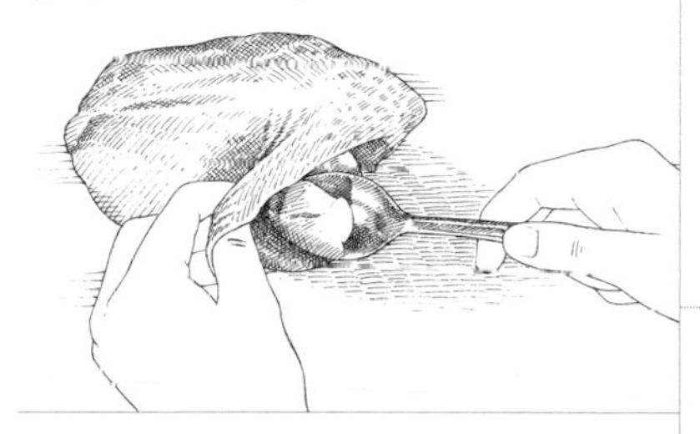

ADD BUTTER BITS TO UNCOOKED EGGS FOR OMELETS

Whisking a tablespoon of cold, diced butter into the eggs before cooking is the secret to a soft, creamy omelet. Without butter, the proteins in egg whites form tight, cross-linked bonds, yielding a dense, rubbery version of the French classic. But with our method, the eggs cook as the butter melts and disperses, coating the proteins and stopping them from linking.

ADD COLD BUTTER TO PAN SAUCES

Swirling a tablespoon or two of cold butter into a pan sauce right before serving adds both richness and body. (Cold, firm butter resists separation, while the water in softened butter separates more easily and can lead to a broken emulsion.) Cut the butter into tablespoon-size chunks so that it melts quickly.

USE COLD—NOT SOFTENED—BUTTER FOR PASTRY

Good, light pastry and biscuits depend on distinct pieces of cold, solid butter distributed throughout the dough that melt during baking and leave behind pockets of air. To keep the butter cold during mixing, we use a food processor, but you can also grate frozen butter into the dry ingredients using the large holes of a box grater.

ADD BUTTER BEFORE DAIRY IN MASHED POTATOES

If the dairy is stirred into the hot cooked potatoes before the butter, the water in the dairy will combine with the potatoes' starch, making them gummy. When melted butter is added first, the fat coats the starch molecules and prevents them from reacting with the water in the dairy. The result? Smoother, more velvety mashed potatoes.

SIMPLE BUTTER RECIPES

GARLIC COMPOUND BUTTER
MAKES 4 TABLESPOONS

Using fork, beat 4 tablespoons softened unsalted butter, ½ teaspoon finely grated lemon zest, 1 tablespoon minced fresh parsley, 1 minced garlic clove, ⅛ teaspoon salt, and pepper to taste in small bowl until combined. Serve as a topping on steak, pork chops, or fish.

FOOLPROOF HOLLANDAISE SAUCE
MAKES ABOUT 2 CUPS

Whisk 12 tablespoons softened unsalted butter and 6 large egg yolks in large bowl set over medium saucepan filled with ½ inch of barely simmering water (don't let bowl touch water) until mixture is smooth and homogeneous. Slowly add ½ cup boiling water and cook, whisking constantly, until thickened and sauce registers 160 degrees, 7 to 10 minutes. Off heat, stir in 2 teaspoons lemon juice and ⅛ teaspoon cayenne. Season with salt to taste. Serve immediately over prepared asparagus or eggs Benedict.

BROWN BUTTER SAUCE
MAKES ABOUT ¼ CUP

Melt 4 tablespoons unsalted butter, cut into 4 pieces, in small traditional skillet over medium-low heat. Cook, swirling constantly, until butter is dark golden brown and has nutty aroma, 1 to 3 minutes. Remove pan from heat and let stand 1½ minutes. Add 1 tablespoon lemon juice, 1 tablespoon minced parsley, and salt and pepper to taste; swirl pan to combine. Let milk solids settle to bottom of pan, about 10 seconds. Drizzle liquid over gnocchi, mushrooms, steak, or fish, leaving as many solids behind as possible.

WHITE BUTTER SAUCE
MAKES ABOUT ⅔ CUP

Bring 3 tablespoons dry white wine, 2 tablespoons white wine vinegar, 1 tablespoon minced shallots, and pinch salt to boil in small saucepan over medium-high heat. Reduce heat to medium-low; simmer until reduced by two-thirds, about 5 minutes. Whisk in 1 tablespoon heavy cream. Increase heat to high; add 8 tablespoons cold unsalted butter, cut into 4 pieces. Whisk vigorously until incorporated and sauce is thick and pale yellow, 30 to 60 seconds. Remove from heat; serve immediately with fish or vegetables.

COOKING GREENS 101

We've blanched, steamed, stir-fried, and sautéed enough greens over the years to know that some taste best cooked quickly over a high flame, while others benefit from slow, gentle heat. To pair the right leaf with the right cooking method, follow our thoroughly tested guidelines.

STORING

If you're buying greens in advance, we recommend storing them in an open plastic produce bag or zipper-lock bag. In tests, we've found that trapped gases and too much constriction encourage rotting.

CLEANING

To ensure that every bit of dirt and grime gets washed off our greens, we trade the smaller confines of a salad spinner for a clean sink full of water, where there is ample room to swish the leaves. Unless you're stir-frying the greens, don't bother patting or spinning them dry; a little water clinging to their leaves helps them cook.

Gently swish greens under water to loosen grit. Give dirt several minutes to settle to bottom before gently lifting greens into colander to drain. Repeat if necessary to remove all dirt.

MEASURING

Recipes often call for cups of "loosely packed" greens. Here's how to make sure you don't overdo it: Drop greens by the handful into a measuring cup and then gently pat down, using your fingertips rather than the palm of your hand.

PREPPING

MATURE SPINACH

Curly spinach has thick stems that should be removed before cooking. Grasp each leaf at base of stem and pull stem from leaf.

GREEN, RED, AND SAVOY CABBAGE

1. Cut cabbage into quarters and cut away hard piece of core from each quarter.

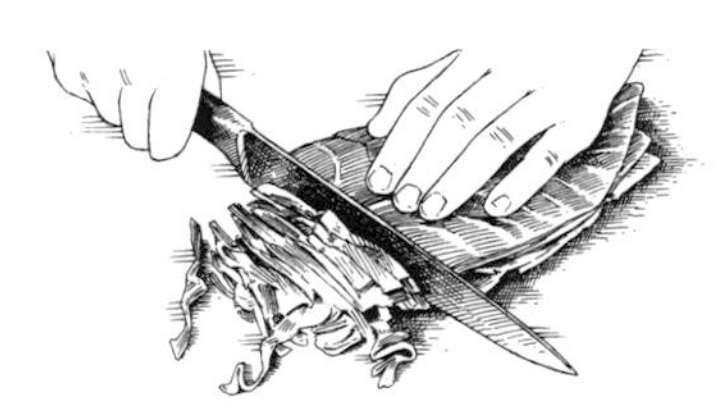

2. Separate quarters into manageable stacks; press each stack to flatten. Cut stacks crosswise into thin strips.

KALE AND COLLARD GREENS

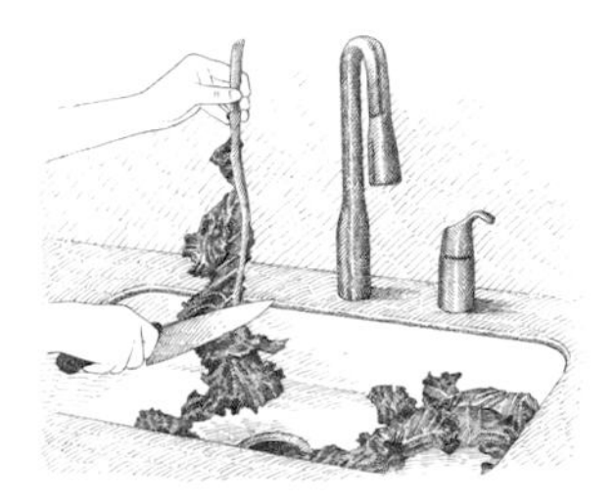

1. Hold each leaf at base of stem and use knife to slash leafy portion from either side of tough stem.

2. Then, stack several washed leaves, roll into cigar shape, and coarsely chop.

SWISS CHARD AND BEET, MUSTARD, AND TURNIP GREENS

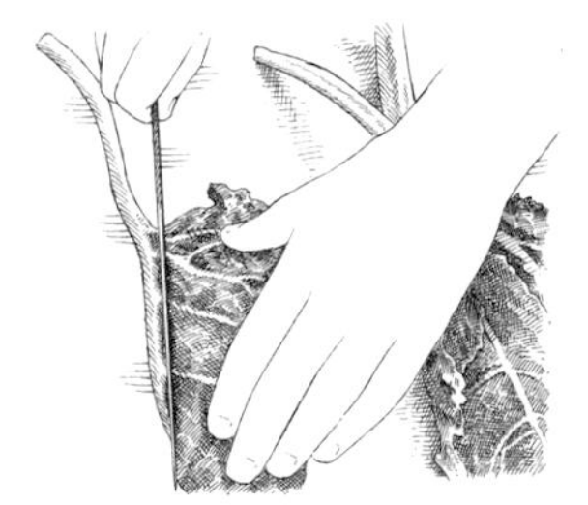

Fold leaves in half. Cut along edge of rib to remove thickest part of rib and stem.

BOK CHOY AND NAPA CABBAGE

1. Trim bottom inch from head. Wash and dry leaves and stalks. Cut away leafy green portion from stalk.

2. Cut each stalk in half lengthwise, then crosswise into strips.

3. Layer leaves in manageable stacks; cut stacks crosswise into thin strips.

FIVE WAYS TO COOK GREENS

STIR-FRY

BEST FOR: Bok Choy and Napa and Savoy Cabbage

WHY USE IT: Stir-frying over high heat lightly browns the greens, enhancing flavor while preserving some crunch.

BASIC METHOD: Heat oil in nonstick skillet (preferred to wok when cooking on flat-top burner) over high heat. If using bok choy or napa cabbage, add sliced stalks and cook briefly. Add aromatics and cook briefly, then add 1½ pounds thinly sliced leaves and cook until tender, about 1 minute.

GIVE STALKS A HEAD START

Unlike many other greens, bok choy and napa cabbage contain both edible stalks and edible leaves. We add the stiffer stalks to the pan first, cooking them until crisp-tender and just starting to brown before adding the more delicate leaves.

SAUTÉ

BEST FOR: Mature Spinach, Swiss Chard, and Beet Greens

WHY USE IT: The relatively high heat cooks down medium-tender, high-moisture greens before they have a chance to get soggy.

BASIC METHOD: Heat garlic in oil in Dutch oven over medium-high heat. Add 2 pounds damp greens and cook, tossing with tongs, until wilted, about 2 minutes for spinach and 5 minutes for Swiss chard and beet greens.

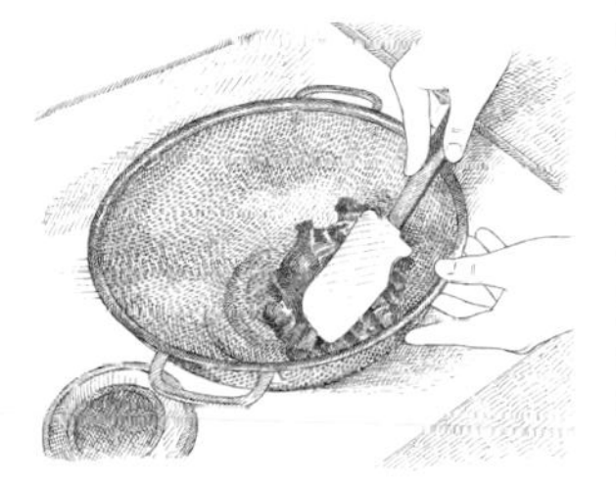

QUICK SQUEEZE

While sautéing evaporates most of the greens' moisture, we like to transfer hot greens to a colander in the sink and gently press them against the side to remove any excess water before serving.

SLOW-BRAISE

BEST FOR: Kale, Collards, and Mustard and Turnip Greens

WHY USE IT: This one-pot method slow-cooks assertive greens in a small amount of liquid. The long cooking mellows the bitterness of the greens more than pan-steaming and yields a more tender texture. To ensure that the greens don't taste watery, we increase the heat at the end of cooking to evaporate excess liquid.

BASIC METHOD: Cook onions in oil in Dutch oven until softened. Add 2 pounds damp chopped greens and cook until beginning to wilt. Add 2 cups braising liquid, cover, and cook over medium-low heat until tender, 25 to 35 minutes for kale and turnip and mustard greens and 35 to 45 minutes for collards. Uncover, increase heat to medium-high, and cook until pot is almost dry.

WHICH METHOD WORKS FOR WHICH GREEN?

GREEN	TEXTURE	COOKING METHOD
Beet Greens	Medium-Tender	S
Bok Choy	Crisp, High Moisture	SF
Collards	Sturdy	SB, PS
Green Cabbage	Crisp, High Moisture	QB
Kale	Sturdy	SB, PS
Mustard Greens	Sturdy	SB, PS
Napa Cabbage	Crisp, High Moisture	SF
Red Cabbage	Crisp, High Moisture	QB
Savoy Cabbage	Crisp, High Moisture	QB, SF
Spinach (mature)	Medium-Tender	S
Swiss Chard	Medium-Tender	S
Turnip Greens	Sturdy	SB, PS

Key: PS=Pan-Steam; QB=Quick-Braise; S=Sauté; SB=Slow-Braise; SF=Stir-Fry

QUICK-BRAISE

BEST FOR: Green, Red, and Savoy Cabbage

WHY USE IT: Cooking cabbage in a small amount of flavorful liquid preserves its bite. This method also creates a flavor exchange with the cooking liquid and builds complexity. Adding butter to the liquid deepens cabbage flavor and improves texture.

BASIC METHOD: Melt 2 tablespoons butter in Dutch oven; add 1 pound thinly sliced cabbage and ½ cup braising liquid. Simmer, covered, until cabbage is wilted, about 9 minutes.

NINE IS A MAGIC NUMBER

Cabbage notoriously gives off an unpleasant odor when it cooks due to the breakdown of the leaves' cell walls, which releases sulfur-bearing flavor compounds. The key to minimizing that smell is all in the timing: We've found that about nine minutes of braising is just long enough to tenderize the sturdy leaves but brief enough to avoid producing an overabundance of sulfurous odor.

PAN-STEAM

BEST FOR: Kale, Collards, and Mustard and Turnip Greens

WHY USE IT: Pan-steaming quickly wilts assertive greens while preserving some of their pungent flavor and hearty texture.

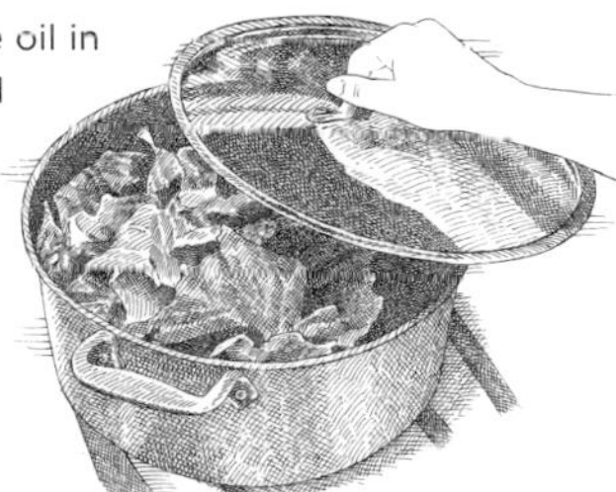

BASIC METHOD: Heat garlic in olive oil in Dutch oven over medium heat. Add 2 pounds damp chopped greens (lots of water should still cling to leaves), cover pan, and cook until wilted, about 7 to 9 minutes for kale and turnip and mustard greens and 9 to 12 minutes for collards.

CANNED DICED TOMATOES

A great can of diced tomatoes offers flavor almost as intense as ripe, in-season fruit—that's why it's one of the most important staples in the test kitchen pantry. But supermarket shelves are teeming with different brands of diced tomatoes, so what should you buy? To make sense of the selection, we gathered 16 widely available styles and brands and tasted them plain and in tomato sauce, rating them on tomato flavor, saltiness, sweetness, texture, and overall appeal. Two samples came in on top in both tastings. What set these apart? A number of factors influenced our findings. Geography may play a factor in good flavor; our top-ranked tomatoes were grown in California, where the dry, hot growing season develops sweet, complex flavor (the losers were from the Midwest and Pennsylvania). More important is that the ripe tomatoes are processed quickly to preserve fresh flavor. Additives also affected the balance of flavors and texture—some tomatoes were too sweet or too acidic from the amount of citric acid, others were bland from lack of salt or too chewy from the firming agent, calcium chloride. Tomatoes are listed in order of preference; sodium and sugar are per ½-cup serving.

RECOMMENDED

HUNT'S Diced Tomatoes
PRICE: $1.99 for 28 oz.
INGREDIENTS: Tomatoes, tomato juice, less than 2% of: salt, citric acid, calcium chloride
SODIUM: 310mg **SUGAR:** 3g **PH:** 4.01
PEELING PROCESS: Steam
COMMENTS: Tasters deemed these tomatoes "fresh" and "bright," with a "sweet-tart" flavor and "juicy," "firm, crisp-tender chunks." When commenting on the sauce, they liked the "concentrated," "bright," and "acidic" tomato flavor, "tender, small-to-medium-sized chunks," and "beautiful texture."

MUIR GLEN Organic Diced Tomatoes
PRICE: $2.69 for 28 oz.
INGREDIENTS: Organic tomatoes and tomato juice, sea salt, naturally derived citric acid and calcium chloride
SODIUM: 290mg **SUGAR:** 4g **PH:** 4.23
PEELING PROCESS: Steam
COMMENTS: These tomatoes tasted "sweet," "but in a natural way, unlike others," said tasters, with "fruity," "fresh" flavor. Tasters noted a choppy, irregular dice, though pieces were "juicy." In sauce, the tomatoes were "sweet" with a "robust," "pleasing" flavor.

RECOMMENDED WITH RESERVATIONS

DEL MONTE Diced Tomatoes
PRICE: $1.33 for 14.5 oz.
INGREDIENTS: Tomatoes, tomato juice, salt, calcium chloride, citric acid
SODIUM: 200mg **SUGAR:** 4g **PH:** 3.87
PEELING PROCESS: Proprietary
COMMENTS: Tasters said these tomatoes were "firm and meaty with lots of fresh flavor." For some, though, the dice was too big: "the size of Texas." Others found them a bit "chewy." In sauce, the tomatoes were "bright" with "rich tomato flavor," though some tasters judged them "too acidic."

RECOMMENDED WITH RESERVATIONS *(continued)*

CONTADINA Petite Cut Diced Tomatoes
PRICE: $1.79 for 14.5 oz.
INGREDIENTS: Tomatoes, tomato juice, tomato puree, salt, calcium chloride, citric acid
SODIUM: 250mg **SUGAR:** 4g **PH:** 4.06
PEELING PROCESS: Proprietary
COMMENTS: Many tasters liked the "sweet, clean flavor" and "nice, soft texture" of these tomatoes. But a few complained of "uber-sweetness" and felt the dice was "too small" and "stringy." The tomatoes fared better in a sauce, receiving comments such as "good chew" and "nice all around."

CENTO Petite Diced Tomatoes
PRICE: $2.59 for 28 oz.
INGREDIENTS: Fresh red ripe tomatoes, tomato juice, salt, calcium chloride, naturally derived citric acid
SODIUM: 220mg **SUGAR:** 3g **PH:** 4.18
PEELING PROCESS: Lye
COMMENTS: When tasted plain, these tomatoes were called "mealy," "like stewed tomatoes," with "the texture of canned peaches" and a slightly "stale," "chunky-ketchup" flavor. But in sauce, they won praise for their "bright flavor," though tasters thought they broke down too much.

NOT RECOMMENDED

CONTADINA Diced Tomatoes
PRICE: $1.99 for 14.5 oz.
INGREDIENTS: Tomatoes, tomato juice (tomato puree, water), salt, citric acid, calcium chloride
SODIUM: 200mg **SUGAR:** 4g **PH:** 4.16
PEELING PROCESS: Proprietary
COMMENTS: These tomatoes received a few positive comments and many negative, such as "too bland" and "very watery and artificial taste." A too-firm texture and too-acidic flavor led one taster to write: "Styrofoam city with citric acid." When describing the sauce, tasters noted "so-so" flavor and "very inconsistent"texture.

TOMATO PASTE

Tomato paste is the backbone of many of our recipes, providing deep, rich tomato flavor. Even in some non-tomato-based recipes, like beef stew, tomato paste acts as our secret ingredient because it's naturally full of glutamates, which bring out subtle flavors and savory notes. Could a better-tasting brand have an even bigger impact? We sampled 10 top-selling brands plain, cooked on their own, and cooked in marinara sauce. When we sampled our lineup uncooked, tasters were split between brands that tasted bright and acidic, like fresh tomatoes, and those with deep "cooked" tomato flavor. Many downgraded brands for dried herb notes. In the end, while better tomato pastes improved the taste of the marinara, no one brand ruined the dish. Tomato pastes are listed in order of preference.

RECOMMENDED

GOYA Tomato Paste
PRICE: $0.70 for 6 oz.
INGREDIENTS: Tomatoes
SODIUM: 25mg per 2-tablespoon serving
SUGARS: 5g
COMMENTS: "Rich, bold, and complex," Goya offered "peppery kick" and "bright, robust tomato flavor." Tasters liked its sweetness, yet found it well balanced.

PASTENE Fancy Tomato Paste
PRICE: $0.59 for 6 oz.
INGREDIENTS: Tomato pulp
SODIUM: 20mg **SUGARS:** 3g
COMMENTS: Uncooked, this paste had "light and clean," "herbaceous, grassy" tomato flavor. That quality carried over to cooked paste, which tasters described as "acidic, almost lemony." Some tasters objected that the paste was "not sweet enough," but in marinara found it "bright and balanced."

CONTADINA Tomato Paste
PRICE: $0.79 for 6 oz.
INGREDIENTS: Tomatoes
SODIUM: 20mg **SUGARS:** 3g
COMMENTS: "Pleasant and floral," especially in the marinara sauce, Contadina tomato paste was "fresh, balanced, what I'm looking for," one taster said, with a "strong tomatoey flavor." However, others found it "sweet upfront, with an acidic finish," and many deemed it "too acidic."

RECOMMENDED WITH RESERVATIONS

RIENZI Tomato Paste
PRICE: $1.00 for 6 oz.
INGREDIENTS: Tomato paste
SODIUM: 60mg **SUGARS:** 4g
COMMENTS: "Tinny and raw-tasting" straight out of the can, Rienzi mellowed when cooked to provide "sweet," "tangy," "good tomato flavor." In marinara, it had "decent body and depth."

HUNT'S Tomato Paste
PRICE: $0.75 for 6 oz.
INGREDIENTS: Tomato paste, salt, spices, natural flavors, citric acid
SODIUM: 105mg **SUGARS:** 4g
COMMENTS: While tasters enjoyed Hunt's "concentrated, deep-tomato punch," many objected that its "strong oregano" and "Italian spices" drowned out the tomato taste. In marinara, it was a hit: "Tastes like it was cooked longer."

RECOMMENDED WITH RESERVATIONS *(continued)*

REDPACK Tomato Paste
PRICE: $0.63 for 6 ounces
INGREDIENTS: Tomatoes, citric acid
SODIUM: 20mg **SUGARS:** 3g
COMMENTS: "Raisiny" and "fruity" straight from the can, cooked Redpack struck tasters as weakly flavored. As one put it, "Nothing offensive here, though not very tomatoey." In marinara, it was "mild, smooth" but "could be a tad sweeter."

HUNT'S Tomato Paste No Salt Added
PRICE: $0.75 for 6 oz.
INGREDIENTS: Tomato paste, spices, natural flavors, citric acid
SODIUM: 15mg **SUGARS:** 4g
COMMENTS: Uncooked, this paste "tastes like ketchup," and has a "bitter aftertaste." After cooking, we deemed it "nothing special." In marinara, it had "bold" flavor but a "tinny" aftertaste.

CENTO Tomato Paste
PRICE: $0.50 for 6 oz.
INGREDIENTS: Tomatoes
SODIUM: 25mg **SUGARS:** 5g
COMMENTS: "This tastes exactly like what I expect tomato paste to taste like," one taster noted, "concentrated tomatoes." Cooked, however, it became "a bit flat," and in marinara the paste was "too sweet," leaving the marinara "lackluster" with "no tomato oomph."

MUIR GLEN Organic Premium Tomato Paste
PRICE: $1.59 for 6 oz.
INGREDIENTS: Organic tomato paste and naturally derived citric acid
SODIUM: 35mg **SUGARS:** 3g
COMMENTS: Tasters found this to be "basic paste, but a little salty" and "uninspiring" uncooked. After cooking it was "not sweet at all," and while "the smell was great, the taste was not so much." In marinara, it was "a little tinny."

AMORE Double Concentrated Tomato Paste
PRICE: $3.49 for 4.5 oz.
INGREDIENTS: Tomato paste, salt
SODIUM: 173mg **SUGARS:** 5.3g
COMMENTS: Uncooked, Amore tasted "harsh, sweet, and overly stewed," "coppery and extremely acidic." Cooking developed its "intensely tomatoey and complex" profile. Despite the "double concentrated" billing, Amore recommends that you use the same amount as you would of other tomato pastes.

YELLOW MUSTARD

Yellow mustard is a versatile condiment; it's as much at home on a hot dog as it is in potato salad, barbecue sauce, salad dressing, or marinades for chicken or pork. To determine which yellow mustard is best, we tasted seven nationally available brands plain and with steamed hot dogs. Yellow mustard is made from white (also called yellow) mustard seed, which is flavorful but doesn't cause the nasal burn of brown or black mustard seed. Our tasters wanted to actually taste the mustard seed; the two brands they judged to have the most mustard flavor both list mustard seed high up in their ingredients. The amount of salt was also key, with mustards with the least sodium scoring higher. Why? Vinegar adds so much pungency, these yellow mustards didn't need extra seasoning; indeed, too much salt threw the flavors out of balance. Mustards are listed in order of preference; sodium is per 1-teaspoon serving.

RECOMMENDED

ANNIE'S NATURALS Organic Yellow Mustard
PRICE: $3.79 for 9 oz. **SODIUM:** 55mg
INGREDIENTS: Distilled white vinegar from corn, mustard seed, turmeric, paprika, cloves, sea salt
COMMENTS: Tasters praised the "good balance of heat and tang" of Annie's, but what truly set it apart was the "richer mustard flavor." Two factors that helped push it to the top of the chart: Mustard seed is listed second among its ingredients, and the sodium is relatively low. As one taster summed up, "Legit."

GULDEN'S Yellow Mustard
PRICE: $1.89 for 12 oz. **SODIUM:** 55mg
INGREDIENTS: Vinegar, mustard seed, salt, spices, turmeric, paprika, garlic powder
COMMENTS: Tasters deemed this "very well balanced" mustard pleasantly "zesty" and "spicier than typical yellow mustard." Its low sodium fit the profile of all our preferred mustards. Tasters also liked Gulden's "slightly grainy" texture and "nice thick consistency."

FRENCH'S Classic Yellow Mustard
PRICE: $2.49 for 14 oz. **SODIUM:** 55mg
INGREDIENTS: Distilled vinegar, water, #1 grade mustard seed, salt, turmeric, paprika, spice, natural flavors, garlic powder
COMMENTS: More than one taster likened the "very bright," "sharp" flavor and "silky," "thin" consistency of this ubiquitous brand to "ballpark mustard." It is very acidic; a few tasters favorably compared its briny flavor to pickles.

WESTBRAE Natural Yellow Mustard
PRICE: $2.39 for 8 oz. **SODIUM:** 75mg
INGREDIENTS: Water, grain vinegar, organic mustard seed, turmeric, salt, spices
COMMENTS: Tasters judged Westbrae "not too strong" and "a good basic mustard for kids." It has a "nice mustard flavor," and the "very smooth" texture is "great." Most tasters praised it as "acidic and bright," although a few found it "too vinegary."

RECOMMENDED WITH RESERVATIONS

PLOCHMAN'S 100% Natural Mild Yellow Mustard
PRICE: $2.39 for 19 oz. **SODIUM:** 55mg
INGREDIENTS: White distilled vinegar, water, #1 grade mustard seed, salt, turmeric, onion powder, spices, natural flavoring
COMMENTS: Some tasters disputed the "mild" moniker, finding this "very tangy" mustard "too vinegary." The mysterious "natural flavoring" on the ingredients list might be to blame for the "fruity" flavors a few tasters noticed and found out of place. Still, most rated Plochman's "not bad" with "decent mustard flavor."

BEAVER BRAND Classic Yellow American Picnic Mustard
PRICE: $3.50 for 12.5 oz. **SODIUM:** 75mg
INGREDIENTS: Water, white distilled vinegar, mustard seed, salt, sugar, soybean oil, turmeric, garlic, spices, xanthan gum, annatto, calcium disodium EDTA (retains product freshness), citric acid, natural flavor
COMMENTS: "Sweet" and "balanced," according to most of our tasters. Some, however, picked up on flavors that, although not unpleasant, don't belong in yellow mustard: "fennel," "curry," and "caraway." "Complex but not in a good way," said a taster who'd noted those peculiar flavors.

NOT RECOMMENDED

EDEN Organic Yellow Mustard
PRICE: $2.33 for 9 oz. **SODIUM:** 80mg
INGREDIENTS: Organic apple cider vinegar, water, organic yellow mustard seed, Eden sea salt, organic turmeric, organic paprika, organic garlic
COMMENTS: "Very little discernible mustard flavor." "Just vinegar and salt—where's the mustard?" "Sour and winey." "Obviously unbalanced." "It tastes like old pickle water and sweat."

RED WINE VINEGAR

As with balsamic vinegars, the number of red wine vinegars in the condiment aisle has exploded in the past decade. Given the variety available, we decided to take a look at red wine vinegars and asked tasters to sample 10 brands plain, in a simple vinaigrette, and in pickled onions. In the plain tasting, we assumed that tasters would be partial to the vinegars that were sweet and less harsh. In fact, the favorite in this round fell right in the middle of the rankings for sweetness and harshness. Tasters, it seemed, liked full flavor and a little sharpness. However, in the vinaigrette, some of the harsher vinegars were experienced as relatively sweet due to the presence of sugar in the vinaigrette, which heightened the sweet taste of the strong, highly acidic vinegars. Less acidic vinegars, on the other hand, were pushed into the background, with the stronger extra-virgin olive oil and mustard masking their flavor. This told us that a good vinegar needs some muscle in the form of acidity to hold its own in a recipe. In the end, tasters preferred vinegars with crisp red wine flavor balanced by stronger than average acidity and subtle sweetness; they also liked vinegars that were a blend of multiple varieties of grapes, as this creates a more complex flavor. Vinegars are listed in order of preference.

RECOMMENDED

LAURENT DU CLOS Red Wine Vinegar
PRICE: $5.99 for 16.9 fl. oz. (35 cents per oz.)
ACIDITY: 6.12%
SUGAR: None detected
TYPE OF GRAPE: Vinifera, red and white
COMMENTS: "Good red wine flavor" won the day for this French import. Tasters liked the "nicely rich," "well-balanced," and "fruity" flavor that came through in the pickled onions, and they praised the "clean, light, pleasant taste" and "subtle zing" it added to the vinaigrette.

POMPEIAN Gourmet Red Wine Vinegar
PRICE: $3.99 for 16 fl. oz. (25 cents per oz.)
ACIDITY: 5.14%
SUGAR: 0.5%
TYPE OF GRAPE: Concord
COMMENTS: Tasters were enthusiastic about this "very mild, sweet, pleasant" red wine vinegar with "tang" that was in "harmonious balance." It was "not harsh at all," but had a "bright, potent taste" with "really pleasing red wine flavor."

RECOMMENDED WITH RESERVATIONS

SPECTRUM NATURALS Organic Red Wine Vinegar
PRICE: $5.99 for 16.9 fl. oz. (35 cents per oz.)
ACIDITY: 6.06%
SUGAR: None detected
TYPE OF GRAPE: Concord/Vinifera-type grapes
COMMENTS: Tasters praised our former favorite supermarket brand's "winy" and "fruity" taste with "buttery" and "briny" undertones, but it stumbled in the pickled onions, inspiring remarks about its "watery," "thin," and "wimpy" flavor.

HEINZ Gourmet Red Wine Vinegar
PRICE: $3.99 for 12 fl. oz. (33 cents per oz.)
ACIDITY: 5.32%
SUGAR: None detected
TYPE OF GRAPE: Concord
COMMENTS: Tasted on its own, this domestic red wine vinegar was deemed "bright and sweet with good red wine flavor." Once cooked, however, a few tasters noticed a "sour, almost fermented taste" that was "too harsh" to let the wine flavor through.

RECOMMENDED WITH RESERVATIONS *(continued)*

HOLLAND HOUSE Red Wine Vinegar
PRICE: $2.89 for 12 fl. oz. (24 cents per oz.)
ACIDITY: 5.2%
SUGAR: 0.3%
TYPE OF GRAPE: Concord
COMMENTS: Some tasters liked its "tart," "fruity," and "cherry/nectarine" notes, but this vinegar also received the most complaints about its "acetone" or "nail polish remover" smell and taste.

REGINA Red Wine Vinegar
PRICE: $2.49 for 12 fl. oz. (21 cents per oz.)
ACIDITY: 5.2%
SUGAR: None detected
TYPE OF GRAPE: Vinifera
COMMENTS: Distinguishing itself with its perceived sweetness, this vinegar with "berry" and "floral" notes didn't offend, nor did it wow tasters, whose comments included "middle-of-the-road quality" and "no zip or zing."

COLAVITA Red Wine Vinegar
PRICE: $2.99 for 17 fl. oz. (18 cents per oz.)
ACIDITY: 6.3%
SUGAR: 0.9%
TYPE OF GRAPE: Vinifera
COMMENTS: Some tasters appreciated this vinegar's "winy and sweet" flavor and "nice balance" with "just the right tang." Others, however, found it "harsh," "sour," and "sharp" with a "saccharine aftertaste."

STAR Red Wine Vinegar
PRICE: $2.39 for 12 fl. oz. (20 cents per oz.)
ACIDITY: 5.08%
SUGAR: None detected
TYPE OF GRAPE: Vinifera
COMMENTS: This vinegar had a "bright and zippy" presence in vinaigrette and a "refreshing bite" in the pickled onions, but its lack of "real red wine taste" allowed the acidity to prevail, making it harsh for some.

BEEF BROTH

When we first sampled beef broth over 10 years ago, we were disappointed and vowed to avoid it where possible. To find out if any of today's broths could provide a suitable stand-in for homemade, we tasted 13 different broths, stocks, and bases. After a plain tasting, the top eight contenders were sampled in French onion soup and gravy. Two winners received votes for beefiest of the bunch; one brand listed nearly 20 ingredients (many of them processed additives), while the other listed just eight ingredients. The runner-up went the route of low-cost, factory-engineered flavor, with additives such as beef extract and beef powder; savory-flavor boosters such as tomato paste and yeast extract; and corn syrup solids and soy lecithin for body. The winner included concentrated beef stock, a pile of vegetables, and only one processed additive: yeast extract. Broths are listed in order of preference; sodium and protein are per 1-cup serving.

RECOMMENDED

RACHAEL RAY Stock-in-a-Box All-Natural Beef Flavored Stock (made by Colavita)
PRICE: $4.95 for 32 oz.
SODIUM: 480mg **PROTEIN:** 3g
INGREDIENTS: Concentrated beef stock (contains: beef stock, sea salt, yeast extract), vegetable stock (carrot, celery, onion, leek, natural flavor)
COMMENTS: "Steaky" with "thick, gelatin-like body," this was the only product to achieve reasonably beefy flavor in soup and gravy without a slew of processed additives. Its primary ingredient—concentrated beef stock—contains twice as much meat as regular beef stock and is amplified by only one additive: glutamate-boosting yeast extract.

COLLEGE INN Bold Stock Tender Beef Flavor
PRICE: $3.99 for 32 oz.
SODIUM: 730mg **PROTEIN:** 7g
INGREDIENTS: Beef stock, beef extract, contains less than 1% of the following: natural flavors, vegetable juices, salt, sugar, tomato paste, yeast extract, dextrose, corn syrup solids, beef powder, beef fat, potassium chloride, mono- and disodium phosphate, soy lecithin, gum arabic, caramel color, thiamine hydrochloride
COMMENTS: Singled out for its "strong aroma of roasted bones" and fairly "robust" flavor, this broth—full of beef derivatives and flavor-boosting additives—tasted "nicely beefy" and "well balanced" in onion soup, though it became "very salty" when reduced in gravy.

RECOMMENDED WITH RESERVATIONS

SWANSON Cooking Stock Beef Flavor
PRICE: $2.99 for 26 oz.
SODIUM: 500mg **PROTEIN:** 4g
INGREDIENTS: Beef stock, contains less than 2% of the following: yeast extract, sea salt, natural flavoring, honey, salt, onion juice concentrate, tomato paste, beef fat, carrots, cabbage, beef extract, onions, celery, celery leaves, parsley
COMMENTS: Though this broth scored high in the gravy test with "decent beef flavor," tasters detected slightly "sour" and "bitter" flavors in the plain tasting as well as in the soup.

RECOMMENDED WITH RESERVATIONS *(continued)*

PROGRESSO 100% Natural Beef Broth Flavored
PRICE: $3.69 for 32 oz.
SODIUM: 850mg **PROTEIN:** 1g
INGREDIENTS: Water, beef broth, sea salt, autolyzed yeast extract, sugar, natural flavor, salt, evaporated cane juice, beef tallow, spices, onion powder, beef, garlic powder, gelatin
COMMENTS: More than 25 adjectives were used to describe this high-salt broth; however, "beefy" was used sparingly. Cane juice brought out the onions' sweetness, rendering the French onion soup "sweet and bland."

REDI-BASE Beef Base
PRICE: $7.95 for 8 oz. (makes 2½ gallons)
SODIUM: 690mg **PROTEIN:** 1g
INGREDIENTS: Roasted beef with natural juices, salt, yeast extract (contains salt, caramel color, and barley gluten), sugar, beef extract, onion powder, caramel color, rendered beef fat, potato flour, chicken fat, flavors, maltodextrin, natural flavors (contains soybean), disodium inosinate, sodium guanylate
COMMENTS: In 2006, this brand topped our ranking, our only complaint being that tasters found the gravy salty. This time around tasters found it had comparatively faint meaty flavor.

NOT RECOMMENDED

WOLFGANG PUCK Organic Beef Flavored Broth
PRICE: $3.42 for 32 oz.
SODIUM: 660mg **PROTEIN:** 1g
INGREDIENTS: Organic beef broth [water, beef broth, maltodextrin, pureed vegetables (carrot, celery, onion), salt, cane juice solids, natural flavor, caramel color, soybean oil, potato starch, vegetable flavor (celeriac concentrate), tomato paste]
COMMENTS: "Sweet," "mild," "boring." This brand steered clear of yeast extract and all other flavor potentiators except for tomato paste. The result was a watery broth.

NONFAT GREEK YOGURT

In recent months, sales of Greek yogurt have jumped 160 percent. Where once only one or two brands were available, supermarkets now carry nearly a dozen brands with a variety of fat levels. To find out if any of these brands lived up to the hype, we sampled 10 different nonfat plain Greek yogurts. Some yogurts were stiff, others watery. Flavors ranged from bland to lightly tangy to strongly sour. A little research into the yogurt-making process helped us understand these variations. The major difference between ordinary yogurt and Greek-style yogurt is that true Greek yogurt is strained to remove most of its liquid whey; the result is a thicker yogurt that is higher in protein. But some manufacturers are using shortcuts, such as skipping the straining and adding gelatin or pectin to accomplish a thicker, creamier product. Our tasters caught on and downgraded these yogurts for their gelatinous texture. Greek yogurts are listed in order of preference; protein is per 6-ounce serving.

HIGHLY RECOMMENDED

OLYMPUS Traditional Greek Nonfat Yogurt Strained, Plain
PRICE: $1.99 for 6 oz. **PROTEIN:** 15g
INGREDIENTS: Grade A pasteurized nonfat milk, yogurt culture
COMMENTS: This yogurt—the lone Greek import—won raves for its "smooth, fatty," "seriously creamy" consistency and "pleasantly tangy," well-balanced flavor. In sum: "Hard to believe it's nonfat."

RECOMMENDED

VOSKOS Greek Yogurt Plain Nonfat
PRICE: $2.69 for 8 oz. **PROTEIN:** 18g
INGREDIENTS: Grade A pasteurized skim milk, live and active cultures
COMMENTS: Though a bit on the runny side for some tasters, this "creamy" yogurt was "bright, clean, and rich," with the kind of "nice tang" and "complex flavor" that you'd "expect from Greek yogurt."

BROWN COW Greek Yogurt 0% Fat, Plain
PRICE: $0.99 for 5.3 oz. **PROTEIN:** 17g
INGREDIENTS: Cultured pasteurized nonfat milk. Contains live active cultures.
COMMENTS: Most tasters found this Greek-style relative of our favorite regular plain yogurt "very thick," "super silky," and "smooth." Many noted that its "good, rich tang" reminded them of sour cream and cream cheese. Others found this sample "a bit too acidic."

DANNON Greek Plain 0% Fat
PRICE: $1.39 for 5.3 oz. **PROTEIN:** 17g
INGREDIENTS: Cultured Grade A nonfat milk. Contains active yogurt cultures.
COMMENTS: Most tasters agreed that this yogurt's consistency was "ideal": "thick, smooth, and lush." One happy taster even called it "a guilty pleasure" and compared it to ice cream. Still, others felt its richness wasn't enough to temper its "super-duper sour" flavor and "slightly chalky aftertaste."

RECOMMENDED *(continued)*

OIKOS Organic Greek Yogurt 0% Fat, Plain
PRICE: $1.99 for 5.3 oz. **PROTEIN:** 17g
INGREDIENTS: Cultured pasteurized organic nonfat milk. Contains live active cultures.
COMMENTS: This Greek-style offering from the folks at Stonyfield Farm boasted "lots of tang," a quality that some found "distracting." Texture-wise, this product was on the "watery" side, with a "puddle-y" consistency.

FAGE Total 0% Greek Strained Yogurt
PRICE: $1.99 for 6 oz. **PROTEIN:** 15g
INGREDIENTS: Grade A pasteurized skimmed milk, live active yogurt cultures
COMMENTS: Unlike other samples, this well-known Greek brand (by the way, it's pronounced "fa-yeh"), which now produces yogurt in the U.S., met no criticism for excessive tanginess. In fact, most tasters found it a tad "muted." Others described it as "nice and creamy, with just enough tang to remind you, 'Yes, this is yogurt.'"

RECOMMENDED WITH RESERVATIONS

CHOBANI Greek Yogurt Plain Nonfat
PRICE: $1.25 for 6 oz. **PROTEIN:** 18g
INGREDIENTS: Cultured pasteurized nonfat milk. Contains live active cultures.
COMMENTS: While some tasters found this yogurt's texture "buttery" and like "clotted cream," others deemed it "ricotta-like." Several tasters also inquired about the missing "tang," noting that it "would work to cool down a spicy dish" but wasn't worth eating on its own.

NOT RECOMMENDED

ATHENOS Greek Strained Nonfat Plain Yogurt
PRICE: $3.29 for 16 oz. **PROTEIN:** 16g
INGREDIENTS: Cultured pasteurized nonfat milk
COMMENTS: As we like to say in Boston, this sample from Kraft was "wicked sour." The texture was "wrong," too. Tasters described it as "smooth" but "runny," "thin," and "on a par with regular yogurt."

PANCAKE MIX

Americans spend more than $250 million a year on pancake mixes. To find the best one, we rounded up 16 pancake mixes (choosing buttermilk flavor when possible), tasting our way down to eight. We prepared the pancakes according to package instructions and served them plain, with syrup on the side. Not surprisingly, tasters liked pancakes with a flavorful balance of sweetness and tang—that is, pancakes that were well seasoned with sugar and salt. But texture proved just as important as flavor, maybe even more so: Tasters preferred light, fluffy pancakes. Squat, tough pancakes with little height and fluff were downgraded substantially. So what's the secret to the best texture? Our top two mixes require the addition of vegetable oil, plus milk and egg, to reconstitute the batter. Oil affects texture by helping to govern how the air bubbles (from the leavener) are retained during cooking. Other mixes call for butter or compensate with partially hydrogenated vegetable oil, which creates soft, but not fluffy, pancakes. Mixes are listed in order of preference; sodium and sugar are per ⅓-cup mix.

RECOMMENDED

HUNGRY JACK Buttermilk Pancake and Waffle Mix
PRICE: $2.39 for 32 oz.
INGREDIENTS: Enriched bleached flour, sugar, rice flour, baking powder, buttermilk, less than 2% of: partially hydrogenated soybean oil, salt, calcium carbonate, corn starch, iron, niacin, vitamin B6, riboflavin, thiamin mononitrate, folic acid, vitamin B12
THE COOK ADDS: milk, oil, egg
SODIUM: 630mg **SUGARS:** 5g
COMMENTS: Tasters practically leaped out of their chairs to praise the "extra fluffy" and "wonderful, thick, light" texture. Said one: "Looks and tastes like a dream of a homemade pancake." For flavor, it scored just behind our runner-up, Aunt Jemima.

AUNT JEMIMA Original Pancake and Waffle Mix
PRICE: $2.69 for 32 oz.
INGREDIENTS: Enriched bleached flour, sugar, leavening, salt, calcium carbonate
THE COOK ADDS: milk, oil, egg
SODIUM: 740mg **SUGARS:** 7g
COMMENTS: The industry-leading brand edged out Hungry Jack by a hair for flavor (but ranked second for texture). This Auntie includes more sugar and salt than any other manufacturer—to her advantage. "Are you sure this came from a box?"

RECOMMENDED WITH RESERVATIONS

CARBON'S Golden Malted Original Pancake & Waffle Flour
PRICE: $10.99 for 33 oz.
INGREDIENTS: Enriched wheat flour, corn flour, leavening, malt powder, salt, sugar, buttermilk, artificial flavor
THE COOK ADDS: egg, whole milk or buttermilk, melted butter
SODIUM: 380mg **SUGARS:** 0g
COMMENTS: Astute tasters picked up on the pleasant "malt" and "cornmeal" flavors and were generally pleased with how these cakes tasted (even though they contain no sugar). Tasters weren't as fond of the "flat, gummy, and dense" texture.

RECOMMENDED WITH RESERVATIONS *(continued)*

KRUSTEAZ Light & Fluffy Buttermilk Complete Pancake Mix
PRICE: $2.29 for 32 oz.
INGREDIENTS: Enriched bleached flour, sugar, leavening, soy flour, dextrose, partially hydrogenated soybean and cottonseed oils, buttermilk, salt, mono and diglycerides, eggs
THE COOK ADDS: water
SODIUM: 373mg **SUGARS:** 6g
COMMENTS: Our tasters enjoyed the "slightly sweet," "mild" flavor of these pancakes, which have the third most sodium and second most sugar of all mixes in the lineup. But texture—which tasters panned as "dense and dry" and "rubbery"—pushed Krusteaz down our rankings.

MRS. BUTTERWORTH'S Buttermilk Complete Pancake & Waffle Mix
PRICE: $2.59 for 32 oz.
INGREDIENTS: Bleached wheat flour, sugar, dried buttermilk, leavening, defatted soy flour, less than 2% of: dextrose, partially hydrogenated soybean oil, isolated soy protein, salt, dried whole eggs, calcium carbonate, nonfat dry milk, natural and artificial flavor, mono and diglycerides
THE COOK ADDS: water
SODIUM: 450mg **SUGARS:** 6g
COMMENTS: Tasters knocked the artificial aroma of these pancakes, comparing it to "vanilla candles" and "pancake-scented Febreze." They described the flavor as "very sweet" and "like marshmallows." The "high-rising," "fluffy" texture was a plus.

BISQUICK Original Pancake and Baking Mix
PRICE: $2.99 for 40 oz.
INGREDIENTS: Enriched flour bleached, partially hydrogenated soybean and/or cottonseed oil, leavening, dextrose, salt
THE COOK ADDS: milk, eggs
SODIUM: 410mg **SUGARS:** 1g
COMMENTS: These "exceptionally bland" pancakes scored no better than average across the board. Tasters couldn't muster any strong feelings about either flavor or texture, with one commenting, "It could be a lot worse."

MACARONI AND CHEESE

Sales of macaroni and cheese (both boxed mixes and frozen dinners) have risen 25 percent over the past four years, and new brands and varieties have exploded onto the market. We wanted to know, are they any good? We conducted two preliminary taste-offs of several available varieties of Kraft and Annie's (Kraft alone has 50 kinds), then added other brands, including two frozen dinners. We carefully followed package instructions, microwaving the frozen dinners (much quicker than baking), and started tasting, ultimately finding just three brands we would even consider eating. The so-called "cheese sauce" was one of several features that distinguished winners from losers. Our favorite reinforced its sauce with blue and cheddar cheeses, and all our top choices used liquid sauce, which was creamy and suitably clingy. Macaroni and cheese brands are listed in order of preference.

RECOMMENDED

KRAFT HOMESTYLE Macaroni & Cheese Dinner Classic Cheddar Cheese Sauce
PRICE: $2 for 12.6-oz. bag
TOTAL COOKING TIME: Approx. 20 minutes
TYPE OF CHEESE SAUCE: Liquid
THE COOK ADDS: 2 percent milk, unsalted butter
COMMENTS: The best of the 11 Kraft varieties we tried and the best overall, this creamy, flavorful macaroni tasted the most like homemade. Tasters really liked the breadcrumb topping and praised the "thick" sauce for its "real" cheese flavor.

KRAFT VELVEETA Original Shells & Cheese
PRICE: $2 for 12-oz. box
TOTAL COOKING TIME: Approx. 10 minutes
TYPE OF CHEESE SAUCE: Liquid
THE COOK ADDS: Nothing
COMMENTS: This cheese flavor was strong and rich, the sauce nice and thick. Many of our tasters instantly recognized the distinct taste of Velveeta. Some complained that the cheese became waxy if it sat around.

RECOMMENDED WITH RESERVATIONS

ANNIE'S Deluxe Shells & Real Aged Cheddar
PRICE: $3.99 for 11-oz. box
TOTAL COOKING TIME: Approx. 12 minutes
TYPE OF CHEESE SAUCE: Liquid
THE COOK ADDS: Nothing
COMMENTS: The small shells sometimes clumped, cooking unevenly. Tasters liked the initial cheddar flavor, but many detected an off-putting aftertaste.

NOT RECOMMENDED

STOUFFER'S Macaroni & Cheese Family Size
PRICE: $5.99 for 40-oz. box
TOTAL COOKING TIME: 23 minutes in the microwave, 75 minutes in 375-degree oven
TYPE OF CHEESE SAUCE: Already incorporated
THE COOK ADDS: Nothing
COMMENTS: Some tasters praised the good cheddar flavor; others tasted only salt. Our biggest gripe? "Smushy," "gloppy" texture. We used the microwave for speed.

NOT RECOMMENDED *(continued)*

BACK TO NATURE Macaroni & Cheese
PRICE: $2.19 for 6.5-oz. box
TOTAL COOKING TIME: Approx. 8 minutes
TYPE OF CHEESE SAUCE: Powdered
THE COOK ADDS: Low-fat milk, unsalted butter
COMMENTS: Despite the addition of milk and butter, tasters found this brand "pasty" and "powdery," with cheese that was "chemical-y," strangely "sweet," and wan. As one taster put it, "It was as if the mac and cheese was depressed."

KRAFT Macaroni & Cheese Dinner Original
PRICE: $1.15 for 7.25-oz. box
TOTAL COOKING TIME: Approx. 8 minutes
TYPE OF CHEESE SAUCE: Powdered
THE COOK ADDS: Margarine, 2 percent milk
COMMENTS: "The Cheesiest" was plastered across the box, but this classic mac and cheese was everything but. Tasters jotted down "sweet," "bitter," "fake," "fishy," "sour," and more—but nary a "cheesy." Kraft may eat up 80 percent of the dry macaroni-and-cheese market, but this blue box we all know from childhood was just plain awful.

PASTA RONI Cheddar Macaroni
PRICE: $1.59 for 5.3-oz. box
TOTAL COOKING TIME: Approx. 16 minutes
TYPE OF CHEESE SAUCE: Powdered
THE COOK ADDS: Nothing
COMMENTS: Easy-peasy to make: You bring water to a boil, add the pasta and seasoning packet, simmer, and let stand. No draining, no fuss, and . . . oops, no flavor! The cream-colored powder turned a disturbing neon yellow. Also disturbing—the flavorless, "rubbery, mushy mass" of "hideous orange elbows."

BANQUET Macaroni & Cheese Meal
PRICE: $1.25 for 8-oz. box
TOTAL COOKING TIME: 6 minutes in the microwave, 28 minutes in 350-degree oven
TYPE OF CHEESE SAUCE: Already incorporated
THE COOK ADDS: Nothing
COMMENTS: This heat-and-eat frozen dinner was "bland" and "squishy" with a "weird plastic" aftertaste. Described as "flabby" and with zero cheese flavor, the closest compliment was "Tastes like a Cheez Doodle."

CREAMY PEANUT BUTTER

Scan the peanut butter aisle at your supermarket and you'll find dozens of different brands and options. But no option seems to be taking up space like the "natural" peanut butters (which sometimes are more than just peanuts and salt). We set out to find the best creamy peanut butters, and gathered a number of both conventional and natural butters, some of which mimic conventional peanut butter with naturally hydrogenated palm oil. Tasters sampled 10 brands plain, in peanut butter cookies, and in a spicy satay sauce. When it came to great peanut butter, tasters made it clear that texture was paramount. The peanut butters had to be smooth, creamy, and spreadable; they also had to have a good balance of sweet and salty flavors. Peanut butters are listed in order of preference.

RECOMMENDED

SKIPPY Peanut Butter
PRICE: $2.39 for 16.3 oz. (15 cents per oz.)
TOTAL SUGAR: 10.7% **SALT:** 1.25%
INGREDIENTS: Roasted peanuts, sugar, hydrogenated vegetable oils (cottonseed, soybean, and rapeseed) to prevent separation, salt
COMMENTS: In a contest that hinged on texture, tasters thought this "smooth," "creamy" sample was "swell" and gave it top honors, both plain and baked into cookies. Its rave reviews even compensated for a slightly "weak" nut flavor that didn't come through as well as that of other brands in the pungent satay sauce.

JIF Natural Peanut Butter Spread
PRICE: $2.29 for 18 oz. (13 cents per oz.)
TOTAL SUGAR: 11.5% **SALT:** 0.61%
INGREDIENTS: Peanuts, sugar, palm oil, contains 2% or less of salt, molasses
COMMENTS: The big favorite in satay sauce, this peanut butter's "dark, roasted flavor"—helped by the molasses—stood out well against the other heady ingredients and made cookies with "nice sweet-salty balance." Plus, as the top-rated palm oil-based sample, it was "creamy," "thick," and better emulsified than other "natural" butters.

REESE'S Peanut Butter
PRICE: $2.59 for 18 oz. (14 cents per oz.)
TOTAL SUGAR: 9.9% **SALT:** 1.11%
INGREDIENTS: Roasted peanuts, sugar, peanut oil, hydrogenated vegetable oil (contains rapeseed, cottonseed, and soybean oils), salt, molasses, monoglycerides, and cornstarch
COMMENTS: "This is what peanut butter should be like," declared one happy taster, noting specifically this product's "good," "thick" texture and "powerful peanut flavor." In satay sauce, however, some tasters felt that heavier body made for a "pasty" end result.

JIF Peanut Butter
PRICE: $2.29 for 18 oz. (13 cents per oz.)
TOTAL SUGAR: 10.7% **SALT:** 1.26%
INGREDIENTS: Roasted peanuts, sugar, contains 2% or less of molasses, fully hydrogenated vegetable oils (rapeseed and soybean), mono- and diglycerides, salt
COMMENTS: This classic butter lived up to its "creamy, rich" reputation and turned out "nice, chewy" cookies. But some tasters felt the chiles and other ingredients in satay sauce overpowered its "sweet, mellow" flavor.

RECOMMENDED *(continued)*

SKIPPY Natural Peanut Butter Spread
PRICE: $2.39 for 15 oz. (16 cents per oz.)
TOTAL SUGAR: 8.8% **SALT:** 1.26%
INGREDIENTS: Roasted peanuts, sugar, palm oil, salt
COMMENTS: The only other palm oil-based peanut butter to make the "recommended" cut, this contender had a "looser" texture than its winning sibling but still won fans for being "super-smooth." Tasters thought it made an especially "well-balanced," "complex" peanut sauce.

RECOMMENDED WITH RESERVATIONS

PEANUT BUTTER & CO. No-Stir Natural Smooth Operator
PRICE: $4.49 for 18 oz. (25 cents per oz.)
TOTAL SUGAR: 8.7% **SALT:** 0.85%
INGREDIENTS: Peanuts, evaporated cane juice, palm fruit oil, salt
COMMENTS: Though it says "no-stir" on the label, this "stiff" palm oil-enriched peanut butter was "weeping oil" and came across as "greasy" to some tasters. However, it turned out a respectable batch of cookies—"chewy in the center, crisp and short at the edge"—and made "perfectly good" satay sauce.

MARANATHA Organic No Stir Peanut Butter
PRICE: $5.69 for 16 oz. (36 cents per oz.)
TOTAL SUGAR: 9.3% **SALT:** 0.51%
INGREDIENTS: Organic dry roasted peanuts, organic palm oil, organic unrefined cane sugar, sea salt
COMMENTS: On the one hand, this organic peanut butter produced cookies that were "soft and sturdy" yet "moist," with "knockout peanut flavor." On the other hand, eating it straight from the jar was nearly impossible; its "loose," "liquid-y," and "dribbly" consistency had one taster wonder if it was "peanut soup."

PETER PAN Peanut Butter
PRICE: $2.49 for 18 oz. (14 cents per oz.)
TOTAL SUGAR: 10.8% **SALT:** 1.11%
INGREDIENTS: Roasted peanuts, sugar, less than 2% of hydrogenated vegetable oils (cottonseed and rapeseed), salt, partially hydrogenated cottonseed oil
COMMENTS: Though this peanut butter offered an ideally "cushiony, smooth" texture, it also left an "off-putting," "waxy," "stale" aftertaste that, according to some tasters, also plagued the cookies.

MILK CHOCOLATE

Recently, milk-chocolate manufacturers have been taking a cue from the much-hyped dark chocolate market, reformulating recipes and advertising cacao percentages on the label. Is milk chocolate just getting fancy, or is it getting better? We tasted 10 national brands plain and in chocolate pudding. A few samples had the mild, sweet, milky taste expected; others were deeper, cocoa-y, and less sweet—just like dark chocolate. Why so different? Milk-chocolate makers have lots of latitude. Federal standards require milk chocolate to contain at least 10 percent cacao, which is the actual chocolate in the bar. In comparison, dark chocolate, both bittersweet and semisweet, must have at least 35 percent cacao. Interestingly, several brands we sampled would qualify as dark chocolate if not for the presence of milk. Also, manufacturers can choose among cream, whole or reduced-fat milk, and powdered, condensed, or evaporated milk. One brand won for its full chocolate flavor, creamy texture, and moderate sweetness; two runners-up won over dark-chocolate fans. Milk chocolates are listed in order of preference; figures for cacao content also include milk protein (ranging from 4% to 7%), which is difficult for laboratories to isolate.

RECOMMENDED

DOVE Silky Smooth Milk Chocolate
PRICE: $2.79 for 3.53 oz.
CACAO: 36% **SUGARS:** 56.7%
MILK FAT: 7% **COCOA BUTTER:** 24%
COMMENTS: Our old favorite won again. Tasters found Dove "very satisfying" and "super creamy" with a "surprisingly rich chocolate flavor" yet "not overwhelmingly sweet." This chocolate "tastes like more than just sugar and milk," one taster wrote. Said another: "Definitely would eat this, and I only buy dark chocolate."

ENDANGERED SPECIES All-Natural Smooth Milk Chocolate
PRICE: $2.99 for 3 oz.
CACAO: 56% **SUGARS:** 36.6%
MILK FAT: 6% **COCOA BUTTER:** 33%
COMMENTS: A relative newcomer, this brand was "not terribly creamy." But it had "great chocolate taste" that was "intense" with "hints of coffee"—perhaps not surprising given its 56 percent cacao, more than enough to qualify as dark chocolate (with which some tasters compared it). Tasters also praised its "bitter and sweet" but "not too sweet" taste.

GREEN & BLACK'S Organic Milk Chocolate
PRICE: $3.69 for 3.5 oz.
CACAO: 37% **SUGARS:** 55.5%
MILK FAT: 7% **COCOA BUTTER:** 27%
COMMENTS: Tasters found this organic brand "very creamy and not too sweet" with "mild bittersweet notes," in which the "sweetness is balanced with chocolate flavor." It "does not try to hide the fact that it's milk chocolate," wrote one taster approvingly.

LINDT Classic Recipe Milk Chocolate
PRICE: $2.79 for 4.4 oz.
CACAO: 43% **SUGARS:** 51.5%
MILK FAT: 5% **COCOA BUTTER:** 27%
COMMENTS: Tasters liked Lindt (whose namesake invented conching) for its creaminess with a "caramel, nutty" flavor and "balanced sweetness." But a few criticized it as "lacking in chocolate oomph."

RECOMMENDED WITH RESERVATIONS

GHIRARDELLI Luxe Milk Chocolate
PRICE: $3.19 for 3 oz.
CACAO: 36% **SUGARS:** 56.3%
MILK FAT: 7% **COCOA BUTTER:** 26%
COMMENTS: Tasters split: Some liked the creamy texture and milk flavor, calling it "the epitome of creamy, milky milk chocolate." Others said the "sweetness overpowered everything" and the bar tasted "more like caramel or toffee." Concluded one: "Not bad, but not worth the calories, either."

SCHARFFEN BERGER Extra Rich Milk Chocolate
PRICE: $3.99 for 3 oz.
CACAO: 47% **SUGARS:** 46.8%
MILK FAT: 5% **COCOA BUTTER:** 26%
COMMENTS: Despite its "deep chocolate flavor," tasters found Scharffen Berger to be "very bitter and acidic," with "burnt sugar," "kind of chemical-y" off-flavors, and a texture that "could be a little more creamy." Some disliked the "slightly fruity" taste. "Is this really milk chocolate?" one asked.

HERSHEY'S Milk Chocolate
PRICE: $1.99 for 4.4 oz.
CACAO: 36% **SUGARS:** 56.5%
MILK FAT: 7% **COCOA BUTTER:** 23%
COMMENTS: Tasters identified the iconic American brand as "a familiar friend," "like the milk chocolate I ate as a kid." They found it "chocolaty," "rich and pure," but also "a touch grainy" and "waxy." Several criticized it as too sweet. One speculated that it was "more appealing because of memories than quality."

NOT RECOMMENDED

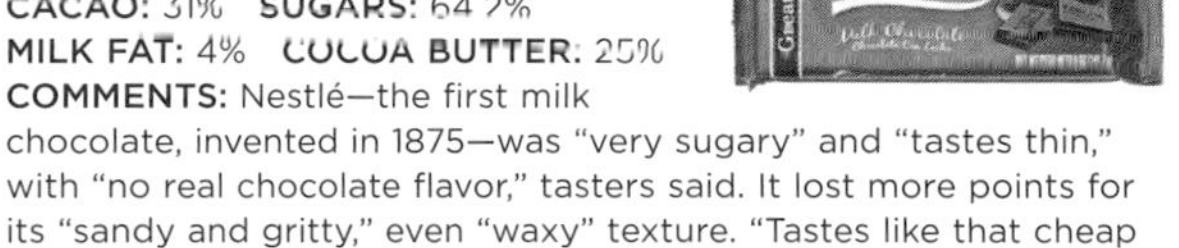

NESTLÉ Milk Chocolate
PRICE: $1.99 for 5 oz.
CACAO: 31% **SUGARS:** 64.2%
MILK FAT: 4% **COCOA BUTTER:** 25%
COMMENTS: Nestlé—the first milk chocolate, invented in 1875—was "very sugary" and "tastes thin," with "no real chocolate flavor," tasters said. It lost more points for its "sandy and gritty," even "waxy" texture. "Tastes like that cheap chocolate you get on sale the day after Easter."

UNSWEETENED CHOCOLATE

The purest form of chocolate, just cocoa solids and cocoa butter (no sugar added), unsweetened chocolate helps deepen chocolate flavor in desserts without adding sweetness. Baker's and Hershey's have been mainstays in the marketplace for more than a century, but these days, there are more options on the shelves. To find out if any of the more expensive "premium" brands could outshine the basic brands, we gathered seven other chocolates and sampled all nine plain and in brownies and chocolate sauce. In the plain tasting, individual flavor nuances came to the forefront; chocolates were described as nutty, fruity, smoky, and coffeelike. Surprisingly, in the brownie and chocolate sauce tastings, some of the more exotic brands fell short, described as "bland" and "nothing special." After analyzing the percentages of cocoa solids and cocoa butter, it was clear that the winner contained more cocoa solids and the least cocoa butter than the rest of the lineup, which explained why it was praised for its richer chocolate flavor. Chocolates are listed in order of preference.

RECOMMENDED

HERSHEY'S Unsweetened Baking Bar
PRICE: $1.99 for 4 oz. (50 cents per oz.)
FORM: Bar **FAT:** 50.30%
COMMENTS: "Straightforward and intense," "likable—like a firm handshake," this supermarket brand bolstered with cocoa was "well rounded and complex" and "rich" with "deep notes of cocoa" in both brownies and chocolate sauce. Tasters appreciated the complexity of its "caramel and coffee flavors," with a "hint of cinnamon."

VALRHONA Cacao Pate Extra 100%
PRICE: $21.95 for 2.2 lbs. (62 cents per oz.) (mail order)
FORM: Block **FAT:** 54.64%
COMMENTS: Tasters praised this chocolate for "intense richness; full, almost coffeelike flavor," and a texture that was "nicely creamy," with a "pleasant" "balance of roasted beans and buttery richness" and "hints of honey." "Not overly bitter," it struck tasters as "very cocoa-y," with "good chocolate thunder, bass tones of chocolate."

SCHARFFEN BERGER Unsweetened Dark Chocolate
PRICE: $9.99 for 9.7 oz. ($1.03 per oz.)
FORM: Bar **FAT:** 55.03%
COMMENTS: This brand containing vanilla beans had "strong" chocolate flavor with "raspberry," "fruity," "raisiny," and "slightly smoky" notes, accenting its "rich," "dark chocolate profile." With one of the highest percentages of fat in the lineup, it was "crazy smooth," with a "lush, creamy" texture in chocolate sauce.

RECOMMENDED WITH RESERVATIONS

GHIRARDELLI Unsweetened Baking Bar
PRICE: $3.79 for 4 oz. (95 cents per oz.)
FORM: Bar **FAT:** 55.35%
COMMENTS: "Mild and a little bitter" with a "tropical" flavor like "banana" or "guava," this mid-ranked chocolate struck tasters overall as "pleasant," with "average chocolate intensity," "not terrible, not great," with "a little bit of chocolate punch at the end, but not enough."

RECOMMENDED WITH RESERVATIONS *(continued)*

CALLEBAUT Unsweetened Chocolate Liquor Disks
PRICE: $16.50 for 2.2 lbs. (47 cents per oz.) (mail order)
FORM: Disks **FAT:** 55.59%
COMMENTS: While it has "really chocolaty flavor," this chocolate had some "harsh," "slightly charred" notes that tasters detected in sauce; in brownies it was "pretty meek, mild," "sandy and sweet," and "way too one-dimensional." In short, an "average sample, a bit too sweet but not bad."

GUITTARD Unsweetened Baking Chocolate
PRICE: $9.95 for 16 oz. (62 cents per oz.) (mail order)
FORM: Disks **FAT:** 53.32%
COMMENTS: "Where's the chocolate?" tasters asked. They described brownies made with this brand as "more sugary than chocolaty," "plain and boring like the brownies I grew up eating from the school cafeteria." In sum: "not a showstopper" and "ho-hum."

BAKER'S Unsweetened Baking Chocolate Squares
PRICE: $3.39 for 8 oz. (42 cents per oz.)
FORM: Bar **FAT:** 52.19%
COMMENTS: Tasters noted that this brand has "some bitterness and complexity, but falls flat pretty quickly," though they did praise its "cinnamon-y" notes and "creamy" texture in sauce. In brownies, a few tasters liked the "cherry undertones," but many felt it suffered from being too sugary. "Tastes like low-end milk chocolate Easter candy," said one taster.

NOT RECOMMENDED

DAGOBA Organic Prima Materia Pure Unsweetened Chocolate
PRICE: $2.69 for 2 oz. ($1.35 per oz.)
FORM: Bar **FAT:** 53.90%
COMMENTS: With a "weird cardboard-y" taste and "flat," "unremarkable" chocolate flavor, a "sour aftertaste," and "sugar-forward" profile, this brand, containing small amounts of milk and soy lecithin, also lost points for a distinct "charcoal," "tobacco," and "smoky" taste, "like licking charred bark" or "an ashtray."

ICE-CREAM BARS

Americans have been eating ice-cream bars for some 90 years. Today, there are dozens of brands, styles, and flavors to choose from. Since milk-chocolate-coated vanilla ice-cream bars are the most popular, we selected six brands from the supermarket and gathered some eager tasters. As it turns out, ice-cream bars are not pure chocolate and ice cream: Most brands use stabilizers, dyes, and artificial flavors in the ice-cream portion, and every brand uses coconut oil in the coating (to reduce chocolate bloom in the freezer), with most brands listing the oil as the first coating ingredient. Because of that, most of the bars had weak or muddled chocolate flavor. By contrast, our two favorite bars list milk chocolate as the first ingredient in the coating, and our top choice supplements it with semisweet chocolate. Interestingly, while prominent chocolate flavor was important to our tasters, vanilla flavor wasn't; neutral or scant vanilla flavor was fine as long as it was clean. Ice cream texture was very important, with thicker, denser ice cream standing up to a thicker shell, both of which we preferred, whether the bar had a stick or not. Light, fluffy ice cream seemed thin and wan to many tasters, and it melted too quickly. Ice-cream bars are listed in order of preference.

HIGHLY RECOMMENDED

DOVE BAR Vanilla Ice Cream with Milk Chocolate
PRICE: $4.39 for three
SERVING SIZE: (1 bar) 74g
CHOCOLATE SHELL THICKNESS: 1.77 mm
COATING: ★★★
ICE CREAM: ★★
COMMENTS: It's no surprise that the winner of our milk chocolate tasting took top honors: Tasters liked the "very chocolaty" and "thick, crunchy chocolate coating," which also happened to be the thickest coating of those we tested. The "thick, creamy ice cream" is "not too sweet," and it complemented the chocolate.

RECOMMENDED

HÄAGEN-DAZS Vanilla Milk Chocolate All Natural Ice Cream Bars
PRICE: $4.39 for three
SERVING SIZE: (1 bar) 83g
CHOCOLATE SHELL THICKNESS: 1.33 mm
COATING: ★★
ICE CREAM: ★★★
COMMENTS: Häagen Dazs was the only brand that listed vanilla extract in its ice-cream ingredients. That list, incidentally, was the shortest among all the brands we tested and included no gums or stabilizers. No wonder "the ice cream was great!" as more than one taster concluded. Unfortunately, full-flavored ice cream overshadowed the weak chocolate flavor.

BLUE BUNNY Big Alaska Bar
PRICE: $2 each
SERVING SIZE: (1 bar) 95g
CHOCOLATE SHELL THICKNESS: .98 mm
COATING: ★★
ICE CREAM: ★★
COMMENTS: Tasters praised this thick ice-cream bar for its "light, crisp chocolate shell" and "creamy, sweet" and "rich" vanilla ice cream. Although the texture was good, the flavor of the chocolate coating was off—perhaps because coconut oil, not chocolate, comes first on the ingredient list.

RECOMMENDED *(continued)*

GOOD HUMOR Milk Chocolate Bar
PRICE: $2.50 for six
SERVING SIZE: (1 bar) 59g
CHOCOLATE SHELL THICKNESS: .88 mm
COATING: ★★
ICE CREAM: ★
COMMENTS: Tasters were familiar with this style of bar from ice-cream trucks: "light, fluffy, airy ice cream," "light, crispy chocolate," very sweet, and a "very clean flavor." While we preferred a thicker, richer bar, most tasters found the Good Humor bar generally acceptable.

RECOMMENDED WITH RESERVATIONS

KLONDIKE Original Vanilla Bar
PRICE: $2.99 for six
SERVING SIZE: (1 bar) 86g
CHOCOLATE SHELL THICKNESS: 1.6 mm
COATING: ★
ICE CREAM: ★★
COMMENTS: "Thick chocolate shell" with "creamy" ice cream that had the right texture. So what was wrong? The flavor of both the ice cream and, especially, the chocolate was ambiguous, our tasters noted. Coffee, butterscotch, toffee, and mocha were among the competing flavors they detected.

NOT RECOMMENDED

HOOD Ice Cream Bars
PRICE: $4.39 for 12
SERVING SIZE: (1 bar) 46g
CHOCOLATE SHELL THICKNESS: .75 mm
COATING: ★
ICE CREAM: ★
COMMENTS: This "thin, sad, and foamy" bar won few fans. Tasters labeled it "generic" and "wimpy" for flavor and texture. The Hood bar was roughly half the size of our winner, and it "melted too fast to taste anything."

LIQUID MEASURING CUPS

The liquid measuring cup is a basic kitchen tool, where accuracy matters more than looks. But when we shopped recently, we were greeted by a variety of innovative new shapes and materials. We selected 15 models and quickly whittled the list to eight. The first ones cut simply weren't accurate. Additionally, some weren't sturdy or heatproof, while others lacked ¼ or ⅓ cup markings, which we consider essential. To test durability, we ran all cups through numerous dishwasher cycles and dropped them on the floor. We downgraded cups that contained Bisphenol A, a controversial material that has been linked to health issues. Measuring cups are listed in order of preference.

RECOMMENDED	PERFORMANCE	TESTERS' COMMENTS
GOOD COOK by Bradshaw International 2-Cup Measuring Cup **MODEL:** 19864 **PRICE:** $3.99 **MATERIAL:** Plastic **BPA:** None **DISHWASHER:** Top rack **MICROWAVE:** Yes	ACCURACY: ★★★ PERFORMANCE: ★★★ DESIGN: ★★★ DURABILITY: ★★	While we'd prefer a cup that feels more substantial, this lightweight, crisply marked model was accurate and easy to read and provided all the measurements we needed—and no more. Most testers found it "easy and basic." And it's cheap.
ARROW Cool Grip 2.5-Cup Measuring Cup **MODEL:** 473812 (00031) **PRICE:** $11.80 **MATERIAL:** Plastic **BPA:** None **DISHWASHER:** Top rack **MICROWAVE:** Yes; 15-minute limit	ACCURACY: ★★★ PERFORMANCE: ★★★ DESIGN: ★★★ DURABILITY: ★★	We liked this simple cup with its easy-on-the-eyes markings and stay-cool handle. Rounded corners made it easy to scrape out sticky honey. One quibble: the manufacturer squeezed in markings right to the rim, where liquids can spill.

RECOMMENDED WITH RESERVATIONS	PERFORMANCE	TESTERS' COMMENTS
OXO Good Grips 2-Cup Angled Measuring Cup **MODEL:** 70981 **PRICE:** $9.99 **MATERIAL:** Plastic **BPA:** Yes **DISHWASHER:** Yes **MICROWAVE:** Yes; 4-minute limit; no fats or oils	ACCURACY: ★★★ PERFORMANCE: ★★★ DESIGN: ★★ DURABILITY: ★★	Comfortable to pour, with an ergonomic handle, oval shape, and sharp, drip-free spout. Angled measurement panels inside the cup, readable from above, were clear to testers, who got accurate results, but they were a nuisance when testers scraped out honey.
WILTON 2-Cup Liquid Measure **MODEL:** 2103-334 **PRICE:** $10.78 **MATERIAL:** Plastic **BPA:** None **DISHWASHER:** Top rack **MICROWAVE:** No	ACCURACY: ★★★ PERFORMANCE: ★★ DESIGN: ★★ DURABILITY: ★★	Accurate, comfortable, and lightweight, its oval shape helped control pouring. We liked the "stepped" design, with each step a measurement, but some testers found the yellow markings hard to read.

NOT RECOMMENDED	PERFORMANCE	TESTERS' COMMENTS
ISI Basics Flex-It 2-Cup Measuring Cup **MODEL:** B 26400 **PRICE:** $8.99 **MATERIAL:** Silicone **BPA:** None **DISHWASHER:** Yes **MICROWAVE:** Yes	ACCURACY: ★★★ PERFORMANCE: ★★ DESIGN: ★ DURABILITY: ★★★	This simple silicone cylinder was soft and pliable—a fatal flaw when boiling liquid turned it overly squishy and too hot to hold. Still, scraping honey out of the smooth, tubular body was easy and testers were able to obtain accurate results.
ZYLISS Mix-n-Measure Measuring Cup Set with Lid (1, 2 & 4 Cup) **MODEL:** 13850 **PRICE:** $19.99 **MATERIAL:** Plastic **BPA:** Yes **DISHWASHER:** Yes **MICROWAVE:** No	ACCURACY: ★★★ PERFORMANCE: ★★ DESIGN: ★ DURABILITY: ★★★	We liked the idea of markings readable from the top or side, but these were printed in such small, busy type that the information was lost on several testers; many also disliked the handle's sharp edges.
EMSA Perfect Beaker with Seal by Frieling **MODEL:** 2206990096 **PRICE:** $12.46 **MATERIAL:** Plastic **BPA:** None **DISHWASHER:** Yes **MICROWAVE:** Yes; 3-minute limit	ACCURACY: ★ PERFORMANCE: ★★ DESIGN: ★★ DURABILITY: ★★	The "perfect beaker" it isn't. The 1-cup marking was short by nearly 1 tablespoon. It was easy to pour from, except when full of boiling water, when the lack of a handle was a true disadvantage.
PYREX 2-Cup Measuring Cup with Read from Above Graphics **MODEL:** 1085812 **PRICE:** $6.49 **MATERIAL:** Glass **BPA:** None **DISHWASHER:** Yes **MICROWAVE:** Yes	ACCURACY: ★ PERFORMANCE: ★★ DESIGN: ★ DURABILITY: ★★★	This redesigned cup was a disaster. Testers struggled to tell if they'd hit the mark and couldn't double-check from the outside (for one thing, markings appear backward); their uncertainty showed up in poor measuring results. The big, conical shape is hard to pour from and eats up storage space. Accuracy was off by 2 teaspoons.

KITCHEN SHEARS

Kitchen shears are the best all-around tool on the counter, useful for any number of tasks, such as cutting up chicken, trimming pie dough, or snipping kitchen twine. We wanted to find a pair that aced every task, with powerful, sharp blades that were easy to maneuver, had slip-resistant, comfortable handles and were easy to clean up. They also had to work for lefties. Testers cut away using seven models priced from $9.95 to $75. Some shears sacrificed comfort for style, with snazzy-looking handles that made hands ache or slipped once they got wet or greasy. We preferred models that allowed us to adjust the tension. If the tension was too tight, cutting became halting and laborious; if too loose, the shears felt flimsy. Shears are listed in order of preference.

HIGHLY RECOMMENDED	PERFORMANCE	TESTERS' COMMENTS
SHUN Classic Kitchen Shears **MODEL:** 1120M **PRICE:** $39.99 **EXTRAS:** Jar gripper, bottle opener, screwdriver, nutcracker **CLEANUP:** Separable blades. Washing by hand highly recommended.	CUTTING: ★★★ COMFORT: ★★★	Thanks to 9-inch, very sharp blades (one with fine micro-serrations; the other deeply grooved ones), breaking down a chicken felt effortless. Large, rubbery handles were comfy, and blades were symmetrical for right- and left-handed use. They come with a lifetime guarantee.

RECOMMENDED	PERFORMANCE	TESTERS' COMMENTS
J. A. HENCKELS INTERNATIONAL Kitchen Shears—Take Apart BEST BUY **MODEL:** 11517-100 **PRICE:** $14.95 **EXTRAS:** Jar and screw cap gripper, nutcracker **CLEANUP:** Separable blades. Dishwasher-safe. 	CUTTING: ★★★ COMFORT: ★★½	Cutting through branches of fresh rosemary or poultry bones felt effortless with these solid, sharp shears. Fine serrations on one side helped blades stay in place when breaking down a chicken. But the handles fit only three fingers, and the blade tension is not adjustable.
MESSERMEISTER 8-Inch Take-Apart Kitchen Shears **MODEL:** DN-2070 **PRICE:** $9.95 **EXTRAS:** Jar gripper, bottle opener, screwdriver, nutcracker **CLEANUP:** Separable blades. Dishwasher-safe.	CUTTING: ★★½ COMFORT: ★★★	The short blades on this ambidextrous model lack serrations, so they sometimes slid on slippery bones. Their separable blades fell apart unexpectedly when opened to as little as 90 degrees. Still, the rubbery handles are roomy and symmetrical, good for a variety of hand types.
WÜSTHOF Come-Apart Kitchen Shears **MODEL:** 5557 **PRICE:** $74.95 **EXTRAS:** Jar gripper, bottle opener, screwdriver, notch for cutting bones **CLEANUP:** Separable blades. Washing by hand recommended. 	CUTTING: ★★★ COMFORT: ★	Thanks to their heft and sharpness, these pricey shears butchered a chicken with powerful, sure strokes. A notch and serrated edge on one blade got a grip on bigger bones. But their weight (nearly a half pound) and blade-heavy balance wore some testers out, and tight stainless-steel handles felt slippery in greasy hands.

RECOMMENDED WITH RESERVATIONS	PERFORMANCE	TESTERS' COMMENTS
MESSERMEISTER Take-Apart Shears **MODEL:** DN-1070 **PRICE:** $14.95 **EXTRAS:** Jar gripper, bottle opener, screwdriver **CLEANUP:** Separable blades. Dishwasher-safe. 	CUTTING: ★★ COMFORT: ★★	These sharp, slim shears (our old favorite) felt secure thanks to rubber-wrapped handles for a comfortable, sure grip. Our gripes? The nonserrated blades sometimes slipped, and lefties found them unsatisfying, if not impossible, to use.
KUHN RIKON Household Shears **MODEL:** 2722 **PRICE:** $16 **EXTRAS:** Herb stripper, rounded "safety" blade tips **CLEANUP:** Separable blades. Washing by hand recommended.	CUTTING: ★★½ COMFORT: ★	These lightweight shears cleaved poultry bones easily thanks to ultra-fine serrations on one blade. However, the hard plastic-wrapped handles proved uncomfortable, the thumbhole pinched, and the tension (which is not adjustable) loosened slightly over the course of testing.

NOT RECOMMENDED	PERFORMANCE	TESTERS' COMMENTS
KUHN RIKON 8-Inch Kitchen Shears **MODEL:** 2705 **PRICE:** $19.99 **EXTRAS:** Bottle opener, herb stripper **CLEANUP:** Not separable. Dishwasher-safe.	CUTTING: ★★ COMFORT: ★	These shears are spring-loaded: The cutting action only involves squeezing them closed. Testers with large, strong hands found them liberating (no holes to shove your fingers into), but smaller, weaker testers struggled. A plastic safety sheath is necessary to keep them closed.

METAL AND PLASTIC SPATULAS

We recently tested nearly two dozen spatulas, both metal and plastic spatulas, from $2 to $38. We started the evaluations with a basic challenge: frying eggs in an 8-inch skillet. Shoveling—and breaking—the delicate eggs in such cramped quarters winnowed the lineup to 10 (five metal and five plastic); these graduated to tests with fresh-baked cookies, pans of lasagna, fluffy pancakes, and oversize hamburgers. To gauge heat resistance and strength, we then tried to melt them and even balance bricks on them. We prefer a spatula with a slim front edge that can easily slip under food. Also, a little stiffness in the spatula head was preferred; spatulas that were too flexible threatened to drop their contents. Both metal and plastic spatulas are listed in order of preference.

Metal Spatulas

HIGHLY RECOMMENDED	PERFORMANCE	TESTERS' COMMENTS
WÜSTHOF Gourmet Turner/Fish Spatula **MODEL:** 4433 **PRICE:** $34.95 **MATERIAL:** High-carbon stainless steel head **FRONT EDGE:** 0.83 mm	**PERFORMANCE:** ★★★ **DESIGN:** ★★★ **STRENGTH:** ★★★	For maneuverability, surgical precision, and crisp, high-end construction, this spatula could not be beat. It supported a 4-pound brick without the slightest slip, and its sharp, gently uptilted front edge could slip under anything and hold it in place.
OXO Good Grips Flexible Turner—Steel BEST BUY **MODEL:** 34491 **PRICE:** $7.99 **MATERIAL:** Spring-steel head **FRONT EDGE:** 0.2 mm	**PERFORMANCE:** ★★★ **DESIGN:** ★★★ **STRENGTH:** ★★½	This slim, gently angled turner looked flimsy, but excelled across the board. Its nicely proportioned head flexes up but not down, so it can support heavy lasagna and burgers (though it dropped the 4-pound brick like a hot potato).

RECOMMENDED	PERFORMANCE	TESTERS' COMMENTS
LAMSONSHARP 2-3-Inch x 4-Inch Flexible Flared Turner **MODEL:** 39546 **PRICE:** $25 **MATERIAL:** High-carbon stainless steel head **FRONT EDGE:** 0.67 mm	**PERFORMANCE:** ★★ **DESIGN:** ★★½ **STRENGTH:** ★★★	This sturdy turner hoisted the heaviest loads without a qualm. We liked its slim, squared-off front edge, which cut layers of pasta and cheese like a sharp knife. But "flexible" was a misnomer; it was too stiff to be our all-purpose pick.
WMF ProfiPlus 12¾-Inch Stainless Steel Slotted Turner **MODEL:** 1871056030 **PRICE:** $17.90 **MATERIAL:** 18/10 stainless steel **FRONT EDGE:** 0.53 mm	**PERFORMANCE:** ★★ **DESIGN:** ★★½ **STRENGTH:** ★★★	We liked this model's slim front edge and sturdy construction. But the curved front corners of the head were inconvenient for scraping a pan or cutting lasagna, and it was too long for perfect control.

Plastic Spatulas

HIGHLY RECOMMENDED	PERFORMANCE	TESTERS' COMMENTS
MATFER BOURGEAT Pelton Spatula **MODEL:** 112420 **PRICE:** $8.23 **MATERIAL:** Exoglass (polyamide plastic) **FRONT EDGE:** 0.92 mm	**PERFORMANCE:** ★★★ **DESIGN:** ★★★ **STRENGTH:** ★★★ **MELTING POINT:** ★★½	Comfortable from any angle, this spatula boasts a thin front edge and moderately flexible head with a slight upward tilt that kept food secure. It melted slightly at 380 degrees, despite the manufacturer's claim that it was heat resistant to 430 degrees.

RECOMMENDED WITH RESERVATIONS	PERFORMANCE	TESTERS' COMMENTS
OXO Good Grips Silicone Flexible Turner **MODEL:** 1071536 **PRICE:** $6.95 **MATERIAL:** Stainless steel head with silicone coating **FRONT EDGE:** 1.72 mm	**PERFORMANCE:** ★★ **DESIGN:** ★★ **STRENGTH:** ★★★ **MELTING POINT:** ★★★	Nicely proportioned, with a comfortable handle and angle similar to those of its steel sibling. The soft silicone coating was impervious to even searing heat—it withstood a temperature of 670 degrees—but made the head far too thick.
PYREX Flexible Turner **MODEL:** 1083742 **PRICE:** $8.95 **MATERIAL:** Nylon **FRONT EDGE:** 1.27 mm	**PERFORMANCE:** ★★ **DESIGN:** ★ **STRENGTH:** ★★★ **MELTING POINT:** ★★	In an 8-inch pan, this turner's super-wide head filled all available space. It also melted into stringy fibers at 353 degrees, despite the manufacturer's claim of 400 degrees. Still, it was nicely flexible and passed more tests than expected.

PARING KNIVES

There are numerous tasks we couldn't accomplish in the test kitchen without a paring knife in hand. From peeling apples and sectioning oranges to trimming away the silver skin on a roast, this small, easy-to-maneuver knife is essential for daily cooking chores. To find the best one, we gathered 10 models and subjected them to a range of tasks to determine their precision; ability to peel around curves; cutting ability, blade strength, and sharpness; user-friendliness and comfort level; and edge retention. In the end, the best paring knives had well-shaped blades with sharply pointed tips and narrow edges, a compact length, a good handle-to-blade balance and weight, and a comfortable grip that felt secure. Knives are listed in order of preference.

HIGHLY RECOMMENDED	PERFORMANCE	TESTERS' COMMENTS
WÜSTHOF Classic with PEtec, 3½-inch **MODEL:** 4066 **PRICE:** $39.95 **WEIGHT:** 2⅛ ounces	PRECISION: ★★★ PEELING: ★★★ CUTTING: ★★★ USER-FRIENDLINESS: ★★★ EDGE RETENTION: ★★½	This razor-sharp knife with "Precision Edge Technology—PEtec" was comfortable and well proportioned. A recent redesign gave it a narrower blade angle of 14 degrees (previously 19 degrees) on each side and a new plastic handle that feels like hard, smooth wood.
HENCKELS Four Star Paring Knife, 3-inch **MODEL:** 31070-080 (Note: -083 is same knife, packaged in box) **PRICE:** $24.99 **WEIGHT:** 1⅝ ounces	PRECISION: ★★★ PEELING: ★★★ CUTTING: ★★½ USER-FRIENDLINESS: ★★½ EDGE RETENTION: ★★★	This knife with a super-sharp edge and 15-degree blade angle would have tied with the winning Wusthof but for its slightly too short 3-inch blade. That said, most testers preferred its "grippier" handle, and our final paper-slicing test showed that it retained its edge a bit better than the Wüsthof.
VICTORINOX Fibrox Paring Knife, 3¼-inch BEST BUY **MODEL:** 40600 **PRICE:** $4.95 **WEIGHT:** ¾ ounce	PRECISION: ★★★ PEELING: ★★★ CUTTING: ★★★ USER-FRIENDLINESS: ★★ EDGE RETENTION: ★★½	At a fraction of the price of the top two knives, this sharp, precise blade is a real bargain—and feels more secure in the hand than its 4-inch sibling. Our only gripe? It's a featherweight compared with other models and feels a bit flimsy and plasticky.

RECOMMENDED	PERFORMANCE	TESTERS' COMMENTS
KUHN RIKON Paring Knife Colori I Nonstick, 3½-inch **MODEL:** 2808 **PRICE:** $10 **WEIGHT:** 1⅛ ounce (without sheath)	PRECISION: ★★ PEELING: ★★½ CUTTING: ★★★ USER-FRIENDLINESS: ★★½ EDGE RETENTION: ★★½	This inexpensive, lightweight knife was comfortable to hold and came with a snug sheath. Its stiff, nonstick-coated blade felt a bit unwieldy for intricate tasks—and the coating itself was generally superfluous—but the cutting edge was razor-sharp and slid through shallots with ease.
DEXTER-RUSSELL V-Lo Paring Knife, 3½-inch **MODEL:** V105-CP **PRICE:** $7.30 **WEIGHT:** ¾ ounce	PRECISION: ★★ PEELING: ★★ CUTTING: ★★ USER-FRIENDLINESS: ★★½ EDGE RETENTION: ★★	While we appreciated this knife's sharp blade, the ribbed, slim-waisted plastic handle and extreme lightweight design divided testers' votes: Those with small hands deemed it "a pleasure to hold," while those with large hands felt that it was "too insubstantial" and "like a toy."
VICTORINOX Fibrox Paring Knife, 4-inch **MODEL:** 40501 **PRICE:** $4.95 **WEIGHT:** ¾ ounce	PRECISION: ★ PEELING: ★★½ CUTTING: ★★½ USER-FRIENDLINESS: ★★ EDGE RETENTION: ★★½	"Nice, sharp" blade. But while the extra ¾ inch on this larger Victorinox twin came in handy for slicing fruit and cheese, it was too much metal for most testers, who complained that the elongated blade felt unwieldy during intricate tasks like hulling berries.

RECOMMENDED WITH RESERVATIONS	PERFORMANCE	TESTERS' COMMENTS
SHUN Classic Paring Knife, 3½-inch **MODEL:** DM0700 **PRICE:** $70 **WEIGHT:** 2⅛ ounces	PRECISION: ★½ PEELING: ★★½ CUTTING: ★★★ USER-FRIENDLINESS: ★ EDGE RETENTION: ★★½	Though wonderfully sharp, this knife was handle-heavy and slick, making it awkward for hand-held cutting tasks like berry hulling. And at nearly twice the cost of our winner—and 14 times the cost of our Best Buy—we just couldn't bring ourselves to shell out for it.

2-SLOT TOASTERS

We wanted a toaster that could make golden-brown toast—and make it snappy. We tried out seven 2-slice toasters priced from $30 to almost $70, toasting dozens of loaves of bread (and piles of toaster pastries, frozen waffles, and bagels). It was quickly evident that not every model was adept at the basic function of making evenly toasted bread and doing so quickly. Most machines toasted single slices of bread unevenly because both slots heat up no matter if you only want one slice; when we made two slices at once, bread emerged more evenly toasted. As for speed, few contenders in our lineup managed to perform quickly and also produce acceptable toast; most couldn't do both. Toasters are listed in order of preference.

RECOMMENDED	PERFORMANCE	TESTERS' COMMENTS
KALORIK Aqua 2-Slice Toaster MODEL: TO20621 PRICE: $59.99 EXTRAS: Bagel, defrost, reheat	SPEED: ★★ EVENNESS: ★★ DESIGN: ★★★ FLAW: None	An all-around good toaster, reliably producing acceptably even toast in just over 2½ minutes. The controls are well marked and intuitive. Glass plates keep the exterior cool.
RECOMMENDED WITH RESERVATIONS	**PERFORMANCE**	**TESTERS' COMMENTS**
CUISINART Countdown Metal 2-Slice Toaster MODEL: CPT-170 PRICE: $69.95 EXTRAS: Bagel, countdown timer, defrost, reheat	SPEED: ★★★ EVENNESS: ★★ DESIGN: ★★ FLAW: Exterior too hot	One of the fastest toasters, at the cost of minor inconsistency between the sides of the toast with one slice; the problem disappeared when both slots were used. One big drawback: The exterior hit a scorching 155 degrees.
BLACK & DECKER 2-Slice Toaster MODEL: T2707S PRICE: $34.99 EXTRAS: Bagel, defrost	SPEED: ★ EVENNESS: ★★ DESIGN: ★★★ FLAW: Too slow	This toaster made perfect toast, but took over a minute longer than some—not bad, until you're running late for work. To get golden toast we had to crank it to the darkest setting, so dark toast was out of the question; the lightest setting merely dried the bread. On the plus side, the exterior stayed cool.
NOT RECOMMENDED	**PERFORMANCE**	**TESTERS' COMMENTS**
HAMILTON BEACH Digital 2-Slice Toaster MODEL: 22502 PRICE: $50 EXTRAS: Bagel, defrost	SPEED: ★★★ EVENNESS: ★ DESIGN: ★★ FATAL FLAW: Uneven toast	Our fastest model was excellent 80 percent of the time, but it was inconsistent, sometimes burning, other times not toasting at all. As testing went on, we found ever-greater color discrepancy between the two sides of toast, and we measured a nearly 100-degree difference in the heating elements.
KRUPS 2-Slice Toaster MODEL: TT6190 PRICE: $59.99 EXTRAS: Bagel, countdown timer, defrost	SPEED: ★ EVENNESS: ★★★ DESIGN: ★★ FATAL FLAW: Slots too small	This toaster had the most even heating, with only a few degrees' difference between the two sides. But it was also one of the slowest. Its controls and countdown timer were easy to interpret. But the slots were too short to fit sandwich bread.
T-FAL AVANTÉ Classic 2-Slice Toaster MODEL: 8746002 PRICE: $29.99 EXTRAS: Bagel, "hi-lift" lever, reheat	SPEED: ★★ EVENNESS: ★★ DESIGN: ★ FATAL FLAW: Slots too small	It boasted fairly even heating and a stay-cool exterior, but the slots were too short for sandwich bread. It lacked a "defrost" setting, which we prefer for frozen waffles or bread. The second lever, to raise hot toast, was superfluous.
WEST BEND 2-Slice Stainless Steel Toaster MODEL: 78002 PRICE: $41.99 EXTRAS: Bagel, defrost, reheat	SPEED: ★★ EVENNESS: ★ DESIGN: ★ FATAL FLAW: Uneven toast	Its steel exterior hit a whopping 144 degrees; the interior heated one side more than 100 degrees hotter than the other, producing very uneven toast. Even on "high," this toaster struggled to color the bread.

TOASTER OVENS

Toaster ovens have come a long way. Many now offer a slew of additional features, such as the ability to act as food dehydrator, bun warmer, or chicken rotisserie, and have the price tag to match. We tested 10 toaster ovens, ranging in price from $60 to a staggering $250, to find the best one. We made single slices of toast (using white bread) on medium and dark settings to evaluate their ability to make toast. We also toasted multiple batches of six slices to evaluate the heating patterns in the ovens. To test cooking performance, we baked lemon cookies, melted cheese on sandwiches, heated frozen pizzas and macaroni and cheese, and roasted chickens. To gauge accuracy, we used a thermocouple to judge how well empty ovens held the standard temperature of 350 degrees. Finally, we considered design and usability. Toaster ovens are listed in order of preference.

HIGHLY RECOMMENDED	PERFORMANCE	TESTERS' COMMENTS
The Smart Oven by BREVILLE **MODEL:** BOV800 XL **PRICE:** $249.95	TOASTING: ★★★ COOKING: ★★★ USER-FRIENDLINESS: ★★★ ACCURACY: ★★★	While the price makes us wince, this well-designed oven aced every test and was simple to use. Food browned and cooked uniformly, whether we were roasting chicken, toasting bread, or melting cheese. Five quartz elements consistently cooled and reheated, producing steady, controlled heat.
RECOMMENDED	**PERFORMANCE**	**TESTERS' COMMENTS**
HAMILTON BEACH Set & Forget Toaster Oven with Convection Cooking BEST BUY **MODEL:** 31230 **PRICE:** $99.99	TOASTING: ★★★ COOKING: ★★ USER-FRIENDLINESS: ★★★ ACCURACY: ★★	Clearly designed control buttons, a helpful electronic display, and an easy-to-understand manual made using this oven a snap. Not quite as accurate as our winner, it still produced golden-brown toast and crisp-skinned roast chicken. Pizza and cookies baked a tiny bit unevenly. We liked its meat probe.
RECOMMENDED WITH RESERVATIONS	**PERFORMANCE**	**TESTERS' COMMENTS**
BLACK & DECKER Digital Convection Oven **MODEL:** CTO6305 **PRICE:** $89.99	TOASTING: ★★★ COOKING: ★★ USER-FRIENDLINESS: ★★★ ACCURACY: ★	This oven's performance was acceptable but a little uneven. Its elements cycled far lower when we set it for 350 degrees. Cookies and chicken browned unevenly, though mac and cheese and pizza were fine; toast was terrific with one slice but a little patchy in multiple batches.
KRUPS 6-Slice Convection Toaster Oven **MODEL:** FBC2 **PRICE:** $149.99	TOASTING: ★ COOKING: ★★ USER-FRIENDLINESS: ★★★ ACCURACY: ★★	A more pared-down version of our previous winner from Krups, which was discontinued, this oven just doesn't measure up to new competition. Ironically, the earlier Krups made decent toast. This time, single slices of toast were its biggest downfall, coloring too much or barely at all.
DUALIT Professional Mini Oven **MODEL:** 89100 **PRICE:** $249.95	TOASTING: ★★ COOKING: ★★★ USER-FRIENDLINESS: ★★ ACCURACY: ★	Solidly built and simple to set, this pricey oven was well lit with a large window—a good thing, since testing confirmed that it ran so hot (cycling as high as 428 degrees when we wanted 350) that we usually had to stand by, ready to yank out the food early, before it overcooked. Still, it cooked evenly and well.
OSTER 6081 Channel 6-Slice Toaster Oven **MODEL:** 6801 **PRICE:** $58.01	TOASTING: ★★★ COOKING: ★★ USER-FRIENDLINESS: ★ ACCURACY: ★★	This was the cheapest model in the lineup, and its slightly tinny feel and badly designed controls made that clear: Knobs are labeled underneath and hard to set without stooping; settings are printed in low-contrast color. But its heat was relatively accurate and the cooking, including toast, was surprisingly above par.
NOT RECOMMENDED	**PERFORMANCE**	**TESTERS' COMMENTS**
CUISINART Convection Toaster Oven **MODEL:** TOB-195 **PRICE:** $179	TOASTING: ★★ COOKING: ★★ USER-FRIENDLINESS: ★★ ACCURACY: ★	Toast turned out light when we wanted it medium or dark, plus it always colored unevenly. Cookies, pizza, and tuna melts also came out with darker patches where they'd been under the elements. Chicken cooked well but made a smoky, greasy mess. Its controls (with 16 buttons!) required multiple steps.

INEXPENSIVE NONSTICK SKILLETS

No matter how gently you treat your nonstick skillet, scratches will eventually mar the pan's surface or the nonstick will wear off, which is why we recommend not spending a ton of money on this pan. To find the best inexpensive nonstick skillet, we tested eight contenders under $60 against our longtime favorite, the All-Clad Stainless 12-Inch Nonstick Frying Pan, $129.99. We tested the nonstick effectiveness of each pan by frying eggs (and recording how many eggs released before sticking occurred) and stir-frying beef and vegetables. To see which pans cooked food evenly and were sizable but easy to maneuver, we made crêpes and frittatas in each. The All-Clad is still a solidly built pan, but we found a winner that cost a fraction of the price. Skillets are listed in order of preference.

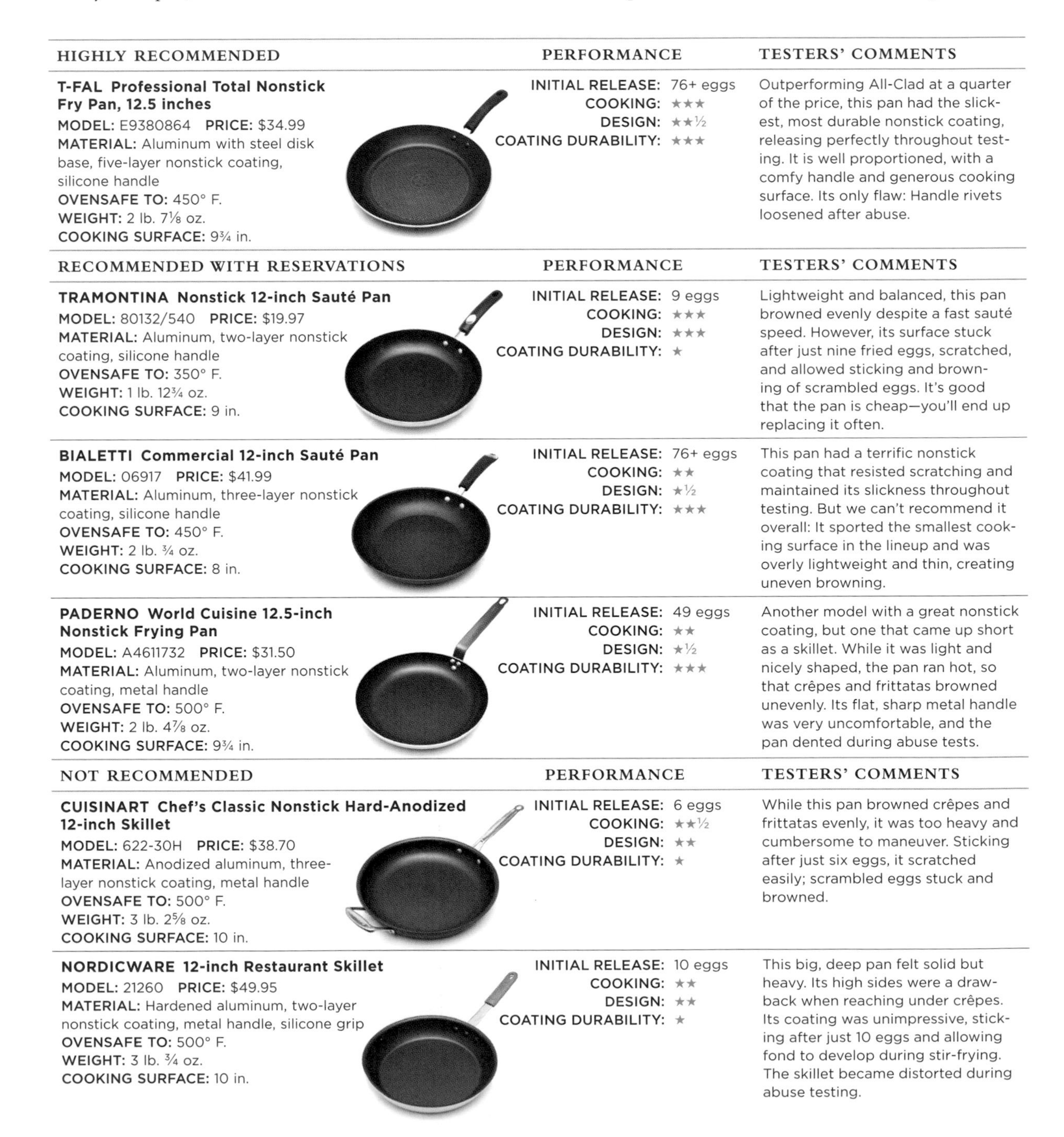

HIGHLY RECOMMENDED	PERFORMANCE	TESTERS' COMMENTS
T-FAL Professional Total Nonstick Fry Pan, 12.5 inches **MODEL:** E9380864 **PRICE:** $34.99 **MATERIAL:** Aluminum with steel disk base, five-layer nonstick coating, silicone handle **OVENSAFE TO:** 450° F. **WEIGHT:** 2 lb. 7⅛ oz. **COOKING SURFACE:** 9¾ in.	INITIAL RELEASE: 76+ eggs COOKING: ★★★ DESIGN: ★★½ COATING DURABILITY: ★★★	Outperforming All-Clad at a quarter of the price, this pan had the slickest, most durable nonstick coating, releasing perfectly throughout testing. It is well proportioned, with a comfy handle and generous cooking surface. Its only flaw: Handle rivets loosened after abuse.
RECOMMENDED WITH RESERVATIONS	**PERFORMANCE**	**TESTERS' COMMENTS**
TRAMONTINA Nonstick 12-inch Sauté Pan **MODEL:** 80132/540 **PRICE:** $19.97 **MATERIAL:** Aluminum, two-layer nonstick coating, silicone handle **OVENSAFE TO:** 350° F. **WEIGHT:** 1 lb. 12¾ oz. **COOKING SURFACE:** 9 in.	INITIAL RELEASE: 9 eggs COOKING: ★★★ DESIGN: ★★★ COATING DURABILITY: ★	Lightweight and balanced, this pan browned evenly despite a fast sauté speed. However, its surface stuck after just nine fried eggs, scratched, and allowed sticking and browning of scrambled eggs. It's good that the pan is cheap—you'll end up replacing it often.
BIALETTI Commercial 12-inch Sauté Pan **MODEL:** 06917 **PRICE:** $41.99 **MATERIAL:** Aluminum, three-layer nonstick coating, silicone handle **OVENSAFE TO:** 450° F. **WEIGHT:** 2 lb. ¾ oz. **COOKING SURFACE:** 8 in.	INITIAL RELEASE: 76+ eggs COOKING: ★★ DESIGN: ★½ COATING DURABILITY: ★★★	This pan had a terrific nonstick coating that resisted scratching and maintained its slickness throughout testing. But we can't recommend it overall: It sported the smallest cooking surface in the lineup and was overly lightweight and thin, creating uneven browning.
PADERNO World Cuisine 12.5-inch Nonstick Frying Pan **MODEL:** A4611732 **PRICE:** $31.50 **MATERIAL:** Aluminum, two-layer nonstick coating, metal handle **OVENSAFE TO:** 500° F. **WEIGHT:** 2 lb. 4⅞ oz. **COOKING SURFACE:** 9¾ in.	INITIAL RELEASE: 49 eggs COOKING: ★★ DESIGN: ★½ COATING DURABILITY: ★★★	Another model with a great nonstick coating, but one that came up short as a skillet. While it was light and nicely shaped, the pan ran hot, so that crêpes and frittatas browned unevenly. Its flat, sharp metal handle was very uncomfortable, and the pan dented during abuse tests.
NOT RECOMMENDED	**PERFORMANCE**	**TESTERS' COMMENTS**
CUISINART Chef's Classic Nonstick Hard-Anodized 12-inch Skillet **MODEL:** 622-30H **PRICE:** $38.70 **MATERIAL:** Anodized aluminum, three-layer nonstick coating, metal handle **OVENSAFE TO:** 500° F. **WEIGHT:** 3 lb. 2⅝ oz. **COOKING SURFACE:** 10 in.	INITIAL RELEASE: 6 eggs COOKING: ★★½ DESIGN: ★★ COATING DURABILITY: ★	While this pan browned crêpes and frittatas evenly, it was too heavy and cumbersome to maneuver. Sticking after just six eggs, it scratched easily; scrambled eggs stuck and browned.
NORDICWARE 12-inch Restaurant Skillet **MODEL:** 21260 **PRICE:** $49.95 **MATERIAL:** Hardened aluminum, two-layer nonstick coating, metal handle, silicone grip **OVENSAFE TO:** 500° F. **WEIGHT:** 3 lb. ¾ oz. **COOKING SURFACE:** 10 in.	INITIAL RELEASE: 10 eggs COOKING: ★★ DESIGN: ★★ COATING DURABILITY: ★	This big, deep pan felt solid but heavy. Its high sides were a drawback when reaching under crêpes. Its coating was unimpressive, sticking after just 10 eggs and allowing fond to develop during stir-frying. The skillet became distorted during abuse testing.

PORTABLE CHARCOAL GRILLS

Whether you grill for two, take your grilling on the road, or just lack the space for a full-size grill, a portable charcoal grill offers the smoky flavors of charcoal grilling in a convenient size. Portable grills come in two styles: Small kettle grills and collapsible models. We gathered six portable grills, priced from $20 to $140, and tested them with burgers, flank steak, and butterflied chickens. Some models were cumbersome to dismantle and transport; others were too heavy. We came to appreciate lightweight grills that didn't require assembly every time we wanted to cook. We preferred grills that fit at least six burgers and three-quarters of a chimney's worth of briquettes; a raised lip also helped, as it kept food from falling off. Grills are listed in order of preference.

HIGHLY RECOMMENDED		PERFORMANCE	TESTERS' COMMENTS
WEBER Smokey Joe Gold **MODEL:** 40020 **PRICE:** $34.70 **COAL CAPACITY:** ¾ chimney **COOKING SURFACE:** Round, 13½ inches in diameter		**COOKING:** ★★★ **PORTABILITY:** ★★ **DURABILITY:** ★★★ **DESIGN:** ★★★	This smaller version of our favorite Weber One Touch Gold Charcoal Grill shares many of its attributes. The ample cooking surface fit six to eight burgers at a time or a 1½-pound flank steak. The domed cover allowed us to grill-roast a butterflied chicken perfectly. Adjustable vents on the cover and on opposite sides of the grill's body gave us plenty of control over the fire.

RECOMMENDED		PERFORMANCE	TESTERS' COMMENTS
FYRKAT Charcoal Picnic Grill by BODUM **MODEL:** 10630 **PRICE:** $49.95 **COAL CAPACITY:** ¾ chimney **COOKING SURFACE:** Round, 13¾ inches in diameter		**COOKING:** ★★½ **PORTABILITY:** ★★ **DURABILITY:** ★★★ **DESIGN:** ★★½	Compact and lightweight for easy transport, this colorful little grill is similar in design to our winner. While the cooking surface easily accommodated a whole butterflied chicken, the lid's dome was too shallow for it. But for high-heat grilling, such as steaks and burgers, this grill performed as well as the winner.

RECOMMENDED WITH RESERVATIONS		PERFORMANCE	TESTERS' COMMENTS
LODGE LOGIC Sportsman's Grill **MODEL:** L410 **PRICE:** $139.95 **COAL CAPACITY:** ¾ chimney **COOKING SURFACE:** 17½ by 9-inch oval		**COOKING:** ★★½ **PORTABILITY:** ★ **DURABILITY:** ★★★ **DESIGN:** ★★	This grill easily fit six burgers but was a little too narrow to accommodate a butterflied chicken. We couldn't grill-roast, either, because the grill has no cover. We did, however, like the draft door to regulate heat, and a flip-down door made it easy to access coals. Made entirely of cast iron, this grill seared beautifully. If only it didn't weigh 32 pounds.
SON OF HIBACHI **MODEL:** B003G73SBW **PRICE:** $69.99 **COAL CAPACITY:** ½ chimney **COOKING SURFACE:** Two 10 by 8-inch rectangles		**COOKING:** ★½ **PORTABILITY:** ★★★ **DURABILITY:** ★★★ **DESIGN:** ★	This grill is a chimney starter and a grill in one: Fill it with coals and use it as a chimney when folded; unfold it to reveal two adjustable cast-iron grates, albeit very small ones. When you're done, fold it up and place the hot grill in its heat-resistant snuff-out pouch—very clever. Unfortunately, this grill held the fewest briquettes and could not fit a whole chicken, nor does it have a cover. Only for small batches of food.
FIRE SENSE Hotspot Notebook Portable Charcoal Grill **MODEL:** 60508 **PRICE:** $27 **COAL CAPACITY:** Full chimney **COOKING SURFACE:** Rectangular, 17 by 12¾ inches		**COOKING:** ★★ **PORTABILITY:** ★★★ **DURABILITY:** ★ **DESIGN:** ★	This grill stands 13½ inches tall but collapses to just 1 inch thick. It has plenty of cooking surface and a high coal capacity, and it easily fit eight burgers. But it doesn't have a cover, making it ill suited for anything other than high-heat grilling, nor does it have a lip, so we found ourselves chasing burgers off the edge of the grill. This model dented and warped during testing.

NOT RECOMMENDED		PERFORMANCE	TESTERS' COMMENTS
BAYOU Classic Fold and Go Charcoal Grill **MODEL:** 400-402 **PRICE:** $20.43 **COAL CAPACITY:** Full chimney **COOKING SURFACE:** Rectangular, 19¼ by 14¼ inches		**COOKING:** ★ **PORTABILITY:** ★★★ **DURABILITY:** ★ **DESIGN:** ★	This grill has the largest cooking surface of all the grills we tested, but no lip or lid. It folds down to just 2½ inches wide, but all the hinges required to collapse it proved cumbersome. More than once, the sides buckled while we were cooking, making the grilling surface unsteady (to say the least). What's more, the grill's sharp edges tore the carrying case.

FOOD PROCESSORS

We've gladly paid top dollar for our favorite food processor, the KitchenAid 12-Cup Food Processor, which costs $180. It slices and chops evenly, cleanly, and quickly and boasts a compact, intuitive design. To find out if any new contenders could beat our favorite, we tested seven models alongside the KitchenAid. A good food processor should have a razor-sharp blade and perform certain core tasks—shredding, chopping, slicing, and grinding—with ease. The ideal machine should also be able to whip up batches of dough—both pastry and pizza—and mayonnaise. After putting each machine through its paces, we came back to our established winner as the one to beat. Food processors are listed in order of preference.

HIGHLY RECOMMENDED	PERFORMANCE	TESTERS' COMMENTS
KITCHENAID 12-Cup Food Processor **MODEL:** KFP750 **PRICE:** $179.99 **BOWL CAPACITIES:** 12 and 4 cups	 GRATING/SLICING: ★★★ CHOPPING: ★★★ GRINDING: ★★★ PASTRY: ★★★ PIZZA DOUGH: ★★ MAYONNAISE: ★★★ EASE OF USE: ★★★ CLEANUP: ★★★	Still the one to beat. It's simple to operate, powerful, moderately priced, and offers ample capacity in an intuitive, compact design. The 4-cup mini bowl is essential for small jobs like whipping mayonnaise and mincing herbs. We disliked the dough blade, finding the regular metal blade far more effective.
RECOMMENDED	**PERFORMANCE**	**TESTERS' COMMENTS**
VIKING Food Processor, 12-Cup **MODEL:** VFP12BR **PRICE:** $334.95 **BOWL CAPACITIES:** 12 and 3 cups	 GRATING/SLICING: ★★ CHOPPING: ★★★ GRINDING: ★★ PASTRY: ★★★ PIZZA DOUGH: ★★★ MAYONNAISE: ★★★ EASE OF USE: ★★★ CLEANUP: ★★	Quiet and powerful, this model rivaled the KitchenAid almost across the board (and bested it in the pizza dough test). But its steep price was a deterrent, as was the manufacturer's recommendation to hand-wash each component. (Note: The bowls and blades emerged unscathed from one dishwasher cycle.) Wheels on the rear of the base are a nice plus for moving it around.
CUISINART Custom 14-Cup Food Processor **MODEL:** DFP-14BCN **PRICE:** $199 **BOWL CAPACITY:** 14 cups	 GRATING/SLICING: ★★ CHOPPING: ★★ GRINDING: ★★ PASTRY: ★★★ PIZZA DOUGH: ★★★ MAYONNAISE: ★★★ EASE OF USE: ★★★ CLEANUP: ★★★	We developed a real appreciation for this user-friendly classic, but came away with a couple of quibbles. First, precutting vegetables into 1-inch chunks (per the manufacturer's recommendation) was tedious, and even then the results were uneven. Second, its feed tube was short—too short for a russet potato, which had to be trimmed extensively to fit into the chute (though once trimmed, the potato sliced perfectly).
RECOMMENDED WITH RESERVATIONS	**PERFORMANCE**	**TESTERS' COMMENTS**
CUISINART Elite Collection 14-Cup Food Processor **MODEL:** FP-14DC **PRICE:** $235.37 **BOWL CAPACITIES:** 14, 11, and 4 cups	 GRATING/SLICING: ★★ CHOPPING: ★★ GRINDING: ★★ PASTRY: ★★★ PIZZA DOUGH: ★★★ MAYONNAISE: ★★ EASE OF USE: ★★ CLEANUP: ★★	Cuisinart's much-anticipated new release may pack power (good for pizza dough), heft, and plenty of extra bowls, but it didn't do anything better than the cheaper, simpler, more compact KitchenAid. Mayonnaise never came out perfectly emulsified, and chopped carrots emerged accompanied by wasted end pieces. The leakproof rubber gasket "SealTight" lid constantly trapped food bits.
HAMILTON BEACH Big Mouth Deluxe 14-Cup **MODEL:** 70575 **PRICE:** $99.99 **BOWL CAPACITY:** 14 cups	 GRATING/SLICING: ★★ CHOPPING: ★★ GRINDING: ★★ PASTRY: ★★★ PIZZA DOUGH: ★★ MAYONNAISE: ★★★ EASE OF USE: ★★ CLEANUP: ★★	On the one hand, this machine's well-labeled blades and lock/unlock indications made it easy to use. (Other brands constantly left us guessing.) On the other, its wide-mouth feed tube was overcomplicated with pop-up lids and double-barreled inserts that were somewhat hard to clean. Performance-wise, it was generally fair across the board.
OMEGA Professional Food Processor, 11-Cup **MODEL:** O660 **PRICE:** $179.95 **BOWL CAPACITIES:** 11 and 4 cups	 GRATING/SLICING: ★★ CHOPPING: ★★ GRINDING: ★★★ PASTRY: ★★ PIZZA DOUGH: ★ MAYONNAISE: ★★★ EASE OF USE: ★★ CLEANUP: ★★★	This model almost cloned the KitchenAid in looks and price—but not performance. Though it turned out perfect bread crumbs, nuts, and mayonnaise, it strained with a double batch of pizza dough. Plus, the curve of its kidney-shaped feed tube was so subtle that we mistakenly put the pusher in backward more than once.

SLOW COOKERS

The winner of our previous slow-cooker testing, made by All-Clad, costs nearly $200. We recently pitted it against six new, less expensive models to see if we could save money without sacrificing performance. We limited our lineup mainly to oval cookers, which can fit a large roast, with capacities of 6 quarts or more, and judged the cookers on design and performance. Six models had programmable timers and warming modes, features we like. We also liked clear glass lids to assess the food as it cooks. Ideally, a slow cooker should produce perfect results on all settings. But when we made pot roast, meaty tomato sauce, and French onion soup, some models variously gave us pot roast with dry, tough meat or juicy, sliceable meat, tomato sauces that were extra-thick or thin and watery, and soup with burnt onions or nicely browned onions. We devised a test to measure the maximum temperatures of the models on high and low settings and found that some just didn't get hot enough, whereas others reached the boiling point; the best models fell somewhere in between. Slow cookers are listed in order of preference.

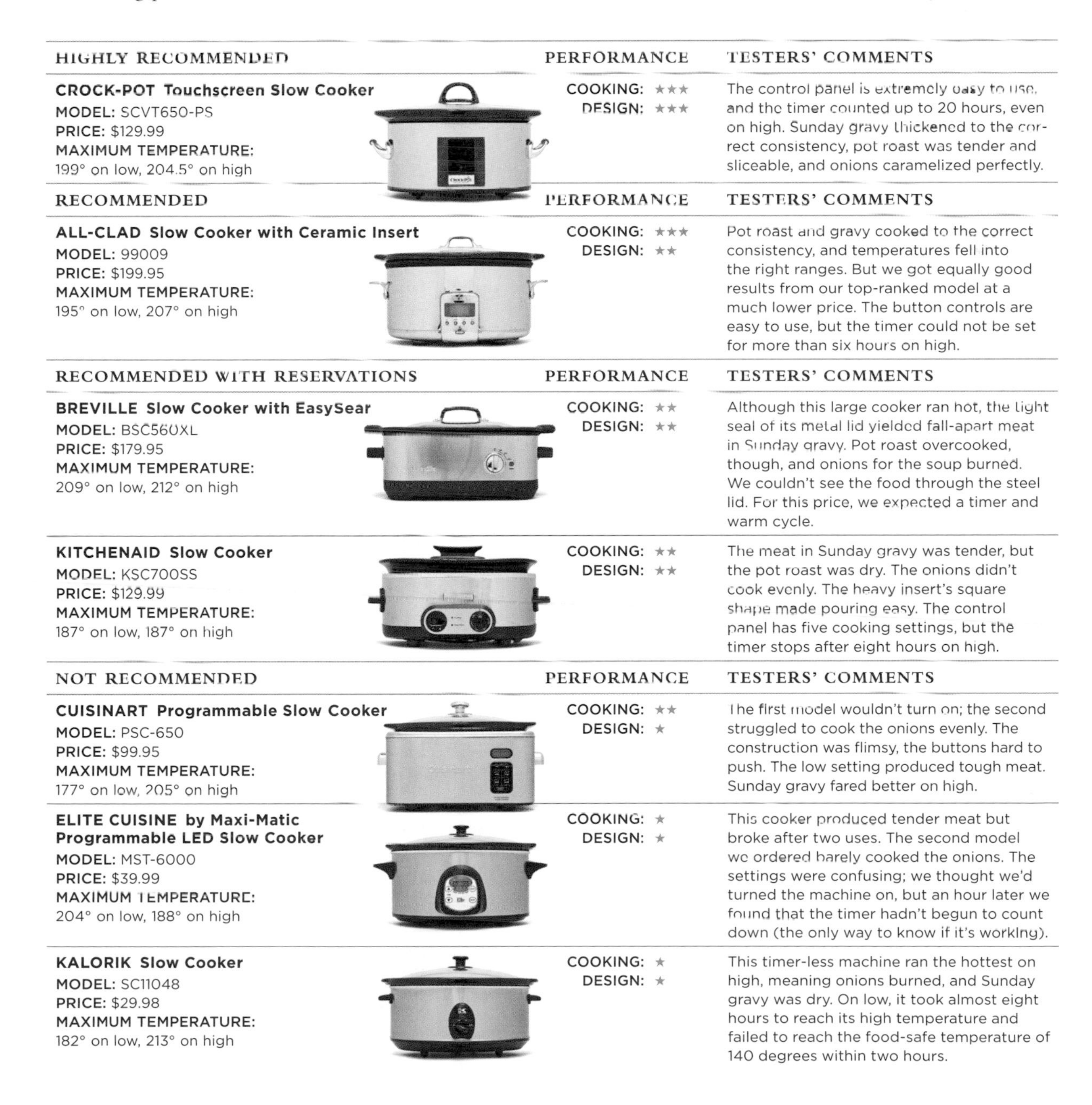

HIGHLY RECOMMENDED	PERFORMANCE	TESTERS' COMMENTS
CROCK-POT Touchscreen Slow Cooker **MODEL:** SCVT650-PS **PRICE:** $129.99 **MAXIMUM TEMPERATURE:** 199° on low, 204.5° on high	**COOKING:** ★★★ **DESIGN:** ★★★	The control panel is extremely easy to use, and the timer counted up to 20 hours, even on high. Sunday gravy thickened to the correct consistency, pot roast was tender and sliceable, and onions caramelized perfectly.
RECOMMENDED	**PERFORMANCE**	**TESTERS' COMMENTS**
ALL-CLAD Slow Cooker with Ceramic Insert **MODEL:** 99009 **PRICE:** $199.95 **MAXIMUM TEMPERATURE:** 195° on low, 207° on high	**COOKING:** ★★★ **DESIGN:** ★★	Pot roast and gravy cooked to the correct consistency, and temperatures fell into the right ranges. But we got equally good results from our top-ranked model at a much lower price. The button controls are easy to use, but the timer could not be set for more than six hours on high.
RECOMMENDED WITH RESERVATIONS	**PERFORMANCE**	**TESTERS' COMMENTS**
BREVILLE Slow Cooker with EasySear **MODEL:** BSC560XL **PRICE:** $179.95 **MAXIMUM TEMPERATURE:** 209° on low, 212° on high	**COOKING:** ★★ **DESIGN:** ★★	Although this large cooker ran hot, the tight seal of its metal lid yielded fall-apart meat in Sunday gravy. Pot roast overcooked, though, and onions for the soup burned. We couldn't see the food through the steel lid. For this price, we expected a timer and warm cycle.
KITCHENAID Slow Cooker **MODEL:** KSC700SS **PRICE:** $129.99 **MAXIMUM TEMPERATURE:** 187° on low, 187° on high	**COOKING:** ★★ **DESIGN:** ★★	The meat in Sunday gravy was tender, but the pot roast was dry. The onions didn't cook evenly. The heavy insert's square shape made pouring easy. The control panel has five cooking settings, but the timer stops after eight hours on high.
NOT RECOMMENDED	**PERFORMANCE**	**TESTERS' COMMENTS**
CUISINART Programmable Slow Cooker **MODEL:** PSC-650 **PRICE:** $99.95 **MAXIMUM TEMPERATURE:** 177° on low, 205° on high	**COOKING:** ★★ **DESIGN:** ★	The first model wouldn't turn on; the second struggled to cook the onions evenly. The construction was flimsy, the buttons hard to push. The low setting produced tough meat. Sunday gravy fared better on high.
ELITE CUISINE by Maxi-Matic Programmable LED Slow Cooker **MODEL:** MST-6000 **PRICE:** $39.99 **MAXIMUM TEMPERATURE:** 204° on low, 188° on high	**COOKING:** ★ **DESIGN:** ★	This cooker produced tender meat but broke after two uses. The second model we ordered barely cooked the onions. The settings were confusing; we thought we'd turned the machine on, but an hour later we found that the timer hadn't begun to count down (the only way to know if it's working).
KALORIK Slow Cooker **MODEL:** SC11048 **PRICE:** $29.98 **MAXIMUM TEMPERATURE:** 182° on low, 213° on high	**COOKING:** ★ **DESIGN:** ★	This timer-less machine ran the hottest on high, meaning onions burned, and Sunday gravy was dry. On low, it took almost eight hours to reach its high temperature and failed to reach the food-safe temperature of 140 degrees within two hours.

BROILER-SAFE BAKING DISHES

Many casseroles prepared in 13 by 9-inch pans are finished under the broiler. But our favorite pan with these dimensions, the Pyrex Bakeware 13 by 9-inch Baking Dish, shouldn't go under the broiler; abrupt temperature changes can cause it to crack or shatter. We gathered seven rectangular broiler-safe baking dishes, looking for a sturdy stand-in, and prepared baked scrod and Chantilly Potatoes. We tested two dishes made of enameled cast iron and five made of ceramic, including two of porcelain, which is lighter, harder, and less porous than many other ceramics. Lightweight porcelain dishes were preferred, as they were easy to carry, even when full. Large, easy-to-grip handles were helpful, and straight sides ensured that the capacity of the baking dish wasn't cut short. Baking dishes are listed in order of preference.

HIGHLY RECOMMENDED	PERFORMANCE	TESTERS' COMMENTS
HIC Porcelain Lasagna Baking Dish **MODEL:** SKU 02-1228-48 **PRICE:** $37.49 **MATERIAL:** Porcelain **SIZE:** 3 quarts **WEIGHT:** 4.35 lbs.	COOKING: ★★★ DESIGN: ★★★	This porcelain baking dish has large handles for secure gripping and straight sides for easy serving. It's deep enough for Chantilly Potatoes, but not so large that the butter burned as we broiled scrod. Finally, it was not too heavy, even filled with potatoes.
RECOMMENDED	**PERFORMANCE**	**TESTERS' COMMENTS**
EMILE HENRY Lasagna Dish **MODEL:** 379632 **PRICE:** $66 **MATERIAL:** Ceramic **SIZE:** 3.8 quarts **WEIGHT:** 5.1 lbs.	COOKING: ★★★ DESIGN: ★★	Potatoes and scrod broiled perfectly in this well-proportioned pan. The dish was easy to transport and clean (although we would have preferred larger handles), and the food came out cleanly from the straight sides.
RECOMMENDED WITH RESERVATIONS	**PERFORMANCE**	**TESTERS' COMMENTS**
LE CREUSET Small Roaster **MODEL:** L2011-3071 **PRICE:** $124.95 **MATERIAL:** Enameled Cast Iron **SIZE:** 2.5 quarts **WEIGHT:** 6.7 lbs.	COOKING: ★★ DESIGN: ★★	Small but hefty, this dish cooked everything evenly and managed to contain the full batch of Chantilly Potatoes. But the combination of narrow handles and cast-iron weight made it difficult to safely slide out from under the broiler.
PILLIVUYT Large Rectangular Baker **MODEL:** 220335 BL **PRICE:** $56.95 **MATERIAL:** Porcelain **SIZE:** 3 quarts **WEIGHT:** 3.3 lbs.	COOKING: ★★ DESIGN: ★★	Small and lightweight, this porcelain dish had thin walls and shallow sides. It was easy to carry and cooked food beautifully. But its curled handles were too small to grip properly with oven mitts—our thumbs ended up in food.
NOT RECOMMENDED	**PERFORMANCE**	**TESTERS' COMMENTS**
CUISINART Chef's Classic Enameled Cast Iron 14-inch Roasting/Lasagna Pan **MODEL:** CI1136-24CR **PRICE:** $59.95 **MATERIAL:** Enameled Cast Iron **SIZE:** 3 quarts **WEIGHT:** 10.5 lbs.	COOKING: ★★ DESIGN: ★	This enameled cast-iron baking dish was the biggest and heftiest of the bunch. Lifting it when it was filled with Chantilly Potatoes was a chore. It was just too unwieldy. Also, although the pan cooked well, the food was too spread out, so we had to pull it out of the oven earlier than expected.
ESPRIT DE CUISINE By Appolia Baking Dish **MODEL:** 540/360A **PRICE:** $60 **MATERIAL:** Ceramic **SIZE:** 3 quarts **WEIGHT:** 4.25 lbs.	COOKING: ★★ DESIGN: ★	The angled-in sides pinched capacity, so the dish was cramped. While the dimensions around the top rim were similar to other dishes', the bottom of the dish measured only 10¼ by 5½ inches. The wavy edge looked nice but made serving difficult.
PIRAL Rectangular Baking Dish **MODEL:** RT320BLCR **PRICE:** $54.95 **MATERIAL:** Terra Cotta **SIZE:** 3 quarts **WEIGHT:** 3.3 lbs.	COOKING: ★★ DESIGN: ★	While food emerged cooked as desired, this dish had no handles, so getting it in and out of the oven was an adventure. Made from terra cotta, it needed to be soaked in water for 6 to 8 hours before its first use. After one use, the bottom appeared bowed.

MUFFIN TINS

Six years ago, we tested muffin tins and decided on two "must-have" features: a nonstick coating and handles for easy gripping. We decided to revisit muffin tins and chose eight nonstick models that all had extended rims or silicone tabs for gripping. To find the winner, the test kitchen baked more than 300 muffins and cupcakes. While the nonstick coatings ensured easy release of baked goods, some coatings were more effective at this than others. To gauge durability, we smeared the tins with béchamel and let it harden overnight; the next day, testers scraped and scrubbed. We also shocked the pans by heating them empty to 500 degrees and then plunging them in ice water to see if any would warp. Muffin tins are listed in order of preference.

RECOMMENDED	PERFORMANCE	TESTERS' COMMENTS
WILTON Avanti Everglide Metal-Safe Non-Stick 12-Cup Muffin Pan MODEL: 2105-3018 PRICE: $13.99	BROWNING: ★★ BAKED GOODS SHAPE: ★★ RELEASE: ★★★ HANDLE DESIGN: ★★★ DURABILITY: ★★★	Wide, extended rims and a raised lip make this tin very easy to grip even with thick oven mitts. Its durable construction withstood abuse, and its nonstick coating consistently released. Browning was acceptably even, though not stellar—but the price sure is right.
NORPRO Nonstick 12-Muffin Cupcake Pan MODEL: 3931 PRICE: $15.99	BROWNING: ★★★ BAKED GOODS SHAPE: ★★★ RELEASE: ★★★ HANDLE DESIGN: ★ DURABILITY: ★★★	This tin had one big drawback: a single extended rim, on a long side, which sloped downward, making it hard to hang on to. However, it browned deeply, baked relatively evenly, and released perfectly.
ANOLON Advanced Bakeware 12-Cup Muffin Pan MODEL: 54710 PRICE: $24.99	BROWNING: ★★ BAKED GOODS SHAPE: ★★ RELEASE: ★★★ HANDLE DESIGN: ★★★ DURABILITY: ★★★	This comparatively expensive tin was a respectable performer, with good "grabability" thanks to generous, well-placed silicone handles and a raised lip around the perimeter.
BONJOUR Commercial Nonstick Bakeware 12-Cup Muffin Pan MODEL: 57086 PRICE: $24.99	BROWNING: ★★ BAKED GOODS SHAPE: ★★★ RELEASE: ★★ HANDLE DESIGN: ★★ DURABILITY: ★★★	Two-toned finish (dark bottom, light top) earned high honors in the cupcake competition, turning out pert little cakes with well-defined edges and even tops. It stumbled releasing blueberry muffins (some berries burnt on), and the handles were not generous.
RECOMMENDED WITH RESERVATIONS	**PERFORMANCE**	**TESTERS' COMMENTS**
FARBERWARE Soft Touch Nonstick 12-Cup Muffin Pan MODEL: 52146 PRICE: $13.95	BROWNING: ★★ BAKED GOODS SHAPE: ★★ RELEASE: ★★★ HANDLE DESIGN: ★★ DURABILITY: ★★	This tin was one of two pans to emerge from the thermal shock abuse test with a very slight warp. Its cupcakes were not impressive and the muffins a bit squat, although they baked fairly evenly and released well.
PYREX Metal Bakeware 12-Cup Muffin Pan with Cover MODEL: 70950044973 PRICE: $25.99	BROWNING: ★ BAKED GOODS SHAPE: ★ RELEASE: ★★★ HANDLE DESIGN: ★★★ DURABILITY: ★★★	Browning was inconsistent. "They look boiled," one tester said about the mottled, pale cupcakes. A ridge line (described by the manufacturer as a "fill" line) marred the shape of the muffins and cupcakes. Too bad, because the wide, four-sided upturned rim was easy to grab. The optional carrying cover is too low to fit our blueberry muffins and frosted cupcakes.
RACHAEL RAY Oven Lovin' Nonstick 12-Cup Muffin Pan MODEL: 54075 PRICE: $19.99	BROWNING: ★★ BAKED GOODS SHAPE: ★★ RELEASE: ★ HANDLE DESIGN: ★★ DURABILITY: ★★	When the going got tough, this tin couldn't take it. Muffins released without incident, but cupcakes stuck. Hardened béchamel stuck so tenaciously we had to use a scraper. Heat discolored the orange silicone handle tabs. Very uneven performance.
USA PANS 12-Cup Muffin Pan MODEL: 1200MF-3 PRICE: $29.95	BROWNING: ★ BAKED GOODS SHAPE: ★★ RELEASE: ★★ HANDLE DESIGN: ★★ DURABILITY: ★	The highest-priced pan proved among the least durable. It warped slightly after thermal shock and clutched béchamel crusts for dear life in spots. The light-colored metal led to very light browning, so if you like deeper color, you will have to extend baking times in this tin.

CONVERSIONS & EQUIVALENCIES

SOME SAY COOKING IS A SCIENCE AND AN ART. We would say that geography has a hand in it, too. Flour milled in the United Kingdom and elsewhere will feel and taste different from flour milled in the United States. So, while we cannot promise that the loaf of bread you bake in Canada or England will taste the same as a loaf baked in the States, we can offer guidelines for converting weights and measures. We also recommend that you rely on your instincts when making our recipes. Refer to the visual cues provided. If the bread dough hasn't "come together in a ball," as described, you may need to add more flour—even if the recipe doesn't tell you so. You be the judge.

The recipes in this book were developed using standard U.S. measures following U.S. government guidelines. The charts below offer equivalents for U.S., metric, and Imperial (U.K.) measures. All conversions are approximate and have been rounded up or down to the nearest whole number. For example:

1 teaspoon = 4.929 milliliters, rounded up to 5 milliliters

1 ounce = 28.349 grams, rounded down to 28 grams

VOLUME CONVERSIONS

U.S.	METRIC
1 teaspoon	5 milliliters
2 teaspoons	10 milliliters
1 tablespoon	15 milliliters
2 tablespoons	30 milliliters
¼ cup	59 milliliters
⅓ cup	79 milliliters
½ cup	118 milliliters
¾ cup	177 milliliters
1 cup	237 milliliters
1¼ cups	296 milliliters
1½ cups	355 milliliters
2 cups	473 milliliters
2½ cups	592 milliliters
3 cups	710 milliliters
4 cups (1 quart)	0.946 liter
1.06 quarts	1 liter
4 quarts (1 gallon)	3.8 liters

WEIGHT CONVERSIONS

OUNCES	GRAMS
½	14
¾	21
1	28
1½	43
2	57
2½	71
3	85
3½	99
4	113
4½	128
5	142
6	170
7	198
8	227
9	255
10	283
12	340
16 (1 pound)	454

CONVERSIONS FOR INGREDIENTS COMMONLY USED IN BAKING

Baking is an exacting science. Because measuring by weight is far more accurate than measuring by volume, and thus more likely to achieve reliable results, in our recipes we provide ounce measures in addition to cup measures for many ingredients. Refer to the chart below to convert these measures into grams.

INGREDIENT	OUNCES	GRAMS
Flour		
1 cup all-purpose flour*	5	142
1 cup cake flour	4	113
1 cup whole wheat flour	5½	156
Sugar		
1 cup granulated (white) sugar	7	198
1 cup packed brown sugar (light or dark)	7	198
1 cup confectioners' sugar	4	113
Cocoa Powder		
1 cup cocoa powder	3	85
Butter†		
4 tablespoons (½ stick, or ¼ cup)	2	57
8 tablespoons (1 stick, or ½ cup)	4	113
16 tablespoons (2 sticks, or 1 cup)	8	227

* U.S. all-purpose flour, the most frequently used flour in this book, does not contain leaveners, as some European flours do. These leavened flours are called self-rising or self-raising. If you are using self-rising flour, take this into consideration before adding leavening to a recipe.

† In the United States, butter is sold both salted and unsalted. We generally recommend unsalted butter. If you are using salted butter, take this into consideration before adding salt to a recipe.

OVEN TEMPERATURES

FAHRENHEIT	CELSIUS	GAS MARK (imperial)
225	105	¼
250	120	½
275	130	1
300	150	2
325	165	3
350	180	4
375	190	5
400	200	6
425	220	7
450	230	8
475	245	9

CONVERTING TEMPERATURES FROM AN INSTANT-READ THERMOMETER

We include doneness temperatures in many of our recipes, such as those for poultry, meat, and bread. We recommend an instant-read thermometer for the job. Refer to the table above to convert Fahrenheit degrees to Celsius. Or, for temperatures not represented in the chart, use this simple formula:

Subtract 32 degrees from the Fahrenheit reading, then divide the result by 1.8 to find the Celsius reading.

EXAMPLE:

"Roast until chicken thighs register 175 degrees."

To convert:

175° F - 32 = 143°

143° ÷ 1.8 = 79.44°C, rounded down to 79°C

INDEX

NOTE: Page references in *italics* refer to photographs

C

D

G

H

I

J

N

O

P

Q

R

S

T

U

V

W

Y

Z